ADVENTURES IN ANTHROPOLOGY

A Reader in Physical Anthropology

William Jerald Kennedy

Florida Atlantic University

West Publishing Company
St. Paul • New York • Boston • Los Angeles • San Francisco

Library of Congress Cataloging in Publication Data

Main entry under title:

Adventures in anthropology

  Includes index.
  1. Physical anthropology—Addresses, essays,
lectures. 2. Archaeology—Addresses, essays,
lectures. I. Kennedy, William Jerald, 1932–
GN60.A39   573   76–28709
ISBN 0–8299–0094–2

To you, of course

Preface

This book is written for those being introduced to the subject matter of physical anthropology for the first time. The more traditional type of article has in many cases been purposefully avoided. Selections have been made with the student in mind, rather than the professional anthropologist. Typically, many readers assume a level of knowledge in the subject that the student has not yet attained. It has been the editor's intent to select articles which go beyond traditional bounds, in the hope that an interest in the field of anthropology can be cultivated. Hopefully, the three R's of any textbook—readability, relevancy, and academic respectability—have been met. At the same time it is the editor's hope that this book may stimulate students in a field of inquiry which marks the beginning of a rewarding and fascinating adventure in anthropology.

I want to thank my many students who have encouraged me to write this text, and West Publishing Company who gave me the opportunity to put this book in print. My deepest appreciation also goes to Drs. Norman Alger, William Maples, and Robert Dailey, whose constructive suggestions regarding the manuscript at various stages were most welcome.

Contents

Part III
Non-Human Primate Behavior

Part IV
Human Diversity

Part V
Early Hominids: Their Evolution And Culture

Part VI
The Evolution Of Homo Erectus, Later Hominids And Culture

Part VII
Archaeology Today

Part VIII
Further Cultural Developments

Part IX
Epilogue

Contributors

The author wishes to thank the following authors for permission to reprint their material.

Irwin S. Bernstein, Ph.D., is Associate Professor and Adjunct Professor of Anthropology at the University of Georgia, Athens, Georgia. He is also Adjunct Professor at the Yerkes Regional Primate Center.

Ralph Bolton, Ph.D., is Associate Professor of Anthropology at Pomona College, California.

Aubrey Burl, Ph.D., is Senior Lecturer in Prehistory at Kingston upon Hull College of Education, Yorkshire, England.

Robert Carneiro, Ph.D., Curator of the American Museum of Natural History, New York, has written numerous articles in scholarly journals and is a recognized authority in the field of cultural anthropology.

Te-K'un Cheng, Ph.D., is Professor of Chinese Studies at the Chinese University, Hong Kong.

Michael D. Coe, Ph.D., is Professor of Anthropology at Yale University. Dr. Coe is author of several books on Pre-Columbian civilizations. He has made a number of important discoveries in the field.

Cyril D. Darlington, Ph.D., is Professor of Botany at Oxford University, Keeper of the Botanic Gardens, and a widely known authority in his field.

Hester Davis, M.A., is State Archaeologist with the Arkansas Archaeological Survey.

Bob Ferguson is working with the Southeastern Indian Antiquities Survey. Nashville, Tennessee.

Robin Fox, Ph.D., is Professor of Anthropology at Rutgers University and co-director of research for the H. F. Guggenheim Foundation.

A. Roberto Frisancho, Ph.D., is Associate Professor of Anthropology at the University of Michigan, Ann Arbor, and Research Associate at the Center for Human Growth and Development.

Thomas P. Gordon, trained in physiological psychology, is at the Yerkes Primate Center Field Station, Lawrenceville, Georgia. He is interested in research measuring hormonal correlates of behavioral events in both nonhuman primates and humans.

Katherine M. Homewood is completing her Ph.D. on the socioecology of the Tana mangabey monkey at the University College, London, while conducting research at the Wellcome Institute of Comparative Physiology.

S. D. Jayakar, Ph.D., Editor of the *Journal of Genetics,* is Research Officer of the Biochemical Evolutionary Genetics Laboratory of the Italian National Research Council at Pavia.

Mary-Claire King, Ph.D., is a research geneticist at the Hooper Foundation of International Health, University of California, San Francisco.

Gina Bari Kolata is a science writer for *Science* Magazine.

Roy Lachman, Ph.D., is a psychologist in the Department of Psychology, University of Houston, Houston, Texas.

William S. Laughlin, Ph.D., is Chairman of the Laboratory of Biological Anthropology, Department of Behavioral Sciences, University of Connecticut, Storrs, Connecticut.

Mary Lewin is science writer for the *New Scientist* magazine.

R. D. Martin, Ph.D., is senior research fellow at the Wellcome Institute of Comparative Physiology, London, England.

Ernst Mayr, Ph.D., author of numerous scholarly articles, is Alexander Agassiz Professor of Zoology at the Museum of Comparative Zoology, Harvard University.

Emil Menzel, Ph.D., is research psychologist at the State University of New York at Stony Brook.

Gary Mitchell, Ph.D., is a psychologist at the University of California, at Davis. His research has been published in a number of scientific journals.

Janet L. Mistler-Lachman, Ph.D., is in the Department of Psychology at the University of Houston, Houston, Texas.

James W. Prescott, Ph.D., is a neuropsychologist and health scientist at the National Institute of Child Health and Human Development, NIH, Bethesda, Maryland.

Michael Raleigh, Ph.D., is on the staff and conducts research at the Neuropsychiatric Institute, University of California at Los Angeles.

William L. Rathje, Ph.D., is Associate Professor in the Department of Anthropology at the University of Arizona.

Vernon Reynolds, Ph.D., is author of numerous articles and papers dealing with primate behavior. Much of his field work has been centered around observing chimpanzees in their natural habitat. He is a professor in the Department of Physical Anthropology at the University of Oxford.

Lawrence H. Robbins, Ph.D., is Associate Professor, Department of Anthropology and African Studies, Michigan State University, East Lansing, Michigan.

Harry Shapiro, Ph.D., is Curator Emeritus of Anthropology at the American Museum and Professor of Anthropology at Columbia University.

Elie A. Shneour, Ph.D., is Professor and Director of Research at Calbiochem, San Diego, California.

Elwyn L. Simons, Ph.D., is Professor of Paleontology and Curator of Vertebrate Paleonotology, Peabody Museum, Yale University. He is an authority on primate and human evolution.

Ralph Solecki, Ph.D., is Professor of Anthropology at Columbia University.

Curt Stern, Ph.D., is Emeritus Professor of Genetics at the University of California, Berkeley and a recognized authority in his field.

Leon Stover, Ph.D., is Professor of Anthropology at the Illinois Institute of Technology, Chicago, Illinois.

William Sullivan is a writer for the *New York Times.*

Phillip V. Tobias, M.D., is an anatomist and Head of the Department of Anatomy at the University of Witwatersland, South Africa.

Ian Tattersall, Ph.D. is James Dwight Dana Fellow in Geology and Geophysics, Yale University and has recently published *Man's Ancestors,* a book on human evolution.

Sherwood L. Washburn, Ph.D., author of numerous articles and books in the field of physical anthropology, is Professor of Anthropology at the Department of Anthropology, University of California, Berkeley.

Allan C. Wilson, Ph.D., is Professor of Biochemistry at the University of California, Berkeley.

ADVENTURES
IN
ANTHROPOLOGY

Introduction

The articles reprinted in this reader will introduce the student to the multifaceted nature of physical anthropology. The current trend in this field is clearly one which is interdisciplinary in focus.

Physical anthropologists have previously worked closely with cultural anthropologists and archaeologists—all profiting considerably from each other's research.

At an increasing rate, major contributions to the discipline are coming vis-à-vis investigations in the fields of genetics, molecular biology, geology, paleontology, primate ethology, and psychobiology.

To a large extent, this will be noted from the list of contributing authors whose expertise is in a variety of disciplines.

Despite the diverse nature of the articles it will be evident that there is an underlying thread of continuity throughout—an emphasis on the evolutionary and comparative approach as well as treatment of the linkages and interplay between the biological and non-biological nature of the human animal.

Many of the articles broaching a particular topic will demonstrate that many central issues are still to be solved; that, in many cases, there are opposing views to now accepted theories.

Part I

Biological Anthropology and Genetics

The following articles comprise a brief encounter with fundamental concepts in the field of biological anthropology—evolution and genetics. A little reflection will suggest a mutual complementarity among selections in this section. Ernst Mayr's article stresses the scientific breakthroughs required and philosophical obstructions removed before a Darwinian concept of evolution through natural selection could be accepted. The so-called "synthetic theory of evolution" is universally accepted in the biological and natural sciences today, yet Washburn's interesting article suggests that certain "facts" of human evolution are still uncertain, and that blind faith in this theory may actually slow down scientific advancement. The work by Curt Stern treats a number of topics dealing with human genetic phenomena—new developments as well as the now classic findings in this field. The final article, by King and Wilson, marks major research advances in the area of molecular biology. The close genetic link, previously established, between chimpanzee and man is noted, along with other data, to suggest that regulatory mutations may best account for the major biological differences between humans and chimpanzees. The reader is encouraged to pursue such additional readings as R. Eckhardt's "Population Genetics and Human Origins", *Scientific American,* January 1972; and "The Biological Nature of Man", by George Gaylord Simpson, *Science,* 152, April 1966, pp. 472-78.

The Nature of
the Darwinian Revolution

The road on which science advances is not a smoothly rising ramp; there are periods of stagnation, and periods of accelerated progress. Some historians of science have recently emphasized that there are occasional breakthroughs, scientific revolutions (1), consisting of rather drastic revisions of previously maintained assumptions and concepts. The actual nature of these revolutions, however, has remained highly controversial (2). When we look at those of the so-called scientific revolutions that are most frequently mentioned, we find that they are identified with the names Copernicus, Newton, Lavoisier, Darwin, Planck, Einstein, and Heisenberg; in other words, with one exception, all of them are revolutions in the physical sciences.

Does this focus on the physical sciences affect the interpretation of the concept "scientific revolution"? I am taking a new look at the Darwinian revolution of 1859, perhaps the most fundamental of all intellectual revolutions in the history of mankind. It not only eliminated man's anthropocentrism, but affected every metaphysical and ethical concept, if consistently applied. The earlier prevailing concept of a created, and subsequently static, world was miles apart from Darwin's picture of a steadily evolving world. Kuhn (1) maintains that scientific revolutions are characterized by the replacement of an outworn paradigm by a new one. But a paradigm is, so to speak, a bundle of separate concepts, and not all of these are changed at the same time. In this analysis of the Darwinian revolution, I am attempting to dissect the total change of thinking involved in the Darwinian revolution into the major changing concepts, to determine the relative chronology of these changes, and to test the resistance to these changes among Darwin's contemporaries.

The idea of evolution had been widespread for more than 100 years before 1859. Evolutionary interpretations were advanced increasingly often

By Ernst Mayr. Reprinted with permission, from *Science*, 176, 2 June 1972, pp. 981-89. Copyright © 1972 by the American Association for the Advancement of Science.

in the second half of the 18th and the first half of the 19th centuries, only to be ignored, ridiculed, or maligned. What were the reasons for this determined resistance?

The history of evolutionism has long been a favorite subject among historians of science (3-5). Their main emphasis, however, has been on Darwin's forerunners, and on any and every trace of evolutionary thinking prior to 1859, or on the emergence of evolutionary concepts in Darwin's own thinking. These are legitimate approaches, but it seems to me that nothing brings out better the revolutionary nature of some of Darwin's concepts (6) than does an analysis of the arguments of contemporary antievolutionists.

Cuvier, Lyell, and Louis Agassiz, the leading opponents of organic evolution, were fully aware of many facts favoring an evolutionary interpretation, and likewise of the Lamarckian and other theories of transmutation. They devoted a great deal of energy to refute evolutionism (7-10) and supported instead what, to a modern student, would seem a less defensible position. What induced them to do so?

It is sometimes stated that they had no other legitimate choice, because—it is claimed—not enough evidence in favor of evolution was available before 1859. The facts refute this assertion. Lovejoy (11), in a superb analysis of this question, asks: "At what date can the evidence in favor of the theory of organic evolution . . . be said to have been fairly complete?" Here, one can perhaps distinguish two periods. During an earlier one, lasting from about 1745 to 1830, much became known that suggested evolution or, at least, a temporalized scale of perfection (12). Names like Maupertuis (1745), de Maillet (1749), Buffon (1749), Diderot (1769), Erasmus Darwin (1794), Lamarck (1809), and E. Geoffrey St. Hilaire (1818) characterize this period. Enough evidence from the fields of biogeography, systematics, paleontology, comparative anatomy, and animal and plant breeding, was already available by about 1812 (date of Cuvier's *Ossemens Fossiles*) to have made it possible to develop some of the arguments later made by Darwin in the *Origin of Species* (6). Soon afterward, however, much new evidence was produced by paleontology and stratigraphy, as well as by biogeography and comparative anatomy, with which only the evolutionary hypothesis was consistent; these new facts "reduced the rival hypothesis to a grotesque absurdity" *(11)*. Yet, only a handful of authors [including Meckel (1821), Chambers (1844), Unger (1852), Schaaffhausen (1853), Wallace (1855)] adopted the concept of evolution while such leading authorities as Lyell, R. Owen, and Louis Agassiz vehemently opposed it.

Time does not permit me to marshal the abundant evidence in favor of evolution which existed by 1830. A comprehensive listing has been provided by Lovejoy *(11)*, although the findings of systematics and biogeography must be added to his tabulation. The patterns of animal distribution were particularly decisive evidence, and it is no coincidence that Darwin devoted to it two entire chapters in the *Origin*. In spite of this massive evidence, creationism remained "the hypothesis tenaciously held by most men of science for at least twenty years before 1859" *(11)*. It was not a lack of supporting facts, then, that prevented the acceptance of the theory of evolution, but rather the power of the opposing ideas.

Curiously, a number of nonscientists, particularly Robert Chambers *(13)* and Herbert Spencer saw the light well before the professionals. Chambers, the author of the *Vestiges of the Natural History of Creation*, developed quite a consistent and logical argument for evolutionism, and was instrumental in converting A. R. Wallace, R. W. Emerson, and A. Schopenhauer to evolutionism. As was the case with Diderot and Erasmus Darwin, these well-informed and broadly educated lay people looked at the problem in a "holistic" way, and thus perceived the truth more readily than did the professionals who were committed to certain well-established dogmas. A view from the distance is sometimes more revealing, for the understanding of broad issues, than the myopic scrutiny of the specialist.

POWER OF RETARDING CONCEPTS

Why were the professional geologists and biologists so blind when the manifestations of evolution were staring them in the face from all directions? Darwin's friend Hewett Watson put it this way in 1860 *(14, p. 226)*: "How could Sir Lyell

... for thirty years read, write, and think on the subject of species *and their succession*, and yet constantly look down the wrong road?" Indeed, how could he? And the same question can be asked for Louis Agassiz, Richard Owen, almost all of Lyell's geological colleagues, and all of Darwin's botanist friends from Joseph Hooker on down. They all displayed a nearly complete resistance to drawing what to us would seem to be the inevitable conclusion from the vast amount of evidence in favor of evolution.

Historians of science are familiar with this phenomenon; it happens almost invariably when new facts cast doubt on generally accepted theory. The prevailing concepts, although more difficult to defend, have such a powerful hold over the thinking of all investigators, that they find it difficult, if not impossible, to free themselves of these ideas. To illustrate this by merely one example, I would like to quote a statement by Lyell: "It is idle . . . to dispute about the abstract possibility of the conversion of one species into another, when there are known causes, so much more active in their nature, which must always intervene and prevent the actual accomplishment of such conversions" *(9, p. 162)*. Actually one searches in vain for a demonstration of such "known causes" and any proof that they "must" always intervene. The cogency of the argument relied entirely on the validity of silent assumptions.

In the particular case of the Darwinian revolution, what were the dominant ideas that formed roadblocks against the advance of evolutionary thinking? To name these concepts is by no means easy because they are silent assumptions, never fully articulated. When these assumptions rest on religious beliefs or on the acceptance of certain philosophies, they are particularly difficult to reconstruct. This is the major reason why there is so much difference of opinion in the interpretation of this period. Was theology responsible for the lag, or was it the authority of Cuvier or Lyell, or the acceptance of catastrophism (with progressionism), or the absence of a reasonable explanatory scheme? All of these interpretations and several others have been advanced, and all presumably played some role. Others, particularly the role of essentialism, have so far been rather neglected by the historians.

NATURAL THEOLOGY
AND CREATIONISM

The period from 1800 to middle of that century witnessed the greatest flowering of natural theology in Great Britain *(5, 15)*. It was the age of Paley and the Bridgewater Treatises, and virtually all British scientists accepted the traditional Christian conception of a Creator God. The industrial revolution was in full swing, the poor working man was exploited unmercifully, and the goodness and wisdom of the Creator was emphasized constantly to sooth guilty consciences. It became a moral obligation for the scientist to find additional proofs for the wisdom and constant attention of the Creator. When Chambers in his *Vestiges (13)* dared to replace direct intervention of the Creator by the action of secondary causes (natural laws), he was roundly condemned. Although the attacks were ostensibly directed against errors of fact, virtually all reviewers were horrified that Chambers had "annulled all distinction between physical and moral," and that he had degraded man by ranking him as a descendant of the apes and by interpreting the universe as "the progression and development of a rank, unbending, and degrading materialism" *(5, p. 150; 16)*. It is not surprising that in this intellectual climate Chambers had taken the precaution of publishing anonymously. Yet the modern reader finds little that is objectionable in Chambers' endeavor to replace supernatural explanations by scientific ones.

To a greater or lesser extent, all the scientists of that period resorted, in their explanatory schemes, to frequent interventions by the Creator (in the running of His world). Indeed, proofs of such interventions were considered the foremost evidence for His existence. Agassiz quite frankly describes the obligations of the naturalist in these words: "Our task is . . . complete as soon as we have proved His existence" *(10, p. 132)*. To him the *Essay on Classification* was nothing but another Bridgewater Treatise in which the relationship of animals supplied a particularly elaborate and, for Agassiz, irrefutable demonstration of His existence.

Natural theology equally pervades Lyell's *Principles of Geology*. After discussing various remarkable instincts, such as pointing and retrieving, which are found in races of the dog, Lyell states: "When such remarkable habits appear in races of this species, we may reasonably conjecture that they were given with no other view than for the use of man and the preservation of the dog which thus obtains protection" *(9, p. 455)*. Even though cultivated plants and domestic animals may have been created long before man, "some of the qualities of particular animals and plants may have been given solely with a view to the connection which, it was foreseen, would exist between them and man" *(9, p. 456)*. Like Agassiz, Lyell believed that everything in nature is planned, designed, and has a predetermined end. "The St. Helena plants and insects [which are now dying out] may have lasted for their alloted term" *(9, p. 9)*. The harmony of living nature and all the marvelous adaptations of animals and plants to each other and to their environment seemed to him thus fully and satisfactorily explained.

CREATIONISM AND
THE ADVANCES OF
GEOLOGICAL SCIENCE

At the beginning of the 18th century, the concept of a created world seemed internally consistent as long as this world was considered only recently created (in 4004 B.C.), static, and unchanging. The "ladder of perfection" (part of God's plan) accounted for the "higher" and "lower" organization of animals and man, and Noah's flood for the existence of fossils. All this could be readily accommodated within the framework of a literal Biblical interpretation.

The discovery of the great age of the earth *(5, 17)* and of an ever-increasing number of distinct fossil faunas in different geological strata necessitated abandoning the idea of a single creation. Repeated creations had to be postulated, and the necessary number of such interventions had to be constantly revised upward. Agassiz was willing to accept 50 or 80 total extinctions of life and an equal number of new creations. Paradoxically, the advance of scientific knowledge necessitated an increasing recourse to the supernatural for explanation. Even such a sober and cautious person as Charles Lyell frequently explained natural phenomena as due to "creation" and, of course, a carefully thought-out creation. The fact that the brain of the human embryo successively passes through stages resembling the brains of fish, reptile, and lower mammal discloses "in a highly interesting manner, the unity of plan that runs through the organization of the whole series of vertebrated animals; but they lend no support whatever to the notion of a gradual transmutation of one species into another; least of all of the passage, in the course of many generations, from an animal of a more simple to one of a more complex structure" (9, p. 20). When a species becomes extinct it is replaced "by new creations" (9, p. 45). Nothing is impossible in creation. "Creation seems to require omnipotence, therefore we cannot estimate it" (18, p. 4). "Each species may have had its origin in a single pair, or individual where an individual was sufficient, and species may have been created in succession at such times and in such places as to enable them to multiply and endure for an *appointed* period, and occupy an *appointed* space of the globe?" (italics mine) (9, pp. 99-100). Everything is done according to plan. Since species are fixed and unchangeable, everything about them, such as the area of distribution, the ecological context, adaptations to cope with competitors and enemies, and even the date of extinction, was previously "appointed," that is, predetermined.

This constant appeal to the supernatural amounted to a denial of all sound scientific methods, and to the adoption of explanations that could neither be proven nor refuted. Chambers saw this quite clearly (13). When there is a choice between two theories, either special creation or the operation of general laws instituted by the Creator, he exclaimed, "I would say that the latter [theory] is greatly preferable, as it implies a far grander view of the Divine power and dignity than the other" (13, p. 117). Indeed, the increasing knowledge of geological sequences, and of the facts of comparative anatomy and geographic distribution, made the picture of special creation more ludicrous every day (11, p. 413).

ESSENTIALISM AND A STATIC WORLD

Thus, theological considerations clearly played a large role in the resistance to the adoption of evolutionary views in England (and also in France). Equally influential, or perhaps even more so, was a philosophical concept. Philosophy and natural history during the first half of the 19th century, particularly in continental Europe, were strongly dominated by typological thinking [designated "essentialism" by Popper (19, 20)]. This presumes that the changeable world of appearances is based on underlying immutable essences, and that all members of a class represent the same essence. This idea was first clearly enunciated in Plato's concept of the *eidos*. Later it became a dominant element in the teachings of Thomism (21), and of all idealistic philosophy. The enormous role of essentialism in retarding the acceptance of evolutionism was long overlooked (22, 23). The observed vast variability of the world has no more reality, according to this philosophy, than the shadows of an object on a cave wall, a Plato expressed it in his allegory. The only things that are permanent, real, and sharply discontinuous from each other are the fixed, unchangeable "ideas" underlying the observed variability. Discontinuity and fixity are, according to the essentialist, as much the properties of the living as of the inanimate world.

As Reiser (24) has said, a belief in discontinuous, immutable essences is incompatible with a belief in evolution. Agassiz was an extreme representative of this philosophy (23). To a lesser extent the same can be demonstrated for all of the other opponents of evolutionism, including Lyell. When rejecting Lamarck's claim that species and genera intergrade with each other, Lyell proposes that the following laws "prevail in the economy of the animate creation . . . Thirdly, that there are fixed limits beyond which the descendants from common parents can never deviate from a certain type; fourthly, that each species springs from one original stock, and can never be permanently confounded by intermixing with the progeny of any other stock; fifthly, that each species shall endure for a considerable period of time" (9, p.

433). All nature consists, according to Lyell, of fixed types created at a definite time. To him these types were morphological entities, and he was rather shocked by Lamarck's idea that changes in behavior could have any effect on morphology.

As an essentialist, Lyell showed no understanding of the nature of genetic variation. Strictly in the scholastic tradition, he believed implicitly that essential characters could not change; this could occur only with nonessential characters. If an animal is brought into a new environment, "a short period of time is generally sufficient to effect nearly the whole change which an alteration of external circumstances can bring about in the habits of a species, . . . such capacity of accommodation to new circumstances is enjoyed in very different degrees by different species" (9, p. 464). For instance, if we look at the races of dogs, they show many superficial differences "but, if we look for some of those essential changes which would be required to lend even the semblance of a foundation for the theory of Lamarck, respecting the growth of new organs and the gradual obliteration of others, we find nothing of the kind" (9, p. 438). This forces Lyell to question even Lamarck's conjecture "that the wolf may have been the original of the dog." The fact that in the (geologically speaking) incredibly short time since the dog was domesticated, such drastically different races as the Eskimo dog, the hairless Chihuahua, the greyhound, and other extremes evolved is glossed over.

LYELL'S SPECIES CONCEPT

Holding a species concept that allowed for no essential variation, Lyell credited species with little plasticity and adaptability. This led him to an interpretation of the fossil record that is very different from that of Lamarck. Anyone studying the continuous changes in the earth's surface, states Lyell, "will immediately perceive that, amidst the vicissitudes of the earth's surface, species cannot be immortal, but must perish, one after the other, like the individuals which compose them. There is no possibility of escaping from this conclusion, without resorting to some hypothesis as violent as that of Lamarck

who imagined . . . that species are each of them endowed with indefinite powers of modifying their organization, in conformity to the endless changes of circumstances to which they are exposed" (9, pp. 155-156).

The concept of a steady extermination of species and their replacement by newly created ones, as proposed by Lyell, comes close to being a kind of microcatastrophism, as far as organic nature is concerned. Lyell differed from Cuvier merely in pulverizing the catastrophes into events relating to single species, rather than to entire faunas. In the truly decisive point, the rejection of any possible continuity between species in progressive time sequences, Lyell entirely agreed with Cuvier. When he traced the history of a species backward, Lyell inexorably arrived at an original ancestral pair, at the original center of creation. There is a total absence in his arguments of any thinking in terms of populations.

The enormous power of essentialism is in part explainable by the fact that it fitted the tenets of creationism so well; the two dogmas strongly reinforced each other. Nothing in Lyell's geological experience seriously contradicted his essentialism. It was not shaken until nearly 25 years later when Lyell visited the Canary Islands (from December 1853 to March 1854) and became acquainted with the same kind of phenomena that, in the Galapagos, had made Darwin an evolutionist and which, in the East Indian Archipelago, gave concrete form to the incipient evolutionism of A. R. Wallace. Wilson (18) has portrayed the growth of doubt which led Lyell to publicly confess his conversion to evolutionism in 1862. The adoption of population thinking by him was a slow process, and even years after his memorable discussion with Darwin (16 April 1856), Lyell spoke in his notebooks of "variation *or* selection" as the important factor in evolution in spite of the fact that Darwin's entire argument was founded on the need for *both* factors as the basis of a satisfactory theory.

LYELL AND UNIFORMITARIANISM

It is a long-standing tradition in biological historiography that Lyell's revival of Hutton's theory of uniformitarianism was a major factor in the eventual adoption of evolutionary thinking. This thesis seems to be a great oversimplification; it is worthwhile to look at the argument a little more critically *(25)*. When the discovery of a series of different fossil faunas, separated by unconformities, made the story of a single flood totally inadequate, Cuvier and others drew the completely correct conclusion that these faunas, particularly the alternation of marine and terrestrial faunas, demonstrated a frequent alternation of rises of the sea above the land and the subsequent reemergence of land above the sea. The discovery of mammoths frozen into the ice of Siberia favored the additional thesis that such changes could happen very rapidly. Cuvier was exceedingly cautious in his formulation of the nature of these "revolutions" and "catastrophes," but he did admit, "The breaking to pieces and overturning of the strata, which happened in former catastrophes, show plainly enough that they were sudden and violent like the last [which killed the mammoths and embedded them in ice]" *(26,* p. 16). He implied that most of these events were local rather than universal phenomena, and he did not maintain that a new creation had been required to produce the species existing today. He said merely "that they [modern species] did not anciently occupy their present locations and that they must have come there from elsewhere" *(26,* pp. 125-126).

Cuvier's successors did not maintain his caution. The school of the so-called progressionists *(27)* postulated that each fauna was totally exterminated by a catastrophe at the end of each geologic period, followed by the special creation of an entirely new organic world. Progressionism, therefore, was intellectually a backward step from the widespread 18th-century belief that the running of the universe required only occasional, but definitely not incessant, active intervention by the Creator: He maintained stability largely through the laws that He had decreed at the beginning, and which allowed for certain planetary and other perturbations. This same reasoning could have easily been applied to the organic world, and this indeed is what was done by Chambers in 1844, and by many other devout Christians after 1859.

Catastrophism was not as great an obstacle to evolutionism as often claimed. It admitted, indeed it emphasized, the advance which each new creation showed over the preceding one. By also conceding that there had been 30, 50, or even more than 100 extinctions and new creations, it made the concept of these destructions increasingly absurd, and what was finally left, after the absurd destructions had been abandoned, was the story of the constant progression of faunas *(28)*. As soon as one rejected reliance on supernatural forces, this progression automatically became evidence in favor of evolution. The only other assumption one had to make was that many of the catastrophes and extinctions had been localized events. This was, perhaps, not too far from Cuvier's original viewpoint.

The reason why catastrophism was adopted by virtually all of the truly productive leading geologists in the first half of the 19th century is that the facts seemed to support it. Breaks in fossil strata, the occurrence of vast lava flows, a replacement of terrestrial deposits by marine ones and the reverse, and many other phenomena of a similar, reasonably violent nature (including the turning upside down of whole fossil sequences) all rather decisively refuted a rigid uniformitarian interpretation. This is why Cuvier, Sedgwick, Buckland, Murchison, Conybeare, Agassiz, and de Beaumont, to mention a few prominent geologists, adopted more or less catastrophist interpretations.

Charles Lyell was the implacable foe of the "catastrophists," as his opponents were designated by Whewell *(29)*. In his *Principles of Geology (9),* Lyell promoted a "steady state" concept of the world, best characterized by Hutton's motto, "no vestige of a beginning—no prospect of an end." Whewell coined the term "uniformitarianism" *(30)* for this school of thought, a term which unfortunately had many different meanings. The most important meaning was that it postulated that no forces had been active in the past history of the earth that are not also working today. Yet, even this would permit two rather different interpretations. Even if one includes supernatural agencies among forces and causes, one can still be a consistent uniformitarian, provided one postulates that the Creator continues to reshape the world actively even at the present. Rather candidly, Lyell refers to this interpretation, accepted by him, as "the perpetual intervention hypothesis" *(18,* p. 89).

Almost dimetrically opposed to this were the conclusions of those who excluded all recourse to supernatural interventions. Uniformitarianism to them meant simply the consistent application of natural laws not only to inanimate nature (as was done by Lyell) but also to the living world (as proposed by Chambers). The important component in their argument was the rejection of supernatural intervention rather than a lip service to the word uniformity.

It is important to remember that Lyell applied his uniformitarianism in a consistent manner only to inanimate nature, but left the door open for special creation in the living world. Indeed, as Lovejoy *(11)* states justly, when it came to the origin of new species, Lyell, the great champion of uniformitarianism, embraced "the one doctrine with which uniformitarianism was wholly incompatible—the theory of numerous and discontinuous miraculous special creations." Lyell himself did not see it that way. As he wrote to Herschel *(31)*, he considered his notion "of a succession of extinction of species, and creation of new ones, going on perpetually now . . . the grandest which I had ever conceived, so far as regards the attributes of the Presiding Mind." There is evidence, however, that Lyell considered these creations not always as miracles, but sometimes as occurring "through the intervention of intermediate causes" thus being "a natural, in contradistinction to a miraculous process." By July 1856, after having read Wallace's 1855 paper, and after having discussed evolution with Darwin (16, April 1856), Lyell had become completely converted to believing that the introduction of new species was "governed by laws in the same sense as the Universe is governed by laws" *(18,* p. 123).

Only the steady-state concept of uniformitarianism was novel in Lyell's interpretation. The insistence that nature operates according to eternal laws, with the same forces acting at all times was, from Aristotle on, the standard explanation among most of those who did not postulate a totally static world, for instance, among the French naturalists preceding Cuvier. Consequently, acceptance of uniformitarianism did not, as Lyell himself clearly demonstrated, require the acceptance of evolutionism. If one believed in a steady-state world, as did Lyell, uniformitarianism was incompatible with evolu-

tion. Only if it was combined with the concept of a steadily changing world, as it was in Lamarck's thinking, did it encourage a belief in evolution. It is obvious, then, that the statement "uniformitarianism is the pacemaker of evolutionism," is an exaggeration, if not a myth.

But what effect did Lyell have on Darwin? Everyone agrees that it was profound; there was no other person whom Darwin admired as greatly as Lyell. *Principles of Geology,* by Lyell, was Darwin's favorite reading on the *Beagle* and gave his geological interests new direction. After the return of the *Beagle* to England, Darwin received more stimulation and encouragement from Lyell than from any other of his friends. Indeed, Lyell became a father figure for him and stayed so for the rest of his life. Darwin's whole way of writing, particularly in the *Origin of Species,* was modeled after the *Principles.* There is no dispute over these facts.

But, what was Lyell's impact on Darwin's evolutionary ideas? There is much to indicate that the influence was largely negative. Knowing how firmly Lyell was opposed to the possibility of a transmutation of species, as documented by his devastating critique of Lamarck, Darwin was very careful in what he revealed to Lyell. He admitted that he doubted the fixity of species, but after that the two friends apparently avoided a further discussion of the subject. Darwin was far more outspoken with Hooker to whom he confessed as early as January 1844, "I am almost convinced . . . that species are not (it is like confessing murder) immutable" *(14,* p. 23). It was not until 1856 that Darwin fully outlined his theory of evolution to Lyell *(18,* p. xlix). This reticence of Darwin was not due to any intolerance on Lyell's part (or else Lyell would not have, after 1856, encouraged Darwin so actively to publish his heretical views), but rather to an unconscious fear on Darwin's part that his case was not sufficiently persuasive to convert such a formidable opponent as Lyell. There has been much speculation as to why Darwin had been so tardy about publishing his evolutionary views. Several factors were involved (one being the reception of the *Vestiges*), but I am rather convinced that his awe of Lyell's opposition to the transmutation of species was a much more weighty reason than has been hitherto admitted. It is no coincidence that Darwin finally began to write his great work within 3 months after Lyell took the initiative to consult him and to encourage him. Lovejoy summarizes the effect of Lyell's opposition to evolution in these words: "It was . . . his example and influence, more than the logical force of his arguments, that so long helped to sustain the prevalent belief that transformism was not a scientifically respectable theory" *(11)*. I entirely agree with this evaluation.

UNSUCCESSFUL REFUTATIONS OWING TO WRONG CHOICE OF ALTERNATIVES

Creationism, essentialism, and Lyell's authority were not, however, the only reasons for the delay in the acceptance of evolution; others were important weaknesses in the scientific methodology of the period. There was still a demand for conclusive proofs. "Show me the breed of dogs with an entirely new organ," Lyell seems to say, "and I will believe in evolution." That much of science consists merely in showing that one interpretation is more probable than another one, or consistent with more facts than another one, was far less realized at that period than it is now *(32)*.

That victory over one's opponent consists in the refutation of his arguments, however, was taken for granted. Cuvier's, Lyell's, Agassiz's, and Darwin's detailed argumentations were all attempts to "falsify," as Popper *(33)* has called it, the statements of their opponents. This method, however, has a number of weaknesses. For instance, it is often quite uncertain what kind of evidence or argument truly represents a falsification. More fatal is the frequently made assumption that there are only two alternatives in a dispute. Indeed, the whole concept of "alternative" is rather ambiguous, as I shall try to illustrate with some examples from pre-Darwinian controversies.

We can find numerous illustrations in the antievolutionary writings of Charles Lyell and Louis Agassiz of the limitation to only two alternatives when actually there was at least a third possible choice. Louis Agassiz, for instance, never seriously considered the possibility of true evolution, that is, of descent with modification.

For him the world was either planned by the Creator, or was the accidental product of blind physical causes (in which case evolution would be the concatenation of such accidents). He reiterates this singularly simple-minded choice throughout the *Essay on Classification (10)*: "physical laws" versus "plan of creation" (p. 10), "spontaneous generation" versus "divine plan" (p. 36), "physical agents" versus "plan ordained from the beginning" (p. 37), "physical causes" versus "supreme intellect" (p. 64), and "physical causes" versus "reflective mind" (p. 127). By this choice he not only excluded the possibility of evolution as envisioned by Darwin, but even as postulated by Lamarck. Nowhere does Agassiz attempt to refute Lamarckian evolution. His physical causes, in turn, are an exceedingly narrow definition of natural causes, since it is fully apparent that Agassiz had a very simple-minded Cartesian conception of physical causes as motions and mechanical forces. "I am at a loss to conceive how the origin of parasites can be ascribed to physical causes" (*10,* p. 126). "How can physical causes be responsible for the form of animals when so many totally different animal types live in the same area subjected to identical physical causes?" (*10,* pp. 13-14). The abundant regularities in nature demonstrate "the plan of a Divine Intelligence" since they cannot be the result of blind physical forces. (This indeed was a standard argument among adherents of natural theology.) It never occurred to Agassiz that none of his arguments excluded a third possibility, the gradual evolution of these regularities by processes that can be daily observed in nature. This is why the publication of Darwin's *Origin* was such a shock to him. The entire evidence against evolution, which Agassiz had marshaled so assiduously in his *Essay on Classification,* had become irrelevant. He had failed completely to provide arguments against a third possibility, the one advanced by Darwin.

The concept of evolution, at that period, still evoked in most naturalists the image of the *scala naturae,* the ladder of perfection. No one was more opposed to this concept than Lyell, the champion of a steady-state world. Any finding that contradicted a steady progression from the simple toward the more perfect refuted the validity of evolution, he thought. Indeed, the fact that mammals appeared in the fossil record before birds, and that primates appeared in the Eocene considerably earlier than some of the orders of "lower" mammals were, to him, as decisive a refutation of the evolutionary theory as was to Agassiz the fact that the four great types of animals appeared simultaneously in the earliest fossil-bearing strata.

The assumption that refuting the *scala naturae* would refute once and for all any evolutionary theory is another illustration of insufficient alternatives. Lyell was quite convinced that the concept of a steady-state world would be validated (including regular special creations), if it could be shown that those mechanisms were improbable or impossible which Lamarck had proposed to account for evolutionary change.

But there were also other violations of sound scientific method; for instance, the failure to see that both of two alternatives might be valid. In these cases, the pre-Darwinians arrived at erroneous conclusions because they were convinced that they had to make a choice between two processes which, in reality, occur simultaneously. For example, neither Lamarck nor Lyell understood speciation (the multiplication of species), but this failure led them to opposite conclusions. When looking at fossil faunas, Lamarck, a great believer in the adaptability of natural species, concluded that all the contained species must have evolved into very different descendants. Lyell, as an essentialist, rejected the possibility of a change in species and therefore he believed, like Cuvier, that all of the species had become extinct, with replacements provided by special creation. Neither Lamarck nor Lyell imagined that both processes, speciation and extinction, could occur simultaneously. That the turnover of faunas could be a balance of both processes never entered their minds.

FAILURE TO SEPARATE DISTINCT PHENOMENA

A third type of violation of scientific logic was particularly harmful to the acceptance of evolutionary thinking. This was the erroneous assumption that certain characteristics are inseparably combined. For instance, both Linnaeus and Darwin assumed, as I pointed out at an earlier occasion *(34)*, that if one admitted the *reality* of species in nature, one would also have to postulate their immutable *fixity*. Lyell, as a good essentialist, unhesitatingly endorsed the same thesis: "From the above considerations, it appears that species have a real existence in nature; and that each was endowed, at the time of its creation, with the attributes and organization by which it is now distinguished" *(9, p. 21)*. He is even more specific about this in his notebooks *(18, p. 92)*. That species could have full "reality" in the nondimensional situation *(34)* and yet evolve continuously was unthinkable to him. Reality and constancy of species were to him inseparable attributes.

IMPACT OF THE ORIGIN OF SPECIES

The situation changed drastically and permanently with the publication of the *Origin of Species* in 1859. Darwin marshaled the evidence in favor of a transmutation of species so skillfully that from that point on the eventual acceptance of evolutionism was no longer in question. But he did more than that. In natural selection he proposed a mechanism that was far less vulnerable than any other previously proposed. The result was an entirely different concept of evolution. Instead of endorsing the 18th-century concept of a drive toward perfection, Darwin merely postulated change. He saw quite clearly that each species is forever being buffeted around by the capriciousness of the constantly changing environment. "Never use the word(s) higher and lower" *(35)* Darwin reminded himself. By chance this process of adaptation sometimes results in changes that can be interpreted as progress, but there is no intrinsic mechanism generating inevitable advance.

Virtually all the arguments of Cuvier, Lyell, and the progressionists became irrelevant overnight. Essentialism had been the major stumbling block, and the development of a new concept of species was the way to overcome this obstacle. Lyell himself eventually (after 1856) understood that the species problem was the crux of the whole problem of evolution, and that its solution had potentially the most far-reaching consequences: "The ordinary naturalist is not sufficiently aware that, when dogmatizing on what species are, he is grappling with the whole question of the organic world and its connection with a time past and with man" (*18*, p. 1). And, since he came to this conclusion after studying speciation in the Canary Islands, he added: "A group of islands, therefore, is the fittest place for Nature's trial of such permanent variety-making and where the problem of species-making may best be solved" (*18*, p. 93). This is what Darwin had discovered 20 years earlier.

SPECIAL ASPECTS OF THE DARWINIAN REVOLUTION

No matter how one defines a scientific revolution, the Darwinian revolution of 1859 will have to be included. Who would want to question that, by destroying the anthropocentric concept of the universe, it caused a greater upheaval in man's thinking than any other scientific advance since the rebirth of science in the Renaissance? And yet, in other ways, it does not fit at all the picture of a revolution. Or else, how could H. J. Muller have exclaimed as late as 1959: "One hundred years without Darwinism are enough!" *(36)?* And how could books such as Barzun's *Darwin, Marx, Wagner* (1941) and Himmelfarb's *Darwin and the Darwinian Revolution* (1959), both displaying an abyss of ignorance and misunderstanding, have been published relatively recently? Why has this revolution in some ways made such extraordinarily slow headway?

A scientific revolution is supposedly characterized by the replacement of an old explanatory model by an incompatible new one *(1)*. In the case of the theory of evolution, the concept of an instantaneously created world was replaced by that of a slowly evolving world, with man being part of the evolutionary stream. Why did the full acceptance of the new explanation take so long? The reason is that this short description is incomplete, and therefore misleading, as far as the Darwinian revolution is concerned.

Before analyzing this more fully, the question of the date of the Darwinian revolution must be raised. That the year 1859 was a crucial one in its history is not questioned. Yet, this still leaves a great deal of leeway to interpretation. On one

hand, one might assert that the age of evolutionism started even before Buffon, and that the publication of the *Origin* in 1859 was merely the last straw that broke the camel's back. On the other hand, one might go to the opposite extreme, and claim that not much had changed in the thinking of naturalists between the time of Ray and Tournefort and the year 1858, and that the publication of the *Origin* signified a drastic, almost violent revolution. The truth is somewhere near the middle; although there was a steady, and ever-increasing, groundswell of evolutionary ideas since the beginning of the 18th century, Darwin added so many new ideas (particularly an acceptable mechanism) that the year 1859 surely deserves the special attention it has received. Two components of the Darwinian revolution must thus be distinguished: the slow accumulation of evolutionary facts and theories since early in the 18th century, and the decisive contribution which Darwin made in 1859. Together these two components constitute the Darwinian revolution.

The long time span is due to the fact that not simply the acceptance of one new theory was involved, as in some other scientific revolutions, but of an entirely new conceptual world, consisting of numerous separate concepts and beliefs *(37)*. And not only were scientific theories involved, but also a whole set of metascientific credos. Let me prove my point by specifying the complex nature of the revolution: I distinguish six major elements in this revolution, but it is probable that additional ones should be recognized *(32)*.

The first three elements concern scientific replacements:

Age of the Earth

The revolution began when it became obvious that the earth was very ancient rather than having been created only 6000 years ago *(17)*. This finding was the snowball that started the whole avalanche.

Refutation of both Catastrophism (Progressionism) and of a Steady-state World

The evolutionists, from Lamarck on, had claimed that the concept of a more or less steadily evolving world, was in better agreement with the facts than either the catastrophism of the progressionists or Lyell's particular version of a steady-state world. Darwin helped this contention of the evolutionists to its final victory.

Refutation of the Concept of an Automatic Upward Evolution

Every evolutionist before Darwin had taken it for granted that there was a steady progress of perfection in the living world. This belief was a straight-line continuation of the (static) concept of a scale of perfection, which was maintained even by the progressionists for whom each new creation represented a further advance in the plan of the Creator.

Darwin's conclusion, to some extent anticipated by Lamarck, was that evolutionary change through adaptation and specialization by no means necessitated continuous betterment. This view proved very unpopular, and is even today largely ignored by nonbiologists. This neglect is well illustrated by the teachings of the school of evolutionary anthropology, or those of Bergson and Teilhard de Chardin.

The last three elements concern metascientific consequences. The main reason why evolutionism, particularly in its Darwinian form, made such slow progress is that it was the replacement of one entire *weltanschauung* by a different one. This involved religion, philosophy, and humanism.

The Rejection of Creationism

Every antievolutionist prior to 1859 allowed for the intermittent, if not constant, interference by the Creator. The natural causes postulated by the evolutionists completely separated God from his creation, for all practical purposes. The new explanatory model replaced planned teleology by the haphazard process of natural selection. This required a new concept of God and a new basis for religion.

The Replacement of Essentialism and Nominalism by Population Thinking

None of Darwin's new ideas was quite so revolutionary as the replacement of essentialism by population thinking (19-23, 38). It was this concept that made the introduction of natural selection possible. Because it is such a novel concept, its acceptance has been slow, particularly on the European continent and outside biology. Indeed, even today it has by no means universally replaced essentialism.

The Abolition of Anthropocentrism

Making man part of the evolutionary stream was particularly distasteful to the Victorians, and is still distasteful to many people.

NATURE OF THE DARWINIAN REVOLUTION

It is now clear why the Darwinian revolution is so different from all other scientific revolutions. It required not merely the replacement of one scientific theory by a new one, but, in fact, the rejection of at least six widely held basic beliefs [together with some methodological innovations (32)].

Furthermore, it had a far greater relevance outside of science than any of the revolutions in the physical sciences. Einstein's theory of relativity, or Heisenberg's of statistical prediction, could hardly have had any effect on anybody's personal beliefs. The Copernican revolution and Newton's world view required some revision of traditional beliefs. None of these physical theories, however, raised as many new questions concerning religion and ethics as did Darwin's theory of evolution through natural selection.

In a way, the publication of the *Origin* in 1859 was the midpoint of the so-called Darwinian revolution rather than its beginning. Stirrings of evolutionary thinking preceded the *Origin* by more than 100 years, reaching an earlier peak in Lamarck's *Philosophie Zoologique* in 1809. The final breakthrough in 1859 was the climax in a long process of erosion which was not fully completed until 1883 when Weismann rejected the possibility of an inheritance of acquired characters.

As in any scientific revolution, some of the older opponents, such as Agassiz, never became converted. But the Darwinian revolution differed by the large number of workers who accepted only part of the package. Many zoologists, botanists, and paleontologists eventually accepted gradual evolution through natural causes, but not through natural selection. Indeed, on a world-wide basis, those who continued to reject natural selection as the prime cause of evolutionary change were probably well in the majority until the 1930's.

Two conclusions emerge from this analysis. First, the Darwinian and quite likely other scientific revolutions consist of the replacement of a considerable number of concepts. This requires a lengthy period of time, since the new concepts will not all be proposed simultaneously. Second, the mere summation of new concepts is not enough; it is their constellation that counts. Uniformitarianism, when combined with the belief in a static essentialistic world, leads to the steady-state concept of Lyell, while when combined with a concept of change, it leads to the evolutionism of Lamarck. The observation of evolutionary changes, combined with essentialist thinking, leads to various saltationist or progressionist theories, but, combined with population thinking, it leads to Darwin's theory of evolution by natural selection.

It is now evident that the Darwinian revolution does not conform to the simple model of a scientific revolution as described, for instance, by T. S. Kuhn *(1)*. It is actually a complex movement that started nearly 250 years ago; its many major components were proposed at different times, and became victorious independently of each other. Even though a revolutionary climax occurred unquestionably in 1859, the gradual acceptance of evolutionism, with all of its ramifications, covered a period of nearly 250 years *(37)*.

Notes

1. T. S. Kuhn, *The Structure of Scientific Revolutions* (Univ. of Chicago Press, Chicago, 1962).

2. S. Toulmin, *Boston Stud. Phil. Sci.* 3, 333 (1966); I. Lakatos and A. Musgrave, Eds., *Criticism and the Growth of Knowledge* (Cambridge Univ. Press, Cambridge, England, 1970), reviewed by D. Shapere, *Science* 172, 706 (1971).

3. To cite only a few: L. Eiseley, *Darwin's Century* (Doubleday, New York, 1958); B. Glass, O. Temkin, W. L. Straus, Jr., Eds., *Forerunners of Darwin, 1745-1859* (Johns Hopkins Press, Baltimore, 1959); J. C. Greene, *The Death of Adam* (Iowa State Univ. Press, Ames, 1959); W. Zimmer-

mann, *Evolution, Geschichte ihrer Probleme und Erkenntnisse* (Alber, Freiburg, West Germany, 1953); J. C. Greene, "The Kuhnian paradigm and the Darwinian revolution in natural history," in *Perspectives in the History of Science and Technology,* D. H. D. Roller, Ed. (Univ. of Oklahoma Press, Norman, 1971); M. T. Ghiselin, *New Lit. Hist.* 3, 113 (1971).

4. G. de Beer, *Charles Darwin* (Doubleday, Garden City, N.Y., 1964).

5. C. C. Gillispie, *Genesis and Geology* (Harvard Univ. Press, Cambridge, Mass., 1951; rev. ed., Harper & Row, New York 1959).

6. C. Darwin, *On the Origin of Species by Means of Natural Selection* (1859).

7. G. Cuvier, *Essay on the Theory of the Earth* (Edinburgh, ed. 3, 1817); much of it is an implicit refutation of Lamarck's ideas.

8. W. Coleman, *Georges Cuvier, Zoologist* (Harvard Univ. Press, Cambridge, Mass., 1964).

9. C. Lyell, *Principles of Geology* (John Murray, London, 1835), vols. 2 and 3 (I have used ed. 4). Important for British biology because it was the first presentation of Lamarck's theories to the English-speaking world (Book III, chap. I-XI). Darwin had previously heard about Lamarck from R. E. Grant in Edinburgh in 1827 [see *(4,* p. 28)].

10. L. Agassiz, *Essay on Classification* (Little, Brown, Boston, 1857; reprint, Belknap, Cambridge, Mass., 1962).

11. A. O. Lovejoy, "The argument for organic evolution before the *Origin of Species,* 1830-1858," in *Forerunners of Darwin, 1745-1859,* B. Glass, O. Temkin, W. L. Straus, Jr., Eds. (Johns Hopkins Press, Baltimore, 1959), pp. 356-414.

12. A. O. Lovejoy, *The Great Chain of Being* (Harvard Univ. Press, Cambridge, Mass., 1963), Lecture 9.

13. The authorship of the anonymously published *Vestiges of the Natural History of Creation* (1844) did not become known until after the death of Robert Chambers [M. Millhauser, *Just Before Darwin* (Wesleyan Univ. Press, Middletown, Conn., 1959); see also *(5,* chap. 6)]. A sympathetic analysis of the *Vestiges,* that does not concentrate on Chambers' errors and his guillibility, is still wanting [F. N. Egerton, *Stud. Hist. Phil. Sci.* 1, 176 (1971)].

14. F. Darwin, Ed., *Life and Letters of Charles Darwin* (Sources of Science Ser. No. 102; reprint of 1888 ed., Johnson Reprints, New York 1969), vol. 2.

15. H. Fruchtbaum, "Natural theology and the rise of science," thesis, Harvard University (1964).

16. A. Sedgwick, *Edinburgh Rev.* 82, 3 (1845).

17. F. C. Haber, in *Forerunners of Darwin, 1745-1859,* B. Glass, O. Temkin, W. L. Straus, Jr., Eds. (Johns Hopkins Press, Baltimore, 1959), pp. 222-261.

18. L. G. Wilson, Ed., *Sir Charles Lyell's Scientific Journals on the Species Question* (Yale Univ. Press, New Haven, Conn., 1970).

19. K. R. Popper, *The Open Society and its Enemies* (Routledge & Kegan Paul, London, 1945).

20. D. Hull, *Brit. J. Phil. Sci.* 15, 314 (1964); *ibid.* 16, 1 (1965).

21. Aristotle is traditionally included among the essentialists, but newer researches cast considerable doubt on this. There is a growing suspicion that much of the late medieval thought labeled as Aristotelianism, had little to do with Aristotle's actual thinking. See for instance, M. Delbrück, in *Of Microbes and Life,* J. Monod and E. Borek, Eds. (Columbia Univ. Press, New York, 1971), pp. 50-55.

22. E. Mayr, in *Evolution and Anthropology: A Centennial Appraisal* (Anthropological Society of Washington, Washington, D.C., 1959).

23. _____. *Harvard Labr. Bull.* 13, 165 (1959).

24. O. L. Reiser, in *A Book that Shook the World,* R. Buchsbaum, Ed. (Univ. of Pittsburgh Press, Pittsburgh, Pa., 1958).

25. It is impossible in the limited space available to give a full documentation for the refutation of this thesis [see W. Coleman, *Biology in the Nineteenth Century* (Wiley, New York, 1971), p. 63].

26. G. Cuvier, *Essay on the Theory of the Earth,* R. Jameson, Transl. (Edinburgh, ed. 3, 1817). It is frequently stated that Cuvier believed in large-scale creations, necessary to repopulate the globe after major catastrophes, and this may well be true. However, I have been unable to find an unequivocal statement to this effect in Cuvier's writings [see also (*8,* p. 136)].

27. Progressionism was the curious theory according to which evolution did not take place in the organisms but rather in the mind of the Creator, who—after each catastrophic extinction—created a new fauna in the more advanced state to which His plan of creation had progressed in the meantime. This thought was promoted in Britain particularly by Hugh Miller (*Footprints,* 1947), Sedgwick (*Discourse,* 1850), and Murchison (*Siluria,* 1854), and in America by L. Agassiz (*Essay,* 1857); see *(3).*

28. The difference between catastrophism and uniformitarianism became smaller, as it was realized that many of the "catastrophes" had been rather minor events, and that contemporary geological phenomena (earthquakes, volcanic eruptions, tidal waves, glaciation) could have rather catastrophic effects [S. Toulmin, in *Criticism and the Growth of Knowledge,* I. Lakatos and A. Musgrave, Eds. (Cambridge Univ. Press, Cambridge, England, 1970), p. 42].

29. [W. Whewell] *Brit. Critic* 9, 180 (1831); *Quart. Rev.* 47, 103 (1832). For a full discussion of catastrophism see *(5).* A new interpretation of the traditional geological theories which Lyell opposed is given by M. J. S. Rudwick, "Uniformity and progression," in *Perspectives in the History of Science and Technology,* D. H. D. Roller, Ed. (Univ. of Oklahoma Press, Norman, 1971), pp. 209-237.

30. The term uniformitarianism was applied to at least four different concepts, and this caused considerable confusion, to put it mildly. For recent reviews see R. Hooykaas, *Natural Law and Divine Miracle* (E. J. Brill, Leiden, the Netherlands,

1959); S. J. Gould, *Amer. J. Sci.* 263, 223 (1965); C. C. Albritton, Jr., Ed., "Uniformity and simplicity," *Geol. Soc. Amer. Spec. Pap. No. 89* (1967); M. S. J. Rudwick, *Proc. Amer. Phil. Soc.* 111, 272 (1967); G. G. Simpson, "Uniformitarianism," in *Essays in Evolution and Genetics* (Appleton-Century-Crofts, New York, 1970), pp. 43-96. The most important interpretations of uniformitarianism are: the same processes act now as in the past, the magnitude of geological events is as great now as in the past, and the earth a steady-state system.

31. Mrs. Lyell, Ed., *Life, Letters and Journals of Sir Charles Lyell* (John Murray, London, 1881), vol. 1, pp. 467-469 (letter of 1 June 1836 to J. W. Herschel).

32. Darwin's *Origin* was one of the first scientific treatises in which the hypothetico-deductive method was rather consistently employed [M. Ghiselin, *The Triumph of the Darwinian Method* (Univ. of California Press, Berkeley, 1969)]. Equally important, and even more novel, was Darwin's demonstration that deterministic prediction is not a necessary component of causality [M. Scriven, *Science* 130, 477 (1959)]. Perhaps this can be considered a corollary of population thinking, but it is further evidence for the extraordinary complexity of the Darwinian revolution.

33. K. R. Popper, *The Logic of Scientific Discovery* (Hutchison, London, 1959).

34. E. Mayr, Ed., *The Species Problem* (AAAS, Washington, D.C., 1957), p. 2.

35. F. Darwin and A. C. Seward, Eds., *More Letters of Charles Darwin* (reprint of 1903 ed., Johnson Reprints, New York, 1971), vol. 1, p. 114.

36. H. J. Muller, "One hundred years without Darwinism are enough," *School Sci. Math.* 1959, 304 (1959).

37. It remains to be determined to what extent a similar claim can also be made for some of the physical sciences, for instance, the Copernican revolution.

38. In all recent discussions of natural selection, the assumption is made that the concept traces back to the tradition of Adam Smith, Malthus, and Ricardo, with the emphasis on competition and progress. This interpretation overlooks the point that the elimination of "degradations of the type" as the essentialists would call it, does not lead to progress. For the typologist, natural selection is merely the elimination of inferior types, an interpretation again revived by the mutationists (after 1900). Darwin was the first to see clearly that a second factor was necessary, the production of new variation. (This leads to population thinking.) Selection can be creative only when such new individual variation is abundantly available.

39. I greatly benefited from stimulating discussions with S. J. Gould and F. Sulloway, who read a draft of this essay, and from a series of most valuable critical comments, received from Prof. L. G. Wilson, which helped me to correct several errors. My own interpretation, however, still differs in some crucial points from that of Prof. Wilson. Some of the analysis was prepared while I served as Visiting Fellow at the Institute for Advanced Study, Princeton, N.J., in 1970.

The Evolution Game

"We have met the enemy and they are us" (Pogo).

Twenty-five years ago Dr. Paul Fejos, then Director of the Wenner-Gren Foundation for Anthropological Research, suggested that I go to Africa to see fossils and study contemporary Primates. As a result, I found myself visiting Raymond Dart at the University of the Witwatersrand and later, Robert Broom in Pretoria. I have never forgotten how Dart welcomed me into his office and immediately showed me the fossils in his collection. As a student I had heard that it was often very difficult to gain access to original specimens, but no such barrier existed in South Africa, either in Johannesburg or Pretoria. Professor Dart showed me the latest finds and animatedly discussed their meaning. As I was examining the specimens and he was calling my attention to critical points, his tone of voice suddenly changed from excitement to frustration. He pointed to a manuscript on his desk. It had been rejected for publication. I urged Professor Dart to send the paper to the *American Journal of Physical Anthropology*. The editor, T. Dale Stewart, accepted the contribution.

This experience made a deep impression on me. In the study of human evolution, with all the problems of fragmentary specimens, uncertain dates, and theoretical disagreements, where does editorial responsibility end and censorship begin? To make sure that Professor Dart's views got a fair and much more extensive hearing, Dr. Fejos arranged for him to come to the United States. If there had only been a Wenner-Gren Foundation 20 years earlier at the time of the Taung controversies, the correctness of Dart's point of view might have been recognized much sooner.

These events came vividly back to my mind when Phillip Tobias asked me to contribute to his volume, honouring Raymond A. Dart. I will always remember his generosity, hospitality, and his determined courage in presenting his points of view.

By Sherwood L Washburn. Reprinted with permission of Academic Press, Inc., from *Journal of Human Evolution*, 2, 1973, pp. 557-61 Copyright © by Academic Press, Inc.

But the questions of the right to publish and of editorial responsibility are parts of a much wider question. Why was not the original discovery at Taung welcomed, rather than great efforts going into the attempt to prove that it had little to do with human evolution? And later on why was it believed that the pelvis could not have belonged with the skull or that a creature with a small brain could not have made stone tools? In retrospect, I think that it is clear that the general theories of human evolution held prior to the long series of discoveries in South and East Africa made it very difficult for many to adjust to the new information. Rather than the theories being in a form which accelerated the understanding of human evolution, they took a form which tended to create personal controversies and retard progress.

As MacLean (1970) has pointed out, emotion inevitably becomes a part of science because of the construction of the human brain. In commenting on attempts to be completely objective he states, "The irony of all such attitudes is that every behavior selected for study, every observation and interpretation, requires subjective processing by an introspective observer" (p. 337). And later, "Emotional cerebration appears to have the paradoxical capacity to find equal support for opposite sides of any question." Surely these problems are maximized in the study of human evolution where facts are few, often ambiguous, and emotions are strong.

In searching for ways to reduce unnecessary controversy, I have come to think that one of the major causes of futile debate is the illusion of certainty, the illusion of science. For example, in concluding his discussion of the Taung skull Keith stated " . . . leave me in *no doubt* as to the nature of the animal to which the skull formed part; *Australopithecus* was an anthropoid ape" (Keith, 1931, p. 115, italics mine). But surely there was room for doubt. After all, the specimen was a juvenile and differed from apes of comparable age, as Keith recognized. What if the conclusions had been stated differently? Suppose Dart had concluded that, with only a skull and no postcranial bones, the odds were 2 to 1 that the specimen represented a form particularly close to man, and suppose Keith had suggested that the odds were the opposite way. Then both might have supported the need for immediate, extensive excavation of the site. The fact is that the controversies took a form which seemed to discredit Dart and delayed, rather than accelerated, the search for additional fossils.

Keith was a wise man, and these remarks are not intended to be critical of him. Later, when more fossils had been found, he changed his mind, and thought that the "Dartians", as he called *Australopithecus*, were the direct ancestors of subsequent forms of men (Keith, 1949). The point is that the form of scientific publication and the kind of conclusions which are expected of a scientist practically force confrontations of the sort which took place between Dart and Keith. In the study of human evolution truth is a very fickle thing, and we need ways of expressing our opinions, but with some qualification so that it is clear how firmly we hold them, and how ready we are to accept change. That is why I suggest that conclusions might be accompanied by odds, and, whenever possible, alternative ways of looking at the data be presented.

One of the reasons that many found it hard to accept *Australopithecus* was that they considered Piltdown a genuine fossil. If this were the case, then the large brain evolved before the human face and teeth. The skull from Taung showed precisely the opposite, a small brain with very human teeth. I believe that it was this theory that the large human brain evolved early (proven by Piltdown and Galley Hill) that made the acceptance of Taung so difficult. Hooton (1931) and Keith (1931) both believed that modern man, Piltdown, and ancient man (Java, Pekin) lived at the same time at the beginning of the Pleistocene. If this view had been correct, then the separations of various human lines well back into the Pliocene would have been necessary. Certainly that was a reasonable point of view, but the problems came from the certainty with which it was held. For example, Hooton wrote, "The finding of fragments of another Piltdown skull of the same type seems to settle the case of the association of the original jaw with the skull . . . " (1931, p. 314). But Hrdlička had written, "In view of all this it must be plain that any far-fetched deductions from the Piltdown materials are not justified" (1930, p. 89). Clearly, when the experts disagreed, it might have been more helpful to put the conclusions in terms of odds, rather than absolute conclusions and for both groups to urge large-scale, supervised excavations.

The essential points are two. First, the controversies took attention away from the necessity for more excavation. They slowed progress toward the solution of the problem (Weiner, 1955). Second, these scientists knew that there would be more finds, progress, and that opinions would be modified. But it was just where they were sure that they were right that they were wrong. Hooton (1946) defended Piltdown with the same zeal with which Weidenreich (1946) attacked the "chimera".

Surely, as one looks back over the controversies on human evolution, particularly as reflected in the life of Raymond Dart (Dart with Craig, 1959), the conviction grows that there must be a better way, a way which reduces the personal controversies and maximizes the support for research and for progress. For example, in retrospect, I have usually agreed with Professor Dart. But I have never found the case for an osteodontokeratic culture very convincing. A few years ago when I published some notes on the subject, it would have been much clearer if I had stated that my opinion was 2 to 1 against the view that most of the bones had been used as tools. This would have shown my opinion, but clearly indicated that there was a very strong possibility that I was wrong. Recently, the studies by Sutcliffe (1970) suggest that, since hyenas sometimes collect bones, the odds might be raised to 10 to 1. But this still states that, in my opinion, Dart may be right, and that a few of the bones may have been used as tools. Again, just as in the case of Taung or Piltdown, the necessary research was not done for many years after the issues had been raised. Our tradition of science and of publication led to acceptance of the osteodontokeratic culture, or to its rejection. Obviously it would have been useful if the issues had been stated in terms of odds, and if there had been agreement on the research which was necessary to shift the odds one way or the other.

In retrospect it seems to me that progress would have come more rapidly and with less controversy if the study of human evolution had been regarded as a game, rather than as a science. The study is a serious game, but the theory of natural selection commits the players to a point of view which is very far from laboratory science. If the course of evolution were determined by reproductive success of populations of long ago, we can only guess at the important events of evolution through reconstruction. It is not the fossil bones as such which are important, but the clues they give about the populations long extinct. These reconstructions contain very large subjective elements, and, if we regard evolution as a game, then this fact must be considered, and we must be explicit as to the rules which are used in the reconstructions. How far we are from agreement on the rules is well shown in Zuckerman's "Myths and Methods in Anatomy" (1966).

It is only an illusion to suppose that there are "facts" upon which we must agree and which force us to some particular theory of human evolution. The danger of the traditional "scientific" approach is that it gives people the illusion of security. For example, in the preceding paragraph, I spoke of a theory of evolution which committed scientists to one way of interpreting the record. But molecular biology has raised the issue of at least some substantial parts of the process of evolution depending on changes which are adaptively neutral. The probability of non-adaptive characters is open again, and how much Darwinian evolution will have to be modified is uncertain.

There are beliefs at the present time which may be barriers to progress, much as the theories of a half a century ago hindered the acceptance of *Australopithecus*. Only a few years ago continental drift was regarded as impossible, and the distribution of fossils was used to prove that this was the case. Today the rates that lands drift have been measured, and continental drift is used to explain the same distributions of fossils which formerly proved that it was impossible. Drift suggests that there may be three major changes in the assumptions about primate evolution. First, it was assumed that the South American Primates were descended from North American prosimians and that the separation from Old World forms must be at least 50 million years, and probably a good deal more. Only last year I heard this "fact" used to prove the impossibility of the much later time which Sarich (1971) had suggested for the separation of

these forms. Sarich suggested that the ancestors of the New World had rafted across the ocean from Africa before the two continents had drifted too far apart. This point of view is now supported by Hoffstetter (1972), who points to a similar African-South American connection for the caviomorph rodents. Continental drift makes it possible to fit the immunological information with a time of origin for the New World Primates which seemed impossible only a short time ago.

A second major change in thinking about Primate evolution which comes with continental drift is the position of Africa in the process. Before approximately 18-20 million years ago, Africa was more separated from Eurasia than traditionally believed. At a later time the Mediterranean basin was a vast area below sea level with numerous fresh water lakes (Hsü 1972). Seven or eight million years ago Africa was not separated, and Primates might have moved freely over vast areas which are now under water. Recently there has been a tendency to emphasize Africa and the African origin of man. But such thinking may be only a reflection of where the fossils have been found and of the influence of present-day geography. Suppose a genus of apes had inhabited the area of what is now India, the Near East, the Mediterranean basin and parts of Europe and Africa. As time proceeded, the area was divided by the flooding of the Mediterranean and desiccation in large areas. Two species of apes persisted in what became a very distinctive faunal area in Africa, and an Indian and Near Eastern species evolved into man. Such a model may fit the facts as well as the African origin one, and in addition accounts for the lack of apes in India. My point is not to argue that this must have been the case, but only to point out that the geography was very different, and the claim that man "must" have originated in Africa may have as little foundation as the earlier one that man "must" have evolved in Asia.

The third major change which comes from both continental drift and potassium-argon method of dating, is the short Pliocene (Van Couvering, 1972). If it was the flooding of the Mediterranean basin 5.5 million years ago which marks the end of the Miocene, then the generally accepted dates for the beginning of the Pliocene (12 million) are much too old. Again it has been argued that a late origin of man was impossible because we "know" that it must have been late Miocene at the very latest and that means more than 10 million years ago. But if a time span of 6-10 million years ago are late Miocene, then it may be possible to reconcile the late time of origin of the human lineage with the palaeontological information. The issue is not who is right or wrong now, but that the traditional origin of the New World Primates from North America, the separation of the present-day African fauna, and the supposed length of the Pliocene all worked together to form a set of objections to the molecular and immunological data. All of this suggests a recent origin of man (whatever that may prove to be in millions of years).

Just as the climate of opinion made it very difficult for the scientific community to accept Professor Dart's claims for *Australopithecus*, so the present climate of opinion makes it hard to include recent advances in the evolution game. And, probably, just as in the case of the Taung skull, the objections are based on "facts" which everyone accepted a few years ago and which are not facts at all.

Again, returning to the paper by MacLean (1970), "Differing groups of reputable scientists, for example, often find themselves in altercation because of diametrically opposed views of what is true. Although seldom commented on, it is equally bewildering that the world of science is able to live comfortably for years, and sometimes centuries, with beliefs that a new generation discovers to be false. How is it possible that we are able to build higher and higher on the foundations of such beliefs without fear of their sudden collapse?" (p. 337). MacLean finds the answer in the peculiar nature of the human brain, an organ which inevitably mixes knowledge (science), with emotion, and which exists only in a social situation, in a moment of human history.

The essential point is that the human brain is the product of a particular evolution. It evolved because it was a successful organ of adaptation. It did not evolve to rationally perceive truth, in any other sense. It is particularly in the study of human evolution where the facts are so few compared to what we all desire that the emotional character of the theories comes to the fore. That is why it is useful to regard the study of human evolution as a game, a game with uncertain rules, and with only the fragments to represent the long-dead players. It will be many years before the game becomes a science, before we can be sure of what constitutes the "facts".

References

Dart, R. A. (with D. Craig) (1959). *Adventures with the Missing Link*. New York: Harper.

Hoffstetter, R. (1972). Relationships, origins and history of the ceboid monkeys and caviomorph rodents. In (Th. Dobzhansky, Ed.), *Evolutionary Biology* 6, 323-347. New York: Appleton-Century-Crofts.

Hooton, E. A. (1931). *Up from the Ape*. New York: Macmillan Company.

Hooton, E. A. (1946). *Up from the Ape*. Revised edition. New York: Macmillan Company.

Hrdlička, A. (1930). *The Skeletal Remains of Early Man*. Smithsonian Miscellaneous Collection 83. City of Washington: Smithsonian Institution.

Hsü, K. J. (1972). When the Mediterranean dried up. *Scientific American* (December), 26-36.

Keith, A. (1931). *New Discoveries Relating to the Antiquity of Man*. London: William & Norgate.

Keith A. (1949). *A New Theory of Human Evolution*. New York: Philosophical Library, London: Watts.

MacLean, P. D. (1970). The triune brain, emotion, and scientific bias. In (F. O. Schmitt, Ed.), *The Neurosciences: Second Study Program*, pp. 336-349. New York: Rockefeller University Press.

Sarich, V. M. (1971). A molecular approach to the question of human origins. In (P. Dolhinow & V. M. Sarich, Eds), *Background for Man*, pp. 60-81. Boston: Little, Brown and Company.

Sutcliffe, A. J. (1970). Spotted hyaena: crusher, gnawer, digester, and collector of bones. *Nature* 227, 1110-1113.

Van Couvering, J. A. (1972). Radiometric calibration of the European Neogene. In (W. W. Bishop & J. A. Miller, Eds), *Calibration of Hominoid Evolution*, pp. 247-271. Edinburgh: Scottish Academic Press.

Weidenreich, F. (1946). *Apes, Giants and Man*. Chicago: University of Chicago Press.

Weiner, J. S. (1955). *The Piltdown Forgery*. London: Oxford University Press.

Wilson, A. C. & Sarich, V. M. (1969). A molecular time scale for human evolution. *Proceedings of the National Academy of Sciences* 63, 1088-1093.

Zuckerman, S. (1966). Myths and methods in anatomy. *Journal of the Royal College of Surgeons of Edinburgh* 11, 87-114.

High Points of Human Genetics

Human genetics is a child of general genetics. It had its origin in Mendel's experiments with the garden pea. Human genetics has profited from advances made in the general field and it has at times added its own contributions to those derived from the studies of many varieties of plants, animals, and microorganisms. In this paper I will discuss a number of topics all dealing with genetic phenomena in man. These topics have been chosen from a large number of possible ones and no specific system underlies their choice. Some of them represent very recent findings, some go back for a hundred years. My method of selection follows Moussorgsky's procedure in his composition "Pictures at an Exhibition." The visitor to the exhibition will choose for study here a large and there a small picture, here a colorful and there a somber mood, and here a sketch and there a detailed painting. Yet, there is a unity to the whole that binds its parts together as high points of human genetics.

CHROMOSOMES

Let us begin with the chromosomes of man. The first time the mammalian chromosomes were pictured was in 1865. In that year the anatomist Henle published drawings of cells from the testes of a cat. Some of these cells exhibited short rod-like structures in their interior, others lacked them. Henle did not attempt to interpret these structures. The process of mitosis was not yet understood and the varying configurations which the content of the nucleus assumes during mitotic cell division were only slowly recognized as successive stages of a dynamic process. The first drawings of *human* cells in stages of division were published in 1879. They showed dividing cells of a tumor, but the drawings were greatly schematized and unsuitable for an analysis of the mitotic events. Five years later, from better preparations, Flemming described and

By Curt Stern. Reprinted with permission, from *The American Biology Teacher,* 37, No. 3, March 1975, pp. 144-49.

pictured mitoses in normal human tissue. Some 20 "nuclear ribbons" long and short, of V, J, and rod-shape were distinguishable.

The structures of the cellular nucleus whose behavior define mitosis had been given various names, such as chromatic elements, caryosomes, primary ribbons, and others. It occurred to the anatomist Waldeyer (1888) to coin a new word: *chromosome.* "If this designation is useful in practice," he stated, "then it will be assimilated into the language. If not may it soon fall into oblivion."

Now a new question arose: How many chromosomes are altogether typically present in a human cell? No one had counted them, not even Flemming. In 1898, however, Flemming went back to the only slide left to him after nearly 20 years and, with improved optics and cautious hesitation, concluded that somatic cells have certainly more than 22 and probably less than 28 chromosomes and that 24 seemed to be the true number.

There were many who were not convinced that the number of human chromosomes had been definitely established. Numbers as low as 8 and as high or higher than 40 were reported by successions of investigators. The most thorough investigations of their time indicated that the chromosome number of man was 48 in the female and either 47 or 48 in the male. For several decades the textbook answer to "how many chromosomes has man?" was "48 or 47"; but in 1956 it was proven that this answer was wrong. Tijio and Levan had made cultures of human embryonic tissue. Their superb preparations showed beyond a doubt that the correct answer is "46."

Why did it take a century until a count of chromosomes finally established to everyone's satisfaction that the number is 46? The cytologists of that era were among the leaders of biology. Why then did the actual number of human chromosomes escape them? It must seem strange to a noncytologist and even to cytologists used to the large chromosomes of grasshoppers, lilies, and indeed most multicellular organisms that the number of human chromosomes had not been settled many years prior to 1956. It was a matter of technique which accounted for the delay. The chromosomes of warm blooded animals are relatively numerous and crowded in a small nuclear volume. After use of standard fixation techniques, they not only lie on top of one another in the optical axis of the microscope but often clump together. Even an experienced microscopist will frequently be unable to decide whether at certain places he has one single bent chromosome before his eyes or two straight ones. The way out of these ambiguities involved some simple experimentation. Pretreatment of the cells with hypotonic solutions enlarges the nucleus durng mitosis so that chromosomes are distributed over a greater area than normal, and a simultaneous pretreatment with colchicine contracts the chromosomes. Thus, the occurrence of optical overlaps of chromosomes is greatly reduced.

I have told the story of the chromosome number of man in some detail to show the obstacles which may have to be overcome even in deciding simple issues. Was it worth the effort which finally succeeded in establishing the number 46? It was satisfying to know the truth, but the truth did not appear important. Yet it took only three years until it was shown that knowledge of the chromosome number of man included the key to an understanding of the origin of the most frequent single specific birth defect in man—Down's syndrome, formerly called mongolism. Infants exhibiting the manifold anatomical features of this syndrome and the variable but severe mental deficiencies have 47 chromosomes. Numbering the chromosomes of a normal individual according to size from 1 to 23, each normal person has two chromosomes of each kind adding up to 46. The 47th chromosome, which distinguishes a Down's individual from normal, is of the class number 21—a fact which has been the basis for sometimes calling Down's syndrome 21-trisomy.

Down's syndrome is not the only abnormality which is characterized by an abnormal number of chromosomes. There are men with 47 chromosomes, one of which is an extra X chromosome, and there are women with only 45 chromosomes, lacking one of the two X chromosomes which are present in normal females. Many other abnormal chromosome constitutions have been found in abnormal infants, most of whom are physically and mentally severely abnormal.

The knowledge that Down's syndrome is due to the presence of an extra chromosome does not lead immediately to means of preventing or curing the syndrome. One can foresee, however, that progress in this direction will be furthered.

SOMATIC CELL HYBRIDS

Geneticists have often regretted the fact that crosses between different species, particularly taxonomically distant species, usually do not succeed. Had I been asked whether one can cross man and mouse, I would have smiled wisely and listed many arguments against the possibility of such a cross. These arguments would have included discussion of fertilization and development. If I had been offered a bet that hybridization between man and mouse is possible I would not have hesitated to accept it. I would have lost! One cannot fertilize human eggs with mouse sperm, or mouse eggs with human sperm, but one can fuse somatic cells of one species with somatic cells of another. The somatic hybrid cells in such cases have a nucleus which contains the sum of the human and mouse chromosomes, $46 + 40 = 86$. The cells can divide and give rise to a strain of hybrid cells. In hindsight the success of somatic hybridization is not so surprising. The chromosomes of man and mouse, indeed of all eucaryotic species, are very similar in biochemical make-up. The cytoplasm of the fusing cells of the hybridizing species must be similar in many respects. Why should one not think of the cytoplasm as a good culture medium in which the chromosomes grow and replicate? They do so, indeed, although there are impediments in the way.

In tissue cultures of the hybrid cells the latter lose chromosomes, resulting in cells with a variety of chromosome mixtures and numbers. From there, cell cultures have been obtained that possess all mouse chromosomes but only one or a few human chromosomes. In a specific test all cells died that did not have a gene for the enzyme thymidine kinase. Cytological inspection showed that all surviving cells contained at least one human chromosome number 17. The ability to form thymidine kinase is thus dependent on a gene located in chromosome 17.

Somatic cell hybrids thus can be used to assign genetic markers to their specific chromosome. This may appear a laborious method to determine the location of genes in specific chromosomes. When one considers the slowness of progress in the assignment of specific genes to their specific chromosomes, one is greatly impressed by the wholesale determination of gene localization by means of somatic cell hybrids. It may be pointed out, however, that these gene-chromosome assignments tell us only that a specific gene is localized somewhere in a specific chromosome but they do not enable us to construct a chromosome map on which the gene occupies a specific locus.

ASCERTAINMENT

At this point we shall leave consideration of chromosomal aspects of human genetics and look at two high points which involve statistical and population genetical features. Shortly after the turn of the century it had become clear that albinism in man is due to a recessive gene, inherited in typical Mendelian manner. Ideally one would expect in this case that the marriage of two heterozygous parents would result in a 3:1 ratio of normal to albino offspring. It was obvious that chance would see to it that the 3:1 ratio would not be found among the offspring of every individual pair of parents. If, for instance, there are four children in each family, one family may have four nonalbino children and no albino; another family may have 3 normal and 1 albino child; and still another family may have 2 normal and 2 albino children and so on till finally all four children would be albinos. Thus there are some families in which the 3:1 ratio actually would appear and other families in which too many or too few albinos would be found. It was expected that pooling the data from many families should result in an average value of three normal to one albino out of four children, that is, 25% albinos.

HARDY-WEINBERG EQUILIBRIUM

When Bateson, the British fighter for Mendelism, pooled the data on the frequency of albinos obtained by various investigators he found that the average frequency of homozygous recessives from matings of normal parents to one another

persistently is higher than 25%. He could not account for the discrepancy between expectation and observation although he hinted at the explanation. It remained to the German physician Weinberg to furnish the full explanation. He recognized that there are two kinds of matings which result in normal offspring only. One kind would have parental genotypes AA x AA, or AA x Aa which cannot produce any aa children since their genotypes do not lead to homozygosity for albinism. The other kind of matings which result in normal offspring only would be the kind Aa x Aa which is capable of producing aa children but in which chance is responsible for the absence of albino children. By pooling only the offspring of all unions which resulted in at least one albino, one leaves out of consideration the offspring of those other unions which by chance resulted in nonalbino offspring only. When the offspring of these unions are added to the pooled data one finds indeed that the observed ratio of normals to albinos agrees with expectation since the higher than 3:1 ratio in the raw data is transformed by the addition of the normals to a ratio of 3:1.

Weinberg was not only the first student of human genetics who realized the biases which selection of data may introduce; he also invented methods of correcting for these biases in the ascertainment of data.

The work of the early geneticists of this century dealt primarily with inheritance in individual families. More recently much attention is being paid to population genetics which deals, as the name indicates, with inheritance in groups of individuals. Mendel himself had considered a problem in population genetics. Starting with a single individual heterozygous for a gene, A^1A^2 and assuming self-fertilization as it occurs in peas, Mendel asked the question, What kinds of genotype and in what proportions will they be found in successive generations of the offspring of the A^1A^2 parent? Mendel showed that the resulting population would vary from one generation to the next. Thus the first uniform generation A^1A^2 would be replaced by a second generation of 3 genotypes $A^1A^1:2A^1A^2:A^2A^2$ in the proportion 1:2:1, the second generation by the same genotype in the proportion 3:2:3 and after n generations in the proportion 2n-1:2:2n-1.

In cross fertilizing species, different results

were expected. What they were was demonstrated by a famous mathematician in answer to a thoughtless question of a distinguished statistician. On 28 February 1908, Bateson's colleague R. C. Punnett gave a lecture before the Royal Society of Medicine in London entitled "Mendelism in Relation to Disease." In the discussion which followed the lecture and which is reported in the printed *Proceedings* the well known statistician G. H. Yule referred to some of the figures illustrating the Mendelian cases which puzzled him very much. He commented:

Assuming that brown . . . eye color was dominant over blue, if matings of persons of different eye colors were random . . . it was to be expected that in the population there would be three persons with brown eyes to one with blue; but that was not so . . . The same applied to the examples of brachydactyly. The author said brachydactyly was dominant. In the course of time one would expect . . . to get three brachydactylous persons to one normal, but that was not so.

Now it was the occasion for Punnett to be puzzled. He reworded, somewhat inaccurately, Yule's comments as "Mr. Yule wondered why the nation was not slowly becoming brown-eyed and brachydactylous . . . " and replied "so it might be for all he knew but this made no difference to the mode of transmission of eye color or brachydactyly." Punnett, however, did not feel content with his own comment. On his return to Cambridge he at once sought out the mathematician G. H. Hardy whom he knew well. "Knowing that Hardy had not the slightest interest in genetics I [Punnett] put my problem to him as a mathematical one. He replied that it was quite simple and soon handed to me the now well-known formula . . . Naturally pleased at getting so neat and prompt an answer I promised him that it should be known as Hardy's Law—a promise fulfilled in the next edition of my *Mendelism*."

The essence of Hardy's findings is the constancy of the distribution of the three genotypes *AA, Aa,* and *aa* whatever the frequencies of the two alleles may be. Specifically Hardy showed through two examples that the proportion of brachydactylous persons, if the trait is dominant, will have no tendency whatever to increase and, if it is recessive, would have no tendency to decrease.

It has been said that nature yields answers only to correctly formulated questions. Hardy's solution to Yule's difficulty shows that wrong questions may sometimes be fruitful also.

Hardy's Law remained known under this designation until 1943 when it was realized that, independently of Hardy and indeed at least six weeks prior to Hardy's involvement in genetics, Weinberger had presented the equivalent formula before the Society for Natural History in Stuttgart. The names of both the discoveries are now attached to the population formula: the Hardy-Weinberg Law.

BIOCHEMICAL GENETICS

Gene action at the molecular level includes transcription of DNA into RNA, translation of RNA into amino acid sequences, as well as the biochemistry of subsequent chains of reactions. Normal and mutant genes can be used as probes which enter into the chemical reactions at specific stages in the development of the individual or in experimental tissue cultures. Let us consider a few examples. The first is the genetics and biochemistry of Tay-Sachs disease (infantile amaurotic idiocy). Infants with this condition show developmental retardation during the first months of life which is followed by paralysis, dementia, and blindness, with death in the second of third year of life. The genetic basis is a recessive gene *(t)*. It affects the activity of hexosaminidase, an enzyme which is involved in the metabolism of complex fatty substances called gangliosides. When the overall activity of hexosaminidase is measured no significant difference in the activity is found in three genotypes *TT, Tt,* and *tt*. When the enzyme is partitioned into two components, A and B, it is found that all three genotypes uniformly have high activity of component B but different activities of component A. Affected infants seem to lack A enzyme, normal homozygotes have high enzyme A activity, and heterozygotes are intermediate. Hexosaminidase assays can be made early in pregnancy with fetal amniotic fluid cells. This permits early diagnosis of the homozygous recessive genotype.

A fascinating inborn error of development is the syndrome of testicular feminization. It consists in the development of a phenotype which externally is typically that of a normal female. Internally, however, instead of ovaries, testes are present as well as derivatives of the wolffian ducts. The affected individuals are XY as in normal males. The syndrome is clearly genetic. Females carrying the gene are normal in having two X chromosomes and their phenotype is that of normal females, but males carrying the gene are feminized.

It might have been suspected that the paradoxical contrast between internal presence of testes and external feminine appearance was due to secretion of abnormal male sex hormone. It was found, however, that this hormone, testosterone, is normal. In male embryos it is converted by a hydroxylase to dihydrotestosterone. In testicular feminization the hydroxylase is absent so that no dihydrotestosterone is formed. As a result the embryo fails to respond to the testicular hormone and develops as a phenotypical female.

In recent years immunological phenomena have attracted the attention of a variety of investigators including immunogeneticists. Here we shall not cite some of the remarkable findings made in the molecular analysis of immunological phenomena but outline an example of genetically based immunological interaction between mother and child. It concerns the gene *R* and its role in often causing a hemolytic disease of newborn babies. Typically the disease affects only infants whose mother has the genotype *rr* for absence of an Rh antigen and who themselves are *Rr* and do form the Rh antigen. The disease is the result of a mother-child interaction during pregnancy. Some of the fetus' blood with Rh antigen finds its way into the mother's blood where it stimulates the production of anti-Rh antibody. This antibody does not harm the blood cells of the *rr* mother since they lack the Rh antigen. When, however, the antibody finds its way back to the blood of the fetus an immunological reaction between the antibody and the red cells of the fetus may take place, resulting in the newborn's disease.

When more than 30 years ago the causes of the hemolytic disease were recognized, ways were found to cure the illness, such as giving certain types of blood transfusions. Many, but by no means all, lives were saved that way and research was undertaken to prevent any initial illness rather than to treat children who already were sick.

For months C. A. Clarke, his wife, and his group in Liverpool had puzzled over the problem. Then, Clarke relates, one night he was awakened by his wife who said, "Give them anti-Rh." Irritated by being disturbed in deep sleep, he replied: "It is anti-Rh we are trying to *prevent* them from making," and went to sleep again. The next morning, however, the idea made sense. If, at the right time, anti-Rh is given to a pregnant *rr* women it will destroy any Rh-positive blood cells that she might acquire across the placenta from an Rh-positive fetus. The right time for this procedure, it became apparent, is a short period around the time of the child's birth. During most of the pregnancy not enough red cells leak from the child to the mother to stimulate the production of anti-Rh antibodies. Most of the leakage occurs shortly before or during birth. Injection of anti-Rh within up to 72 hours after birth will result in destruction of leaked Rh positive cells before they have a chance to lead to anti-Rh production by the mother. Use of the method of anti-Rh injection has practically reduced the danger of Rh disease to zero. The method represents a striking example of the collaboration of different branches of knowledge, Mendelian analysis, immunology, and physiology in solving problems affecting human health.

BARR BODIES AND DOSAGE COMPENSATION

Twenty-five years ago Barr and Bertram noticed that many cell nuclei of some cats possess a special, small, stainable body that is not present in most nuclei of other cats. The cats with the "Barr body" were females, those without it males. It was soon established that human females, like cats, have Barr bodies while human males lack them. Later cytological evidence showed that the Barr body constitutes one of the two X chromosomes of the female. Instead of uncoiling during the stage between two consecutive mitoses, this chromosome remains condensed and appears as the Barr body. There is much evidence that a condensed chromosome is not active. This means that of the two X chromosomes of a female only one is active. In males which have only a single X chromosome this chromosome is active and no Barr body is present.

At the chromosome level males and females are distinguished by the total number of X chromosomes, the "doses of X chromosomes" being respectively 1 and 2. At the genetic activity level the two sexes are alike since there is a cellular mechanism, inactivation of one of the X chromosomes of the female, which compensates for the different doses of the X-chromosomes in males and females.

THE SINGLE-ACTIVE-X THEORY

The single-active-X theory, often called after its foremost architect the Mary Lyon Theory, is supported by a large and increasing body of evidence. Females heterozygous for a recessive X-linked gene often are mosaics composed of regions exhibiting the effects of the recessive allele and regions showing the effects of the dominant genes. This suggests that in some embryonic cells the X chromosome with the dominant gene, and in other embryonic cells the X-chromosome with the recessive gene, has been inactivated. Furthermore, the fact that the mosaic areas are large indicates that the determination as to which X chromosome will form a Barr body is made early in development and that, once established, it is irrevocable.

An example of the mosaicism of females heterozygous for an X-linked recessive gene is that for "anhidrotic ectodermal dysplasia." In males this gene reduces greatly the number of sweat glands and causes very incomplete development of the teeth. Heterozygous females have large patches of skin without or with low numbers of sweat glands as well as jaws mosaic for normal and abnormal teeth.

A particularly impressive further example of evidence for the single-active-X chromosome theory concerns the behavior of the enzyme G-6-PD in electrophoresis. There are two variants of this enzyme, designated A and B. Tissue cultures from females heterozygous for both A and B all show an intermediate electrophoretic pattern but when a number of tissue cultures were studied whose cells had each been derived from

a single cell forming a "clone" it was found that none of them had both A and B while the nine clones consisted of three A and six B. In other words, in three clones the single active X was A and in six clones it was B.

The formation of Barr bodies as well as the single active-X chromosome determination are examples of genetically based cellular control mechanisms. Such mechanisms play a role in the fundamental processes of developmental genetics.

BEHAVIORAL GENETICS

It is found in every population, human or non-human, that the individuals vary from each other in many ways. Often the differences within a population are small, sometimes they are striking, in form and function, in static properties and in behavior. How much of this variation is based on differences of genotypes? How much is based on differences in environmental agents which influenced the development of individuals? How much is due to interactions of genetic and environmental functions? These questions have probably been asked as long as human beings have existed. There are no absolute answers. Two persons may be different in some traits for purely genetic reasons while two other persons may be different in these same traits for environmental reasons. Or, two persons may be alike genetically but unlike phenotypically.

The latter situation applies in most general terms to identical twins. It yields to an unconditional statement of fact: all differences between identical twins are the result of environmental influences which impinged at some stage in the development of the twins. For other situations no a priori statement can be made regarding the partitioning of the variance into genetic and environmental causes. The general patterns of genetic and environmental contributions to the variability of "traits" in human populations apply to physical traits as well as mental ones. In the latter case we speak of behavioral genetics. Let us consider a few examples.

There is a rare syndrome named after Lesch and Nyhan which affects male children and which consists of constantly recurring series of slow movements of the hands and feet, severe mental deficiency, compulsive aggressive behavior towards others, and extreme self-destruction by chewing of lips and fingers. This abnormal behavior is associated with excessive purine synthesis leading to a type of gout. It is caused by deficiency of an enzyme that participates in purine metabolism. The whole syndrome is the effect of an X-linked recessive gene. This extreme of antisocial gene-dependent behavior suggests that other genotypes may be instrumental in the causation of lesser degrees and different types of deviant behavior.

We are now acquainted with a number of phenomena which provide unequivocal evidence for genetic determination of mental performance within the more or less normal range. For example, deviations from the normal sex-chromosome number result in some lowering of mental function. Many persons with such unbalanced chromosomal constitutions are normal, and only statistical comparisons show that on the average they are somewhat lower in mental ability. Among these kinds of individuals are women with only one X chromosome and women with three X chromosomes as well as men with XXY constitution. It would have been difficult to prove the genetic basis of some of these slight impairments of mental performance had they not occurred as by-products of readily recognizable chromosome aberrations. The discovery of the genetic basis under these circumstances justifies the conviction that other genotypes more difficult to analyze are involved in similar slight variations in mental function.

Progress in behavioral genetics extends to mental illness, particularly schizophrenia. It has been known for many years that the frequency of schizophrenia in close relatives of affected individuals is increased over that in control populations. This information by itself is subject to either a genetic or an environmental interpretation. The increased frequency of the disease in relatives could be due to the fact that relatives have similar genotypes which make them predisposed to the disease. Alternatively, the increased incidence of the disease in relatives could be interpreted as a consequence of environmental factors which also are more similar in relatives than unrelated controls.

In order to determine whether there is a genetic component in schizophrenia some specific methods were used. One of these methods consisted in a comparison of individuals all of whom had been born to schizophrenic mothers with a carefully matched control group of individuals whose mothers had not been affected. Both groups of individuals had been placed soon after birth into adoptive or foster homes. The question asked was this: Will the children of affected mothers after having reached adulthood show a rather high frequency of schizophrenia as compared to the offspring of control mothers, or will those frequencies be lower? The data strongly point to the first alternative. Notwithstanding the rather similar environments from early life of the children of affected mothers and those of healthy mothers, the adult offspring of the affected mothers was significantly more frequently schizophrenic than that of the controls. This points to a genetic component of the disease.

In a similar study cases were found in vital statistics records of individuals who as infants had been placed in adoptive homes and who later had developed schizophrenia or related disorders. In this study the frequencies of the illness in the biological and the adoptive relatives of the index cases were determined. The data showed that the frequencies in the biological relatives were significantly higher than in a control group consisting of the relatives of unaffected adopted individuals.

This kind of evidence for a genetic component of schizophrenia does not yield unequivocal information on the type of inheritance which is involved in the trait under consideration. It establishes the involvement of genetic factors.

GENETICS SERVING HUMANITY

Human genetics is a foremost example of science serving humanity. Initially, human genetics had to lay the groundwork of systematic knowledge of the genetics of its unique organism, man. Once attained, specific areas of human genetics became the domain of human genetics counseling. If, for instance, a child suffering from Tay-Sachs disease had been born to a pair of parents, a genetic counselor was able to predict to the parents that the probability of a recurrence of this fatal disease in any subsequent infant was 1 in 4 or 25%. Again, if a child bearing the signs of Down's syndrome had been born, the counselor could predict a much lower incidence that a later born child would be affected than in the Tay-Sachs example. In the case of Down's syndrome the counselor could go further. He knew from established evidence that chromosomally there are two main kinds of Down's syndrome. The relatively frequent kind shows the presence of a typical free supernumerary chromosome 21. In the less frequent kind the supernumerary is not free but is permanently translocated to some chromosome other than 21. Down's syndrome caused by the presence of a free third chromosome 21 only very rarely occurs more than once in a kinship. By contrast the translocated chromosome represents a built-in mechanism for the reconstitution of a third chromosome 21. Study of the chromosome 21 in affected persons permits a decision as to whether a recurrence of the syndrome is very unlikely or whether allowance should be made for the likelihood of recurrence.

In the past human genetic counseling has usually been given in terms of probability. In recent years a method has been worked out which in many instances provides certainty. This method, called amniocentesis, consists of withdrawing some fluid from the amniotic sac which surrounds the fetus in a pregnant woman. The fluid contains cells derived from the fetus which can be cultured and studied to determine the presence or absence of a biochemical marker or of a chromosomal abnormality. In Tay-Sachs disease the presence of the enzyme hexosaminidase A assures with certainty normality of the develop-

ing child while absence of the enzyme implies certainty of the child's abnormal fetal constitution. Similarly, the visible presence of a third chromosome 21 signifies to the parents with certainty that a Down's syndrome child is developing.

What can be done with these facts? The answers to this question vary. If the cytological or biochemical diagnosis is that the child will be normal, the concern of the parents supposedly facing a high risk of producing an abnormal offspring can be relieved. If the diagnosis reveals an affected fetus, then a therapeutic termination of pregnancy would be advocated by many persons, including many parents and many physicians. However, there are legal, ethical, and psychological considerations which are not judged uniformly by different individuals or groups of persons. The borderline between those who are in principle in favor of abortion of fetuses destined to develop into severely abnormal children and those who in principle condemn it is not sharply drawn and is subject to change with changes of the climate of opinion.

Human genetics' service to humanity of course is not limited to amniocentesis and counseling. It deals with the immense manifoldness by means of which a single cell may develop into a specific human being, with the potentiality of sex determination, with effects of radiation and of chemical agents on mutation, with selection in populations, with critical awareness of problems of eugenics and dysgenics, and many others. Human genetics adds perspectives to our explorations of man. It gives us a modicum of choice in our future where none existed before.

Our Close Cousin, the Chimpanzee

Until recently many biologists assumed that the evolution of organisms was based predominantly on mutations in the genes coding for proteins (that is, the structural genes). Another possibility, however, is that mutations in genes that control the expression of the structural genes play the major part in adaptive evolution. In this article we argue that comparative studies with chimpanzees and human beings provide evidence showing that the evolution of organisms may depend predominantly on regulatory mutations.

During the past decade many biologists participated in the development and application of biochemical methods for comparing the genes of different species. These methods include the comparison of nucleic acids by annealing techniques and the comparison of proteins by electrophoretic, immunological and sequencing techniques. The only two species which have been compared by all of these methods are chimpanzees and humans. This pair of species is also unique because of the thoroughness with which they have been compared at the organismal level (that is, at the level of anatomy, physiology, behaviour and ecology). This therefore presents a good opportunity for finding out whether the various biochemical estimates of gene resemblance are consistent and whether the molecular and organismal estimates of resemblance agree.

The most direct method available for comparing chimpanzee and human genes is DNA hybridisation, a technique that measures the similarity between different DNA's. Several researchers have measured the thermal stability of chimpanzee-human hybrid DNA formed in the laboratory. Each hybrid DNA molecule contains one human strand annealed to one chimpanzee strand. The two strands in the hybrid DNA dissociate into single strands at a temperature that is about 1.1°C lower than the dissociation temperature of human DNA. This indicates that human and chimpanzee DNA differ in nucleotide sequence by only 1.1 per cent. In other words, a strand of human DNA that is 3000 nucleotides long (and capable of coding for a sequence of 1000 amino acids), differs in nucleotide sequence at about 33 sites from the equivalent chimpanzee strand.

Another method involves comparison of human proteins with their counterparts in chimpanzees. There are three ways of comparing the amino acid sequences of such proteins: direct chemical determination of the amino acid sequences, a tedious and expensive procedure; micro-complement fixation, which provides immunological distances linearly correlated with degrees of sequence difference; and electrophoresis.

PROTEIN SIMILARITIES

Immunological and amino acid sequence comparisons have been made with a wide variety of proteins from the two species. At about 19 of the 2633 amino acid sites compared, chimpanzees have a different amino acid from humans. The average degree of sequence difference between chimpanzee and human proteins, according to this approach, is seven substitutions per thousand amino acid sites. Electrophoresis of more than 40 diverse proteins provides a similar estimate, about eight substitutions per thousand amino acid sites. Both estimates indicate that the average human protein is more than 99 per cent identical in amino acid sequence to its chimpanzee homologue.

The DNA hybridisation experiments show that there may be more sequence difference at the *gene* level than at the *protein* level: individual amino acids are coded for by a triplet of nucleotide bases, yet the experiments show that for every amino acid sequence difference observed, about four nucleotide differences occur in DNA. There are at least two reasons for this discrepancy: first, some nucleotide differences do not lead to amino acid substitutions because of redundancies in the genetic code; second, and more pertinent to this argument, other nucleo-

By Marie-Claire King and Allan C. Wilson. Reprinted with permission of the authors and *New Scientist,* from *New Scientist,* 3 July 1975, pp. 16-18. This article first appeared in *New Scientist,* London, the weekly review of science and technology.

tide differences occur in regions of the genome that do not code directly for proteins.

We have found that human and chimpanzee genes are remarkably similar compared with the resemblance between genes of other pairs of species. This is evident from both DNA and protein studies. As the DNA data in Table 1 show, the

Table 1. DNA comparisons made by examining the thermal stability of hybrid double strands

Species compared	Percent sequence difference in DNA	Level of taxonomic difference
Human with chimpanzee	1.1	Family
Two species of mouse (Mus)	5	Species
Two species of frog (Xenopus)	14*	Species
Two species of fly (Drosophila)	19	Species

*Information supplied by Glenn Galau and Eric Davidson of Cal Tech.

chimpanzee-human difference is far smaller than that between species within a genus of mice, frogs or flies. Protein comparisons yield similar results, as illustrated in Figure 1, which is based on studies with scores of species pairs. At the gene level, chimpanzees and humans are as similar as a pair of sibling species.

In anatomy and way of life, however, humans and chimpanzees differ far more than do sibling species. Because of these major differences at the organismal level, taxonomists put the two species not only in separate genera, but in distinct families. So it seems that molecular and organismal methods of evaluating the chimpanzee-human difference yield quite different conclusions.

EVOLUTIONARY SEPARATION

An evolutionary perspective further illustrates the contrast between the results of the molecular and organismal approaches. Since the last common ancestor of the two species lived, the chim-

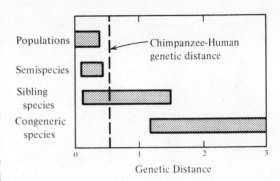

Figure 1. The genetic distance between humans and chimpanzees compared with other organisms, based on protein data. One genetic distance unit means there is an average of one electrophoretically detectable substitution per polypetide. Semispecies are not full species because limited gene flow occurs between them. Congeneric species belong to the same genus

panzee lineage has evolved slowly relative to the human lineage, in terms of anatomy and adaptive strategy. This concept is illustrated in Figure 2. However, phylogenetic analysis of sequence comparisons among chimpanzees, humans and other primates indicates that the two lineages have undergone approximately equal amounts of sequence change in their macromolecules. Hence the major adaptive shift which took place in the human lineage was probably not accompanied by accelerated DNA or protein sequence evolution.

Such a finding is by no means peculiar to the case of hominoid evolution. Although this may seem astonishing and perplexing, it appears to be a general rule that structural genes evolve no faster in rapidly evolving lineages than in slowly evolving ones. Frogs, for example, are an extremely conservative group in terms of organismal evolution; yet their genes have changed as fast as those of placental mammals, whose rates of organismal evolution have been very rapid. Findings like this lead us to question the evolutionary significance of sequence changes in structural genes.

What then is the genetic basis for evolutionary change at the organismal level? Organismal evo-

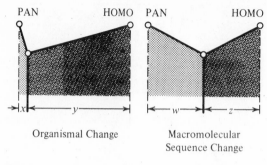

Figure 2. The contrast between biological evolution and molecular evolution since the divergence of the human and chimpanzee lineages from a common ancestor. The top diagram shows that zoological evidence indicates that far more biological change has taken place in the human lineage *(y)* than in the chimpanzee *(x)*. Protein and nucleic acid evidence indicate that as much change has occurred in chimpanzee genes *(w)* as in human genes *(z)*—bottom diagram

lution might result from regulatory mutations; that is, mutations modifying the activity of structural genes without affecting their nucleotide sequences. According to this hypothesis, small differences in the time of activation or in the level of activity of a single gene could in principle influence considerably the course of embryonic development. The organismal differences between chimpanzees and humans would then result chiefly from genetic changes in a few regulatory systems, while amino acid substitutions in proteins would rarely be a key factor in major adaptive shifts. The idea that regulatory mutations have had a major role in human evolution is consistent with the old observation that adult humans resemble foetal apes in some respects. The retention of foetal patterns of gene expression during childhood may have played an important part in evolving such human features as our large brain, our small jaws and canine teeth, our naked skin and even our upright posture.

Regulatory mutations may be of at least two types. First, mutations can occur in the nucleotide sequence of the regulatory genes. Such mutations can affect dramatically the production, though not the amino acid sequences, of a group of enzymes under the control of a given regulatory gene. Second, the order of genes on chromosomes may change owing to inversion, translocation, duplication or deletion of genes, or to fusion or fission of chromosomes. These changes in chromosome organisation bring genes into new relationships with one another. Altered patterns of gene expression sometimes result from such chromosomal mutations.

Evolutionary changes in gene order occur frequently. Microscopic studies of fruit fly, Drosophila salivary chromosomes show, as a general rule, that no two species have the same gene order. Furthermore, there is a parallel between rate of gene rearrangement and rate of anatomical evolution in the three major groups of vertebrates that have been studied in this respect, namely birds, mammals and frogs. Gene rearrangement may therefore be an important source for evolutionary changes in gene regulation.

Although humans and chimpanzees have rather similar chromosome numbers, 46 and 48 respectively, the arrangement of genes on chimpanzee chromosomes differs from that on human chromosomes. Only a small proportion of the chromosomes have identical banding patterns in the two species. The banding studies indicate that at least ten large inversions and translocations and one chromosomal fusion have occurred since the two lineages diverged. Further evidence that humans and chimpanzees differ considerably in gene rearrangement merges from studies in which a purified nucleic acid fraction was annealed to chromosomes *in situ;* the chromosomal sites at which annealing occurred were distributed quite differently in the two species, indicating different gene arrangements on the chromosomes.

TWO TYPES OF EVOLUTION

We propose that there are two types of molecular evolution. One is sequence change within structural genes; this process is not tightly geared to organismal evolution and tends to go on relentlessly at about the same rate in all organisms. The second process consists of changes in patterns of gene expression, brought about in many cases by rearrangement of genes; this process parallels and underlies organismal evolution. According to this proposal, chimpanzee and human genes are remarkably similar because the two species diverged rather recently whereas the large organismal differences are due to rapid regulatory evolution in the human lineage.

Biologists are still a long way from understanding gene regulation and so far only a few cases of regulatory mutations are known in mammals. When the regulation of gene expression during embryonic development is more fully understood, however, molecular biology will contribute more significantly to our understanding of the evolution of whole organisms, including ourselves.

Part II

Up from the Apes

The following articles focus on the evolution of the primates. The initial article, co-authored by Raleigh and Washburn, discusses the appearance of early man and major physical changes, especially of the brain, in response to certain selective pressures. Eventually, human socio-cultural evolution outpaces the biological changes, creating potential problems today. The writers point to the relationship of research in the fields of molecular biology and behavioral studies, noting that insights can be gained via these findings, especially in the transition from hominoid to human status. Martin's interesting account of the ascent of the primate order points to the evolutionary relationships that exist among the living primates even today. Despite each group having its own separate evolutionary history, there are many primitive features that were shared by the ancestral primates, such as, being essentially arboreal in their habitat and possessing hands and feet adapted for grasping. Simons' article sheds new light on the probable course of primate evolution by his findings in Egypt of various Oligocene primate species. The final two articles focus on evolution as well. Kolata's is of interest as it shows how the study of physical anthropology converges with cultural anthropology. The study of present day hunters and gatherers like the !Kung Bushmen aids the anthropologist in interpreting the life styles of early human populations. R. Fox's contribution is a thought-provoking article dealing with the evolution of sexual behavior, which he sees as an end product of human evolution, through the process of natural selection. Methodologically, reliance is on analogies with non-human primate behavior. An interesting reading to supplement this section is "The Casts of Fossil Hominid Brains," R. Holloway, *Scientific American,* July 1974, pp. 106-15.

Ascent of the Primates

Ever since Thomas Huxley joined forces with Charles Darwin to establish the theory that monkeys, apes, and humans evolved from a common stock, the order Primates has attracted special attention from scientists of many disciplines. Field studies of these fascinating mammals have often had as a focus the hope that they may throw some light on human evolutionary history. Efforts by researchers to identify ecological and behavioral factors relating to the evolution of the primates have resulted in a vast amount of new information about man's distant relations.

Textbooks customarily divide the primates into two main groups: Prosimians (lemurs, lorises, and tarsiers) and simians (monkeys, apes, and man). As their name implies, the prosimians are generally regarded as more primitive than the simians and, in some way, as their forerunners. Certainly, the evolutionary lines leading to modern prosimians branched off some time before the split took place between the monkeys, apes, and eventually, man. The "primitive" status of the prosimians, however, has often been taken too literally, and the evolution of the primates has been widely discussed as if present-day simians were actually derived directly from living prosimians.

It is only over the last two decades that the prosimians have been comprehensively studied in their own right, with an emphasis on their behavior under field conditions, rather than being treated as a largely uniform collection of primitive primates. In fact, recent study has emphasized that there is a tremendous variety in both structure and behavior in the living prosimians, which have undergone extensive evolutionary change since they parted company with the line leading to the modern simians.

Modern geographic distribution and fossil evidence indicate that the primates have always inhabited tropical or subtropical areas. One can therefore conclude that the primates generally

By R. D. Martin. Reprinted with permission, from *Natural History* Magazine, March 1975, pp. 53-60. Copyright © 1975 by the American Museum of Natural History.

are not adapted to continuous low temperatures and the added burden of marked seasonal variations in food availability. This is true of all the prosimians and of the New World monkeys today, although a few of the Old World simians (some species of monkeys and man) have recently managed to spread out into colder climatic zones. Among the prosimians, the lemurs, constituting three-quarters of the surviving prosimian species, are now confined to Madagascar. Their closest relatives, the bush babies, pottos, and angwantibos occur on mainland Africa, with two outlying loris species living in the Indian region and in southeast Asia. The tarsier is extremely limited in distribution, occurring only in rain forest areas on some islands in Southeast Asia.

Another major characteristic of the surviving prosimians is the predominance of nocturnal habits, contrasting with the typically diurnal habits of monkeys, apes, and man. (Only one simian, the South American owl monkey, is nocturnal.) Recent research indicates that there was probably a two-way split in the early stages of primate evolution, giving rise to the lorises and lemurs on one hand and the tarsiers and simians on the other. The former have retained the primitive mammalian characteristic of a moist, naked patch of skin, or rhinarium, surrounding the nostrils and joining the upper lip—these animals have been designated "strepsirhines." The latter, having lost this feature, have hairy skin between the nostrils and the upper lip—these have been assigned the name "haplorhines."

This seemingly trivial morphological characteristic, associated with the sense of smell because the rhinarium is related to the Jacobson's organ, may provide a clue to some of the fundamental factors that have governed the evolution of all primates. It can be reasonably suggested, for example, that the ancestral mammals were nocturnal, with an adaptive emphasis on smell rather than sight, and that this way of life was retained in the arboreal primates prior to the two-way split leading to modern primates (strepsirhines and haplorhines).

After this split, the lemurs and lorises generally remained nocturnal with a well-developed sense of smell, while the haplorhine ancestors of the tarsiers and simians became diurnal at an early stage of their evolution. (There are good reasons to believe that the eyes of the common ancestor of the tarsier and the owl monkey were primarily adapted for diurnal life and that the enormous eyes of these two modern species have been reconverted for nocturnal vision.) The shift to diurnal life in the early tarsiers and simians would have favored the greater development of the brain, one of the main characteristics distinguishing the two halves of the primate evolutionary tree.

Given that nocturnal life seems to be associated with slow expansion of the brain in mammals generally, we can see why the lemurs and lorises are more primitive, over-all, than the tarsiers and simians, and why the tarsiers (secondary nocturnal forms apparently derived from a diurnal ancestor) are in many respects intermediate.

Among the lemurs and lorises, only the large Madagascar lemur species (for example, ringtailed and sifaka) are diurnal in habits. The remaining lemur species (mouse, dwarf, and sportive lemurs) are nocturnal, as are all members of the loris group (bush babies, pottos, angwantibos, and lorises). In short, only a quarter of the surviving strepsirhine species are diurnal.

Using the argument that a widespread character in an animal group is more likely to be ancestral than a trait occurring in only a few representatives, we can conclude that the ancestor of the lemurs and lorises was probably nocturnal. The inference that the lemurs and lorises are all derived from a nocturnal ancestor is further strengthened by the fact that all lemurs and lorises, whether nocturnal or diurnal, have a reflecting layer, or tapetum, behind the retina, which doubtless evolved as an aid to nocturnal vision. Also, the reflective material of the tapetum consists of the same substance, riboflavin crystals, in those bush babies and lemurs that have so far been examined by scientists.

If, on the basis of this evidence, it is accepted that the lemurs and lorises are descendants of a nocturnal stock, it follows that the living nocturnal species are likely to be closer to the ancestral condition. Hence, study of the nocturnal forms should prove particularly valuable in interpreting the morphology and behavior of early primates. Luckily, the reflecting tapetum is of great

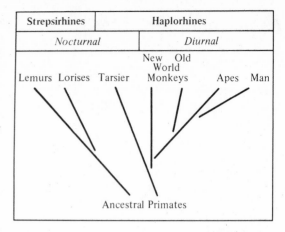

Figure 1. An important split probably occurred during the early stages of primate evolution. The lorises and lemurs (strepsirhines) retained primitive mammalian morphological features adaptive for a nocturnal existence. The other primate groups (haplorhines) lost these features and evolved diurnal habits. The tarsier, which is considered an intermediate form, has evolved back to a nocturnal life.

value here; an observer moving through the forest at night with a head lamp can locate and follow these animals by keeping a continuous lookout for the reflections of their eyes.

In recent years, intensive field studies have been carried out on individual species by zoologists Jean-Jacques Petter, Pierre Charles-Dominique, Marcel Haladile, Simon Bearder, and the author. As a result, some information is now available for two-thirds of the approximately twenty nocturnal lemur and loris species. Data on the small-bodied mouse lemurs and bush babies is of special value, since the ancestral primate was probably also small-bodied and similar in many of its basic behavioral and structural characteristics. A preliminary review of that information reveals several new insights into the behavior of the nocturnal primates and the evolution of the primate group in general.

Virtually all primates except man are arboreal at least part of the time, and virtually all primates other than man have both hands and feet with the thumbs and big toes widely spread and adapted for grasping. Certainly all the living prosimians are essentially arboreal; only the ring-tailed lemur *(Lemur catta)* spends a significant proportion of its time on the ground. Again, taking the most widespread characteristics as indicative of the primitive condition, the ancestral primate was probably also arboreal, with grasping hands and feet.

Study of mouse lemurs and the smaller bush babies shows how such an adaptation may have been important during the early history of the primates. These small-bodied, nocturnal primates are typically active in what has been called the "fine branch niche," moving about with great agility in tangles of creepers, thin stems, and fine branches. Obviously, the larger-bodied lemurs and lorises must move around on broader supports, but it is in the fine branch niche that the small-bodied ancestral primates, like the smallest of their living descendants, probably circulated. In such an environment, they could move with greater ease than many arboreal competitors.

A versatile combination of grasping and leaping in a tangle of fine supports would have favored many of the developments of primate evolution. Increased visual accuracy would have been required for leaping among a great variety of supports, and a visual memory would have been of great benefit. Development of vision would have involved expansion of the brain and refinement of cortical association areas in order to link vision with other sensory and motor components. The variation in diameter and orientation of the supports used would also have encouraged the development of a fine tactile sense and sophisticated feedback systems for control of the skeletal musculature. The nocturnal prosimians even have relatively larger, more forward-facing eyes than other nocturnal mammals, and the visual and motor areas of their brains are comparatively well developed. In other mammal groups, which developed adaptations primarily for branch running, claws were at a premium and leaping was less favored. Clawed branch runners do not require such versatile visual and motor systems and, consequently, have comparatively smaller brains.

The high, pointed cusps and simple cusp arrangements of the molar teeth of early mammal fossils indicate that the ancestral mammals sub-sisted largely on small animal prey, such as insects, for which shearing was more important than grinding. In the primates there seems to have been a general shift to the inclusion of more plant food in the diet. The lower cusps and increasing complexity of the molar teeth of early primate fossils indicate that the ancestral primate probably had a mixed diet of small animals and plant products, such as fruit, as is now the case with the living mouse lemurs, dwarf lemurs, bush babies, and lorises. Such a diet, however, is only common among small-bodied mammals—larger species usually have a more specialized diet. Because of their higher metabolic rate, small-bodied mammals must feed on items that readily yield large quantities of energy. Larger mammals, on the other hand, can exploit food sources, such as leaves, that provide a slower energy turnover. Also, it has been shown with bush babies, angwantibos, and pottos that—regardless of body size—only a standard quantity of insects is captured in the course of a night. This indicates that there is usually an upper limit on insect hunting.

With the larger lemurs there has been an increased emphasis on plant food, and several species are exclusively vegetarian. The sportive lemur specializes in a leaf diet to such an extent that it reingests feces derived from the cecum so that the products of bacterial action can be absorbed during a second passage of the vegetable matter through the gut.

The bizarre aye-aye *(Daubentonia madagascariensis)* has become specialized in an entirely different direction. This large-bodied lemur has a thin middle finger on each hand and rodent-like, continuously growing incisors used in the extraction of wood-boring larvae, a major constituent of its diet.

Such specializations in diet have in all cases been associated with pronounced modifications of the dental apparatus and the digestive tract. Only the smaller-bodied nocturnal lemurs and lorises, which now exhibit a mixed diet of readily accessible small animal prey and plant products, have retained basically primitive dentitions. They all have molar teeth with essentially simple cusp patterns and a dental formula of two incisors, one canine, three premolars, and three molars on each side of the upper and lower jaws. Since dental formulas are typically reduced in mammalian evolution, while molar cusps typically become more complex in arrangement, the common ancestor of the lemurs and lorises probably had this maximum dental formula and simple molar teeth.

In fact, all of the small-bodied nocturnal lemur and loris species have a peculiar modification of the lower anterior dentition in that the crowns of the two canines and four incisors are all inclined horizontally to form a six-tooth "scraper." This can also be seen in more robust form in some of the larger lemurs, such as the ring-tailed; but in species such as the indri or aye-aye the dental formula has been reduced and the tooth scraper has been modified.

All lemurs and lorises use the lower anterior teeth for grooming, and this has been widely regarded as the major function of the tooth scraper, although most other mammals engage in grooming without requiring such specialization of their dental apparatus. Field studies of the smaller nocturnal forms have shown that there is another function that is at least as important and probably more influential. All of these species include plant gums in their diet, and the tooth scraper is used to scoop away fresh collections of gum from certain trees night after night. In some species, such as the mouse lemur *(Microcebus murinus)*, gums are only a minor part of the diet during at least part of the year, while in others, gums are a major dietary component throughout the year. The fork-crowned lemur *(Phaner furcifer)* and the needle-clawed bush baby *(Euoticus elegantulus)* feed mainly on gums, with a small supplement of insects, and they have the largest tooth scrapers—relative to skull size—among the nocturnal strepsirhines.

Obviously the supplementation of the diet with gums could have been an important factor in the evolution of the tooth scraper, and the use of this device for grooming could have developed as a secondary feature. For a primate evolving in any subtropical area with marked alternating wet and dry seasons, the ability to obtain gum in the absence of abundant fruit and insect food would represent a valuable advantage. The presence of this specialized dental apparatus in many lemurs and lorises is just one example of an independent evolutionary specialization that has not occurred among the haplorhine tarsiers and simians.

The lemurs and lorises also differ markedly from the tarsiers and simians in their reproductive biology. Whereas the tarsiers and simians have a highly invasive type of placentation, the lemurs and lorises have the least invasive type found among the placental mammals. In the tarsiers and simians, the outermost embryonic membrane is eventually bathed directly in maternal blood from the uterine vessels, following breakdown of the uterus lining. With lemurs and lorises, by contrast, no such breakdown of the internal uterine wall occurs.

Coincident with this, a female tarsier or simian of any given body weight will give birth to an infant weighing almost three times as much as the infant of a lemur or loris mother of similar body weight. This explains several observations of differences in reproductive behavior between these two groups of primates. Whereas the tarsiers and simians typically have only one infant at a time, which is carried on the mother's fur from birth onward, some of the smaller-bodied lemurs and lorises—such as the mouse and dwarf lemurs and the Senegal bush baby—may have twins or triplets and give birth to their babies in nests. Such species carry the infants by mouth when necessary; this is possible because of the infants' smaller size with respect to their mothers.

Presumably, nests are also necessary to keep the tiny infants of the smallest species warm during the night. With most of the larger lemur and loris species, no nest is used, and there is usually only one infant at each birth, which clings to the parent's fur. Nevertheless, the large-bodied aye-aye builds an enormous nest, and the variegated lemur typically gives birth to twins, which are left in a nest of some kind. This may reflect retention of the ancestral condition from the small-bodied common ancestor of the lemurs and lorises. Here it is reasonable to conclude that the small-bodied ancestors of the lemurs and lorises had two or three tiny offspring and built nests, at least for breeding, whereas the ancestors of the tarsiers and simians, with their single, larger offspring, did not do so.

In addition, it is likely that in a subtropical zone with marked seasonality there might have been a selective advantage in developing relatively lightweight infants as an adaptation to the mothers' limited food supply. Thus, the reproductive evidence correlates with the evidence of the gum-collecting tooth scraper as adaptations enabling a small-bodied lemur or loris to cope with strictly seasonal conditions.

Some important new information has also emerged with respect to the social life of nocturnal prosimians. These primates have often been described as solitary in contrast to the typically gregarious simians. Although nocturnal prosimians are not often seen moving and feeding in groups, they have well-established patterns of social life involving overlapping home ranges in which communication between individuals is insured by occasional encounters, vocalizations, and scent marking. There seems to be a general pattern in which certain males have large ranges, each overlapping the ranges of several females. This has been observed with mouse lemurs, sportive lemurs, various bush baby species, pottos, and angwantibos. A similar arrangement may also occur with the tarsier. In some cases the females actually sleep in groups during the daytime, and they may occasionally be joined by males. Since the sex ratio at birth for prosimians generally is usually one to one, there are often excess, peripheral males excluded from direct contact with females.

Such a basic pattern may well have existed with the nocturnal ancestral primates and would have provided a starting-point for the emergence of more complex, gregarious social behavior in the diurnal primates. This interpretation is supported by the gregarious social behavior exhibited by those lemurs that, like the simians, have become diurnal in habits. The ring-tailed lemur, for example, lives in social groups of about two dozen individuals, which move, feed, and sleep together. Indeed, there are many parallels between ring-tailed lemurs and baboons in the broad aspects of their social behavior.

Thus, contrary to what is often assumed, the origin of gregarious patterns of social behavior of diurnal primates may well have been in a harem network rather than in a pair-bonding system. In fact, family groups or groups containing equal numbers of adult males and females are relatively uncommon among diurnal primates, whereas the tendency to harem formation and relegation of excess males to the periphery is widespread.

In this, and many other features, small-bodied nocturnal primates such as the mouse lemur and the smaller bush babies seem to have remained close to the ancestral primate condition. The reason for this is that they have probably remained in an ecological framework similar to that in which the earliest primates evolved. Moving in the fine branch niche, feeding on a mixed diet of small animal prey and accessible plant products, and relying on versatility for survival, the early primates were stamped with certain characteristics that influenced the subsequent course of primate evolution.

Nevertheless, one must not forget that even bush babies and mouse lemurs have continued to evolve from this ancestral condition. The early primates had smaller brains than any living species, and their motor and visual systems were surely less sophisticated. Even bush babies and mouse lemurs are not, therefore, primitive primates, although they have apparently retained many characteristics that are close to the ancestral primate condition.

Hunting the "Dawn Apes" of Africa

Almost all of the existing knowledge of the Old World ancestors of apes, men and monkeys is based on 28 to 35-million-year-old fossils from the Fayum desert of Egypt. Marine mammals were reported from these beds in 1879, but the varied and exotic series of land mammals was not found until about 1900. The six recent Yale University expeditions have uncovered fossilized fragments which shed new light on the origin and evolution of African mammals, including man's forerunners. Among the latter are bones of the oldest undoubted great ape and the first relatively complete upper jaws of Oligocene apes, together with fossils of monkey relatives. Until now, the oldest known upper jaws of any higher primates specially related to man dated back to a comparatively recent 19 million years ago.

The first light on the early age of mammals in the "dark continent" was shed by reports resulting from several paleontological collecting expeditions sent to the area mainly in the decade after 1900. During this period fossils of four genera and species of ancient Egyptian "apes" were found and named: *Parapithecus, Propliopithecus, Apidium* and *Moeripithecus*. Species of the first two of these primates were established on relatively complete mandibles. These were widely figured in books on paleontology and human evolution, and came to serve as the basis for almost all discussions of the origin of the higher primates, or "Anthropoidea." The type species of *Moeripithecus* and *Apidium*, on the other hand, were based on jaw fragments with few teeth. The scantiness of the remains of the latter two limited scientific discussion of their affinities.

Curiously enough, however, no further productive field research on this early African primate fauna was undertaken until the Yale University expedition began in 1960. Perhaps this inactivity was due to the relative lack of success

By Elwyn L. Simons. Reprinted with permission, from *Discovery* (Peabody Museum, Yale University), 4, No. 1, 1968, pp. 19-32.

of earlier expeditions in finding smaller vertebrate remains. Small fossils are seldom preserved in coarse river-deposited sands and gravels; before 1960 only about 20 pieces of mammals of cat size or smaller had been found in the Fayum. As a result, for more than half a century virtually all consideration of the initial stages of man's ancestry, and that of apes, was based on the fragmentary evidence of the parts of four different lower jaws from Egypt. Two of these dentally resembled apes, the other two, monkeys.

Among the most important accomplishments of the Yale expeditions was the discovery of many new fossil ape specimens. Linking forms demonstrated that *Moeripithecus markgrafi* was not really a distinct genus but should be considered as a species of *Propliopithecus*. Much more important than this, however, was the recovery of numerous specimens of a new and relatively large ape, *Aegyptopithecus zeuxis*, and a much smaller and distinctive form, *Aeolopithecus chirobates*, both named by Simons in 1965. Together all these might popularly be termed the "dawn apes".

With such fragmentary material to work on as existed before the Yale expeditions, scientists varied in the interpretations of the evolutionary meaning of these remains of early higher primates. Certain partly misleading ideas about these earliest-known close relatives of man were proposed initially and then continued to be quoted and requoted in textbooks. Thus discussions of hominoid origins departed farther and farther from the facts. Apparently only a few persons ever bothered to study the original dawn ape fossils at Stuttgart, Germany, and consequently *Parapithecus* was often said to foreshadow Hominidae (the taxonomic family of man), *Propliopithecus* thought to be an early gibbon, and *Moeripithecus* was taken as a possible monkey forerunner. Actually, none of these suppositions has subsequently proven correct.

To clarify the status of some of these important fossils the author organized and directed the six recent paleontological Yale expeditions to Egypt. Apart from recovery of more or better primate remains another major objective of the Fayum expeditions was to study the environment in which these ancient apes lived. Comparison of fossil plants and animals with their living relatives often helps paleontologists determine the broad environmental conditions within which prehistoric species flourished. To understand how our ancient forerunners lived it is particularly important to understand their ecological setting.

By combining information on the Fayum fossil primates with interpretation of their environment, questions such as the following can receive at least partial answers. How recently were the ancestors of both men and apes still tree dwellers? When did the latest common ancestors of man and the apes, particularly the African apes, exist? What are the relationships of Oligocene apes and monkeys to later forms?

ANCIENT MAN IN THE FAYUM

The Fayum "bone fields" (which have revealed all we know of the Oligocene life of the African continent) are situated in an arid desert about 65 miles southwest of Cairo and along the northern margin of the Fayum Depression at the eastern edge of the Sahara. Not only is this area of importance in the study of the history of African land mammals but the region is of considerable interest to archaeologists as well. The interaction of man and environment along the shores of brackish Lake Qarun has long been in progress. In fact, the region itself takes its name from an ancient Egyptian word for lake, *phiom*.

After the Fayum depression had been formed, probably by wind erosion in the Pliocene or early Pleistocene, a large lake developed in the area, fed by occasional Nile floods spilling in from the east. This great tamarisk-lined lake abounded in wild fowl and fish. Hippopotamus and gazelle grazed along its reedy shores and ostrich stalked the uplands. Today the dry margins of this former lake are littered with the bones of these animals and of the stone tools of several successive levels of habitation by Stone Age hunters. About 4000 years ago the Fayum region achieved great importance due to the irrigation projects of Amenemhat I and his successors of the XII Dynasty. These ancient Egyptians temporarily stabilized the diminishing lake level by regulating the natural canal from the Nile at Lahún. A network of canals branching from this main source watered the southern margin of the depression and early established the Fayum

province as the richest agricultural region of Egypt after the Nile delta.

In Ptolemaic times irrigation projects and further exposure of arable clays of the lake temporarily allowed establishment of agricultural cities on the north shore. Now the long abandoned ruins of these cities project raggedly from the horizons of the Fayum bone fields. In this desert modern paleontologists occasionally come across Graeco-Roman coins and even the bones and teeth of these classical Egyptian agriculturists.

A roadway largely made of petrified wood is another relic of the ancient Egyptians. This apparently was used to transport blocks of basalt on sleds from the lava flow at the top of the cliffs to a point near the north shore of the lake where the quarried materials could have been removed by boat. Although untrodden for almost 4000 years, parts of it look as if they had been completed yesterday. This road has more than historical significance. If the approximate time of its construction could be determined, much could be learned about the rate and manner of recent desert erosion by wind and water through study of the effects of flash flooding and sand blasting of the petrified wood pavement of this roadway.

DEPOSITION OF THE SEDIMENTS

Today the Fayum fossil sites are easily reached by road from Cairo in 2½ hours, a far cry from the week-long camel-caravan treks by early Fayum paleontological expeditions. Turning off from the main Cairo-Medinet el Fayum road in the vicinity of the Ptolemaic ruins of Kom Oshim, a desert track winds about 18 miles in a northwesterly direction to the main Oligocene fossil localities. The fossil sites are distributed throughout a distance of about 20 miles upon a broad bench running along a northeast-southeast line. This is the upper of two benches lying between the lower cliffs along the north shore of Lake Qarun (about 140 feet below sea level) and a continuous series of cliffs or escarpment called Jebel Qatrani ("Tar Hills") rising to a height of over 1100 feet. In the center of this upper bench the Yale University groups have pitched their main field camp.

The fossil-bearing sediments of the Jebel el Qatrani Formation were deposited by a river or rivers flowing from the south. Beginning in early Oligocene times, deposition of riverine and estuarine sands and clays upon the Eocene ocean deposits of the region was locally accelerated. In the central part of the fossil wood zone, 600 to 650 feet of continental sediments accumulated. With the passage of time the northern margin of the African continent, which was then situated about 140 miles to the south of the present Mediterranean coastline, was gradually built northward by silt from these sources.

A TROPICAL FOREST

The plant and animal fossils contained in these ancient riverlain deposits show that the Oligocene environment of the northern coast of Africa contrasted sharply with conditions in the region today. The richest fossil beds contain numerous trunks of trees often as long as 30 meters (98 feet). Although some early geologists speculated that "removal" of branches from these trunks indicated that these trees had been brought down flooded rivers from forest lands many hundreds of miles to the south, there is considerable evidence against this conjecture. Tropical forest trees typically have straight boles with few branches except at the crown in the canopy. Such trees after waterlogging in stream channels soon lose roots and branches, and so reach the condition seen in the Fayum logs without much transport. Moreover, many of the small vertebrate remains are too delicate to have been moved far among gravels. Many of these also belonged to animals whose present-day relatives dwell in forested regions, so it seems unlikely that the fossil logs and the vertebrate bones were derived from different areas. Although impressions of leaves from these trees have not been preserved in the Fayum sands, a number of seed pods have. Studies of the seed pods and of the types of wood represented have helped determine the forest flora. Altogether the picture indicated by these plant remains is of a tropical gallery forest which flourished in or very near the Fayum region in Oligocene times. Since the region adjoined the shore there were probably also areas of open savannah or coastal plains.

In addition, this type of environment is indicated by the fish and land vertebrates which are found as fossils in these same sediments. The majority of fossils occur in stream-channel deposits which range in composition from fine sands to gravels. Primarily, the fossils consist of disassociated skeletal elements which have been moved to their final resting place by water. The individual elements (jaw, limb-bones, teeth, etc.) are generally assorted by size, the smaller vertebrate remains occurring in the fine sands, and, particularly with the mammals, the larger accumulated in the gravels.

In the finer sands and gravels fish bones are abundant. The commonest of these are the spines of freshwater "upside-down" catfish and the tooth plates of lungfish. The rarity of shark teeth and dental batteries of rayfish suggest that the Fayum Oligocene beds were deposited in fresh water but near the coast. These stream channels vary in width from one or two feet to large lenses 30 or 40 feet wide which were once broad gravel bars. Upon these were stranded the bones of primitive elephant ancestors together with those of many other large vertebrates, particularly bones of the giant *Arsinoitherium* (a four-horned plant eater which was about the size of the modern African white rhinoceros).

In the search for fossil primates and the other small vertebrates the *Arsinoitherium* bone beds proved unrewarding for they contain large bones almost exclusively. Since these were practically the only deposits worked by paleontologists at the turn of the century the early Fayum collections produced very little knowledge of small Oligocene mammals. Fortunately Yale scientists found that such "microfaunal" remains are abundant in certain of the finer sands. Among the smaller of these remains are lower jaws of insectivores, bats and rodents, none of which is much more than a centimeter long. Most of the mammal skulls are damaged and the bones of a single individual are almost never found together. This is probably due not only to their having been moved by water, but also to their having been pulled about by the catfish, turtles, crocodiles and other predators which inhabited those sluggish Oligocene streams.

Thus in picturing the environment of the dawn apes one can imagine that they lived in the forest canopy, as most generalized primates, such a lemurs, bush-babies, marmosets, etc., do today. A misjudged leap between branches overhanging a stream or an incautious visit to the waterside could have resulted in fatal attacks from aquatic enemies. An indication of the inexperience of these ancient primates is that the degree of tooth eruption in their jaws shows that most were not adult. In fact only one of the many dozens of jaws now known is of an old individual with an advanced stage of tooth wear.

One further ecological deduction about the environment of the dawn apes may be indicated by the rarity of members of the small mammal fauna other than primates and rodents. This may mean that the undergrowth near the Oligocene streams was too dense or too wet to maintain an abundance of small mammals. However, the primates and rodents which are the common faunal elements might have reached such relatively inaccessible river banks through the forest canopy.

LOCATING FOSSIL CONCENTRATIONS

Each main type of fossil occurrence presents problems to the vertebrate paleontologist. The process of locating bone concentrations and extracting the fossils from the rock varies greatly from one country to another. In the Fayum there is no problem of seeing a maximum of rock exposure as there is no cover of vegetation. Even so, spots where there are concentrations of small vertebrate remains rich enough to warrant extensive excavation are extremely rare. An added complication is that the main rock type is a loose sand or "sandstone" which is only occasionally consolidated. In excavations the sand tends to slump back into the quarry or be blown into the "bone pits" by the wind. Thus, digging for fossils is not too practical.

Strong winds blowing across the desert are common and were a perpetual annoyance to earlier collectors and to our first expeditions. We found, however, that even the winds could be put to use in collecting—an unusual method of recovering fossils. It is only necessary for us to remove the "desert pavement" (a gravel cover consisting mainly of larger fragments of chert, lava and quartz which have resisted wind and water erosion). When this crust is gone the wind scours along the surface and a constant swirl of blowing sand gradually erodes the quarry face. In general, the fossils are not moved by the wind so that after a storm, collectors can harvest the quarry face.

Cementing with one of the newer types of plastic resins is particularly important for fossil mammal jaws from these sediments for, unlike most vertebrate bones of equal antiquity, there has been little mineralization, or penetration of the bone by hardening minerals carried in by ground water. Since these fossils have not thus been "permineralized" they are exceedingly fragile. The light buff and whitish colors of the fossil bones are very close to those of the surrounding sands and gravels. It takes a practiced eye to locate the smaller fossils even on well blown-off surfaces.

CONTEMPORARIES OF THE DAWN APES

What other animals were contemporaries of the dawn apes? Among the reptiles were giant land-tortoises similar to those which exist today mainly on islands such as the Malay Archipelago and on the Galapagos Islands. In the past, such giant tortoises have often occurred in association with tropical forest faunas. They are found, for instance, in the Miocene and Pliocene deposits of the Siwalik Hills of north India and much later in association with the apeman *Homo erectus* in the middle Pleistocene beds of Java. Africa today is still a haven for giant tortoises of the genus *Testudo,* two species of which rival the island forms and those of the Fayum Oligocene in size.

Turtles and crocodiles were abundant in the sluggish streams. In addition to broadnosed crocodiles, similar to the modern African species, the ancient Fayum was also inhabited by false gavials of the genus *Tomistoma.* These crocodilians possessed long narrow snouts adapted for fish-eating. Today, members of this genus ony inhabit fresh-water swamps and rivers in the tropical forests of Borneo and the Malay Peninsula. Although classified as an unusual crocodile these animals closely resemble the modern Indian gavials of the Ganges and other

Indian rivers. The presence of both these crocodilians indicates that the Fayum Oligocene environment was that of a warm, well-watered lowland.

The land mammals of these 28 to 35 million-
year-old Egyptian deposits presented a very different picture of the fauna of Africa than that
which we know today. There were no animals related to antelope, water buffalo, giraffe, rhinoceros, leopard, lion, jackel or hyena, or indeed to
many others of the characteristic African mammals of the present day, such as aardvark, drom-
edary, or zebra. Such animals first reached Africa much later in Tertiary times. Instead of such
mammals, there existed types of carnivores and
herbivores which had evidently developed in the
continent independently, arising from some
early Tertiary colonization that terminated with
the isolation of Africa from Eurasia by the ancestral Mediterranean or "Tethys" sea. In any
event, the majority of the mammals of the Fayum Oligocene are so different from their contemporaries elsewhere in the world that any
early Tertiary routes of migration from Europe
or Asia must have been transitory at best. Even
the Fayum primates and rodents, members of
mammalian orders which elsewhere have evidently been able to cross open seaways by clinging to drifting masses of vegetation, are not
much like those of the world outside Africa.

Although many of the most striking groups of
modern African vertebrates are missing here,
the Fayum fossils show that numerous, less conspicuous modern mammals originally arose in
Africa. These include insect eaters such as the
hedgehog-like tenrecs, now surviving only in
Madagascar, and elephant shrews, a character-
istically African group.

The rodents in these deposits belong to one
characteristic group named phiomyids from
their having been originally discovered in the
Fayum. The jaws of these ancient rodents resemble those of rats and squirrels in general
form, but whether they were ground-dwelling or
arboreal species is not certain. Fossils from the
miocene of eastern Africa show that phiomyids
had by then become abundant and diversified,
and were adapted to a variety of habitats from
trees to subterranean tunnels. Although phiomyids are the only rodents known from the African Oligocene and were still the dominant group

in the Miocene, by now they have been largely
replaced by rodents which migrated in from
Eurasia later on. Today the only presumed descendants of the phyiomids are the African Cane
Rats and Rock Rats, which inhabit many different environments in sub-Saharan Africa.

Perhaps the most important mammalian radiation to take place was that which produced
three related orders: the elephants, sea cows and
the hyraxes (also called dassies or rock conies).
Outwardly hyraxes look vaguely like wood-
chucks or overgrown guinea-pigs but, as with
elephants, there are upper tusks and on each toe
a small but distinct hoof. Apparently the main
early introduction of plant-eating placentals into
Africa consisted of some unknown but generalized Paleocene member or members of an ancient mammalian order (Condylarthra). From
such a postulated source there apparently arose
during the unknown early stages of African
mammalian evolution six major groups of large
mammals all of which occur in the Fayum fossil
fields. This is the earliest known occurrence of
most of these groups. They are:

1. Arsinoitheres or embrithopods.

2. Hyracoids (hyraxes or conies)

3. Mastodonts (terrestrial proboscideans)

4. Moeritheres (affinities with both sea cows
and mastodonts)

5. Barytheres (affinities uncertain)

6. Sirenians (sea cows)

In future Yale Fayum expeditions one of our
most important objectives will be to bring to
light the unknown earlier stages of African
mammal evolution. Eocene land deposits apparently exist in the western desert of Egypt to
the southwest of the Fayum.

The Largest Fayum Mammals

Perhaps the strangest of these plant-eating
mammals are the arsinoitheres, which have
never been found outside the Fayum. These were
the largest mammals of the African Oligocene,
some standing about seven feet high at the hips,
the head and forequarters being carried somewhat lower than the hind. These ungainly
beasts, perhaps somewhat inappropriately
named for the beautiful Queen Arsinöe, second

wife of Ptolemy II and later the patron goddess of the Fayum, are so little like any other type of mammal that they are placed in their own order, Embrithopoda. There were four sharp horns on the head in males. The horn-cores of these were more rounded and apparently less dangerous in the females. In some males the horn cores of the front pair are over 20 inches long. These appear to have had some sort of horny sheath over them which must have extended the length of the anterior horns, to at least three feet and perhaps as much as five. The neck muscle attachments are powerfully developed and the body heavily built. Consequently great force could be put behind ramming and tossing with these horns. In fact they are as formidable as any defensive weapon to have evolved among the Mammalia. Presumably the horns were used in rutting combat between the males as well as for defense against the contemporary hyaenodont carnivores and crocodilians. Their sturdy limbs and broad spreading feet seem to indicate an adaptation to moving about in soft soil and marshy terrain.

The tooth structure of arsinoitheres could be derived from a pattern preserved from early times in hyraxes, to which they are related. The latter in their turn are the most varied group of herbivores of the African Oligocene, perhaps ecologically equivalent to the antelopes of Africa today. Although present-day species of hyrax are small—never bulkier than a dachshund—some of their Oligocene relatives were at least the size of a Malay tapir. The Fayum hyracoids ranged from this size down to animals only a little larger than present day species.

The earliest relatives of elephants known anywhere appear in the Fayum fauna in the form of small mastodonts of the genus *Paleomastodon*. Anatomical studies indicate that this group is related to the hyraxes, but even by Oligocene times the two stocks had diverged markedly. During the 19th century, paleontologists were puzzled by the question of where the huge and exotic proboscideans had arisen. It was difficult to relate them to any of the early Tertiary groups of mammals known from Europe and North America and it was clear that their origins lay outside these continents. All that was known was that they were widespread throughout the northern hemisphere by Miocene times. Therefore

when, about the turn of the century, members of the Egyptian geological survey first reported primitive elephants in the North African Oligocene, this discovery was widely heralded. In fact the search for more of these primitive elephants gave considerable impetus to the early Fayum expeditions. As one contemporary scientist put it, "North Africa became the storm-center of paleontology."

At about the same time as *Paleomastodon* was discovered, two other quite bizarre proboscidean relatives were first reported. These were the tapir-sized *Moeritherium* and a much larger elephant-sized form, *Barytherium*. Both these large mammals were amphibious. They are first found in the Eocene marine sediments which underlie the continental deposits of the Egyptian Oligocene. *Moeritherium* also occurs in the higher continental deposits but by then *Barytherium* had disappeared. Species of these two genera show resemblances to each other and to the sea cows (Order Sirenia), also represented in the African Fayum by species of the genera *Eotherium* and *Eosiren*. All these proboscideans and the related sea cows indicate adaptations to well-watered lowlands, with vegetation-clogged rivers grading into sluggish deltaic streams and brackish estuaries where the moeritheres and sea cows grazed.

THE FAYUM PRIMATES

In addition to numerous jaws now recovered indicating the existence in the African Oligocene of at least nine primate species, a collection of several isolated skull and limb bone fragments has been made, culminated by the recovery of a partial skull of *Aegyptopithecus*. In general terms these show what Oligocene Anthropoidea were like but, except on grounds of size it is not possible to associate particular skeletal fragments with one or another of the known species.

What does the known anatomy of the Fayum primates tell us? Four parts of frontal (forehead) bones of different sizes all show that the dawn apes had comparatively narrow snouts between the eyes, some forebrain expansion and relative reduction of olfactory lobes. These correlate with predominance of the visual sense over the

Figure 1.   Order Primates (Fayum forms in bold letters).

I.   Suborder Prosimii (Lower Primates or prosimians: lemurs, lorises, tarsiers)
II. Suborder Anthropoidea (Higher Primates or simians)
   A. Infraorder Platyrrhini (New World monkeys)
   B. Infraorder Catarrhini (Old World; more advanced monkeys, apes, man)
     1. Superfamily Parapithecoidea (**Apidium, Parapithecus;** perhaps belongs in the following group)
     2. Superfamily Cercopithecoidea (advanced Old World monkeys, such as baboons, macaques, langurs)
     3. Superfamily Hominoidea (most advanced primates)
       a.   Family Oreopithecidae (*Oreopithecus)*
       b.   Family Pongidae (fossils **Propliopithecus** [including **Moeripithecus**], **Aegyptopithecus, Aelopithecus, Dryopithecus, Pliopithecus,** possibly **Oligopithecus;** living forms: gibbons, chimpanzee, orangutan, gorilla)
       c.   Family Hominidae (man and his most recent fossil ancestors: *Ramapithecus, Australopithecus, Homo*)

olfactory in higher primates. Moreover, in all four specimens, the left and right frontals are fused into one bone along the mid-line, as is also true in the newly reported skull of *Aegyptopithecus.* These two bones remain separate in nearly all lower primates or prosimians at least until old age. But frontal fusion at an early individual age is characteristic of higher promates or Anthropoidea. One of the new Fayum primate frontals appears to belong to a sub-adult, as indicated by the striated texture of the bone. Nevertheless the specimen has completely fused frontals.

The limb skeleton is poorly known but some of the toe bones and ankle bones have been recovered as well as the humerus and ulna of the forelimb. Taken together these postcranial remains indicate a structural grade intermediate between lemurs and Old World higher primates. This morphological grade is best seen today in various South American monkeys.

One additional find of interest in the main primate quarry (I) were the tail bones of primates. Because of their size these might belong with one of the larger Oligocene primate species which on dental grounds are clearly hominoids. Previously living and fossil apes were characterized as tailless, but in tracing back their evolution, they must ultimately, of course, have had tailed ancestors. Perhaps these large tail bones from the Fayum indicate that this was so for Oligocene apes. Moreover, it has recently been shown from the size of the spinal canal in sacral vertebrae of the Miocene gibbon *Pliopithecus* that this early ape also had a long tail. Thus as we gain better knowledge of early apes the old distinction between tailless apes and the tailed monkeys breaks down.

The nine African Oligocene primate species so far discerned belong to at least two primate families. One of these, Parapithecidae, contains only the fossil genera *Parapithecus* and *Apidium;* the other, Pongidae, contains the fossil genera *Propliopithecus, Aeolopithecus, Aegyptopithecus, Dryopithecus* and *Pliopithecus,* as well as modern gibbons, orangutan, chimpanzee and gorilla. One further genus, *Oligopithecus,* is of uncertain placement.

Oligopithecus

Oligopithecus savagei has a molar morphology close to that of the Eocene prosimians of the family Omomyidae, while on the other hand this species is classifiable as a member of Anthropoidea or higher primates. As such, it has the most generalized tooth structure of any anthropoidean. It comes from the lowest level in the Fayum Oligocene section from which a primate of definite locality is known. Therefore, it is almost certainly the oldest Fayum primate.

Parapithecus

This genus and *Apidium* are the most abundant of African Oligocene primates and a prominent element in the African fauna of that time.

The genus and species *Parapithecus fraasi*, based on a lower jaw containing all but three teeth, was discovered in the Fayum in 1908 and described by the famous German paleontologist Max Schlosser in 1910. Judging from the size of this jaw, *Parapithecus* was about the size of a tarsier or a squirrel monkey.

In the last three field seasons a number of jaws of a second and larger species of *Parapithecus* have been found in Egypt by Yale expeditions. With these additional materials it is possible to resolve some of the problems raised by the enigmatic structure of the first known jaw of *Parapithecus*. *P. fraasi* was for 50 years the only recognized evidence of the African early Tertiary primate family Parapithecidae, to which subsequently *Apidium* also proved to belong. Several hypotheses about the relationships of *P. fraasi* were presented during these five decades, but wide-ranging conclusions could not and cannot safely be based on a single fragmentary mandible.

The jaws of *Parapithecus* and *Apidium* found since 1962 in the Egyptian Oligocene show that these primates had the tooth size, arrangement and number of the New World monkeys and that, unlike those in prosimians, the two sides of the lower jaw were solidly grown together at the front even in the young. This characteristic, called symphyseal fusion, is typically present in juvenile Anthropoidea. Thus the new material of *Parapithecus* shows that the relationships of these animals may be close to Old World higher primates and perhaps to monkeys or to the extinct Italian primate *Oreopithecus bambolii*.

Apidium

The first specimen of *Apidium phiomense* was described in 1908. Originally, however, it was not definitely recognized as a primate. As a result, not as much has been said about its relationships to later primates as is the case for the other Fayum primates. Some early students thought that it might be near the ancestry of the cercopithecoid monkeys. More recently scientists have held that it might be related to pigs or to certain archaic mammals other than primates. In 1960 I suggested the possibility that it had affinities with the strange Miocene-Pliocene primate *Oreopithecus*. The recent discoveries include over 50 lower, and several upper, jaws of *Apidium*. These show that the animal is definitely a primate, short-faced, and, like *Parapithecus*, had the same number of teeth as the New World monkeys, i.e., there were four more bicuspids or premolars than any Old World primate now has—one in each side of each jaw. An excellent facial fragment found in January 1967 shows that the eyeball was enclosed in a socket of bone behind, a feature not matched in any prosimian.

Propliopithecus

Propliopithecus haeckeli, also named by Max Schlosser in 1910, was discussed by him and by many later students as an ancestral gibbon. Nevertheless, there are several dental differences from gibbons, and the tooth rows and jaws show few pongid specializations. For instance, the front premolars are not elongated as in apes and monkeys, the canines are small and the three molars subequal in size rather than as in most apes where the second molars are much larger than the first. Moreover, the front teeth or incisors appear to have been placed vertically rather than jutting forward as they usually do in apes and monkeys. All these and a few other more technical details resemble these characters of Hominidae (the family of man) more than they do apes. In fact, some have thought tooth and jaw structure in *Propliopithecus* shows that apes with hominid features had already differentiated by early Oligocene times. Nevertheless, these features could also exist if *Propliopithecus haeckeli* a small-faced, generalized, arboreal species in which the large canines, slicing premolars, etc., that are typical of later Old World higher primates had not yet arisen. If this is so, it may be interpreted as more representative of the basal stock from which sprang the common ancestry of the apes and man.

Some of the new undescribed primate fossils from the Fayum, particularly a series of isolated teeth from one of the quarries near the middle of the continental section, show structural intermediacy between *P. haeckeli* and *Aegyptopithecus*. Since *P. haeckeli* comes from lower in the section than does any of the material of *Aegyptopithecus* (discussed below), perhaps there was sufficient time for a species of *Propliopithecus* to have differentiated to the level of a new genus, in this case *Aegyptopithecus*. If, as the preliminary evidence indicates, this is what happened, then it is more reasonable to conclude that the hominid-like features of *Propliopithecus* are due to its primitiveness and not to its having had special relationship with the origin of the family of man. As is well known to students of the fossil record, Hominidae is a very late-appearing mammalian family. Notwithstanding a few recent papers it cannot be documented as having existed prior to the late Miocene, perhaps 14 million years ago when a species of the genus *Ramapithecus* occurred in East Africa, India and China. *Ramapithecus* is accepted by many as a hominid on the grounds of dental similarity to the Pleistocene hominid *Australopithecus* and Pleistocene-Recent *Homo*. For those who do no accept *Ramapithecus* as a hominid the family has hardly any Tertiary record.

Moeripithecus

Another of the dawn apes from the Fayum described by Schlosser was *Moeripithecus markgrafi*. This species is based on a type specimen which consists of a jaw fragment of a young animal with only the first and second molar preserved. It has proved to belong to a distinct species of *Propliopithecus* but not to a separate genus.

Aeolopithecus

Aeolopithecus chirobates, a new kind of Fayum Oligocene primate, was described and named by the author in 1965. The distinctive type, the only specimen, comes from Yale Quarry I. The type of *Aeolopithecus* consists of both branches of a lower jaw, fused at the front and carrying all of the teeth except the incisors, whose sockets are present. This is a relatively complete specimen as Egyptian Ologocene primates go, but unfortunately chemical corrosion during burial has removed enamel from all tooth surfaces. *Aeolopithecus* has relatively huge canines with stout roots, a large anterior premolar and quite small third molar. The decrease of jaw depth toward the rear and the outline of the chin cross-section

in this form suggest that it may have affinities with modern gibbons.

Aegyptopithecus

This species is perhaps the most significant find of the Fayum expedition. The new skull, about 28 million years of age, is older by 8 or 10 million years than the oldest previously known ape skull. Also, although incomplete, it is better preserved than are any other Tertiary hominoid crania. Numerous dental similarities between this species and the 16-20 million-year-old apes of East Africa suggest that it was in or near their ancestry. These in turn may well be close to the ancestry of the modern apes and man. *Aegyptopithecus zeuxis* is the largest of the African Oligocene primates (about as big as a gibbon), and is almost twice the size of species of *Aeolopithecus, Apidium,* and *Parapithecus*.

Aegyptopithecus possessed the distinctive dental features of early apes. Closure of the eye socket is nearly as complete as in modern apes and man, and frontal bones are fused.

CONCLUSION

Considered as a group, much about the probable course of primate evolution can be learned from the many specimens of the dawn apes now known. Various of these Egyptian Oligocene species can be interpreted as showing relationships to earlier and later Old World primates.

In closing it is perhaps well to bear in mind that none of the dawn apes and monkeys needs necessarily be close to the ancestry of any living primates—African or otherwise. Scientists even today know almost nothing of the first half of the Age of Mammals in Africa and have only scanty faunal samples from this continent during Oligocene and Miocene times. Many African Early Tertiary primate species must have existed about which we know nothing and some of which may have been more directly related to living man and his relatives than any we now know. The search for these is one of the exciting challenges to geobiologists of the future.

Human Behaviour
and the Origin of Man

Modern man is distinguished by his ability to talk, walk bipedally, and manufacture tools skilfully. These fundamental abilities are expressed in every human society and, because of their universality, their importance is often minimized. By comparing these behaviours with their counterparts in monkeys and apes, however, it can be seen that they are major adaptations. By speaking, for example, man is able to convey a great deal of information. He can communicate about past and future events and is able to organize the activities essential to man's way of life. In contrast, monkeys and apes are limited to communicating about their internal states. Fear, anger and contentment are readily expressed, but there is little reference to the external environment. One can imagine what human behaviour would be like if man were restricted to this type of communication.

The behaviours characterizing man have extensive biological bases and it is this special biology that permits man to acquire readily the behaviours that make him human. A human child easily learns to speak because he has the necessary neurological base and vocal tract, while a chimpanzee, even one raised in a human home an diligently tutored, cannot be taught to speak. Intensive training cannot compensate for the absence of the biological features critical to speech development. In a similar fashion, bipedal walking and skilful manufacture of tools are impossible without man's unique biology.

While it is biology that makes human behaviour possible, behaviour and its biological basis have evolved in a complex feedback relationship. In man's history, natural selection favoured the behavioural patterns that distinguish man from his apelike relatives. This can be illustrated by considering the evolution of speech. Some thousands of years ago, man's ancestors began communicating by a code in sounds. Improved communication enabled these early men

to hunt, gather food, elude predators, and, very important, to organize group activities more effectively than had been done earlier. Those individuals whose biology permitted them to engage more readily in these behaviours were likely to live longer and produce more offspring. Since biological structures result from an interplay between the genetic base and the environment, the proportion of individuals possessing the genes responsible for these structures increased. Gradually the genetic basis for the biological foundation of speech was incorporated into the human gene pool. Today all human populations possess genes that programme large areas of the brain for participation in speech behaviour.

The fundamental human adaptations of walking, talking and tool-using evolved at very different times. Evolution is clearly a continuous process with no major discontinuities, but to facilitate discussion, it is convenient to divide man's evolution into four stages: the transition from ape to man, earliest man, ancient man, and modern man.

THE TRANSITION
FROM APE TO MAN

Molecular biologists have shown recently that man is much more closely related to the chimpanzee and gorilla than to any other kind of primate. Quantifiable and repeatable, the techniques of molecular biology have been applied to a large number of molecules including DNA, some of the blood proteins and several enzymes. According to the molecular information, man and chimpanzee are more closely related than 'horse-donkey, water buffalo-cape buffalo, cat-lion or dog-fox' [1].[1] These conclusions suggest that man and ape shared a common ancestor as recently as 6 million years ago. This is less than a tenth of the time primates have existed [2].

From an evolutionary perspective, man is a very recent phenomenon. The view that there is a particularly close relationship between man and the African apes is not new. It is identical with the pre-evolutionary *scala naturae* and with the classic evolutionary view of Darwin and Huxley.

By Michael Raleigh and S. L. Washburn. Reprinted with permission of UNESCO, from *Impact of Science on Society*, XXIII, No. 1, 1973, pp. 5-13.

[1]The figures in brackets refer to the references at the end of this article.

The striking similarity between man and the apes is also apparent in the field studies of free-ranging primates. Chimpanzee behaviour is far more similar to human behaviour than to that of monkeys. In fact, many of the activities which have previously been considered unique to man have now been observed in wild chimpanzees [3]. The results of recent behavioural studies may be summarized in three major groups.

First is the matter of tool use. Chimpanzees use objects to a much greater extent than any other non-human animal. Studies of chimpanzees show that they use sticks and branches in agonistic displays, fishing for termites, and gathering honey and fire ants. Stones are thrown in aggressive interactions and, additionally, are utilized to crack nuts. Chimpanzees use leaves for cleaning themselves and for sponging and scooping water which has collected in crevices of trees. In the wild, chimpanzees have been observed employing a wide variety of objects for play. Limited as these activities may be from a human standpoint, they constitute considerably more object use than has been noted in any other animal.

Besides Hunting, Chimps use Gestures

Second is the fact that chimpanzees engage in hunting. Studies show that they hunt small mammals. This activity may involve both planned and unplanned attacks: occasionally chimpanzees fortuitously stumble across immature gazelles; sometimes the hunting is an organized activity involving several co-operating males.

Third concerns the use of gestures by chimpanzees. These gestures are remarkably human. When begging, chimpanzees hold their palms upward, sometimes placing an arm around the shoulders of another animal. Many of the similarities in gestures result from similarities in anatomy. This is apparent in stretching the arms to the sides, balancing in the same way, and in folding the arms. The similarity is very striking when chimpanzees jump—leaping from the hind legs, swinging their arms and landing on their hind legs, all in an amazingly human fashion.

The findings of molecular biology and behavioural studies complement each other and fun-

damentally alter our view of the problems associated with the origin of man. Many of the traditional studies relating to the problems of coming to the ground, the origin of hunting, the development of walking, and the rise of complex tool using need to be re-evaluated.

Traditionally, the origin of man has been considered the problem of how an arboreal animal came to the ground. The molecular data, however, show that the human lineage has a relatively short antiquity while the field studies demonstrate that chimpanzees and gorillas live on the ground and walk on their knuckles. Consequently, insight into the origin of man's locomotor adaptation is more likely to come from posing the question of how a ground-living knuckle-walker became a biped rather than by focusing attention on the transition of an arboreal ape to a ground dweller [4].

The suggestion that our ancestors were once knuckle-walkers is supported by the fact that man still occasionally employs this position. Obviously man's legs are so long that he cannot normally use the knuckle-walking position, but there are times when this position is employed—in line-ups, for example, for the American version of Rugby football. So even though human knuckle-walking is uncommon, it is anatomically possible. Some millions of years ago when arms were longer and legs shorter, it might have been part of the normal behaviour repertoire of our ancestors.

EARLIEST MAN'S FIRST ARRIVAL

In the past several years, palaeontologists and archaeologists have been discovering fossil remains at a tremendous rate. These discoveries show that earliest man first appeared more than 4 million years ago and survived until about 1 million years ago. His colonies inhabited the savannahs of eastern and southern Africa. By comparing the remains of earliest man with the bones of chimpanzees and modern man, scholars have demonstrated that the hip bones of these earliest men were shaped very much like those of modern man [5].

This suggests that these proto-humans (or prehominids) were able to walk bipedally and that their hands were free for making tools, carrying materials and defending themselves. In contrast to the very human pelvis, however, the brain was only a third of the size of contemporary man's. In light of this evidence, it is likely that most of man's distinguishing features (including intelligence, skilful use of complex tools, and language) evolved in the last million years—long after the human line had separated from that leading to the contemporary apes.

Equally intriguing are the cultural remains of these early humans. Some of their artefacts, such as simple pebble tools, are more than 3 million years old. Although crude, these tools must have enhanced the possibility of escaping from predators and increased the efficiency of hunting.

Furthermore, since we know that chimpanzees make any tools from materials such as wood, that could not be preserved for 2 million years, it is reasonable to infer that the stone objects represent only a small fraction of the tools earliest man produced. In contrast to the later stages of human evolution when cultural change was quite rapid, the early tools persisted in their unrefined form for more than 1 million years [6]. None the less, it was the success of a way of life, based on object-using, that enabled a knuckle-walker to evolve into a biped.

THEN ANCIENT MAN APPEARS ON STAGE

Emerging about 1 million years ago, ancient man evolved from earliest man and differs from him in several important anatomical and behavioural characteristics. Anatomically, the most noticeable change is the doubling of the brain size. In conjunction with this more human brain, there were major behavioural alterations. Unlike the earlier pebble tools, the stone tools that ancient man made were complex and varied. These tools are very difficult to reproduce and their presence demonstrates that ancient man developed far more skill than earliest man.

Hunting was a major activity of ancient man, with large animals, such as elephants, frequently being killed [7]. This kind of hunting would have been impossible without a high degree of planning and co-operation. Caves in China re-

veal that ancient man used fire, perhaps for the purposes of driving out cave bears, warming himself, or cooking his food.

Because of these behavioural alterations, ancient man's way of life was certainly more human than that of earliest man. The progressive changes produced a very successful species that occupied the entire Old World. Nevertheless, man's unspecialized hunting way of life persisted for several hundred thousand years.

Material progress was very slow. The making of particular kinds of tools, such as hand axes, persisted for long periods of time; these tools have been found distributed over huge geographic areas. Archaeological evidence of this kind suggests that ancient men had not attained a fully human intellectual capacity.

NEXT TO ARRIVE IS MODERN MAN

With the advent of anatomically modern man about 40,000 years ago, the rate of cultural evolution accelerated dramatically. Within a period of a few thousand years, man invented new kinds of weapons and tools. Elaborate artwork, agriculture and boatmaking made their appearance. Man invaded the Arctic and peopled the New World.

This cultural explosion may have been made possible by the evolution of language in its modern form. The extensive anatomical base for language implies that there must have been a long period of evolution in which simple speech behaviour evolved in a feedback relation with neural and articulatory structures. Several scholars believe that all contemporary languages began evolving from a single language about 40,000 years ago, earlier forms of man probably having utilized a much less effective type of communication. Speech, with its capacity to convey tremendous amounts of information, probably did not appear until the final stage of human evolution.

The interrelation of human behaviour and human biology has changed slowly over millions of years, culminating in the evolution of contemporary man. This evolutionary heritage has profound consequences for human societies because the biological basis of human nature evolved under conditions that no longer exist. In the world of prehistoric man, people lived in small, permanent social groups. Most people were born, reached maturity, and died in the same social group. Most likely there were fewer than 100 members in these groups and each person was familiar with everyone else.

On the basis of skeletal remains, it appears that most of our forebears died young and few people survived much more than thirty years. Food was secured by hunting for animals and gathering plants, but this arrangement supported only sparse populations. As in the case of the hip bones which help form the pelvis, the human brain evolved as an adaptation to these conditions. Because the brain was designed for life in a world that has vanished, its abilities are limited in a peculiar fashion. Despite this the brain has been viewed as an infallible organ of rational thought. This idea, in turn, has produced unnecessary confusion about the nature of man. In the remainder of this article, we would like to consider the implications of viewing human biology in general, and the brain in particular, as adaptations to these primitive conditions.

SELECTIVE LEARNING: WALKING AND THROWING

Man easily learns the kinds of behaviour that were important during his evolution. The feedback relation between successful behaviour and biological structures produced brains that learn certain behaviours far more easily than others. Human beings learn to walk proficiently, but few learn to swim effectively because walking was important during human evolution and swimming was not. Throwing and hunting represent two behaviours that were critical in the history of man and their acquisition illustrates what is known as the ease of learning principle [8].

Powerful throwing is anatomically possible only for apes and man. As zoo visitors observe, chimpanzees can throw accurately both underhand and overhand. Behavioural studies of free-ranging chimpanzees, however, indicate that they throw only when displaying or attacking. In a natural environment, a chimpanzee's throwing is not rewarded or encouraged and these animals do not develop their potential for throwing.

In contrast, man readily learns to throw powerfully because it is a socially rewarded activity. Unlike a chimpanzee, man practises throwing; attainment of skill requires a tremendous amount of repetition. Whether one throws spears, stones, or baseballs is determined by one's particular culture, but in every society the skill is learned in play. It is remarkable how many games include throwing and how pleasurable it is for the individuals involved. Throwing has been of great adaptive importance in hunting and fighting and, like other formerly important behaviours, it was encouraged by man's social circumstances. Thus, even such an apparently simple action as throwing depends on anatomical structures, the brain, and social encouragement.

In a similar fashion, hunting has been so important in man's development that people easily learn to enjoy hunting—even when there is no apparent, reasonable reward. Many people will hunt or fish at great effort and expense despite no economic need and negligible results. The American Government, for instance, has for many years raised fish and game for the pleasure of hunters; these expenditures go unquestioned. Unless taught otherwise, men enjoy the emotions of the chase and the kill as manifested by the use of light tackle or arms to enhance the illusion of struggle and achievement.

While hunting is not an innately programmed activity, it represents a class of behaviours which can be learned with great facility. It is difficult to prevent man from learning to like to hunt, especially in societies where hunting is frequently the centre of play activities. As in throwing, hunting is learned because in times past it was highly rewarded. Just as the role of an actor is meaningless without the play, so human behaviour has no meaning without human society.

HUMAN BIOLOGY LAGS WHILE CULTURE EXPANDS

In the cases of hunting and throwing, evolution has produced accord between biology and previously effective behaviours. Evolution has also adapted the human mind to that earlier world, however, where hunting and throwing were crucial activities. For more than 99 per cent of his career, man has lived in a world of small tribal societies; only very recently has dramatic cultural change altered this situation. Human biology has not kept pace with the accelerating cultural revolution, for the human mind is still biologically designed to function in the world of primitive man.

Living in such a world, the human brain makes a series of fundamental assumptions—that man lives in a small, flat, simple universe, where there is no place for scientific explanation. Causes are thought to be the actions of spirits or gods; nature is personified, and natural events such as floods are explained as resulting from the whims of supernatural beings. The forces governing nature are assumed to operate by the same standards that govern conscious human behaviour.

In the physical and biological sciences, this primitive view of the world has been replaced. For science, every dimension of reality is new. These conceptual revolutions result from the techiques of science rather than the development of more intelligent human beings. The notions of time, space and causation that are so commonplace in science differ unbelievably from the concepts of the primitive world. Man's primitive mind can comfortably deal, for example, with periods of time of about 100 years but it cannot appreciate the difference between 100,000, 10 million, and 100 million years. The century span is the time during which man can continue to appreciate events on an emotional level. Science, on the other hand, works with vast quantities of time which are determined by objective techniques such as radiometric dating. To scientists, 30 million years is a manageable amount of time.

Even in science, the changes that freed man from the primitive world are very recent. Belief in spontaneous biological generation was abandoned about a century ago. Some of the understanding of the nature of dreaming is a product of only the last twenty years. Although recent, science's liberation from the primitive world and its beliefs has had a major impact on society. Had science retained the concepts of the ancient world, the germ theory of disease would never have developed and leeches would not have given way to the pharmacological industry.

HUMAN MINDS DEVISE SOCIAL INSTITUTIONS

Contrasting with the precepts of science are the social institutions of man, for these still reflect the values of that simpler world. Consequently, man's notions about religion, law, and political systems persist. In every society, institutionalized religion has many social and psychological functions. Although these functions transcent the realm of biology, all religions are based on the way the untrained human mind deals with the problems of nature and causes. Without the singularity of the human mind there could be no religions.

Man's view of his political systems is also a product of this brain. In the age of nuclear weapons, political systems that free man from the primitive world are desperately needed. Yet the human mind is adapted to life in a world where small tribes constantly fought their neighbours. Without seeing one's political institutions as virtuous, desirable and necessary, it would be difficult to survive in this world. Consequently, it is not surprising that attempts to replace the old order with institutions which rationally distribute territory and resources among the world's populations are adamantly opposed by large blocks of people. Under the conditions of the primitive world, social institutions such as religions and political systems which relied heavily on one powerful leader were adaptive, but today these arrangements may no longer be needed nor desirable. They may, indeed, be as outmoded as belief in spontaneous generation.

Aggressive individual behaviour is another manifestation of man's evolutionary heritage. Until quite recently, aggression was a necessary component of most human societies. It functioned to ensure order within a tribe and to fend off raiding neighbours. From our ancestors, modern man inherited the hormonal and neurological factors that enabled him to be aggressive. As a result, while man does not *have* to learn to be aggressive, he is *very likely* to do so. Traditional European society is a vivid illustration of this point, where aggression permeated the entire culture. Actions which were damaging to the individual were used in child rearing, in school, in sports, and in personal disputes: they were regarded as the natural way to guide the young and settle issues. For centuries, torture was commonplace and executions were important public events.

In our time, man's inclination towards aggression probably does not account for the institution of war but, from an evolutionary point of view, it is difficult to understand how war could have been so common and exalted if man had not been highly aggressive. As in religion, aggression can be understood only when it is viewed as a situation produced by cultural and biological change over time, as a product of evolution.

It is by recognizing his potential for aggression that man can begin to control human aggressivity. There is no definite amount of aggression that has to be released in one's lifetime. Rather, the amount is determined by an individual's life situation. Consequently, unless he alters his prescientific customs, man cannot hope to avoid paying a great price in terms of individual conflict and international war.

CRITERIA FOR TOLERATING DIFFERENCES IN BEHAVIOUR

The notion that man easily learns those behaviours which have been important in his history is crucial to the evolutionary approach to human nature. Man readily learns to be religious, to be aggressive, and to be social. The social learning is complex and it is easy to learn social relations with the near and the few, for these are the dimensions of primitive society. It is far more difficult to acquire comparable feelings for the many and the remote. A clear case where the standards of behaviour tolerated in a distant country would never have been allowed near home is the war in Viet-Nam—how many Americans would permit the declaration of a free fire zone in Ohio?[2]

In another way, the evolutionary data may be applied to a developing social institution. At present, many millions of people are spending a

quarter of their lifetime in school. This is a completely new social situation and there is much concern about its psychological costs. Studies of non-human primates show that learning takes place in a social situation that represents the antithesis, to cite a case, of the American educational system. These studies indicate that early experience is overwhelmingly important, especially when the species matures as slowly as man does.

At first, learning occurs in emotional, closely interpersonal situations, and later it is motivated by clearly defined objectives. Because learning is enjoyable, repetition is ensured until the skills are mastered. Peers are very important in the transmission of education, and the rewards of education are highly specific and immediately important. American schools operate contrary to all that is known about how primates learn. Formal American education begins too late and is set in a cold, impersonal environment. Great importance is attached to words, rather than action. Discipline, not play, is a major feature of the system. Peers are excluded from the role of teacher, and the goals are clear neither to the teacher nor to the student. All natural learning situations have been eliminated from the activities of the school; it would be difficult to devise a worse system for educating human beings.

One of the purposes of evolutionary studies is to view man in a new perspective. Whatever future there may be, the actors in the new social system will be endowed with the peculiarities of man's further evolutionary heritage. For any society, the profound consequences of this fact cannot be overemphasized.

The physical and biological sciences have created a new world of technical possibilities for human behavioural improvement far beyond the imaginings of our ancestors. Hopefully, biology and the study of human evolution can help to free man from the limitations of the primitive world so that he may flourish in the world of the future.

[2]A free fire zone is a combat target area where artillery or aircraft may direct their fire at known or suspected installations or troop movements without specific authorization as in the case of the opposite, 'observed fire' situation. The zone is posted with signs advising local inhabitants of the peril.

References

1. Doolittle, R. F.; Mross, G. A. Identity of chimpanzee with human fibrinopeptides. *Nature,* vol. 225, 1970, p. 643-55.

2. Sarich, V. M. A molecular approach to the question of

human origins. In: P. Dolhinow and V. M. Sarich (eds.), *Background for man.* Boston, Mass., Little, Brown, 1971.

3. Van Lawick-Goodall, J. *In the shadow of man.* Boston, Mass., Houghton Mifflin, 1971.

4. Washburn, S. L. *The study of human evolution.* Eugene, Oreg., University of Oregon Press, 1968.

5. Pilbeam, D. *The ascent of man.* New York, N.Y., Macmillan, 1972.

6. Clark, J. D. *The prehistory of Africa.* London, Thames & Hudson, 1970.

7. Howell, F. C. *Early man.* New York, N.Y., Time Inc., 1965.

8. Hamburg, D. A. Emotions in the perspective of human evolution. In: P. Knapp (ed.) *Expression of the emotion of man.* New York, N.Y., International Universities Press, 1963.

The Evolution
of Sexual Behavior

Human sexual behavior is as much the end product of evolution as human sexual anatomy. But while the idea that the body has evolved has become familiar, we are only beginning to understand the implications of extending to behavior the same kind of analysis that has proved successful with flesh and bone. Indeed, it must seem at first glance that this is an impossible task. The evolution of human anatomy can be studied from the various fossil forms that have been discovered, and the gradual transition from ape man to true man can be discerned with some accuracy. But there is only the sketchiest idea of what these creatures were *doing*, so is it possible to ask about the evolution of their behavior?

Nevertheless, it is known that there must have been such an evolution. In the same way as there was a gradual transition from apelike to manlike form there must have been a similar gradual transition from apelike to manlike function. Man's body testifies to the first change—as any simple comparison of man with other primates will show. To what extent does his behavior testify to the second?

At least one school of zoologists would claim that the study of the evolution of behavior can be more instructive than that of the evolution of anatomy. The science of ethology—defined by one of its practitioners as the "biological study of behavior"—which has flourished under the leadership of such men as Konrad Lorenz in Germany and Niko Tinbergen in Britain, is one of the youngest branches of zoology. Its stance is neo-Darwinian, and in essence it points up the fact that natural selection operates on the performance of the animal. Structure therefore evolves in order that the creature may function in ways that give it selective advantage in the struggle for survival.

In the case of certain gross motor activities this may seem obvious: speed enables animals to chase and to flee, et cetera. But the ethologists have concentrated mainly on the *signaling* abilities of animals, showing how these social signs serve to enhance threat behavior, inhibit aggression, attract mates and so on. The point about these signals—whether they be structural, such as bright coloring, or purely behavioral, such as specific postures—is that they evolved by the process of natural selection and hence have become part of the genetic repertoire of the animal.

When a black-headed gull is defending its nesting site during the breeding season the presence of any other animal is clearly threatening to it. Male and female black-headed gulls look pretty much alike; so even when a prospective mate lands on the site, the male's aggressive instinct of territorial defense is aroused. However, if the female does not stare at the male but turns her head aside, then the male's aggression is inhibited and the preliminaries of mating become possible.

This looking-away gesture of the gull is only one of many in its total ethogram of postures and gestures, which are as much a part of its genetic endowment as feathers and wings—and just as necessary to its survival and success. The ethologists have found that by careful comparison of closely related species, they can arrive at answers to the question, Why does this particular species behave in this particular way?

Ethologists have, until very recently, confined their attention to lowlier forms of life, such as birds, fish, and small mammals. In these the genetically based behaviors are easy to ascertain. But what of the more complex, higher mammals—and what of man?

Some very careful studies of man's primate cousins over the past decade have produced much-needed comparative material from closely related species. But these species prove to be much more complex than the little creatures familiar to ethology. It is not that they are without genetically programed predispositions, but that their range of behavior is extended by programing to take more advantage of their learning ability than is the case with lower forms.

At the pinnacle of this development stands man, with the greatest learning capacity of all animals. His behavior has evolved, it is true, but this evolution has been toward greater flexibility. To put it paradoxically: man's greatest instinct is the instinct to learn. It is therefore natural to man to be unnatural—to go beyond nature and supplement the genetically endowed predispositions of behavior with cultural forms not built into the chromosomes.

This has been regarded by some observers as the ultimate stumbling block to our understanding of human behavior on ethological lines. And it is true that if the methods of the ethologists are rigidly stuck to, only a limited amount will be learned about man. Nevertheless, things are not so black. What the flexible learning ability of man allows him to do is extend the range of his behavior, but only within well-defined limits. His genetic behavioral inheritance lays down for him a limited number of things to do, but he can vary enormously the ways in which he does them.

For example, as with many other animals, man prefaces the formation of a stable mating arrangement with some form of courting activity. The form of this activity, however, can be extremely varied, and consists of a great many postures, gestures, and sounds that are traditional rather than genetic. The black-headed gull can look away and do a few other things, but it cannot write sonnets, dance the frug, or wear an engagement ring. The difference can perhaps be expressed in a metaphor: animal behavior is like filling in a form; in some animals there are a lot of instructions on the form but only a limited space for answers, while in other animals there is the same number of instructions but the space for answers is large and the range of possible answers is wide. It is not that animals have instincts while man does not, but that man can do more things about his instincts than other animals.

What kinds of evidence exist for looking at the basic sexual behavior of man as the end product of a long process of natural selection? There is the fossil record; the social behavior of related species; the social behavior of the creature itself. With a judicious survey of the evidence from these three sources, it should be possible to reconstruct the evolution of human sexual behavior. (I am confining this analysis to heterosexual behavior.)

It may seem absurd, but perhaps the greatest gap is in the information on the natural sexual behavior of man. A great deal of the knowledge here is inferential; very little is known about sex, despite man's seeming obsession with it. But at a fairly gross level there is enough known to start with, even if the knowledge is not of the detailed kind that the ethologist would need. What, then, are some of the main characteristics of human sexual behavior?

There is the striking fact of the absence of an oestrous cycle in the female: she does not go into heat. This fact is usually phrased as "permanent sexual receptivity" in the human female—which may seem a little extreme and over-optimistic. Such evidence as there is on female receptivity indicates that it is at its height just before and just after menstruation. This is curious in that the peak in other primates comes halfway between menstrual periods—that is, during ovulation. In other words, most non-human primate females are most receptive at the time when they are most likely to conceive, while the human primate female is most receptive when she is least likely to conceive. There may be the evolution of some kind of birth-control device lurking here, but it is difficult to see this as being very efficacious unless the female determines the timing of intercourse according to her own physiological state of readiness—an interesting but unlikely theory.

The lack of heat goes along with the lack of a breeding season. This is not peculiar to man, but it does put him into the category of primates that have continual sexual activity. True, there are birth peaks in most societies, which shows that breeding is to some extent seasonal (in Christian countries the peak comes nine months after Christmas, as a rule), but there is no rutting season as such in man. This year-round activity is probably also connected with another feature—namely, the high level of sexual activity and the drive for novelty and variety in sexual experience. Compared, say, with the gorilla, man exhibits a level of sexual activity that is quite phenomenal.

Insofar as the end product of sexual activity is offspring—and in man this is not always the case—the "breeding pair" is the most typical unit for this purpose. Like many fish, birds, and mammals that establish "pair bonds," man does not just mate promiscuously and then leave the female to rear the young. Rather he tends to associate regular sexual activity and at least some degree of emotional attachment with the rearing of offspring.

One way of looking at this—favored, for example, by Desmond Morris—is to see the "pair bonding" phenomenon among animals duplicated in man by the process of "falling in love"—a behavioral mechanism for keeping the pair together. Other observers (including this one) see more of a contractual element in the male-female relationship when it comes to the business of forming a family and rearing children. Love and marriage may go together like a horse and carriage, but let us not forget that the horse has to be broken and harnessed.

Strong bonds between mated pairs are certainly common enough in *Homo sapiens,* but this is by no means the whole story. These bonds are not necessarily the result of a primitive pair-bonding instinct and, indeed, seem extremely variable in intensity. They are primarily an adolescent phenomenon and obviously have to do with giving impetus to the breeding process. But once this is under way the relationship becomes complex indeed, and the bond between the pair is as much an outcome of their role as parents as of their role as lovers. The "tenacity of the pair bond," which Morris seems so anxious to establish, is as much a tenacity of the parental bond as anything else. There are obviously good evolutionary reasons for this. But the bond is not exclusive; there is no reason why it should be; and there are many reasons why it could not have been.

The starting point for the analysis of the biological evolution of any human social behavior is obvious: the brain. Apart perhaps from the precision grip of the hand and the bones and muscles devoted to the striding walk, this is man's only major biological specialization.

The question that must then be asked is the familiar one of chicken or egg. Did the growth of the brain lead to the capacity for greater social complexity, or vice versa? I think the answer is undoubtedly that, as certain kinds of animals developed complex social systems as weapons in the struggle for survival, there was pressure in the direction of selecting out those animals with the best brains. These were the animals better able to cope with the complexities of life in a so-

cial group. But in our particular family of animals, the primates, what kind of social system was involved?

Here another of our three kinds of evidence must be introduced: the social behavior of primates. This is, as might be expected, enormously varied. But certain constant features stand out in those primates that, like man, have an organized social system, and particularly in those that, again like man, have spent a considerable portion of their evolution outside the forest environment in which the earliest primates were nurtured. Typical examples are the baboons and macaques.

A baboon group usually comprises about forty animals that wander about in search of food, always keeping together. This cohesion is of enormous advantage to animals like these, living as they do in open savanna and subject to attacks from predators. A single baboon is not much of a match for the big cats, but a group of baboons stands a pretty good chance of beating off attacks with concerted action.

The social system, however, is anything but democratic. Power in the group lies with the biggest and most successful of the males. These (never more than about six in number, however large the total group) stay at the center with the females and young. Around this central core will wander a number of "cadets"—young males who are candidates for membership in the hierarchy. At the edge of the horde are the "peripheral males"—unsuccessful and immature animals who have not yet made it. Many never will. Some even wander off and become solitaries—the drop-outs of the monkey rat race. These peripheral males act as first line of defense and a kind of living radar for the group. The big males of the hierarchy are the ultimate deterrent; they also keep order within the group, and are especially solicitous of the welfare of the young.

This is a very sketchy account of a "typical" society of ground-dwelling primates. What are its dynamics? How do young males get into the hierarchy and what is the significance of this? The significance is overwhelming in terms of the evolution of the group because *it is only the males of the hierarchy that do the breeding.* While the cadets and peripheral males may get a chance to copulate with a female during her infertile periods, only the hierarchical males mate with the females at the peak of oestrus—that is, during ovulation. Therefore, only these males are going to pass on genes to the next generation. It is of tremendous significance, then, to know what characterizes these successful males.

Before answering this question it must be noted that there is another form of terrestrial primate society that has to be reckoned with: the form represented by baboons living on dry desert savanna, as opposed to those living in woodland savanna. The desert horde is not divided into the components just described, but rather into a series of polygamous families in each of which one male collects a number of females (usually four) and monopolizes these the whole time. Here also, however, there are the unsuccessful males at the edge waiting to get in. How do they do it, and who succeeds?

Not to put too fine a point on it, it is the smart ones who make it. But what constitutes smartness? Basically, it is the ability to control and time responses—to understand the consequences of one's actions. The British ethologist Michael Chance has described the process as "equilibration"; thus, an animal caught between the desire to copulate with an oestrous female, on the one hand, and the desire to escape attack from a dominant male, on the other, must be able to inhibit his sexual response and bide his time. If he fails to do so often enough, he will, at worst, be either killed or driven out, or, at best, fail to ingratiate himself with his superiors and thus will not be tolerated by them. The stupid animal, then, one that blunders about, following without foresight the dictates of his lustful and aggressive appetites, will never make it to the top. The cunning animal, on the other hand, that can forgo present indulgence in anticipation of future reward, will be more likely to get there.

Of course, he has to have other qualities. He must be sociable and able to co-operate, or the big males will not accept him. He must also be acceptable to the females, it seems; hence his capacities as a baby minder (and the rank of his mother) are important. Besides possessing these charming attributes, he must also be tough and aggressive in order to assert his rights as a hierarchy member. It is easy to see the evolutionary advantages of such a process. It is a breeding system that puts at a premium those qualities in the male most advantageous to the survival of the group.

If this kind of social system was, in fact, typical of man's ancestors, then it provides some powerful clues concerning the evolution of the brain. Clearly, it was those animals with the best brains who were going to do the breeding, and each generation would see a ruthless selection of the best-brained males, with the dumbest and weakest going to the wall. And it was the *controlling* aspects of the brain that were being so strongly selected. The more the emotions of aggression and lust came under cortical control, the better chance the animal had of surviving and passing on his genes to the next generation.

But the expanding brain had to cope with other things besides sex and aggression. Predominant among these were the use of tools and the development of language. Large areas of the cerebellum are concerned with the control of the hand, and the growth of this center must have been a response to the demands of toolmaking. Control over the emotions was one thing; control of the environment through tools and weapons was, however, equally important. Selection favored the controlled and *skillful* animal. It also favored the animal that could *communicate* best. Up to a point, a series of nonlinguistic signals will do; but after a certain point of social complexity is reached, co-operation is impossible without a more flexible code. Large areas of the brain, then, are devoted to speech.

Many commentators have stressed these two aspects of brain evolution, but few have taken the breeding problem seriously. Yet without this component the major puzzle in brain evolution remains unanswered: How did the hominid brain manage to evolve so quickly? About a million years ago, the brain of one of the earliest recognizable hominids (the family that includes man and his extinct relatives and ancestors) was little larger than that of the chimpanzee. Within that million years it trebled in size—an almost unprecedented rate of evolution.

Now, whatever the pressures in favor of a larger, "thinking" brain exerted by the demands for better technicians and speakers, the question still remains: By what kind of breeding system were these newly acquired traits so quickly de-veloped? Given that the prespeech and pretools system had, built into it, the breeding mecha-nisms we have described, we only have to add that the successful breeders needed to be elo-quent and skillful, as well as controlled. The sys-tem would then ensure that these were the males who passed on the essential genes, and the rapid (in evolutionary terms) development of the large forebrain would be a certainty.

This suggests that throughout the evolution of the hominid lines that eventually led to *Homo sapiens*, the social system was one in which the majority of the breeding was done by a minority of the males, with the least successful males being largely shut out of the breeding sys-tem—in other words, a system based on the polygyny of the powerful. And note that this polygyny has not to do primarily with sexual ap-petite. It has to do with dominance and the rela-tion of males to males. The survival value of the system is obvious.

And now comes the most controversial and difficult of the three kinds of evidence: the fossil record. It is possible to know that the model of the society of the ground-dwelling primates is applicable to human evolution only if it can be shown that the model plausibly fits the earliest of man's ancestors. It has been established that the hominid line evolved from monkeylike forms that moved from forest to savanna, and hence must have been in some ways like contemporary savanna-dwelling primates. Those earlier homi-nids of a million years ago on the East African savanna were elementary hunters, and this trait increased in complexity and importance as time went by. Hence, to the qualities that went into being a dominant male must be added skill in hunting. Indeed, it may have been the pressures of the chase that accelerated the demand for more advanced tools and speech.

Some writers have seized upon the fact that man's earliest manlike ancestors were hunters, in order to "prove" many things about the changes from the apelike to the human in sexual behavior. But it must be remembered that the changes did not occur overnight, and that there was much in the old vegetarian ape that was use-ful to his omnivorous successor. Some things certainly changed. The female presumably came to be less and less under the control of the oes-trous cycle, and the "permanent sexual receptiv-ity" phenomenon emerged.

It has been suggested that this happened as a result of the pressures exerted by the need for co-operative hunting. Hunters need a fixed home base. The females stay in this base with the young; the males return and provision them—a practice unheard of among vegetarian primates, but common for example, among hunting carnivores, such as wolves. It has been argued that with such a system the old primate dominance hierarchy could not operate, since this depended on females coming in and out of heat and being monopolized by the top males during ovulation; if the males had to be away a good deal of the time, this would not work.

What is more, if the male needed a female to work for him—cooking, skinning, gathering vegetable food, et cetera—he would want her "attached" for more of the time than just when she was feeling sexy. Similarly, she would want the constant attention of the male for provision-ing herself and her young. If she were constantly available for sexual intercourse, this would be more likely to happen. The high level of sexual-ity would make the relationship more rewarding to the partners and hence keep them bonded. Thus many features of human sexuality would emerge as responses to the demands of the hunt-ing situation.

This is fine until it is pushed one step further, as it usually is, and the evolving hominid is cred-ited with instinctive tendencies to form monoga-mous nuclear families. I never cease to be amazed by the ingenuity of speculative writers in their efforts to prove that deep in man's nature is a *Saturday Evening Post* family: Dad, Mom, and the kids. Their assertiveness on this point has often a rather frantic air to it, and what they never do is ask what the consequences would have been if our earliest protohuman ancestors had allowed fair shares for all in the mating game. It seems unimaginative, to say the least, to pin these enterprising creatures down to dreary monogamy.

The point here is that none of the features of human sexuality that have developed are incom-patible with a breeding system based on the rela-tive dominance of a few males. If a male can at-tach one female to him for the reasons ad-vanced, he can attach several just as easily, provided he can maintain his harem against all comers. Insofar as only a minor part of the food intake of hunters is animal protein and something approaching 80 per cent is vegetable, then a small army of root diggers and berry pickers may well have been an advantage to a male.

It can never be known exactly what kind of mating institutions characterized the transitional ape man. But it is possible to ask: In order for the critical developments in the evolution of the brain to take place so quickly, what kind of breeding system must have been in operation? The answer is: one that would rapidly select out the animals with the better brains and pass on their genes to the next generation. And, concomitantly, one that would push to the peripheries of the breeding system animals lacking the qualities of intelligence and control. Some kind of hierarchical system with differential access to females would solve this problem, and seems to me to be the only candidate. If every male had been allowed the chance to contribute equally to the gene pool—as would be the case in a monogamous system—man might never have made the *sapiens* bit and been forever stuck as *Homo stupidus:* promising, with his speechlike grunts and crude tools, but not really in the top league.

I have considered only the male contribution to brain development here because it is the most obvious. But, lest I be accused of prejudice, we should look at the female's role. Was she simply a passive mechanism for passing on the genes of the big-brained, dominant males?

It could well be, but there is a chance that she actively helped the process along. I have mentioned that the rank of a male's mother may affect his chances of getting into the hierarchy. The son of a high-ranking female can be kept near the center of the group by his mother, where the big males will learn to tolerate him—a help when he comes to make his bid for membership. If this is a crucial criterion for membership in the hierarchy—and we are not sure that it is—then the qualities that go into being a high-ranking female, insofar as they involve cortical control of sex, may well contribute to the development we have envisaged.

They may also help to account for the gradual loss of hormonal influence over sexual receptivity in the female that led to the loss of the oestrous cycle. The female was no longer subject to periodic sexual mania during which she solicited any male in sight; she had gradually come to control her own responses in the same way as the male. It may well be, in fact, that this permanent sexual receptivity in the female was a by-product of the general processes mentioned earlier, rather than a result of the pressures introduced by hunting. To answer this question more thoroughly it would be necessary to know what qualities went into being a dominant female. All that can be said is that they were not necessarily the same qualities that went into being a dominant male.

But it is not desirable to take only one primate system as the model. Those polygamous primates that live on the arid savannas form "harems," in which several females are permanently attached to a male who monopolizes them throughout the year, despite oestrus and seasonal breeding. Some observers have claimed that the hominids passed through a similar stage of development, since, during the forging time of their existence—the Pliocene—there was extreme drought, and they must have adapted to these dry conditions in much the same way as contemporary desert-dwelling baboons. Of course, the creatures discussed here were not baboons but ape men; still, the baboons do rather knock on the head the idea that there could not have been stable family groups within the protohominid band as long as the females were subject to periodic sex mania and breeding was seasonal. There is no doubt, however, that permanent mating of a human kind is facilitated by the fact that the human female, in a sense, comes into heat at puberty and stays there—at a moderate level of sexual excitement—for most of her life.

There are several forms of breeding hierarchy possible, given an animal that lacks the oestrous cycle, and we cannot know which of these prevailed. Indeed, various groups of evolving hominids may have tried them all. Some may even have tried monogamy. What matters is not the actual institutional form, but the differential access to the females.

The fact that permanently receptive females were more or less permanently attached to dominant males would simply make life harder for the young males who wanted to get into the hierarchy, and would increase the demands for better equilibration—for greater control and inhibition. It would be unlikely under these conditions that some males would be absolutely barred from breeding (although it could well happen), but some would be *less likely* than others to contribute significantly to the genetic endowment of the group.

The criteria of dominance would, of course, differ as the creature became progressively more "human," but they would be basically much the same as among the primates. Hence the unsuccessful male would have to be controlled, cunning, co-operative, attractive to the ladies, good with the children, relaxed, tough, eloquent, skillful, knowledgeable, and proficient in self-defense and hunting. Depending on the nature of the group, some of these qualities might have been emphasized more than others.

With the advent of agriculture and the fighteningly rapid growth of population densities over the past ten thousand years, things have changed. But the animal coping with these changed conditions is the end product of hundreds of thousands of years of intensive selection in which, if this hypothesis is correct, differential access to mates was of crucial importance. And this *must* have left its mark on our behavior.

A brief look at the incest taboo will complete the roster of current sexual facts and their evolution. Many observers have put the taboo on incest at the heart of human social development. Animals are incestuous; man is not. This, then, is the great breakthrough. Many reasons have been given for this, and all assume that the taboo is *imposed*. But it is highly probable that it is, in fact, a natural development.

As far as we can tell from nonhuman evidence, there is for example, little incest between mother and son. The mother is to her son a dominant animal, and mating requires that the female partner be subdominant. If a young male manages to get into the hierarchy, he may or may not mate with his sisters. On the other hand, the possibility of fathers mating with daughters is quite high. The frequency of occurrence of incest in human society is exactly paral-

lel. This fits our picture of sexual relations evolving in a dominance framework.

It follows that with the stabilization of mating relationships, equilibration would have been more in demand. Particularly in the case of the growing "boy," it would have been important to control any sexual approaches toward mothers and sisters who were under the control of a dominant male or males; he also would have had to inhibit aggressive advances toward the latter. Hence neural mechanisms evolved to this end.

The young hominid met his first and most intensive trial of controls in the immediate family circle, but he was learning them as they applied to *all* dominant males and their females. Freud, although perhaps right about some of the evolutionary processes that led to incest taboos, was wrong about locating them exclusively in the nuclear family. The Oedipus complex has to do with the relationship of young subordinate males to older dominant males—not just sons to fathers.

The sum total of all these processes was a creature capable of control and of guilt—the mechanism that lets the individual know it has broken the rules. As the controlling elements of the brain came to dominate the appetitive elements, the evolving hominid could depend less on instinct as a guide to action. D. H. Lawrence, it seems, was wrong: sex really is in the head.

If differential access to mates is the secret of it all, how does this help us to understand our own behavior? It has been argued that man is tenaciously monogamous; but this monogamy, if we are honest, is more apparent than real. It is very rare for men of power, wealth, and influence to confine their sexual activities to one woman. Although the majority of males in a population are confined to one woman at a time, those in a position to accumulate more seem to do so. These may be straight wives, as in overtly polygamous societies, or they may go under other names. A "big man" is one who has access to many females, or is credited with such access, or who controls a large number. They may not be mates, but we know that only a high-prestige man can run even a chaste harem. How far up the pecking order is a man with one wife, two full-time secretaries, twenty typists, and the girl who comes in to do his manicuring? I can think of professors with a modest haul of, say, one wife, one secretary, one research assistant, two teaching assistants, several members of a research team, and four part-time typists. The gathering unto males of females as a sign of status must surely emanate from deep down there in the cunning brain.

Another factor that must be an end product of the processes discussed is the difference between male and female sexual behavior in *Homo sapiens*. Because the equilibration process was predominantly directed toward the male, we might expect that he is more readily conditionable in matters of sex than the female—that most males are more easily made to feel guilty about sexual matters.

Men are caught between their inherited tendencies to promiscuity and dominance, and the necessities of regularized mating; women, between the same promiscuous tendencies and the pulls toward security for self and offspring that can usually be obtained only by at least a show of fidelity. This is another product of the dominance process wherein the status of the male is measured by his control over females.

If this control is challenged, then the "owner's" self-esteem suffers. It is noticeable that it is usually women who are *punished* for unfaithfulness. Thus the other curiosity of male behavior—sexual jealousy—is part and parcel of the scheme.

In any event, the doctrine that male and female differences in sexual behavior are simply the result of the learning of different sex roles needs careful examination in the light of the evolutionary evidence. Also, the notion that male-female relationships can be totally explained by pair-bonding tendencies that never quite evolved properly (Desmond Morris again) should be treated skeptically.

The point here is that human sexual behavior is the product of enormously complex evolutionary processes. It is no good taking fragments of this behavior and trying to explain them by *ad hoc* hypotheses, however entertaining. The only theory worth aiming at is one that will account for *all* the basic emotions—dominance, love, guilt, tenderness, parental affection, jealousy, security, lust, fidelity, novelty, and many others. Such a theory must take account of the difficult evolutionary problems that we have raised.

There are obviously many confused issues here. I have been able to outline only a fraction of the complexities, have glossed over many extremely complicated issues, and missed others completely. So, if nothing else, perhaps I have put the interested reader on guard against those who seek to exploit the obvious interest of this topic by offering intellectual short cuts to solutions. As I have said, some things we can never know, and it is dishonest to pretend that answers are possible; but other things can be settled with a fair degree of approximation to the truth—given time, patience, and hard work.

Human Evolution: Life-Styles and Lineages of Early Hominids

Primates that walked upright and are believed to be ancestors of human beings lived in Africa at least 3 million years ago. Because these early hominids have no living counterparts, anthropologists are trying to reconstruct their history from an ever-expanding collection of fossils and artifacts. Many now believe that the early hominids had behavior patterns that are distinctive characteristics of human beings. Moreover, some anthropologists postulate that at least two lineages of early hominids existed between 1 and 3 million years ago, but only one lineage survived and evolved into human beings.

According to evolutionary theory, early hominids evolved from apes and then into human beings who, for most of their past, have been hunter-gatherers. Some anthropologists, then, are trying to understand the cultural history of early hominids by making analogies with present-day nonhuman primates and hunter-gatherers. Traits that distinguish hunter-gatherers from nonhuman primates are being analyzed to see whether they may have been traits of the early hominids. And behavioral patterns shared by both non-human primates and hunter-gatherers are now believed to have been found among early hominids.

Human beings are different from all other animals because they alone leave behind an archeological record of their behavior, according to Glynn Isaac of the University of California at Berkeley. People leave tools, weapons, and other artifacts along with animal bones at their home bases. By analyzing which of these items occur at archeological sites and how they are distributed, investigators have been able to study activities and cultures of people who lived in the Stone Age. Now, artifacts have been found along with fossils of the early hominids, and, hence, Isaac believes, archeologists are realizing that they can study, in a similar way, the distinctly

By Gina Bari Kolata. Reprinted with permission, from *Science*, 187, 14 March 1975, pp. 940-42. Copyright © 1975 by the American Association for the Advancement of Science.

human component of activities of these beings.

Mary Leakey of Oduvai Gorge, Tanzania, and other investigators found stone tools and animal remains along with fossils of early hominids in East Africa. The animal remains intrigue the archeologists because they include bones from animals varying in size—as small as those of mice and as large as those of elephants. This is evidence that early hominids ate meat regularly and ate very large animals and indicates, Isaac believes, that the behavior of early hominids was different from the behavior of apes and chimpanzees. Chimpanzees and other such primates eat meat only occasionally and, when they do eat meat, consume animals much smaller than themselves.

Stone tools found with fossils of early hominids are considered good evidence that they were different from other primates. The functions of the various tools cannot always be determined; but, since tools are often found along with animal bones, many anthropologists believe that at least some of the tools were used to cut up meat. The patterns of distribution of these tools may also be significant.

Both Leakey and Isaac, working at different sites in East Africa, compared sites occupied at earlier dates to those occupied later, and discovered that the number and diversity of stone tools was greater at the sites occupied later. Isaac speculates that this could mean that more stone tools were made at later times, that sites were occupied for longer periods or were visited more often at later times, or that the later hominids developed better containers for carrying stones to the sites where tools were made.

John Yellen of the Smithsonian Institution in Washington, D.C., who studies the !Kung hunter-gatherers of Botswana, believes that some of the patches of artifacts found along with animal bones and hominid fossils in East Africa resemble camp sites of the !Kung. He emphasizes that both !Kung camp sites and some of the sites of early hominids are characterized by nonrandom distributions of material. At !Kung sites, this distribution indicates that different activities took place at different areas of the camp. Isaac also believes that the early hominids had camp sites or home bases. He suggests that the early hominid groups were, like hunter-gatherer groups, organized around such sites where they regularly shared food—another behavior pattern not found to any significant degree among nonhuman primates.

Alan Mann of the University of Pennsylvania, Philadelphia believes that early hominids differed significantly from other primates because they had a delayed period of physical maturation. He studied the rate that their teeth developed by x-raying jaws from fossils of children. Molars that are beginning to develop but have not yet erupted can be seen in x-ray pictures. Mann found that the teeth of early hominids erupted slowly—at a rate typical of tooth eruption in people rather than apes or chimpanzees. Since the rates at which teeth erupt are linked to rates at which skeletons develop, Mann proposes that the early hominids had a slow rate of skeletal growth. This slow growth rate, he concludes, may indicate that young hominids evolved to have long periods of dependency on adults because the hominids had an adaptive pattern that demanded more learned behavior.

THE IMPORTANCE OF PLANT FOODS

While most archeologists recognize the probable importance of plant foods to the early hominids, a popular misconception has arisen of these beings as "killer apes"—the carnivorous male hunters who brought home huge carcasses to their dependent females and offspring. This scenario is questioned by Adrienne Zihlman and Nancy Tanner of the University of California at Santa Cruz. They point out that both hunter-gatherers such as the !Kung and primates such as chimpanzees rely on plant foods rather than on meat for most of their calories and nutrients. And plant foods are usually gathered by females who, far from being dependent on the males, are crucial to the survival of the group. Moreover, social groups of primates such as chimpanzees and of hunter-gatherers such as the !Kung are not tightly structured units, organized around bonds between males and females. Instead these groups have variable compositions; the members of the groups disperse and aggregate according to ecological conditions and the groups are structured around bonds between mothers and their offspring and among siblings. By anal-

ogy, early hominids were likely to have had similar diets, organizational flexibility, and social bonds, Zihlman and Tanner believe.

No definitive evidence of the social structure of early hominid groups can be obtained. However, Tanner and Zihlman contend that it is most likely that plant foods rather than meats were of the greater importance to hominids. The early hominids had enormous cheek teeth, and these, according to many anthropologists, were probably used to grind plant roots, seeds, and tubers.

Early hominid fossils exhibit a great deal of variability. Adults ranged in size from about 3 to 6 feet (1 foot = 0.3 meter) tall, according to Milford Wolpoff of the University of Michigan, Ann Arbor, and various hominids differed greatly in their cranial capacities and the sizes of their cheek teeth. Analyses of this variability have led to a controversy among anthropologists as to whether the fossils represent more than one lineage of hominid.

According to Wolpoff and his colleague C. Loring Brace, there was only one lineage of early hominid. They reason that because of the small sample of the fossils of hominids that lived in East and South Africa between 1 and 3 million years ago, the data are insufficient to permit a distinction between different hominid lineages. Wolpoff and Brace believe that the early hominids appear to be more similar to than different from each other. They attribute the morphological variability among the early hominids to differences between males and females and to natural variations among members of a population and between populations. To postulate more than one lineage of hominids, they contend, is to raise more problems than can be resolved.

If two lineages of hominids lived in the same area, say Brace and Wolpoff, they would compete with each other for food and other resources. This competition would result in one of three outcomes: the extinction of one lineage, the dislocation of one population, or niche divergence—that is, the exploitation of different resources by members of the different lineages. The first two possibilities, they believe, can be ruled out. The two lineages apparently lived together in East Africa, at least, for 1 million years or more. The third possibility—that the hominids occupied different ecological niches—

they believe is not yet proved. Hominids, Brace and Wolpoff explain, were probably like human beings in that they were able to utilize a wide variety of resources. This ability would have been enhanced by their propensity to make and use tools, to protect each other from predators, and to share food and communicate.

The argument that hominids of different lineages would have had to exploit different ecological niches is controversial, however. Alan Walker of Harvard University in Cambridge, Massachusetts, is among those who claim that niche divergence is not a reasonable issue in early hominid evolution. He cites numerous examples of closely related species that live in the same areas. Niche separation need not be specified in these cases because it is a theoretical construct and, as such, is not precisely mirrored in the field. Moreover, Walker proposes that those who go by the fossil record are more likely to err in the direction of counting fewer species than existed. Since closely related species often have nearly identical skeletons, Walker believes that the extreme diversity of early hominids is indicative that more than one lineage existed.

David Pilbeam of Yale University in New Haven, Connecticut, and Stephen Gould of Harvard University are proponents of a hypothesis that there were two lineages of early hominids in Africa. According to these investigators, individuals of one of the two lineages evolved only in the direction of greater size and they eventually died out. The other lineage evolved so that the individuals became larger, had a proportionately larger cranial capacity, and had smaller cheek teeth. This lineage, Pilbeam and Gould propose, subsequently evolved into human beings.

When an animal evolves to grow larger, different parts of its anatomy change in different ways. For example, limb bones become relatively thicker, and the ratio of brain weight to body weight becomes smaller. In order to argue that one lineage of early hominids—classified by many anthropologists as Australopithecines—evolved only to become larger, Pilbeam and Gould had to define how parts of an animal's body change to scale when it grows. They focused on changes in cranial capacities and cheek teeth areas.

HOW THE HOMINIDS GREW

The way in which cranial capacities change to scale as primates grow larger has been determined. It turns out that, if cranial capacities increase proportionately with increases in body sizes, then the graph of cranial capacity plotted as a function of body weight will be a straight line with a slope of about 0.66. Australopithecines fall into three size classes. When estimates of cranial capacities were plotted as a function of body weights for these three sizes of hominids, Pilbeam and Gould obtained a line with slope about 0.66.

A second lineage of hominids, according to the scheme devised by Pilbeam and Gould, is represented by the genus *Homo*. A hominid of this genus—which has been called *Homo habilis*—lived in East Africa at the same time as the Australopithecines lived there. (Those who believe that there was only one lineage of early hominids do not distinguish between the Australopithecines and *Homo habilis*.) Pilbeam and Gould propose that *Homo habilis* was morphologically different from the Australopithecines and that it evolved into *Homo erectus* and then into *Homo sapiens*. When they plotted the rate of increase of cranial capacity of the *Homo* lineage, Pilbeam and Gould obtained a straight line with slope of about 1.73. A similar analysis of cheek teeth areas led these investigators to conclude that cheek teeth areas of Australopithecines increased proportionately as these animals increased in size. Cheek teeth areas of the *Homo* lineage, on the other hand, evolved to be both relatively and absolutely smaller.

D. Carl Johanson of Case Western Reserve University in Cleveland, Ohio, has recently acquired data on early hominids that may support the hypothesis that there were two lineages of these animals. Johanson has found fossils of hominids that lived in Ethiopia 3.5 million years ago, were most likely bipedal, and had small cheek teeth in relation to the sizes of their skeletons. He speculates that these fossils represent the oldest known specimens of the *Homo* lineage and that the *Homo* lineage had, then, diverged from the Australopithecines more than 3 million years ago.

WHAT DO THE CHANGES MEAN?

The tendency for cranial capacities of the *Homo* lineage to increase as these beings evolved is generally considered to indicate increased intelligence. Interpretations of the decreases in the areas of cheek teeth as the hominids evolved are more speculative. Pilbeam and Gould and Wolpoff and Brace suggest that the smaller teeth could indicate that members of the *Homo* lineage had a decreased dependence on roots and tubers for food and increased dependence on meat. And this may mean that the diet of members of the *Homo* lineage was more like that of hunter-gatherers, who eat meat regularly, than like that of nonhuman primates, who rarely eat

meat. Various anthropologists also suggest that and increased use of tools for processing plant foods before they were eaten may help account for a decreased need for large cheek teeth in members of the *Homo* lineage.

Some anthropologists are skeptical of the arguments advanced by Pilbeam and Gould favoring the hypothesis that there were two lineages of early hominids. Wolpoff and Brace, for example, point out that, not only did Pilbeam and Gould fit curves to sets of three data points but, in five out of six of their data points, at least one of the variables is a guess. Pilbeam and Gould sympathize with such objections but, they write, "in a field as important yet as bereft of data as this one, one must work with what one has."

Part III

Non-Human Primate Behavior

The study of non-human primate behavior is of major interest to the anthropologist and students of man regarding questions concerning the origin and nature of human behavior. The following articles have been selected to illustrate the scope of primate behavior studies, especially as they relate to adaptive success and evolutionary reconstruction. Katherine Homewood's ecologically oriented paper illustrates how the life ways of one Old World monkey, the Tana mangabey, is intricately related to the fluctuating forest-riverine habitat. The article by Bernstein and Gordon presents an interesting thesis regarding the function of aggression in primate groups and how it may be vital to the establishment and regulation of primate sociality and society itself. The Mitchell selection illustrates the value of primate research and how insights into human problems are acquired from such work. In this case, the primate studies focus on early social deprivation and its relationship to violence. The articles by Menzel and the Lachmans deal with primate communication, but from different vantage points. Both authors give recent findings which demonstrate the chimpanzee's "cognitive capacity" for language. Emil Menzel, on the one hand, discusses the chimpanzee's "natural" communication system, showing it to be extremely effective in conveying information about the presence, direction, location and relative desirability of distant goal. The Lachmans, by contrast, explore recent findings regarding language acquisition by primates and conclude that appropriate criteria must be made by the investigator when demonstrating language capabilities and making any comparisons with human language. As a precautionary note, the final article by Reynolds raises questions concerning previous findings of primate ethologists and their observation of animals in the wild. The Gombe reserve "wild chimpanzee" studies by Jane Van Lywick-Goodall are a case in point. Are these animals truly wild or, in view of the fact they have been artifically fed, is their "natural" behavior altered? For an additional insight into primate communication the reader may profit from Gordon Hewes' article, "Primate Communication and the Gestural Origin of Languages," *Current Anthropology,* 14, Nos. 1-2, February-April 1973, pp. 5-12. Of especial interest when read with Reynolds' article is Teleki's "The Omnivorous Chimpanzee", *Scientific American,* January 1973, pp. 33-42.

Monkey on a Riverbank

The Tana is Kenya's longest river, rising from the eastern flanks of the Aberdare Range and entering the Indian Ocean more than 500 miles away. For most of its course it flows through a semidesert of scrub vegetation, but as it nears the sea and rainfall and humidity rise, groundwater seepage from the river is sufficient to support a narrow, 40-mile-long strip of patchy forest and woodland.

Here in northeastern Kenya, the river meanders across a flood plain up to five miles in width, building banks of sandy levees by continuous deposition. When seasonal rains in the catchment area around Mount Kenya are sufficiently heavy, the river overflows, flooding the plain. The swollen waters may burst through weakened banks and narrow meander loops, carving new channels and leaving cutoff levees and oxbow lakes.

The forests, which thrive best on the soil type and water conditions of the raised riverside levees, are thus subject to the vagaries of an unstable river course. As a result, the vegetation is a continually changing mosaic—areas newly exposed to colonization, young forests of a few colonizer species, mature diverse forests, and dying or degrading forests, cut off at any of these stages by a change in the river course. The patches of forest, each no more than a few acres, are linked by stretches of woodland, bush, and grassland, which grow on soils that are poorer, less permeable, and more subject to flooding.

This is one of Kenya's richest wildlife areas. Such forest species as red duikers, waterbuck, and bushbuck are found here throughout the year. Two rare primate subspecies, the red colobus monkey *(Colobus badius rufomitratus)* and the Tana mangabey *(Cercocebus galeritus galeritus)* are found here and nowhere else.

The Tana mangabey is an attractive, hitherto little-known monkey with fawn-gray fur and a semiprehensile tail, which it carries in a characteristic questionmark pose.

By Katherine M. Homewood. Reprinted with permission, from *Natural History* Magazine, January 1975, pp. 68-73. Copyright © 1975 by The American Museum of Natural History.

Living in the small patches of gallery forest on the Tana River, the mangabey population—an estimated 500 to 1,500 individuals—is some 1,000 miles distant from its nearest relatives, the subspecies *C. galeritus agilis* and *C. galeritus chrysogaster*, which inhabit the riverine forests of the Congo Basin. This curious geographic distribution of *C. galeritus*, together with the absence of the species from all nonriverine but otherwise apparently suitable forest, indicates that the three races are relics of a once widely spread population, now specifically dependent on gallery forest conditions.

On the Tana River, an expanding human population is progressively destroying this habitat. A two-year field study of the mangabey population was carried out in an attempt to explain their presence in these forests and to assist in their conservation.

Various features of their morphology, ecology, and behavior appear to place the Tana mangabeys intermediate between savanna baboons and monkeys of the genus *Cercopithecus*, such as guenons and monas. Tana mangabeys are slightly larger than *Cercopithecus* monkeys and have longer muzzles with stronger dentition, but none of these traits is as marked as in baboons. Mangabeys have characteristic pads of bare skin on their rumps (ischial callosities) fused in the midline in males as in baboons. They are semiterrestrial, at home on the forest floor or 100 feet up in the tree canopy. Restricted to forest and bush, mangabeys occasionally travel through open country to get from one wooded patch to another, but not for such long distances or as regularly as baboons. Tana mangabeys live in groups of thirteen to thirty-six individuals—smaller than most baboon groups—but under certain conditions groups may temporarily come together to form aggregations of fifty to sixty individuals.

Within a group there are one to six adult males and about twice as many adult females. Surplus adult and large subadult males spend comparatively little time with the group, making up a floating population of peripheral, solitary males, which spend some of their time near their group of origin, some near neighboring groups, and much of it wandering and feeding alone. This continues unless, by overpowering a resident male, they find a place in an established group.

The ranging pattern of any one group of mangabeys depends on its habitat type. Because of the peculiar conditions dictating vegetation growth, patches of forest along the Tana River vary greatly in terms of abundance, composition, and distribution of plant species. Some forest patches contain a wide diversity of species; in others, individual plant species may be dominant over wide areas, giving a very low diversity. In the latter case, the monkeys often vary their range seasonally according to the distribution of food resources. One study group of fourteen individuals foraged over an area of some 100 acres of single-species-dominated woodland, showing a distinct seasonal pattern in their ranging and little overlap with adjacent groups. In another diverse forest, a group of thirty-six individuals ranged over a 37-acre tract, which they shared with another group of at least twenty monkeys. Population density thus varies from less than one to more than six mangabeys per five acres. These figures, together with the total area of forest inhabited, give a total population estimate of 500 to 1,500 surviving Tana mangabeys.

The semiterrestrial mangabeys have access to a wide range of food sources; they are, in fact, highly opportunistic feeders, eating more than 100 different items from more than 50 different plant and animal species—mainly fruits, seeds, and insects, as well as leaves and flowers, bark, tree gum, and wild honey. They occasionally catch and eat small vertebrates, such as frogs and lizards, and have been observed dining on ground squirrel. Their powerful jaws and teeth enable them to strip and eat such tough items as bark and palm nuts, and their dexterity in gripping and handling small objects makes them efficient insect foragers.

The social behavior of the Tana mangabey shows certain characteristic features. At dawn, and occasionally later in the day, the adult males issue loud vocalizations audible at distances of more than half a mile. During the dry season, this appears to be a spacing mechanism, and the groups tend to avoid each other. Occasionally an aggressive interaction occurs at a territorial boundary. Typically the adult and large subadult males of both groups advance toward the boundary, take to the canopy, and perform a series of circuits with loud calls and stiff-legged leaps from branch to branch. This display of noise and crashing foliage may develop into a chase, with a male of one group attempting to catch and bite a male of a rival group. The females and young do not participate in these relatively rare intergroup interactions. During the rainy season, however, the pattern changes. The same long-range vocalizations are given, but their spacing effect is no longer evident. Neighboring groups have several times been observed approaching each other and coming together to form temporary aggregations of fifty to sixty individuals—although intermingling between individuals of different groups is rare. This behavioral flexibility allows efficient exploitation of locally and seasonally varying food sources, so important in this shifting mosaic system.

Within the group, the adult males show a dominance hierarchy. One male may tend to be more aggressive and displace the others from choice feeding or resting positions and proximity to estrous females. Females and young are subordinate to males, and when approaching or passing a dominant male, they invariably "present" (assume a precopulatory posture) as a gesture of greeting or submission. Adult male presenting is rare but has been observed. In order to displace another male, it usually suffices for a dominant animal to simply approach a subordinate, and the latter will move away. In a more intense situation, facial expressions may be used as a threat. Eyebrows are raised and the mangabey's white eyelids exposed; the head is lowered and thrust forward, producing an effective aggressive display.

Where the dominance hierarchy is not firmly established or when a new male seeks to join the group, such threats give way to outright chasing, fighting, and biting. A subordinate male that is being threatened may pick up an infant and hold it ventrally as a submissive display.

The leadership of the group of fourteen individuals that I studied changed three times in the course of a year—the first two times because of predation by a 15-foot-long rock python and the last because of the advent of a peripheral male, which established his dominance over the sole remaining adult male.

As in baboons, the adult female mangabey undergoes externally visible changes in the course of her estrous cycle. At the peak of her sexual receptivity she exhibits bright pink swellings on her perineal area. In this state she is very attractive to adult, subadult, and even juvenile males. The attraction is olfactory as well as visual—several times a male was seen approaching and sniffing a branch on which a swollen female had been sitting.

A sexually receptive female mates several times, generally with more than one male, but at the peak of her estrus, the dominant male stays close and discourages other males. The full swelling lasts for about a week and then shrinks. If the female has not conceived, she may come into estrus again. The whole cycle lasts about twenty-eight to thirty days. Birth occurs during the sixth month of pregnancy, usually between November and February, with most young born in December or January. In one study group all five adult females gave birth to healthy infants. In a second observation group containing an estimated twelve females, only four gave birth; but in this group there were a large number of young juveniles from the previous birth season. Of the nine infants born in the two groups, eight were still living when the study ended eight or more months following their births.

The newborn infant is covered with a fuzz of grayish fur; it has a bright pink face and hands and large black eyes. An infant is particularly attractive to adult and subadult females, which seek to groom and hold it. For the first couple of months, however, the mother jealously guards her offspring, and only later, when it begins to acquire the dark adult facial pigmentation, will she readily allow others to groom and hold it. By three to four months of age the infant is adventurous, spending less time with its mother, suckling less, and beginning to eat other foods by watching and copying its mother. As it matures to juvenile and subadult, peer relationships become more important, but the offspring still spends more time near its mother than any other adult female.

When the young mangabey is between six and ten months old the mother comes into estrus again, although she still occasionally suckles her infant. Observations of known individuals and the age structure of juveniles in the group indicate that the female doesn't conceive again until about twelve months after the previous birth: the interval between births is often eighteen months to two years. Since a female takes four to five years to reach sexual maturity, this is perilously slow reproduction for an animal close to extinction.

The ecological and behavioral findings of the study demonstrate that the Tana mangabey is specifically adapted to a cyclic, fluctuating ecosystem, such as the gallery forests of the lower Tana River. Since they are semiterrestrial, the mangabeys are capable of open-country travel. They are also behaviorally equipped to visit different areas including the territories of other groups during certain seasons. In a society of long-lived, intelligent primates, this is equivalent to a capacity for exploration that leads to

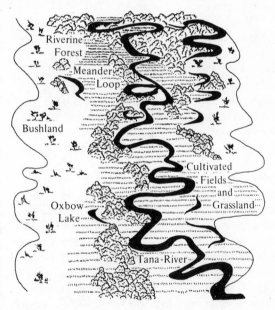

Figure 1. An ecological mosaic of forest patches, grassy fields, and bushland has been created by the unstable course of the lower Tana River. When the river changes direction, cutoff forests die because of a lack of water. Semiterrestrial Tana mangabeys, which inhabit these small forests, respond by colonizing clumps of trees in wetter areas.

the colonization of newly generating stands and escape from dying forests. Population dispersal is facilitated by these physical and behavioral traits.

The mangabeys' opportunistic feeding patterns are also adaptive in an unstable ecosystem. They make use of a wide range of food sources and are physically equipped to eat tough materials. Their semiterrestriality gives them access to virtually all potential foods in the area, and because they are behaviorally adapted to travel, they can exploit distant, seasonal, and locally abundant plant species. Flexible intergroup social behavior also permits an efficient exploitation of fluctuating abundance and distribution of food sources.

Genetic diversity within the various groups may be enhanced by the mobility and sometimes rapid turnover of leading, or dominant, males, despite the potentially isolating conditions of their habitat.

These morphological, ecological, and behavioral characteristics are similar in all three of the long-isolated subspecies of *C. galeritus*, helping to confirm that in a seasonally flooding gallery forest system there is a selective advantage for such an adaptive complex. These rather specialized features, in many ways intermediate between savanna baboons and *Cercopithecus* monkeys have apparently enabled *C. galeritus* to survive in cyclic, fluctuating forest systems, but it may not do as well if forced to compete with more generalized primates in other, stabler environments. The Tana mangabey would be unlikely to survive should the Tana River forests be converted to a stable ecosystem. I found much evidence that this is exactly what is happening.

In many places the river banks have been cleared of natural vegetation by the Pokomo, a riverine tribe that lives by fishing and shifting cultivation. They are not hunters, but as their population steadily expands, they progressively clear more and more of the remaining forest for agriculture. They also fell trees to make dugout canoes and houses. Where large old trees are taken, a valuable and often irreplaceable structural and food element for the mangabeys is lost from the forest.

The Tana flood plain is also inhabited by the Orma, a pastoral tribe that regularly burns off grass and bush to improve the grazing for its cattle. This tends to maintain a fire climax pasture in areas where bush and woodland could have regenerated; it also damages the edges of remaining forests.

Slash-and-burn agriculture and fire climax pastures used to be a consistent part of the dynamic mosaic of the Tana ecosystem. As the river course changed, the villages grew, shifted, and then died, to be reclaimed by forest. During the rapid population increase of the last fifty years, however, destruction has far outstripped regeneration.

In addition, the government of Kenya is implementing a scheme to harness the river for irrigation and hydroelectric power. Among other effects, this will eliminate flooding, drastically diminish the silt load, and level out the highly variable river flow to half the present average. Deprived of its cutting power, the river will be stabilized in its present course. The river regime will be converted from a fluctuating ecosystem with a continuous cycle of development and destruction to a steady one in which any surviving forests will eventually reach stable maturity.

The pattern of an ecosystem is reflected in its component species: for example, a young ecosystem favors pioneer species with prolific reproduction, efficient dispersal, wide environmental tolerance, genetic diversity, and a capacity for opportunistic exploitation. A mature system, on the other hand, has a quality rather than quantity criterion, with restricted reproduction and dispersal. Because a cyclic, fluctuating system such as the Tana's flooding riverine forests is a continuously changing mosaic of soil and water conditions, a shifting combination of pioneer and mature plant associations makes up the vegetative cover.

With control of the Tana River, all this will be changed. The colonizing plant species, with their rapid growth, short lifespan, and quick turnover of shoots, flowers, and seeds will give way to the slow-growing, low-turnover species characteristic of mature forests. Also, the reduced water supply will cause an over-all decrease in the forest vegetation. These changes will, in turn, affect the animal species. The findings of this field study indicate that the Tana River mangabey, with all its adaptations for a cyclic mosaic system, will be the one to suffer most.

Until recently, it seemed that with the steadily encroaching human population, the Tana mangabey would become extinct very quickly. But the Kenya Game Department, together with scientists working in the area, is now organizing a small game reserve in an area of prime habitat and high mangabey density. These rare and beautiful primates and their unique habitat have been given a respite. But unless landuse practices and river management schemes are changed to preserve the Tana gallery forest ecosystem, the mangabey's future remains in doubt.

The Function of Aggression in Primate Societies

Beginning with the earliest studies, investigators of primate social behavior have been struck by the significance of primate aggressive potential and the consequent need for social control of such aggressive potential in socially living animals. Studies directed at describing aggressive behavior and the situations which elicit it, as well as the social mechanisms which control it, were therefore among the first investigations of primate social behavior.

The largest Old World monkeys—drills, mandrills, baboons, and geladas—have the longest and sharpest canine teeth literally rivaling those of the great cats. These monkeys are sexually dimorphic, the males often weighing two or three times as much as the females, and it is the males which have the well-developed canines. Furthermore, the elaborately evolved, lower first premolar and upper canine honing surfaces insure maintenance of a razor-sharp cutting edge. Even the casual zoo visitor cannot help but be awed by the yawning, canine-grinding displays of adult male monkeys, and primate colony managers can readily attest to the effectiveness of such teeth in fights involving adult males.

COMPETITION THEORIES

Quite naturally, then, the focus of many early studies was upon male aggression. Zuckerman (1932) described competitive interactions among hamadryas baboon males at the London Zoo when females were introduced to the colony. The subsequent severe fighting resulted in multiple deaths, primarily female, and Zuckerman analyzed these violent encounters in relationship to primate social structure. It seemed that sexual competition was such a powerful and pervasive social incentive that it might permeate every aspect of group living. As a consequence, the re-

By Irwin Bernstein and Thomas Gordon. Reprinted with permission, from *American Scientist,* journal of Sigma Xi, The Scientific Research Society of North America, 62, May—June 1974, pp. 304-11.

sultant aggressive competition and its control must be central to the organization of primate groups.

Other competitive interactions were explored by Maslow and coworkers (1936, a, b, c, 1940) who noted the variety of expressions given to competitive interactions in different kinds of primates. Carpenter (1954), as a result of his pioneering primate field studies, suggested that the dominance hierarchy so apparent in many primate societies might have as its primary function the control of intragroup and even intergroup aggression. During the years that followed, many investigators worked to explicate the forms of primate aggression, the situations which elicit such aggression, and the social mechanisms which channel and control aggression. Chance and his colleagues (1967, 1970) focused on spatial control mechanisms; others took developmental approaches noting the special status of infants and the possible significance of natal coats as inhibitory cues. Attention which had earlier focused on sexual competition gradually shifted to consider the whole array of incentive situations which theoretically provoked primate aggression.

Because primates were considered to compete for any resource in the environment, it was expected that hungry monkeys would fight over food, thirsty monkeys would fight over water, sexually aroused males would fight over receptive females and, in general, any time more than one monkey sought the same incentive simultaneously, resolution of this conflict was expected to be through some form of aggressive expression. Theories were developed which relegated the function of aggression entirely to such conflict resolution, but the motivating force of competition for incentives began to be doubted when experiments involving the reduction of space or the withholding of food failed to produce more than temporary increases in intragroup conflict (Southwick 1967). Indeed, food deprivation not only failed to increase agonistic frequencies (Rosenblum 1969) but in some cases actually resulted in decreased frequencies of agonistic interactions (Marsden 1972). Studies of animals in the wild under conditions of extreme food deprivation likewise revealed that starving monkeys devoted almost all available energy to foraging, with little remaining for aggressive interaction or any social behavior (Hall 1963). Furthermore, evidence from a variety of primate taxa began to accumulate which indicated that one of the most potent stimuli for eliciting aggression was the simple introduction of an intruder into an organized group (Bernstein 1964b, 1969a, 1971; Kawai 1960; Southwick 1967). Such introductions resulted in far more serious aggression than had been produced in any laboratory experiments contrived to stimulate competition.

INTRODUCTIONS
AND GROUP FORMATION

These studies suggested that unfamiliar conspecifics introduced to one another for the first time showed considerable hostility because, in the absence of a social order, one had to be established to control interanimal relationships. When a new animal was introduced into an existing social organization, the newcomer met even more serious aggression. Whereas in the first case aggression established a social order, in the second case, resident animals mobbed the intruder, thereby initially excluding a new animal from the existing social unit. When several animals were introduced simultaneously, the effect was lessened, if only because the group divided its attention among the multiple targets. If, however, the several animals introduced to a group themselves constituted a social unit, it might be postulated that two social organizations in conflict would constitute the most potent situation. Indeed, in such cases each group may mass and fight the opposing group as a unit, but, again, no individual is subjected to the consequences of mass attack, and the very cohesion of the groups precludes prolonged individual combat as group members come to each other's aid and the focus of activities shifts from area to area. The defeat of one group is marked both by a reduction in aiding and by responding to further aggression solely with submissive signals. The submission of the defeated group, rather than unleashing unchecked aggression on the part of the victorious group, serves to reduce both the intensity and frequency of further attack. Monkey groups therefore seem to be organized primarily to maintain their established social order rather than to engage in hostilities per se.

Studies of introductory techniques in captive group formations (e.g. Bernstein and Mason 1963; Bernstein 1964b, 1969a, 1971; Vandenbergh 1967; Vessey 1971) have revealed certain uniformities among the variety of cercopithecine monkeys studied. Despite the intensity of initial strife and the occasional exclusion of some individuals, almost all of our attempts to form a social unit have proved successful and have revealed similar social mechanisms among these primate groups. Initial high levels of aggressive interaction decline sharply even within the first hour, and the expression of aggression gradually shifts from the most extreme forms of attack to more token expressions and threats. Furthermore, the age and sex of the animals introduced, the number of animals simultaneously introduced, and the age-sex composition of the resident group all clearly influence the original reception.

As part of a series of studies concerned with hormonal correlates of stress and aggression conducted in collaboration with Robert M. Rose, we instituted a systematic exploration of some of these variables. Nearly one hundred planned introductions, reintroductions, and group formations involving rhesus monkeys have clarified the nature of social mechanisms and have permitted us to obtain an understanding of the function of primate aggression in these and other situations (Bernstein et al. in press, a, in press, b).

Moreover, examination of field study literature and our own field work reassured us that these situations and phenomena were not merely the results of the artificial conditions of captivity. To be sure, spatial restriction precludes effective use of some social mechanisms and enhances aggressive encounters. We thus might see more extreme aggression more frequently than under conditions where escape is possible, but severe fighting does sometimes occur under the same sets of circumstances in natural habitats. Whereas troop-to-troop fighting in the wild may routinely follow ritualized patterns as in territorial disputes or similar encounters (Bernstein 1968; Carpenter 1938; Ellefson 1968; Mason 1966), when spatial mechanisms fail, other more violent forms of interaction may prevail (Southwick et al. 1965). Furthermore, inasmuch as the exchange of males is the principal means of genetic exchange among the semi-closed social units common to so many of the primates, the use of confined groups and deliberate introductions only serves to exaggerate natural response patterns and allows specification of their operation.

Considering the well-earned reputation of rhesus monkeys as nearly intractable laboratory animals and the frequency with which they engage in agonistic displays, the choice of subject for study may also be challenged. Fortunately, studies of sooty mangabeys, geladas, green monkeys, and a variety of macaques under the same laboratory conditions produced very similar results (Bernstein 1970).

AGGRESSIVE RESTRAINTS

It was with some trepidation that we approached our first introduction of thirty-six adult male rhesus monkeys into a single enclosure. The vigor of initial encounters seemed to justify our fears, but it soon became apparent that there was an element of restraint even in the most intensive male-to-male fighting. From the onset it was clear that many males selectively displayed submissive behavior to other males even on first encounters. Positive social behavior, such as combining to form mutually supportive alliances, was in evidence even in the first minutes and played a significant role in the establishment of a social order.

Initial fighting seemed unrestrained, but later investigation of the wounds actually inflicted, and consideration of the damage that unmodified canine teeth can inflict, led us to conclude that the male aggression witnessed was not uninhibited. No animal died of wounds, and all the wounds healed spontaneously, without sign of infection. Furthermore, the location of wounds—and their absence on the throat or abdomen—suggested that conspecific male-to-male fighting in rhesus monkeys was in some way limited. The areas injured—shoulders, face, haunches, brows, tails, and even back areas—can all sustain injuries without damage to vital organs. The most vulnerable

areas—throat and abdomen—were uninjured, although opportunity for such injuries certainly existed as animals were sometimes rolled over and appeared helpless to defend themselves against further attack.

The apparent helplessness of a victim in fact appeared to inhibit further attack. Thus, animals no longer attempting to defend themselves were soon subjected to only token aggressive responses. Species-typical responses communicating a submissive role include passive crouching and turning away from the attacker. Such signals combined with the obvious helplessness of a defeated animal to exert an inhibitory influence against further attack. The inhibition is reinforced by the tendency of even the most passive submissive animals to resume resistance when subjected to further real injury. Thus, we have seen defeated males passively accept incisor bites, emitting only grimaces and squeals in response to each nip, but abruptly wheel about and slash when canine teeth were also used in further biting. The sudden turnabout from passive to active defense, albeit still mixed with grimacing and squealing, seemed difficult to explain until analysis of photographic records clearly indicated the use of a canine in bites preceding such defense.

A suggestion of ritualization of fighting was reinforced by watching the fighting patterns of males attacked by females in later studies. Male aggression was so controlled in these cases that at times a small number of females succeeded in completely overpowering male opponents twice their physical size and possessing vastly superior dental armament.

Female monkeys proved themselves formidable opponents in agonistic interactions and, in undisturbed groups, demonstrated more frequent aggressive responses than did males (Bernstein 1970). This difference could be demonstrated for a variety of species and was especially clear when noncontact forms of aggression, such as threatening and chasing, were considered. This suggests that concern for understanding male aggression and the emphasis on its importance has been based more on the consequences of male aggression than its frequency. In undisturbed groups, males may rarely be involved in fighting, but when they are, the results may be apparent for weeks. More important perhaps is the fact that male aggression, both in frequency and intensity, does exceed female aggression in crucial situations. Thus, during group-to-group introductions and group formations, males accounted for almost all the aggression displayed in the first twenty minutes, which included the most serious forms of contact aggression. By the end of the first hour female participation in agonistic episodes had increased, rivaling or exceeding male rates, and forms of contact aggression were superseded by chases, threats, and other noncontact expressions of aggression (Bernstein et al. in press, a, in press, b).

CONTROL ROLES

When an intact natural group is challenged by some external source of disturbance, one or more particular animals in the group will respond in predictable fashion, identified as the "control animal role," most often played by a male (Bernstein 1964a, 1966). This individual may be the last group member to retreat or may otherwise place himself between the source of disturbance and the group. Deliberate challenges to captive groups have revealed that this role behavior is dependent on the presence of the group and also is "expected" by group members who will seek out the control animal when subjected to attack or harassment.

This was experimentally verified by separate testing of the control animal in the presence and absence of his group and by testing the group with the control animal physically restricted in space (Bernstein 1966). Naturally there are limits to any such behavior pattern, and we may regard the headlong flight of all baboons when chased by a lion as not in contradiction to the bluffing behavior of baboon males when confronted by less capable predators (DeVore and Washburn 1963; Rowell 1973).

The same animals which serve control role functions when a troop is threatened by external disturbance are most likely to respond to intra-group sources of disturbance as well. In the event of prolonged or intensive fighting within the group, the control animal may intervene by attacking either participant, attacking a neutral third party, or otherwise making a display of aggression. In any case, the control animal's aggression usually supersedes all other aggression in the group, thus terminating the original fight. The intervention of the control animal thus appears to be part of a role pattern—not truly "aggressively motivated"—whose functions can be satisfied with only a few token gestures.

ELICITING AGGRESSION

But what of the initial fighting within the group? What situations provoke such fighting and what function does such aggression serve? Is aggression ordinarily only a disruptive force that requires elaborate control mechanisms, including the use of aggression to control aggression? Is the "natural" aggression of primates a socially centripetal force that tends to destroy primate societies? Is primate society and sociality only possible when social mechanisms are capable of suppressing this "naturally" disruptive force? Or is it possible that this "excessive" primate aggression is the very force which bonds primates to one another and maintains their primate societies? Before dismissing the last question as heresy, let us look at the evidence and examine some supporting views.

First, although there is irrefutable evidence that primates are at times predators, they are more often prey. For most primates, ultimate safety lies in the trees, but many of the larger species are often on the ground and sometimes far from trees. Although vigilance and rapid flight may still serve a primate well, more active defense against the smaller predators is possible. In these circumstances, one or more of the large troop males, upon discovering a potential predator, may engage in aggressive displays that seem to drive the predator off (DeVore and Washburn 1963).

It should not be inferred that a baboon male, or a coalition of several males, can really defeat an animal such as a leopard in combat, but it is only necessary to postulate that they would inflict injury upon the leopard in a fight. Such injuries can prove fatal for an animal that requires maximum ability every few days to obtain his next meal. There has surely been selection against predators who risk serious injury routinely and, likewise, selection against baboon males who recklessly attack predators such as leopards—for the baboon risks more than just a wound. The net result is a carefully balanced stalemate with a premium placed on alertness and the communication of aggressive threat for the baboon, and on stealth and the search for easier prey on the part of the leopard. By contrast, a lion, at three to five times the body weight of a leopard, can probably dispatch a fair number of male baboons with little personal risk—thus there is no need for a lion to be cautious about attacking boisterous baboons and no gain for baboons who try to bluff lions.

Concerted group aggression against an outside threat thus may serve to preserve the group, and any mechanisms making the expression of such directed aggression more effective would have positive value.

In this case at least, it is the expression of outward-directed aggression, rather than its inhibition, which unites and preserves the society. We might similarly analyze the effect of extragroup aggression directed against conspecifics. Once again, a noisy bluffing display rather than actual combat would be the more desirable expression of spacing mechanisms or the means for resolution of conflict. Bluffing certainly kills fewer members of a species than does intraspecific fighting.

But what of intragroup aggression? How can this ever be anything but disruptive to normal social relations? First, let us examine the circumstances under which we see intragroup agonistic behavior, and simultaneously consider how "normal" social relations are established. Beginning with one of the most common experimental procedures, we might study aggression by throwing one piece of food between two monkeys in a group. At times one monkey may quietly retrieve and eat the food; at other times we may see one monkey aggress against the other. Before assuming this aggression to be competitive aggression, we should realize that it is almost invariably unidirectional—i.e. one animal aggresses and the other flees or otherwise submits. We may explain the absence of aggression in the one case by postulating that dominance hierarchies exist to control aggressive competition. The aggression that does occur thus reflects a failure of the rank structure to completely suppress aggression.

At times, however, we may note that a social "inferior" may take the offered food and do so with apparent impunity. Infants, young juveniles, and favored females may be exceptionally bold in feeding in the immediate proximity of a large male who will not tolerate another male anywhere in the area while he is feeding. Surely his dominance rank must be more securely established with regard to the immature animals, and yet it is they that fail to respect it by the same deference the male's peers show. Rather than invoke special mechanisms to protect females and infants taking such liberties, it might be more parsimonious to explain why intragroup aggression in a wide variety of circumstances is most frequently directed to animals of adjacent rather than distal ranks. Stated another way, we might say that the greater the social rank disparity between two animals, the less frequently we see aggressive encounters.

By way of illustration, a group of juvenile rhesus monkeys instantly deferred to a single large adult male introduced to their group, and the male seldom directed even the mildest forms of aggression against the immature animals while maintaining his alpha rank absolutely (Bernstein and Draper 1964). His superiority was such that the juveniles represented an insignificant threat to his alpha status. Animals of more equal abilities and of near-equal rank are the ones most likely to challenge an established social relationship, and aggression against these potential usurpers may be used to ward off any perceived threat to existing social relationships.

Aggression may, therefore, at times function to curb the upward social mobility of individuals whose success can only be at the expense of those of the next highest ranks in an agonistic dominance hierarchy. Greater frequencies of agonistic interactions among animals of adjacent rather than distal rank have been reported in a variety of primates studied under diverse conditions. It is most readily recognized by significantly higher scores along the diagonals of agonistic matrices organized to reflect a dominance hierarchy (Christopher 1972, Plotnik et al. 1968).

The significance of this mechanism was revealed in a sequence of events leading to the spontaneous reorganization of a pigtail monkey group after years of relatively stable rank relationships. A young male who had achieved third rank in the hierarchy was repeatedly attacked by the second ranking male, who ceased in his attacks as the young male successfully defended himself. However, no reversal in agonistic roles was seen. Instead, the young male was challenged to several fights by the alpha male, who subsequently died of infection. The second male assumed the alpha position, but, because he avoided all agonistic confrontations with the young male, two months later the young male claimed the alpha position and attacked the second male each time he failed to conform to his newly subordinate role. Although the young male had not previously *initiated* any aggression, he now enforced his new position by repeated attacks against his former superior, showing less and less frequent aggression as his former superior showed more and more submission (Bernstein 1969b, 1969c.).

Aggression would therefore seem to be motivated *primarily* by efforts to preserve established social position and to enforce expected patterns of social behavior, rather than resulting from active competition leading to conflict. An individual will fight to maintain his social position and warn all potential usurpers of his readiness to fight. A group of animals will use aggression to preserve an established social order and to maintain role relationships. A society will mobilize all of its aggressive resources for self-preservation.

MAINTAINING SOCIAL ORDER

If the difference between a society and an aggregation lies in the interrelated network of roles in the former, and if these roles are characterized by typical patterns of responses for individuals under specified conditions of social interaction, we may correctly ask how the rules of primate societies are developed and maintained. What enforces these codes of conduct?

The late Professor K. R. L. Hall put it very succinctly when he wrote that one of the most potent stimuli eliciting primate aggression was a perceived violation of the social code (1964). Aggression is then used to maintain the very fabric of primate society. Rather than disrupting social

relationships, aggression serves to enforce regulated social interactions which maintain primate societies.

One other point in Professor Hall's statement should be considered and appreciated. He stressed that it was the *perceived* rather than the *actual* violation of the social code which elicited aggressive response. Thus, no particular response will invariably provoke aggression; it must first be perceived as a challenge to a social relationship. For example, in food competition tests, the alpha male need show little response to group members showing proper deference, he need show no aggression to insignificant juveniles feeding on scraps in his area, but he may be motivated to respond strenuously should it appear that some individual is contesting him for a piece of food he has claimed as his own. The perception of challenge can result from the mere proximity of an animal to the morsel the dominant individual is moving towards. Thus, a rolling piece of food approaching a stationary animal may cause that animal to flee. This apparent paradox of hungry animals fleeing choice food is better understood when one realizes that the animals are avoiding a situation which in the past has provoked the wrath of superiors. When the more dominant individuals no longer seek food, then it is safe for the more subordinate animals to feed freely on the same food previously avoided.

SOCIALIZATION AND SOCIAL ROLES

How then are these social relationships established? Newborn infants enjoy extraordinary toleration and are objects of active interest in primate societies. As the infant grows, its behavior is slowly shaped by the requirements of its group. We may think of this as the socialization process. An infant's weaning experiences certainly will vary in accordance with species membership as well as with the personalities of mothers, but most weaning includes some of the earliest experiences with punishment—"punitive deterence." Such punishment was at first thought to drive the infant from the mother, thus aiding in the separation of mother and child. It was therefore surprising to learn that mother-infant attachment appeared greater in species with more punitive mothers, and that the most punitive mothers within a species had the most dependent offspring (Kaufman and Rosenblum 1969; Jensen et al. 1967). It seemed that baby monkeys sought their mothers for protection and comfort when distressed, even if the mother was the source of the distress.

Longitudinal studies of several groups of Old World monkeys in our laboratory have demonstrated that the bond between mother and infant is not severed at weaning, or even at full maturity. This long association with mother results in close association with siblings, and mother's relationships as well; matriarchal groups can be recognized by persisting high frequencies of social interaction even when as many as four generations are represented. Furthermore, in the pigtail monkey at least, even in the event of the matriarch's death, the association of siblings is not diminished—we still see regular association between the now-adult offspring of several deceased females. It is perhaps noteworthy that strong bonding is particularly evident in our pigtail monkey group—the very spcies which Kaufman and Rosenblum (1969) had described as so punitive in comparison with bonnet macaque groups.

The use of aggression in establishing social bonds is not limited to infant socialization studies. In fact, the same "bizarre" response of approaching the attacker was reported by Kummer as the mechanism by which hamadryas male baboons maintain their females in close proximity (1968). A straying female is attacked by her male unit leader, who subjects her to a ritualized neck bite. Instead of fleeing the male, the female may then be embraced and comforted by the male, the punishment clearly having been in response to her failure to maintain proper social proximity, not distance. Aggression here establishes and maintains a social bond.

In a series of field experiments, Kummer introduced strange hamadryas and anubis females to a troop of hamadryas baboons. The rapid integration of the hamadryas females was not surprising, but anubis females ordinarily live in troops with no particular bond between individual males and females. Although in anubis troops, females usually avoid actively aggressive males, the hamadryas males were successful in training at least some of the anubis females to approach and to maintain proximity in response to male aggressive display. To be sure, there were modifications of the typical hamadryas patterns, but primates are capable of great behavioral plasticity and anubis females could learn the appropriate responses to a hamadryas male's aggressive signals.

Perhaps as an indicator that the male hamdryas behavior is not a unique species attribute, but rather only an extreme form of a common pattern, we should recognize that even in the familiar rhesus monkey, consort pairs make frequent use of aggression to maintain close proximity and stimulate reproductive behavior. Whereas the pair generally shows mutual support in outwardly directed aggression (at times with no apparent target visible), the initial response may be an ambiguously directed threat by the female or the male.

Primate societies are characterized by relatively stable social relationships. However, as animals grow and individuals age and pass from one category to another, their roles in a society change, and social relationships are dynamic. The rules governing social relationships are in part typical of the species and in part determined by past individual histories. The enumeration and etiology of rules governing social conduct in the variety of extant primate societies remain a future challenge. For the present, however, we may predict that a change in social relationships and "expected" social responses will be accompanied by aggressive interactions as individuals resist the change and/or enforce the new rules of behavior governing the relationship. Since a change in relative position is enforced by aggression, one might expect that every illness and injury would represent an opportunity to overthrow a social superior, but animals living in a society depend more on alliances and coalitions rather than on individual fighting skills to maintain their social position. Thus a scrawny old female supported by many generations of offspring and long associations with other females and adult males may maintain a position of unquestioned superiority over young males of much greater fighting ability. So, too, may an old male retain his high rank, eventually losing to a challenger not because of his failing fighting abilities but because of the successful recruitment of support from group members by the challenger. After such a defeat, a new order is established incorporating all animals into a society that recognizes the new relationships (Bernstein 1969b, 1969c).

Infants born into a group are newcomers and intruders, but they represent little direct threat to anybody. The infant's position in the group is entirely dependent upon its alliances, usually consisting of the mother and the coalition of animals who support the mother. These allies of the mother are among the first to contact the new infant and, when the infant begins to move independently, both they and the mother will protect the infant in social conflicts. The infant's socialization then consists of learning its mother's position relative to all others in the group, and in learning which responses will provoke a superior and which will be tolerated. Representing so little challenge to an adult animal in and of itself, it enjoys an initial toleration which gradually declines as the infant matures.

An adult inserted into a group, however, is an immediate challenge. The more capable the individual, the greater the threat it represents to the existing social structure. In the face of this threat, a society can dissolve and allow the newcomer to reorder the group and its social relationships, or it can attack and subdue the threat. Under most circumstances, a group will coalesce to meet such a threat, members supporting one another in repelling the intruder. The group members most threatened will likely be of the same age-sex class as the intruder, but they can usually enlist the rest of the group. An adult male is thus met by resident adult males supported by females and even the immature members of a group. Adult females are challenged by adult females backed by resident adult males and immatures. Immature animals, however, represent little threat to adults, and resident immature animals are so dependent on adult support to maintain their own social position that they seldom attempt direct challenge to gain social position. Thus, very young animals may be incorporated into a group with little incident, sometimes being rapidly adopted by a group member or otherwise accepted into the group (Bernstein et al. in press).

GENETIC EXCHANGE

What of the introduction of a female to an all-male group? Such a female represents little threat to adult males in and of herself, and females introduced to all-male groups in our laboratory have suffered little attack. A female, however, may ally herself with a high-ranking resident male and thus achieve even second-ranking position in a group of adult males, all of which outweigh her and are better equipped for combat. Nonetheless, the female allied to an alpha male will enforce her position by repeated aggression against all lower-ranking males, at first heavily dependent upon her male ally, but gradually acting more and more independently. The full weight of the alliance can thus be brought to bear by any party to an alliance in monkey societies where the individuals have had ample opportunity to learn which animals support which other animals.

In contrast, a male introduced to a group of females is an immediate challenge to all. He may be successful in claiming alpha position and possibly reorganizing the group, or the resident females may resist. In our laboratory groups, the outcome seemed dependent on the breeding season, with males attaining success far more readily then than at other times of the year. It should be remembered that primate societies are only semiclosed breeding units and that species integrity is maintained by genetic exchange between troops, principally by the transfer of males during the breeding season. Thus, the mechanism of genetic exchange runs counter to social mechanisms preserving and protecting social orders by isolation and exclusion.

The net result of these two social mechanisms appears to be that male mobility for the rhesus monkey is largely restricted to the breeding season (Lindburg 1969; Neville 1968), which is also the period of the most significant male wounding (Vandenbergh and Vessey 1968; Wilson and Boelkins 1970). Therefore adult males may be wounded during the breeding season not because of direct competition for receptive females but rather as a consequence of their mobility—from one troop to another. The stimulus for changing troops is imperfectly understood; fully adult prime males with little competition from other males, and with estrous females present, may abandon a troop only to show up later attaching themselves to another troop. Because such males may have been of any previous rank position, we cannot claim that they were "driven out" of their natal troops, nor can we claim that only newly adult or very old males leave, for it appears that adult males may transfer from troop to troop on an average of every three years (Neville 1968). The male joining a new troop need not suffer immediate group attack, for under natural conditions he may follow at a distance and gradually make contact with troop members before being integrated into the troop. The presence of a brother already in the new troop has been shown to appreciably ease acceptance into the troop, thus demonstrating the long-term relationships between siblings and the influence of alliances in troop structure (Sade 1968).

CONCLUSIONS

Aggression can certainly produce damage to an individual, and uncontrolled aggression can destroy a society. It may at times run counter to other biological mechanisms, but aggression is itself a biological mechanism shaped by natural selection into an adaptive force which helps to establish and maintain primate societies. The development of extraordinary male aggressive potential in certian Old World monkeys may function to protect the group from some predators, thus preserving the individual male and other individuals most likely sharing his genetic heritage.

The same aggressive displays may be used in conspecific group competition, or other sources of social disruption, to preserve the group. Minor altercations within a group can be rectified with little effort and, indeed, fighting within a group should result in minimum injury if the group is not to suffer in its ability to survive. With adult males responding to external threats, there is little need for females and juveniles to develop lethal fighting abilities for intragroup aggressive encounters. Indeed, such abilities in females and juveniles may be contraindicated for group survival, especially because there may be ample opportunity for aggression among

group members, and severe wounding of genetically related individuals would surely be rapidly selected against.

But what of the adult males and their fighting potential? Granted their abilities may have evolved as protection against external threats where there is clear positive selective pressure for increased fighting ability in conflicts with genetically unrelated animals. Can we therefore ignore the damage such males may inflict in intragroup fighting? Indeed not, and we may readily recognize a number of independent mechanisms which control primate male intragroup aggression. Some primate groups are organized into one-male units or societies wherein the unit leader faces no serious challenge to his social position from females and juveniles. On the other hand, many primates are organized into multimale units wherein not only may male-to-male fighting occur but the system of alliances may pit females against males. The full expression of male fighting potential could be disastrous to a society in such cases, and numerous checks are apparent, such as ritualization and inhibition in response to social communication. In fact, many communication responses are specifically related to communication of threat and submission, thereby averting direct physical contest. Male fighting-potential is thus limited within the group by established relationships and specific control mechanisms. Its full expression is released primarily in response to serious challenges to the survival of the male or his group.

All this is not to say that the sole function of aggression is to maintain a society, nor is it to be taken as implying that aggression is the primary mechanism maintaining primate societies. Certainly primates are attracted to one another and live as members of social groups as a result of multiple motivational systems, and aggression may be elicited in a variety of situations, at times driving animals apart. In its extreme expression, aggression may threaten the survival of a group or a species, but it is because of the many positive facets of primate aggression that selection has been for control and not for elimination. Ritualized fighting within groups limits the consequences of aggressive encounters, and social mechanisms controlling aggression between groups of conspecifics clearly helps preserve the species. Even with regard to extraspecific aggressive encounters, we have seen that bluffing and display may be positively selected.

Uncontrolled aggression is certainly disastrous to primate societies, but the complete absence of aggression may be equally disastrous. We require a new perspective to view aggression in terms of its biological and sociological functions rather than simply in terms of its extreme direct outcomes. It may not be possible to have a primate society totally devoid of aggression, but by studying its function, expression, and control, we may be better able to limit the undesirable side effects.

References

Bernstein, I. S. 1964a. Role of the dominant male rhesus in response to external challenges to the group. *J. Comp. Physiol. Psychol.* 57:404-06.

_____. 1964b. The integration of rhesus monkeys introduced to a group. *Folia Primatologia* 2:50-63.

_____. 1966. Analysis of a key role in a capuchin *(Cebus albifrons)* group. *Tulane Studies in Zool.* 13(2):49-54.

_____. 1968. The lutong of Kuala Selangor. *Behaviour* 32:1-16.

_____. 1969a. Introductory techniques in the formation of pigtail monkey troops. *Folia Primat.* 10:1-19.

_____. 1969b. Spontaneous reorganization of a pigtail monkey group. In *Proc. Sec. Int. Cong. Primat.* Vol. 1, C. R. Carpenter, ed. Basel: S. Karger, pp. 48-51.

_____. 1969c. Stability of the status hierarchy in a pigtail monkey group *(Macaca nemestrina). Animal Behaviour* 17:452-58.

_____. 1971. The influence of introductory techniques on the formation of captive mangabey groups. *Primates* 12:33-44.

_____. 1970. Primate status hierarchies. In *Primate Behavior: Development in Field and Laboratory Research,* Vol. 1, L. A. Rosenblum, ed. Academic Press, pp. 71-109.

Bernstein, I.S., and W. A. Draper. 1964. The behavior of juvenile rhesus monkeys in groups. *Animal Behaviour* 12:92-96.

Bernstein, I. S., T. P. Gordon, R. M. Rose. Aggression and social controls in rhesus monkey *[Macaca mulatta]* groups revealed in group formation studies. *Folia Primatologia,* in press, a.

_____. Factors influencing the expression of aggression during introductions of rhesus monkey groups. In *Primate Aggression, Territoriality and Xenophobia,* R. Holloway, ed. Academic Press, in press, b.

Bernstein, I. S., and W. A. Mason. 1963. Group formation by rhesus monkeys. *Animal Behaviour* 11(1):28-31.

Carpenter, C. R. 1954. Tentative generalizations on the grouping behaviour of nonhuman primates. *Human Biology* 26(3):269-76.

Chance, M. R. A. 1967. Attention structure as the basis of primate rank orders. *Man* 2(4):503-18.

Chance, M. R. A., and C. J. Jolly. 1970. *Social Groups of Monkeys, Apes and Men.* Dutton, p. 224

Christopher, S. B. 1972. Social validation of an objective measure of dominance in captive monkeys. *Behav. Res. Meth. Instrum.* 4:19-20.

DeVore, Irven, and S. L. Washburn. 1963. Baboon ecology and human evolution. In *African Ecology and Human Evolution,* F. Clark Howell and Francois Bourliere, eds. Aldine, pp. 335-67.

Ellefson, John O. 1968. Territorial behavior in the common white-handed gibbon, *Hylobates lar Linn.* In *Primates,* Phyllis C. Jay, ed. Holt, Rinehart and Winston, pp. 180-99.

Hall, K. R. L. 1964. Aggression in monkey and ape societies. In *The Natural History of Aggression,* J. D. Carthy and F. J. Ebling, eds. Academic Press, pp. 51-64.

Jensen, G. D., R. A. Bobbitt, B. N. Gordon. 1967. Sex differences in social interaction between infant monkeys and their mothers. *Recent Adv. Biol. Psychiat.* 9:283-93.

Kaufman, I. C., and L. A. Rosenblum. 1969. The waning of the mother-infant bond in two species of macaque. *Determinants of Infant Behavior* 4:41-59.

Kawai, Masao. 1960. A field experiment on the process of group formation in the Japanese monkey *(Macaca fuscata)* and the releasing of the group at Ohirayama. *Primates* 2(2):181-253.

Kummer, Hans. 1968. *Social Organization of Hamadryas Baboons.* University of Chicago Press, p. 189.

Lindburg, D. G. 1969. Rhesus monkeys: Mating season mobility of adult males. *Science* 166:1176-78.

Marsden, H. M. 1972. Effect of food deprivation on intergroup relations in rhesus monkeys. *Behav. Biol.* 7:369-74.

Maslow, A. H. 1936. The role of dominance in the social and sexual behavior of infrahuman primates: I. Observations at Vilas Park Zoo. *J. Genet. Psychol.* 48:261-78.

_____. III. A theory of sexual behavior in infrahuman primates. *J. Genet. Psychol.* 48:310-36.

_____. IV. The determination of heirarchy in pairs and in a group. *J. Genet. Psychol.* 49:161-98.

Maslow, A. H., and S. Flanzbaum. II. An experimental determination of the behavior syndrome of dominance. *J. Genet. Psychol.* 48:279-309.

Mason, W. A. 1966. Social organization of the South American monkey, *Callicebus moloch:* A preliminary report. *Tulane Stud. Zool.* 13:23-28.

Neville, M. K. 1968. Male leadership change in a free-ranging troop of Indian rhesus monkeys *(Macaca mulatta). Primates.* 9:13-27.

Plotnik, R., F. A. King, L. Roberts. 1968. Effects of competition on the aggressive behavior of squirrel and cebus monkeys. *Behaviour* 32:315-32.

Rosenblum, L. A. 1969. Interspecific variations in the effects of hunger on diurnally varying behavior elements in macaques. *Brain Behav. Evol.* 2:119-31.

Rowell, T. 1973. *The Social Behavior of Monkeys.* Penguin Books, p. 203.

Sade, D. S. 1968. Inhibition of son-mother mating among free-ranging rhesus monkeys. *Sci. and Psychoanal.* 12:18-37.

Southwick, C. H. 1967. An experimental study of intragroup agonistic behavior in rhesus monkeys *(Macaca mulatta). Behaviour* 28:182-209.

Southwick, C. H., M. A. Beg, M. R. Siddiqi. 1965. Rhesus monkeys in North India. In *Primate Behavior: Field Studies of Monkeys and Apes.* Irven DeVore, ed. Holt, Rinehart and Winston, pp. 111-59.

Vandenbergh, J. G. 1967. The development of social structure in free-ranging rhesus monkeys. *Behaviour* 29:179-94.

Vandenbergh, J. G., and S. H. Vessey. 1968. Seasonal breeding of free-ranging rhesus monkeys and related ecological factors. *J. Reprod. Fert.* 15:71-79.

Vessey, S. H. 1971. Free-ranging rhesus monkeys: Behavioural effects of removal, separation and reintroduction of group members. *Behaviour* 40:216-27.

Wilson, A. P., and R. C. Boelkins. 1970. Evidence for seasonal variation in aggressive behaviour in *Macaca mulatta. Animal Behav.* 18:719-24.

What Monkeys Can Tell Us about Human Violence

Unprovoked violence is one of those aberrations which behavioral science seeks to understand. While it is generally believed that only man attacks his own kind without provocation, laboratory studies have proved that monkeys and apes will do the same, if reared under certain conditions. Over the past several years, I have worked with various research teams studying these pathological behaviors in the rhesus monkey.

Rhesus monkeys are very social animals. In the wild, they live and travel in troops, and social forces greatly influence an infant monkey's development. When we put these animals in the boring and restricted environment of captivity, we can make any individual seem "abnormal." Abnormality is irrelevant unless related to some standard of the normal, and science defines abnormality by comparing two groups of animals, both familiar with the captive testing environment.

Age and sex are also important for labeling behaviors. Like humans, monkeys change as they mature, and many behaviors which seem strange are often normal for a given age. Younger monkeys, for example, are very active, while their elders are more sedentary, spending much time simply scanning the environment with their eyes. The sex influence appears predictable—males seem to be more seriously impaired by adverse rearing conditions than females. A few researchers are even convinced that this is a general law among vertebrates.

SOCIAL ISOLATION STUDIES: A BRIEF OVERVIEW

The "abnormal" behaviors seen in captive animals are mild idiosyncracies compared with the strange symptoms shown by social isolates—animals removed from the mother at birth, and reared in an environment allowing no physical

By Gary Mitchell. Reprinted with permission, from *The Futurist,* published by the World Future Society, P. O. Box 30369 (Bethesda), Washington, D.C. 20014, April 1975, pp. 75-80.

contact with other members of the species. Usually, an isolate is raised in a bare wire cage which permits it to see, hear or smell other animals but which allows no touching, cuddling, sucking, or somatosensory stimulation whatever (wire-cage isolates). Enclosed isolates are animals reared in a totally enclosed environment and having no contact at all with others of their kind.

The study of early somatosensory deprivation did not become prominent until the late 1950s, when the American psychologist Harry Harlow reported his discovery that orphaned baby monkeys form deep emotional attachment to folded pieces of cloth, or "inanimate surrogate mothers." When Harlow compared the time that infant monkeys spent near their source of milk against the time they spent clinging to the surrogate mothers, he discovered warmth and softness—not nourishment—to be the primal bond between infant and mother. Emotionally, said Harlow, nursing is not important because of the milk the infant receives, but because nursing insures frequent and intimate body contact of the infant with the mother. "Certainly, man cannot live by milk alone," said Harlow. "Love is an emotion that does not need to be bottle or spoonfed."

Harlow also demonstrated that a variety of physical sensations, including movement, clinging, sucking, and warmth, underlie the emotional attachment of infant monkeys. His work stimulated a rapid increase of research into the question of early social deprivation among primates.

In the early sixties, William A. Mason studied some near-adult monkeys reared in bare wire cages at the University of Wisconsin Primate Laboratory. These animals were sexually deficient, especially the males. Although aroused by receptive females, the isolate males could not successfully copulate. There were other strange behaviors in these animals as well: They did not groom themselves or each other very often, they fought more, and they physically interacted with uncommon ferocity. The isolated animals also failed to achieve a dominance order; they seemed unable to determine who would be at the top of the pecking order.

Mason concluded that while socially deprived animals showed all the components of normal social behavior (the postures, gestures and vocalizations), they were unable to combine these unlearned cues in a meaningful pattern. He theorized that the abnormal behaviors were caused by a communication deficiency; lacking in social experience, the animals could not send or interpret the signals that monkeys use to communicate with each other.

As a graduate student at the University of Wisconsin, I worked on several research projects which followed in the wake of Mason's discoveries. In one of these studies, Guy L. Rowland raised two groups of monkeys in total, enclosed isolation; one group was isolated for six months after birth, the other for an entire year. These animals were fearful, disturbed, and sexually abnormal when Rowland studied them at 20 months of age. The research team that I participated in followed these monkeys well into their adult lives in an effort to determine whether or not the effects of isolation would persist.

At two or three years of age, the animals continued to display many infantile disturbances. They showed much fear and aggression, very little sexual activity or play, and many idiosyncratic, bizarre movements.

At 44 months of age, the monkeys which had been isolated for a full year were fearful and non-aggressive, though they threatened many attacks. The six-month isolates were both fearful *and* aggressive, often making suicidal attacks against huge adult males, or brutally beating juveniles. Such behaviors are never seen in normally raised monkeys.

Our long-term studies found that the behavior of monkeys reared in isolation gradually changes from cringing fearfulness into prominent displays of hostility in adulthood. This change occurs gradually, but becomes salient around puberty, especially in the males. The longer and more severe an animal's early social isolation, the later in life will this change from fear to hostility occur.

ISOLATES FLIP, PACE, BITE SELVES

Early social isolation evidently decreases normal sex differences. Rhesus males are ordinarily more dominant than females, yet among isolates, male dominance activity decreases, while female dominance remains at about the same levels as normal. Aggressiveness and dominance are quite different types of behavior. Normal expressions of dominance often depend on appropriately *restraining* aggression, and redirecting hostility away from another animal.

The enclosed isolates also engaged in an enormous amount of stereotyped pacing, flipping, jumping, self-clasping and self-biting, and various idiosyncratic, bizarre movements. While stereotyped rocking, pacing, or flipping reflected fear, the bizarre movements varied inversely with fear, and were presumably caused by "events" occurring within the animal.

One of the enclosed isolate males provides a good example of these bizarre movements. Prior to puberty, he would slowly move his right arm toward his head, and upon seeing his own approaching hand would suddenly appear startled by it. His eyes would slowly widen, and he would fear-grimace, threaten, or even bite the hand that was "sneaking up on him." If he did not look directly at the hand, or did not bite it, the hand would continue to creep up on him; his eyes became wider and wider until the hand entirely clasped his face. He would hold this position for a couple of seconds, his eyes agape in terror between the clutching fingers of his own hand.

ISOLATES ARE SEXUALLY MALADJUSTED

We have noted above that monkeys reared in social isolation do not develop a normal sex life. The males, in particular, indulge in excessive, compulsive masturbation, and their sexual relations with other monkeys remain abnormally low in frequency and deviant in form throughout life. While the females are sometimes impregnated by patient and sophisticated males, isolate-reared males have been justifiably described as "totally inept" during attempts to copulate. Isolate males rarely even attempt a mount, and when they do, their efforts are generally directed at the wrong target, such as the side of a female's body Consequently, none of the males manage to reproduce. The isolate females try to avoid males, threaten them, or collapse under the weight of a mount, making the act very difficult to accomplish.

BRUTAL MOTHERS
AND VIOLENT YOUNG

Females raised in isolation later become thoroughly inadequate mothers. B. M. Seay, now at Louisiana State University, conducted the first study of these "motherless mothers." He found that some isolate mothers were brutal, others indifferent, toward their offspring. As a group, the motherless mothers showed less warmth and affection than did normal mothers and punished their young more frequently and more severely. Their infants would have died without human intervention.

Another study found that the infants of socially-deprived mothers show a very high frequency of clasps, pulls, and bites when they interact with other infants. This was the first sign that rearing by motherless mothers facilitates aggression. Longer term studies discovered that near-adolescent males raised by such mothers display a rare penchant for violence and cruelty. They attack other animals without warning or provocation. One such animal bit off the finger of a normal infant monkey. Another motherless-mothered male bit four fingers off the hand of one cage-mate and killed another. Monkeys with a normal upbringing do not exhibit such behavior.

A monkey reared by a motherless mother clearly is likely to become aggressive. But even normally reared monkeys become more aggressive when they are raised by punitive mothers. Early punishment by the mother results later in aggression among her youngsters.

HOPE FOR SOCIAL ISOLATES?

Normal rhesus mothers are very anxious and affectionate toward their first infant, but become more casual and punitive with their later offspring. But these rules do not apply to isolate mothers, who often treat their second infant adequately. To discover whether the first experience with motherhood caused this change, we compared two groups of female isolates: one

group of eight-year-olds and another of four-year-olds. The older monkeys were less aggressive toward infants, whether or not they had previously given birth. This decrease in infant-directed aggression seems to be very much an exception to the rule, for both groups of monkeys remained very aggressive toward their peers.

Male isolates also exhibit an improvement in infant-directed behavior as they mature. Jody Gomber of the California Primate Research Center in Davis paired three one-month-old infant monkeys with 13-year-old male isolates. The deprived males are actually rearing the infants, and while their behavior is sometimes arbitrary, they are certainly not brutal. Play, grooming, and affectionate behaviors have appeared.

This decrease in fear and aggression toward infants indicates that at least some of the devastating effects of early deprivation may be reversible; apparently the animals mellow somewhat with age. However, self-directed biting and bizarre movements do not improve, and the sexual behaviors of adult male isolates remain abnormal. Still, the improvements that are seen give us hope that the persistent pathology of social isolation may not be permanent.

BEHAVIOR OF ISOLATES
ALONE IN THEIR CAGES

Several studies have shown that when animals are removed from isolation, they cannot relate to others of their kind. We studied four rhesus monkeys kept in isolation at the Davis center, to determine when abnormal patterns of behavior are established.

We found that the first month of life is crucially important in the development of many abnormal behaviors. Before the end of the first month abnormal movements of rocking, self-grasping, and autoeroticism had already appeared. Without a mother to restrict their activities or answer distress signals, the isolates displayed more behaviors, both normal and abnormal, at an earlier age than normal animals. Before the isolates were three months old, they could be easily identified because their movements were slow, halting, and careful; this persisted even to seven months, when they climbed more frequently than average.

COMMUNICATION FAILURE:
A STUDY OF LOOKING BEHAVIOR

Infant monkeys like infant humans, stare at the world with wide-open, almost expressionless eyes. As the monkey matures, this wide-eyed stare gives way to nervous glances, which are replaced at a still later age by aggressive stares expressing both fear and interest.

The prolonged eye contact which humans associate with affection, interest, or curiosity, does not play a part in the normal social life of mature monkeys. Normal adult monkeys almost always interpret mutual eye-to-eye contact as a gesture of hostility (not curiosity) and they avoid it at all costs. However, monkeys raised in social isolation seem to lose the mature skill of avoiding eye contact.

At the Davis center we compared the looking behavior of isolates with normal rhesus monkeys in order to discover some of the reasons behind their social inabilities. By viewing films of adult male isolates, we are able to follow closely their visual orientation. Even though the isolates are physically outweighed, and even after they have been beaten in a fight, they often return to the other animal and stare directly into its eyes from as close as two to three inches away. Naturally, this upsets the other monkey, and another fight is almost inevitable. The normal males appear confused by this odd behavior. They repeatedly "face away" and sometimes even resort to fear grimaces and withdrawal, in spite of their proven superiority during the fight.

On the basis of eye contact, it is difficult to determine who threatens first. The normal monkey may actually start the fight by threatening a face which is merely wide-eyed with wonder. Although isolates made the majority of first lunges or attacks, we don't know how the stares were interpreted by the animals, especially the isolates.

ISOLATES SHOW
LIMITED SELF-AWARENESS

Early in life, isolate-reared monkeys cling to and suck on themselves more than do normal monkeys. But somewhere between infancy and adolescence, the animal stops expressing affection toward itself (such as self-clinging and rocking), and becomes self-destructive. These isolated monkeys do not simply dislike themselves; there is evidence that they apparently do not even recognize themselves! Time and again, the isolated animals appear unaware that the parts of the body they are looking at, threatening, or biting, are a part of themselves.

The development of self concepts and self worth among human beings are major topics of interest to contemporary psychologists. Nonhuman primates, and apes even more than monkeys, provide a fertile source of information in this field.

Watching monkeys is a fascinating activity. In the visual exchanges between monkey and man, it becomes very obvious (at least to the human) that we are both primates. Of course, the danger always exists that similar behaviors will be emphasized, and some important difference will be omitted. We can avoid such overgeneralizing by studying several different species within the primate order. When a result can be replicated for many of them, there is a strong chance that it holds true for humans as well.

Early rearing in an isolated environment produces the same severe pathology in all primates so studied. If they are denied the early experiences of skin or fur contact, clinging, and warmth from other animals, primates develop into self-mutilating menaces who are incapable of normal sexual relations. But because the brutality of isolates toward infants appears to wane with age, many researchers are reasonably confident that ways can be found to alleviate the pathology of these animals.

The effects of severe social deprivation may never be totally erased, but the passage of time and interaction with younger animals and peers may make an isolate less socially maladroit and even capable of giving and receiving affection. This could be of signal importance in treating pathology in adult humans and in suggesting ways to forestall the destructive acts of violence-prone adults who were affection-starved and socially deprived as children.

Language in Man, Monkeys, and Machines

Rumbaugh *et al. (1)* claim to have demonstrated language use—reading and sentence completion—in a chimpanzee named Lana. Since numerous investigators are now studying language use in infrahuman organisms, we should keep under continuing review the criteria for evaluating claims that an infrahuman organism is using language. We propose the following: (i) A strong criterion and a weak criterion of language use in nonhumans can be articulated, the choice of criterion depending on the inferences the investigator wishes to make. (ii) By the strong criterion, only *Homo sapiens* presently uses language; by the weak criterion, man, computers, and some chimpanzees use language. The distinction is based on process and product comparisons, respectively. (iii) Lana has not been shown to use language by any criterion strong enough to exclude rats, worms, and any other conditionable animal.

Since man is the only species whose language utilization is unquestionable, man provides the reference point for judging the equivalence of animal performance with language use. The weak criterion asserting weak equivalence requires only that some of the behavioral products of man and nonhumans are apparently similar. For example, if a convincing case can be made that a chimpanzee behaves in a way that requires labeling, syntax, and semantics, the animal can be said to use some language, by the weak criterion, regardless of how the behavior was induced. Strong equivalence, in contrast, requires that the linguistic performance of nonhumans be accomplished by mechanisms similar to those of men. This criterion entails a far heavier burden of evidence; that is, it must be shown that the organism learns its language by mechanisms similar to those of men, makes similar errors, shows a similar developmental pattern, effects its language use by similar neurological structures, and demonstrates any pattern that

By J. L. Mistler-Lachman and R. Lachman. Reprinted with permission, from *Science,* 185, 6 September 1974, pp. 871-72. Copyright 1974 by the American Association for the Advancement of Science.

can be shown to be true of all human languages (that is, linguistic universals). The appropriate criterion must be chosen by reference to the intent of the scientist. If he is interested only in the symbolic capacity of a particular species such as the chimpanzee, the weak criterion suffices and the term language" functions as a useful metaphor. However, if the scientist wishes to relate the animal's performance to that of humans, the strong criterion must be met.

The weak criterion of equivalence is the only one that has heretofore been met in the comparative study of language, because highly structured, carefully controlled training procedures must be introduced to overcome the chimpanzee's lack of vocalization and spontaneous linguistic behavior, short-comings sometimes characterized as trivial. The most successful effort has been that of Premack *(2),* who has trained his chimpanzee Sarah by means of operant techniques. Such training procedures themselves preclude the strong criterion; they are totally unlike the circumstances under which the human child learns language. They require that production and comprehension of symbols and symbol strings be carefully shaped. The animal is reinforced with 100 percent consistency; it is presented with only well-formed strings; and only the well-formed strings for a particular phase of training receive reinforcement. In contrast, human children are inconsistently reinforced; they are presented with ill-formed strings; and their ill-formed productions are often rewarded, especially if they are factually correct *(3).* The training procedure also precludes the opportunity for an animal to make errors similar to those of the human child acquiring language, as well as the opportunity to show the developmental sequence that is universal among human children. However, the weak criterion can be met with non-humans, and Sarah appears to have met it. Premack gives sophisticated evidence of labeling, syntax, and semantics in Sarah's behavioral repertoire. While this is an impressive accomplishment, it does not warrant generalizations to human language use. The measures necessary to overcome Sarah's linguistic shortcomings are too heroic for useful comparisons to be made. A logical equivalent would be verbally instructing a human to swing through trees with the aid of cables, harness, and nets in an effort to study the ontogeny or phylogeny of tree-swinging in simians.

Rumbaugh *et al.* have failed even to meet the weak criterion; they give no convincing evidence of any language use in Lana. There is no evidence that Lana labels. Her performance of different response sequences for different rewards might be called labeling if the rewards obtained were shown to be appropriate to her known drive states (which they were not). But if this is labeling, then rats that discriminate between the response sequences necessary for food and water in a T-maze can be said to be labeling the sides of the maze as "the food side" and "the water side." Similar labeling could be attributed to any lower animal whose responses correlate with its drive states. Second, there is no evidence that Lana uses syntax. A knowledge of syntax implies the capacity for linguistic productivity; the obvious way to test for its presence in Lana would be to teach her a new lexigram—such as *raisin*—and see if she generates the novel string *Please/machine/give/piece/of/raisin* without shaping. Premack's chimp Sarah has apparently performed successfully in such a test; however, the present authors do not report even attempting it. Correct insertion of the new item in the appropriate string could also be used to demonstrate use of semantics. Lana performs the sequence *Please/machine/tickle/Lana*. If she were taught a new relational term such as *hug* and a new object name such as *raisin*, she could be tested for the appropriate placement of these new terms in her old strings. Correct production (without shaping) of *Please/machine/hug/Lana* but not *Please/machine/raisin/Lana* would suggest that she discriminates relational terms from objects. Premack has reported that semantic competence is part of Sarah's repertoire, but there is no evidence for semantic competence in Lana. What capacities can the authors reasonably conclude that Lana has? She can carry out nine or ten partly overlapping response sequences up to seven items long and discriminate those that terminate in reward from those that do not. Lana has definitely learned to perform longer and longer sequences for reward. Training animals to perform longer and longer sequences for rewards is not novel; it has been done with pigeons and even worms, and has a long history in the instrumental conditioning literature. It certainly does not imply language use. The only support for the claim that Lana's performance is "reading" and "writing" of language is in the authors' arbitrary equating of the response sequence to English sentences. There is no evidence that meanings for the terms or syntax for the strings exists anywhere but in the linguistic competence of the experimenters. It is not even clear that Lana utilizes the exact correspondences between response sequences and particular rewards; that she accepted the rewards is unconvincing, since all were positive. The demonstration with Lana has failed in every respect to meet any reasonable criterion of equivalence between Lana's language and man's. Premack's work is linguistically more sophisticated and empirically more convincing. He has successfully met the weak criterion of equivalence, if not the strong one.

By the weak criterion of equivalence, chimpanzees are not the only nonhumans that are linguistically capable. By this criterion, the computer that trains Lana uses language, interpreting Lana's key-press sequences and responding to them. This linguistic performance is limited as computer programs go; there are many programs whose outputs mimic not only some of man's language capacity, but also his abilities to reason, draw inferences, plan, and intend *(4)*. The weak criterion of equivalence is sufficient to establish that the machine using these programs indeed reasons, draws inferences, makes plans, and has intentions. Many behavioral scientists might find such claims less palatable than the assertion that an animal uses language, but their logical status is equally good. Evolutionary arguments can be adduced that the strong criterion will never be met with apes; this is a subject for longer papers *(5)*. However, since a computer program can be written for any process we understand, the strong criterion of language equivalence is potentially attainable with a computer. Thus, the study of human language may be more rapidly advanced by research programs utilizing computers than by those utilizing chimpanzees.

Notes

1. D. M. Rumbaugh, E. V. Gill, E. C. von Glasersfeld, *Science* 182, 731 (1973)

2. D. Premack, *ibid.* 172, 808 (1971).

3. R. Brown and U. Bellugi, *Harv. Educ. Rev.* 34, 133 (1964).

4. H. Simon and L. Siklóssy, *Representation and Meaning: Experiments with Information Processing Systems* (Prentice-Hall, Englewood Cliffs, N.J., 1972).

5. J. L. Mistler-Lachman and R. Lachman, in *The Ontogeny of Language*. P. W. Dixon, Ed. (Univ. of Hawaii Press, Honolulu, in preparation); R. Lachman and J. L. Mistler-Lachman, in *Current Trends in Computer Uses for Language Research*. W. A. Sedelow and S. Y. Sedelow, Eds. (Mouton, The Hague, in preparation).

6. Support by NIH grant MH21488 is gratefully acknowledged.

Natural Language of Young Chimpanzees

Suppose you found yourself in an unknown land populated by strange creatures which are almost human in form, appear highly intelligent, live in well-organised social groups, but do not seem to share any verbal language or sign language in common with us. How would you go about studying their capacity for information processing and social communication? This problem would make for good science fiction; but it is also the problem that faces any scientist who sets out to study chimpanzee communication.

There are at least three different solutions to this problem. Psychologists such as David Premack, Beatrice and R. Allen Gardner, and Roger Fouts would say, "Catch one of the beasts, preferably an infant, take it to the laboratory, and see if you can teach it English or some other system that meets the standards a human linguist would set for real communications". Naturalists would be more inclined to observe what self-trained animals already do with each other in ordinary circumstances. Some naturalists, such as Jane van Lawick-Goodall, Peter Marler, and Jan van Hooff, say, "Watch every movement and listen to every sound that individuals make when they are in company with each other, and try to compile a dictionary of these natural communication signals".

The third group, myself included, would follow the lead of Karl von Frisch and Clarence Ray Carpenter, and say, "Look at the society as a whole and try to discover where it is headed and what are its goals. Then you can say what the individuals might have to communicate about, and ask how they do it". These three approaches to the general problem of communication are of course complementary rather than contradictory; here I shall concentrate on what has been learned by the last approach.

One of the most obvious goals of any mobile group of animals is to get to food without individuals getting lost from each other or being involved in perpetual conflict. After observing the spontaneous travel and foraging of chimpanzees for several years I arrived at the following test procedure for analysing their accomplishments more closely. Six or eight young wild-born chimpanzees, who have lived together at least a year and who have come to form a very compatible and stable social unit, are locked together in a small cage on the border of a large outdoor enclosure. An experimenter then enters the enclosure and hides food or some other object in one or more randomly selected locations.

The next step is to take one of the chimpanzees out from the cage and carry him around the enclosure to show him the hiding places. After this the chimp is returned to his group and the experimenter leaves the scene. Several minutes later all of the chimpanzees are turned loose. Each time the test is repeated, a new set of hiding places is used. Each member of the group who can be carried away from his fellows without raising a big fuss is given the opportunity to serve as the informed animal or (as I call him here) the leader.

When he was released to look for the food the leader almost never searched a false location or missed a baited one by more than a meter or two or researched a place that he had already emptied of food. He also never used the same trail over which we had carried him, unless this was also a very efficient route. In other tests we found he could also remember the type and amount of food that he had seen in each place, and whether or not a snake or other frightening object was also hidden nearby. In sum, the chimpanzees seemed to know the nature and relative positions of most of the objects in the field, and their own position (at any given time) in this scaled frame of reference. As the late Edward Chace Tolman would have said, it was as if the leader had a "cognitive map" of the area and knew how to use it in planning an itinerary.

During the course of their travels, the chimpanzees usually moved as a very cohesive body and the informed animal clearly controlled the move. However, it was clear that the leader was by no means moving independently of his followers. If we tested him alone and thus gave him the opportunity to get all the loot for himself, he usually went nowhere, but begged at us with an

By Emil Menzel. Reprinted with permission, from *New Scientist*, 16 January 1975. This article first appeared in *New Scientist*, London, the weekly review of science and technology.

extended hand or whimpered and tried to open the cage door to release his followers. If the chimps were tested together but for some reason the followers did not follow, the leader took a step or two and stopped and waited, glancing back from one animal to the next. He beckoned with a wave of the hand or a nod of the head, or tapped a preferred companion on the shoulder and "presented" his back to solicit "tandem walking" (with an arm around the waist). Sometimes he walked backward toward the goal while orienting toward the group and pursing his lips in a "pout face".

If all these devices failed, he whimpered and tried to pull preferred companions to their feet, he bit them on the neck until they started to move, or he dragged them along the ground by a leg. If they still did not follow, or tried to engage him in play, he rolled around on the ground screaming and tearing his hair. At this the followers usually ran to the leader, clung to him, and then started to groom him. Once they had placated him the leader usually "gave up" and no longer tried for the food—unless someone else got up, started to walk away from the group, and in the correct direction. The leader then would rise too and travel behind the "followers" as long as their course was accurate. If they started to change course he grimaced and glanced back and forth at them and toward the goal-location, or he ran to them, put a hand on their shoulder, and steered them back on course. Once the group got going well first one animal and then another would glance at his fellows and step up the pace just a little. Soon the whole pack was racing down the field.

Usually the leader went in front, but this was by no means necessary. The followers knew which way to go anyway. Some followers in fact often ran several metres ahead of the leader, sighted back at him periodically, and then raced to search any likely-looking hiding places which lay ahead on the leader's path. In tests where we left a pile of food only partially covered, so that it could be spotted from about five metres, and the leader was given less than complete knowledge of its location, one chimp even developed the strategy of running ahead of the leader and climbing a tree to scan the field from a height.

Did the followers know from the leader's be-

haviour that food, rather than something else, or perhaps just the desire for a stroll, was the object of the leader's travel? In some of our experiments we randomly showed the leader a toy or a snake or an empty pile. There was no question that not only the leader but also his followers knew what, if anything, was out there. Sometimes the leader led the group within 10 metres of a hidden snake and then hooted or barked an alarm, and would go no farther—at which a follower walked over toward the spot at which the leader stared, picked up a stick, and clubbed this place. If we had removed the snake after showing it to the leader (to avoid all possibility that the followers could perceive it for themselves), the animals, after mobbing the previous hiding place, climbed the trees or walked along the fence scanning outside the enclosure—exactly as they would search for a snake that they had all seen crawling along the ground only to disappear from sight.

In contrast, where the hidden object had been food (and we had removed it after showing it to the leader) the whole group searched the hiding place manually with no sign of caution, and with great excitement, as if they all expected food. And if the leader had been shown an empty pile, he usually did nothing unless the others tried to get him going. In some instances the leader led the others over to the empty pile after they had tugged at him, but when the group got over to the pile he sat down and watched as the others dove on the pile and searched through it.

In still other tests we found that if two leaders were shown different hidden goals the group would split up and the leader who was going to the better goal would get the larger following. For example, whichever leader was going to four pieces of food attracted about two followers to every one follower that accompanied the leader who was going to two pieces of food. The leader going to fruit (preferred) attracted more followers than the leader going to vegetables (non-preferred). The leader going to a new toy attracted more followers than the leader going to an old toy.

There was also a clear leadership hierarchy: if their goals were equal, some chimps consistently got a larger following than others. Generally speaking, the preferred leaders were more willing than the nonpreferred leaders to share their spoils. Other characteristics which a chimpanzee had to possess before he attracted much of a following were familiarity (strangers were shunned) and ability to move out independently from others (with perhaps an occasional glance backward to make sure one is being followed).

Could the leader tell the others where to go without actually going there himself? On some occasions a leader started out only to give up for one reason or another and the followers took over and continued 50 metres or more in the correct direction. However, when we tried to test this behaviour formally, by putting the leader with the group for a few minutes and then taking him out and putting him in a separate cage while the followers were turned loose, the results were (as we had predicted) inconclusive. The leader whimpered and the followers went nowhere, but tried instead to open the cage door and release him. In am more inclined to attribute this result to motivational factors than to any failure of communication.

I base this statement on experiments in which we did not show the leader the hidden object, but only gave him a social cue as to its direction. For example, we merely pointed in the appropriate direction manually; or, to use signals that were more like the ones that the chimpanzees themselves used, we took a few steps and leaned forward and acted as if we had seen food. In some experiments we used two piles of food of different size, and used a long walk as a cue for the big food pile and a short walk as a cue for the small pile.

Even though the experimenter had left the enclosure and there had been several minutes delay between his signal and the opportunity to respond, the leader usually set out within 10 degrees of the indicated course. Walking, pointing, and merely orienting visually in a fixed direction were almost equally effective cues. On tests where two food piles were involved the leaders almost always went to the larger pile first; and as in most of our tests their performance was excellent even on the first trial. Control tests, in which we put no food at all or otherwise gave the cue in a false direction, ruled out the possibility that the animals could smell the food or were using cues other than the ones we had intended.

Exactly how far ahead of us in space the leaders could extrapolate I do not know, because our enclosure was too small to test the upper limits of their ability; but it is no less than 80 metres. And regarding the time limit of their ability to remember a social cue of direction, I would estimate it is at least a half hour.

It is, of course, easier to convey directional information than it is to convey the exact location (direction and distance) of an object. However, the chimpanzees did appear to use several different types of cues to pinpoint the exact location. To any student of spatial perception, the most interesting cue was triangulation. If the same animal successively oriented toward the same point in space from several different places (or, alternatively, if several group members simultaneously oriented toward the same point from several different angles) some followers seemed to put these several directional signals together and immediately infer the exact location of the goal.

In sum, the chimpanzees were able, and without any deliberate training on our part, to convey to each other the presence, direction, probable location, and the relative desirability and undesirability (if not the more precise nature) of a distant, hidden goal which no one had directly seen for himself. From my discussion with other primate research workers—particularly Hans Kummer, Jane van Lawick-Goodall, Robert Hinde, and their students—I would be very surprised if at least this much could not be demonstrated for many wild monkeys and apes, if not for pack-living carnivores and for many other animals of different types.

Why have primate field studies thus far reported little or no evidence for communication about the environment? Largely, I suspect, because these studies have not indentified or controlled the goals the animals are responding to, and because, under the influence of Lorenzian ethology, they have restricted themselves to describing the particular signals that individuals make and trying to compile a sort of dictionary of these signals. A dictionary of signals (or "elements") does not necessarily tell us what messages are actually conveyed across a group, for the same signals can take on a totally different meaning according to who gives it and in what context it is given; and the same message can be conveyed with many different ritualised signals, or even with no ritualised signals at all, but merely a glance or a bodily "point" or a nod of the head in the appropriate set of circumstances.

Perhaps various species differ less in how much information individuals can transmit to each other than in how and under what conditions they do it. A big difference between the signal systems of chimpanzees and the signal systems of bees and ants is that chimpanzee leaders do not restrict themselves to any small set of inborn or highly ritualised signals. They can learn to do almost anything they have to do to achieve their over-all objective: to get to distant, hidden goals without having to go it alone. Similarly followers do not have to attend to any one particular signal or nuance of the leader; they need only attend to the general situation closely enough to get the general message. Biologically speaking, it does not matter whether the follower gets his cues from visual, auditory or some other sensory channel, or from the leader, another follower, the environment, or some aspect of interaction thereof. The important thing is that he, too, is able to get to the distant resources without getting lost from the group. And, except in experimentally contrived test situations, there are always many alternative, redundant sources of information regarding the group's goals. Gestural or dance languages could no doubt be learned by wild chimpanzees, but they would still be necessary only to the extent that alternative cues or information processing systems were not sufficient to remove the mismatch between what the leader knows (or desires) and what the follower knows (or desires).

I know of no evidence to date that chimpanzees trained in a humanoid language but otherwise deprived of experience with other chimpanzees—as, for example, in the studies of David Premack and Beatrice and R. Allen Gardner—could tell each other any more than wild chimpanzees are capable of conveying to each other with their "language of the eyes". In my group of chimpanzees, the most dramatic and humanoid-looking signals were made by the most infantile and least efficient leaders, and they decreased markedly as the animals gained experience at leading other chimpanzees.

The leaders who best conveyed the nature, direction, and relative desirability of their goal were those who simply took a few steps "independently" and then glanced back to see what the others were doing; and, finally, they abandoned their own goal and joined another potential leader if he clearly seemed to be more eager and well-oriented than they. As Norbert Wiener said, the ability that two animals have to pick out the moments of each other's special active attention, and to use these moments as cues to the nature of the environment, is itself a "language" as varied in possibilities as the range of impressions that the two animals are able to encompass.

Does the chimpanzee's "natural" system for communicating about the environment reduce, then, merely to unintentional displays of eagerness on the part of the leader, together with the innate tendency of others to follow whoever goes the fastest? I think not. I found in my studies, and Jan van Lawick-Goodall has found in wild chimpanzees, that older animals can actively inhibit most signs of emotion if they so choose, and thus withhold information from each other, if not actually lie. For example, a chimpanzee who has seen food never "automatically" runs to it, grabs for it and stuffs it in his mouth. If a stranger or a dominant is nearby he waits as long as he has to until the coast is clear; or he might even get up, lead the other animal somewhere else, and then (while the follower is otherwise engaged) circle back for the hidden food. Conversely, followers are sometimes very acute in assessing from a deceptive leader's displacement activities and holdings-back what he is up to. The less eager and obvious he *tries* to act, the more closely the followers might keep him under surveillance.

Particularly in the light of what other researchers have disclosed in the last five years about chimpanzee and human information processing, and observations I have described here suggest that chimpanzees perceive the world and interpret each other's behaviour in ways that are not ridiculously different from the ways that we ourselves use, especially when we are silent and nonsedentary. Whether or not untrained chimpanzees have real language as a linguist would define it, they do possess information processing systems, predominantly visually based ones, which are to a considerable degree one of the same form as our own verbal language and which serve the same biological functions.

As David Premack has said, it is as if all of the cognitive structures necessary for grammar are already there not only in proverbal children but also in nonverbal chimpanzees. These subjects do not have to be taught grammatical modes of thought, in the ordinary sense of the word "taught", but only provided with a means for expressing their knowledge to us, their observers, in terms that we can understand. By human standards, or even by the standards of language-trained chimpanzees, self-trained chimpanzees do not *seem* to have a great deal to say; but how much of this result is attributable to their poor communicative ability and how much is due to our limitations as observers is still an open question.

How Wild Are the Gombe Chimpanzees?

How wild are the Gombe chimpanzees? Judging from Geza Teleki's book *'The Predatory behavior of wild chimpanzees'*, and writing as one who has studied truly wild chimpanzees, I would say that they do not appear to be very wild at all. This view is, I think, in line with the view of them one forms from reading some of the works of van Lawick-Goodall (1963; 1967; 1971), and from the films made at Gombe. All these show us in intimate detail the day-to-day lives of the Gombe chimpanzees but destroy any notion one may have had that one is looking at wholly wild animals. The Gombe chimpanzees have recently been described as 'feral' (Tutin 1974); perhaps 'free-ranging' would be a better word to use.

Fortunately for Teleki a recent paper by Wrangham (1974a) does put the issue of predatory behaviour into the perspective of feeding behaviour as a whole. The year described by Teleki in this book, 1968-69, seems to have been the year when tension between the chimpanzees and the baboons at Gombe was at or just past its height, owing to a particular form of banana feeding during 1967-68 which brought large numbers of each species to the Goodall campsite in a highly competitive situation. I have observed a comparable situation, where fruit was given to a group of thirty or more chimpanzees at a couple of dozen food hoppers in a large building at one end of a 30-acre enclosure at the Holloman Air Force Base, New Mexico. Feeding took place early in the mornings and again in the afternoons. As feeding time approached, the number of aggressive interactions rose among this group of otherwise peaceful and friendly animals. Dominant males were especially liable to attack and bite others at this time. During feeding, aggression was less frequent and quite subtle food-sharing interactions between certain males and females, and between adults and youngsters, occurred. After feeding, the animals

drifted off in groups or settled down to groom each other and calm returned to the colony.

It is clear from Teleki's detailed account that the attacks of chimpanzees at Gombe on other species, especially baboons, did not always, or even often, occur actually at the feeding-place or at feeding time. To this extent one cannot *simply* conclude that chimpanzee 'predation' at Gombe is a direct outcome of the competition and hostility arising from the artificial and highly unnatural situation produced by feeding. Yet Teleki clearly describes, on pp. 62-63, an attack by the adult male chimpanzee Mike on the young female baboon Amber as an outcome of, or accompaniment to, feeding tension.

We can be sure that the cases of predation on certain species other than baboons—red colobus monkey, bush pig and bush buck—were not related to the increased boldness and interspecific aggressiveness engendered by the Gombe feeding situations because they occurred before artificial feeding started. But in at least two earlier studies of truly wild, unprovisioned chimpanzees, that of Nissen (1931) and that of Reynolds and Reynolds (1965), there was no evidence at all of predation by chimpanzees. Nissen's study was made in woodland terrain in Guinea, Reynolds and Reynolds' in rain-forest in Uganda.

Kortlandt (1962; 1967) and his co-workers have made extensive studies of chimpanzees visiting food-rich plantation sites and provisioned areas in west and east Africa. They have been concerned to document chimpanzee reactions *to* a predator (stuffed leopard) but have reported no predation *by* chimpanzees. We should note that where this research team has used provisioning to tempt the chimpanzees into camera range for the leopard experiment, conditions differ from those at Gombe in two important respects. First, the provisioning was for short periods only. Second, no other non-chimpanzee species were present to compete for the food. This is clearly a very different situation from the one at Gombe. Albrecht and Dunnet (1971: 101) report no predation by chimpanzees on baboons despite considerable social tension between the two species.

Predation by chimpanzees is thus not a common or frequent event. At Gombe it takes an average of 200 observation hours on males to see

By Vernon Reynolds. Reprinted with permission of the Royal Anthropological Institute of Great Britain and Ireland, from *Man,* 10, No. 1, March 1975, pp. 123-25.

predation (Wrangham 1974*b*), and elsewhere, e.g. in rain-forest, it may not be seen, even if it occurs.

Predatory behaviour has, however, been reported at a site to the south of the Gombe National Park by Kawabe (1966). Kawabe's account of the chasing, killing and carrying away of a redtail monkey by a group of six chimpanzees is thoroughly convincing. There is no mention of feeding, and Kawabe stresses that this incident was an isolated case. Further data on chimpanzee predation are given by Nishida (1974), who reports on seven predatory episodes, involving killing, eating, and carrying away prey species of suni, squirrel, mongoose, bushbaby, redtail and vervet monkey.

Sugiyama (1968) during a six-month study in the same area of the Budongo Forest as that in which Reynolds and Reynolds worked for eight months in 1962 again found no evidence of meat-eating (p. 228). He did, however, include in his report a personal communication from Suzuki to the effect that the latter had seen chimpanzees eat a blue monkey and a black-and-white colobus monkey in Budongo, and the data were later published by Suzuki (1971). Suzuki describes how he saw chimpanzees eating the flesh of (a) a baby chimpanzee, (b) a young blue monkey and (c) a young black and white colobus monkey. In the latter case, although the kill itself was not seen, there was evidence of a chase and a catch. He also describes in some detail the process of meat-sharing among the individuals involved in a catch. Teleki likewise gives data on meat-sharing.

Teleki himself argues that the Gombe predatory behaviour cannot be ascribed to provisioning because (a) it occurred there prior to the onset of regular feeding and (b) because of the reports of Kawabe and Suzuki already discussed. However, both Wrangham (1974*a*) and I feel that Teleki has seriously under-rated the impact of the Gombe feeding technique, especially during the year 1967-68, on chimpanzee-baboon relations and thus on chimpanzee-*baboon* predation.

From all this it follows that great caution needs to be exercised in drawing inferences from the meat-eating habits of the Gombe chimpanzees to those of our hominid ancestors. Such a speculative 'scoop' is not missed by Teleki, nor by Carpenter in his Foreword to the book. Indeed, everything the Gombe chimpanzees do—their 'tool-making' and their use of tools for termite fishing, their use of leaves as 'sponges' or as 'toilet paper'—tends to be seized on rather uncritically by those eager to prove something (what?) about early man.

Teleki's own treatment of the implications of the Gombe data for man is disappointing. He appears to be unaware of the excellent comparative study of predatory behaviour by Schaller and Lowther (1969) though it is highly relevant to the theme of his discussion (pp. 175-77). Nor are there any references in the text to other work on human/hominid origins, though the bibliography is quite extensive. In a book one does expect a fuller discussion than is presented here, and perhaps we can expect one at some future time?

References

Albrecht, H. & S. C. Dunnett 1971. *Chimpanzees in western Africa*. Munich: Piper.

Kawabe, M. 1966. One observed case of hunting behaviour among wild chimpanzees living in the savanna woodland of W. Tanzania. *Primates* 7, 393-6

Kortlandt, A. 1962. Chimpanzees in the wild. *Sci. Am.* 206, 128-38.

———— 1967. Experimentation with chimpanzees in the wild. *Trans. 1st Congr. int. primatol. Soc.*, 208-24.

Lawick-Goodall, J. van 1963. My life among wild chimpanzees. *Nat. geogr. Mag.* 124, 272-308.

———— 1967. *My friends the wild chimpanzees*. Washington: National Geographic Society.

———— 1971. *In the shadow of Man*. London: Collins.

Nishida, T. 1974. Ecology of Wild chimpanzees. In: *Human ecology* (Ohtsuka, Tanaka & Nishida eds.), Tokyo.

Nissen, H. W. 1931. A field study of the chimpanzee. *Comp. Psychol. Monogr.* 8, 1-22.

Reynolds, V. & F. Reynolds 1965. Chimpanzees of the Budongo forest. *Primate behaviour* (ed.) I. DeVore. New York: Holt, Rinehart & Winston.

Schaller, G. B. & G. R. Lowther 1969. The relevance of carnivore behaviour to the study of early hominids. *S. West J. Anthrop.* 25, 307-41.

————, Y. 1968. Social organisation of chimpanzees in the Budongo forest, Uganda. *Primates* 9, 225-58.

Suzuki, A. 1971. Carnivority and cannibalism observed among forest-living chimpanzees. *J. anthrop. Soc. Nippon* 79, 30-48.

Teleki, G. 1973. *The predatory behaviour of wild chimpanzees.* Lewisburg: Bucknell Univ. Press.

———, C. E. G. 1974. Exceptions to promiscuity in a feral chimpanzee community. Paper presented to *5th Congr. Int.* *Primatol. Soc.,* Nagoya.

Wrangham, R. W., 1974*a*. Artificial feeding of chimpanzees and baboons in their natural habitat. *Anim. Behav.* 22, 83-93.

——— 1974*b*. Behavioural ecology of chimpanzees in Gombe National Park, Tanzania. Thesis, University of Cambridge.

Part IV

Human Diversity

The initial selection by S. D. Jayakar presents a population geneticist's approach concerning race and racial classification, treating a variety of structural elements in breeding populations. Clinal variations, geographical isolates and hybrid belts are discussed and usher the reader into the topic of what many people choose to call race. The following article by A. R. Frisancho considers various adaptive mechanisms that are found among contemporary highland and lowland Indian populations in South America which allow them to overcome physiological stress associated with high altitude. "Aggression and Hypoglycemia among the Qolla - A study in Psychobiological Anthropology" has implications for the student of man. Using a psychobiological approach, Ralph Bolton studies a group of Aymara-speaking Indians and brings to light the close interplay of human biology, cultural behavior, and mental illness. While not conclusive, his research demonstrates the aggressive nature of the Qolla, in part, is causally related to a physiological malady, hypoglycemia. On the other hand, Elie Shneour's article stresses the effect that environment has on the individual. Recent research findings suggest nutrition plays a more lasting and far greater role in determining the quality of cognitive abilities than what was previously thought. For the reader interested in pursuing issues in human diversity the following readings are suggested. A classic article by S. Washburn, "The study of Race" is to be found in *American Anthropologist,* 1963, 65, pp. 521-31. Stephen Molnar's *Races, Types and Ethnic Groups,* 1975, Prentice-Hall, is a recent book covering many facets of human diversity in a most readable manner.

Racial Differences in Man: a Population Geneticist's View

In every science, classification is one of the branches of study. Classification in biology, i.e. taxonomy, has interested scientists since ancient times. The importance of Linnaeus in the history of biology demonstrates the essential role of a rational hierarchical system of classification. However, classification is not an end—it is a beginning, and the Linnean classification is important mainly for having provided a sound basis for evolutionary theories, and the next great landmark in biology is the Darwin-Wallace theory of evolution by natural selection. Evolutionary theory provided a new way of looking at living organisms and their relationships to each other. It led to the modern concept of biological species as dynamic entities, continuously changing and interacting with each other, which replaced the old concepts of species as static, fixed, discontinuous groups. The older concepts were typological or morphological, that is the classifications were based on characters of morphology and physiology. The modern concept of species on the other hand is an operational one and takes account of other characters such as behaviour, and above all, genetics—in other words, species are defined on the basis of fertility between individuals of different populations. Let us quote the definitions of species by two authorities on the subject: (a) Mayr (1940)—'groups of actually or potentially interbreeding natural populations which are reproductively isolated from other such groups'; (b) Dobzhansky (1950)—'the largest and most inclusive . . . reproductive community of sexual and cross-fertilising individuals which share in a common gene pool'. These definitions have not been substantially changed since they were given. They are very similar in concept, and to take the most important point contained in both definitions, species consists of populations which are potentially capable of exchanging genes between them. For two individuals to belong to the same species, it is not sufficient that

By S. D. Jayakar. Reprinted with permission of UNESCO, from the *International Social Science Journal*, XXVI, No. 4, 1974, pp. 651-61 Copyright 1974 by UNESCO.

they mate and reproduce—the offspring must themselves be fertile. The concept of a species is then clearly defined, though sometimes difficult to apply rigorously in nature.

The concepts of 'race' and 'subspecies' however still suffer from the disadvantages of being essentially typological. 'Many different meanings have been assigned to the term "race". In the combination "geographic race", it is sometimes synonymous with "subspecies". However in many branches of taxonomy as well as in daily life, the term "race" is used colloquially to designate populations or aggregates of populations within formally recognized species' (Mayr, 1963). Much of the difficulty in the definition of the term 'race' is due to an insufficient knowledge of genetics. This situation is however slowly improving and to quote a recent definition of the term, a race is 'a breeding population of individuals identifiable by the frequency with which a number of inherited traits appear in that population' (Goldsby, 1971). The greater the number of genetic characters we can identify the better we will be able to define races. In the definition of races in the human species, there are unfortunately cultural and political overtones which further complicate the issue.

Populations in biology can be of various types. An ideal population is a closed one, allowing no gene exchange from outside, but completely free gene exchange between all individuals within the population (panmixia). A population can have more or less inflow or outflow of genes from one or several other populations. It can be so large that gene exchange between different parts of it is not complete—in other words, individuals are more likely to mate with each other when they are situated geographically closer to each other than when they are farther. Mayr (1963) identifies three structural elements of populations: (a) clinal variation—a population or a group of adjacent populations showing geographical variation; (b) geographical isolate—an isolated population which has little or no gene exchange with other populations of the species; and (c) hybrid belts—areas where two subspecies have come into contact and given rise to hybrid populations. In order to understand the nature of the variation between and within populations, it is necessary to understand something of population genetics.

What is population genetics? It is the study of how the genes of individuals belonging to a population vary in space and in time, and naturally the study of the factors which influence these variations. The fundamental variable used in population genetics is the gene frequency. Consider for example the ABO blood group system. We know that this sytem is controlled by a set of alleles at a single genetic locus, and the precise mechanism of this control. Thus, given a population which contains these blood groups in certain frequencies, we can estimate with a fair degree of accuracy the frequencies of the various alleles (allelic or gene frequencies) at this locus in this population. If we now take another population more or less related to this one, the gene frequencies in the second one will be more or less different from those in the first. Thus on the basis of differences between gene frequencies we can quantify the difference between these populations. These populations will, however, also differ in their frequencies for other known genetic characteristics, such as the MN and other blood group systems, various enzyme variants, colour blindness, various diseases, etc., where gene frequencies can be estimated. In addition however, they will also vary in other genetic characteristics for which the genetic determination is either unknown, partly known, or is such that it is determined by several different genetic loci and/or the environment; examples of such characters are height, weight, skin colour, body shape, and so on. For such characters, we can measure differences between populations on the basis of statistical frequency distributions of the variable, but depending on how much and what kind of genetic control exists, this kind of comparison will be more or less genetically informative. There are of course other genetic characteristics for which we have not yet learnt to distinguish the various types (phenotypes).

Observed differences in genetic characteristics of populations can be used mainly for two scientific purposes. First, one can, descriptively on the basis of the frequencies of several genetic loci, classify populations as being similar or dissimilar to each other. There are various techniques for doing this. Some of these techniques use a measure of genetic distance between the populations and on the basis of the genetic distances construct phylogenetic trees to describe the interrelationships between the populations. Secondly one can look for correlations of the gene frequencies with elements of the environment in which the populations have evolved. This can lead to the formulation of various hypotheses regarding the causative processes which have led to the establishment of these differences. Differences need not however be always causal—they can often be casual (indeed one school of population genetics believes that they are almost always so). If a population is small at least for some period, because of the fact that when a new generation of small dimensions is produced, sampling variations can produce random differences which can build up in time if the population remains small. Secondly, if a small part of a large population breaks away from this population, and establishes itself far enough away to be reproductively separate from it, the detached part may, again due to sampling variations, be more or less different in its gene frequencies (genetic composition) from the large population. Differences of the former type which are dependent on differences in the environment and which are almost always due to the action of natural selection, are called adaptive, since the population is genetically adapting itself to the conditions in which it finds itself. Differences due to casual processes (random genetic drift) are on the other hand called non-adaptive. It is not always clear whether observed differences between populations are adaptive or not.

There is another way in which non-adaptive changes can take place in a population. This is due to the way in which genes are organized into linear groups—the chromosomes. If two gene loci are closely linked on a chromosome, the changes that take place in the frequencies of the various alleles at these loci are not independent of each other. Hence if adaptive changes are taking place at one of the loci, correlated changes will take place at the other locus, though the latter may be selectively neutral, i.e. the various alleles at it may not have selective advantages or disadvantages with respect to each other; these correlated changes will then be non-adaptive.

Characters can also be correlated for biochemical or for physiological reasons. At the biochemical level, a single gene controls a single protein or part of a protein. Since this protein can be involved in several different pathways of biochemical reactions, the change in a single gene can and usually does produce changes in several different characters. In *Drosophila*, for example, there is a mutant called vestigial, since its most evident effect is to shorten the wings so that the fly is incapable of flying. However the same gene affects several other characters: the balancers, certain bristles, the shape of the spermatheca, the number of egg strings in the ovaries, etc. At the physiological level, the change in a certain character can so modify the physiology of the individual as to produce a secondary effect on other characters. The frizzle mutant in poultry, for example, shows as a primary effect, a change in the shape of the feathers, which are curled. An individual with this phenotype has, because of this feather abnormality, difficulty in thermoregulation and, as a consequence, it develops enlarged heart, spleen, crop, gizzard, pancreas, adrenals and kidneys.

To sum up the role of population genetics, it is the study of intraspecific variation by mathematical methods. Let us examine each of Mayr's structural elements of populations of a species in terms of populations genetics, first for animal species in general and then for man. (The human species must be considered separately since in addition to biological evolution, we must also consider cultural evolution, and since man has a unique means of adaptation to his environment, by using and conserving energy for his own purposes.)

CLINAL VARIATION

When a population is distributed more or less continuously over a geographic area, the genetic constitutions of representative groups at the extremes of this area will be different in many ways. These genetic differences may be either because the environmental conditions at the two extremes are different and the different subpopulations have accordingly adapted to these variations, or it may be that the differences have arisen by chance and are maintained due to the restricted interbreeding (gene flow) between geographically distant regions. If the population is continuously distributed in this area, then the genetic changes are likely to be gradual, and this is the kind of variation which is typically called clinal variation. Examples of such clinal variation are common among warm-blooded animals occupying a sufficiently wide range of latitudes. As one moves towards colder latitudes, there is a steady increase in body size, since this implies a more efficient ratio of heat production to heat loss.

Clinal variation can be seen in man where members of the same race occupy large land masses uninterrupted by geographic barriers such as mountain ranges. There are for instance some genetic differences between northern Italians and southern Italians, as there are between Swedes and Belgians. Of course these differences may be slight compared to those between a Swede and an African pygmy or between a southern Italian and an Italian gypsy, but it is important to remember that in almost all cases the differences are of the same nature and are different only in degree.

GEOGRAPHICAL ISOLATES

Populations belonging to a species, which are, however, reproductively isolated from the main body of the species are expected to be genetically different from the latter. There are at least three possible sources of these differences: (a) at the formation of the isolate, the genetic composition (gene pool) of the founding group may have been considerably different from that of the population from which it derived; (b) random differences are likely to accumulate between these populations and the main population due to independent mutations (which are very unlikely to be the same) and in the absence of gene flow between them; and (c) they are likely to evolve genetical differences due to natural selection. In fact such populations are ecologically different in as much as they are isolated, and if they remain isolated for a sufficiently long period they are potentially new species.

There are numerous examples of such isolated populations in animals. The best known examples are island populations of continental species. For instance, the common European wall lizard, *Lacerta muralis*, has evolved more than fifty races in the Balearic and Pityusas groups of islands though only three races are known on the Iberian peninsula. This is un-doubtedly due mostly to the first two mechan-isms of differentiation mentioned above. How-ever, the fact that in several cases, island popu-lations are identical among themselves, though independently derived from the mainland popu-lation and different from it, points to the im-portance of the third factor.

Many isolated populations existed in man till recent times though they are now fast disappear-ing, partly due to interbreeding and 'accultura-tion' into other populations and partly due to the destruction of their habitat and political rea-sons. Some of these populations have been studied genetically and most of those studies have revealed a notable amount of genetic dif-ferences and in many cases new allelic variants have been found which are not known in any other population.

In addition, due to man's social structure there is another type of isolate popula-tion—those that lie side by side with another population but do not interbreed with them for religious, economic or other reasons. Thus there are several religious groups in the United States which emigrated from Europe two or three hun-dred years ago but have maintained their unity as a breeding group—the same is true for the Parsis in India who migrated there around the seventh century and till recently have remained separated as a separate religion and community. Similarly there is a group of Japanese isolates in Brazil and probably many other such isolated populations. The gypsies in the different parts of Europe are genetically very similar among them-selves, and very different from the local popula-tion.

There is not in man, however, one main body of the species—there are several, and these are usually referred to as 'races'. There are differ-ences of opinion as to how precisely to subdivide the species, and this is due to the tremendous mobility of man even before the era of steam driven engines. The American Indians travelled an enormous distance from somewhere in Central Asia across the Bering Straits and down through North, Central and South America. Man's capacity to migrate has led to various in-tergradations and mixtures between the various groups. There is no doubt, however, that there are large portions of the human population who were reproductively isolated from each other. For example the African, European, Asian (Mongol) and Australoid populations were re-productively isolated from each other till fairly recently, and judging from the genetic differ-ences between them they must have evolved in-dependently of each other for some considerable time (the best estimates are of the order of about 1,000 generations or tens of thousands of years, about one hundred-thousandth of the earth's age). Some anthropologists define, besides these, other groups, such as the people of the Indian subcontinent, as separate races. However, whether a population is defined as a race or as a population within a race, or as an isolated group of that race, is not of importance. The important question, if we wish to classify populations into an evolutionary scheme, is to have some measure of genetic differentiation (genetic distance) be-tween them, which is also to some degree a mea-sure of their time of separation.

Certainly the study of subspeciation and race formation in man is highly complicated due to his complex history—the great migrations, bellic conquest and consequent interbreeding be-tween the two groups involved, slavery, social structure, religion, etc.

HYBRID BELTS

In animal species, these are usually found at an interface between two subspecies or races and consist of populations with various degrees of mixtures between the two. Genetically, as one expects, gene frequencies in these hybrid belts are intermediate between those of the two sub-species. Naturally, depending on the width of the belt, the intergradation and clinal variation can be sudden or gradual. One of the best known examples of a hybrid belt is between the carrion crow and the hooded crow in Europe, where the hybrid belt runs across Scotland, Den-mark, Germany, Austria, and along the Alps to the Mediterranean near the Franco-Italian bor-der. Within the belt, there seems to be a situa-tion which is nearly panmictic, though in other parts, individuals showing characters of both types are extremely rare.

The nature of hybrid belts in man is naturally very different from that in other animals. An obvious example of a situation where we have a large hybrid population between two races is the one in the United States, where, however, the separation between the populations is not geographical but social. The African slaves were brought over in large numbers, and there has been a certain amount of interbreeding between the white colonizers and the blacks descending from the slaves. Though arbitrary social and other prejudices have prevented free intermarriage between the populations there has inevitably been a certain amount of gene flow between the populations, and because of the biased and unbiological definition of any hybrid between the two as 'balck', a large proportion of the genes of an American black can derive from white ancestors. There have been various estimates of the proportion of white genes in the American blacks, but due to the heterogeneity of the white populations contributing to this gene pool and the uncertainty of the origin of the black ancestors, these estimates are not too accurate. The rough estimates which many geneticists have agreed on for the proportion of white genes in the black American population, using gene frequency data, are up to 30 per cent depending on which part of the United States one considers.

Analogous situations have arisen in various other parts of the world, and in some cases there have been successive waves of conquest and interbreeding, for example on the Indian subcontinent, which is a complicated hybrid area of several different populations and races, but unfortunately little is known of the origin of the populations which contributed to it, except for the European colonizers. Complicated racial mixtures exist also in many South and Central American countries and among the white populations in the United States.

To sum up the concept of races within species, then, they consist of populations which are geographically isolated, but have no fertility barriers, that is, members of two different races can not only produce fertile offspring but these in turn can breed with both races. Within such populations, there is geographic variation. When two geographically separated populations come into contact, they give rise to populations in which genetic characters of both parent populations are combined.

It is important at this stage to discuss the variation we are talking of. Until the last century, biological variation referred mainly to external morphology and physiology. Since then, however, many biochemical differences have been discovered; first the blood groups, and in more recent times several different types of protein variations. Such variations have now been studied in man as well as in other animals. They can be studied fairly easily by means of their biophysical properties (for example electrophoresis) or by their antigenic or other biochemical properties. Variations in external morphology, though often genetic in nature, depend on a number of interacting genes and on environmental differences. The precise genetic differences between individuals or populations cannot therefore be directly inferred from observed differences. Protein variations are, on the other hand, almost always simple in their genetic determination. Differences between two individuals can therefore be directly related to the differences in the alleles they carry at a particular genetic locus. Differences between populations can be measured by means of differences in gene frequencies at the locus. This is informative, since whatever the nature of the selection process or random genetic drift involved, the final effect is on the gene pool. Naturally some of these genes that can be studied by biochemical or biophysical methods are not related in any way to characters of external morphology, and are not directly related to known physiological parameters, but they are in some cases related to phenotypic variations on which selection can operate.

As we have said before, all genetic differences between populations are not adaptive. Can we recognize those changes which are not adaptive? Most often we cannot, and this is one of the central problems of population genetics today. As in many scientific fields, there are two sides of the argument: (a) unless a particular difference between two populations can be shown to be related to the environment, and explained on the basis of the environmental differences to have been caused by them, the differences should be considered non-adaptive; (b) unless the gene differences concerned can be shown to be neutral in their effects, they should be considered of selective value, since any gene difference is likely to cause some phenotypic change and its frequency is therefore likely to change adaptively. As in most such cases, the answer probably lies somewhere in between.

As for differences in external morphology, we know that some of them are adaptive, but even in cases where such differences can be explained on the basis of environmental factors, there are exceptions which cannot always be explained away as something which proves a rule. The characters of external morphology which have interested physical anthropologists are the most evident ones: height, weight, body shape, skin colour, facial characteristics, properties of the hair, etc. A well-known example of a character of external morphology which is of adaptive value is body shape. It has often been stated as a general rule in animal physiology that populations living in colder climates have a body shape that gives a greater body volume/body surface ratio, since the rate of metabolism depends on the former and the rate of loss of body heat on the latter. This is no doubt true to a large extent but other factors also play a role. The fact that people living in tropical forests are usually of small height is certainly not casual. Thus several different factors interact to produce a body shape which is adapted to the environment. Further, morphological characters can show a certain plasticity and respond differently to different conditions. Thus, Japanese brought up in the United States are significantly taller than those brought up in Japan. This difference is not genetic. The same genetic constitution reacts differently to different environments, and in particular, in this case to the different diets habitual in the two countries. People living in high altitudes, in extreme cold, in deserts, and other such extreme conditions are certainly adapted to them in some way. Part of this adaptation may be behavioural, the dress of the Saharan peoples, for example. Part of it is certainly genetic, either due to the shifting of the mean of certain physiological characteristics, or due to a more plastic expression of the phenotypes. An extensive study of adaptation in man has been undertaken in the Human Adaptability Program of the International Biological Programme.

There is another kind of variation which shows, besides individual variations, clear differences between populations—behaviour. Little or nothing is known about the genetics of behaviour in any organism, let alone in man. There are two main reasons why the genetics of behaviour have not been studied till now: (a) it is often quantitative in nature, and adequate methods of statistical analysis are not available for the meagre data that are available; (b) it is highly dependent on upbringing and the environment in general, and it is therefore difficult to separate the genetic contribution of one's parents from that due to the fact that one is brought up by them.

There are two human characteristics which have given rise to much controversy recently, namely skin colour and intelligence. So let us examine them in particular. Skin colour shows some variation within human populations but this variability is negligible in comparison to that between populations. Further there is a high correlation between skin colour and environment in that people in lower latitudes are darker than those living in more temperate climates. In particular, African populations and Australoid populations are very dark skinned. This correlation would indicate that there is natural selection for skin colour, and several hypotheses have been put forward for the mechanism of this selection. The first is that dark skin is a protection against the ultra-violet fraction of sunlight; the second is that it regulates the amount of absorption of vitamin D from the ultra-violet light—both too little and too much vitamin D assimilation is harmful; and there are others. Whatever be the explanation the Mongoloid populations have not evolved dark skins. The explanation of this is simple—they have developed a keratinized horny layer of the skin as a protection (Lerner, 1968). There are also differences in skin colour between different regions of Europe; those living in lower latitudes being again darker than the more northern ones. Some of these differences are not genetic, but there is a certain genetic component too. A Swede is more likely to suffer sunburn and freckle than a Sicilian. We can conclude then that skin colour is very probably an adaptive difference. The genetics of skin colour have not been worked out, and there are certainly several genetic loci involved, five or more. Naturally the hybrid populations which make up the American blacks are hybrid for these gene loci too, that is they must have gene frequencies at these loci which are intermediate between those of the two parent populations.

Let us now turn to intelligence. The standard method of judging individual intelligence is the measurement of the Intelligence Quotient (IQ), which is computed by scoring an individual on a series of tests of various sorts of mental ability and combining the scores into one coefficient, which is then compared with the distribution of the coefficient in the general population of that age group to judge whether a child is intelligent and to obtain a measure of his 'intelligence'. The tests selected for measurement of IQ are those which correlate fairly well with scholastic ability in European and white American children. If we think of how complicated a simple biological phenotype like height or weight is to analyse genetically, we should be very suspicious of the use of the IQ as a suitable phenotype for genetic studies. Nevertheless IQ has shown to have a genetic component. The obvious thing to do next is to try and identify those tests which have a high genetic component and which can be more easily analysed genetically. The only tests for which results have been reported, to my knowledge, is the 'spatial ability test', for which the authors have reported a sex-linked component (Bock and Kolakowski, 1973; Hartlage, 1970). Such specific abilities are in my opinion much more suitable for genetic analysis than IQ. With some luck, one may even be able to work out the genetics of such capacities in some detail. Naturally these specific abilities, more than most other variables are likely to have undergone selection and adaptation for certain environments in which they evolved. More likely since some of them are of considerable survival value in our species. Obviously, however, the abilities that are required for forest life are not the same as those necessary for surviving on the steppes. Different populations are likely to have different kinds of abilities in their various environments.

It is fairly clear then that populations are different both for skin colour and for specific mental abilities. Is there any correlation between any of these specific abilities and skin colour? None

has so far been demonstrated. It is highly unlikely, since dark skin in itself is shared by a number of very different populations from highly varied environments. It would be as senseless as to talk of a correlation between skin colour and stature—look at the Mbuti pygmies and the Watutsi.

The American blacks are descended from slaves transported to the United States and from white immigrants from Europe. It is not clear as to exactly where the slaves were brought from, though certainly some of them came from West Africa. The present black population contains up to 30 per cent of genes of European origin and more than 70 per cent are of African origin. No doubt the selection pressures they were exposed to were much different than in Africa and not much different to those in Europe, but any way selection has only had about twenty generations in which to operate, and this is a very small period in evolutionary time.

It is an established fact that American blacks do badly at IQ tests, as it is an established fact that they do better at certain sports. The first fact is interpreted by several people to mean that blacks are of 'inferior intelligence'. One could develop a battery of tests at which blacks would perform better than whites. To jump from the differences in IQ results to conclusions of general application regarding racial differences in intelligence is unjustified. The line of argument in reaching this conclusion must run as follows: (a) the IQ measures intelligence; (b) black-skinned people show lower IQ; (c) therefore the blacks are less intelligent. There are flaws in each one of these logical steps. First, IQ does not measure intelligence, if at all a concept like 'intelligence' can be measured. It is a combined score for certain mental abilities selected in a particular culture in a particular context—scholastic ability. Second, it has yet to be demonstrated that objectively sound comparisons show higher achievement by whites than by blacks with a similar background. The number of social factors influencing IQ measurement is increasing constantly. Katz (1968) for example shows how the test performance can be influenced by the colour of the person administering the test, by what the subjects are told beforehand about their intellectual capacities and by their need for approval. Third, even if we are measuring something which measures general mental ability and the blacks and whites from 'similar backgrounds' show different abilities, so what? It is highly unlikely that skin colour *per se* has anything to do with it. There are no other examples of correlation between superficial characters and behavioural characters. All we can say is that there are morphological and behavioural differences between the populations which are partly genetic and partly environmental. To base a scientific argument of racial superiority on such differences is unobjective; to base a policy of education on it is sheer folly to say the least and highly dangerous.

References

Bock, R. Darrell; Kolakowski, Donald. 1973. Further evidence of sex-linked major-gene influence on human spatial visualizing ability. *Am. J. hum. Genet.*, Vol. 25, No. 1.

Dobzhansky, T. 1950. Mendelian populations and their evolution. *Am. Nat.*, Vol. 84, p. 401.

Goldsby, Richard A. 1971. *Race and races.* New York, N.Y., Macmillan.

Hartlage, L. C. 1970. Sex-linked inheritance of spatial ability. *Percept. motor Skills*, Vol. 31, p. 610.

Katz, Irwin. 1968. Some motivational determinants of racial differences in intellectual achievement. In: Margaret Mead, Theodosius Dobzhansky, Ethel Tobach and Robert E. Light (eds.), *Science and the concept of race.* New York and London, Columbia University Press.

Lerner, I. Michael. 1968. *Heredity, evolution and society.* San Francisco, Calif., Freeman.

Mayr, E. 1940. Speciation phenomena in birds. *Am. Nat.*, Vol. 74, p. 249.

_____. 1963. *Animal species and evolution.* Harvard, Mass., Belknap Press.

Functional Adaptation to High Altitude Hypoxia

During their conquest of the Incas of Peru, the Spaniards were the first to notice that high altitude environments could have adverse effects on the normal functioning of people accustomed to living at low altitudes *(1)*. In 1590, the chronicler Jose de Acosta, in his *Historia Natural y Moral de las Indias*, gave the first clear description of mountain sickness experienced by lowland natives sojourning at high altitudes *(1)*. Three centuries later, Jourdanet *(2)* and Bert *(3)* began their scientific observations of the effects on man of high altitudes and low barometric pressures. Since then, the study of the mechanisms whereby man adapts to the pervasive effects of high altitude hypoxia has been the concern of both biological and social scientists.

There is little doubt that man can adapt to oxygen impoverished environments—witness the large number of populations living at high altitudes. In becoming so adapted, the organism develops a variety of coordinated mechanisms that have been investigated intensively in recent decades, both at high altitudes and in low pressure chambers. In this article I describe the various adaptive mechanisms that enable both the lowland and the highland native to overcome the hypoxic stress of high altitudes and to attain physiological homeostasis under the conditions of high altitude hypoxia.

THE NATURE OF HYPOXIC STRESS

The Low Pressure of Oxygen.

The biological problem of adaptation to high altitude hypoxia depends mainly upon the partial pressure of oxygen in the atmosphere which decreases proportionately with an increase in altitude. The oxygen reaches the cells of man through the combined functions of the respiratory, Cardiovascular, and hematological systems

By A. R. Frisancho. Reprinted with permission, from *Science*, 187, 31 January 1975, pp. 313-18. Copyright © 1975 by the American Association for the Advancement of Science.

that facilitate passage of gas molecules from the atmosphere to the tissues. When the tissues receive insufficient oxygen, a physiological condition called "hypoxia" develops. Hypoxia can be produced by any physiological, pathological, or environmental condition that interferes with the oxygen supply to the tissues. For example, certain defects in the cardiopulmonary system can produce the condition known as anemic hypoxia. Hypoxia can also be produced by atmospheric conditions, for example, contamination of the air with carbon monoxide or other gases that displace oxygen, or by normal depletion of oxygen in the atmosphere such as occurs at high altitudes.

The amount of oxygen in the atmosphere, 20.93 percent, remains constant up to an altitude of 110,000 meters. However, because air is compressible, the number of gaseous molecules it contains is greater at low altitudes than at high altitudes and the barometric pressure, which depends upon the molecular concentration of the air, thus also decreases with an increase in altitude. This is the fundamental problem of high altitude hypoxia: the oxygen in the air at high altitudes is less concentrated and, consequently, is at a lower pressure than it is at low altitudes.

At sea level the barometric pressure is 760 millimeters of mercury and the partial pressure of oxygen (pO_2) is 159 mm-Hg (corresponding to the 20.93 percent of oxygen at 760 mm-Hg). At 3500 m (11,840 feet) the barometric pressure is reduced to 493 mm-Hg and the pO_2 is 103 mm-Hg; that is, at an altitude of 3500 m the oxygen has about 35 percent less pressure than at sea level. At 4500 m the pO_2 is decreased by as much as 40 percent (to 91 mm-Hg) with respect to the pO_2 at sea level (Fig. 1). Because of this decrease in pO_2 in the ambient air, the pO_2 of the air reaching the trachea and the alveoli is also reduced and this, in turn, reduces the amount of oxygen that is available to the tissues.

The decrease in pO_2 at high altitudes causes a reduction in the oxygen saturation of the arterial blood because the proportion of oxyhemoglobin formed depends on the pO_2 in the air reaching the alveoli. Thus, if the pO_2 of the ambient air is 159 mm-Hg and in the alveoli it is 104 mm-Hg, as it is at sea level, the hemoglobin in the arterial blood is 97 percent saturated with oxygen. On

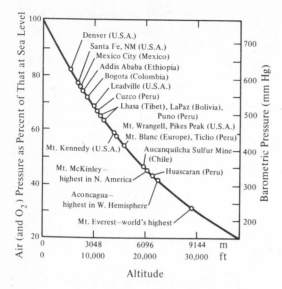

Figure 1. Barometric pressure and oxygen pressure at high altitudes. With an increase in altitude there is a percentage decrease in the air and oxygen pressure. Modified from Folk *(66)*.

the other hand, if the pO_2 of the ambient air is 110 mm-Hg and in the alveoli it is 67 mm-Hg, as occurs at an altitude of 3000 m (9840 feet), the hemoglobin in the arterial blood is only 90 percent saturated. This means that at an altitude of 3000 m there is a decrease of 10 percent of oxygen for each unit of blood that leaves the lungs. Between an altitude of 4000 and 5000 m, this decrease might reach as high as 30 percent.

Symptoms of High Altitude Hypoxia

The initial symptoms of high altitude sickness include shortness of breath, respiratory distress, physical and mental fatigue, rapid pulse rate, interrupted sleep, and headaches intensified by activity. There may also occur some slight digestive disorders and in some cases a marked loss of weight. In other cases the individual may feel dyspnea, nausea, and vomiting. In very rare cases at altitudes above 4500 m there may occur a diminution of visual acuteness, painful menstruation, and bleeding of the gums. While some individuals appear to be predisposed to high altitude sickness, others may feel only mild effects that can be overcome with acclimatization.

Among those individuals who appear to be predisposed to mountain sickness, some may lack the ability to become acclimatized and may develop chronic mountain sickness *(4)*.

The effects of high altitude hypoxia also depend on physical and biological factors. Some physiological effects may be evident at 1500 m (4920 feet). Under rest conditions at this altitude there may not be any effects, but during physical activity hypoxia effects may become evident. Between 2000 and 3000 m (6500 to 9840 feet) the effects of hypoxia are felt during both rest and physical activity. Above 3000 m the physiological effects become increasingly evident and unavoidable and the physiological limits of human tolerance to high altitude hypoxia appear to be reached at 8545 m (33,000 feet).

ADAPTIVE PATHWAYS

The various adaptive mechanisms triggered by exposure to high altitudes are directed toward increasing the availability of oxygen and increasing the pressure of oxygen at the tissue level. This is accomplished through modifications in (i) pulmonary ventilation, (ii) lung volume and pulmonary diffusing capacity, (iii) transportation of oxygen in the blood, (iv) diffusion of oxygen from blood to tissues, (v) utilization of oxygen at the tissue level.

Pulmonary ventilation

Upon exposure to high altitude hypoxia, lowland natives show, both at rest and during exercise, a progressive increase in pulmonary ventilation that may reach as much as 100 percent of the values at sea level *(5-8)*. Such hyperventilation is both adaptive and nonadaptive. It is adaptive because it increases the pO_2 at the alveolar and arterial levels and consequently increases the diffusion gradient between the blood and the tissues *(5, 8, 9)*. It is nonadaptive because it decreases the partial pressure of carbon dioxide (pCO_2) at the alveolar level and, if this is not compensated for, it may change the pH of the blood from a normal (pH 7.4) to an alkaline state (pH>7.4) and result in alkalosis. Such alkalosis is prevented by rapid active removal of bicarbonate from the cerebrospinal fluid *(10)* and blood. This mechanism, which lowers the pH of the medullary chemoreceptors in relation to any given pCO_2, resets the level at which the arterial pCO_2 is regulated by changing the relation between the pCO_2 and the response of the medullary chemoreceptors to pH. In this manner the original homeokinetic relationship between the pH of the cerebrospinal fluid and the blood is restored to sea level values. It is the maintenance of this equilibrium that enables the lowland native to sustain an increased ventilation at high altitudes without the risks of alkalosis or hypocapnia.

As shown by recent analyses *(11)*, in both the lowland and the highland native the magnitude of the increase in pulmonary ventilation during exercise is directly proportional to the increase in altitude. However, at a given altitude, as shown in Fig. 2, the pulmonary ventilation of the lowland native (sojourning on a short-term or long-term basis at high altitudes) is invariably higher than that of the high altitude native *(12-18)*.

In summary, acclimatization to high altitude in the lowland native is associated unquestionably with an increase in pulmonary ventilation. In the highland native, however, acclimatization to high altitude is accompanied by a lesser increase in pulmonary ventilation. Since the increase in pulmonary ventilation permits the newcomer to maintain an increase in pO_2 at the alveolar level and an increase in arterial oxygen saturation *(11)*, it would appear that a hyperventilatory response is critical to the acclimatization of the newcomer. However, after acclimatization occurs, the increase in pulmonary ventilation reaches a plateau, probably reflecting the operation of other adaptive mechanisms.

Lung Volume and Pulmonary Diffusing Capacity

Upon initial exposure to high altitude hypoxia, the vital capacity and residual lung volume of lowland natives is reduced, but after about 1 month of residency at high altitudes, such subjects attain values which are comparable to those they had at low altitudes *(19, 20)*. The oxygen pulmonary diffusing capacity of lowland natives remains unchanged at high altitudes when compared to the capacity attained at sea level *(21, 22)*.

In contrast, highland natives have a larger lung volume, and especially a larger residual lung volume (volume of air remaining in lungs after maximum expiration), than subjects from low altitudes, when adjustments are made for differences in body size *(12, 23-25)*. Studies indicate that the enlarged lung volume of the high altitude native is attained through a rapid and accelerated development *(24, 26)*. During childhood at low altitudes, growth in lung volume is associated with the proliferation of alveolar untis and the consequent increase in alveolar surface area *(27)*: among children raised at high altitudes, the rapid growth in lung volume is probably also associated with these factors. Studies invariably indicate that the pulmonary diffusing capacity of the highland native is systematically greater than that attained by lowland natives at low altitudes *(22. 28)*. Since the mm-

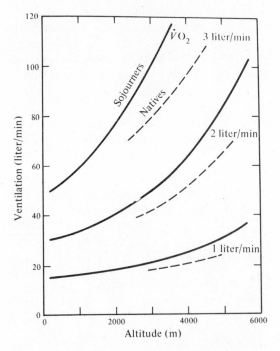

Figure 2. Pulmonary ventilation (BTPS) in relation to altitude in lowland and highland natives measured at rest and at three levels of exercise. (VO_2, maximum volume of oxygen consumed.) Adapted from Lenfant and Sullivan *(11)*.

pulmonary diffusing capacity is related in part to the alveolar surface area, the enhanced pulmonary diffusing capacity of the highland native is probably due to his having a greater alveolar area and an increased capillary volume.

In a recent investigation designed to determine the mechanisms of functional adaptation to high altitude hypoxia *(18, 25)*, the forced vital capacity (maximum amount of air expired after maximum inspiration) of lowland subjects and high altitude natives was measured (see Table 1). The results demonstrated that lowland natives who were acclimatized to high altitude during growth, when adjusted for variations in body size, attained the same values of forced vital capacity as the highland natives. In contrast, lowland natives (Peruvian and white U.S. subjects) acclimatized as adults had significantly lower vital capacity than highland natives. It was thus postulated that the enlarged lung volume of the highland native is the result of adaptations occurring during growth and development *(18)*.

This hypothesis is supported by experiments conducted on animals. Various studies *(29-32a)* demonstrate that young rats after prolonged exposure to high altitude hypoxia (3450 m) ex-

hibited an accelerated proliferation of alveolar units, and an accelerated growth in alveolar surface area and lung volume. In contrast, adult rats after prolonged exposure to high altitude hypoxia did not show changes in alveolar quantity and lung volume *(32)*. These findings suggest that in experimental animals and in man the enlarged lung volume at high altitude is probably mediated by developmental factors.

Transport of Oxygen in the Blood

The major function of the hemoglobin in the red blood cells is to transport oxygen from the lungs to the tissues. At high altitudes, in response to the insufficient amount of oxygen, the bone marrow is stimulated by an erythropoietic factor to increase the production of red blood cells *(33)*. For this reason, at altitudes above 4000 m, both lowland and highland natives have normal red blood cell counts ranging from 5 to 8 million per cubic millimeter compared to 4.5 million at low altitudes *(34, 35)*. Along with the increase in the red blood cells, the hemoglobin is augmented so that at high altitudes the averages range from 17 to 20 grams per 100 milliliters

Table 1. Covariance adjustment of forced vital capacity (adjusted for age, weight, and height) among subjects tested at high altitudes. *F*, variance ratio values; S.E., standard error; NS, not significant. After Frisancho *et al. (25)*.

N	Group	Forced vital capacity (ml)	
		Mean	S.E.
	Subjects tested at 3840 m		
40	High Altitude natives	4830.3	69.9
13	Sea level subjects acclimatized as adults	4504.6	122.1
F ratio		5.19	*P* < .02
	Subjects tested at 3400 m		
20	High altitude natives	4990.3	128.6
12	Sea level subjects acclimatized during growth	5055.0	121.5
F ratio		0.36	NS
10	White U.S. subjects acclimatized as adults*	4573.9	231.6
F ratio		5.53	*P* < .02

*When compared with the high altitude natives tested at 3840 and 3400 m.

compared to the 12 to 16 g/100 ml at sea level *(34)*. In this manner, the oxygen carrying capacity of the blood at high altitudes is increased.

Diffusion of Oxygen from Blood to Tissues

For the oxygen to be utilized, it must reach the cell mitochondria through a process of physical diffusion, and the rate of such diffusion depends on the pO_2. Because the oxygen is consumed as it goes through successive tissue layers, the pO_2 rapidly declines, and the more distance the oxygen has to travel, the greater the drop in the pO_2. At high altitude, where the pO_2 of the ambient air is already low, the organism must respond by shortening the distance the oxygen has to travel. This is accomplished by the opening up of existing and new capillaries. Through microscopic studies of experimental animals it has been found that the number of open muscle capillaries at high altitudes is increased by more than 40 percent compared to the number at low altitudes *(36-38)*. A very important effect of the increased capillary bed is that it increases the blood perfusion and, thus, oxygen is more readily diffused per unit time into tissue despite the lowered oxygen tension of the blood before it reaches the capillaries *(39)*. Since among highland natives the muscle myoglobin concentration is also increased *(40)*, this, coupled with the increased capillarization, must certainly enhance the diffusion of oxygen at high altitudes.

Another mechanism which at high altitudes facilitates the diffusion of oxygen from the blood to the tissues is that shown by a rightward shift in the dissociation curve for oxygen and hemoglobin *(8, 41, 42)*. This shift results from a decrease in the hemoglobin affinity for oxygen. This decrease appears to be related to an increase in intraerythrocytic 2,3-diphosphoglycerate *(8, 42, 43)*.

At a given pO_2, the percentage of oxygen in the hemoglobin of venous blood is significantly lower at high altitudes than at sea level. Because of this difference, among lowland and highland natives, the proportion of the available oxygen that is delivered to the tissues is greater at high than at low altitudes *(8, 41)*. However, the relative effectiveness of this mechanism is not well defined yet.

Utilization of Oxygen

The last step in the process of adaptation to hypoxia involves variations in the rate of oxygen utilization and generation of energy at the cellular level. On the basis of studies on guinea pigs it has been postulated that at high altitudes glycolysis (anaerobic) proceeds by way of the pentose phosphate pathway rather than the Embden-Meyerhof pathway *(44)*. The advantage of the pentose pathway appears to be related to the fact that no additional adenosine triphosphate (ATP) is required to generate glyceraldehyde triphosphate as is necessary in the Embden-Meyerhof pathway. According to this mechanism *(44, 45)*, at high altitudes, by relying on the pentose phosphate pathway, the organism saves energy (ATP) or produces more chemical energy with the same oxygen consumption. This hypothesis is supported by the finding that the activity of oxidative enzymes in the sartorius muscles is greater at high altitudes than at sea level *(44)*. For example, in homogenates of whole cells the reduced diphosphopyridine nucleotide-oxidase system, the reduced triphosphopyridine nucleotide-cytochrome c reductase, and the transhydrogenase are significantly more active in the highland than in the lowland native *(44)*. Thus, it appears that among highland natives the chemical and morphological characteristics related to energy utilization and energy production are qualitatively and quantitatively different from those of lowland natives. It is not known whether such characteristics may be acquired by lowland natives residing for long periods at high altitudes.

CARDIOVASCULAR TRAITS

Pulmonary Circulation

Histological studies have demonstrated that after the first month of postnatal development, children born at high altitudes show a thickening of the muscular layer and muscularization of the pulmonary arteries and arterioles that resembles the development of the fetal pulmonary vascular tree *(46)*. These characteristics contribute to the increased pulmonary vascular resistance or pulmonary hypertension in the high altitude resident and native *(47-49)*. Based on studies of steers, the hypothesis has been that pulmonary hypertension at high altitudes would favor a more effective perfusion of all the pulmonary areas, and, therefore, increase the effective blood-gas interfacial area of the alveoli *(50)*. In this manner, perfusion of the entire lung coupled with an increased vascularization would enhance the diffusing capacity of the lung and should decrease the difference between the arterial and the alveolar blood. These changes would permit a more effective oxygenation of the arterial blood. However, one cannot assume that pulmonary hypertension would necessarily decrease the arterial-alveolar gradient in man, and the application of this hypothesis to the adaptation of human beings to high altitudes remains to be proved.

As a result of the increased pulmonary resistance or hypertension, the right ventricle of the heart of the high altitude resident and native is enlarged, as shown by anatomical and electrocardiographic studies *(51, 52)*. The enlargement of the right ventricle may also be related to the high prevalence of patent ductus arteriosus among highland natives *(53)*. Hence, because of the pressure differential between the aorta and pulmonary artery, the work of the right ventricle of the heart may be increased. The high incidence of patent ductus arteriosus may be a consequence of fetal and newborn hypoxia and may also be one of the sources of the pulmonary hypertension. Lowland natives with patent ductus arteriosus also commonly suffer from right ventricular hypertrophy and pulmonary stenosis.

Although pulmonary hypertension and right ventricular hypertrophy may occur at all ages in both highland and lowland subjects in their native environments, these characteristics are accentuated among subjects exposed to insufficient supplies of oxygen during childhood and adolescence *(47, 48, 52, 54)*. These findings demonstrate the influence of developmental factors in the acquisition of the cardiovascular characteristics of highland dwellers.

Cardiac Output

Upon initial exposure to high altitude hypoxia, the resting pulse rate of the lowland native increases rapidly from an average of 70 beats per minute to as much as 105 beats per minute. This increase is associated both with a generalized increase in sympathetic activity and with an abrupt augmentation of the resting cardiac output *(55, 56)*. With acclimatization, the cardiac output declines so that in about a week it equals or is below that attained at sea level *(57, 58)*. This decline in cardiac output appears to be associated with a decrease in heart rate which usually remains above sea level values *(57)*. The cardiac output of highland natives during rest and exercise was found to be equal to that of lowland natives at sea level *(49)*. Therefore, the oxygen requirements of the body appear to be met by greater oxygen extraction rather than greater blood flow at high altitude.

Systemic Circulation

Various studies indicate that the systemic blood pressure in adult highland natives is lower than it is in lowland natives at sea level *(47, 59-61)*. Among highland natives, the frequency of systemic hypertension and ischemic heart disease is also significantly lower than among lowland natives at sea level *(61)*. Furthermore, recent studies *(60)* indicate a lowering of 10 mm-Hg or more in systolic and diastolic pressures in lowland subjects who resided for a long time (2 to 15 years) at high altitude.

The etiology of these differences has not been completely determined. Because exposure to high altitudes results in increased vascularization *(36, 38, 41, 62)*, it is possible that the prevalence of low blood pressure at high altitude may be related to the reduction in peripheral vascular resistance to blood flow. In other words, lowering of blood pressure may be considered a by-product of tissue adaptation to high altitude hypoxia.

WORK CAPACITY

Lowland Newcomers to High Altitudes

During severe exercise the metabolic requirements for oxygen increase drastically so that all the processes involved in the transport, delivery, and utilization of oxygen are required to work at their maximum. For this reason, the effects of high altitude hypoxia are most evident during periods of hard work. Measurements of an individual's work capacity indicate the degree of success of the various adaptive responses made by the organism.

It is generally agreed that the maximum oxygen intake per unit of body weight (or aerobic capacity) during maximal acitvity is a measure of the individual's work capacity because it reflects the capacity of the working muscles to utilize oxygen and the ability of the cardiovascular system to transport and deliver oxygen to the tissues. Studies of newcomers to high altitudes demonstrated a reduction in aerobic capacity of from 13 to 22 percent *(6, 15, 16, 20, 63)*. The maximum aerobic capacity of fit lowland natives at high altitudes, when expressed as a percentage of the values obtained at sea level, declines by 3.2 percent for every 300 m (1000 feet) ascended beyond 1500 m (5000 feet) *(15)*. In contrast, the aerobic capacity of highland natives is comparable to that attained by lowland natives at sea level *(6, 14-17, 64)*.

Developmental Response

To determine the influence of developmental factors on functional adaptation to high altitude, my co-workers and I recently conducted an investigation on aerobic capacity *(18)*. This study (see Table 2) demonstrated that lowland natives when acclimatized to high altitude during childhood and adolescence attained an aerobic capacity and pulmonary ventilation that was equal to that of the highland natives. Furthermore, in both groups the volume of air ventilated per unit of oxygen consumed, the increase in heart rate, and the volume of oxygen consumption per pulse rate are highly comparable.

In contrast, lowland natives (Peruvian and U.S. subjects) when acclimatized to high altitudes as adults attained significantly lower aerobic cacapacities and higher pulmonary ventilation than the highland natives. Similarly, these lowland subjects attained a significantly higher ventilation ratio and lower heart rate than the highland natives.

The extent to which developmental factors influence the attainment of aerobic capacity at high altitudes is illustrated in Fig. 3. These data show that, among lowland natives acclimatized to high altitudes during growth and development, the attainment of aerobic capacity is directly related to age at migration and length of residency. In contrast, when subjects were acclimatized to high altitudes as adults, age at mi-

Table 2. Physiological data of Peruvian and U.S. subjects during work on a bicycle ergometer at high altitude. Values are means ± standard deviations. After Frisancho *et al. (18)*.

	Peruvians			U.S. subjects acclimatized as adults (N = 10)
	Highland native (N = 20)	Acclimatized as young (N = 23)	Acclimatized as adults (N = 10)	
Maximum volume of O_2 consumed (ml kg^{-1} min^{-1})				
46.3 ± 5.0	46.0 ± 6.3	38.0* ± 5.2	38.5* ± 5.8	
51.2 ± 5.8†	50.1 ± 5.4†	42.3* ± 5.0†	41.6* ± 5.6†	
Maximum pulmonary ventilation (liter/min)‡				
138.5 ± 22.4	139.7 ± 17.9	165.0* ± 17.2	175.3* ± 25.5	
Ratio of maximum pulmonary ventilation to maximum O_2 consumed				
51.3 ± 6.5	50.7 ± 5.4	64.4* ± 7.2	75.5* ± 7.9	
Maximum heart rate (beat/min)				
196.1 ± 6.6	193.2 ± 6.5	192.6* ± 6.0	187.2* ± 7.9	
Volume of O_2 consumed per heart beat (ml/beat)				
13.9 ± 1.8	14.4 ± 1.7	11.1 ± 0.6	14.6 ± 2.4	

* Significantly different from highland native at $P < .01$ level.
† Related to fat-free weight.
‡ Corrected for body temperature and pressure, saturated (BTPS).

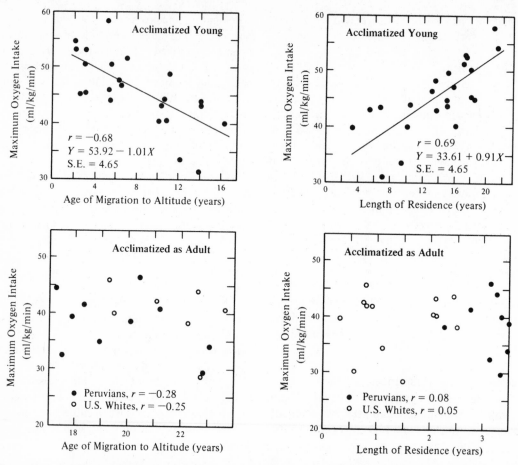

Figure 3. Influence of developmental adaptation on aerobic capacity at high altitude. Among subjects acclimatized to high altitudes during the developmental period, age at migration and length of residency are significantly correlated with aerobic capacity, while this is not the case when the subjects are acclimatized as adults.

Adapted from Fisancho *et al. (18).*

gration and length of residency did not influence the attainment of aerobic capacity. In other words, from these investigations it appears that the attainment of normal aerobic capacity at high altitudes is influenced by adaptations occurring during the developmental period *(18).*

CONCLUSIONS

The various adaptive mechanisms that enable both the lowland and highland native to overcome the hypoxic stress of high altitudes are summarized in Fig. 4. In both lowland and highland natives, adaptation to the low availability of

oxygen at high altitudes results in the operation of a variety of coordinated mechanisms oriented toward increasing the supply of oxygen to the tissue (Fig. 4). However, the lowland native uses different paths from the highland native to acclimatize to high altitudes. While both the lowland and the highland native utilize the increase in oxygen carrying capacity of the blood, and augmented capillarization to acclimatize, it is mainly the lowland native who utilizes the increase in pulmonary ventilation. That acclimatization of highland natives does not depend on hyperventilation is perhaps due in part to their enlarged lung volume that facilitates the receiv-

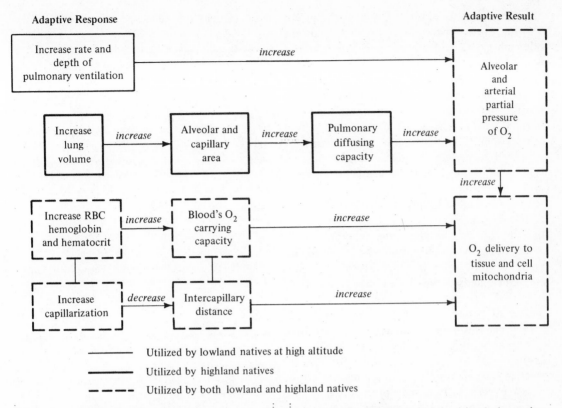

Adaptive Response   **Adaptive Result**

Figure 4.   Schematic representation of the adaptive pathways elicited by high altitude hypoxia. Adaptation to high altitude hypoxia results in the operation of a series of coordinated mechanisms oriented toward increasing the oxygen supply at the tissue level. The lowland and the highland native use different paths to acclimatize to high altitude hypoxia. While systems for the increase in oxygen carrying capacity of the blood and augmented capillarization are operative in both the lowland and the highland native, the increase in pulmonary ventilation is utilized mostly by the lowland native, RBC, red blood cell.

ing of an adequate oxygen supply at the alveolar level. The low dependence on hyperventilation in spite of arterial hypoxemia in the highland native would suggest a difference in the reactivity of the peripheral chemoreceptors.

Recent investigations suggest that the acquisition of an enlarged lung volume and chest size *(24, 25, 65)* and attainment of normal aerobic capacity *(18)* at high altitude are influenced by developmental factors. Studies on cardiac morphology *(47)* indicate that the enlarged right ventricle of the heart that characterizes the high altitude native is acquired during development. Thus it is suggested that the differences between the highland and the lowland native in physiological performance and morphology are due, in part, to adaptations acquired during the developmental period.

During growth and development, environmental factors are constantly conditioning and modifying the expression of inherited potentials. The influence of the environment on the organism depends on the type of stress imposed and especially on the age at which the individual is subjected to the stress. Hence, the respective contribution of genetic and environmental factors varies with the developmental stage of the organism and, in general, the earlier the age, the greater the influence of the environment. For these reasons, it would be surprising if developmental processes did not influence the functional performance and morphology of the high altitude native. At present, however, the extent to which this conclusion is applicable to the other physiological traits of the highland native is not known. For example, it appears that the attainment of low systemic blood pressure at high altitudes does not depend on developmental factors because it can be acquired by lowland natives residing for long periods at high altitudes *(60)*. Similarly, the mechanisms by which high altitude hypoxia induces the development of the characteristics of the highland native are not known.

Because high altitude hypoxia affects the major physiological processes it is conceivable that it may also influence the functional processes not only during growth but also during aging. Because aging in general results in a decreased capacity of the oxygen transport system, functional processes during aging may be expected to be affected at high altitudes to a greater extent than they are at sea level. Studies of human adaptation to high altitudes during aging would thus help to elucidate the various mechanisms whereby man overcomes the stress of low oxygen supply, such problems being of major importance to both lowland and highland populations. Therefore, future endeavors should be oriented to fill this gap in our knowledge.

Notes

1. R. H. Kellogg, *Physiologist* 11, 37 (1968).

2. D. Jourdanet, *in Les Altitudes de l'Amerique Tropicale Comparees au Niveau des Mers au Point de Vue de la Constitution Medicale* (Bailliere, Paris, 1861).

3. P. Bert, in *La Pression Barometrique: Recherches de Physiologie Experimentale* (Masson, Paris, 1878).

4. M. C. Monge and C. Monge C., in *High Altitude Diseases: Mechanism and Management* (Thomas, Springfield, Ill., 1966).

5. H. Rahn and A. B. Otis, *J. Appl. Physiol.* 1, 717 (1949).

6. R. F. Grover *et al., ibid.* 22, 555 (1967).

7. J. T. Reeves, R. F. Grover, J. E. Cohn, *ibid.*, p. 546; S. C. Sorensen and J. W. Severinghaus, *ibid.* 25, 211 (1968); *ibid.*, p. 217; *ibid.*, p. 221.

8. J. D. Torrance *et al., Respir. Physiol.* 11, 1 (1970/71).

9. C. Lenfant, J. D. Torrance, C. Reynafarje, *J. Appl. Physiol.* 30, 625 (1971).

10. J. Severinghaus and L. Carcelen, *ibid.* 19, 319 (1964); J. W. Severinghaus, R. A. Mitchell, B. W. Richarson *ibid.* 18, 1155 (1963).

11. C. Lenfant and K. Sullivan, *N. Engl. J. Med.* 284, 1298 (1971).

12. A. Hurtado, *Handb. Physiol.* 4, 843 (1964).

13. ____, T. Valásquez, B. Reynafarje, H. Aste-Salazar, *U.S. Air Force School of Aviation Medicine Rep. 56-104.* Randolph Air Force Base, Tex. (1956); B. Balke, *Am. J. Cardiol.* 14, 796 (1964); W. P. Lahiri and J. S. Milledge, *Nature (Lond.)* 207, 610 (1965); S. Lahiri, J. S. Milledge, H. P. Chattopadhyay, A. K. Bhattacharyya, A. K. Sinha, *J. Appl. Physiol.* 23, 545 (1967).

14. T. M. Valásquez, in *The Physiological Effects of High Altitude*, W. H. Weihe, Ed. (Pergamon, Oxford, 1964).

15. E. R. Buskirk, J. Kollias, R. F. Akers, E. K. Prokop, E. Picon-Reátegui, *J. Appl. Physiol.* 23, 259 (1967).

16. J. Kollias, E. R. Buskirk, R. F. Akers, E. K. Prokop, P. T. Baker, E. Picon-Reátegui, *ibid.* 24, 792 (1968).

17. R. B. Mazess, *Hum. Biol.* 41, 494 (1969).

18. A. R. Frisancho, C. Martinez, T. Valásquez, J. Sanchez, H. Montoye, *J. Appl. Physiol.* 34, 176 (1973).

19. H. Rahn and D. Hammond, *ibid.* 4, 715 (1952); S. M. Tenney, H. Rahn, R. C. Straud, J. C. Mithoefer, *ibid.* 5, 607 (1952); F. Ulvedal, T. E. Morgan, Jr., R. G. Cutler, B. E. Welch, *ibid.* 18, 904 (1963); J. L. Shields, J. P. Hannon, C. W. Harris, W. S. Platner, *ibid.* 25, 606 (1968).

20. C. F. Consolazio, H. G. Johnson, L. O. Mataush, R. A. Nelson, G. J. Isaac, *U.S. Army Med. Res. Nutr. Lab. Rep. No. 300* (1967).

21. F. Kreuzer and P. Van Lookeren Campagne, *J. Appl. Physiol.* 20, 519 (1965).

22. A. C. DeGraff, Jr., *et al., ibid.* 29, 71 (1970).

23. A. Hurtado, T. Valásquez, C. Reynafarje, R. Lozano, R. Chavez, H. Aste-Salazar, B. Reynafarje, B. Sanchez, J. Muñoz, *U.S. Air Force School of Aviation Medicine Rep. 56-1.* Randolph Air Force Base, Tex. (1956).

24. A. R. Frisancho, *Hum. Biol.* 41, 365 (1969).

25. ____, T. Valásquez, J. Sanchez, *ibid.* 44, 583 (1973).

26. A. Hurtado, *Am. J. Phys. Anthropol.* 17, 137 (1932).

27. M. S. Dunnill, *Thorax* 17, 329 (1962).

28. T. Valásquez and E. Florentini, *Arch Inst. Biol. Andina.* Lima 1, 179 (1966); J. E. Remmers and J. C. Mithoefer, *Respir. Physiol.* 6, 233 (1969); J. S. Guleria, J. N. Pande, P. K. Sethi, S. B. Roy, *J. Appl. Physiol.* 31, 536 (1971).

29. P. H. Burri and E. R. Weibel, *Respir. Physiol.* 11, 247 (1971).

30. D. Bartlett, Jr., and J. E. Remmers, *ibid.* 13, 116 (1971).

31. D. Bartlett, in *Regulation of Organ and Tissue Growth*, R. Goss, Ed. (Academic Press, New York, 1972).

32. P. H. Burri and E. R. Weibel, in *High Altitude Physiology: Cardiac and Respiratory Aspects*, R. Porter and J. Knight, Eds. (Churchill, Livingstone, London, 1971).

32a. E. L. Cunningham, J. S. Brody, B. P. Jain, *J. Appl. Physiol.* 37, 362 (1974).

33. C. Reynafarje, J. Ramos, J. Faura, D. Villavicencio, *Proc. Soc. Exp. Biol. Med.* 116, 649 (1964); P. H. Abbrecht

and J. K. Littell, *J. Appl. Physiol.* 32, 54 (1972).

34. A. Hurtado, C. F. Merino, D. Delgado, *Arch. Int. Med.* 75, 284 (1945).

35. C. F. Merino, *Blood* 5, 1 (1950); G. R. Fryers, *Am. J. Physiol.* 171, 459 (1952); A. Anthony and J. Krieder, *ibid.* 200, 523 (1961); K. R. Reissman, *ibid.* 167, 52 (1951); C. Reynafarje, R. Lozano, J. Valdivieso, *Blood* 14, 433 (1959).

36. E. L. Becker, R. G. Cooper, G. D. Hathaway, *J. Appl. Physiol.* 8, 166 (1955).

37. E. Valdivia, M. Watson, C. M. Dass, *Arch. Pathol.* 69, 199 (1960).

38. S. Cassin, R. D. Gilbert, E. M. Johnson, *U.S. Air Force School of Aerospace Medicine. SAM-TR-66-16* (1966): S. M. Tenney and L. C. Ou, *Respir. Physiol.* 8, 137 (1970).

39. H. Rahn, In "Life at high altitudes," *Pan Am. Health Organ. Sci. Publ. No. 140* (1966), p. 2.

40. J. B. Wittenberg, *J. Gen. Physiol.* 49, 57 (1965); B. Reynafarje, *J. Appl. Physiol.* 17, 301 (1962).

41. H. Aste-Salazar and A. Hurtado, *Am. J. Physiol.* 142, 733 (1944).

42. C. Lenfant, J. D. Torrance, E. English, C. A. Finch, C. Reynafarje, J. Ramos, J. Faura, *J. Clin. Invest.* 47, 2652 (1968); M. Rorth, S. Nygaard, H. Parving, *Scand. J. Clin. Lab. Invest.* 29, 329 (1972); G. J. Brewer, J. W. Eaton, J. V. Weil, R. F. Grover, in *Red Cell Metabolism and Function*, G. Brewer, Ed. (Plenum, New York 1970).

43. L. G. Moore, G. Brewer, F. Oelshlengel, in *Hemoglobulin and Red Cell Structure and Function*, G. J. Brewer, Ed. (Plenum, New York, 1972), p. 397.

44. B. Reynafarje, in "Life at High Altitudes," *Pan Am. Health Organ. Sci. Publ. No. 140* (1966), p. 40.

45. B. Reynafarje, thesis, Universidad Nacional Mayor de San Marcos, Lima, Peru (1971).

46. J. Arias-Stella and M. Saldana, *Med. Thorac.* 19, 484 (1962); J. Arias-Stella and H. Kruger, *Arch. Pathol.* 76, 147 (1963).

47. D. Peñaloza, F. Sime, N. Banchero, R. Gamboa, J. Cruz, E. Marticorena, *Am. J. Cardiol.* 11, 150 (1963).

48. F. Sime, N. Banchero, D. Peñaloza, R. Gamboa, J. Cruz, E. Marticorena, *ibid.*, p. 143.

49. N. Banchero, F. Sime, D. Peñaloza, J. Cruz, R. Gamboa, E. Marticorena, *Circulation* 33, 249 (1966).

50. R. F. Grover, J. T. Reeves, D. H. Will, S. G. Blount, *J. Appl. Physiol.* 18, 567 (1963).

51. A. Rotta, A. Canepa, A. Hurtado, T. Valásquez, R. Chavez, *ibid.* 9, 328 (1956); J. Arias-Stella and S. Recavaren,

Am. J. Pathol. 41, 55 (1962); D. Peñaloza, J. Arias-Stella, F. Sime, S. Recavaren, E. Marticorena, *Pediatrics* 34, 568 (1964); C. Harris and J. E. Hansen, *Am. J. Cardiol.* 18, 183 (1966).

52. D. Peñaloza, N. Banchero, N. Sime, R. Gamboa, *Biochemical Clinics No. 1, The Heart* (Reuben Donnelley, New York, 1963), p. 283.

53. E. Marticorena, D. Peñaloza, J. Severino, K. Hellriegel, *Memorias del IV Congreso Mundial de Cardiologia, Mexico* (1962), I-A, p. 155.

54. J. Arias-Stella and S. Recavaren, *Am. J. Pathol.* 41, 55 (1962).

55. J. A. Vogel and C. W. Harris, *J. Appl. Physiol.* 22, 1124 (1967).

56. J. Stenberg, B. Ekblom, R. Messin, *ibid.* 21, 1589 (1966).

57. K. Klausen, *ibid.*, p. 609.

58. B. Saltin *et al.*, *ibid.* 25, 400 (1968); L. H. Hartley *et al.*, *ibid.* 23, 839 (1967).

59. M. C. Monge, *Meteorol. Monogr.* 2, 50 (1954); A. Chavez, thesis, Universidad Nacional Mayor San Marcos, Lima, Peru (1965).

60. E. Marticorena, L. Ruiz, J. Severino, J. Galvez, D. Penaloza, *Am. J. Cardiol.* 23, 364 (1969).

61. L. Ruiz, thesis, Universidad Peruana Cayetano Heredia, Lima, Peru (1973).

62. J. Martini and C. R. Honing, *Microvasc. Res.* 1, 244 (1969).

63. B. Balke, in *Science and Medicine of Exercise and Sports*, W. R. Johnson, Ed. (Harper, New York, 1960); D. B. Dill, L. G. Myhre, D. K. Brown, K. Burrus, G. Gehlsen, *J. Appl. Physiol.* 23, 555 (1967); J. Faulkner, J. Kollias, C. Favour, E. Buskirk, B. Balke, *ibid.* 24, 685 (1968).

64. R. W. Elsner, A. Bolstad, C. Forno, in *The Physiological Effects of High Altitude*, W. H. Weihe, Ed. (Macmillan, New York, 1963); P. T. Baker, *Science* 163, 1149 (1969).

65. A. R. Frisancho, *Am. J. Phys. Anthropol.* 32, 401 (1970).

66. G. E. Folk, *Introduction to Environmental Physiology* (Lea & Febiger, Philadelphia, 1966).

67. I thank Mrs. Kathleen Font and Laura Bakken for their assistance in the preparation of this manuscript. Supported in part by grant HB-13805 from the National Institutes of Health and by grant GS-37542X from the National Science Foundation. Various phases of the present investigation were conducted in cooperation with the Institute of Andean Biology of the National University of San Marcos of Peru and the International Biological Programme of the United States.

Aggression and Hypoglycemia Among the Qolla: A Study in Psychobiological Anthropology[1]

In a series of important writings published more than ten years ago, Anthony F. C. Wallace (1960, 1961a, 1961b, 1961c, 1962) suggested that specialists in the field of culture and personality expand the scope of their interests and incorporate new theoretical perspectives into their thinking. He recommended that anthropologists devote more attention to two significant, though neglected, problem areas: (1) the relation between culture and cognition, and (2) the biological bases of cultural behavior and mental illness. In reviewing Wallace's proposals, LeVine (1963:110) noted that these writings "constitute a challenge to the culture and personality fields to consider rival biopsychological theories for the interpretation of data rather than drawing exclusively upon the one theoretical framework derived from psychoanalytic sources," and he concluded by saying, "It seems unlikely that investigators can continue to ignore biological and cognitive factors in cross-cultural studies of personality."

During the past decade anthropologists have responded to one of Wallace's challenges; and one of LeVine's predictions has proven to be accurate. We have witnessed the emergence of a major emphasis on the study of cognition, and, at the same time, we have seen a "decline in popularity" of psychoanalytic work among anthropologists (Pelto 1967). However, Wallace's other challenge has not been taken up. Biological factors in social and cultural behavior and in mental illness have not been widely explored. With some notable exceptions, psychobiological approaches to problems in culture and personality continue to be neglected. In this paper, I shall attempt to demonstrate the utility of a psychobiological approach to culture and personality by applying it to a traditional problem in psychological anthropology.

By Ralph Bolton. Reprinted with permission, from *Ethnology*, XII, No. 3, July 1973, pp. 227-57.

In the research reported herewith, I set out to discover the roots of social conflict among the Qolla Indians of Peru.[2] Since I was unable to account for the forms and intensity of aggressive behavior found on the basis of social and cultural factors alone, I directed my attention to an examination of the possible biological factors which might be responsible for the apparently irrational aspects of Qolla agonistic behavior. Consequently, this study is intended as a contribution to the explanation of the nature and etiology of the so-called Aymara personality and the aggressive behavior of Andean peoples. By providing a partial solution to that question, I shall endeavor to show that we have advanced our theoretical understanding of a problem of considerably broader concern throughout the behavioral sciences, the causes of aggression.

AYMARA PERSONALITY

Generalizations about the outstanding characteristics of Qolla social behavior are largely contained in the corpus of literature which deals with the Aymara personality. Table I presents a list of the salient features of social behavior and personality attributed to the Aymara-speaking Qolla by eight different scholars. Although the terms employed by different observers are not always identical, in general the descriptions are consistent with one another and are compatible with the interpretation of high aggressiveness and pervasive hostility among the Qolla.

"In the anthropological literature," as Pelto (1967:151) has pointed out, "these Andean highlanders are portrayed as perhaps the meanest and most unlikable people on earth." In fact, the Aymara-speaking Qolla in recent years have been cited by numerous textbook writers (e.g., Barnouw 1963, 1971; Harris 1971) as the classic example of a people with an extreme modal personality configuration dominated by excesses of hostility and aggressiveness. With the exception of Plummer (1966), most authorities agree with this evaluation. It can be traced back as far as the sixteenth century, when Padre Martín de Murúa (1946), a Mercedarian friar, described the Qolla as *"brutos y torpes,"* words which in English can be glossed as "irrational, cruel, uncivilized, stupid, dull."

Table 1. Behavioral and Personality Traits Attributed to Aymara-Speaking Qolla

Paredes	Forbes	Bandelier
distrustful	submissive	distrustful
pessimistic	reflective	submissive
doubtful of everything	silent	neglectful
expect only the bad	cruel	gruff
fearful	highly suspicious	malicious
no creative impulses	intense hate	quarrelsome
submissive	distrustful	rancorous
hostile	non-communicative	dishonest
self-pitying		cruel
		pugnacious

Carter	La Barre	Romero
anxious	apprehensive	reticent
hostile	crafty	silent
submissive	treacherous	melancholic
utilitarian	violent	distrustful
deceitful	hostile	no imagination
vengeful	turbulent	cruel
fatalistic	sullen	no aspirations
miserly	humble	emotionally
distrustful	melancholic	unstable
little appreciation for	submissive	
original thought	pugnacious	
boastful	bad humor	
	emotionally unstable	

Tschopik		Squier
anxious		sullen
hostile		cruel
irresponsible		morose
submissive		jealous
disorderly		vindictive
utilitarian		

See Tschopik (1951) for details on Paredes, Forbes, Squier, Romero, Bandelier and La Barre; and see Carter (1965, 1966, 1968).

The Qolla, as I have observed them, tend to swagger, especially when inebriated, and at such times they frequently indulge in monologues describing their own ferocity while laughing at the puniness of their enemies. *"Noqa q'ari kani, karaho,"* they shout, gesticulating wildly in the air, as if in the face of the person being insulted. "I am a man, dammit! You, you are nothing but a dog, an ass, excrement!" While there is a concern for displaying masculinity it would be inaccurate to claim that the Qolla possess a full-blown *machismo* complex.

Qolla informants sometimes attested that going to law over insignificant damages to crops, for example, was necessary to prevent future recurrences. One must defend oneself. A Qolla man must be strong enough to deter potential encroachments on his sexual and economic rights by other members of his society. In the prevention of such infringements a reputation for fierceness might be valuable. Credibility is gained by a demonstration of willingness to react vigorously, regardless of the costs, when anyone dares to infringe, even by accident. Indeed, a small amount of "irrational" touchiness might add to the effectiveness of one's stance.

In reality the Qolla do not have an ethic which extols violence or aggressiveness. Instead their moral code demands of them charity, compassion, and co-operation with all men. Informants were quite adamant in their insistence upon the importance of Christian virtues. Neither persistent probing nor my most skillful cajoling interrogation could budge informants in the slightest from a rigid adherence to a series of moral imperatives by which men are to be guided at all times. Often, during such interviewing sessions but in a different topical context, informants would illustrate how they had reacted to situations in which the code could be thought to apply. While the informants rarely perceived the discrepancy between their own conduct and the conduct called for by the code, the disparity was enormous. In their moral discourse the Qolla set exorbitantly high standards for themselves, and that they fail to meet those standards is not surprising. But that they should fail so miserably is strange.

In the end I came to agree with several informants who gave answers to my questions about why people killed one another, slaughtered each others' animals, burned their crops, fought with them, and so forth. They insisted: "Such behavior is not rational. A rational person could not do things like that! *No es racional, pues.*" Study of the conflict case file which I compiled seemed to suggest that in that event, the "irrationality" of Qolla peasants was causing much trouble in the village of Incawatana.

Several anthropologists have tried to account for the behavioral syndrome attributed to the Qolla. LaBarre has been the major proponent of what can be called the "domination hypothesis." In a series of articles (cr. LaBarre 1965,

1966), he has offered the notion that the antisocial behavior and attitudes of the Aymara-speaking Qolla are a result of hundreds of years of domination. This hypothesis carries a certain plausibility, but it suffers from a failure to specify the mechanism by which such domination, whether Inca, Spanish, or mestizo, becomes translated into hostility and aggression within the villages. It also fails to describe the variables which form part of the domination concept.

LaBarre (1965: 29) notes that "from our earliest knowledge of them, the Aymara have had an authoritarian, power-stratified society such as is not uncommonly found among people of considerable agricultural development." He continues (ibid., p. 30):

> We know something of the results in behavior and morale from experiments of psychologists with varying 'autocratic' and 'democratic' organization of groups to advance our hypothesis: if the Aymara, as evidenced in their folktales (and indeed throughout the rest of their culture), are apprehensive, crafty, treacherous, violent and hostile, one reason for this may be that such a character structure is an understandable response to their having lived under rigidly hierarchic, absolutist, tyrannical economic, military and religious controls for perhaps as long as a millennium.

Without denying that historical causes might be at work in contributing to the personality of the Qolla, LaBarre's argument is suspect for several reasons. First, the experiments to which he alludes have little relevance. They were carried out presumably in more or less democratic homes and communities with children obviously not accustomed to an "autocratic" atmosphere. Second, looking at life from within the village rather than from the vantage point of an outside observer, a case can be made for the reverse of absolutism, rigid hierarchy, and external tyranny. Life within Qolla villages is anarchic. The situation was succinctly summed up by one of my informants when he said "We suffer from too much freedom!" If an authoritarian societal structure has produced an authoritarian character structure, then, as my informant's statement implies, the lifting of controls could be as much a source of anxiety and hostility as the controls themselves, or perhaps more so. It is difficult to see how the domination hypothesis can accommodate both hierarchy and anarchy domination and the release from domination, as the causes of Qolla behavior and attitudes.

There is another sense, however, in which domination by the Incas, then Spaniards, and finally mestizos may have contributed to the development of Qolla behavior patterns. As Murra (1968) has pointed out, previous to the exogenous conquests, each of the Qolla states controlled vast areas encompassing many different ecological zones. These states were not fractionated into communities along contemporary lines. If this is the case, then it may be that pre-Incaic residents of Qolla territory enjoyed a healthier diet and access to more resources than the modern Qolla. If true, then an inadequate diet, possibly one of the causes of the physiological condition which produces aggression, could be attributed to conquest of the region by outside forces.

Harris (1971: 577), too, has argued in favor of the domination hypothesis. He writes that, "As in the case of the Chimborazo of Ecuador, the temperament of the Aymara reflects a historic process of sustained deprivation at the hands of both Indian and Spanish ruling classes." In discussing Andean xenophobia, Harris (1971: 478) asserts that "hostility and fear are adaptively correct responses" to outsiders. He does not indicate the extent to which he believes that intra-village, interpersonal aggression and hostility are "adaptively correct responses."

Barnouw (1963) used the Aymara personality to illustrate the complexities involved in trying to unravel the network of etiological factors contributing to the development and maintenance of an extreme modal personality. He listed (Barnouw 1963: 15-16) a series of factors which he suggested might enter into the etiology.

High altitude, excessive drinking and coca chewing, combined with unsanitary homes, inadequate clothing, poor diet, and much sickness—is there any wonder that the Aymara are unhappy? Yet these are not the only factors that may be responsible for their alleged character traits. There is also the historical background of these people and their social relationships with the Mestizos toward whom they play a submissive role.

After surveying his list of possible causes, Barnouw recognized the inadequacy of some of them. For example, he states that altitude may not be a significant factor; after all, the Nepalese and Tibetans also live at high altitudes and do not have the same reputation. Indeed, it is possible that, taken individually, any one of these factors might be refutable.

In essence, then, we find two closely related hypotheses in the literature to account for Aymara aggressiveness: (1) the domination hypothesis, which emphasizes the role of social subordination in the etiology of the Aymara personality, and (2) the environmental-harshness hypothesis, which places emphasis on a series of stress factors found in the culture, society, and physical environment of the Qolla.

In this paper I shall suggest that it is social and physical stresses in the Qolla environment that promote aggressiveness through their combined effects on the physiological condition of individuals subjected to them. I shall argue that problems of glucose homeostasis are causally related to aggressiveness. In examining the terms in Table I, one finds that aggressiveness is the most frequently mentioned trait, although the concept is often tagged by other descriptive terms. In accounting for Qolla aggressiveness, consequently, I hope to explain in large part the distinctive feature of the Qolla or Aymara personality. The hypothesis which I am proposing may be called the "hypoglycemia hypothesis."

AGGRESSION IN INCAWATANA

Varieties of Aggression

Before proceeding to a discussion of the major forms of aggressive behavior in Incawatana, I wish to define two terms which I shall be using. Aggression, following Berkowitz (1962), is behavior whose goal is the injury of some object. Aggressive, aggressivity, and aggressiveness refer to response tendencies involving aggression. From this definition is excluded the more general idea of self-assertiveness which is sometimes part of the definition of aggressiveness. Not all self-assertion involves aggression in the sense intended by the definition used here. Included, however, is the notion of intention. It is the intention of an aggressive person to do harm to some other person or object.

Not all oppositional behavior involves the intention of injury. Consequently, a broader concept is needed, and I shall use the term "agonistic" to designate behavior which symbolizes or expresses opposition on the part of one social entity (i.e., person or group) toward another social entity or entities. In other words, agonistic behavior may communicate opposition, but it does not necessarily consist of any intention to injure on the part of the behaving entity.

Qolla aggression can assume any of a bewildering multiplicity of behavioral forms. In specific behavioral instances it may be difficult to decide whether or not the behavior involved should be classified as aggression, since intent may or may not be present. Most of the types of behavior which I shall discuss below do qualify as aggression rather than merely agonistic behavior in at least a high percentage of all instances for which information is available to us. I shall discuss only those forms of behavior which the Qolla themselves consider to be the most serious types of aggression occurring in the village.

Litigation is an important activity in Incawatana. Villagers readily complain to local-level and district-level authorities when they feel that someone, including a member of their nuclear family, has aggressed against them. Only those forms of aggression considered trivial are permitted to pass without resorting to third parties such as the *tenientes,* who are the principal mediators in village disputes. Although the *tenientes* and other village authorities have almost no power to impose settlements to disputes, they do provide a setting in which grievances can be aired and differences resolved.

For the past fifteen years, village authorities have kept records of disputes, carefully noting the details of complaints brought before them. The documents are retained by the authority who hears the cases as evidence, in the event that such information might be needed in later disputes involving the same litigants. For two years I systematically searched the village for these documents, which I borrowed from their owners and copied. On the basis of this material, combined with data obtained through interviews, I constructed the conflict case file which was mentioned above. The file does not contain the complete universe of disputes. In cases of lesser significance to the litigants, written records are not always drawn up. A few villagers had lost some documents to thieves or fire. Nevertheless, I estimate that for the decade from 1961 through 1970 I was able to obtain information on at least 60 per cent of all publicly processed cases. We find that during that period an average of 80 cases per year came to our attention for the village of Incawatana (population 1,200).

Most conflict cases do not deal with only one instance of agonistic behavior. In fact, usually a variety of differing forms occur as part of a sequence of actions. One form of agonistic behavior leads to escalating agonistic interaction; or, just as often, some form of nonagonistic interaction is transformed into an escalating agonistic sequence. For example, when X's sheep wander or are driven into Y's field, Y may shout to X to remove the animals. X, in turn, may shout back, adding an insult directed against Y. Y then runs up and hits X, inflicting a wound. X threatens to kill Y and Y leaves the scene, but not without first snatching X's coca bag or scarf. The hearing convened to hear such a case would have to deal with each of these acts: insults, threats assault, property damage, and theft. The rights and wrongs on each side of the dispute would have to be carefully balanced in order to achieve a harmonious settlement of the case.

The major complaint category in the conflict case file is one called "fights and injuries." Violent encounters are commonplace, and the person who receives even the slightest wound in a scuffle is quite likely to sue for damages. In many cases wounds are serious. More than two hundred cases in the file involve fights and injuries, thus indicating a marked involvement in a competitive style based on physical skill (Sutton-Smith and Roberts 1964).

While most cases involving fights or large-scale brawls also include insults, not all cases of insulting escalate to fighting. Consequently, the second most important category of aggressive behavior in the file deals with insults alone. Although the Qolla define the concept of insult rather broadly, minor insults are not brought before the authorities. Interestingly, it is considered an insult to the hearer when a man walks along shouting "I am a man," since the implication of that oft-heard phrase is that other men are not men. The Qolla tend to be constantly on guard against slights and insults, and they often twist someone's seemingly innocent statement into an occasion for retorting with an insult. People "err in choosing words," it is said.

Stealing ranks just below insulting in frequency in the file. To some extent, of course, stealing might be viewed as agonistic behavior but not aggression. Certainly theft has utilitarian overtones and sometimes committed primarily because the thief desires the object stolen. But quite often in Incawatana, as elsewhere in the Andes (see Gade 1970), theft does involve the intent to injure and must be classified as aggression. Or the thief may be retaliating for some earlier agonistic action by his victim. This can most readily be seen in instances when the object stolen has no value to the thief, such as the victim's draft card. But even in many cases in which the stolen object has potential value, the choice of victim indicates that more than utilitarian objectives are at stake in the crime.

Damages to crops, the next most frequent offense category, can be intentional or unintentional. Shepherds may deliberately fail to control their herds, allowing the animals in their charge to eat from neighboring fields. In some cases of crop damage, intent to injure is safely inferred, for example, when a man methodically uproots his enemy's potato plants before they have produced any tubers.

Difficulties in classification of cases are inherent in the next category, failure to pay debts or fulfill contracts. A peasant may refuse to pay a debt because he lacks the money to do so. Frequently, however, his failure to pay is an act of aggression against the creditor, who must go to great lengths to recover outstanding loans.

Another major category involves threats. These may be directed against the person or his property or both. Sometimes the wording is subtle—e.g., *"Vas a ver"* ("You'll see")—but at other times it is brutally blunt. While it is easy to overlook insults by a drunk, threats are taken very seriously.

Other types of agonistic behavior are less prominent in Incawatana, although when they occur they are considered serious. The miscellaneous group of cases includes rape, arson, abor-

tion, slander, and land ownership disputes. Of course, many forms of agonistic behavior and aggression are engaged in extensively but are not dealt with by the authorities under normal circumstances. For example, while adultery is widespread, retaliation against the participants is more likely to take the form of spouse-beating than litigation. Finally, although low in terms of relative frequency, homicide is an important form of aggression, and I now turn to a detailed discussion of homicide in Incawatana.

Homicide in Incawatana.   Homicide is strongly disapproved of, receiving greater condemnation than any other form of behavior with the possible exception of incestuous intercourse between mother and son, father and daughter, and *compadre* and *comadre* (ritual kin). Nevertheless, in conversations with me, villagers were quick to accuse one another of homicidal acts; and regardless of the actual rate of homicide in Incawatana, there is a widespread assumption that literally dozens of fellow villagers are murderers.

For several reasons, I have chosen to employ homicide as my indicator of societal levels of aggressiveness. First, in almost all societies homicide is regarded as one of the most serious forms of aggression. Second, homicide rates have been calculated for numerous societies, thus providing us with data against which to compare the Qolla rate. Third, because of the gravity and relative infrequency of homicide, statistics for homicide tend to be more accurate than those for other kinds of aggressive behavior. To be sure, measuring homicide rates still involves many potential pitfalls; but, I would argue, these rates can serve as a rough indicator of the level of aggressiveness in a society.

Calculating the homicide rate for Incawatana is complicated by the fact that the population base to use is not obvious. One must distinguish three categories of individuals in the population of a "village": (1) resident members actually in residence at the time of population count; (2) resident members of the community who are temporarily absent for purposes of working, visiting, studying, etc.; and (3) nonresidents who are still considered to be members of the community by virtue of close ties of kinship and property, even though they are residing elsewhere because of a permanent job or marriage to an outsider. On the basis of estimates of the average population in each of these categories during the 25-year period 1945-1969, I calculated the homicide rates given in Table 2. The rate which is probably most comparable to rates calculated for other societies is A.1. in Table 2; in other words 55 homicide victims per year per 100,000 population. This figure measures the number of victims in a geographically limited area with respect to the total stable population in the area. Data in Table 2 include only those cases for which the evidence, both from documents and interviews with villagers, was consistent and generally accepted as true by everyone.

If one compares this rate with rates for other societies, one discovers that the Qolla do indeed have an extremely high homicide rate. Not one country for which data are available has a rate as high as the Qolla: national rates range between .3 and 34.0 per 100,000 population (Wolfgang and Ferracuti 1967: 274-275). Nor does any African tribe reported on in Bohannan (1967) have such a high rate: these fall between 1.1 and 11.6 homicides per 100,000 population. In a few districts of Colombia the rate is as high as 63 per 100,000, and in some areas of Mexico rates as high as 82.8 have been reported. Friedrich (1964) notes that during one year the village of Acan had a rate of 200.

It might be argued that my method of gathering data has inflated the rate for Incawatana. But even if one counts only prosecuted homicides, one finds that the rate is high, 20 per 100,000. No estimate for the Qolla as a whole exists in the literature. However, Cuentas (1966) has provided information which allows us to calculate the rate for the province of Huancané (Peru) during five years in the 1950s, and that rate is approximately 15 homicides per 100,000, a figure reasonably close to the rate for Incawatana, since Cuentas counted only prosecuted cases. Additionally, Andrée Michaud (personal communication), an anthropologist who studied a village near Incawatana, found the rate in that village to be at least as high as the one for Incawatana.

These high rates for the Qolla have implications which I cannot deal with in the present context, but I would like to mention the broad ramifications of this type of aggressive behavior within the village. During the 25-year period

Table 2.   Homicide Rates and Numbers for 25 Years, 1945-1969, Involving Residents and Members of the Village of Incawatana.

	Number	Rate
A. Incawatana Victims of Homicide		
1. Resident members, killed inside confines of the village	11	55.0
2. Absentee resident members, killed outside the village	4	80.00
3. Non-resident members, killed outside the village	5	100.0
4. Combination of 1-3, i.e., all persons considered members of Incawatana	20	66.7
B. Incawatana Offenders, Homicide Cases		
1. Resident members prosecuted for involvement in homicide	13	65.0
2. Resident members formally accused of involvement in homicide	19	95.0
3. Resident members suspected of involvement in homicide but not accused nor prosecuted	13	65.0
4. Resident members who in fact probably participated in homicide	21	105.0

(Note: the rates are calculated for a hypothetical population of 100,000.)

under consideration, Incawatana consisted of approximately 220 households, which are the solidary units in Qolla society. More than 20 per cent of all households contain, at present, an adult member who has been deprived of at least one parent, child, spouse, or sibling through homicide. An additional 10 per cent of all households have a living adult member who has been formally accused of murder or who has probably participated in an act of homicide; therefore, over 30 per cent of all Incawatana households contain an adult member whose parent, child, spouse, or sibling has been involved as an offender in a homicide case. It can be seen, then, that an impressive proportion—above 50 per cent—of all Incawatana adults have had some form of participation in the events surrounding at least one homicide. Since retaliation against the murderer requires self-help activities by the dead person's kinsmen and their action-sets, homicide may in any single case generate considerable participation in the post-homicide events by a large segment of the village. The effects of an act of homicide are widely felt throughout the community in this small-scale society. Violence produces more violence.

Aggression Rankings in Incawatana

Not everyone in Incawatana participates in equal measure in the agonistic interaction which takes place in the village. When discussing aggression with informants and when reviewing the case file, we found that the names of some villagers appeared more frequently than those of others. Some names cropped up only rarely, and then in the context of minor troubles rather than serious ones. The remainder of this work is based on this differentiation. I have tried to support the conclusion, reached by earlier ethnographers, that the Qolla are aggressive. Now I would like to proceed to another question, specifically, "Why are some Qolla peasants more aggressive than others?" By explaining differences in aggressiveness within Qolla society, I hope to provide part of the answer to the larger question, "Why are the Qolla aggressive?" Since a large proportion of the aggression in Incawatana is accounted for by the activities of its most aggressive citizens, if we understand what causes them to be aggressive, then we should have a better understanding of the causes of the level of aggressiveness in Qolla society as a whole.

It became apparent early in our field work that it would be impossible to have a detailed acquaintance with all 1,200 residents of the village. Consequently, I decided to concentrate on aggression by males. This approach seemed advisable for several reasons. First, we could more readily interview males than females without arousing suspicions of our intentions. Second, the most serious forms of aggression seem to be engaged in primarily by males. This is not to imply that aggression by females is not important. It is our impression that quite often the actions of women provide the stimulus for male aggression. For example, a drunken woman may run around insulting neighbors, thus provoking more serious aggression such as a fight, between the households' male residents. Male aggression is more likely to lead to action before the authorities; and since most of our behavioral data was generated by examining records of legal proceedings and interviewing participants in these affairs, we could get more and better data on males.

Another reason for our decision to deal primarily with male household heads was that time-depth comparability is important and could not be achieved using youths or children. However, 248 subjects were still too many to include for interviewing and other procedures, even though more elaborate statistical work would be possible with a larger sample. Therefore, we selected a 50 per cent random sample of male household heads, chosen equally from all seven sectors of the community, in order to achieve a kinship and residential balance.

When we collected physiological data, only 66 of the 124 subjects were available for testing (see below). In order to obtain a measure of the aggressiveness of these 66 subjects, I had them ranked by key informant raters. The raters were given a set of cards with the name of one subject written on each card. The raters were instructed to place these cards in order, starting with the most aggressive individual on the upper left corner of the table and ending with the least aggressive individual on the lower right corner. Raters were given as much time as they needed to complete the task.

Table 3. Intercorrelation of Aggression Rankings for a Sample of Incawatana Household Heads.

		1	2	3	4	5	6
1	1st Rater's 1st Ranking	X	.57	.62	.56	.50	.50
2	1st Rater's 2nd Ranking		X	.50	.46	.39	.52
3	2nd Rater's 1st Ranking			X	.92	.72	.75
4	2nd Rater's 2nd Ranking				X	.68	.72
5	3rd Rater's 1st Ranking					X	.78
6	3rd Rater's 2nd Ranking						X

The instructions to the raters were designed to get at the concept of aggressiveness in the broadest fashion. Since all three raters understood Spanish, the instructions were first given in that language and then supplemented with a Quechua rephrasing of the statement. They were told to base their judgments on questions such as who likes to fight a lot, who gets into lots of trouble, who is nasty and ill-tempered—who is aggressive, in short. The raters had no difficulty in understanding the instructions.

The raters worked completely independently of each other, carrying out their assignments in different rooms under supervision. Each rater performed the task of rating twice, the second session following the first by several hours. (Part of the interval was occupied with rating the same subjects on other traits, such as wealth and indulgence in alcoholic beverages.) Consequently, the sample was rated on aggressiveness a total of six times. The intercorrelations of these ratings are given in Table 3.

An analysis of the correlations in Table 3 shows that this indicator of aggressiveness has a moderately high degree of reliability if the first rater's ratings are eliminated. The first rater was not consistent with himself on the rating-rerating, nor with the other raters. The correlations of the rating-rerating scores for the second and third raters, on the other hand, are acceptably high, .92 and .78 respectively. Moreover, the average correlation for ratings three through six is satisfactory at .76. Since the reliability of the first rater's scores is low, I excluded his ratings from the final aggressiveness scale, which consists of the combined scores of the other four rat-

ings. I used the Spearman rho.

To some extent, the ratings probably reflect the likes and dislikes of the raters. An additional source of inconsistency is time. Although the raters were instructed to make their judgments on the basis of how the person had acted during the past ten years, it is difficult to know whether or not they took into account the entire period. While the trait of aggressiveness is undoubtedly somewhat stable, individuals do not maintain a constant level of aggressive behavior, and I suggest that individuals pass through what might be called "agonistic careers" during which their levels of aggressiveness may rise or fall. The theoretical basis for this suggestion is to be found below.

The aggressiveness scores of the subjects ranged from 7 (highly aggressive) to 263 (nonaggressive), while the theoretically possible range was from 4 through 264.

Validation of the Rankings. Although it has been shown that the indicator of reputational rankings for aggressiveness is acceptably reliable, the question can still be raised about the appropriateness of this indicator. I would defend the use of this measure on the following grounds. I am interested, first of all, in naturally occurring aggression rather than experimentally induced aggression; therefore, I need an indicator which measures aggressiveness as demonstrated in natural settings rather than in the laboratory. Further, I am interested in inferring aggressiveness from overt behavior, and to do this a greater time span than would be possible in experimental sessions is desirable. Certainly some sort of "objective" measure could be found, such as frequency of involvement in fights or lawsuits. However, an objection to a more precise indicator of that type can be offered, which is that the form aggressive behavior takes may vary from one person to another. Therefore, one might not make an accurate inference about general aggressiveness by limiting the indicator to narrow behavioral types. The reputational method of ranking subjects can be improperly used, of course. However, I feel that its utilization is warranted in the village context. The raters were extremely familiar with the persons they rated. They have known the subjects throughout a lifetime. They are constantly hearing information about the behavior of these subjects, including their intimate behavior within the nuclear family, through the extensive gossiping which is part of everyday life in Incawatana. If a man beats his wife or hits his children, the neighbors hear it and soon everyone knows about it. The "character" of almost every adult resident of Incawatana is known to every other adult villager. It is even better known by men in positions of authority, since they interact frequently with most of the villagers and are strategically situated to hear more gossip. The two most reliable raters have occupied authority positions repeatedly over the past ten years.

It might be desirable, however, to examine the validity of the aggressiveness indicator by comparing it to more "objective" measures of aggressive behavior as well as other "subjective" indicators. I pointed out earlier that, during our two years in the village, the villagers rather readily accused one another of homicidal acts. Our field notes show that 15 out of the 66 subjects in our sample were so accused at one time or another. Table 4 shows how these accusations were distributed with respect to the aggression rating done by the key informants.

The aggression ratings, then, tend to correspond to our information on homicide accusations, data built up over the two-year period of our research. Seven of the fifteen subjects accused of homicide are included in the top fourth of the subjects in aggression ranking, while only one person accused of homicide lies within the bottom fourth of the aggression rankings.

Another check on the validity of the aggression rankings can be made through an examina-

Table 4. Homicide Accusations Compared to the Aggression Ratings.

Aggression Rankings (grouped by fourths)	Number of Subjects Accused of Homicide
1 (high aggression)	7.0
2	3.5
3	3.5
4	1.0

(The 3.5 figure is a result of one subject falling at the median with respect to aggression scores. Note that the end quartiles contain one less subject each than the middle quartiles.)

tion of litigation. The results of that check are presented in Table 5, where participation is classified into three categories—plaintiff, defendant, and miscellaneous—plus a combined category which includes only cases involving the subject as plaintiff or defendant. The subjects rated high in aggression have higher rates of participation in litigation than do those ranked low. This finding occurs regardless of whether the subject is involved as a plaintiff, defendant, or in a miscellaneous capacity, which includes witnesses, guarantors and public officials. Interestingly, the high aggressors are involved in cases more as defendants than as plaintiffs while the low aggressors have a higher involvement in cases as plaintiffs than as defendants.

The miscellaneous category reflects a number of factors which are operating. First, it shows that low aggressors not only are not involved as principals in cases, but they also tend not even to attend judicial hearings. The extreme disparity of involvement in these cases in a miscellaneous capacity, however, is largely explained by the fact that I have included in this category participation as an authority. There is a strong tendency for persons holding official positions to be ranked among the most aggressive in the village. Several interpretations can be found for that fact. First, only extremely aggressive individuals could handle the job of settling disputes, since such work requires that the authority be strong, vigorous, and willing to engage in threats and violence in order to deal with highly aggressive individuals. Second, public officials are in a po-

Table 5.   Participation in Litigation Compared to Aggression Ratings for the Subjects in the Sample.

Aggression Rankings (grouped by fourths)	Average Number of Cases			
	Plaintiff	Defendant	Combined	Miscellaneous
1 (high aggressors)	4.4	6.8	11.2	25.3
2	3.2	3.9	7.1	15.9
3	3.9	3.2	7.1	15.1
4	2.5	1.9	4.4	2.1

sition where they must engage in behavior which is seen as aggressive or at least agonistic, and therefore the raters would tend to rank them high, regardless of their general level of aggressiveness.

I noted earlier that the case file included an average of 80 cases per year for the village of Incawatana, or approximately one case for every three households. But that figure does not provide an indication of the true level of litigation involvement, as many cases involve multiple plaintiffs and multiple defendants. We find that the subjects in my sample averaged 7.2 cases each over the past decade. When one considers that the case file includes only about 60 per cent of the actual number of cases, it can be surmised that the villagers are involved on the average in one case of litigation per year. The range of differential participation is from a low of zero cases through more than four cases per year; or in other words, for the ten-year period, a range of no involvement in litigation through about 40 cases. This range mirrors almost precisely the range of scores obtained in the key informant ratings.

In this section of the paper I have attempted to document the forms of aggression in Incawatana and the range of differentiation among the villagers. In the next I shall endeavor to explain part of the biological basis of Qolla aggressiveness.

THE HYPOGLYCEMIA HYPOTHESIS

The Physiology of Aggression

In recent years research on the physiology of

aggression has advanced our understanding of the biological dimensions of this type of behavior. For excellent discussions of this, the interested reader should consult Moyer (1971, 1972), Boelkins and Heiser (1970), Mark and Ervin (1970), Storr (1968), Clemente and Lindsley (167), Wolfgang and Ferracuti (1967), Klopper (1964), Buss (1961), and Scott (1958).

For more than half a century fairly accurate information about the physiological effects of anger has been in circulation. While the details have been refined over the years, in 1915, Cannon presented a scheme involving the basic effects of anger on the organism, e.g., increase in the pulse rate, rise in level of blood glucose, increased breathing rate, and reduction in digestive processes. These are all means of preparing the organism for physical exertion such as fighting. Many of the effects of anger are the results of changes in the output of numerous hormones. In particular, it has been found that anxiety and anger are potent stimuli in the elicitation of adrenal secretions (Klopper 1964).

However, when one turns from an examination of the effects of anger or aggression on the organism to the physiological causes of aggression or anger, not only is evidence more difficult to find, but there is also considerable disagreement among biological scientists.

The mapping of brain structures associated with aggressive behavior is quite advanced, and there is less disagreement on this topic than on some others. Studies of brain functioning, done by recording electrical activity in the brain, the removal of parts of the brain (ablation), and stimulation with chemicals or electric current, have indicated those structures of the brain which are important in the activation or inhibition of aggressive behavior, not only in lower animals but in man as well.

The disagreement centers on whether or not the acknowledged circuits in the brain which are associated with aggressive behavior can fire in the absence of an external stimulus. Moyer (1971:62) has proposed that the neurological systems which are involved in aggression can exist at any point in time in one of three states: (1) inactive and insensitive, i.e., "cannot be fired by the usual stimulation that will provoke attack," (2) sensitized but inactive, i.e., due to the absence of an appropriate stimulus, and (3) spontaneously firing even in the absence of the appropriate stimulus.

If spontaneous firing of the aggression systems in the brain occurs in the absence of an external stimulus, the cause could be related to changes in the internal environment of the neurologically relevant structures, particularly hormonal and blood chemical levels. One finds, however, that the evidence for this is not substantial, at least in studies on human subjects. To date there is information which supports the notion that hypo- and hyperfunction of both the adrenals and thyroid are implicated in increased irritability. Additionally, the evidence increasingly favors the hypothesis that sex hormone balances lead to increased or decreased aggressivity. Although considerable work has been done on the relationship of the adrenal medullary hormones, especially epinephrine and norepinephrine, to aggression, and while it is clear that these hormones tend to be excreted as part of an emotional disturbance, it is not clear that they are among the direct causes of aggression or that they can lead to the spontaneous firing of neural mechanisms (Moyer 1971:47).

Finally, there is the possibility that a causal relationship exists between blood glucose levels and the level of aggressiveness of an organism, i.e., what I have called the "hypoglycemia hypothesis." According to Moyer (1971:100):

Hypoglycemia, from whatever cause is, in many cases, associated with tendencies to hostility and is another dysfunction in the blood chemistry which evidently sensitizes the neural substrates for aggression. There has, unfortunately, been relatively little systematic study of this relationship.

Aggression and Hypoglycemia: The Hypothesis

In spite of the paucity of research which probes the relationship between glucose levels and aggressiveness, the idea presented in this hypothesis is not new. Wilder (1947:126) reviewing the state of knowledge at that time dealing with this hypothesis, concluded that:

we are probably standing here at a beginning rather than at an end of a new scientific approach to the problem of crime, and that many and careful investigations will be necessary in order to establish the proper place of this problem within the framework of criminology and correctional medicine.

The careful studies on hypoglycemia were not forthcoming during the next two decades; physiologists did not delve into this question nor conduct the careful investigations which Wilder thought would follow. Moyer (1971:100) has noted that while Wilder had compiled a "remarkable amount of evidence," his paper was "much neglected."

The studies which Wilder reviewed were primarily of two kinds: (1) those which dealt with personality manifestations of insulin-induced hypoglycemia and (2) those which presented case materials, particularly evidence connecting hypoglycemia with specific aggressive (usually criminal) acts. Wilder (1947:109) listed numerous types of crimes which had been committed "either under the influence of insulin or in a state of spontaneous hypoglycemia," including:

disorderly conduct, assault and battery, attempted suicide and homicide, cruelty against children or spouse, various sexual perversions and aggressions, false fire alarms, drunkenness, embezzlement, petty larceny, willful destruction of property, arson, slander, violation of traffic regulations.

He surveyed other studies which presented evidence of higher rates of hypoglycemia among psychotics than found in nonpsychotic populations.

Two studies published since Wilder's review indicate further support for the association of hypoglycemia and hyperirritability and aggression. Gyland (cited in Fredericks and Goodman

1969) reported that 89 per cent of 600 hypogly-cemic patients suffer from irritability and that 47 per cent of these patients were unsocial, aso-cial, or antisocial. Salzer *(ibid.)* noted that 45 per cent of hypoglycemic patients are extremely ir-ritable and 22 per cent engage in unsocial or an-tisocial behavior.

During recent years, the discussion of hypo-glycemia and its effects has undergone a drastic change of venue, from the medical and psychiat-ric journals cited by Wilder to popular books on medicine, e.g., Martin (1970), Fredericks and Goodman (1969), and Abrahamson and Pezet (1951). Since these books contain sweeping claims about the evils of hypoglycemia and the vast number of ailments which can be elimi-nated by curing it, e.g., neurosis, alcoholism, al-lergy, chronic fatigue, and insanity, it has ac-quired the status of a fad disease and has be-come the center of cult-like attention within the United States. Thus, while one finds informa-tion about hypoglycemia in numerous places, the literature on aggression, regardless of disci-plinary provenance, neglects this factor almost completely. In anthropological writings I have encountered one reference to hypoglycemia in relation to aggression. LeVine (1961) points out that hypoglycemia may be a biopsychological factor in the causation of social conflict.

The hypoglycemia hypothesis can be formu-lated in several ways. On the one hand, it can be stated in the following manner: the lower the fasting blood glucose level the worse the hypo-glycemia and the greater the aggressiveness. It was my realization that the level of blood glucose among Andean Indians generally is low which led me to test the hypothesis. Monge and Monge (1966:19) state, "Low blood glucose concentra-tion is characteristic of the high-altitude na-tive." Carlos Monge, Sr. (1968) reported specific readings to support this contention.

My own first formulation of the hypothesis reads as follows: above a critical minimum level of glucose concentration in the blood, there is an inverse relationship between the levels of blood glucose and the levels of individual involvement in aggressive and hostile behavior, particularly in the range of subnormal and low-normal levels of blood glucose. The novel aspect of this formu-lation is the notion that the relationship may be curvilinear rather than linear. This modification of the earlier hypothesis by Wilder seems neces-sary in view of the fact that individuals with very bad cases of hypoglycemia enter into comas and, presumably previous to reaching that level, suf-fer a reduction in aggressive tendencies due to diminution of energy. At the upper end of glu-cose levels within the normal range there is no reason to expect differences in aggressiveness; therefore, I conclude that the hypothesis is most applicable in the subnormal and low-normal range. Once one gets into the range of high levels (diabetes) the problems change. Since I did not expect to find much diabetes in the Andes, I did not formulate the hypothesis to take into account the high levels.

However, before testing the hypothesis, I dis-covered in the literature additional information which forced me to revise the hypothesis. Ap-parently, symptoms of hypoglycemia appear not so much as a result of specific fasting levels as in response to various changes in blood glucose concentrations and to the speed with which the level drops after the level has been raised by the ingestion of food. According to this formulation, then, hypoglycemia is defined as present when the glucose concentration drops below the nor-mal fasting level by ten or more milligrams per 100 milliliters of blood within four to six hours after the ingestion of food. (Details are in next section.) Consequently, the hypoglycemia hy-pothesis which I am testing can be stated in the following manner: there is a curvilinear relation-ship between the amount of drop in blood glu-cose during the administration of a Glucose Tolerance Test and the level of aggressiveness of an individual, with high levels of aggressiveness occurring in the range of mild hypoglycemia, i.e., a drop in glucose by 10 to 25 mg. per 100 ml. below fasting level. Moreover, it is suggested that the relationship is causal in nature, with moderate glucose deprivation causing aggressiv-ity.

Further explication of the hypothesis will be provided below, but first I shall describe the methods used to test the hypothesis in Incawa-tana.

Physiological Data Collection Methods

The standard diagnostic indicator of hypoglycemia is the shape of the curve obtained from the Glucose Tolerance Test. In this test the subject fasts for twelve hours before the beginning of the analysis, usually overnight. In the morning the first blood sample is drawn while the subject is still in a fasting condition. Immediately thereafter he is given orally 50 grams of sugar in solution. The second and third blood samples are taken at half-hour intervals. After that, samples are taken every hour for four hours or more. Formerly, a laboratory was generally required to handle the analysis of these blood samples for their glucose content; however, reagent strips, produced by the Ames Company and marketed under the brand name "Dextrostix," are now available, permitting on-the-spot analysis. The strips require merely one drop of blood per sample, and this can be drawn by the finger-prick method. Using Dextrostix, a drop of blood is drawn and placed directly on the reagent at the tip of the plastic strip. The blood is washed off exactly one minute later, during which time the color of the reagent part of the strip changes to one of a number of shades of blue or grey, depending upon the amount of glucose which the blood contains. The strip is then compared to a color chart and the corresponding number (or, if necessary, the interpolation) is read off. The number indicates the milligrams of glucose per 100 milliliters of blood.

The collection of physiological data to test the hypoglycemia hypothesis was carried out at the end of our field work in the nearby town of Qochapata. It was necessary to take the subjects out of Incawatana in order to control them during the required fasting period. Community leaders accepted the task of convincing and delivering to us the subjects from our sample of adult males. Community leaders were paid for their work on the project, and each participating subject received payment in cash and foodstuffs for undergoing the test. Additionally, everyone was provided with a free medical examination and medicines for diagnosed ailments. In this way we obtained Glucose Tolerance Test information for 66 persons from our sample of 124 heads of families. Since 25 men from that sample were working in Puno or were temporarily away from Incawatana for some other reason at the time of the testing, we obtained 67 per

cent of those available; 33 either were not contacted or refused to participate in the test. The testing took place on three consecutive days with subjects arriving in the late afternoon and leaving the next day just before noon. Everyone was accommodated in one large hall and kept inside as much as possible after arriving, so that they could be watched by my assistants and the community leaders. After the evening meal subjects were instructed not to eat again until given permission. The evening meal consisted of a close approximation to the normal peasant supper of soup and tea.

In the morning the subjects arose at six o'clock, and from that point on they were carefully watched to prevent eating. Urine samples were collected and blood samples taken, as indicated above: 6:00, 6:30, 7:00, 8:00, 9:00, and 10:00 were the starting times for running the subjects through the line, using the same order each time. We were unable to extend the testing to an additional one or two sample periods for two reasons: we did not have a sufficient supply of Dextrostix, and the subjects began to complain after being pricked for the third time. Thus we felt it wise to stop at the four-hour limit, even though our results would have shown greater proportions of hypoglycemia had the test been extended longer.

The fingerpricking was done by student nurses from the Puno nursing school. All readings of glucose level were done by Ms. Leigh Gates, a British registered nurse who works in the district. She was not acquainted individually with the subjects from Incawatana. After reading the color chart, she dictated results to me. I might add that at this time the aggression rankings had not yet been performed by the key informants.

We cannot be certain that complete control was maintained at all times over all subjects. The room was too large and we had too many subjects at one time to keep an eye on all of them. It is possible that a few subjects did ingest food or coca during the fasting period. (The two persons whom we caught munching on something they had hidden in a pocket both proved to have severe hypoglycemia and so felt a strong need to cheat on the fasting requirement.) The first morning, by good fortune, my wife spied the village candy salesman as he was breaking out his wares and was about to begin to sell sugar-ball candies to the subjects! He was stopped in time.

Because the village leaders allowed all twelve subjects on the second day of testing to wander outside the building during the test, we became suspicious of the results of the GTT for that day. An analysis of the data for that day revealed that by the fourth hour the glucose levels of 91.5 per cent of those subjects had risen above the fasting level, in some cases substantially. It is possible for the level to be above the fasting level at the end of the test, but very rarely does this happen to be a substantial rise. For the other two days' tests the glucose levels rose in only 20 per cent of the cases. Therefore, in the analysis which follows, the subjects tested on the second day are not included. Rather than attempt to eliminate those subjects definitely suspected of having cheated, it was felt better to eliminate the tests of everyone run on that day. We did not have problems controlling the subjects on the first and third days.

All subjects who began the test completed it. Co-operation was excellent. There was some grumbling on the first day about the finger-pricking. I explained hypoglycemia to the participants, but they were not given details about the hypothesis. Several subjects indicated symptoms of severe hypoglycemia during the test, e.g., headache, faintness, and perspiration. They were carefully watched to prevent more dangerous manifestations. They were able to complete the four-hour version of the GTT, but it is doubtful that they would have lasted much longer. Although I shall rely primarily on the GTT in the analysis which follows, each subject was given a medical examination by one of the two participating physicians, Drs. José Sardon and Miguel Neyra. The help of these physicians, I might note, was important not only in order to obtain data from the physical examinations, but also to lend legitimacy to the testing in the eyes of the villagers.

A Test of the Hypothesis

In the analysis of the relationship between aggressiveness ranking and scores on the GTT, I consider a rise in glucose at the end of the four hours or a drop of 5 mg. or less to be "normal,"

i.e., as indicating that the subject had no hypoclycemic tendencies: A drop of 10 to 25 mg. indicates that the subject has "mild hypoglycemia" and a drop greater than 25 mg. will be considered indicative of a case of "severe hypoglycemia."

When one contrasts the subjects who are moderately hypoglycemic with the other subjects, reducing Table 6 to 2×2 form for purposes of statistical analysis, one finds that the null hypothesis can be rejected ($x^2 = 6.12$, $p < .02$); there is a statistically-significant relationship between aggression ranking and the change in blood glucose levels during a four-hour Glucose Tolerance Test. Moreover, the evidence seems to corroborate the idea that mild or moderate hypoglycemia is associated with high aggressiveness. Twelve of the thirteen highest-ranked aggressors, 84.6 per cent of the highest quartile, have glucose homeostasis problems, and eleven of the thirteen appear to have mild hypoglycemia.

Indeed, inspection of Table 6 reveals the fact that glucose homeostasis problems are widespread among the residents of Incawatana. Fully 55.5 per cent of these men appear to have hypoglycemia, and only 44.5 per cent have normal reactions to the GTT. I have not encountered reliable data on other societies with which to compare this finding, but undoubtedly this rate is high. (Estimates for the United States range from 2 to 30 per cent, but the latter figure is considered highly exaggerated by most medical researchers.) To be sure, it is not possible to infer from this case study alone that the level of aggression in a society will be related to its rate of hypoglycemia. However in this village at least, glucose homeostasis problems and high aggressiveness do coincide.

On the basis of this test, it is difficult to evaluate the curvilinear aspect of the hypoglycemia hypothesis. Only 7 (13 per cent) of the subjects were found to have severe hypoglycemia. These cases do seem to indicate that curvilinearity is present, for while 65.2 per cent of the mild hypoglycemia subjects fall into the top half of the aggression rankings, only 42.9 per cent of the subjects with severe hypoglycemia are among the top aggressors. It is true that the cases of severe hypoglycemia are few. Nevertheless, additional

Table 6. Distribution of Blood Glucose Conditions in the Sample Population According to Aggressiveness Ranks.

Aggression Rankings (grouped by fourths)	Normal Glycemia		Moderate Hypoglycemia		Severe Hypoglycemia	
	N	%	N	%	N	%
1 (high aggressors)	1	7.7	11	84.6	1	7.7
2	8	57.2	5	35.7	1	7.1
3	7	50.0	4	28.6	3	21.4
4 (low aggressors)	8	61.5	3	23.1	2	15.4

support for curvilinearity is to be found in the mean scores for aggressiveness. The grouped aggressiveness means are as follows: Normal Glycemia—157, Mild Hypoglycemia—112, and Severe Hypoglycemia—162. While there is no difference between the subjects with severe hypoglycemia and those with normal glucose reactions to the GTT, those with mild hypoglycemia definitely tend to rank high in aggression. Figure 1 shows the curve which is produced when the means for the aggressiveness rankings are plotted against the change in blood glucose during the four-hour GTT.

Correlations between aggressiveness rankings and the results of each reading in the GTT were carried out. The results seem to suggest that the drop at the end of the GTT is not the only important aspect of the test with respect to aggressiveness. Rather, it seems that the rapidity of the decline in blood glucose is significant. The highest correlation (.42) occurs at the 8:00 A.M. reading. Apparently those who are able to maintain high glucose levels during the early phase of the test are the least likely to be aggressive. I also tested the original hypothesis in which fasting glucose levels were related to aggressiveness; that hypothesis, however, must be rejected since there is no difference in the fasting glucose means of high and low aggressors. An analysis of deviant cases was carried out, too, but I cannot present that material in this paper.

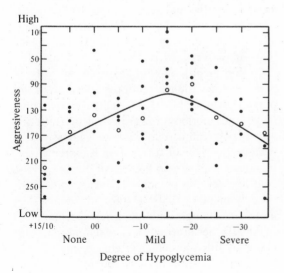

Figure 1. Plot of Data Points and Means of Aggressiveness Rankings with Respect to Blood Glucose Condition According to the GTT.

Discussion of the Results

It has been demonstrated above that there is an association of blood glucose reactions on the GTT and levels of aggressiveness among the Incawatana subjects of our study. Moreover, the data conform to the prediction of our hypothesis. The interpretation to be placed on these results, however, is not self-evident. I have argued that the glucose reactions are causally related to aggressiveness at least in certain ranges of reaction to the GTT. In other words, while the glycemic reaction is important in causing an individual to be ranked among the highest aggressors in the village, it does not account for the aggressiveness placement or rank of the subjects relative to one another if they have identical reactions to the GTT. Those with normal blood glucose are not likely to be extremely aggressive, and the glucose factor does not seem to account for their position within the bottom three quartiles. Whether a normal glycemic subject falls into the second quartile rather than the third or fourth depends on many other factors, some of which are perhaps biological in nature. Moyer (1972:6), for example, argues that "there are many kinds of aggression and each has a different physiological basis . . ."

Given the association of glycemic reactions and aggressiveness, it is possible to arrive at a number of different conclusions about the meaning of the association and the mechanisms which might be involved in mediating between glucose levels and aggressiveness. At the present time I can merely point out some plausible interpretations.

Adequate functioning of the brain depends upon that organ's receiving a sufficient supply of both oxygen and glucose. Presumably the normal fasting glucose level is adjusted to meet the high fuel requirements of the brain. It is quite likely that when the glucose level drops below the normal fasting level, brain requirements are not being met and normal brain functioning is impaired.

Hypoglycemia may cause the individual to become irritable, thus lowering the threshold for aggression release by appropriate stimuli in the environment. On the basis of our evidence it is not possible to decide whether environmental stimuli are necessary for the release of aggression. Our impression is that Qolla individuals do go "spoiling for a fight" on occasion. One could call almost anything within the village a "stimulus" to aggression. The person may see the field of an enemy and begin insulting him, even in his absence; or as he passes a certain house he may insult the owner, not because the latter is his enemy but *por gusto* (for the hell of it).

There are other ways in which hypoglycemia may be considered an indirect rather than direct cause of aggressivity. If the activation of neural circuits in the aggression system of the brain is facilitated by low glucose concentrations or their rapid change, or if hormones essential to such activation are released under conditions of hypoglycemia, then hypoglycemia may be an indirect cause of aggression. If research on epinephrine and norepinephrine, as well as on other hormones, leads to conclusions about the significance of these substances in causing aggression, then a low glucose level, or one that falls too rapidly, plays a role by stimulating the release of these hormones. Moyer (1972:17-18) points out that there "is good evidence for example, that brain chemistry of aggressive animals (isolated mice) is different from that of normals," including differences in turnover rates of serotonin, norepinephrine, and dopamine; and he suggests that aggression may be caused by the endocrine changes which lead to "direct or indirect sensitization or activation of particular brain systems."

Another means by which hypoglycemia might increase aggressiveness is as follows. If one postulates that the human organism attempts to maintain glucose levels at or above the nominal level, which seems to be the case, then when blood glucose falls below the nominal level, processes occur which will raise the glucose level. In the normal, healthy organism those processes are internal metabolic processes. If, however, these metabolic processes are not operating properly, e.g., because of adrenal exhaustion or liver disease, then behavioral and emotional means might be sought to produce the same effects. The individual may find that by becoming angry or by expressing aggression his glucose level is raised. Anger—the fight-flight reaction—may serve as a stimulus to sluggishly operating glands and organs. Consequently, a person's aggression is reinforced because of the physiological feeling of well-being which accompanies the emotions or aggressive actions. In this way hypoglycemia may lead to aggressiveness because this type of stimulation is extremely effective as a short-run booster of glucose levels. And, in fact, the peasants of Incawatana occasionally mention that fighting "makes one feel better." Although the topic is too speculative to pursue further at this time, it is tempting to suggest that this physiological change may be the basis for persisting notions about the cathartic effects of aggression.

Consequently, it can be seen that aggressive behavior may become part of the set of mechanisms which are involved in glucose homeostasis. To be sure, this solution to problems of glucose homeostasis, while markedly effective in the short run, is detrimental to the organism if continued for any length of time. While it is probably maladaptive for the individual, it has potential eufunctional consequences, too, if, for example, it leads to spacing out or increased access to scarce resources important for an adequate diet. I shall discuss this topic below.

It remains possible to suggest that the direction of causality is the reverse of the one I have postulated. Since the present study is based on correlational data, the hypothesis that aggressiveness causes hypoglycemia must be entertained. All the clinical evidence, to be sure (e.g., the effects of insulin-induced hypoglycemia), suggests that hypoglycemia causes aggressiveness and irritability rather than *vice versa*. Although I have been stressing the priority of hypoglycemia, quite clearly there must be interaction between hypoglycemia and aggressiveness. Moreover, within limits there may very well be a reciprocally amplifying or oscillating interaction. That is, hypoglycemia causes the individual to act aggressively. In doing so, and thus becoming the target for aggression as well, the individual's hypoglycemia worsens, at least to the point where hypoglycemia becomes extreme, when, perhaps, the individual either dies or withdraws for a slow recuperation. "Hypoglycemic careers" and "agonistic careers" are undoubtedly closely meshed. Since our study is not diachronic, we cannot resolve the issue of priority with our data. But we strongly suspect that the total stress load, rather than aggression *per se*, is the starting point for hypoglycemia and hence for the developmental sequence of interplay between hypoglycemia and aggressiveness.

THE SYSTEMIC CONTEXT OF HYPOGLYCEMIA AND AGGRESSION

For the most part, the hypoglycemia hypothesis does not contradict the earlier hypotheses dealing with Qolla aggressiveness, i.e., the domination hypothesis and the environmental-harshness hypothesis. In essence, we believe that the hypoglycemia hypothesis goes beyond the previous explanations by pinpointing the physiological mechanism through which the social,

cultural, and environmental factors presented in those hypotheses have their effect on aggressiveness levels among the Qolla. I must emphasize that hypoglycemia is only one of the many variables responsible for high aggressiveness. At the same time, I must also emphasize that the etiology of hypoglycemia is exceedingly complex and poorly understood. Without any doubt, however, it can be said that the factors suggested by previous hypotheses about the Aymara personality explain only part of the variance in aggressiveness rankings.

In this section of the paper I shall relate the hypoglycemia hypothesis to the factors suggested by Barnouw to explain the Aymara personality. Instead of merely listing these items, I shall offer a tentative model of the "bio-aggression system" of the Qolla. Detailed evidence to support my argument will be presented elsewhere (Bolton 1973). Nevertheless, it is hoped that this brief discussion will enable the reader to understand the context in which the hypoglycemia hypothesis must be located.

In Figure 2, I have outlined the major components in the bio-aggression system of the Qolla. The basic postulate with which I am working, of course, is that the biological and ecological factors influencing aggressiveness in Incawatana do so by contributing to the development of hypoglycemia. In order to evaluate this hypothesis, it is necessary to work through the system item by item. Essentially this means evaluating the potential stressors' effects on hypoglycemia and on aggressiveness.

Population growth in Incawatana has resulted in a low per capita resource base, especially with respect to the major form of productive property, land. Overpopulation requires the peasants to use the available land intensively. Fallowing is not possible. Because of a lack of pastures and other sources of feed, villagers are able to raise few animals. Land is overutilized, and villagers are not able to fertilize their fields properly. Both of these conditions lead to depletion of the soil. Per capita food production is low as the result of three major factors: the scarcity of land, the absence of essential nutrients in the soil, and the capricious weather which brings hail, drought, floods, and winds, all of which ruin crops, year after year.

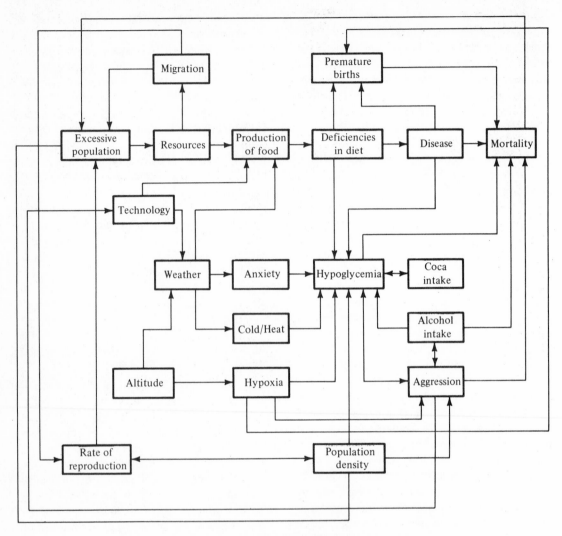

Figure 2. A Model of the Bio-Aggression System of the Qolla.

Inadequate food production has several effects. First, it leads to emigration by many villagers. Some people migrate and remain away from home permanently. Others spend several months each year earning cash by engaging in menial occupations in nearby cities. Migration solves part of the food shortage problem. Permanent migration reduces the burden of an excessive population. Both temporary and permanent migrants frequently send foodstuffs and other items back to their families in the village.

Inadequate food production results in dietary deficiencies of numerous kinds, including probably hypocaloric intake and low protein intake as well as low intake of essential vitamins, e.g.,

A, B complex, and C, and minerals, e.g., calcium. Some of these deficiencies are undoubtedly periodic in nature rather than constant throughout the year. Different age and sex categories may be differentially exposed to these deficiencies. (For information on diet consult Schaedel 1967, Thomas 1970, and Picón 1968.) Dietary deficiencies are thought to have several important consequences. First, they contribute directly to the development of hypoglycemia. Spontaneous attacks of hypoglycemia can occur when an individual has not eaten an adequate meal, or one high in carbohydrates, and then expends large amounts of energy. Second, dietary deficiencies produce other diseases which are associated with hypoglycemia, i.e., diseases such as cirrhosis of the liver. Third, dietary deficiencies may be partly responsible for the high rate of premature births found in the region (Leigh Gates, personal communication).

Premature births, miscellaneous diseases, and hypoglycemia all contribute to a high mortality rate for the village. The high mortality, in turn, prevents the problem of overpopulation from becoming more acute than it already is. Premature births tend to be associated with hypoglycemia in the infant (McClung 1969), which may then be prolonged into adulthood if the subsequent postnatal environment itself is deficient.

The unpredictable weather of the region causes considerable anxiety in the villagers (Tschopik 1951). This anxiety, plus the extremes of temperature at this altitude (12,000 feet above sea level), may be stressful and thus promote the development of hypoglycemia.

Hypoxia, too, may serve as a stressor and may be partly responsible for the widespread hypoglycemia in Incawatana residents. But this question is complex. The data (Baker 1969) seem to suggest that permanent residents at high altitude have attained an adaptation which permits equivalent or higher levels of oxygen consumption than is normal for sea-level subjects. However, it may be that not all individuals in the Andes are equally adapted to the hypoxic conditions. An individual might in fact be overadapted or underadapted to the hypoxic environment. If a person is overadapted, he would necessarily burn more glucose at a faster rate than is considered normal elsewhere. Thus he might more readily experience glucose deficits, particularly if nutrition is poor and if he encounters other forms of stress. If a person is underadapted, the low oxygen pressure would serve as stressor and possibly lead to the eventual deterioration of the adrenal glands and from there to the development of hypoglycemia. One or both of these situations may exist (cf. Van Liere and Stickney 1963). Picón (1962, 1963, 1966) has been studying the effects of chronic hypoxia on carbohydrate metabolism, comparing groups of subjects at sea level and at high altitudes in Peru. His studies show that there are important differences in metabolic processes between the two groups. Among his findings is the fact that

during the intravenous GTT the blood glucose concentration diminishes more rapidly in high-altitude subjects than in sea-level ones, and that the initial hyperglycemic response to glucose is less pronounced in the high-altitude subjects. It was pointed out above that the highest correlation between aggressiveness and glucose levels occurred when the glucose level in the GTT had dropped by the time of the fourth glucose reading, two hours after the beginning of the test. Consequently, the rapidity of the drop seems to be related to both altitude and aggressiveness. Unfortunately, it is not known what causes this rapid drop among high-altitude natives.

I have suggested that there is a reciprocal interaction between coca chewing and hypoglycemia. The person with hypoglycemia becomes hungry and chews coca to dull his hunger pains and to provide himself with energy. The coca has immediate effects in raising the glucose level, probably by stimulating the transformation of glycogen stores, but it probably has long-term detrimental effects which complicate glucose homeostasis problems for the individual who chews. (See Buck *et al.* 1968a and 1968b for a discussion of the relationship between coca chewing and health.) Alcohol, too, provides the individual with quick energy, raising glucose levels; but according to some sources the craving for alcohol is itself produced by hypoglycemia (Tintera 1955, 1956, 1966). The high alcohol consumption may contribute to diseases such as fatty liver or cirrhosis which also are factors in the etiology of hypoglycemia.

Hypoglycemia leads to high involvement in aggression. Aggression has significant effects of several kinds. First, aggression increases the mortality rate. It has a direct effect because of the high homicide rate and indirect effects due to the debilitation occasioned by wounds received in fights. Aggression is a factor which influences some people to migrate to the cities where, according to informants, life is more peaceful. Aggression causes villagers to eye one another with suspicion and prevents them from co-operating with one another, especially on projects which could have a feedback effect on the productivity of the community. For example, it is possible to use smudging techniques during nights when frost falls during the growing season. This technique can prevent damage to crops, but the villagers have found it too difficult to organize this type of communal activity. Therefore, the technology which is available for increasing food production is not employed.

Finally, population growth has resulted in a high population density in Incawatana. High density has an effect on the aggression level, both directly and indirectly. High density is associated with increased rates of interaction and, thus, an increase in the likelihood that an agonistic encounter will occur. We hypothesize that it contributes to the development of hypoglycemia as well. It is difficult to test this hypothesis because the residential units in Incawatana are almost equally spaced throughout the available territory; consequently, there is not much differentiation within the village in terms of distances between houses. However, there are differences between villagers with respect to the distance from their house to a major path. Here we find that there is a correlation between distance and hypoglycemia (.289), indicating that those subjects who live close to a major path are more likely to suffer from hypoglycemia. The correlation between path distance and aggressiveness is considerably lower and not significant (.102). This topic has been well studied in rat populations and other animals (cf. Hall 1969, Deevey 1960, Christian and Davis 1964, Calhoun 1962). But little is known about the physiological effects of population density and crowding in humans. The results for Incawatana suggest that some measures of density are associated with hypoglycemia. Indeed, in some respects, one must consider the bio-aggression system which I have outlined here to be closely related to the population control systems discussed by ethologists concerned with the effects of crowding and density. In part at least, hypoglycemia and aggression appear to be linked with many of the same variables which would have to be included in a model of population system for Incawatana. I shall deal with this problem at greater length in another work.

The question remains: do these stressors cause aggression directly or do they produce an effect indirectly, i.e., by causing hypoglycemia first? Since we were unable to measure all the variables in this model, we can provide only a tentative answer to this question. Multiple re-gression analyses using dietary and spatial factors as independent variables lead to the conclusion that these two categories of items, essentially high density and protein deficiency, account for 20 per cent of the variance in levels of hypoglycemia. We obtained a multiple correlation of .45, significant at the .05 level. In contrast, when we used aggression as the dependent variable, we did not obtain a correlation which was statistically significant. In other words, these results do suggest that dietary and spatial factors influence aggression levels primarily through their effect on the glycemic condition of our subjects.

CONCLUSION

In this paper I have presented a test of the hypoglycemia hypothesis. On the basis of that test a number of conclusions can be drawn. First, we have demonstrated that there is an association between hypoglycemia and aggressiveness among the Qolla Indians of Peru. Analysis of the factors which contribute to the development of hypoglycemia indicates that previous explanations for the Aymara personality were not so much wrong as incomplete. The hypoglycemia hypothesis subsumes the earlier hypotheses.

Second, we have demonstrated that hypoglycemia is a widespread physiological condition in this Andean population. The discovery of this fact opens up many research possibilities. We will want to have detailed studies of the relationship between coca chewing and hypoglycemia and between alcohol consumption and hypoglycemia. Numerous ethnographers have mentioned that Andean peasants seem to be able to live with greater cognitive inconsistency than other peoples. What are the consequences of hypoglycemia for other psychological processes such as perception, memory, and cognition? In the literature it has often been reported that high altitude has an effect on dreaming; is this effect due to hypoxia, to hypoglycemia, or to both?

This research has implications beyond the Andes. Although the Qolla seem to be extremely aggressive, they are not unique. I suggest that the question of peasant personality generally should be looked at again. Many of the same factors which serve as stressors for the Qolla are present in most peasant societies. Is it possible that hypoglycemia is found in other peasant societies as well? It might be fruitful to re-analyze the situations found for other aggressive peoples, too, such as the Yanomamö. Or, one might examine the differences between pastoralists and agriculturalists, testing the hypothesis that hypoglycemia might be a factor which explains differences in aggressiveness (see Edgerton 1971). I cannot neglect to suggest that further research on this topic might be carried out in American ghettos and other poverty areas where high levels of stress are found.

Since the present study provides the first large-scale test of the hypoglycemia hypothesis, we will need replication, and we will need to have controlled experiments before we can proceed to work out all the implications of this finding.

In conclusion, it seems to me that instead of engaging in useless debates over instincts and imperatives, anthropologists must take up Wallace's challenge. We must explore the biological bases of cultural behavior and personality. It is to be hoped that the new directions in human biology discussed by Holloway and Szinyei-Merse will promote an integrated approach to problems which can only be solved through the application of both cultural and biological viewpoints. Holloway and Szinyei-Merse (1972:146-147) have noted that

there is a tendency to forget just how biological life is. Indeed, a newer emphasis is developing, away from that of the past century—which had the great value of showing the biologist how important culture is for understanding human behavior—to that of indicating how important our biological heritage is for sane, moral, adaptive human behavior. The synthesis between these approaches to human existence and improvements is surely close at hand. We no longer believe it reasonable for cultural anthropologists to simply consider the biological realm as some sort of constant, profitably ignored so that social variables alone can be studied.

By applying a psychobiological approach to the problem of Qolla aggression, I have tried to show that a better understanding of the forms and intensity of that kind of human behavior has been attained.

Notes

1. An earlier draft of this paper received the Stirling Award in Culture and Personality Studies presented at the 71st annual meeting of the American Anthropological Association in Toronto, Canada, December 1, 1972. Field work among the Qolla was carried out from December, 1968, to January, 1971, with the financial assistance of the Foreign Area Fellowship Program. A grant from the Latin American Studies Program of Cornell University paid for the collection of the physiological data employed in this article. For this support I am extremely grateful. Among the many people who contributed to the successful completion of this research, I would like to express my appreciation especially to John M. Roberts, Bernd Lambert, Leigh Gates, Miguel Neyra, José Sardón, Charlene Bolton, and the people of Incawatana. A brief version of this article was presented to the 1972 annual meeting of the Southwestern Anthropological Association in Long Beach, California.

2. Details on Qolla culture are provided in my forthcoming monograph. I should explain my usage of the terms "Qolla" and "Aymara." Qolla culture is an Andean subculture found in the area around Lake Titicaca in Peru and Bolivia. On the basis of linguistic criteria alone, the Qolla have often been divided into Quechua and Aymara. In essence, however, one is dealing with a single Andean subculture, which should be referred to as Qolla rather than Aymara. Incawatana, the village which I studied, is located in the Quechua-speaking zone of the Qollao.

Bibliography

Abrahamson, E. M., and A. W. Pezet. 1951. Body, Mind and Sugar. New York.

Baker, P. T. 1969. Human Adaptation to High Altitude. Science 163: 1149-1156.

Barnouw, V. 1963. Culture and Personality. Homewood, Illinois.

_____. 1971. An Introduction to Anthropology: Ethnology, V.2. Homewood, Illinois.

Berkowitz, L. 1962. Aggression: A Social Psychological Analysis. New York.

Boelkins, R. C., and J. F. Heiser. 1970. Biological Base of Aggression. Violence and the Struggle for Existence, ed. D. Daniels, M. Gilula, and F. Ochberg. Boston.

Bohannan, P., ed. 1967. African Homicide and Suicide. New York.

Buck, A. A. *et al.* 1968a. Health and Disease in Four Peruvian Villages: Contrast in Epidemiology. Baltimore.

_____. 1968b. Coca Chewing and Health: An Epidemiologic Study Among Residents of a Peruvian Village. American Journal of Epidemiology 88: ii, 159-177.

Buss, A. H. 1961. The Psychology of Aggression. New York.

Calhoun, J. B. 1962. Population Density and Social Pathology. Scientific American 206: ii, 139-148.

Carter, W. E. 1965. Aymara Communities and the Bolivian Agrarian Reform. Social Science Monograph No. 24. Gainesville, Florida.

_____. 1966. Factores socio-económicos en el desarrollo de la personalidad Aymara. Proceedings of the XXXVI International Congress of Americanists 3: 367-381.

_____. 1968. Secular Reinforcement in Aymara Death Ritual. American Anthropologist 70: 238-263.

Christian, J. J., and D. E. Davis. 1964. Endocrines, Behavior, and Population. Science 146: 1550-1560.

Clemente, C. D., and D. B. Lindsley, ed. 1967. Aggression and Defense. UCLA Forum in Medical Sciences 7 (Brain Function, v. 5) Berkeley.

Cuentas Gamarra, L. 1966. Apuntes antropólogicos sociales sobre las zonas aymaras del dpto. de Puno: Corpuno, Departamento de Integración Cultural.

Deevey, E. S. 1960. The Hare and the Haruspex: A Cautionary Tale. Yale Review 49: 161-179.

Edgerton, R. B. 1971. The Individual in Cultural Adaptation: A study of Four East African Peoples. Berkeley.

Fredericks, C., and H. Goodman. 1969. Low Blood Sugar and You. New York.

Friedrich, P. 1964. El homicidio político en Acan. Revista de Ciencias Sociales 8: i, 27-51.

Gade, D. W. 1970. Ecología del robo agrícola en las tierras altas de los Andes centrales. América Indígena 30: 3-14.

Harris, M. 1971. Culture, Man, and Nature. New York.

Hall, E. T. 1969. The Hidden Dimension. Garden City, New York.

Holloway, R. L., and E. Szinyei-Merse. 1972. Human Biology: A Catholic Review. Biennial Review of Anthropology 1971, ed. B. J. Siegel, pp. 85-166. Stanford.

Klopper, A. 1964. Psysiological Background to Aggression. The Natural History of Aggression, ed. J. D. Carthy and F. J. Ebling, pp. 65-72. New York.

LaBarre, W. 1965. Aymara Folklore and Folk Temperament. Journal of the Folklore Institute 2: 25-30.

_____. 1966. The Aymara: History and Worldview. The Anthropologist Looks at Myth, ed. J. Greenway, pp. 130-144. Austin.

LeVine, R. A. 1961. Anthropology and the Study of Conflict: Introduction. Journal of Conflict Resolution 5: 3-15.

_____. 1963. Culture and Personality. Biennial Review of Anthropology 1963, ed. B. J. Siegel, pp. 107-145. Stanford.

Mark, V., and F. R. Ervin. 1970. Violence and the Brain. New York.

Martin, C. G. 1970. Low Blood Sugar: The Hidden Menace of Hypoglycemia. New York.

McClung, J. 1969. Effects of High Altitude on Human Birth. Cambridge.

Monge M., Carlos. 1968. Man, Climate, and Changes of Altitude. Man in Adaptation: The Biosocial Background, ed. Y. Cohen, Chicago.

Monge M., Carlos, and Carlos Monge C. 1966. High-Altitude Diseases: Mechanisms and Management. Springfield, Illinois.

Moyer, K. E. 1971. The Physiology of Hostility. Chicago.

_____. 1972. A Physiological Model of Aggression: Does It have Different Implications? Paper presented at the Houston Neurological Symposium on Neural Bases of Violence and Aggression.

Murra, J. F. 1968. An Aymara Kingdom in 1567. Ethnohistory 15: 115-151.

Murua, Fray Martin de. 1946. Historia del origen y genealogia real de los reyes Incas del Peru. Madrid: Biblioteca Missionalia Hispanica.

Pelto, P. 1967. Psychological Anthropology. Biennial Review of Anthropology, 1967, ed. A. Beals and B. Siegel, p. 151. Stanford.

Picón-Réategui, E. 1962. Studies on the Metabolism of Carbohydrates at Sea Level and at High Altitudes. Metabolism 11: xi, 1148-1154.

_____. 1963. Intravenous Glucose Tolerance Test at Sea Level and at High Altitudes. Journal of Clinical Endocrinology and Metabolism 23: xii, 1256-1261.

_____. 1966. Insulin, Epinephrine, and Glucagon on the Metabolism of Carbohydrates at High Altitude. Federation Proceedings 25: iv, 1233-1239.

_____. 1968. Food Requirements of High Altitude Peruvian Natives. High Altitude Adaptation in a Peruvian Community, ed. P. T. Baker *et al.* Pennsylvania State University, Occasional Papers in Anthropology 1.

Plummer, J. F. 1966. Another Look at Aymara Personality. Behavior Science Notes 2: 55-78.

Schaedel, R. P. 1967. La Demografía y los recursos humanos del sur del Peru. Mexico: Instituto Indigenista Interamericano, Serie de Antropología Social 8.

Scott, J. P. 1948. Aggression. Chicago.

Storr, A. 1968. Human Aggression. New York.

Sutton-Smith, B., and J. M. Roberts. 1964. Rubrics of Competitive Behavior. Journal of Genetic Psychology 105: 13-37.

Thomas, R. B. 1970. El Tamaño pequeño del cuerpo como forma de adaptación de una población quechua a la altura. Paper presented at the 39th International Congress of Americanists, Lima.

Tintera, J. W. 1955. The Hypoadrenocortical State and Its Management. New York State Journal of Medicine 55: xiii, 1868-1876.

_____. 1956. Office Rehabilitation of the Alcoholic. New York State Journal of Medicine 56: xxiv, 3896-3902.

_____. 1966. Stabilizing Homeostasis in the Recovered Alcoholic Through Endocrine Therapy: Evaluation of the Hypoglycemia Factor. Journal of the American Geriatrics Society 14: ii, 126-150.

Tschopik, H., Jr. 1951. The Aymara of Chucuito, Peru (v. 1,

Magic). Anthropological Papers of the American Museum of Natural History 44, pt. ii. New York.

Wallace. A. F. C. 1961a. Culture and Personality. New York.

———. 1961b. Mental Illness, Biology and Culture. Psychological Anthropology, ed. F. Hsu, pp. 255-294. Homewood, Illinois.

———. 1961c. The Psychic Unity of Human Groups. Studying Personality Cross-Culturally, ed. B. Kaplan, pp. 129-163. Evanston.

———. 1962. Culture and Cognition. Science 135: 351-357.

Wallace, A. F. C., and J. Atkins. 1960. The Meaning of Kinship Terms. American Anthropologist 62: 58-80.

Wilder, J. 1947. Sugar Metabolism in Its Relation to Criminology. Handbook of Correctional Psychology, ed. R. Lindner and R. Seliger, pp. 98-129. New York.

Wolfgang, M. E., and F. Ferracuti. 1967. The Subculture of Violence. London.

Van Liere, E. J., and J. C. Stickney. 1963. Hypoxia. Chicago.

Nutrition, Race, and Intelligence

The human brain is the culmination of almost three billion years of evolutionary history. It represents the most complex structure in creation and is the site of man's supremacy in the animal kingdom. The fossil record discloses that increased brain size has been the most striking sustained trend shown in hominid (family of man and his ancestors) evolution. A large brain must have conferred a clear advantage, and through the ages this attribute must have afforded greater opportunities for survival than did a small brain. [13, p. 114] While at first glance it might have been difficult to tell *Australopithecus* from a contemporary ape, since both could walk on two feet in an upright position and had opposable thumbs and stereoscopic vision, they nevertheless differed in at least this fundamental respect. *Australopithecus* and his descendants had larger brains and overwhelmingly higher intelligence than had the apes that were contemporary with them. The modern adult chimpanzee's average cranial capacity is less than 400 cc (cubic centimeters), the orangutan's is slightly greater than 400 cc, and the modern gorilla's exceeds 500 cc. By contrast, the cranial capacity of the fossil *Australopithecus* was about 500 cc, of *Homo erectus* more than 900 cc, and that of modern man averages 1,400 cc. [13, p. 30]

These data, however, must be interpreted with some caution; cranial capacity is not synonymous with brain volume, and is only a useful approximation of brain size. Brain weight today varies over wide limits, and size can no longer be used as a determinant of intelligence. Some very stupid people have large brains, and some brilliant ones have small brains.

The mature human brain contains about 11 billion nerve cells imbedded in a matrix of housekeeping cells, the neuroglia, whose number exceeds 100 billion. It is these nerve cells

By Elie Shneour. Reprinted with permission, from *The Science Teacher*, 41, No. 9, December 1974, pp. 22-25.
"Nutrition, Race and Intellect" by Elie Shneour, from *The Malnourished Mind* by Elie Shneour. Copyright © 1974 by Elie Shneour. Reprinted by permission of Doubleday & Company, Inc.

which perform the functions we associate with intelligence, consciousness, memory, biological control, and integration. Nerve-cell proliferation is complete at birth, and none of these cells are replaced thereafter. One of the earliest recognizable primordial tissues in the human embryo is the neural plate. This first evidence of brain development appears by the eighteenth day of pregnancy. This means that to generate the required 11 billion nerve cells by the end of gestation requires the production and differentiation of an average of 20,000 nerve cells *per minute* during this period. [10]

The growth of the human brain during gestation is one of the earliest, most rapid, and most extensive developments of the whole organism. After birth the brain continues to grow at a much faster rate than the rest of the body, so much so that by the time a child is four years old his brain has reached 90 percent of its adult weight, while the rest of his body has barely made it to the 20 percent mark. [6] During this critical period of rapid growth, much more than just an increase in weight is involved. The structures making up the brain undergo complex and profound changes in anatomy, chemistry, and physiology. The following table [11] shows the extraordinary growth of the human brain: It shows that while the rate of brain growth is highest before birth, the weight of the human brain nearly triples during the first year of life. This outstanding growth rate is not shared with any other mammal and provides a clue to the important role which the nutritional requirements must play during this early period.

Table 1.

Newborn	340 g
6 months	750 g
1 year	970 g
2 years	1,150 g
3 years	1,200 g
6 years	1,250 g
9 years	1,300 g
12 years	1,350 g
20 years	1,400 g

The inescapable conclusion, therefore, is that the human brain is most vulnerable to inade-

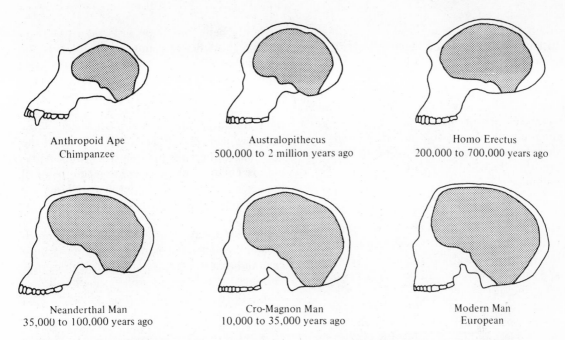

Anthropoid Ape
Chimpanzee

Australopithecus
500,000 to 2 million years ago

Homo Erectus
200,000 to 700,000 years ago

Neanderthal Man
35,000 to 100,000 years ago

Cro-Magnon Man
10,000 to 35,000 years ago

Modern Man
European

Figure 1. The major steps in hominid evolution. A modern anthropoid ape skull silhouette is shown for purposes of comparison. Note the size of the cranial cavities and the slant of the face silhouettes.

Adapted by permission of Doubleday.

quate nutrition during the earliest period of life. Furthermore, the evidence available on the subject suggests that the entire course of human existence may be largely determined by the nutrition received during that time. The logistic problem of providing the nutritional requirements begins shortly after conception and culminates in the development of the placenta. Prenatal nutrition of the embryo, which becomes the fetus when it acquires a human resemblance after six weeks, takes place through the placenta. This is a disc-shaped temporary organ in which the blood vessels of the fetus and those of the mother come together in an intertwined mass without joining. Nutrients, oxygen, hormones, and waste products are exchanged by diffusing from one blood-vessel system to the other. A malnourished mother may be unable to keep up fetal demands for essential nutrients. The classic work of R. A. McCance and E. M. Widdowson demonstrated that a growing organism is extremely sensitive to variations in nutrition, and that malnourished rats, for example, would be permanently stunted even if they later received an adequate diet, while overnourishment would

result in permanently larger animals. [9] That the placenta was involved was demonstrated by J. K. Stephan and B. F. Chow at Johns Hopkins University [12] and by M. Winick at Cornell University. [14] Malnourished mothers produced smaller and lighter placentae than did adequately fed mothers. S. Zamenhof at the University of California at Los Angeles first showed that depriving pregnant rats of protein resulted in a reduced number of brain cells in the offspring. [16, 17] This was confirmed by Dr. Winick, who made the striking observation that newborn animals from deficient placentae also had fewer brain cells. On the other hand, Dr. Zamenhof was able to raise very bright rats, animals that he calls "rat Einsteins," by providing abundant and well-balanced food. Perhaps the most remarkable observation he made was that female rats born to malnourished mothers could not produce adequate placentae, even if they were well-nourished during their entire adult lives. Their offspring exhibited the classic evidence of malnutrition, including a reduction in brain-cell numbers. [18] This work supports the finding of J. J. Cowley and R. D. Griesel in

South Africa that the effect of prenatal malnutrition on rat mental development could affect growth and development into the second generation. [3] Thus malnutrition, an environmental influence, can produce effects very similar to those of hereditary origin. These experiments were carried out mainly with animals rather than human beings for obvious reasons, but there is ample clinical evidence available to suggest that the conclusions are equally applicable to human children.

J. A. Churchill of Wayne State University examined poor black pregnant women and their children and was able to observe a definite relationship between the amounts of amino acids in the mothers' blood streams during pregnancy and the birth weights and skull volumes of their offspring. [2] Mothers who had a low level of these substances in their blood streams as a result of a protein-deficient diet bore children who weighed less and had significantly smaller skulls than those of mothers whose blood had a higher level of amino acids. Since the duration of pregnancies was about the same for all women tested, premature births played no role in these results. The relationship between low birth weight and mental retardation had been known for a long time, but the interpretation usually given was that premature birth was an important cause of mental retardation. This kind of explanation, while probably valid in part, obscured the effect of malnutrition on subsequent mental retardation. In fact, a number of investigators showed that some of the most severely mentally retarded children were the least premature.

L. C. Eaves of the University of British Columbia reported on the IQ test scores of children with a low birth weight. The results of this 18-month study with 502 children showed that those with low birth weight consistently scored lower than normal children. Socioeconomic status played an important role in these IQ deficiencies and became even more significant with increasing age. At six months of age the IQ difference between normal and malnourished children was only 5 points. The spread increased to 17 points by age 4. However, when the low-birth weight children were contrasted with normal children of comparable socioeconomic background, the normal children still performed significantly better on these tests than did their birthweight-deficient counterparts. [5] This observation, confirmed by other investigators, is of capital importance. It suggests that socioeconomic status alone does not account for differences in the IQ test performance of these children, and that the prenatal environment must therefore have played an important role in the outcome. Children born small at term, or premature children, do not seem to reach their full biological potential, no matter how well they are fed in later years. Such investigators as C. M. Drillien at the University of Edinburgh showed that there is among these children a much greater incidence of mental and physical handicap, and that the severity of the difficulties rises strikingly with decreasing birth weight. [4] Less than 1 percent of the normal children were found to exhibit mental deficiencies. But an astounding 54 percent had these problems with a birth weight of 3 pounds or less. A vast amount of research work has also been done with twin births. It has been abundantly demonstrated that nutrients generally do not reach each twin equally during the prenatal period, and that the smaller of the twins almost always exhibits a lower mental potential, as determined by IQ tests.

In the chain of evidence linking early life malnutrition to brain development, a report of M. Winick and P. Rosso of Cornell University Medical College is particularly significant. [15] Examining 19 brains from Santiago, Chile, children who died accidentally, they found that while the brains of well-nourished Chilean children contained the same number of cells as those of well-nourished U.S. children, those of severely malnourished children who weighed less than 4.4 pounds at birth had as much as a 60 percent reduction in their braincell numbers.

Numerous studies exist which relate chronic early-life malnutrition to lowered performance on IQ tests. The word "chronic" is emphasized, because there is also good evidence that even severe acute malnutrition during pregnancy and in the early years of life may cause no long-term damage to cognition. It is primarily the chronically poor of the world, the disadvantaged minorities, who are the most likely long-term victims of chronic malnutrition with all its tragic consequences.

Investigators have grappled for years with the question of heredity versus environment on human cognition. Some of the arguments presented in support of one over the other have reached the point of sanctimonious absurdity. The following three cases will illustrate the reason why such arguments are logically self-defeating:

1. A child is born with the inborn error of metabolism disease phenylketonuria (PKU), which has a clearly defined genetic origin. If left untreated, PKU leads to irreversible mental retardation. However, if the child is fed a diet free of the amino acid phenylalanine, his chances of growing up with normal mental faculties are excellent.

2. A fetus with genetic potential for normal development is growing in its mother's womb. During the third month of pregnancy, the mother is infected by the rubella (German measles) virus. The child is born with severe and permanent defects.

3. An adult with light skin migrates to a sunny southern climate and an outdoor occupation. His skin darkens considerably. Another person with dark skin moves to a northern environment and a sedentary job. His skin eventually appears no darker than the light-skinned person before the move south.

Other factors being equal, how would the relative influence of heredity and environment on the outcome of the three examples just cited be assessed? It is this dilemma which confronts those who consider the emotionally charged issue of race and intelligence. Clearly there are many more variables to be analyzed in this instance than in any of the three cases just cited. It seems clear that chronic malnutrition is a major environmental factor in considering the issue as a whole. The problem begins with what is meant by "race" and by "intelligence."

The word "race" has almost always been used to define a group of human beings who are sociologically related. The modern trend is to define race biologically. The two often coincide, but they are not synonymous. A biological definition of race states that members of a given human group share biological characteristics that make it possible for that group to be differentiated from another group. This does *not* mean, however, that one group can be considered superior to another because of such characteristics. All men are created equal, but they are not all alike. And at the root of this diversity lies the assurance of human survival. But diversity is often confused with inequality. The essential point to remember in this context is that mankind belongs to a single species which has been derived from a common stock. The biological differences exhibited by human beings are due to a combination of genetic and environmental factors. There exist no human groups to which the attribute of "pure race" can be assigned. Human hybridization has been going on for a very long time, and no human being alive today would have got where he is without his parents' having mixed their genes together on his behalf.

Intelligence is even more difficult to define. The psychologist Harold J. Butcher has pointed out that the word "intelligence" is a noun, and that nouns refer to things. [1] Intelligence is not a "thing," but rather a sophisticated abstraction for the way people behave. Intelligence is made up of a wide variety of attributes which individuals possess in varying degrees. Some people have the ability to visualize concepts in three dimensions and can become outstanding architects or sculptors, yet may be very poor at manipulating mathematical abstractions. Others have outstanding verbal facility, yet may be unable to write a declarative sentence even with extraordinary effort. All intelligence-test designers, beginning with Alfred Binet, recognize this problem. They attempt with varying success to probe a variety of factors which appear to correlate with their understanding of what cognitive faculties are. The misleading simplicity and attractive numerical expression of the IQ (intelligence quotient) test, and its predictive effectiveness in assessing education or job potential, very quickly caused enthusiasm for it to overshadow the severe limitations that responsible psychologists had warned against. W. M. Littell emphasizes that these tests have no adequate rationale and that they are yet to be placed on a firm theoretical foundation. [8] Arthur Jensen states that intelligence, like electricity, is easier to measure than to define. He also points out that all major studies in this field have been based on the observation of white European and North American populations, and that knowledge of intelligence in different racial and cultural groups within these populations (e.g., black populations in the United States), is nonexistent. [7] While IQ tests do not necessarily measure intelligence accurately, they are, properly used, a useful research tool and deserve further study and development. IQ scores may be valid for a given human group at a given time and place only. There is no such thing as a universal IQ determination; therefore, such numbers cannot be used to measure intelligence once and for all for people tested. Finally, while the issue of race and intelligence cannot be dismissed out of hand, the truth is that most conclusions drawn by scientists and others on the subject are devoid either of scientific validity or educational significance. It is far more productive to examine those controllable factors which are likely to affect cognitive potential. Chronic early life malnutrition, a probable cause of cognitive deficiencies, is one such factor which deserves attention.

References

1. Butcher, H. J. *Human Intelligence, Its Nature and Assessment*. Methuen & Co., London. 1968. P.22.

2. Churchill, J. A., *et al.* "Relationships of Maternal Amino Acid Blood Levels to Fetal Development." *Obstetrics and Gynecology* 33:492; 1969.

3. Cowley, J. J., and R. D. Griesel. "The Effect on Growth and Behavior of Rehabilitating First and Second Generation Low-Protein Rats." *Animal Behavior* 14:506-517; 1966.

4. Drillien, C. M. *The Growth and Development of the Prematurely Born Infant*. Williams and Wilkins, Baltimore. 1964. P.215.

5. Eaves, L. C., *et al.* "Developmental and Psychological Test Scores in Children of Low Birth Weight." *Pediatrics* 45:9; 1970.

6. Harris, J. A., *et al. The Measurements of Man*. University of Minnesota Press, Minneapolis. 1930.

7. Jensen, A. R. "How Much Can We Boost I.Q. and Scholastic Achievement?" *Harvard Educational Review* 39:1-123; 1969.

8. Littell, W. M. "The Wechsler Intelligence Scale for Children, A Review of a Decade of Research." *Psychology Bulletin* 57:132-62; 1960.

9. McCance, R. A., and E. M. Widdowson. In *Protein Metabolism*. F. Gross, Editor. Springer-Verlag, Berlin. 1962. P.109.

10. Noback, C. R. *The Human Nervous System*. McGraw-Hill Book Co., New York. 1967. P.65.

11. Shneour, E. A. *The Malnourished Mind*. Anchor Press, Doubleday & Co., New York. 1974. P.27.

12. Stephan, J. K., and B. F. Chow. "The Fetus and Placenta in Maternal Dietary Restriction." *Federation Proceedings* 28:915; 1969.

13. Tobias, P. V. *The Brain in Hominid Evolution*. Columbia University Press, New York. 1971. P.114.

14. Winick, M. "Cellular Growth in Intrauterine Malnutrition." *Pediatric Clinics of North America* 17:69-77; 1970.

15. Winick, M., and R. Rosso. "The Effects of Severe Early Malnutrition on Cellular Growth of the Human Brain." *Pediatric Research* 3:181-184; 1969.

16. Zamenhof, S., E. Van Marthens, and F. L. Margolis. "DNA (Cell Number) and Protein in Neonatal Brain: Alteration by Maternal Dietary Protein Restriction." *Science* 160:322-323; 1968.

17. Zamenhof, S., L. Grauel, and E. Van Marthens. "Study of Possible Correlation between Prenatal Brain Development and Placental Weight." *Biology of the Neonate* 18:140; 1971.

18. Zamenhof, S., E. Van Marthens, and L. Grauel. "DNA (Cell Number) in Neonate Brain: Second Generation (F_2) Alteration by Maternal (F_0) Dietary Protein Restriction." *Science* 172:850; 1971.

Part V

Early Hominids* — Their Evolution and Culture

In recent years many significant discoveries in Africa and Asia have advanced our understanding of our human forebears, as articles in this section attest. New questions generated by recent findings continue to arise and many answers relating to hominid evolution remain elusive. Certainly controversy on varied issues surrounding fossil man and his culture is as great as ever. This section deals with some of these varied issues and topics. Simons and Tattersall discuss the complex of adaptive features associated with Ramapithecus in presenting the transition from hominoid to hominid stage of evolution in the primate order. The initial australopithecine find in 1924 and many subsequent discoveries have placed this genus in a key position as regards hominid evolution. The article by Tobias deals with this genus and treats its significance in light of recent data. The selection by Robbins deals with fossil hominids found in a remote region of Africa, the Turkana District of Kenya. Archaeological data from early times to the recent past are considered. This section concludes with Laughlin's "Hunting: An Integrating Biobehavior System and its Evolutionary Importance", which examines the role of hunting and the part it played in human evolutionary development. The reader wishing to pursue his interest in this topic may find David Pilbeam's *The Ascent of Man — An Introduction to Human Evolution,* MacMillan Co., 1972, of interest.

*The term hominid implies human-like characteristics to the exclusion of apes. In evolutionary terms hominid refers to those primates who diverged from the ape-like hominoids to form the human evolutionary line.

Origin of the Family of Man

"He who rejects with scorn the belief that the shape of his own canines, and their occasional great development in other men, are due to our early forefathers having been provided with these formidable weapons, will probably reveal, by sneering, the line of his descent."

"The early male forefathers of man were probably furnished with great canine teeth; but as they gradually acquired the habit of using stones, clubs, or other weapons for fighting with their enemies or rivals, they would use their teeth less and less. In this case, the jaws, together with the teeth, would become reduced in size."

—Charles Darwin, *The Descent of Man,* 1874.

The problem of the origin and evolution of Man is of perennial interest to scientists and laymen alike, but only recently have we begun to discern a mechanism to explain the evolutionary developments which fossil finds recovered over the last forty years have made apparent. In this article we intend to discuss briefly the fossil evidence relevant to the evolution of the human face and dentition, and to indicate the types of inference which may be made from this evidence. Our discussion will be confined to these features not because they are necessarily the most important and instructive parts of the anatomy of man and his relatives, but because paleontological investigation is inevitably concerned with those parts of the body preserved in the fossil record. Teeth and jaws, the former with their hard enamel coating, and the latter with their dense compact bone, are the most robust structures of the body and constitute the overwhelming bulk of the fossil record of many groups of extinct mammals. In the case of the fossil record of Man's forebears, the critical period of evolution between about 14 and 3 million years ago is represented only by jaws and teeth.

The human face and dentition forms a remarkable and unique adaptive complex—one that is in striking contrast to those of man's closest living relatives, the great apes (chimpanzee,

By E. Simons and Ian Tattersall. Reprinted with permission, from *Ventures,* Magazine of the Yale Graduate School, XI, No. 1, Spring 1971, pp. 47-55.

gorilla and orangutan), which retain a type of dentition apparently little modified from that which must have characterized the common ancestor of the apes and man. In the latter the tooth rows, and the face, are greatly abbreviated from front to back. The anterior teeth of man (the canines and incisors) are small, and have been integrated, as David Pilbeam of the Yale Anthropology Department has pointed out, into a single slicing unit. The posterior teeth (the premolars and molars) are comparatively broad and are shortened from front to back. The faces of apes, on the other hand, are long, reflecting a much greater tooth-row length, while their canines, especially those of the males, are enormously developed relative to those of man. Ape incisors are likewise typically enlarged.

In the characteristics induced by their usage, too, the teeth of apes differ from those of man. Apes (particularly the frugivorous chimpanzee and orangutan) use their incisors in food preparation, juicing soft fruits between their mobile lips and the front teeth. The incisors of apes thus generally receive much heavier wear than do those of man; the only exception to this seems to lie among certain groups of eskimos, who use their incisors in the preparation of animal skins. The shortening of the human tooth-rows is further emphasized during life by a phenomenon known as "mesial drift"; during powerful chewing, stresses are set up in the jaws which lead to the resorption of bone in front of each tooth, and deposition behind them. This shifting forward of the teeth is accompanied by wear at the contact points between adjacent teeth, and dental material is lost, thus abbreviating the tooth-rows still further. Although this "interstitial wear," as it is called, does occur in some apes, and can be found in old individuals, the process takes place much faster among primitive humans and prehumans and can readily be identified in individuals which have only slightly worn grinding (occlusal) surfaces on their teeth.

The oldest known fossil form whose dentition shows the complex of features, inherited and acquired, which characterizes man, is known as *Ramapithecus,* a name given it in 1934 by the Yale paleontologist G. Edward Lewis. *Ramapithecus* occurs primarily in deposits in North India and Kenya which are believed to have been laid down between 10 to 14 million years ago. The cheek-teeth of this short-faced animal, in contrast to those of contemporaneous apes, are steep-sided, with broad, relatively flat occlusal surfaces. They are closely packed together as a result of mesial drift and interstitial wear, and show a marked gradient of increasing wear on their occlusal surfaces from back to front. The implication of this is either that a more abrasive diet or more powerful chewing than that typical of the apes promoted faster wear, or that, as in man today, the eruption sequence of the molars was extended over a longer period of time, or a combination of both of these phenomena. Most strikingly, the canines and incisors were reduced in size, although the shape of the canine is reminiscent of that of its contemporaries among the apes. This last similarity is, however, only to be expected if *Ramapithecus* had been relatively recently derived from an animal classifiable as an ape.

A similar complex of features is to be found in the case of *Australopithecus*, a form descended from *Ramapithecus*, or a close relative, and known in Africa from about five to about one million years ago. There is more than one species of *Australopithecus*, and a good deal of variation between these species, but it is sufficient to point out here that they are all characterized to a greater or lesser extent by diminution of the anterior, and enlargement of the posterior, teeth. One group, in particular, possesses greatly expanded or "molarized" premolar teeth; the expansion of the cheek-teeth took the form of broadening, rather than lengthening, in order that the shortness of the face could be preserved. Later members of Hominidae, the zoological family of man, of which man is the only living representative, possess dentitions which are virtually identical to ours; they are, indeed, classified in our own genus, *Homo*.

In which other groups of mammals can we find a dental-facial complex characterized by emphasis on the grinding teeth and reduction of the facial skeleton? Strangely enough, among the elephants, whose fossil record reveals a very steady process through time of facial shortening and deepening in concert with elaboration of the grinding teeth. In fact, modern elephants have lost all their non-molar teeth other than a pair of upper incisors, retained in the form of tusks.

This development correlates with two highly significant features: the elephants' diet of tough herbage, and the fact that, like hominids, elephants do not depend on cropping (or shredding, or juicing) front teeth for the gathering and processing of vegetable food. Hominids convey food to their mouths with their hands, while elephants employ their trunks for this purpose.

The facial shortness of hominids and elephants is related to simple mechanical advantage in forms whose pattern of mastication involves strong horizontal grinding movements. For the purposes of a simplified analysis, the jaws may be viewed as a lever system, with the articulation between the skull and lower jaw as the fulcrum. Shortening of the face, bringing the bitepoint closer to the fulcrum, will reduce the resistance arm of the lever system, while the power arm is maximised by raising the articulation and moving the masses of the primary jaw-closing muscles forward. Since the efficiency of the lever system depends on the ratio of the length of the power arm to that of the resistance arm, maximal efficiency is achieved by the elephant-hominid arrangement.

Over the years a number of hypotheses have been propounded as to the critical change which set man's early ancestors on an evolutionary course divergent from that of the apes. Among these are: (1) the adoption of an upright bipedal posture, perhaps to allow the animals in question to see over tall savannah grasses, or to permit the efficient carrying of food; (2) the invention of tools; (3) the acquisition of language; (4) the development, for generally unstated reasons, of a large brain; and (5) the rather droll possibility, put forward before World War II by the Italian paleontologist Giuseppe Sera and more recently by the noted zoologist Sir Alistair Hardy, that the distinctive features of man are derived from a recent aquatic ancestry.

Recently, however, Clifford Jolly has proposed an alternative model for hominid origins which, even if more prosaic than most of those mentioned above, is a great deal more consistent with what we know of the origins of mammalian groups generally. Jolly's model is based on an analogy with the gelada baboon, perhaps the most terrestrial of all primates other than man himself. This animal, which today survives in the treeless high Semyen country of Ethiopia, was once widespread throughout Africa. In the gelada, as in the hominids, and particularly in many of the early fossil forms, the masticatory musculature is shifted forward, and the face deepened. The molar teeth of the gelada baboon possess expanded occlusal surfaces which, although they initially have a complex crown pattern, rapidly wear flat. The incisor teeth, again in analogy with the early hominids, are reduced. These features all appear to be correlates of a diet of small, tough morsels, the items of which are conveyed to the mouth via the hands. The flatness of the teeth can be explained in terms of their "grain-milling" effect, whereby small, hard particles are rolled between opposing teeth until their point of weakness is found. A diet of this type provides a good explanation for another feature of early hominid teeth: the thickness of their hard enamel covering. The cusps on the occlusal surface of early hominid cheek-teeth are frequently entirely composed of enamel, in consequence of which wear produced during chewing tended to reduce the teeth to flat surfaces. In cases where the enamel is less thick, perforation of this layer, with the consequent exposure of the softer dentine beneath, results in the formation of a series of basins on the tooth surface. This is the type of wear typically seen in apes; the relatively raised enamel edges so formed act as additional shearing edges for cutting vegetation.

Further similarities in the wear-patterns of gelada and hominid teeth lie in the wear gradient along the molar row already referred to in connection with *Ramapithecus*. In the case of the gelada the sharp increase in wear from back to front correlates with its exceptionally abrasive diet, but in the case of early hominids it was probably due in much greater degree to the delayed eruption sequencing of the teeth. It is known that the eruption of the third molars ("wisdom teeth") coincides in time with the attainment of skeletal maturity, so from dental wear it is possible to postulate that the delayed maturation characteristic of modern man was already present in his early ancestors. Further light has been thrown upon this subject by Alan Mann, who has studied the eruption sequence of the *Australopithecus* dentition by using radiographic techniques as well as by the examination of wear patterns. This study clearly demonstrated that, as in modern man, the period of development in *Australopithecus* was greatly extended, although the average age at death of an *Australopithecus* individual was little more than 18 years, and few individuals survived to the age of 40. Mesial drift, too, is evident in the gelada; as we have seen, this is a correlate of powerful chewing, but it also serves to provide an uninterrupted grinding surface and to prevent the formation of gaps within which food particles might lodge and serve as sites for the formation of cavities.

Although the canine teeth of living gelada baboons are not small in males, despite being reduced relative to those of other modern baboons, most of its extinct relatives, some of which attained sizes far greater than that of any present-day monkey, possessed relatively small canines. The origin of the reduced human canine is a question which has fascinated anthropologists for many years, and, following Darwin's speculation, it was popular to suppose that it was associated with the introduction of tool-use. However, canine reduction began among hominids many millions of years before we have any evidence that tools were made, and it seems much more reasonable to infer that the hominid canine was reduced, and also changed in morphology, so that it could form part of a biting complex. This explanation also has the advantage of providing a positive explanation of canine reduction, rather than relying on the theoretically questionable assumption of atrophy. The problem then becomes not "why do hominids have small canines?", but "why do apes have large ones?". As we have seen, male apes have much larger canines than do their female consorts and since male apes have been observed using their long canines to shred and strip vegetable matter, it has been supposed that canine size may correlate with diet. But male and female apes share the same diet, so this is unlikely unless males have to ingest a much greater volume of food, or unless they feed more dramatically on larger, more resistant stalks and branches.

Another theory is that since it is male apes which concern themselves with the defence of the social unit, and among which most intragroup aggression occurs, the size of their canines is related to these aggressive functions. This may indeed be so, but in fact apes have rarely been observed to use their canines in fighting, and it is clear that their social organisation is designed to reduce intra-group aggression to a minimum, potential fights being avoided by the adoption of stereotyped display behavior. At one time "yawning", the type of display in which large canines are most fully revealed, was interpreted as a component of aggressive display, but it is now thought that such behavior may in fact be more plausibly associated with ambivalent motivational states. This question must therefore remain unresolved at present.

Independent support for the small-object-feeding model of hominid origins comes, surprisingly enough, from among the lemurs, generally regarded as being among the most lowly of primates. Isolated for upwards of 50 million years on the island of Madagascar, the lemurs ("prosimian" or "lower" primates), evolved into a strikingly diversified array of forms, some of the most interesting of which have become extinct since the arrival, some 1,000 or 1,500 years ago, of man on Madagascar. *Hadropithecus,* currently under study by one of us, is the most advanced of these recently extinct forms. This animal bears in its dentition all the hallmarks of the gelada complex—high crowned, rapidly-worn and closely-packed grinding teeth with initially complex occlusal surfaces, together with greatly reduced canines and incisors—but possesses in addition a skull which is, especially in the facial region, far more reminiscent of that of man than is the skull of the gelada.

As the illustration shows, the face of *Hadropithecus* is deep, and short from front to back; it is, in fact, the shortest face of any mammal apart from man. The temporal muscle is shifted far forward, and the ascending ramus of the lower jaw vertically oriented. *Hadropithecus* therefore shares with man, to a far greater extent than does the gelada, the biomechanical advantages mentioned above. Studies of stress resolution in the skull of *Hadropithecus* projected for the future are also expected to show that the shortness of the face in this animal and the relation of this part of the cranial skeleton to the braincase are also, at least partially, related to the increased efficiency of force resolution during mastication.

Extrapolating from this postulated feeding behavior of early hominids, we can suggest a possible course of human emergence. *Ramapithecus,* the earliest known hominid, comes from deposits some 10 to 14 million years old, and has faunal associations which show it to have probably lived in a predominantly forested environment. *Australopithecus,* however, the earliest known representative of which is some five million years old, has been recovered from sites which represent environments ranging from open wooded savannah to dry grassland. Yet both forms show essentially similar feeding mechanisms. Evidently, then, early hominids, presumably the descendants of a strictly arboreal stock, were first tempted to the forest floor by food items of high nutritive content which occurred there. Primary among these would have been grains, tubers, roots and, possibly, meat. Only subsequently would hominids have moved to the forest fringes, then out into the open plains, in search initially of the same type of foodstuffs.

Traditionally, scientists have tended to assume that those features which today we take to be distinctively "human"—for instance uprightness, tool-making, possession of a large brain, language—would be those which would be found to characterize early hominids. This was one of the primary reasons why in the early years of this century the large-brained but fraudulent Piltdown "fossil" hominid was accepted as a human ancestor while, a decade later, the first, small-brained, skull of *Australopithecus* was almost unanimously rejected as a human ancestor by the scientific world. There is no evidence, however, that interpretations of the hominid fossil record leading to such conclusions are based on anything more than wish fulfillment on the part of their authors; the more prosaic hypothesis outlined above is far better in accord with both the fossil record of the hominids and with what is known of the origin of mammalian families in general.

The Taung Skull Revisited

When a rock containing a small fossil skull came into the hands of Raymond Dart, a young Australian anatomist, half a century ago, man's ideas about his own evolution were destined to change. Excavated by a miner from a lime works at Taung, a village about 400 miles southwest of Johannesburg, South Africa, the skull was embedded in calcified cave earth, or breccia. It reached Dart at the University of the Witwatersrand in Johannesburg, and for six weeks he chipped away the rock until—just before Christmas, 1924—he exposed the nearly complete skull of a child. With the uncovering of this fossil, Dart opened a series of controversies about human evolution that continues today.

The Taung fossil included the greater part of an endocranial cast (the impression of the interior of the brain case), a superbly preserved facial structure including both jaws, all twenty of the milk teeth, and the first of the permanent teeth to erupt—the upper and lower first molars.

Nothing like it had ever before been discovered. Scientists had dreamed of finding a "missing link," a fossil that might show features intermediate between those of apes and men. To Dart, the Taung skull showed just such features. It was a hitherto unprecedented amalgam of apelike and manlike features. He called the species to which the creature had belonged *Australopithecus africanus: austral,* meaning "southern"; -*pithecus* from the Greek -*pithekos,* meaning "monkey" or "ape."

His claims for the discovery were relatively modest as the wisdom of hindsight now shows. The fossil's structural features led Dart to claim that the creature was a higher primate belonging to an extinct ape species that had a number of features similar to those of man. The environment of Taung, the treeless verge of the Kalahari Desert, and the associated animal remains led Dart to ascribe to *Australopithecus* a way of life different from that of any extant for-

By Phillip V. Tobias. Reprinted with permission, from *Natural History* Magazine, December 1974, pp. 38-43. Copyright © 1974 by the American Museum of Natural History.

est-dwelling ape and approaching more closely that of early man.

A storm of controversy greeted the announcement, and his claims evoked arguments that were not settled until the lapse of twenty-five years and the discovery of many new australopithecine fossils in South and East Africa had produced a most compelling body of evidence. Yet, as early as 1925, Dart had had the insight, the vision, and the courage to assert that *Australopithecus* from Taung vindicated Charles Darwin's 1871 claim that Africa would prove to be the cradle of mankind.

In 1925 the prevailing climate of opinion about man's descent pointed to Asia, not Africa, as the birthplace of mankind. Just thirty-five years earlier, a Dutch surgeon and anatomist, Eugène Dubois, had found a fossilized skullcap, a thighbone, and sundry other remains in central Java, to which he had given the name *Pithecanthropus erectus,* upright ape-man of Java. The discoveries made by Dubois in Java between 1889 and 1895 helped to establish the belief that Asia had been the scene of homonid emergence.

At about the same time, China began to yield some tantalizing relics. Among various fossil fragments found in a Chinese drugstore, one specimen had been recognized as a fossil hominid tooth and traced to a cave near the village of Choukoutien. This led paleontologists to excavate the cave where they found fossil hominid bones, thus making China a possible source of human ancestors. The work of Davidson Black and, later, of Franz Weidenreich was subsequently to prove the former existence of Peking Man *(Homo erectus),* a close relative of Java Man.

The preconceived theories of man's origin were heavily weighted against the suggestion of the little-known young anatomist from the unlikely end of Africa. Not only was Dart's discovery made in the wrong part of the world; it was the wrong kind of creature.

Scientists of the time believed that the progressive enlargement and increasing complexity of the brain had been the chief element in the advance of some ancestral apes toward hominid status. The evolution of the teeth and the locomotor apparatus (pelvis, lower limbs, limb joints, ligaments, and muscles) supposedly evolved at the same rate as did the brain. Fanciful illustrations of slouching cave men with large teeth and projecting canines have perhaps not done justice to these imagined creatures. Presumably the spark of human genius was already present in these forefathers despite the gore-dripping manners and the "brutish" and "beastly" habits commonly ascribed to them.

Few propagated the view of the primacy of the brain more assiduously and convincingly than Dart's old teacher and former fellow-Australian, Sir Grafton Elliot Smith. As head of the Institute of Anatomy at University College, London, Elliot Smith had played a major role in giving Dart his first serious research opportunity in England and in getting a fellowship for him to study in the United States. Undoubtedly, Elliot Smith did much to inculcate in Dart the view that the brain was the focus of evolutionary advancement of both primates and man.

But when the principal actor strode onto the stage, the audience gasped. He was not at all what had been expected. The Taung skull had a *small* brain of apish dimensions, and its canines did not project like an ape's but were reduced like a human child's. The confusing creature's posture was appreciably more erect than that of modern apes judging by the relatively forward position of the orifice in the base of the skull through which the spinal cord passes. The Taung individual's teeth as well as its locomotor apparatus appeared to be in the vanguard of hominization, while the brain itself was lagging—at least in size.

The fossil from Taung forced Dart away from the teachings of his old mentor and to the realization that brain enlargement was not the first step in human evolution. Of course, size is not everything, and Dart drew attention to features of the endocranial cast that pointed to a human-like reorganization of the brain substance itself. It looked more like a miniature human brain than an immature ape brain.

With the Taung fossil defying all expectations, Dart's claims proved a hard pill for most scientists to swallow and caused them to argue for decades over the merits and demerits of according hominid status to the species Dart called *Australopithecus africanus*.

While Dart's discovery forced him to defy the

doctrines of the day, basing his claims on a child's skull made his mission much harder. The state of eruption of the fossil's teeth was typical of a six-year-old modern human or a four-year-old modern chimpanzee. Perhaps the Taung child was about five years old when he died.

Had the first *Australopithecus* discovered been an adult, Dart's task of convincing an incredulous world would have been far easier as the full characteristics of a hominid do not appear until puberty. Yet Dart read the signs of mankind in the child, while the rest of the world waited to be convinced by the discovery of an adult hominid.

The wait lasted twelve years. In 1936, Robert Broom, one of Dart's colleagues and supporters, discovered a skull of an adult *Australopithecus* at Sterkfontein, not far from Johannesburg. Later finds and analyses confirmed that the australopithecines were indeed on the pathway to hominization. Dart's own work suggested that these creatures began using and making tools, an ability that implies a dependence upon cultural activities. As well as biological inheritance by genes, *Australopithecus* was beginning to rely upon a social heritage, the passing of collective wisdom through teaching and example.

Today there are hundreds of specimens of early hominids that have been wrested from the earth at five locations in South Africa, three in Tanzania, six in Kenya, and two in Ethiopia. The total number of individuals represented by the growing stockpile of fossils now runs to several hundred. Fossil teeth alone number well over 1,000. Vertebrae, pelves, and limb bones have supplemented skulls and teeth. Our ideas about these early hominids become more complete every year. Already we know that more than one kind of creature existed.

Paleontologists are now able to compare specific bones of one fossil group with those of other fossil groups, later man, and apes. They can also study the form and size of the brains and the development of teeth.

The australopithecines had small brains and large premolars and molars. But even within this genus of the Hominidae, there are two or three species. One species had a light frame, slender muscles, a small jaw, and, in contrast, fairly large incisors and canines. This gracile species is usually called *Australopithecus africanus*.

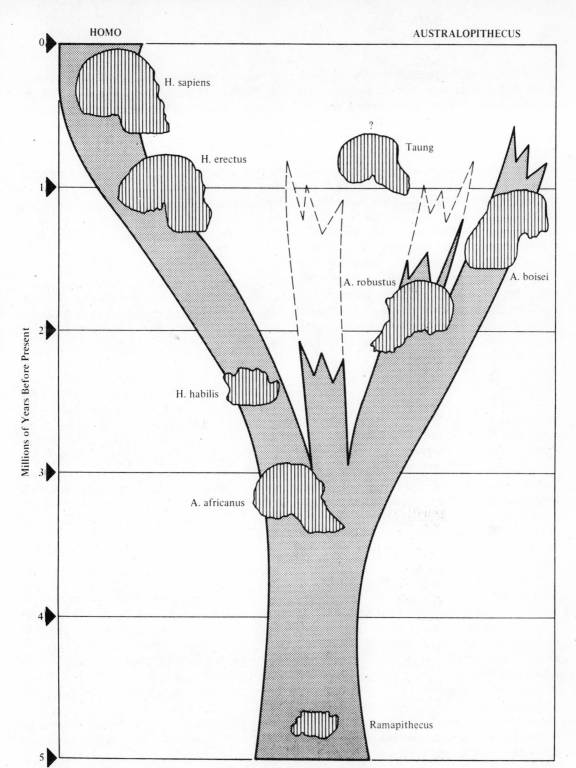

Figure 1. Paleontologists have traditionally dated the Taung child's skull at about 2.5 million years and have classified the fossil as that of a gracile australopithecine, the hominid species that evolved to modern man. But because recent geologic evidence suggests that the skull is less than one million years old, the Taung child may have been one of the last of the robust australopithecines, another hominid species whose million-year old remains were discovered in East Africa.

Another australopithecine species, although probably not taller, was sturdier. Its front teeth were on the small side, but its molars and premolars were very large indeed; also its jaws were much heavier, its muscles more beefy, and its body weight almost certainly greater. To this robust kind of ape-man scientists have given the name *Australopithecus robustus*. In East Africa, the robust form reached such hefty and Herculean proportions that some regard it as representing another species called *Australopithecus boisei*. The two robust australopithecines, however, are fairly closely related to each other.

Specimens of another early hominid have features that distinguish them from *Australopithecus*. More particularly, their brain cases are enlarged (both absolutely and in relation to their medium-sized bodies) 50 to 70 percent above those of *Australopithecus africanus*. The associated limb bones suggest that they may have been even better adapted to standing upright and walking on two legs than was *Australopithecus*. There is evidence that although australopithecines began to use tools, this other early hominid was the first to make stone tools systematically and with a consistent pattern.

Paleontologists have thus classified it as belonging to *Homo*, the hominid genus to which modern man *(Homo sapiens)* belongs. One kind of early *Homo* is named *Homo habilis*, another is the extinct *Homo erectus*, and the third, the extant *Homo sapiens*.

With six possible species of hominids—three of *Australopithecus* and three of *Homo*—and with five of these six species extinct, which of them were our ancestors? A study of the anatomy may provide answers to this question, although it is essential to know the time periods in which each fossil group existed to gain a clearer picture of man's evolution.

Dating used to be matter of sheer guesswork. From the fossil animal bones found along with the hominids at a particular site like Sterkfontein, one could say that this site contained an older, or earlier, fauna than that of Kromdraai, another hominid site in South Africa. Scientists could not tell, however, how much earlier, although guesses were plentiful. Recently, new techniques have made more precise dating possible.

The first important conclusion is that hominid fossils date back at least five million years, although relics older than three million years are scanty and come from only two or three sites. South and East Africa, however, have provided substantial numbers of fossils that are three million years old or less. Any hypothesis about what happened earlier than three million years ago is bound to remain uncertain until more fossils are unearthed from these depths of time.

Although not all of the six species existed at the same time, for a very large part of the period between one and three million years ago, a gracile form and a robust form of hominid coexisted in Africa. If all the known early hominids are plotted according to species, area, and time, a pattern of populations emerges. From this pattern, a phylogeny, or family tree, of man takes shape.

The tree's upper branches are more certain than its trunk, which various scientists have drawn with different lengths. Some suggest a relatively short trunk with its roots placed some five to eight million years ago. This view is supported by the evidence that the protein molecules and the DNA of man and the chimpanzee are astonishingly similar, suggesting that they diverged fairly recently. As we have few good hominid fossils from this period, the theory remains unconfirmed.

Others propose a longer hominid family tree trunk with roots that go further back in time. In this commonly held view, the gracile lineage was ancestral and can be traced back to some higher primates called *Ramapithecus*, which lived in India and Africa about twelve to fourteen million years ago in the Miocene epoch. Another view regards the robust lineage as ancestral and places its roots in a species of *Gigantopithecus*, which existed in India about twelve million years ago.

The missing links in the chain of evidence lie in the rock strata deposited between twelve million and three million years ago. The next crucial breakthrough in our understanding of hominid origins will certainly result from discoveries in those ancient layers of Miocene and Pliocene rocks.

In the branches of the hominid family tree, the evidence suggests that by three million years ago, the ancestral *Australopithecus* had given rise to the first members of *Homo*. Disproportionate enlargement and restructuring of the brain and the presence of the first stone tools mark the emergence of this wholly new and freakish trend in hominid evolution leading to man.

About the same time or soon after, the ancestral hominid gave rise to another line of development. An increasing dependence on larger and larger premolars and molars with accompanying hypertrophy of the jaws and the chewing muscles marked this species. In South Africa, this trend attained modest proportions in *Australopithecus robustus;* in East Africa it reached a crescendo in the aggrandized *Australopithecus boisei*. Both of these closely related robust lineages seem to have died out about one million years ago and apparently made no contribution to modern man. On the other hand, the early *Homo* of three to two million years ago subsequently carried the trend of cerebral increase still further, giving rise to *Homo erectus* between two and one million years ago. Between 500,000 and 100,000 years ago, *Homo erectus* gave way to *Homo sapiens*.

Australopithecus africanus, in this view, spawned two major offshoots—*Homo* and the robust lineages. Did the gracile australopithecine itself persist alongside these two sets of possible competitors? There is little or no trace of such persistence—except perhaps for the Taung child.

Until recently, there was little real information about the age of any of the South African australopithecine caves. None of the five sites in the Transvaal and Cape Province contained undisturbed materials suitable for radioisotope dating; however, the faunal remains discovered with the australopithecine remains at each site could indicate the relative ages—the oldest and the youngest—of the hominid fossils. In East Africa, paleontologists have correlated the faunal remains with potassium-argon dates enabling them to describe the kinds of pigs and elephants living at each stage during the past five million years. By comparing fossils of similar species found in South African sites with those of East Africa, they have been able to infer that the fauna of Makapansgat and Sterkfontein in the Transvaal corresponded to that living in Kenya

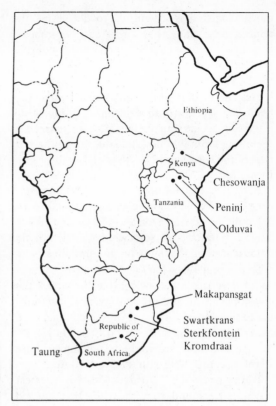

two and a half to three million years ago. Similarly, the fauna accompanying the Swartkrans australopithecines matches the East African fauna of about two million years ago. Such comparisons have not yet proved possible for Taung because the fauna there, save for baboons, is relatively sparse.

For many years paleontologists regarded Taung as the oldest of the five South African sites. Yet the evidence for this view was slender, based mainly on sketchy samples of small mammals. Lawrence Wells of Cape Town has questioned the traditional view for nearly a decade and has concluded from his studies of the Taung fauna that the Taung site is more recent than was believed. It could indeed be contemporary with the youngest of the other four South African sites. Until recently his view was overlooked by most paleontologists, who continued to regard Taung as the oldest South African australopithecine site.

Two new lines of evidence within the past year have strongly confirmed Wells's view. Timothy C. Partridge, a young South African geomorphologist, has attempted to determine the approximate date that the *Australopithecus*-bearing limestone caves opened to the exterior. By gradual extension of underground cavities in the limestone formations, hastened by roof collapses and erosion of the land surface, subterranean caves acquire an external opening. Only after this occurs can surface-derived materials, including animal bones and soil, fall to the bottom of the cave and begin the process of breccia formation.

Partridge has found that the Makapansgat cave opened 3.7 million years ago; Sterkfontein, 3.3 million; and Swartkrans, 2.6 million. Partridge's dates are all somewhat older than the dates placed on the fauna in the same sites.

That is precisely what one would expect. For it would have taken a considerable time *after* the caves opened for the breccia layers to accumulate to the level at which the pigs, elephants, and australopithecines were found. His dates, although stormily received by geologists, are therefore compatible with the faunal dates.

Taung provided Partridge with his greatest surprise; he found that the cave had opened within the past 900,000 years. This astonishingly recent date confirms Wells's claims that the Taung fauna points to a much younger age than was formerly believed.

In another recent study, Karl Butzer of the University of Chicago has meticulously restudied the sequence of geologic events at Taung and, by comparing them with sequences elsewhere, has concluded that the Taung deposit may be younger than that of Swartkrans and Kromdraai.

If these claims prove correct and the date of the opening of the Taung cave is indeed more recent than 900,000 years ago, the age of the Taung australopithecine skull could well be less than 800,000 years. It may be only three-quarters of a million years old, for it came from a part of the Taung breccia appreciably higher than, and therefore younger than, the oldest breccia formed after the opening of the cave. This would make the Taung skull the latest surviving australopithecine in Africa.

In East Africa, the most recent australopithecine deposits are those of Peninj in northern Tanzania and Chesowanja in central Kenya.

Both have been dated to just over one million years old. Both, incidentally, have yielded fossilized bones of robust australopithecines, evidence that the robust hominid lineage survived long after the gracile australopithecines gave way to *Homo*.

Does the recent age of Taung change its status? Most paleontologists have classified the gracile hominids of Sterkfontein and Makapansgat as belonging to the same species as Taung—*Australopithecus africanus*. Yet the new evidence of the recency of the Taung skull places two million years between it and the earalier gracile ape-men of Sterkfontein and Makapansgat.

There are several possibilities to explain this wide interval. While *Australopithecus africanus* was evolving into *Homo* in East Africa, a southerly branch of the species may have persisted in South Africa for another couple of million years as a relict population of living fossils. Or perhaps, by chance, the later hominid finds dated to the two-million-year interval just do not include any gracile australopithecines.

For a number of years I have questioned whether it is correct to assign the juvenile Taung and the gracile hominids of Makapansgat and Sterkfontein to the same species. The prepubertal status of Taung makes comparison with the adult and adolescent specimens of those other sites difficult. The only permanent teeth that can be compared are the upper and lower first molars, while there are not many milk teeth from either the gracile or the robust australopithecines that can be compared with the Taung teeth. So I worried about whether Taung was or was not the same kind of creature.

The young date of Taung has justified my worries. If a gap of two million years really exists between the Taung skull and the others and if they are in the same lineage, how are we to account for this lengthy survival of the species when all around were hominizing into *Homo* or specializing into *robustus*?

At the chronological level to which Taung has now been provisionally assigned, the only other hominids known are the last of the robust australopithecines and *Homo erectus*. Was Taung a third surviving hominid contemporary with these others, as our existing views maintain? I suggest rather that it could represent one or the other of the two well-known groups of hominids that were its contemporaries. Clearly, brain size and facial and dental morphology would rule out Taung's being *Homo erectus*. There remains the last of the robust hominids. The hypothesis that Taung represents a juvenile robust australopithecine would recognize what the fossil record suggests—the early extinction of the gracile australopithecines, not long after some of their populations had evolved into early *Homo*.

The suggestion that Taung may belong to the robust line is the subject of a new heated controversy, just as it was half a century ago. But argument, rhetoric, and vituperation will not solve the problem. Only a new and meticulous study of the Taung skull, in comparison with the other early hominid juveniles now available from both South and East Africa, will permit Dart's child of 1924 to show itself in its true colors.

These days, when I look at the Taung skull in my laboratory. I imagine I detect a light Mona Lisa-like smile—or is it a smirk?—crossing its million-year-old, fifty-year-old, five-year-old face. The child of Taung must have chuckled in 1924 at the preconceived notions his frail bones had overthrown. Just so, in my mind's eye he laughs again in 1974, as big, grown men grapple anew with his mystifying identity.

Archeology in the Turkana District, Kenya

For many years scientists have noted that northwest Kenya was likely to be a very important area for archeological research. In particular, the Turkana District, which connects East Africa with the Sudan and Ethopia, has long intrigued scholars *(1)*. Nevertheless, because of the remoteness of the region, very little systematic fieldwork has been done there. Recent investigations, however, are shedding much new light on the area *(2)*. In this article, I review the archeological sequence and present original data bearing on the cultural relations between East Africa and the middle Nile Valley during the Holocene.

THE TURKANA ENVIRONMENT

Turkana is sharply demarcated by the Rift Valley escarpment on the west and Lake Rudolf on the east (Fig. 1). Within this natural corridor connecting the Sudan to East Africa is a sun-parched landscape of flat plains broken by low volcanic ranges. The central part of Turkana is a desert, with a sparse cover of vegetation, areas of shifting sand dunes, and an annual rainfall of less than 6 inches. In a general way, the remainder of the Turkana District can be described as semidesert. The two major exceptions to this description are the tops of the higher mountain ranges and the main river valleys, where dense fringing vegetation is found.

Judging from the desert conditions and the present scarcity of big game animals, Turkana would appear to have been a marginal subsistence area for Stone Age hunter-gatherers or Iron Age agricultural peoples. However, Turkana has only recently become a desert. Much of the deterioration of the landscape is due to the combination of overgrazing and the strong, daily winds that sweep back the sand from the retreating shoreline of the lake. I have asked many Turkana elders about conditions during their

By L. Robbins. Reprinted with permission, from *Science,* 176, 28 April 1972, pp. 359-66. Copyright © 1972 by the American Association for the Advancement of Science.

boyhood and during their fathers' times. Without exception, the countryside of southcentral Turkana, now extremely desiccated, was said to have been greener, and big game animals abundant. There was grass where there is none today, and animals such as buffalo, giraffe, zebra, rhinoceros, and elephant were found where they are no longer evident. This picture of recent change in southcentral Turkana is duplicated for parts of northern Turkana in the records of various military and early scientific expeditions *(3)*.

Further in the past, there is a very long record of environmental change in the Pleistocene. Although there are no rivers draining Lake Rudolf today, a Nilotic fauna attests to former connections with the Nile's drainage system. Geological and faunal evidence indicates that the ancient lake extended into the Lotigipi Depression in northern Turkana and was drained by the Sobat River, a tributary of the Nile *(4)*. Ancient beachlines can be found as much as 10 miles to the west of the present lakeshore and over 300 feet above the present water level of the lake. These beaches are often characterized by an abundance of archeological remains.

EARLY MAN: THE DAWN OF TOOL-MAKING

In recent years, the Lake Rudolf basin has been yielding spectacular finds about early man. Remains of early hominids have been discovered at Omo in southern Ethopia, in the East Rudolf area, and in Turkana *(5, 6)*.

With regard to the Turkana finds, Australopithicine remains were found at two sites. The oldest fragment was found at Lothagam (2.55°N, 36.4°E) and is believed to date back about 5.5 million years, or to the Pliocene *(7)*. This is the earliest Australopithicine on record. At Kanapoi, which is about 35 miles from Lothagam, an Australopithicine fragment was discovered by Patterson *(6)*. The age of Kanapoi has recently been re-evaluated, and it is now believed to date back about 4 million years, or to Late Pliocene times.

The absence of stone artifacts in Turkana's very extensive Pliocene beds, which are about 4 to 8 million years old, and the appearance in

East Rudolf of well-made stone tools, which are about 2.6 million years old, indicate that archeologists are closing in on the dawn of recognizable technology. It appears that formalized stone tool-making was initiated between 3 and 4 million years ago.

In Turkana, pebble tools of the Oldowan type can be found on the surface in many localities, but the age of these tools is open to question. In fact, some of these implements have been found in Late Stone Age, post-Pleistocene contexts in association with pottery *(8)*. It is interesting that these oldest of technological items were among the most successful inventions, for they continued to be manufactured throughout the entire Stone Age.

HAND AXES—
ANCIENT OR RECENT?

In the 1930's, scholars were intrigued by the possibilities of relating the ancient beaches of the East African lakes to the European Pleistocene glacial sequence *(9)*. It was reasoned that high water levels of lakes resulted from increased rainfall during Pleistocene pluvial episodes in East Africa. Fuchs, working in Turkana, used archeological evidence as one means for dating the ancient lake beds of Lake Rudolf according to the pluvial sequence *(10)*. Since tools described as Chellean and Acheulian were found on the ancient lake deposits, he reasoned that the beds dated to pluvial episodes of the Middle Pleistocene. Assumptions of this type, in which geological events are determined on the basis of artifacts, can lead to a confusion of the evidence. Beaches considered to be Pleistocene have recently surprised workers in the field with pottery in situ and Holocene radiocarbon dates.

Whereas many of the artifacts found on the ancient beaches of Lake Rudolf resemble hand axes, they are not, in fact, Pleistocene in origin. Along the old lake beds in central Turkana, it is possible to find bifacially flaked tools, that, at first glance, closely resemble hand axes. However, having collected a full range of these surface artifacts from Holocene lake beds, I find that about 10 percent of them would pass for hand axes, while the remaining 90 percent are clearly different (Fig. 2, Nos. 1, 2). These tools

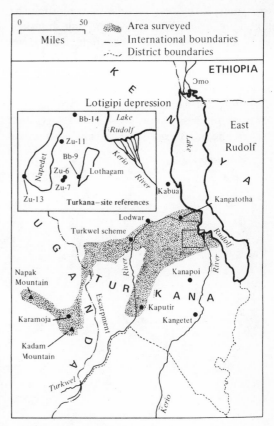

Figure 1.   Map of the area surveyed.

resemble West African Neolithic hoes *(11)*. At this point, I do not claim that the tools are related to the West African finds, nor that they functioned as hoes, but they are most likely post-Pleistocene in origin. Further evidence of the recentness of hand axe-like tools comes from the Omo, where three hand axes were recovered from river sands and gravels coeval to Kibish formation member IVa, which has been radiocarbon dated back about 8900 years *(12)*.

No Acheulian sites have been excavated in Turkana, although sites have been reported for Ngakoriangora Mountain and the adjacent southern Sudan *(13)*. I have found occasional hand axes in central Turkana, but have not yet seen a hand axe in situ there. One possible explanation for the sporadic occurrence of hand axes and the lack of well-defined sites follows: during Middle and Probably Upper Pleistocene times, an enlarged Lake Rudolf would have been an attractive place for Stone Age hunter-gatherers. Some of the early beaches surrounding the lake were, in all likelihood, camping, hunting, and watering areas for Acheulian man. However, according to Walsh, some of the earlier beach levels have been eroded by the water level's rising to 220 feet in the Holocene *(14)*. Therefore, the early sites may well have been destroyed by erosion and the tools redeposited. Hence, the hand axes occur as isolated finds on the same surface where the more recent Late Stone Age peoples have also left behind their flaking debris.

THE UPPER PLEISTOCENE

The Acheulian is followed by a period of regional specialization in the prehistoric cultures of sub-Saharan Africa. One of the best known of

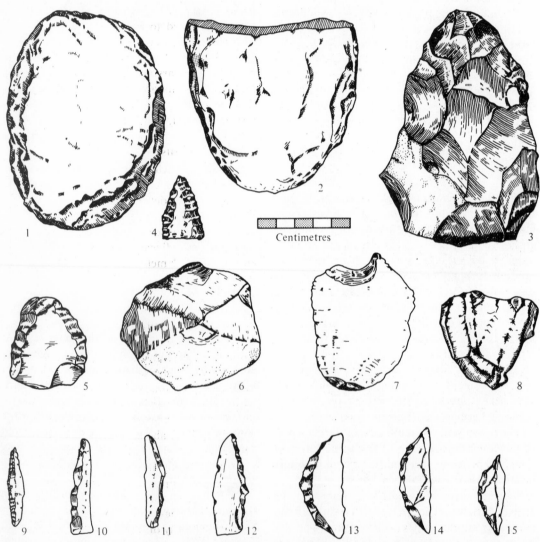

Figure 2.   Stone artifacts: (1, 2) bifacial tools of probable Holocene origin, Zu-12, Zu-6; (3) core ax, Zu-13; (4) bifacial point, Bb-9; (5) prepared core, Zu-7, northwest quadrant, 2 to 10 centimeters deep; (6) chopper, Zu-7, northwest quadrant, 2 to 10 centimeters deep; (7) notched flake, Zu-7, northwest quadrant; (8) blade core, Zu-12; (9) blade backed from two directions, Zu-11; (10, 11) backed blades, Zu-11; (12) backed blade, Zu-12; (13-15) large crescents, Zu-12. All artifacts are lava except (4), which is chert. Proveniences are surface, unless stated otherwise.

the new, Upper Pleistocene regional variants is the Sangoan industry, which has been dated back 46,000 to 37,000 years. The Sangoan industry is often considered one of the earliest adaptations to tropical forest conditions in Africa. The characteristic heavy-duty tools are believed to have been used for woodworking, and sites are distributed in the low-lying riverine and lacustrine areas of Central Africa.

In Turkana, the Sangoan industry appears to be represented at a number of localities. Here again, no sites have been fully excavated, and there are no available radiocarbon dates. Whitworth, for example, has reported Sangoan artifacts from near the Kabua waterhole in central Turkana [15]. Tools described as crude hand axes were found on the surface of ancient lake sediments. In adidition to the artifacts, human skeletal material described as Neanderthaloid was recovered from the site. An Upper Pleistocene age has been suggested for the skeletal material, largely on the basis of faunal remains and the proximity of surface artifacts believed to be Pleistocene in origin [16]. However, oral tradition and archeological evidence indicate that most of the animals positively identified at Kabua survived until quite recently in Turkana. In addition, a range of Late Stone Age microliths and Holocene bone harpoon points were found on the surface at Kabua. For the above reasons, the exact age of the Kabua hominid is still unresolved.

We have discovered one possible Sangoan locality at site Zu-13, just west of the Napedet hills [17]. The tools, which were recovered from the surface, include core axes, choppers, push planes, and heavy-duty scrapers (Fig. 2, No. 3). All of these finds resemble the heavy-duty tools found on Sangoan sites. An outstanding feature of this site is the approximately 141 stone circles arranged in four arc-shaped complexes. According to Turkana elders, the circles may represent an ancient, pre-Turkana site, an Ethiopian outpost, or a colonial military camp. Excavations have not yet resolved this problem because there is little identifiable artifactual debris in the circles.

The Lupemban industries, derived from the Sangoan, existed in Central Africa during Late Pleistocene times (from approximately 36,000 to 14,000 years ago) and are also described as adaptations to the tropical forest. Typical artifacts are lance points, which are possibly derived from the earlier Sangoan core axes. Some writers have attributed bifacial points found on the surface in Turkana to the Lupemban [15]. However, I have found isolated points resembling both Lupemban and Stillbay artifacts in central Turkana on the surface of lake beds that are clearly Holocene. The example shown in Fig. 3 (No. 4) was recovered from the surface of lake sediments dated to about 8230 years ago [18]. Another point was recovered from the surface of sands overlying shell beds dated to approximately 6010 years ago [19]. While it is possible that these points are Late Pleistocene artifacts that were subsequently reused, it is best not to attribute broad, regional cultural affinities to a little-known area on the basis of the typology of a few stone points [20].

As for other Upper Pleistocene industries, I have located a site (Zu-7) eroding from a blowout east of Napedet. Much to my regret, there is no way to date site Zu-7 in absolute years because of the absence of material that can be dated by the radiocarbon method. However, the site is about 2 meters lower in elevation than nearby Holocene lake sediments dated to approximately 7960 years ago [21]. This suggests that the material could be Late Pleistocene. In addition, the artifacts were generally more heavily weathered and larger than comparable samples collected from the Holocene sediments. At Zu-7, a 1-meter square was completely excavated, in quadrants, from the surface to a depth of 15 centimeters, where the material was solidly embedded. Approximately 900 lava artifacts were recovered, about 10 percent of which were formally shaped tools. The implements were characterized by heavy-duty scrapers (25 percent) and choppers (25 percent) (Fig. 2, Nos. 5–7). Blades and microliths were absent at this site, whereas they were present with varying frequency on many of the surrounding, later sites. In terms of the stone technology represented, the assemblage provides a perfect ancestral candidate for many of the Holocene industries in the same area. Holocene industries are often characterized by choppers and scrapers, but also include several important new items: blades, microliths, pottery, and, in some cases, bone points.

THE EARLY HOLOCENE

The Early Holocene includes much of the Late Stone Age (Fig. 3). While each geographical area deserves its own special terminology, a shift toward more intensive exploitation of local food resources is evident in many areas of the prehistoric world after the close of the Pleistocene. For example, one finds specialized fishing peoples utilizing the lakes and rivers more fully than ever before, while other groups are specialized as intensive gatherers of particualr kinds of seeds, nuts, wild grasses, and so on. Archeologically, this period of increased local specialization is often marked by the proliferation of microliths, which reflect the use of composite tools, as well as grinding stones and pottery.

In Turkana, Late Stone Age industries are very well represented and exceedingly diverse in

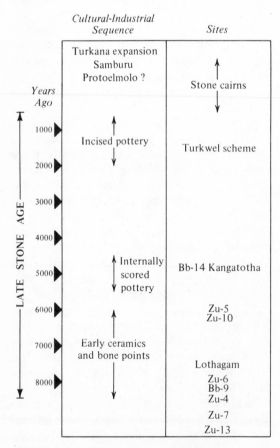

Figure 3. Suggested chronology for
             southcentral Turkana.

character. Those who study African prehistory have traditionally defined these complexes on the basis of similarities and differences in the stone tools found at various sites. Characteristic tool types define a complex as Wilton, Capsian, and so on. Unfortunately, these entities are sometimes treated as distinct cultures, as if different ethnic groups were involved. While "Wilton equals prehistoric Bushman" might be a good equation for some areas, it could be misleading for others, particularly where the human skeletal morphology is not Boskopoid *(22)*. It would be easy to distinguish, on the basis of tool typology, four or five Late Stone Age industries for central Turkana alone. Some sites have a great many microlithic tools, while others have large blades and few microliths. Still others have more flake tools and choppers. Preliminary observations suggest that much of this variation in lithic assemblages is a result of the fact that the tools were functionally specific for certain tasks and activities, as well as dependent on the kinds of raw materials available.

I believe that the pottery, rather than the lithics, will be the more sensitive indicator of chronological, spatial, and, possibly, real ethnic relations. The pottery associated with Late Stone Age industries in Turkana is richly varied in terms of design style and general level of sophistication. Although much of the material comes from surface surveys and has not yet been fully studied, the following information on the early ceramics is important *(23)*.

I have discovered pottery that is surprisingly old for East Africa. At site Zu-4, near Lothagam, I have excavated stamped pottery from a shell bed dated back about 8420 years *(24)*. This early date is supported by evidence from site Zu-6, where stamped and single wavy line sherds have been excavated from Holocene lake beds dated back approximately 7960 years *(21)*. In addition to the above, I have excavated over 800 undecorated sherds from Lothagam. Some of these sherds have been found in lake deposits dated back about 7500 years, although the main complex is later *(25)*. The dates cited relate very well to the Omo Valley sequence established by Butzer *et al. (26)*. The Omo data suggest that the general time span for the pottery corresponds to the maximum stage and subsequent regression of Holocene Lake Rudolf from Kibish formation member IVa.

My evidence proves beyond any doubt that pottery was being used in sub-Saharan Africa before the arrival of food production techniques. The data indicate that at least three different styles of pottery were present at an early food-collecting horizon in southcentral Turkana. As far as I know, neither of the two decorated styles has a counterpart elsewhere in East Africa. However, some of this pottery is similar to material from the Nile Valley settlement of Early Khartoum in the Sudan *(27)*. The ceramic resemblances are strongly reinforced by stylistic similarities in the barbed bone points found in both areas. For example, the unique point in Fig. 4 (lower right) has the same cross-hatching that some Khartoum points have.

Archeologists have long recognized that the Khartoum adaptation, which was based upon the intensive exploitation of riverine and lakeside resources, extended far into the moister Holocene environments of the Sahara *(28)*. My data confirm the fact that the Late Stone Age peoples of Lake Rudolf shared in that adaptive pattern. The great density of sites, along with the early ceramic diversity and the radio-carbon dates, suggests that the Lake Rudolf basin was an early center for this cultural adaptation.

The general way of life associated with the early Holocene cultural pattern in Turkana centered on intensive fishing. People exploited the rich resources of an enlarged and fresher lake. In the Lothagam area, this lake was fresh enough to support at least eight different kinds of mollusks, whereas only one form is found in the modern lake *(29)*. The people speared or harpooned large Nile perch in the shallows with their ingeniouly fashioned bone and ivory points. They also caught several kinds of catfish, including *Clarias, Synodontis,* and *Bagras.* The more than 300 bone and ivory artifacts that were discovered attest to the importance of fishing equipment in the technology. At Lothagam, these points were associated with a fauna that was almost entirely fish *(30)*. In addition to the fish, the marshy lake edge offered soft-shelled turtle, crocodile, cane rat, and hippopotamus. The diet was supplemented by the meat of animals such as wart hog, zebra, buffalo, reedbuck, dik-dik, topi, hartebeest, and giraffe *(31)*.

The people of this period buried their dead in a flexed position on sand spits close to the water's edge, a custom similar to that of the El-molo tribe in East Rudolf. I have not found any elaborate grave goods in the excavations, although there are occasional sherds and chipped stone artifacts. Perhaps this implies a relatively egalitarian social structure. One individual appears to have met a violent death—a small, sharp, stone flake was found embedded between his ribs.

The available information suggests that this way of life spanned much of the early Holocene. Bone harpoon points have been recovered from Kibish IVa sediments dated back about 9100 years, and I have excavated from site Zu-10 wavy line pottery dated back approximately 6200 years *(26, 32)*. Just how long this cultural pattern continued after the latter date has not yet been determined. The Turkana oral tradition indicates that a distinct fishing people occupied the lakeshore near Lothagam sometime before 1800. Perhaps these were the ancestors of the Elmolo, a modern lakeside fishing tribe first observed on the eastern shore in 1888 *(33)*. Before this time, the Elmolo, who fish with iron harpoons, were widely distributed along the east shore of Lake rudolf, and it is reasonable to believe that they inhabited the western shore before the expansion of the modern pastoral peoples and the introduction of firearms.

THE EMERGENCE OF FOOD PRODUCTION

The stages of high water levels of Lake Rudolf in the Holocene may, in part, correlate with a moist episode that is reflected in radiocarbon-dated pollen profiles as far apart as Sacred Lake on Mount Kenya and various localities in the Sahara *(34)*. Between 5000 and 6000 years ago, portions of the Sahara were favorable enough to support groups of people who kept domestic stock. It is believed that desiccation of the Sahara encouraged the spread of pastoralism and, presumably, food cultivation into new areas. It was probably about this time that the idea of food production began to filter down from the

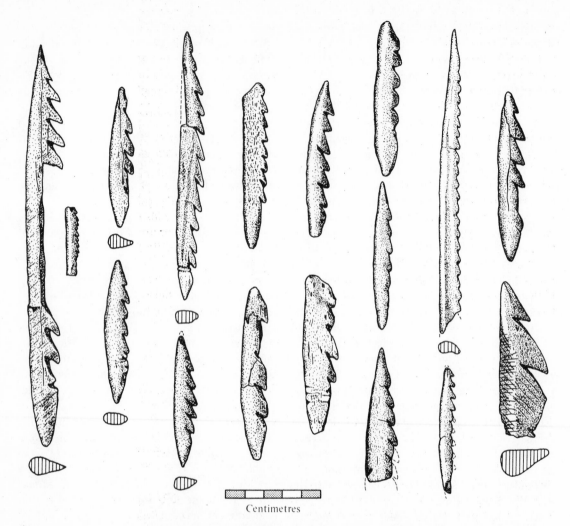

Centimetres

Figure 4.   Bone artifacts from Lothagam, with range of variation. Surface of shell beds dated to approximately 7500 years ago. The lower right specimen has Khartoum-style decoration.

north. Precisely when and where food production entered East Africa remains to be established *(35)*.

Thus far, no sites with bones of domestic animals or with direct evidence of cultivation have been reported for Turkana.

Pottery characterized by internal scoring and basketwork-like impressions on the exterior is widely distributed between the lower Turkwel and Kerio river valleys (Fig. 5, No. 3). Elsewhere in Kenya this material, which has been termed Gumban A, was linked with the stone bowl culture and was presumed to indicate the beginning of food production in East Africa. However,

Cohen has shown that, in the reported sites, there are no dates available for the Gumban A, nor are there any actual associations with stone bowls *(35, 36)*. At Kangatotha, on the lower Turkwel, I have found Gumban A pottery on the surface of lake sediments dated back 4800 years *(37)*. I have also found this pottery, as well as sherds of other kinds of pottery, on the surface of site Bb-14, which is located south of Kangatotha, overlooking the Lorengalup River. Here the setting strongly suggests that the sherds have been eroding out from the deposits. An archeological feature consisting of solid lumps of charred clay was definitely eroding from the site.

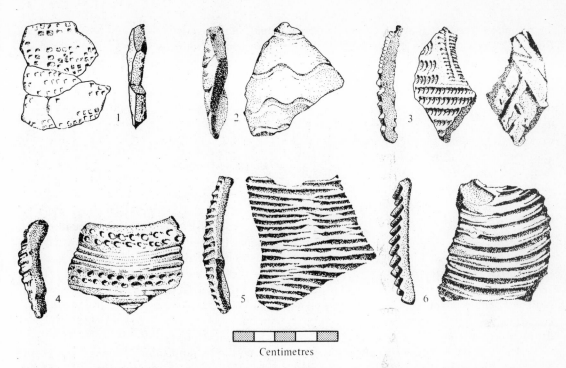

Figure 5. Pottery: (1) stamped, Zu-6, 10 to 20 centimeters deep; (2) single wavy line, Zu-6, 30 to 40 centimeters deep; (3) scored, Zu-4, surface; (4) incised rim, Turkwel scheme, embedded in surface sands; (5, 6) incised, Turkwel scheme, embedded in surface sands.

This feature has been radiocarbon dated to 5020 years ago, a date that is in close accord with the Kangatotha date *(38)*. If these dates are applicable to the scored pottery, then the pottery is much earlier than one might have suspected. It is possible that the Turkana material could be derived from earlier forms of stamped pottery in the Lake Rudolf basin. To the north, in the Omo area, impressed pottery has been found in sediments dated back about 5450 years *(39)*.

Gumban sherds are found in conjunction with a variety of tool complexes. At Kangatotha, for example, the pottery occurs on the same surface with fine microlithic tools made from chert and chalcedony agates. These artifacts, which do not appear to be culturally mixed or derived from secondary deposits, could easily belong in a Wilton assemblage. Just to the east of Napedet, there is a very large and homogeneous surface site (Zu-11) with numerous scored sherds, as well as sherds of other styles of pottery. This site is characterized by a uniform stone industry featuring lava blades, and an associated wild game fauna. The two lithic complexes mentioned above are very different typologically, but they may not represent different traditions of toolmaking. Instead, they may reflect the kinds of activities carried out at the respective sites and the raw materials available for making tools. In only one instance was there found a stone bowl at a site yielding scored sherds.

The Gumban sherds are frequently found on the edges of shallow, natural depressions that even today are transformed into sizable temporary ponds after one of the infrequent rainstorms. After a rainstorm, grass germinates quickly, and the Turkana move their stock into the area for grazing and watering. The modern situation suggests that a slight increase in precipitation would transform the environment into one that could support a sizable population based on food production. The Kangatotha sites are not far from the Turkwel Delta, whose sorghum has been cultivated by the Turkana since at least 1888 *(33)*. Millet occurs in a wild state in nearby southwest Ethiopia *(40)*. This tempts me to speculate that the earlier Turkwel River folk were also cultivators. There is, however, no direct archeological evidence for this.

The water level of the lake fell from the Kibish IVb after about 3000 years ago *(4)*. From that time until about 15000 years ago, the archeological events are inadequately known. In northwest Turkana, along the escarpment, there is a scatter of patinated, Late Stone Age chert artifacts that may belong to this period. The hills along the escarpment receive more rainfall and were undoubtedly favorable areas for retreat during drier episodes.

THE STONE AGE— IRON AGE TRANSITION

A final tradition of the Late Stone Age is associated with a variety of incised pottery that is distinguished by parallel grooves (Fig. 6, Nos. 4–6). This pottery is widely distributed on surface sites, from near the escarpment in western Turkana to the Kerio Delta. I have found similar incised sherds as far north as the Kidepo Valley in Northeast Uganda and as far west as Napak Mountain near the Karamoja-Teso border. Wilson has recently stated that this pottery is linked through oral evidence with a people known as the Oropom, who inhabited much of the area before the expansion of the modern Paranilotes (Nilo-Hamites) *(41)*. The Oropom were essentially a Late Stone Age people who raised stock and cultivated plants.

The incised pottery, then, evidently spans a considerable length of time and offers a unique opportunity to bridge the gap between the Late Stone Age and oral history. In southern Karamoja, I have excavated sherds of this type from a site just below Kadam Mountain, where they were associated with microlithic tools and iron. Apparently the pottery was in use when iron was being introduced to what was otherwise a Late Stone Age technology. In central Turkana, the ware is densely distributed near the Turkwel irrigation scheme, where radiocarbon evidence suggests it dates back about about 1500 years *(42)*. This is consistent with other Early Iron Age dates for East Africa.

Little can be said about the settlement patterns in Turkana on the basis of these transitional Stone Age-Iron Age sites. Most of the evidence comes from the base of inselbergs, rock shelters, and open sites. There are certainly no signs of large-scale settlements in Turkana. However, the general distribution pattern of the sherds does indeed suggest cultural unity over a very wide area.

THE RECENT PAST

If my data for adjacent Karamoja also apply to Turkana, the flaked stone technology was very likely replaced by iron by the 17th century. On Kadam Mountain, a microlithic, Late Stone Age industry has been excavated, including iron artifacts at the Rangi site in layer 2, which appears to date to the 15th century. In the same area, at Kaupokwalot cave, a test pit that was radiocarbon dated to the 17th century yielded iron, but lacked stone artifacts *(43)*.

According to an Ethiopic document, a people called Galla moved through the Lake Rudolf area and crossed into Ethopia between approximately 1522 and 1530 *(44)*. Huntingford suggests that these people contributed to the development of the Paranilotes *(44)*. Perhaps their influence also helped to bring an end to the Stone Age.

Although undated, the rock engravings from the Kangetet area of south Turkana could be related to the origin of the modern, pastoral Paranilotes. The engravings include a circle bisected by a central cross *(45)*. I have seen the same design painted in a dung mixture on a rock shelter in northeast Karamoja. According to a local elder, the circle represents a cattle enclosure and the designs are still made today by travelers who pass the ceremonial rock. In addition to the Kangetet engravings, there are other engravings close to the south end of Lake Rudolf which show camels and wild game. The presence of camels suggests that the engravings were executed by a people who were acquainted with domestic stock. However, the engravings in all likelihood pre-date the arrival of the Turkana, who have no known tradition of engraving stone and who apparently had no camels when they entered the west Rudolf area *(46)*. No rock paintings have been described for Turkana, although I have been told that paintings exist on the remote northern part of the Mogila range and I have seen paintings of giraffes on Kadam Mountain in southern Karamoja (47).

There are also in Turkana numerous stone burial cairns that postdate the Stone Age. According to tribal elders, some of these are recent, while others belong to the Samburu, and still others are attributed to more ancient peoples. Before the expansion of the Turkana tribe in the 19th century, parts of southern Turkana District were inhabited by the Samburu. Oral evidence suggests that the Samburu lived in the Lothagam area at about 1800. They were driven back by the Turkana some time before 1888; Teleki and von Höhnel encountered substantial settlements of Turkana living near the Kerio Delta in that year (33).

The expansion of the Turkana tribe represents the concluding event in an area containing one of the longest prehistoric sequences known anywhere in the world. Where did the Turkana come from? The most prevalent oral tradition suggests that they split from the Jie tribe and moved into the area west of Lake Rudolf from above the Rift Valley escarpment. Another Turkana legend, striking in its parallel to evolutionary theory, states that the first men emerged from the water and descended from nonhuman primates. Some elders call this place of origin Endikerrio, described as a forested area surrounding a large body of water. Indeed, the most recent evidence for early man suggests that perhaps the Lake Rudolf basin was the Endikerrio for mankind.

Notes

1. V. E. Fuchs, *Georg. J.* 86, 114 (1935).

2. Fieldwork was generously supported by NSF grant GS-2642 and the African Studies Center, Michigan State University. I thank the Government of Kenya and the Institute of African Studies, University of Nairobi, for facilitating this research. I thank M. E. Robbins, S. McFarlin, S. R. Munyao, H. R. Munyao, J. I. Ebert, S. Muteti, P. Jaffe, J. Yellen, and the Turkana of Kakamat and Lothagam for field assistance. In addition, I thank the following for contributing to the research: J. D. Clark, A. H. Jacobs, B. M. Fagan, G. Mandahl-Barth, B. Verdcourt, R. J. Clarke, J. Walsh, K. W. Butzer, B. Patterson, G. Nyerwanire, B. Grahame, and K. Thomson.

3. For example, in 1898 Sanderson's Gulf, located near the northwest end of Lake Rudolf, was an estimated 36 miles long and about 6 to 7 miles wide [H. H. Austin, *Among Swamps and Giants in Equatorial Africa* (Pearson, London, 1902), p. 194]. The 1932-33 French expedition to Omo found the gulf completely dry [C. Arambourg, *Mission Scientifique de l'Omo* (Museum of Natural History, Paris, 1947), p. 188].

4. K. W. Butzer, *Nature* 226, 425 (1970).

5. F. C. Howell, *ibid.* 223, 1234 (1969); R. E. F. Leakey, *ibid.* 226, 223 (1970).

6. B. Patterson and W. W. Howells, *Science* 156, 64 (1967).

7. _____, A. K. Behrensmeyer, W. D. Sill, *Nature* 226, 918 (1970).

8. M. D. Leakey, *ibid.* 212, 579 (1966).

9. E. Nilson, *Geogr. An.* 13, 249 (1932).

10. V. E. Fuchs, *Phil. Trans. Roy. Soc. Ser. B* 229, 219 (1939).

11. O. Davies, *West Africa before the Europeans* (Methuen London, 1967), pp. 205-216.

12. K. W. Butzer, personal communication.

13. P. A. Robins, personal communication. The site is located about 12 miles northwest of Kangatotha on Fig. 1. D. Abrams, "An Acheulean assemblage from the Omo River basin" (paper presented at the American Anthropological Association annual meeting, San Diego, Calif., 1970).

14. J. Walsh and R. G. Dodson, *The Geology of Northern Turkana* (Mines and Geological Department of Kenya, Report No. 82, 1969).

15. T. Whitworth, *S. Afr. Archaeol. Bull.* 20, 75 (1965).

16. _____, *ibid.* 21, 138 (1966).

17. The letters in the site designation refer to grid units in the Kenya map system.

18. Mollusk sample N-1102 dated by Rikagaku Kenkyusho to 8230 ± 180 years ago for site Bb-9. All dates quoted for this laboratory are based on a half-life of 5568 years. Dates for the Lake Rudolf shells may be too old in terms of true age, for reasons cited by K. W. Butzer, F. H. Brown, and D. L. Thurber [*Quaternaria* 11, 15 (1969)]. Other evidence concerning variations in the amount of carbon-14 in the atmosphere is discussed by M. Stuiver [*Nature* 228, 484, (1970)].

19. Mollusk sample N-1101 is dated to 6010 ± 155 years ago for site Zu-5, which is located between Lothagam and Napedet.

20. Stone-Age aritifacts are commonly collected by Turkana children, who are fond of playing games with brightly colored stones. As a result, small circles of chert and obsidian artifacts resembling features of archeological significance are frequently encountered on the surface. The children use these stones to represent imaginary domestic stock, or for an *omweso*-type game.

21. Mollusk sample N-813 is dated to 7960 ± 140 years ago at site Zu-6.

22. For criticism of the concept of the Boskop physical type see G. P. Rightmire, *Amer. J. Phys. Anthropol.* 33, 164 (1970). A reconstruction of a fossil *Homo Sapiens* skull from

site Bb-9 is forthcoming in T. W. Phenice [*Hominid Fossils: An Illustrated Key* (Brown, Dubuque, Iowa, 1972)].

23. Observations pertaining to the pottery sequence were first based on a seriation analysis, following the methods described by C. W. Meighan [*Amer. Antiq.* 25, 203 (1959)], W. S. Robinson [*ibid.* 16, 293 (1951)], and G. W. Brainerd [*Ibid.*, p. 301]. The sequence was then confirmed by radiocarbon dates.

24. Mollusk sample N-110 is dated to 8420 ± 165 years ago. Pottery was recovered from 10 centimeters below the level that yielded the carbon-14 sample.

25. Shell sample UCLA-1247 E, quoted as 5610 B.C. ± 1000 years by D. W. Phillipson [*J. Afr. Hist.* 11, 1 (1970)].

26. K. W. Butzer, F. H. Brown, D. L. Thurber *Quaternaria* 11, 15 (1969).

27. A. J. Arkell, *Early Kartoum* (Oxford Univ. Press, London, 1949).

28. _____ and P. J. Ucko, *Cur. Anthropol.* 6, 145 (1965); J. de Heinzelin, *Sci. Amer.* 206, 105 (June 1962).

29. *Corbicula africana, Corbicula artini, Mutela nilotica, Melanoides turberculata, Caelatura rothschildi, Caelatura chefneuxi, Biomphalaria stanleyi,* and *Cleopatra bulimoides* were identified by B. Verdcourt and G. Mandahl-Barth (personal communication) in Holocene beds at Lothagam, which have been dated back about 7500 years.

30. L. H. Robbins, *Azania* 2, 69 (1967).

31. B. M. Fagan, in *The Late Stone Age Fishing Settlement at Lothagam, Northern Kenya*, L. H. Robbins, Ed. (Michigan State Univ. Museum, Ann Arbor, in press).

32. Charcoal sample N-812 is dated to 6200 ± 125 years ago for site Zu-10, which is located between Lothagam and Napedet. The sample was excavated from a stain believed to be the remnants of a hearth.

33. L. von Höhnel, *Discovery by Count Teleki of Lakes Rudolf and Stefanie* (Longmans, London, 1894).

34. E. M. Van Zinderen Bakker, *Palaeobotanist* 15, 128 (1966); J. A. Coetzee, *Nature* 204, 564 (1964).

35. Domestic cattle and a Late Stone Age industry have been dated to between 2910 ± 110 years and 2690 ± 80 years ago at Prospect Farm, Nakuru District, Kenya [M. Cohen, *Azania* 5, 27 (1970)]. Domestic stock have also been dated to the first millennium B.C. at the Narosura site, Narok District, Kenya [N. Chittick, *Azania* 4, 189 (1969)].

36. Gumban A is included in J. E. G. Sutton's pottery class B for the Kenya highland [*S. Afr. Archaeol. Bull.* 19, 27 (1964)].

37. Sample of *Etheria elliptica* dated to 4800 ± 100 years ago is quoted in K. S. Thompson [*Breviora* 243, 1 (1966)].

38. Sample N-814 is dated to 5020 ± 220 years ago.

39. K. W. Butzer, personal communication.

40. J. D. Clark in *Background to Evolution in Africa*, W. W. Bishop and J. D. Clark, Eds. (Univ. of Chicago Press, Chicago, 1967), pp. 613-615.

41. J.G G. Wilson, *Uganda J.* 34, 125 (1970).

42. Charcoal sample N-909 is dated to 15000 ± 100 years ago.

43. Rangi-bone sample N-863 is dated to 510 ± 105 years ago. This sample is believed to be the most reliable of three post-1500 A.D. dates because of its position under a large boulder. Kaupokwalot-Charcoal sample N-865 was dated to 330 ± 105 years ago.

44. G. W. B. Huntingford, in *History of East Africa*, R. Oliver and G. Matthew, Eds. (Oxford Univ. Press, London, 1963), p. 76.

45. R. C. Soper, *Azania* 3, 2 (Fig. 1-d) (1968).

46. P. H. Gulliver, *The Family Herds* (Routledge, London, 1955), p. 260.

47. L. H. Robbins, *Uganda J.* 34, 79 (1970).

Hunting: An integrating Biobehavior System and Its Evolutionary Importance

Hunting is the master behavior pattern of the human species. It is the organizing activity which integrated the morphological, physiological, genetic, and intellectual aspects of the individual human organisms and of the population who compose our single species. Hunting is a way of life, not simply a "subsistence technique," which importantly involves commitments, correlates, and consequences spanning the entire biobehavioral continuum of the individual and of the entire species of which he is a member.

That man achieved a worldwide distribution while still a hunter reflects the enormous universality of this kind of behavioral adaptation. The corollary fact that he practiced hunting for 99 per cent of his history indicates the significance of two neglected aspects: (1) hunting is a much more complex organization of behavior than is currently admitted under the traditional "subsistence technique" categorization, and (2) the intellectual and genetic repertoire of the animal developed in this behavioral regime both permitted and enabled the recent acquisition of civilization to be a rapid acquisition and to be developed independently by hunting peoples in different parts of the world.

The total biobehavioral configuration of hunting includes the ethological training of children to be skilled observers of animal behavior, including other humans. The process itself includes five distinguishable components whose combinations and permutations are certainly varied, but with recurrent and widely distributed commonalities.

Hunting is an active process which puts motion and direction into the diagram of man's morphology, technology, social organization,

By William Laughlin. Reprinted from *Man the Hunter,* eds. Richard B. Lee and Irven Devore (Chicago: Aldine Publishing Company, 1968), by permission of the editors and the publisher. Copyright © 1968 by The Wenner-Gren Foundation for Anthropological Research, Inc.

and ecological relations. Hunting involves goals and motivations for which intricate inhibition systems have been developed. Hunting has placed a premium upon inventiveness, upon problem solving, and has imposed a real penalty for failure to solve the problem. Therefore it has contributed as much to advancing the human species as to holding it together within the confines of a single variable species. A study of hunting removes the tedious ambiguity contained in many current discussions of the importance of tools, whether tool use means that tools use humans or that humans use tools.

HUNTING AS AN INTEGRATING SEQUENCE BEHAVIOR PATTERN

Hunting may profitably be analyzed as a sequence pattern of behavioral complexes. This analysis recognizes the ordered interdependencies of the diverse constituent elements of hunting and it also provides a comparative basis for evaluating the functions and intensities, their similarities and dissimilarities, in radically different cultures. As defined here, hunting consists of five series of patterned activities, beginning early in childhood and extending through the life of the individual engaged in hunting. These five behavior complexes consist of (1) programming the child, (2) scanning or the collection of information, (3) stalking and pursuit of game, (4) immobilization of game, including the killing or capture of game, and (5) retrieval of the game. Although more complexes might be added, such as those concerned with the distribution of game and its various uses, none can be subtracted without impoverishing an appreciation of hunting.

In overall perspective, both for the individual and for the evolution of mankind, this behavior system has had an integrating function. It has served as an integrating schedule for the nervous system. Hunting is obviously an instrumental system in the real sense that something gets done, several ordered behaviors are performed with a crucial result. The technological aspects, the spears, clubs, handaxes, and all the other objects suitable for museum display, are essentially meaningless apart from the context in which they are used. They do not represent a suitable place to begin analysis because their position in the sequence is remote from the several preceding complexes.

Programming Children

Three indispensable parts of the hunting system are programmed into the child beginning early in life. These are the habit of observation, a systematic knowledge of animal behavior, and the interpretation and appropriate action for living with animals and for utilizing them for food and fabricational purposes. Owing to the fact that in many cultures various animals are endowed with souls, that there are animal beings as well as human beings, the killing and eating of animal beings may be fraught with spiritual hazards (Rasmussen, 1929, p. 56). Appropriate behavior toward animals is prominently based upon familiarity with animal behavior and includes ways of living peacefully with animals, of maintaining a discourse with them, as well as the appropriate behaviors, the highly coordinated movements of the hunter proceeding toward a kill, and appropriate social behavior where other hunters are involved. Within a single community it is possible to arrange the hunters in a rank order in terms of their efficiency or productivity. It is sometimes possible to relate lack of success to inadequate training as well as to the other sources of ineptitude. This is especially apparent where the child has been removed from his village during the crucial years, or where the child has been raised by a grandmother or other nonhunter who was not able to provide the necessary tuition.

A general statement embracing the styles, modes, and mechanisms of neurological patterning in childhood has been provided by Gajdusek:

Phylogeny has already patterned the view of the physical world which a child will receive in the structure of the sense receptors: eyes, ears, nose, taste buds; tactile, temperature, and pain receptors; and proprioceptors. The cultural milieu, however, can determine the schemata of thought and the modes of handling of these sense perceptions as well as it determines the quality and the quantity in which they impinge upon the infant and child. There is a vast number of neurological functions of the central nervous system which different cultures have programmed in their own specific ways by the unique environment they provide for the growth and development of their children. These include the style of neuromuscular coordination in fine and gross movements, even at the level of speech and eye movements; styles of posture, gait, stance, climbing and swimming, etc.; modes of nonverbal communication including gesture and dance; use of language, at times polylinguality; the form of the body image; sense of time, space, rhythm, and tone; color sense and acuity of smell and taste, hearing and vision; conceptions of quantity and number, methods of counting (some nonverbal), and processes of reconning and computation; styles of symbolic representation in play or drawing; patterns of sexual responsiveness and behavior; mnemonic mechanisms; and even methods and mechanisms of imagery and imagination, reverie, trance, and dream (1963, p. 56).

It is useful to realize, as D. A. Hamburg has noted (1961, p. 281) that even the autonomic nervous system is not autonomous but rather that it is substantially under central nervous control. Unfortunately we do not have the full span of physiological and neurological observations on a longitudinal, or cross-sectional, series of children for a single hunting community. However, we do have a body of observations, variously rich or sparse, on comparatively gross activities, and in these we can see the way in which children are progressively trained to become active hunters. We can see the end products, the overt manifestations of deeper and more subtle maturational alterations of the nervous system. Our major problem here is to determine what programming, what childhood instruction, is essential and indispensable to subsequent hunting behaviors.

In any community of hunters it is possible to find general exercises that prepare the child for active hunting but many fewer that involve a specific commitment. Probably all forms of exercise are of some value, but only a few have demonstrable relevance in the sense that they are a necessary and specific prerequisite. Beginning with the different practices for the two sexes which are maximized in hunting groups, a series can be assembled. Thus, those practices leading to use of spear throwers, boomerangs, bows and arrows, lances, boat handling, sledding, harpooning, etc., are ordinarily restricted to males or males are clearly favored in systematic instruction. Nevertheless, there is little data bearing on the question of how much instruction is necessary in childhood. The best preparation for throwing a spear as an adult hunter is probably throwing one at an earlier age, but how early or how many practice hours are required is not amenable to quantified estimate. The bow and arrow is in common use among many hunters—Pygmies, Bushmen, Eskimos, various American Indians, Andamanese, Chuckchee, to name only enough to illustrate considerable diversity in the technology and use, however, most observers agree that these hunters are mediocre or indifferent as archers. They hunt effectively with their equipment, but, they compensate for lack of accuracy at appreciable distances, perhaps more than twenty or thirty yards, by spending their time getting closer to the animal. In brief, these hunters clearly spend more time and attention in utilization of their knowledge of animal behavior than in improvement of their equipment or of its use. This generalization, if well founded, probably constitutes an important aspect of primitive hunting and provides a scale for comparisons between groups.

Children were taught to close the distance between themselves and their quarry by sophisticated stalking methods that depended more upon comprehensive observation, detailed ethological knowledge and an equally detailed system of interpretation and action, than upon the improvement of their equipment and the addition of ten or twenty yards to its effective range. In fact, one may pass from this generalization to another and suggest that the very slow improvement in technology, clubs, spears, throwing boards, bows and arrows, as indicated by the archeological record, was contingent upon success in learning animal behavior. It was easier or more effective to instruct children in ethology, to take up the slack by minimizing their distance from the animal prey, than to invest heavily in equipment improvement. The rapid advances in archery of the last fifteen years reflect an application of technological methods to archery equipment that clearly did not arise from a need

to depend upon such equipment for any important portion of the annual food supply.

The difference between specifically programmed and generally programmed prerequisite childhood exercises for hunting in adulthood is epitomized in the tendon lengthening exercises for Aleut children, designed for hunting from the kayak, contrasted with their general exercises. These former focused on the shoulder joint of the throwing arm, on the low back, and on the posterior region of the knee joint.

Very early in childhood, apparently as early as beginning to walk, the male child was placed in a sitting position on a flat surface or on a stool with his heels on another stool or box. His preceptor, a father, uncle, or grandfather, stood behind or to the side of him and pulled his throwing arm up and over behind his back. This was done gently and intermittently, often with a little song or rhythmic susurration, so that several excursions were made rather than one prolonged excursion. This exercise created greater mobility at the shoulder joint and specifically enabled the arm to move farther backward and to come directly forward in a flat, vertical plane. As a consequence, the arm functioned as a longer lever than in those persons who cannot rotate their arm backward without moving it progressively to the side of the body at the same time. A spear or harpoon could be thrown farther, more easily, and from a greater variety of positions available to the seated kayak hunter.

The second and related exercise stretched the tendons and ligaments of the low back. The seated child, legs extended in front, was pushed forward by a hand applied to the back. This exercise specifically anticipated the considerable strain placed on the low back while paddling or throwing when seated in a kayak.

The third exercise of this series consisted of depressing the knees of the seated child so that the tendons on the posterior of the leg, especially the semimembranosus and the semitendinosus tendons in particular, were stretched. As a consequence the person was enabled to sit with legs extended for long periods of time and to operate efficiently.

These three specific exercises were reinforced with various games. In one, the child sat on the ground, legs extended, and threw a dart at a small wooden model of a whale suspended from a flexible withe. Two boys played this game, each facing the other and with his own whale target.

An example of a non-specific exercise of general value to a kayak hunter but with no specific relevance to kayak hunting, is that of finger-hanging. The young child was suspended from a ceiling beam of the house by his fingers. His preceptor then withdrew and the child hung until he was forced to drop. He dropped to the floor, an earth floor covered with dried grass. The exercise was intended to strengthen the fingers and to teach the child to fall on his feet with ease and agility.

The peculiar monopoly which the Aleuts and Koniags held on sea-otter hunting and the corollary fact that no European ever became a successful kayak sea-otter hunter, may be traced in part to their childhood training, both the physical and the behavioral aspect. Many Europeans have learned to paddle kayaks, and many have learned to hunt sea mammals, but extremely few, possibly five, ever became kayak hunters. Aleuts and Koniags were transported from their homeland to alien waters off California and Japan by their Russian administrators, because of their non-duplicable skills in sea-otter hunting. The point in citing this well-known history is that it reflects some of the consequences of a complex hunting achievement which is demonstrably and specifically related to childhood training. While kayak hunting represents a rare technological achievement, the use of the throwing board enjoyed a much wider distribution about the world. Certainly one factor in the failure of the throwing board to diffuse from Eskimos to contiguous groups of Indians is that an essential portion of the complex rested in child training practices. It was not a trait, like the axe, the bow and arrow, or the rifle, which could be easily used by adults.

A fear of kayaks, as found among the Eskimos of Wainwright (Nelson, in press), must be distinguished from the relatively localized "kayak fear" found in west Greenland. The possible relationship of the disease, "kayak fear," to inadequate child training has not been explored. The inability of adult hunters to perform normally is a generic category for investigation

and might well be especially rewarding in revealing defects in childhood programming.

Scanning

Scanning includes the collection of information on where to hunt, what to hunt, and the scheduling of a hunt. The choice of animals to be hunted and the areas which will be searched reflect sophisticated knowledge concerning the behavior of animals, environmental conditions, and other commitments of the hunter to partners or to the portion of the community which depends upon him. His need for food and fabricational materials may outweigh several other considerations. The independence of scanning and its role may be seen in the common practices conducted prior to the pursuit or stalking of detected animals.

For several days prior to the actual detection and pursuit of an animal or herd the hunter may search an area for signs. Frequently he gets this information from other hunters. He must first find what animals are in the territory and the actual tracks, feces, and browsed plants may provide him with the information he needs. The presence of one animal may signal the presence of another so that the hunter is encouraged to continue with this inspection even if he has not actually sighted the animal he wants. He may sight the animal, or a herd, but wait for it to move into a better position, perhaps closer to camp or in a valley where more can be killed than in the open.

In scanning, the knowledge of tracks and indications of animals generally is the paramount feature and obviously the complex which utilizes previously learned observational information concerning animal behavior. The time invested in this portion of the hunting sequence is usually far greater than for any other portion except for the childhood programming.

The scanning and identification problem is quite different for the marine mammal hunter. He must proceed to the most likely area and then search for the interrupting profile of the mammal when it comes to that horizon (Laughlin, 1967). He may first proceed to a mummy cave and ask for help from the hunters interred there who still maintain an active part in the affairs of living people, and he certainly utilizes the information provided by watchmen, those who sit on vantage points and scan the sea, and upon the weather prognosticators. A man of meteorological sophistication, an "astronome" may even be included in a party of kayak hunters (Heizer, 1960, p. 133).

Choices of hunting routes may involve various sorts of divining, whose effect is to randomize the routes or areas searched. This is based on the fact, well known to the primitive hunter, that animals learn the habits of humans and adjust their behavior accordingly.

The religious elements which pervade the preparation are multitudinous and need only be called to mind here. Cleansing rites and special clothing are ubiquitous. They importantly reflect the reciprocal nature of the interaction between those beings in the animal world and those in the human, or stated less egocentrically, the contingent relations between animal beings and human beings (Marsh, 1954; Hallowell, 1960).

Stalking

Stalking and pursuit of game ordinarily begins once the animal has been sighted. Attention then shifts to getting as close to the animal as necessary for an effective shot. In much of hunting, however, there is no sharp line of demarcation between these two portions of the sequence pattern. The hunter may commit himself to a particular animal or herd without having actually seen it. There may be ample evidence that a particular animal is being followed, and the animal may be aware of the pursuit without an actual visual sighting. The hunter and the hunted may smell each other, they may hear each other, they may see each other's tracks, and the animal may actually be attracted to its human pursuer by his urine. Following a polar bear for one or two days, running down a horse over a three-day period, and certainly some of the desert hunting in Australia and in the Kalahari involves a long pursuit and relatively short period for killing.

The hunter is concerned with the freshness of the track and the direction in which he is moving. He wants all possible information on his quarry's condition; its age, sex, size, rate of travel, and a working estimate of the distance by which the animal leads him. In the final stages, when he is closing with the animal, the hunter employs his knowledge of animal behavior and situational factors relevant to that behavior in a crucial fashion. For all birds, animals, and fish the hunter must estimate flight distance, the point at which they will take flight or run away. Conversely, with animals that are aggressive, he needs to interpret any signs, raising or lowering of tail, flexing of muscles, blowing, or salivation, etc., that indicate an attack rather than a flight. In many cases the animal is intentionally provoked to attack. The variations are innumerable.

One useful generalization of the problem faced by the hunter is that he wants to get as close as possible for the best possible shot but he would rather have a poor shot than none at all. The enormous labor and skill that is expended in approaching the animal, often hours of lying on the ground waiting for a change in direction of wind or in the position of the animal, testifies to the crucial importance of stalking.

The technological equipment of most primitive hunters is such that their quarry is usually shot at relatively short distances, usually less than thirty feet for harpoons, bows and arrows, and spears. Even the one generalization about the minimum distance for the best shot must be qualified because the hunter may want the maximum distance compatible with his weapon, in order to provide time for a second shot. Some animals tend to continue in the direction they were traveling after they are shot. Other animals have a tendency to simply stand and bleed, if not frightened by sight or smell of the hunter. The point here is simply that the enormous range and complexities of animal behavior; the influence of situational factors depending upon time of day, sex, age, nutritional state, degree of excitation, being in the company of a mate, with or without young, etc., these factors must all be read into the decision-making machinery of the hunter.

Hunting with high-powered rifles and telescopic sights, and to a lesser extent with modern archery equipment, is substantially different from the hunting of primitive man. In a general fashion, the better the technological equipment the less intimate knowledge of animal behavior is required. Getting close to an animal represents the major investment of the primitive hunter and explains the extensive attention given to childhood programming and to the location of game.

Immobilization, Killing and Capture

The vast majority of animals taken by primitive hunters are not killed outright or are not killed upon initial contact. More often they are wounded, stunned, or immobilized to a degree that renders them incapable of rapid or prolonged flight. Even with the use of poisons the larger mammals may live on, traveling slowly, for one or more days. The Pygmy elephant hunter does not expect his quarry to fall over immediately after the first puncture, but he does expect to be able to induce hemorrhaging that will impair the functioning of the elephant and simplify tracking. In other cases the hunter intentionally avoids killing the animal for very practical reasons. An Eskimo may wound a bear and then drive him down to a stream where he can be killed and boated home. If inland on a small island, the Eskimo may wound the bear and walk him over to the edge of the island, then dispatch him and roll him into the sea where he can be floated and towed away. In many cases it is practical and highly desirable to save an enormous amount of labor, the backpacking of some 1,200 pounds through difficult country, by wounding the animal and heading him in the preferred direction.

Capture of animals may be an objective and done for many different reasons. One important reason is the need to secure living specimens for study and child instruction, commonly categorized as "pets" in the literature. Live animals may be desired for decoys, and of course live animals may be used for various ritual purposes. Birds may be taken for training in hunting or fishing (cormorants, falcons, etc.), or simply kept as a source of feathers. From the enormous range of methods of taking the quarry it is obvious that immediate and outright killing is only one of many variations. The extensive use of snares, traps, and pitfalls in itself testifies to the concern with capture rather than immediate killing.

Retrieval

Retrieval of game represents the end point of the hunting complex pattern, it is the object of those things which have preceded it. Within the retrieval complex are included the immediate details of retrieving a floating seal or walrus, and of getting it secured to the kayak, or to an umiak, or an ice cake so that it can be cut up. Many items of material culture naturally fall in here and retrieving hooks for securing floating animals before they sink are prominent among them. This complex category broadens out to include the dressing and preparation of the animal for return to the camp or village. Finally, the activities involved in this complex extend ultimately to the distribution and use of the game, and ultimately the return of some of the materials back into earlier portions of the sequence system. A flow chart shows the routes by which some of the materials return to participate again in the system (Fig. 1). The most obvious is the capture of an animal to be used for instruction of children in animal behavior. Thus, the entire system is activated in proper sequence and reverts to flow again into the system.

The intellectual requirements for appropriate behavior in this portion of the system still depend in part upon those that were prerequisite to the preceding four portions. However, there is a qualitative difference. An animal must be expertly drawn in accordance with the anatomy of the animal, the various fabricational and nutritional uses of the animal, with attention to size requirements that affect carrying it back to the camp, and to social factors such as some desired portions, horns, tail, forward flipper, or fluke meat, for persons of relevant status. Attention shifts over to anatomy rather than behavior, to material characteristics, to the fabricational and dietary qualities of the animal. Some portions may be eaten immediately, and some may be employed in a ritual observance to insure affability of the animal spirit. Hides are carefully removed if they are intended for fabricational use and their cutting is in accord with a particular use. Thus, if a sealskin is to be used for a line, it must be slipped, in tubular fashion, off the carcass so that a continuous, circumferentially spiral line can be cut. But if the seal is to be fed to dogs, or its skin to be used for clothing, or

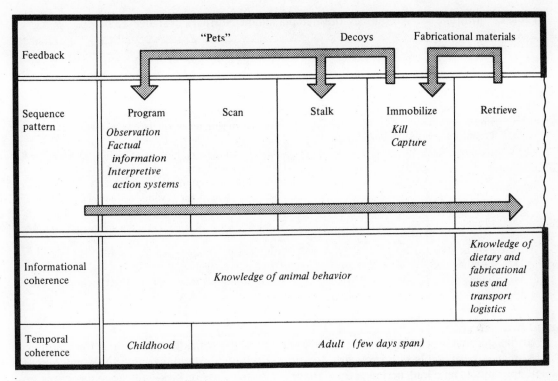

Figure 1. The process of hunting.

both, it is drawn quite differently. A worldwide survey indicates great differences in the utilization of animal tissues. Some people use the intestines and pericardium, others discard them or feed them to dogs (Table 1). The same animal has different meanings for different peoples and this extends far beyond its rank order in their list of food preferences.

Women and dogs have been the principal beasts of burden since Paleolithic times and these are not universally available for the reason that women are not always at the site of killing and butchering, and many people did not breed dogs suitable for packing. Where long distances and large amounts of meat are involved, a village may move to the animal. Elephants and whales, unless juvenile or easily floated, usually become community projects. It is interesting that, excepting the sled and dog traction, both comparatively recent, the only mechanical advantage accessible to primitive man was water transport. The retrieval flow pattern for the Eskimo or Aleut who harpoons a seal, tows it home behind his kayak, and eats all the meat, con-trasted with the sledging Eskimo who harpoons a seal, carries it home on a sled, and then shares it with the dogs, is enormous.

The kayak-hunter can tow much greater weights more easily, than can the sledgers. The kayak-hunter can use the hide of his quarry to make the kayak with which he hunts the beast. Marine hunters use more of the products of the animals they hunt than do terrestrial hunters, and they use them more advantageously. Esophagus, intestines, and pericardia are of little use to most hunting groups as fabricational materials, yet they account for an appreciable part of the clothing of some northern peoples.

THE PHYSICAL SUPERIORITIES OF MAN

Pound for pound, man is a tough, durable, strong, and versatile animal. To the extent that comparisons between species have validity, he is superior in overall physical performance to all or most other mammals. This physical superiority is intimately related to his hunting habit.

Table 1. Multiple use of resources. (Eumetopia jubata [Northern or steller sea lion.])

Part of Animal	Partial List of Uses
1. Hide	Cover for kayak and umiak; line for harpoon
2. Flesh	Food, for humans
3. Blubber	Food: eaten with meat, rendered for oil
4. Organs (heart, liver, spleen, kidney)	Food
5. Bones	Ribs for root diggers, humerus for club, baculum for flaker
6. Teeth	Decorative pendants
7. Whiskers	Decoration of wood hunting hats and visors
8. Sinew	Back sinews used for sewing, lashing, cordage (less desirable than sinew of whale or caribou)
9. Flippers	Soles used for boot soles; contents gelatinized in flipper and eaten
10. Pericardium	Water bottle, general-purpose container
11. Esophagus	Parka, pants, leggings of boots, pouches
12. Stomach	Storage container (especially for dried salmon)
13. Intestines	Parka, pants, pouches

It has become a common routine to observe that man is born helpless and remains dependent upon others for a long period of time, that he is a generalized animal lacking the specializations that characterize other species, and this re-citation often leads to the observation that man is physically weak and defenseless because he is dependent upon culture. This in turn provides the argument for the implication that evolution took place in the past and that the rapidity and pervasiveness of cultural evolution has supplanted physical evolution. A more realistic and holistic view is the recognition of the biobehavioral continuum that characterizes the development of each individual (Ginsburg and Laughlin, 1966). The dichotomy between biology and culture, between cultural learning and its neurological base, has been historically conducive to the denigration of man's physical abilities.

In fact, human beings are remarkably versatile, durable, and strong in their physical constitution. As Haldane has observed, only man can swim a mile, walk twenty miles, and then climb a tree (Haldane, 1956, p. 5). The full list of man's physical superiorities, when compared with other mammals, must include his ability to run rapidly and to run long distances. One need only cite the conquest of the four-minute mile and long-distance running of various Indian tribes. Tarahumara endurance runners have

been scientifically studied and the results confirm and extend various anecdotal accounts. Participants in kick-ball races may cover up to 100 miles in 24 hours (Balke and Snow, 1965). That Indians can run down horses and deer is well known, by pacing the animal, keeping him moving, and taking advantage of the tendency of many ungulates to move in an arc by traversing the chord. The Indian hunter who is running down an animal makes use of his own physical superiority and his knowledge of the animal's behavior.

In pulling strength, humans compare favorably with adult chimpanzees. In ability to carry loads, humans regularly display abilities superior to the donkey, and this superiority is demonstrated at high altitudes as well. Loads of sixty pounds are commonly carried and the literature abounds with examples of porters carrying loads in excess of their own body weight.

Functional flexibility permitting a wide range of movements and postures, best seen in young children, acrobats, gymnasts, ballet dancers, wrestlers, swimmers, and divers, is unequivocally superior to other mammals. The closest approach to human flexibility as a whole is probably found in the orangutan and in the spider monkeys, the latter having the advantage of a prehensile tail. However, these contenders are lacking in the fine motor control of the hand and of a specialized foot. Nor can they swivel their heads as far or as easily as humans. They do not have the ability to milk a cow, a manual feat requiring a subtle succession of digital closure, and as runners or weight bearers they cannot even be entered in the lists.

Man's sensory apparatus is excellent. His vision is acute and of course includes color vision. It is exceeded only by that of various birds. His auditory acuity compares well with other animals and is a prime factor in his hunting abilities. His olfactory abilities do appear to be more limited than those of some other species, polar bears for example, but it is adequate to facilitate hunting. The external integument of humans is remarkably tough. Many groups live their entire lives without benefit of clothes and this includes groups living in areas as stressful and divergent as Australia, Tierra del Fuego, the Congo, and the Kalahari Desert. The fallacious idea that man lost his body hair as a consequence of wearing clothes, still recited as a demonstrated fact (Glass, 1965, p. 1254), is easily disposed of by the examples of hirsute and naked hunters, the Australian aborigines, and of glabrous and naked hunters, the Bushmen. Human skin tans well and is far more durable than that of many other mammals. One may speculate on the role hair has played in human evolution, but a tough skin has been a distinct advantage in a large variety of recurrent situations to the primitive hunter.

Considerable physiological tolerance, an unsurpassed ability to adapt to environmental stresses of which high altitude is most prominent, is surely one of man's major physical superiorities. Few animals, rats and dogs, to cite undomesticated and domesticated examples, compare with humans in this respect. A review of all the areas in which members of our species live serves to indicate our great physiological plasticity. No other single species lives at high and low altitudes, extremely hot and extremely cold climates and in all the combinations of humidity, light and darkness that compose the panel of human habitats.

Among the many other superiorities enjoyed by the human animal is a dental and alimentary system that permits a truly omnivorous diet. Humans can tolerate a large number of plants and animals and can adapt to diets that are composed totally of flesh or of plant foods. Additionally, they can continue work under conditions of deprivation.

When the superior memory and learning abilities of man is included, and the use of tools, language, and other elements of the biobehavioral matrix in which man operates, the remarkable versatility of the human animal becomes even more apparent. However, this should not obscure the basic fact that viewed solely from the standpoint of anatomy, physiology, and neurology man enjoys many superiorities compared with other species. A man can run down a horse in two or three days, and then decide whether to eat it, ride it, pull a load with it, wear it, or worship it.

SIMPLICITY OF BASIC TECHNOLOGY

The common weapons and related devices used in stalking and in the immobilization of game animals is basically simple and elementary. Over the million or more years in which man has evolved as a hunter, it is probable that the vast majority of mammals, birds, and fish have been killed with clubs, stones, knives, and spears or simply strangled with the hands or in a snare or noose. Examination of the archeological record, even that of Upper Paleolithic big-game hunters, is not impressive except in virtuosity of flaking or in other artistic variations. Diagonal flaking of a spear point has no demonstrable advantage over parallel flaking, and fluting offers no discernible advantage over unfluted points.

As Boas observed, "As soon as a reasonably long shaft allowed an attack from a point beyond the reach of the teeth and paws of the animal, hunting became safer" (Boas, 1938, p. 254). The spear, used as a lance or cast, was certainly a major step forward, and has persisted for some hundreds of thousands of years. Nevertheless, it is basically a simple invention, and the spearthrower, still in use by some Eskimos and Australian aborigines, is similarly an uncomplicated device. The bows and arrows in use by most primitive hunters were not impressive for their cast, their distance, nor their accuracy. An examination of the variety of arrow releases and their geographical distribution (Wissler, 1926, pp. 30–40) serves to reinforce the idea that cultural styles in the construction and use of various tools and weapons have only limited relevance to the potential efficiency of the weapon. As previously suggested, the enormous variety of harpoon heads that have been used to harpoon the same species of seal, or the variety of fishhooks that are used to catch the same species of fish, illuminates the basic fact that the hunter invests more heavily in knowledge of the behavior of the animals, in methods for approaching them or attracting them close to him, than in increasing the range or firepower of his weapons.

A substantial amount of hunting reveals the way in which animals can be easily approached under suitable conditions; and then dispatched with a club or a spear. Many animals are killed while asleep. Obviously the most ferocious beast in the world is utterly harmless while asleep, or hibernating. Walrus, who are often victors in combat with polar and brown bears, are frequently taken while asleep. Screening noises are prominently utilized in many forms of hunting. During storms, the sea otter hauls upon shore. The Aleuts approached them with ease at this time owing to the animals' inability to hear the approaching hunters, and simply clubbed them (Elliott, 1886, pp. 142–43). To a significant extent, young animals fall in the same accessible category as sleeping animals. The archeological and ethnographic record is unambiguous on the fact that the vast majority of mammals killed are immature or subadult. This reflects the population profile of many species, but it also represents a preference on the part of the hunter. The largest and oldest animals are more difficult to kill or capture, they do not taste as good as younger ones, their hides are often scarred and therefore less desirable for clothing, and they may even be avoided for frankly conservational and for religious considerations.

Driving animals, whether into a net, a pit, over a cliff, or within range of concealed hunters, is again obviously simple so far as the technology is concerned, but considerably more complex with reference to the coordination required of the persons conducting this part of the hunt. The signalling system used by Aleut and Koniag kayak hunters when employing a surround method reflects the solution of a problem in communication where spoken language would frustrate the combined efforts of the hunters. The positions of the paddle of the first man to sight the quarry provided ample cues to the other hunters. The many ways in which group hunting provided an effective means of scanning, stalking, and killing, and at the same time placed a premium upon precisely coordinated social organization, simultaneously reveals the importance of alternate forms of communication between the participants. Brief, silent, inconspicuous, and unambiguous cues are absolutely necessary in such operations. Though the technological sophistication of many poisons is considerably advanced beyond the handax and club, the use of poisons also illustrates the point that much programming must precede the killing complex (Linné, 1957). The development of effective poisons importantly demonstrates the basic inventiveness of primitive hunters.

Among the great inventory of hunting technology is the ancient and widespread bolas. Its principle, common to the bull-roarer sling and centrifuge alike, is simple enough for women and children to manipulate and helps explain some of their substantial contributions to the hunting economy.

The point of drawing attention to the simplicity of the basic technology is of course to draw attention to the sophistication of the complexes preceding the actual use of the weapons. In a very real sense the hunter is taking a final examination with a mortal demerit for failure. It is the preceding period of learning that enables him to perform adequately.

HUNTER'S SOPHISTICATED KNOWLEDGE OF BEHAVIOR AND ANATOMY

There is ample documentation, though surprisingly few systematic studies, for the postulate that primitive man is sophisticated in his knowledge of the natural world. This sophistication encompasses the entire macroscopic zoological world of mammals, marsupials, reptiles, birds, fish, insects, and plants. Knowledge of tides, meteorological phenomena generally, astronomy, and other aspects of the natural world are also well developed among some primitive peoples. There are genuinely large variations between groups with reference to the sophistication and extent of their knowledge, and to the areas in which they have concentrated. Empiricism is not at all uncommon, and inventiveness similarly recurs in widely separated areas with only remote or no discernible historical connections. Having previously discussed these topics (Laughlin, 1961, 1963), I will here only cite the relevance of this sophistication to the hunting behavior system and to its significance for the evolution of man.

Hunters are extremely knowledgeable concerning animal behavior and anatomy for a variety of reasons. Hunting is their profession and this requires such knowledge. They recite events of hunting, they discuss endlessly the weather and its effects on ice conditions, or on the moss on which caribou feed; they make predictions on the numbers of various animals based on weather conditions and its effects on animals and plants that serve as food for carnivores and grazers. Their conversations often sound like a classroom discussion of ecology, of food chains, and trophic levels.

The accuracy of their information is attested by their success in hunting and by comparisons with scientific studies of behavior and anatomy and systematics. In discussing the species concept of the local naturalist, Ernst Mayr includes the opinion of primitive natives:

Some 30 years ago I spent several months with a tribe of superb woodsmen and hunters in the Arfak Mountains of New Guinea. They had 136 different vernacular names for the 137 species of birds that occurred in the area, confusing only two species. It is not, of course, pure coincidence that these primitive woodsmen arrive at the same conclusion as the museum taxonomists, but an indication that both groups of observers deal with the same arbitrary discontinuities of nature (1963, p. 17).

The consultation of native hunters by naturalists extends well back into the nineteenth century. The naturalist Chamisso who visited Unalaska as early as 1817 published a detailed study of whales in which he depended upon the local Aleuts who carved wooden models of each of the whales and provided various information about each of them (Chamisso, 1824).

The ubiquity of sophisticated information among hunters is probably of more importance for interpreting the development and consequences of such information than the unusual and rare achievements that may occasionally be associated with such knowledge. The preparation of mummies and intentional autopsy of the dead to find out why they died are expectable developments where there is the appropriate context and concern.

The Tungus, described in detail by Shirokogorov (1935), compare favorably with Eskimos and even with the Aleuts (Marsh and Laughlin, 1956). They are good gross anatomists, their ideas on physiological functions are based on their observations, they are good naturalists, and they are concerned to acquaint themselves with the behavior and the anatomy of animals or birds not well known to them, capturing live specimens for this specific purpose and for pets for the instruction of children. "He [the Tungu] is interested in the comparative study of bones and soft parts of the body and he comes to form a good idea as to the anatomical similarities and dissimilarities in animals and even man" (Shirokogorov, 1935, p. 73).

As previously indicated, the sources of Aleut anatomical knowledge can be partitioned into five categories: (1) the study of anatomical structures; (2) a rational medicine and physical culture; (3) dissection of human bodies; (4) true comparative anatomy, focused on the sea otter; and (5) the manufacture of dried mummies (Laughlin, 1961, pp. 157-60). The first, second, and fourth categories appear most ubiquitous. The daily butchering and drawing of animals leads to knowledge about them, and to the extent that internal tissues are used for food or fabricational purposes, the knowledge may be considerably detailed. Hunters are well aware of the affinity between man and other animals, and they all have relevant exercises designed to condition the hunter. A good deal of information inevitably obtains for human biology stemming first from the need for assistance or intervention at birth.

If primitive hunters are compared with ethologists, some common procedures are obvious, and though the goals may rapidly diverge, they are neither antipathetic nor wholly dissimilar. Drawing upon an important position paper of the ethologist, G. P. Baerends, the common element is immediately apparent. "Starting from detailed description of behaviour, ethologists study the factors that underlie their causation, their genetic basis and their ontogeny" (Baerends, 1958, p. 466). The Bushmen, Pygmies, or Aleuts have the detailed description of behavior well in hand, with the emphasis probably on motor systems. Their knowledge of physiology, genetics, and allied disciplines is clearly inadequate to sustain their interests in causation. To my knowledge, no one has inquired into primitive definitions of units of behavior, and how behavior elements enter into their taxonomic groupings. Such studies could only be conducted among hunters who are actively engaged in hunting, not upon reservation natives who have access only to memory.

GENETIC MECHANISMS IN HUNTING SOCIETIES

The nature of the hunting behavior system early imposed conditions on mating behavior both within and between groups. These conditions have had important influences on genetic mechanisms at any given time, and on trends in human evolution over long periods of time in the history of our species. In succinct form, the most salient generalizations applicable to contemporary or recent hunting societies with a focus on big-game hunting, and which can be extrapolated into earlier times, are these: (1) They are small in numbers, with low effective population size. The nature of a hunting economy does not ordinarily permit the aggregation of large numbers of people in one place at one time. The high population density of marine hunters such as the Eastern Aleuts was achieved by multiplication of the number of demes, less so of the size of demes. Most bands tend to be genetic units, with the obvious exception of Australian bands which tend to be exogamous, in which case the tribal units are the important genetic units. (2) Their populations are isolated and the constituent demes are isolated in varying degree, the ideal condition for maximum evolutionary opportunity as demonstrated by Sewall Wright. (3)

The inbreeding effect is usually present and inbreeding is common. This may contribute to rapid action of selection by increasing the number of homozygotes (that would otherwise be undetected). (4) Differential fertility favors headmen, chiefs, or especially successful hunters. They have more wives and more children in proportion to other hunters. Their reproductive success has been a major factor in the evolution of intelligence and will be discussed in more detail. (5) There is a high frequency of accidental deaths. Though the causes of death are poorly known, it does appear that wild animals, disease, and starvation, in various combinations, are prominent among the causes of death of subadults and adults. The category of wild animals may be matched or exceeded by intertribal fights, cannibalism, and related human disaffections. (6) There is a short life span. Although the data are poor and probably over estimate longevity, twenty years is probably a more accurate estimate for a generation than 25. Outstanding exceptions may be found and the contrast between short-lived Eskimos in the Canadian Arctic and much longer-lived Eastern Aleuts has likely been duplicated in a number of places and times (Laughlin, 1963b, p. 638). (7) There is high infant mortality. This again prominently varies with the richness of the exploitational area and the technological sophistication of the people. Infanticide plays an extremely important role. When stillbirths and miscarriages are considered, the genetic wastage may be extremely high. (8) There are frequent population bottlenecks. Annual fluctuations in food supply are common, especially for people hunting migratory animals. Related to the annual cycles of the animals are those of environmental conditions. Dramatic annual alterations occur in desert areas where increase or decrease in water supply involves multitudinous correlative changes, and in arctic regions where water is replaced with ice. Meager storage facilities make it impossible to utilize the common superabundance, for example of caribou, much later in the year. Populations appear to adjust to the lower limits of food resources. During periods of privation the practice of abortion, infanticide, exposure of elderly and infirm persons, and "voluntary death" may further reduce the population size.

Bottlenecks provide opportunity for inadequate sampling between generations. (9) *Founder's Principle:* New communities or demes are often founded by only a few migrants, and these may be closely related. The genetical importance of such partitioning of the gene pool is recognized in the concept of "founder's principle" (see Mayr, 1963, p. 211). The founders carry a small fraction of the genetical variation of the total population. Some authors identify "founder's principle" with random genetic drift. This kind of migrant sampling has been extremely important in human evolution and may therefore be worth separate itemization. (10) There has been fusion of remnant groups. R. H. Osborne has noted that the fusion of surviving groups following a severe bottleneck has an effect similar to recurrent selection. The resulting recombinations may represent an improvement over either of the parental contributors. (11) Gene flow is predominantly from central to marginal populations. Marginal populations do not ordinarily feed back to central populations.

Two points of special importance to the relationship between the hunting behavior pattern and human evolution are seen in (a) the population characteristics of such hunting groups leading to diversity, and (b) those favoring the evolution of intelligence. The opportunities for random variation and for the development of differences between groups are maximized in these groups. Small, isolated populations, with many subdivisions, frequently strained through genetic bottlenecks, and with migrant sampling ("founder's principle") as a major form of moving into new territories and new continents constitutes the ideal conditions for rapid evolution, when viewed over long time periods, and for the accumulation of many chance differences. In examining the mechanism of human raciation, and especially the role of isolation and migration, G. Lasker provides the relevant comment:

Race formation seems to be a continual process. Although there is no reason to doubt that it has operated on man, natural selection has not been satisfactorily demonstrated as a significant factor in racial differentiation. It is more plausible that small groups would come to differ racially by the purely random process of primarily endogamous mate selection. Subsequent rapid increases in population size

based on cultural advantages or historical opportunities could be responsible in the main for the kind of racial pattern manifest today (1960).

High intergroup diversity is a characteristic of the human species which is closely related to the group size, isolation, and generational and migrational sampling inadequacies of hunting groups. To the isolating factors, those of culture as such, of distance and of distributional pattern, the common result of inhibition of gene flow over distance, of dilution of frequencies outward from centers are especially effective. As Shapiro has remarked, "Thus although some cross-cultural miscegenation is an ancient phenomenon and can occur in a variety of ways, the isolating effects of culture are on the whole predominant" (1957, p. 24).

A major function of culture is that of maximizing the welfare of its members and therefore minimizing and screening contacts with nonmembers. The more cultures there are, the more diffusion barriers there are to gene flow. This is especially important over distance. Contemporary racial diversity has been enhanced by the distributional patterns imposed by the hunting system. In fact, viewing the genetic diversity of our species from the question of why it did not break into separate species, we find that our knowledge of what holds the species together is not well studied. Mayr has remarked, "The essential genetic unity of species cannot be doubted. Yet the mechanisms by which this unity is maintained are still largely unexplored. Gene flow is not nearly strong enough to make these species anywhere nearly panmictic. It is far more likely that all the populations share a limited number of highly successful epigenetic systems and homeostatic devices which place a severe restraint on genetic and phenotypic change" (Mayr, 1963, p. 523). The human species fits this problem and deserves the kind of study necessary to elucidate the ways in which its unity has been maintained.

The rewards accruing to superior hunters within a community throw light on the evolution of intelligence. The headmen, chiefs, or leaders are generally excellent hunters. Their excellence in hunting depends in part on intelligence, which, however defined, is a multigenic trait with moderate to high heritability. The headmen have more wives than other members and consequently more children, and thus contribute differentially to the succeeding generation. This process can be demonstrated for contemporary hunters and its projection into earlier times provides a major insight into the way in which the hunting system has favored the evolution of intelligence.

The Xavante Indians of Brazil illustrate this mechanism. "As befits the chief, he had more wives (five) than any other member of the tribe" (Neel *et al.*, 1964, p. 94). This man had 23 surviving offspring and in descending order of wives, one man had four wives and six offspring, four men had three wives and thirteen offspring, ten men had two wives and 23 offspring, and 21 men had one wife and 24 offspring. Thus, the leader has produced over 25 per cent of the surviving offspring.

The Anaktuvuk Eskimos of Alaska, a small inland group of some 78 caribou hunters, illustrate the disproportionate contributions of a superior hunter. One elderly but able hunter, one of the founders of the isolate, had seven children of whom six had the blood group gene B. Five matings from these children produced ten children of whom eight had at least one gene for blood group B. Thus, he had contributed to some 20 per cent of the total living population (Laughlin, 1957).

It is possible to generalize on headmen from the existing literature. As a rule they appear to be well informed, to have better memories, more equipment or material goods, more wives including access to women who may not formally be their wives, to be above average in physical constitution, and—directly as a consequence of their superior hunting abilities—to have a better food supply than those less well endowed. A multitude of consequences follow. The wife, or wives, of a headman are better fed and more likely to carry a pregnancy to full term, and any infants are likely to be better fed and therefore more likely to survive to reproductive age than those infants that are less well fed.

Crow has suggested that it would be easier, by selection, to change the intellectual or other aptitudes of a population than to change the incidence of disabling diseases or sterility. "This is not to say that there has not been some selection for intelligence in the past, but it has surely been much less intense than that for fertility, for example" (Crow, 1961, p. 429). This is certainly true, but I would suggest that there has been a constant selection for intelligence and that it has been sufficient to prepare the species for a relatively rapid shift over to civilization where assortative mating tracks based on culturally defined interests in very large populations take over the role of selecting for intelligence and aptitudes.

EVOLUTIONARY ASPECTS

Hunting played the dominant role in transforming a bipedal ape into a tool-using and tool-making man who communicated by means of speech and expressed a complex culture in the infinite number of ways now known to us. The evolutionary importance of hunting can be demonstrated by a combination of nutritional, psychological, and anatomical (including neurophysiological) aspects of our contemporary behavior, with the fossil and archeological record, and with primate comparisons.

Three things are essential to this thesis. One, that hunting is a complex sequence behavior pattern beginning in childhood. Two, the nutritional advantages of a carnivorous-omnivorous diet extend into several aspects of life ranging from childhood dependency and longer period for learning over to the increased territorial mobility permitting occupation of any place in the world. Three, hunting behavior is prior, psychologically, to the use and manufacture of tools. In brief, what the tools were used for, how they could be made to serve the objectives of the hunter, what the hunter was doing that he needed tools, and what he was doing that developed the mind that conceived the design of tools, that executed their manufacture, and that employed them and revised them, these are the important considerations. Tools provide a thermometer for measuring intellectual heat generated by the animal, they are not the source of heat. There is of course a constant feedback so that tool use contributes to the patterning of the brain, thus becoming both subject and object in both a neurological and philosophical sense. For these reasons I stress the importance of the behavior first, and the relevance and importance of tools second. Tools did not make the man, man made tools in order to hunt.

The nutritional advantages of a carnivorous-omnivorous diet, its correlates and its consequences are well attested (Oakley, 1961; Spuhler, 1959; Washburn and Avis, 1958). Spuhler has presented the most succinct itemization in a context with six other preconditions for the beginning of culture: accommodative vision, bipedal locomotion, manipulation, carnivorous-omnivorous diet, cortical control of sexual behavior, vocal communication, and expansion of the association areas in the cerebral cortex. A large supply of compact animal proteins, high in caloric values, concentrated and packaged in a container suitable for transport, its own skin, provides a basis for food sharing, for the differentiation of functions in a family unit, for the long dependency of human children, and such a food supply facilitates migration and it provides more time in which to accomplish other things. Plant-eating primates, gorillas for example, must procure a much larger bulk of shoots, leaves, and stems to have an equivalent caloric value, and they must spend a much longer period each day in eating their vegetarian diet (Schaller, 1963, pp. 149–68). They do not share food. One can only remark that if such vegetarians did want to share food they would need baskets or wheel-barrows. The amount of information which must be exchanged between plant eaters is small compared with that needed in group-hunting of large animals, wolves for example. Equally to the point is the lack of challenge or psychological stimulation involved in plant eating. Plants do not run away nor do they turn and attack. They can be approached at any time from any direction, and they do not need to be trapped, speared, clubbed, or pursued on foot until they are exhausted.

The value of plant food in sustaining a hunting population during periods when meat is in short supply, and the value of invertebrates that can be collected by simple methods, for example the crucial use of sea urchins collected in the intertidal zone by Aleuts, cannot be overlooked. It is however the focus on hunting moving game that has organized the structure and functioning of humans, not the casually collected foods.

Washburn has remarked (Washburn and Avis, 1958, p. 433) that hunting has had three important effects on human behavior and nature: psychological, social, and territorial, and he has summarized by indicating that after bipedalism came the use of tools, the hunting habit, increase in intelligence and, finally, the animal we know as man (p. 435). This is a coherent and synoptic view which is well documented. However, the priority of the hunting habit before the use of tools should be considered as a necessary sequence. Bipedalism was a necessary precondition, but at least two apparently well differentiated species, *Australopithecus robustus* and *A. africanus,* and possibly a third, "Homo habilis," to use the names of three groups of uncertain taxonomic status, were bipedal, and only one appears to have continued along the line leading into man. The possibility that desiccation led to a dietary change requiring carnivorism for the Australopithecines is well known, and the possibility that *A. robustus* remained primarily a vegetarian and became extinct is equally well known. The archeological evidence is ambiguous and whether both of these lines used tools and made tools is uncertain. If *A. robustus* was a vegetarian, it is difficult to imagine what he was doing with tools. On the other hand, tools became useful to a bipedal hunter because they do facilitate killing and the reduction of the dead animal for food and fabricational purposes.

Dental morphology is of little help. Gorillas have very large canines and high cusps compared to humans, and they are vegetarian. Humans can and do eat everything from leaves to meat and bones with no detectable correlaton between the diet and their dental morphology. In fact, humans the world over promptly remove their cusps and fissural patterns by normal attrition during childhood so that it is difficult to find a readable fissural pattern in an adult male or female primitive. Chipped teeth are found in Eskimos and in Aleuts, in keeping with their extensive chewing on bones and bone splinters, and the use of their teeth for fabricational purposes. Deducing what humans have eaten with their teeth is comparable to deducing what they have held in their prehensile hand.

At what point in the continuous line leading to man we choose to apply the label *human* is subjective in the extreme. Because of the necessity of childhood instruction for hunting, the overall integration of posture, vision, hand, communication, and brain required for hunting behavior, I would suggest that this was the crucial adaptation and therefore provides a meaningful criterion for so labeling the organism who had achieved this level of organization.

CONCLUSIONS AND SUMMARY

The overall evolutionary efficacy of hunting as a master integrating pattern of our species is illustrated in many ways. Man successfully evolved with a simple technology over hundreds of thousands of years; he migrated into all the continents and climes; he solved all the local problems of adaptation with ingenuity and inventiveness. These feats are climaxed by the relative rapidity with which he developed civilizations and, equally important, that he as a hunter was converted to civilized man independently in different continents. He was obviously preadapted and even predisposed to civilization.

The inherent ingenuity of primitive hunters, of marginal peoples generally, can be attested by citing inventions and by examining the great heterogeneity of marginal peoples (Lowie, 1952). It is commonplace to cite the inventions of various peoples, but I think it more instructive to assemble them within the context of an historical tradition rather than cut across cultures gleaning exotic examples. Two points of interest result: the inventions listed are confined almost entirely to material devices and particular peoples have been more inventive than is generally appreciated. The kayak with three-piece keelson of the Aleuts, the snow dome house of the Arctic Eskimos, the double-purchase pulley, screw-thread, slit goggle, visor, three-legged stool, etc., of the Aleut-Eskimo stock is matched by their development of human anatomical knowledge, their knowledge of natural phenomena, prominently including animal behavior, and by their systems of navigation on sea and land. Goggles and stools are well known, however; the nonmaterial inventions are not. The material things remain clever devices until the intellectual context of their invention and use is comprehended. Where primitive hunters have not invented material devices that capture the attention of observers, they are less often credited with inventiveness and their knowledge

in those areas in which they invested their time and interest is underestimated.

The psychological differences between hunters contrasted with farmers and livestock breeders has properly been emphasized (Clark and Piggott, 1965, pp. 157-59). However, it should be noted that primitive hunters domesticated the dog, probably more than once, and this may have provided a model for the domestication of other animals. As I have suggested previously, hunters capture animals for use as pets and a major use is the instruction of children in animal behavior. Domestication of the dog ranks as a great achievement in the investigation of wolf behavior and subsequently in animal breeding.

The theory of cultural advance offered by Ginsburg and Laughlin (1966), suggesting that crossing the biobehavioral threshold leading to civilization depended upon the important ingredient of assortative mating tracks within large populations, is an explanation of how existing variability can be recombined and repackaged without the addition of new genetic materials or of outside intervention.

Man's life as a hunter supplied all the other ingredients for achieving civilization: the genetic variability, the inventiveness, the systems of vocal communication, the coordination of social life. It could not provide the large and dense population size nor the internal genetic restructuring attendant upon the establishment of assortative mating tracks whereby the frequency of matings between persons sharing culturally defined interests and talents could be maximized. The basic anatomical structure, the neurophysical processes, and the basic patterns of behavior had been so successfully organized and integrated by the attention given to the lifelong study of behavior and anatomy and the other portions of the total sequence pattern that rapid and extensive changes could take place. While learning to learn, man, the hunter, was learning animal behavior and anatomy, including his own. He domesticated himself first and then turned to other animals and to plants. In this sense, hunting was the school of learning that made the human species self-taught.

In the final analysis we return to the informational requirements of the hunting system for the development of the individual. Hunting must be learned by children and the children must learn by observation and by participation the habit of critical observation, the facts concerning animal behavior, and the appropriate responses. It is insufficient to tell children about animal behavior and anatomy; it must be prorammed into them in a far more integrated fashion. A corollary point which applies to hunting groups and their history clearly is that a simple technology does not indicate simple-mindedness. We know a good deal about the magnitude of the task accomplished with simple tools, the hundreds of thousands of years of successful human evolution. We know therefore that the major information investment went into the nervous system and the non-material aspects of the highly adaptive hunting cultures.

References

Baerends, G. P. "The Contribution of Ethology to the Study of the Causation of Behavior." *Acta Physiologica et Pharmacologica Neerlandica.* 7 (1958), 466–99.

Balke, Bruno, and Clyde Snow. "Anthropological and Physiological Observations on Tarahumara Endurance Runners." *American Journal of Physical Anthropology* (n.S.), 23 (1965), 293–301.

Boas, Franz. "Invention." In F. Boas et al. (Eds.), *General Anthropology.* Boston, London: D.C. Heath, 1938.

Chamisso, Adelbertus De. "Cetaceorum Maris Kamtschatici Imagines, ab Aleutis e ligno fictas, Adumbravit Recensuitque." Verhandlugen der Kaiserlichen Leopoldnisch-Carolinischen Akademie der Naturforscher (Breslaw and Bonn), 4(1) (1824), 249–62 (*Nova Acta.* 12, pt. 1).

Clark, J. Graham D., and Stuart Piggott. *Prehistoric Societies:* New York: Alfred A. Knopf, 1965.

Crow, James F. "Mechanisms and Trends in Human Evolution." *Daedalus.* 90(3) (1961), 416–31.

Elliott, Henry W. *Our Arctic Province: Alaska and the Seal Islands.* New York: Scribner's, 1886.

Gajdusek, D. Carleton. "Ethnopediatrics as a Study of Cybernetics of Human Development." *American Journal of Diseases of Children.* 105 (1963), 554–59

Ginsberg, Benson E., and William S. Laughlin. "The Multiple bases of human adaptability and Achievement: a Species Point of View." *Eugenics Quarterly.* 13 (3) (1966), 240–57.

Glass, Bentley. "The Ethical Basis of Science." *Science.* 150 (3701) (1965), 1254–61.

Haldane, J. B. S. "The Argument from Animals to Men: an Examination of its Validity for Anthropology." *Journal of the Royal Anthropological Institute of Great Britain and Ireland.* 86 (1956), 1–14.

Hallowell, A. Irving. "Ojibwa Ontology, Behavior, and World View." In Stanley Diamond (Ed.), *Culture in History: Essays in Honor of Paul Radin.* New York: Columbia University Press, 1960.

Hamburg, David. "The Relevance of Recent Evolutionary Changes to Human Stress Biology." In S. L. Washburn (Ed.), *Social Life of Early Man.* Chicago: Aldine Publishing Company, 1961.

Heizer, Robert F. "The Aleut Sea Otter Hunt in the Late Nineteenth Century." *Anthropological Papers of the University of Alaska.* 8 (2) (1960), 131–35.

Lasker, G. W. (Ed.). *The Processes of Ongoing Human Evolution.* Detroit: Wayne State University Press, 1960.

Laughlin, William S. "Blood Groups of the Anaktuvuk Eskimos, Alaska." *Anthropological Papers of the University of Alaska.* 6 (1) (1957), 2–15.

_____. "Acquisition of Anatomical Knowledge by Ancient Man." In S. L. Washburn (Ed.), *Social Life of Early Man.* Chicago: Aldine Publishing Company, 1961.

_____. "Primitive Theory of Medicine: Empirical Knowledge. In Iago Galdston (Ed.), *Man's Image in Medicine and Anthropology.* Institute of Social and Historic Medicine, Monograph 4 (1963a), 116–40. New York: The New Academy of Medicine.

_____. "Eskimos and Aleuts: their Origins and Evolution." *Science.* 142 (3593) (1963b), 633–45.

_____. "Human Migration and Permanent Occupation in the Bering Sea Area." In D. M. Hopkins (Ed.) *The Bering Land Bridge.* Stanford: Stanford University Press, 1967.

Linne, Sigvald. "Technical Secrets of American Indians." *Journal of the Royal Anthropological Institute of Great Britain and Ireland.* 87 (2) (1957), 149–64.

Lowie, Robert H. "The Heterogeneity of Marginal Cultures." In Sol Tax (Ed.), *Selected Papers of the 29th International Congress of Americanists.* 3 (1952), 1–7. Chicago University of Chicago Press.

Marsh, Gordon H. "A Comparative Survey of Eskimo-Aleut Religion." *Anthropological Papers of the University of Alaska.* 3 (1) (1954), 21–36.

Marsh, Gordon H., and William S. Laughlin. "Human Anatomical Knowledge among the Aleutian Islanders." *Southwestern Journal of Anthropology.* 12 (1) (1956), 38–78.

Mayr, Ernst. *Animal Species and Evolution.* Cambridge: Belknap Press (Harvard University Press, 1963).

Neel, James V., F. M. Salzano, P. C. Junqueira, F. Keiter, and D. Maybury-Lewis. "Studies on the Xavante Indians of the Brazilian Mato Grosso." *American Journal of Human Genetics.* 16 (1) (1964), 52–140.

Nelson, Richard King. In press "Alaskan Eskimo Exploitation of the Sea Ice Environment." *Technical Notes of the U.S. Arctic Aeromedical Laboratory* (Fort Wainwright, Alaska).

Oakley, Kenneth P. "On Man's Use of Fire, with Comments on Tool-making and Hunting." In S. L. Washburn (Ed.), *So-

cial Life of Early Man. Chicago: Aldine Publishing Company, 1961.

Rasmussen, Knud. "Intellectual Culture of the Hudson Bay Eskimo, I: Intellectual Culture of the Iglulik Eskimos." *Report of the fifth Thule Expedition, 1921–24,* 7 (1). Copenhagen: Gyldendalske Boghandel, 1929.

Schaller, George B. *The Mountain Gorilla: Ecology and Behavior.* Chicago: University of Chicago Press, 1963.

Shapiro, Harry L. "Impact of Culture on Genetic Mechanisms." *In The Nature and Transmission of the Genetic and Cultural Characteristics of Human Populations.* New York: Milbank Memorial Fund, 1957.

Shirokogorov, S. M. *Psychomental Complex of the Tungus.* London: Kegan Paul, Trench, Trubner, 1935.

Spuhler, J. N. "Somatic Paths to Culture." In J. N. Spuhler (Ed.), *The Evolution of Man's Capacity for Culture.* Detroit: Wayne State University Press, 1959.

Washburn, Sherwood L., and Virginia Avis. "Evolution of Human Behavior." In Anne Roe and G. G. Simpson (Eds.), *Behavior and Evolution.* New Haven: Yale University Press, 1958.

Wissler, Clark. *The Relation of Nature to Man in Aboriginal America.* New York: Oxford University Press, 1926.

Part VI

The Evolution of Homo Erectus, Later Hominids and Culture

The initial article by Shapiro brings to light some intriguing facts associated with the disappearance of Sinanthropus remains from China. The selection by Sullivan gives an account of a recent fossil find in France which may bridge the gap between Homo erectus and Neanderthal man. Despite opposing views on the subject, the article by Solecki argues strongly for Neanderthal as an ancestor of present day Homo sapiens sapiens. Using contemporary ethnographic data derived from the !Kung Bushmen of South Africa, the final article of this section provides clues to the origins of numerous social and demographic changes that may have taken place when people went from a hunting-gathering style of life to one based on farming and herding. The reader may wish to see F. C. Howell's *Early Man,* Revised edition, (New York: Time-Life Books, 1967) for additional coverage.

The Strange Unfinished Saga of Peking Man

In 1941 Peking man disappeared. At least a half-million years ago he had lived in China, near Peking. Like all other extinct forms of man, no tradition of his former existence had survived among his successors, for "racial memory" is no help in tracing the record of human evolution. And then, for a little more than a decade, beginning in 1926, he made a gradual reappearance from oblivion in a blaze of publicity. First, a couple of teeth, and later, bits and pieces of his fossilized skull and skeleton, until about 40 individuals of this long lost population could be identified. As the fragments were found, they were widely and copiously reported in the press, the first time to my knowledge that so general and popular an interest had been displayed in the discovery of the traces of human evolution. Perhaps the Scopes trial had something to do with this, at least in the United States, for it was in 1925 that William Jennings Bryan and Clarence S. Darrow, with their arrays of distinguished authorities, had staged the last major public debate on the validity of evolution, particularly human evolution. As a result, the public was aware of the issue and receptive to fresh evidence relating to it.

In scientific circles the discovery of Peking man caused great excitement. In a short time he became the subject of a series of learned articles and papers, which quickly and firmly established his significance as an outstanding landmark in the hominid procession. For the Chinese, his relics took on the value of crown jewels.

The report from China in 1941 of the loss of these precious fossils spread rapidly around the world, particularly to those scientific centers where human evolution is of major interest. At first, it seemed incredible because since the publication in the nineteenth century of Darwin's *Origin of Species*, fossils—as the sole tangible evidence of evolution—had taken on a kind of

By Harry L. Shapiro. Reprinted with permission, from *Natural History* Magazine, November 1975, p. 8 Copyright © by The American Museum of Natural History.

sanctity. They were the rare fragments of the successive worlds of the past and the keys to understanding the forms that life took in its tireless and unending adaptation to the environment. And among these relics none had a more immediate interest than those that traced the course of human evolution. If an institution was lucky enough to own any of these fossils, it protected them with special care. Permission to handle and examine them was granted only to qualified experts. Since their scientific value had come to be recognized, there had never been such a disaster.

Nowhere was the loss more devastating than at the American Museum of Natural History. Here, Franz Weidenreich, the scientist then most deeply involved with Peking man, was writing his definitive study of the fossils. Since 1934, he had been studying them in China. Although Japan had been at war with China since 1937, in the summer of 1941 Japanese forces threatened to take complete control of the Peking area, and Weidenreich was forced to abandon his laboratory there and seek haven in New York. Reluctantly, he left the fossils in Peking. For at least seven years they had been his major, indeed his sole, scientific concern. The only physical, tangible records of them that he took with him were casts, photographs, and drawings.

The American Museum of Natural History was involved in another way with these famous fossils. In fact we may, in a sense, claim to have had some small share in the chain of events that led to their discovery. In 1921, the Museum's Dr. Walter Granger, chief paleontologist of the Central Asiatic Expedition organized by Roy Chapman Andrews, was in Peking. In that year he joined Dr. J. G. Andersson, a Swedish geologist associated with the Geological Survey of China, on a trip to Choukoutien, some 25 miles southwest of Peking. Granger was not permitted to pursue any independent investigations there since the Central Asiatic Expedition had made an agreement with the Chinese government not to carry on any scientific work in North China.

Andersson had made an earlier trip to Choukoutien in 1918, but this second trip with Granger proved to be much more profitable. A number of fossils of various animals were located, and a promising site for further study and exploration was identified. The prospects were good enough to warrant continued work. Dr. Otto Zdansky, who was a young assistant to Dr. Andersson, was assigned the task of exploring further the resources of Choukoutien.

What led Andersson and Granger to Choukoutien in the first place is an interesting bit of paleontological sleuthing. For years European paleontologists had known that one likely source for the "discovery" of fossils was the traditional Chinese drugstore where peasants sold the "dragon bones" they found in their fields. In the Chinese pharmacopoeia, dragon bones were a standard item. Ground and powdered, they were prepared as specifics by the local medical practitioners. What the peasants did not know, and the peleontologists did, was that the dragon bones were often fossil fragments of extinct animals. As far back as 1901, Dr. K. A. Haberer had found a fossilized tooth in one of these drugstores, and it had been reported as human by Prof. Max Schlosser in 1903. But fossils discovered secondhand in drugstores have only a limited value since they lack the documentation needed for their orientation in time and association with other forms of life. They are of use, however, in suggesting to the experts that where they were found, other fossils are likely to be discovered for more precise reconstruction. Choukoutien is only one of a number of sites found by tracing dragon bones back to their lairs. Years later Prof. Ralph von Koenigswald, a distinguished geologist and student of early man, found the famous *Gigantopithecus* molar teeth in a Canton drugstore.

While these preliminary investigations were going on at Choukoutien in the early 1920's, there was a young Canadian in the wings ready to step forward and take a leading role. This was Davidson Black, professor of anatomy at the Peking Union Medical College, one of the best known in China and one generously supported by Rockefeller Foundation funds. Interested in human evolution, Black was attracted to China because he had become convinced that it was a potentially rich source of fossil evidence for the reconstruction of the hominid odyssey through time. Black had already collaborated with Andersson in writing reports on the human remains found in several prehistoric sites discovered by the latter. And he had achieved recognition as an authority on human skeletal remains.

In 1926, things began to happen. Toward the end of that year both Andersson and Black announced a most unexpected discovery: two fossil teeth, a premolar (bicuspid) and a third upper molar, from Choukoutien were found to be unmistakably human. The teeth were in a collection of fossils sent by Andersson's assistant, Zdansky, to Uppsala, Sweden, for identification.

Black, in reporting the find in *Nature,* cited both Zdansky and Andersson as placing these human relics in the Upper Pliocene because of their association with various extinct mammals. This would have put man in China at least two million years ago—at that time an extreme date for early man. But Black left open the possibility that the fossils might be only from the early Quaternary, some one million years ago. He concluded, "Whether it be of late Tertiary or of early Quaternary age, the outstanding fact remains that, for the first time on the Asiatic continent north of the Himalayas, archaic hominid fossil material has been recovered, accompanied by complete and certain geological data. The actual presence of early man in eastern Asia is therefore now no longer a matter of conjecture."

In that year—1926—the evidence for what was then called early man was very sparse. Some thirty years before, Dr. Eugene DuBois had found the skull cap and leg bone of *Pithecanthropus erectus* in Java. The only other early hominid that had come to light was *Australopithecus africanus,* reported in 1925 from Africa by Prof. Raymond Dart. But its status was still far from clear. Many authorities were not yet ready to accept it as a true hominid. And even Dart, in spite of Robert Ardrey's much later reportage in *African Genesis,* was not altogether clear on the significance of his discovery. The very name he gave this fossil, *Australopithecus africanus*—the southern monkey from Africa—reveals his uncertain, even ambivalent, evaluation. Thus the appearance of early man in China took on a special significance.

When we recall the turmoil that was tearing China apart in the mid-twenties, it seems incredible that Chinese and foreign scientists were able to pursue their delving into the ancient past of this ancient nation. The war lords, who were battling each other and disrupting the life of the country, and the growing antipathy toward foreigners and their treaty ports, fade into a kind of irrelevant background to the drama of the discovery of this earlier population of man. While to many of the Chinese the digging at Choukoutien must have appeared as an unrealistic mania if they even knew of it.

Despite all this, in 1927 Black organized a systematic exploration of Choukoutien, which seemed warranted by Zdansky's discovery of the fossil human teeth. At the very end of this field season, another tooth was found. Black promptly announced its discovery and ventured to give it a generic name, *Sinanthropus pekinensis* (Chinese man from Peking), thus suggesting that it was distinct from other types of man. To some experts the evidence seemed rather slim for the reconstruction of a wholly new genus of man. But Black was in part justified by the discovery in 1928 of a juvenile skull that settled all doubts.

In the succeeding years new finds, many made by Black's assistant, W. C. Pei, came to light and greatly enriched the documentation of this new variety of man. In 1931, I visited Black in his laboratory at the Peking Union Medical College. I watched him meticulously cleaning newly discovered fossils in a cloud of fine dust sprayed out by the dental drill he was using to remove encrustations on the bones. After his tragic and untimely death in 1934, it was reported that inhalation of this dust had contributed to it. Before he died, Black published some reports on the fossils that continued to be laid bare by the unceasing excavations, but the definitive studies were still in the future.

These fell to the lot of Prof. Franz Weidenreich who was appointed in late 1934 to replace Black. Weidenreich, an internationally known German scientist who had made important contributions in hematology and anatomy, had later in his career become fascinated by the problems of human evolution. He had written a report on the Ehringsdorf skull, a Neanderthaloid skull found in Germany, and various other papers dealing with the problems of early man. In 1934 he had left Germany, where his Jewish origins would have become a hazard, to accept a visiting professorship in anatomy at the University of Chicago.

At the end of 1934, he was offered the post recently left vacant by Black's death. The opportunity to settle in Peking where he could pursue investigations in the center of his interests was too attractive to refuse. He took active charge of the scientific investigations at Choukoutien until the Japanese occupation of China finally forced a cessation of all work at Choukoutien and obliged Weidenreich to leave Peking and the laboriously accumulated fossil remains of Peking man.

Why, one wonders, did not Weidenreich take the fossils with him? He knew that the Peking Union Medical College, where the fossils were kept, had thus far escaped Japanese raiding of its treasures because it was technically American property, and Japan and the United States were not yet at war. But the prospects for their future safety already looked bleak. The record is clear that he was deeply concerned with this problem. The options open to him and to the officials in charge of the Cenozoic Research Laboratory were these: they could put the fossils in a secret vault or some other hiding place in Peking, thereby avoiding the danger of shipping them out of a country in turmoil; they could dispatch them to some quieter section of China where they could be protected (Southwest China was such an area considered by the director); or they could send them out of the country altogether. Shipment to the United States was seriously considered. In a letter written January 10, 1941, to Dr. Henry Houghton, director of the Peking Union Medical College, Drs. W. H. Wong and T. H. Yin weighed the merits of the second and third choices. They concluded that in view of the practical difficulties of sending the fossils to the Geological Survey Station in Southwest China, it might be wiser to allow Weidenreich to carry them with him to some institution in the United States, despite the understanding with the Rockefeller Foundation that anything excavated at Choukoutien must remain in China.

A letter dated July 11, 1941, from Weidenreich to Wong summarizes a great deal of discussion and correspondence on the disposition of the fossils: "We arrived at the conclusion that it involved too great a risk to take the originals as part of my baggage. If they were discovered by the customs control in an embarkation or transit port, they could be confiscated. In addition, it had to be taken into account that the objects are too valuable to expose them to an un-protected voyage in so dangerous a time. Con-sidering all the pros and cons, we decided, at least for the moment, it would be wise to leave the originals where they are now, that is, in the safe of the Cenozoic Research Laboratory in the building of the Department of Anatomy at the P.U.M.C." He went on to say that Rockefeller Foundation authorities in New York agreed, but that if conditions deteriorated further, the matter could be reconsidered.

I remember talking with Weidenreich on the matter, and I recall that the decision not to risk shipping the fossils in his private baggage was made after he failed to convince the U.S. ambas-sador and the commanding officer of the Marine Corps in Peking to send them out in official bag-gage. This would have avoided the red tape of customs regulations.

At any rate, nothing was done during those crucial months of 1941. And Weidenreich left China, taking with him beautifully prepared casts, photographs, and detailed drawings he would require for the completion of his study of Peking man.

The opus *The Skull of Sinanthropus Pekinen-sis* appeared in 1943. It was a major study and provided specialists throughout the world with a definitive description and assessment of this an-cestral population of man. When Black first recognized and named Peking man, he identi-fied it as a distinct type of hominid living in the early Quaternary or Pleistocene and he was con-vinced that the population played a role in the evolution of *Homo sapiens*. As later finds and Weidenreich's study showed, Peking man cer-tainly was primitive. He had a brain capacity slightly under 1,100 cc., roughly 250 to 350 cc. less than modern man and about 200 cc. greater than *Pithecanthropus*, the only other early hominid generally accepted at that time. The brain capacities of both *Pithecanthropus* and *Si-nanthropus* were well above the average for apes, which ranges from 350 to 550 cc. The form and shape of the skull of Peking man showed traces of apelike characters. The brow was low and retreating, with a heavy, bony ridge above the eyes. Although much more capacious than that of any ape, the skull was still, by *Homo sapiens* standards, poorly filled out and traces of ridges still, remained. The jaw, too, was primi-tive, lacking a true manlike chin. The teeth, however, were definitely human, with reduced canines and lacking the gap, or diastema, in front of the upper canine where, in ape jaws, the projecting canine of the mandible can be fitted when the jaw is closed. Peking man, as esti-mated from his limb bones, was short—about 5 feet, 1½ inches.

One problem that surfaced early was the rela-tionship that Peking man bore to the then only other generally accepted early man—*Pithecan-thropus*. Black's identification of his finds as a distinct group was challenged by the distin-guished anatomist Le Gros Clark, who claimed that both *Sinanthropus* and *Pithecanthropus* belonged to the same species. A minor contro-versy between Clark and Weidenreich on this point proved of little consequence since they were fundamentally in agreement. Weidenreich, in his study, recognized the close relationship of the two types and compared their distinguish-able differences to the racial distinctions among various groups of mankind today.

The dating of Peking man has never been as conclusive as one would like. One difficulty is that estimates on dates of the Pleistocene have varied with new geologic interpretations. Another difficulty is the precise placement of Peking man in the Pleistocene by associating him with extinct animals whose time spans are also subject to variation. At present, scientists generally agree that Peking man lived in the mid-Pleistocene (somewhat later than Black's estimate), probably during the second glacia-tion. One interpretation extends the Pleistocene period for two million years, which would date Peking man back about one million years. On a more conservative scale, Peking man lived 500,000 years ago. These dates may be modified as new data become accessible. Even now, recent paleomagnetic studies by Allen Cox suggest that Peking man might be dated at 650,000 years ago.

Since Weidenreich's time, another important reorientation has occurred that has affected the attitude toward *Sinanthropus*. This is the recent accumulation of australopithecine and related fossils from Africa. The first of these, although known to Weidenreich, played no part in his as-sessment of Peking man, since he and many others regarded it as rather apelike. Today the relative abundance of these hominids has clarified the picture. They are a much earlier form of manlike creature and existed as far back as four to five million years ago. Thirty to forty years ago *Sinanthropus* and *Pithecanthropus* looked very primitive to our eyes; now, contrasted with the far earlier African forms, they are well-developed hominids, very close to *Homo sapiens.*

A gap remains between Peking and modern man. Weidenreich and others have filled it in with Neanderthal man, whom they regard as the logical transitional stage between the two, just as *Sinanthropus* and *Pithecanthropus* partly fill the evolutionary sequence after the African australopithecines.

Weidenreich was also struck by a number of anatomical characteristics of the Peking skull and dentition that are remarkably similar to those found among the Chinese and other Mongoloids today, but that are rare or nonexistent in other racial groups. From these comparisons he concluded that Peking man, if not the exclusive ancestral group of the living Mongoloids, must have played a major role in their evolution. He envisaged human evolution toward *Homo sapiens* going on simultaneously in various parts of the world, thus leading to some extent to the production of the geographic distinctions that exist among modern man.

When word reached us in December, 1941, that the Peking fossils had disappeared, the manner of their loss was uncertain. Conflicting accounts trickled through. Appeals to official sources in Washington for more reliable information were completely fruitless. One thing was clear: the Peking Union Medical College authorities had reconsidered what to do to insure the safety of the fossils as war between Japan and the United States became increasingly imminent, with its threat to American institutions such as the Peking Union Medical College. One story was that the fossils were packed in boxes and shipped to the coast to be transferred to the S.S. *President Harrison.* As the lighter with its precious cargo was being unloaded, it somehow tilted and the boxes slid into the harbor and were lost.

Another story, which made a bit more sense and which we tended to accept, was this. Shortly before Pearl Harbor, the Peking Union Medical College officials approached the U.S. Embassy for aid in transferring the fossils to the United States, since by then any other plan seemed impractical. The Embassy assigned a number of boxes containing the specimens to the charge of the last group of U.S. Marines to be evacuated before the Japanese took over all installations in Peking. The story went on to relate that en route to Tientsin, the train bearing the marines and their baggage was halted by Japanese troops who ransacked the luggage, including the boxes containing the fossils. As a result, they were scattered and lost.

Another version of this, reported by *The New York Times* on January 5, 1952, relates that the then commanding officer of the Marine contingent at Peking, Colonel Ashurst, had sent the fossils in footlockers to Chinwangtao where they arrived safely. According to this account, the train with its freight, including the footlockers, was captured by the Japanese.

Since this took place at the outbreak of hostilities with Japan, there was little hope of discovering the truth or of recovering any of the apparently dispersed fossils. We reluctantly resigned ourselves to the situation.

After the war, Weidenreich, stimulated by a success story in which Dr. Walter Fairservis (presently associated with the American Museum and a professor at Vassar College) played the chief role, tried again in 1947–48 to determine the circumstances of the loss and the possibility of finding the missing specimens. Shortly after the war had ended, Fairservis, a former student and a friend of mine, had written to me from Japan where he was engaged as a lieutenant in the Foreign Liaison Service of the U.S. Army. In his letter he asked if he could do anything for me while he was there. Mostly in jest, I suggested he try to find the Solo skull that the Japanese had stolen from Professor von Koenigswald's collection in Java when he was sequestered in a prison camp for the duration of the war. When, a short time later, I received a request from Washington for a description of this late Javanese fossil, I imediately, but almost increduously, began to suspect that Fairservis was on the trail of something. Two days before Christmas of 1946, he met me at the elevator of the Museum, bearing a box in his arms. He had been sent on a ship, rather than on a plane, from Japan to insure the safe delivery of the lost "ewe lamb" to von Koenigswald, who was at that time a guest in my laboratory. Fairservis had found the skull of Solo man in the Japanese emperor's Household Museum.

Encouraged by this fantastic success, Weidenreich tried to get Fairservis assigned to the Peking mystery. But unfortunately nothing could be arranged. I do not know why interest could not be aroused in Washington. Possibly the precarious situation of Chiang Kai Chek's Kuomintang government was the discouraging factor.

Another reverberation set off by the loss of the Peking fossils reached Dr. Weidenreich late in 1945. In November of that year, Frank Whitmore, a staff geologist with the U.S. Army in Tokyo, wrote the following to Dr. Tilly Edinger at Harvard: "November 8—We have just recovered at Tokyo University a collection of bones and artifacts from the famous *Sinanthropus pekinensis* site at Choukoutien, near Peking. Also the original records of Davidson Black's research there. Also the complete original plans of the excavation and their financial records 1927–1938. We want to return all this to its owner, Peking Union Medical College, and today I'm going to scour around to see how best it can be done." Two weeks later Whitmore wrote in more detail: "But speaking of publicity the *Sinanthropus* deal is really hot stuff. . . . I went out to Tokyo University where the collection was, and saw Professor H. Suzuki about it. He said he didn't know anything about it. I asked him the same question again . . . and he said, well, he *had* heard of it but didn't know where it was. I asked him a third time, and he hissed—said he'd go and look around. He was back in five minutes with the collection, which includes some chipped stones and blacked antlers, found with the *Sinanthropus* bones, and many more advanced implements and ornaments from higher levels in the Choukoutien cave. . . ."

The bones and artifacts that Whitmore found at Tokyo were from a late level at Choukoutien and were presumably not considered precious enough to be shipped off with the *Sinanthropus* fossils. But this discovery in Tokyo confirmed the fears that the fossils would have been taken by the Japanese if they had been left in Peking. And the last minute effort to move them to a safer lodging now was clearly well justified.

Yet, in the light of Dr. Whitmore's success in recovering some of the Choukoutien material, the safer course might have been to have left the fossils in Peking. In that case they would have been collected by the Japanese as rare booty and transferred with every caution for their safety and preservation to Tokyo where Dr. Whitmore might have recovered them. As a final thought on this course: What if our atomic bomb had exploded over Tokyo instead of Nagasaki?

One other version of the fate of the relics of Peking man surfaced in March, 1951, eighteen months after the Communist government had taken over China. It involved me in a very personal and totally unexpected way. At that time, the Communist press printed a story that charged The American Museum of Natural History with secretly acquiring and storing the fossils. As chairman of the Department of Anthropology, this placed me in a questionable position. The item was picked up by newspapers around the world, and *The New York Times* carried the account. I immediately issued a complete denial, which *The New York Times* printed. In the following year the same story was broadcast from China at least two more times. I didn't bother to deny the later versions since the repetitions began to look like convenient propaganda. And I assumed that any reasonable colleague reading such nonsense would realize the absurdity and futility of such an allegation. What could one do with such world-famous specimens if they had been illicitly acquired? Any exhibition or scientific use of them would have been like exhibiting a stolen Mona Lisa. And surely they had no aesthetic appeal that might have gratified my solitary enjoyment of them.

I did uncover a clue, however, to the way this story may have originated. Shortly before Weidenreich died, he had been visited in his laboratory by a well-known English paleontologist, Prof. D. M. S. Watson. Watson told me that on his return to London he had invited some of his graduate students to tea in his office, where he described some of the interesting things he had seen in the collections at The American Museum of Natural History. He mentioned that he had called on Weidenreich, who had shown him the skull of Peking man. Watson later explained to me that inadvertently he had not made it clear to the students that Weidenreich had shown him casts of Peking man, not original fossils. One of the young men, a German with Communist leanings, later left London and went to China. Watson concluded that his former student told some Chinese paleontologists that Watson had seen Peking man in the United States—not knowing that the skull was only a plaster replica.

In the decades since their disappearance, we had, I think, all become more or less reconciled or resigned to the irretrievable loss of the original Peking fossils and felt that the true story of their fate would never be established. Some slight softening of the blow has occurred in the past decade by the renewed excavation of the Choukoutien site by the Chinese, who have uncovered some new fossils of Peking man. But those are only a small fraction of the number in the original collection.

And then in April of this year we received a telephone call at the Museum from the office of Dr. William T. Foley, a distinguished heart specialist in New York City. Mr. Herman Davis, his assistant, was inquiring about Fairservis and his attempts to investigate the loss of the fossils back in 1947–48. He wanted the name of the officer with whom Fairservis had corresponded. This led to the totally unexpected and dramatic announcement that Dr. Foley was the Marine officer to whom the fossils had been assigned for transfer out of China to the United States in December, 1941, and that Mr. Davis had handled the boxes containing the specimens. These two men knew firsthand what had happened. Now, 30 years after the event, Dr. Foley, writing an account of his involvement with Peking man for his memoirs, was checking information. I immediately arranged a visit to Dr. Foley's office on East 68th Street to get the details of what had occurred. The gist of that story follows; the details are recorded on tape.

Early in December, 1941, just before hostilities broke out between Japan and the United States, Dr. Houghton, director of the Peking Union Medical College, conferred with Colonel Ashurst, who was in charge of the U.S. Marines

in the Peking area, about shipping the fossils out of the country. Colonel Ashurst and the entire Marine detachment in the Peking area were scheduled to leave for Manila on December 9. Dr. Foley, then a Marine medical officer stationed at Tientsin and a research fellow at the medical college, would have accompanied the detachment to Manila in any case. But since he had spent three years on duty in China and his term was up, he was scheduled to proceed from Manila to his home in New York City. For that reason, Colonel Ashurst had ordered Dr. Foley to carry with him in his personal baggage the endangered fossils.

Although Dr. Foley had seen some of the fossils being packed in large glass jars and placed in standard footlockers at Peking, he was in Tientsin when the operation was completed and ready for shipment. Some of these boxes were labeled as his personal luggage with his name attached to them. Some, it appears, carried the name of Colonel Ashurst. I have been unable to discover the basis for such a division or the reason for it. In any event, the footlockers bearing the names of these two officers were sent as personal luggage directly to Chinwangtao, the port city where the S.S. *President Harrison* was expected to pick up passengers for Manila.

Mr. Davis, then a pharmacist's mate in the U.S. Navy, was stationed with seveneen Marines in Dr. Foley's unit at Camp Holcomb in Chinwangtao. He was asked by Dr. Foley to receive the boxes sent in his name to Chinwangtao and take care of them as personal baggage. On December 8, the day after Pearl Harbor, Davis had already unloaded Foley's baggage and piled it in his room at the camp. That morning they were surrounded by Japanese soldiers, a Japanese cruiser appeared in the harbor, and overhead, six Japanese planes were sighted. The Japanese called on Davis and his companions to surrender. But in the tradition of the Marines they at first refused and were preparing to resist. Davis had stacked the Foley baggage as a nest with his machine gun on top, ready for use, unaware of the danger to the fossils if shots were exchanged. It ended quietly, however, because after radioing to Peking, they were ordered to surrender.

Before herding the marines off to Tientsin,

where they were to be temporarily imprisoned, the Japanese permitted each man to take a single bag of personal belongings. Their remaining boxes and trunks were to be sent on later. Davis had no idea that the Foley baggage, which was among the goods left behind, contained fossils, since he had not opened any of Foley's luggage. A week or two later, the Japanese deposited among the imprisoned marines at Tientsin a jumble of personal effects, all mixed up. They had opened the boxes left behind, ransacked them, and sent on the personal clothing and other effects, which Davis then sorted out, unaware that the fossils had not been forwarded. Davis is of the opinion that whatever fossil specimens the Japanese may have found would have been discarded in the vicinity of the Camp Holcomb buildings.

Dr. Foley told me that on the day war broke out, he had been immediately placed under arrest. He was transferred to the Marine barracks for about a week, but was then permitted to return to his house in the British Concession and allowed semidiplomatic status, which gave him the freedom of the city. Sometime later he received from Chinwangtao boxes labeled with his name. Some of these contained personal effects, others he recognized as boxes assigned to him from Peking.

I asked Dr. Foley why the boxes bearing his name were delivered, apparently intact, while the boxes belonging to the marines from Camp Holcomb had been opened and rifled, and their contents delivered in mixed-up bundles. He replied that he had opened his personal boxes and found that several skulls he kept as anatomical specimens, as well as a Chinese Buddha figure, were missing. The footlockers assigned to him from Peking, he had not examined. That the boxes had been sent to him but not to the marines he attributed to the customary Japanese courtesy and respect for rank.

Faced as he was with the prospect of internment, which in fact came shortly and lasted for four years, Dr. Foley decided to distribute the footlockers from Peking bearing his name in various depositories for safekeeping. Some went to the Swiss Warehouse and the Pasteur Institute in Tientsin and some were placed with Chinese friends on whom he could rely.

Subsequently Colonel Ashurst, Dr. Foley, and their fellow officers lost their diplomatic status and were declared prisoners of war. They were all shipped to a prison camp near Shanghai, where they took their luggage, including one footlocker carrying Ashurst's name that was for some reason considered by the colonel to contain the most precious of the fossils. These items were stored in a warehouse at the camp. While they were at this camp, the Japanese made another search of the baggage, apparently, in Dr. Foley's opinion, looking for *Sinanthropus* remains. But the marines had managed to conceal the box and it was not disturbed by the Japanese. They were still successful in safeguarding the box when they were moved to another camp at Chung Wan nearer to Shanghai.

Then in June 1945, the prisoners and their effects were transferred once again. This time to Fungtai, near Peking. Again their luggage was searched, and once again the box escaped detection. But at the end of the war this box, which had survived so many moves and so many hazards, disappeared. The last that Dr. Foley saw of it was when he and Colonel Ashurst parted company, the former sent to an iron mine in northern Japan and the latter to Hokkaido. Colonel Ashurst died a few years after the end of the war.

What then actually happened to Peking man? The obvious answer is, We don't know. But the accounts of Dr. Foley and Mr. Davis have clarified the circumstances of the disappearance and have now given us a set of options for further search. The possibilities, with varying degrees of likelihood, are these. Some of the fossils might still be miraculously discovered at Camp Holcomb, where the Japanese soldiers ransacking the baggage of the marines might have opened some of the footlockers sent from Peking and discarded what could have appeared to them to be worthless junk. A more likely possibility would be the safety of the boxes Dr. Foley consigned to the Swiss Warehouse, the Pasteur Institute, and to his friends in Tientsin, if these establishments and homes still exist and have not been emptied and put to other uses by the Chinese, and their contents irretrievably dispersed. Would Chinese soldiers clearing out such structures have been any more sophisticated in the scientific value of fossils than their Japanese predecessors? That leaves the single box that Colonel Ashurst and Dr. Foley had cherished for four years. If it was taken over at long last by the Japanese when Colonel Ashurst was transferred to Hokkaido, and if it still contained some of the fossils, the chances are good that they would have been carefully preserved by them. It is obvious from Whitmore's discovery of Choukoutien specimens in Tokyo and from the persistent search of Dr. Foley's baggage that the Japanese were eager to lay their hands on the famous fossils.

It might, at this point, be asked why worry about the fate of these fossils. New ones representing the early Peking population have been found and other are likely to be exhumed in the future. Can't these replace the lost ones? The answer is that such a site as Choukoutien is not inexhaustible. More fossils may well come to light there, but it is most unlikely that a series as large and representative as the original one will be available. Moreover, any loss of this kind is a tragedy and a serious deprivation to the study of the emergence of man. The publications on the original specimens, good as they are, may well need revision in the future as new methods and data become available. For this there is no substitute for the specimens on which they were based.

But when all this is said, there remains the very human reaction to a baffling question. If we knew incontrovertibly that the fossils were destroyed and are unrecoverable, we would, I think, reconcile ourselves to the situation. But as long as there is a shred of hope, some of us will continue to do what we can to save the lost remains from slipping, through neglect, back into the anonymity from which they had once been laboriously rescued.

The Life and Times of Man 200,000 Years Ago

The view from the entrance of the cave was awesome. Massive glaciers filled the valleys of the mountains—the Pyrenees—to the south. Across the treeless plains one could see vast herds of wooly rhinoceroses and archaic horses. There were scatterings, as well, of archaic cattle, caribou and deer.

Below the cave mouth a bluff descended to a river—today it's called the Verdouble—which flowed from a narrow gorge it had cut in the limestone bedrock. Among the willows along the stream were hints of a panther, waiting for the unwary to come for water.

Sometimes, too, a bear or a band of wolves would come along the river, the wolves on the lookout for wild pig, rabbits or other easy prey. A few elephants could be seen in the distance and occasionally an ominous reddish cloud warned of a storm that could carpet the cave with dust and sand, for the region then was arid.

But what was the nature of the human face that looked out upon this scene, some 200,000 years ago? Until a discovery made this summer in the cave, no skull of this period had been recovered with its facial structure intact. And the new skull, it has been found, represents a race of men not previously identified.

This new addition to the family of man would certainly have chilled the spines of the more faint-hearted residents of today's world. His forehead sloped sharply back from enormous eyebrows. His massive jaws were well adapted to masticating the raw flesh of his diverse hunting trophies—revealed by the bones found with his own remains.

From a few jawbones that previously were the only clues to the nature of this ancient European, one could have guessed that he was more primitive than his successor, Neanderthal Man. He represented a major epoch in the development of man—from the ape-like African of a

By W. Sullivan. Reprinted with permission, from *The New York Times,* 7 October 1971. Copyright © 1971 by the New York Times Company.

million years ago ... to the Peking Man and Java Man of 400,000 to 500,000 years ago ... to Neanderthal Man of 90,000 years ago, and modern man (represented archeologically by the Cro-Magnon Man of Europe).

Each earlier stage in this process of development was more "primitive" in a variety of respects. Even Neanderthal, the last before modern man, was so ape-like that when the skull was first discovered, it was taken to be a relic of some terrible birth defect.

That was in 1856, before man's evolution from lower species was generally accepted. The skull was in a cave in the valley of Germany's Neander River (in Old German: the Neanderthal). But since then such skulls have been found across Europe as far distant as the Middle East.

The Neanderthal skull was marked by prominent eyebrow ridges and it was considerably prognathous—its jaw protruding well forward. However, it now appears that the men who inhabited the region during the long period before the Neanderthal were even more primitive in these respects. Although the encrusting sand has only been partially dissected away from the new-found skull, it can be seen that the eyebrow ridges are enormous and the facial angle is even more prognathous.

And the brain case seems much smaller. Despite his brutish appearance, Neanderthal Man, on the average, seems to have had a brain somewhat larger than that of modern man. Some have argued that he needed more brains than we to survive the ice age with only crude stone tools and stone axes.

While the rear part of the new skull is missing, it is so pinched in and narrow, behind the eyes, that it resembles the small, elongated brain case of Peking Man. Yet the new skull lacks the central ridge which ran from the forehead back across the crown of Peking Man's skull.

The discoverers of the skull are sure of its age, and that of two massive jaw bones unearthed at roughly the same depth in the cave floor, because they were found with bones of animals associated with the earliest stage of the next-to-last ice age—a small wolf, a robust panther, four species of extinct rodents and a horse peculiar to that period.

The cave—as large as a grand ballroom—was apparently inhabited by clans of nomads whose dependence on group hunting helped stimulate the development of speech and social structure. Some 20 times during this period some 200,000 years ago—representing, perhaps, only a few centuries—the cave was occupied and its floor accumulated human and animal bones as well as crudely chipped axe heads and other weapons made largely of quartz. Between each occupancy, dust storms buried the debris, offering a clean floor to the next occupants. The total depth of these deposits amounts to several yards.

They were laid down in a dry, cool, steppe-like climate. At some levels, however, there were rivulet furrows, indicating rainy periods. Above that was a layer of consolidated coarse gravel typical of a polar climate, perhaps representing the height of that ice age, known as the Riss. On top of that was a rocky crust rich in iron and manganese formed when the climate was warm and dry. This was presumably the warm period between the last two ice ages, and it was this crust that preserved the deeper remains for posterity.

The newly-discovered skull is now at the Faculty of Sciences at the University in Marseilles and late this month will be brought to the laboratory of Professor Jean Piveteau at the University of Paris, one of the world's leading authorities on early man. It was discovered by a team, led by Henry deLumley and his wife, Marie-Antoinette deLumley, that for several years has been systematically excavating the cave.

Probably no part of the world has revealed so much about the proto-human creatures of this period as southern France. Because the limestone bedrock is easily eroded or dissolved by flowing water, numerous caverns penetrate the walls along its river channels. These provided shelter and some security from predators before man learned to build.

Much is now known about the later inhabitants of this region, the Cro-Magnon, whose skulls are virtually indistinguishable from those of modern man. These were the cave painters and they developed great skill in chipping beautifully summetrical spearheads.

They appeared there some 35,000 years ago, apparently replacing the Neanderthals either by competition or conquest. Whence they came is a major mystery.

In any case, the newly-found skull should throw light on the ancestry of Neanderthal. Its discoverers believe, from what they can see already of its features, that it will show that those inhabiting the world during the Neanderthal period evolved along several independent lines.

As the ice sheets advanced and retreated, man and the animals that he hunted were driven hither and yon. But how these enforced migrations led finally to the rise of Homo sapiens remains uncertain.

Neanderthal is not an Epithet but a Worthy Ancestor

The top of a skull was perched on the edge of the yawning excavation in the huge cavern. At first it was difficult to realize that we had before us an extreme rarity in human paleontology.

Except for its heavy brow ridge, the skullcap looked like a gigantic egg, soiled and broken. When fully exposed on the narrow excavation shelf, it was an awesome sight—obviously the head of a person who had suffered a sudden, violent end. The bashed-in skull, the displaced lower jaw and the unnatural twist of the head were mute evidence of a horrible death.

As we exposed the skeleton which lay under a heavy burden of stones, we had confirmation that this individual had been killed on the spot by a rockfall. His bones were broken, sheared and crushed on the underlying stones. A large number of rocks must have fallen on him within a split second, throwing his body backward, full-length down the slight slope while at the same time a block of stone severed his head and neck from his trunk.

Among his remains there were small concentrations of mammal bones, which might have been rodent nests. But it is equally possible these bones were dropped there as part of a funeral feast for the dead.

This was "Nandy," as we called him, a member of the species *Homo neanderthalensis* who had died about 48,000 years before. In the scientific literature he is referred to as Shanidar I, because his were the first adult human remains that we identified as Neanderthal from a cave near the village of Shanidar high in the mountains of Kurdistan in northern Iraq.

Large, airy, and conveniently near a water supply, Shanidar Cave is still a seasonal home for modern Kurdish tribesmen, as it has been for various groups of men for thousands upon thousands of years. I had led our expedition to Shanidar Cave in a search for cultural artifacts from the Old Stone Age in this part of Kurdis-

By Ralph Solecki. Reprinted with permission, from *Smithsonian* Magazine, May 1971, pp. 21-27. Copyright © 1971 by Smithsonian Institute.

tan, Iraq. Human remains, much less Neanderthal remains, were not the goal, yet altogether in four expeditions from 1951 to 1960 we uncovered nine Neanderthal skeletons.

Laboratory studies of these remains continue to this day and the results are bringing the Neanderthals closer to us in spirit and mind than we would ever have thought likely.

The Neanderthals have been a nettling problem ever since the first find was made more than 100 years ago. This was the famous faceless skull and other skeletal parts found during quarrying operations around a cave in the Neander Valley not far from Düsseldorf in Germany. Primarily through the writings of one man, Marcellin Boule, who was a greatly respected Frenchman in the field of human paleontology, the owner of the Neander skull was soon cast in the role of a brutish figure, slow, dull and bereft of sentiment.

Although we now know much more about Neanderthal man—there have been at least 155 individuals uncovered in 68 sites in Europe, the Near East and elsewhere—he still seems to hang in space on the tree of human evolution. Some anthropologists feel that he had reached a "dead-end" branch on this tree. In any case, his time span on Earth (about 80,000 years) was more than double that of modern man who replaced him, but roughly one-tenth of the time span of *Homo erectus* who preceded him.

AN ABUNDANCE OF NEANDERTHALS

The classical hypothesis, now abandoned, was that Neanderthal man was an ancestral stage through which *Homo sapiens* passed. A second theory is that Neanderthal man was a species apart from *Homo sapiens*, contemporary but reproductively isolated, as donkeys are from horses. The third is that Neanderthal man was a subspecies of early *sapiens*, forming a geographic race. On the whole, the evidence appears to indicate that the Neanderthal did not gradually change into *sapiens*, but was replaced by invading *sapiens*. The greatest difficulty for human paleontologists is that there is a real scarcity of skeletal finds to which they can point with confidence as *sapiens* of an age comparable to that of the Neanderthals.

There was, however, no scarcity of Neanderthals at Shanidar Cave. Prior to the discovery of Nandy, or Shanidar I, we had recovered the remains of an infant. It was later identified as Neanderthal by our Turkish colleague, Dr. Muzaffer Senyürek of the University of Ankara. When it was found, we had little reason to suspect that it was a Neanderthal child.

But not so with Nandy. "A Neanderthal if I ever saw one," is the comment in my field notes for the day of April 27, 1957, the day we found him. Although he was born into a savage and brutal environment, Nandy provides proof that his people were not lacking in compassion.

According to the findings of T. Dale Stewart, the Smithsonian Institution physical anthropologist who has studied all the remains of the Shanidar Neanderthals (except for the Shanidar child), Shanidar I lived for 40 years, a very old man for a Neanderthal—equivalent to a man of about 80 today. He was a prime example of rehabilitation. His right shoulder blade, collar bone and upper arm bone were undeveloped from birth. Stewart believes that his useless right arm was amputated early in life just above the elbow. Moreover, he must have been blind in his left eye since he had extensive bone scar tissue on the left side of his face. And as if this was not enough, the top right side of his head had received some damage which had healed before the time of his death.

In short, Shanidar I was a distinct disadvantage in an environment where even men in the best condition had a hard time. That Nandy made himself useful around the hearth (two hearths were found close to him) is evidenced by his unusually worn front teeth. Presumably, in lieu of his right arm, he used his jaws for grasping. But he could barely forage and fend for himself, and we must assume that he was accepted and supported by his people up to the day he died. The stone heap we found over his skeleton and the nearby mammal food remains show that even in death he was an object of some esteem, if not respect, born of close association against a hostile environment.

The discovery of Shanidar I was for us a major, and unexpected, event. The discovery, about a month later on May 23, of Shanidar II was overwhelming.

The initial exposure was made by Phil Smith, then a Harvard University graduate student, who laid bare the great eye sockets and broken face of a new Neanderthal. My first impression was of the horror a rockfall could do to a man's face. The lower jaw was broken, the mouth agape. the eye sockets, crushed out of shape by the stones, stared hollowly from under a warped heavy brow ridge, behind which was the characteristic slanting brow of the Neanderthal.

From later reconstruction of the event, we determined that Shanidar II was killed by a relatively minor rockfall, followed closely by a major rockfall that missed the dead man. His demise did not go unnoticed by his companions. Sometime after the tumult, thunder and subsiding dust of the crashing rocks, they returned to see what had happened to their cave mate. It looks as though a small collection of stones was placed over the body and a large fire lit above it. In the hearth we found several stone points, and several split and broken mammal bones nearby that may have been the remains of a funeral feast. It appears that, when the ceremony was at an end, the hearth was covered over with soil while the fire was still burning.

As with the first two adults, Shanidar III was found in the course of cleaning and straightening the profile of an excavation. It was as if some Near Eastern genie was testing my alertness by tucking away the skeletons on the borders of the excavation proper.

Like the other two, Shanidar III had been accidentally caught under a rockfall and instantly killed. One of his ribs had a strange cut. X rays taken at Georgetown University Hospital revealed that he had been wounded by a rectangular-edged implement of wood and the wound had been in the process of healing for about a week when he died. Most likely, he had been disabled in a conflict with unfriendly neighbors and was recuperating when he was killed. Clearly, the dangers of the caveman's life were by no means shut out when he crossed the portal to his airy home.

On August 3, 1960, during our fourth and last season at Shanidar, we uncovered the fragile and rotted bones of Shanidar IV. While Stewart exposed these remains, I started to explore the stones and soil near the place where three years before we had found Shanidar III. Parts of his skeleton were missing and unaccounted for in our collection.

In my first trowelings, several animal bones turned up. One did not look like an animal bone; it looked human. Later I encountered a rib bone that Stewart authenticated as human, but it was not until I uncovered a human molar tooth that we confirmed the presence of Shanidar V. This was becoming too much.

Within four days we found several other bones of this fifth Neanderthal including the scattered fragments of the skull. It appeared that he too was killed by a rockfall, perhaps the same one that killed Nandy.

There was yet another discovery to be made. Stewart was clearing around the southern side of Shanidar IV when he encountered some crushed pieces of a humerus near the skull. "It does't make sense," said Stewart, "not in anatomical position." His immediate reaction was that he hated to think that there was yet another Neanderthal in the cave. Furthermore, there were already two humeri for Shanidar IV, the correct number, and now a third: Here was Shanidar VI.

In the space of only five days we had discovered three Neanderthal skeletal groups. Before us were the vast problems of preserving, recording and transporting the remains safely to the Iraq Museum in Baghdad. In the course of feverishly carrying out these activities, we discovered—in some loose material associated with Shanidar VI—more bones which later proved to from yet another Neanderthal, Shanidar VII. These two, VI and VII, were females. We also retrieved some bones of a baby.

The skeleton remains of IV (a male), VI, VII and the baby (VIII) all appeared to lie in a niche bounded on two sides by large stone blocks. The nature of the soft soil and the position of the stone blocks leads me to believe that a crypt had been scooped out among the rocks and that the four individuals had been interred and covered over with earth. The child had been laid in first; the two females next, perhaps at a later time. The remains of these three were incomplete. Shanidar IV, the adult male, received the main attention of the burial. Probably, to make room for Shanidar IV, the bones of the others were disturbed.

As part of the archaeological routine, I had taken soil samples from around and within the area of Shanidar IV and Shanidar VI, as well as some samples from outside the area of the skeletal remains. These were sent for pollen analysis to Mme. Arlette Leroi-Gourhan, a paleobotanist in Paris.

Under the microscope, several of the prepared slides showed not only the usual kinds of pollen from trees and grasses, but also pollen from flowers. Mme. Leroi-Gourhan found clusters of flower pollen from at least eight species of flowers—mainly small, brightly colored varieties. They were probably woven into the branches of a pine-like shrub, evidence of which was also found in the soil. No accident of nature could have deposited such remains so deep in the cave. Shanidar IV had been buried with flowers.

Someone in the Last Ice Age must have ranged the mountainside in the mournful task of collecting flowers for the dead. Here were the first "Flower People," a discovery unprecedented in archaeology. It seems logical to us today that pretty things like flowers should be placed with the cherished dead, but to find flowers in a Neanderthal burial that took place about 60,000 years ago is another matter and makes all the more piquant our curiosity about these people.

Regarding their livelihood, we can certainly say the Neanderthals of Shanidar were hunters/foragers/gatherers. They most likely made a seasonal round of their wilderness domain, returning to shelter in Shanidar Cave.

The animals they hunted are represented in the cave by the bones of wild goat, sheep, cattle, pig and land tortoise. More rare are bear, deer, fox, marten and gerbil. It should be noted that the most common animals represented are the more docile type, the gregarious herbivorous mammals. It is likely that the Neanderthals caught them by running them over cliffs in herds or, conceivably, by running them into blind canyons where they could be slaughtered. There are several such canyons within easy striking distance of Shanidar Cave.

COMMUNAL LIFE
IN A CULTURAL BACKWATER

The picture of the lone stalker cannot be ruled out in the case of the Neanderthal but, since these people lived in a communal setting, it would be more natural for them to have engaged in communal hunting. And the fact that their lame and disabled (Shanidar I and Shanidar III) had been cared for in the cave is excellent testimony for communal living and cooperation.

By projecting carbon 14 dates that we have received for certain portions of the cave, I estimate that its first occupation was at most about 100,000 years ago. For perhaps 2,000 generations, over a period of some 60,000 years, we think that groups of Neanderthals—probably numbering 25 members at a time—made their seasonal home in Shanidar Cave. Preliminary findings from the analysis of pollen samples show that, through the long history of their occupation of the cave, the climate vacillated from cool to warm.

Yet throughout the period, the Neanderthals changed little in their means of adapting to these climatic changes. Their tool kit remained much the same throughout: It included their flaked stone tools identified as a "typical Mousterian" industry of points, knives, scoopers and some perforators, all struck off from locally derived flint pebbles. Only a few fragments of bone tools were found. With this meager tool kit Neanderthal man was able to survive and prosper in his own way.

Shanidar seems to have been a kind of cultural backwater, a "refuge" area bypassed by the stream of history because of the remoteness of the area—a condition still reflected in the Kurdish tribal compartmentalizations of today.

Then, around 40,000–35,000 B.C., the Neanderthals were gone from Shanidar Cave, replaced by a wave of *Homo sapiens* whom we have called Baradostians. We have no skeletal remains of these people but ample evidence that they possessed a brand new stone tool kit. Using the same raw materials available to their predecessors, the Baradostians used the Upper Paleolithic technique of flint-knapping, striking off blades which were used as blanks for tools. They had more stone tool types, a variety of bone

tools and they also possessed a woodworking technology such as the Neanderthals never had. Probably they used elaborate wood-carving stone tools to fashion traps and more advanced kinds of hunting apparatus and with this equipment they pursued much the same kind of game animals (mainly goats) as their extinct Neanderthal predecessors had.

By 35,000 B.C., the Neanderthals seem to have disappeared from the world altogether and we may well ask, what did Upper Paleolithic *Homo sapiens* have that the Neanderthals did not have? To my way of thinking, there were probably two things that weighed heavily in the balance. One was language. Jacquetta Hawkes, the English student of language and prehistory, feels that although the Neanderthal was a skilled toolmaker, his tool kit shows a conspicuous lack of invention and adaptability. He was probably handicapped because he did not develop a fully articulate and precise language. This was the new weapon which we think his Upper Paleolithic replacement possessed and used to make a tool kit so diversified that in the graver category he had more working edges than master cabinetmakers are accustomed to working with today. With his greater articulateness, he was able to describe and demonstrate the details of the manufacture of these stone tools to his people, including the children who were to carry on the group's activities.

The second critical cultural achievement of Upper Paleolithic man, in my opinion, is his ability to keep track of events for the future. Alexander Marshack, a research fellow at Harvard, has provided us with this recent and powerfu insight into prehistoric man. Thousands of notational sequences have been found on engraved bones and stones dating as far back as at least 30 millennia. These markings have been puzzled over or guessed about by archaeologists since the time they were first discovered more than 100 years ago. Marshack has determined that they served Upper Paleolithic man as a kind of farmer's almanac tied in with a lunar notational count. Some are illustrated with the natural history of the events, giving the possessor of the object a mnemonic device reminding him when to expect the change of seasons and the movements and dispersal of game.

AN ANCESTOR OF
SYMPATHETIC CHARACTER

In short, this was of tremendous economic advantage to Upper Paleolithic man, and it gave him a control over his environment and destiny such as was evidently denied to his predecessor, the Neanderthal.

So, men with these remarkable abilities and all that flowed from them overtook and presumably eliminated the Neanderthals. We have long thought of the Neanderthals as ultimate examples of the Hobbesian dictum that the life of a primitive man is "nasty, brutish and short." They have been characterized as having a near-bestial appearance with an ape-like face in profile, a thick neck, stooped shoulders and a shuffling gait. But now it appears that they were actually very similar to *Homo sapiens* in skeletal structure. Stewart's study of the Shanidar Neanderthals led him to the conclusion that below the head there was not too much difference between these early men and modern man. Of course, one cannot deny the bulging prominent eyebrows and the heavy coarse-featured face of the Neanderthal in general, though Anthropologist Earnest Hooton once said: "You can, with equal facility, model on a Neanderthaloid skull the features of a chimpanzee or the lineaments of philosopher."

His own biological evolution is something man really does not have conscious control over. But his culture, his social and religious life, is something else. In the millions of years of evolution that began with the ape-like hominids of Africa it is among the Neanderthals that we have the first stirrings of social and religious sense and feelings: the obvious care with which the lame and crippled were treated, the burials—and the flowers. Flowers have never been found in prehistoric burials before, though this may simply be because no one has ever looked for them. And to be sure, only one of the burials in Shanidar Cave yielded such evidence. But the other buried there could have died during the wrong season for flowers, since death knows no season

The Neanderthal has been ridiculed and rejected for a century but despite this he is still our ancestor. Of course we may still have the privilege of ridiculing him, but in the face of the growing evidence, especially in the light of the recent findings at Shanidar, we can not actually reject him. And what person will mind having as an ancestor one of such sympathetic character, one who laid his dead to rest with flowers?

!Kung Hunter-Gatherers: Feminism, Diet, and Birth Control

If results from recent studies of the !Kung* people apply to other societies, anthropologists may now have some new clues as to the social, dietary, and demographic changes that took place during the Neolithic Revolution when people forsook lives of hunting and gathering and began to farm and to keep herds of domestic animals. The !Kung have lived as hunters and gatherers in the Kalahara Desert of South Africa (Fig. 1) for at least 11,000 years; but recently they have begun to live in agrarian villages near those of Bantus. Investigators who are documenting this change find that, among other things, the settled !Kung women are losing their egalitarian status, the children are no longer brought up to be nonaggressive, and the size of the !Kung population is rapidly increasing rather than remaining stable.

The !Kung's very existence is anomalous since they have lived by hunting and gathering since the Pleistocene. In his archeological studies, John Yellen of the Smithsonian Institution in Washington, D.C., finds artifacts from Late Stone Age hunter-gatherers, of about 11,000 years ago, at the same water holes where modern !Kung set up camp (Fig. 2). According to Yellen, these prehistoric hunter-gatherers even hunted the same animals as the contemporary !Kung, including the nocturnal springhare which must be hunted by a special technique because it spends its days in a long deep burrow.

As recently as 10 years ago, many of the !Kung still lived by hunting and gathering. Now, however, less than 5 percent of the 30,000 !Kung live in this way; the remainder live in agricultural villages. This period of rapid social change

*The exclamation point refers to an alveolarpalatal click. The tongue tip is pressed against the roof of the mouth and drawn sharply away, producing a hollow popping sound.

By Gina Bari-Kolata. Reprinted with permission, from *Science*, 185, 13 September 1974, pp. 932-34. Copyright © 1974 by the American Association for the Advancement of Science.

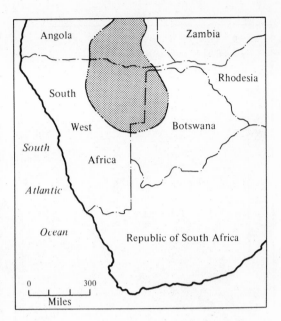

Figure 1. Location of the !Kung in South Africa.

coincided with extensive study of these people by numerous investigators throughout the world and from many disciplines.

It is difficult to distinguish between changes due to settling down and changes due to acculturation to Bantu society. Investigators have drawn on extensive long-term studies of the nomadic !Kung in their documentation of the effects of the !Kung's adoption of an agrarian life, but cannot conclusively state the causes of these effects.

One aspect of the settled !Kung society that has aroused considerable interest among social scientists is the role of women. Patricia Draper of the University of New Mexico reports that !Kung women who belong to the nomadic bands enjoy higher status, more autonomy, and greater ability to directly influence group decisions than do sedentary !Kung women. This loss of equality for the agrarian women, Draper believes, may be explained in terms of the social structure of nomadic, as compared to sedentary, groups.

Draper postulates that one reason for the higher status of !Kung hunter-gatherer women is that the women contribute, by gathering, at least 50 percent of the food consumed by a band. Since food gathered by women is so important to

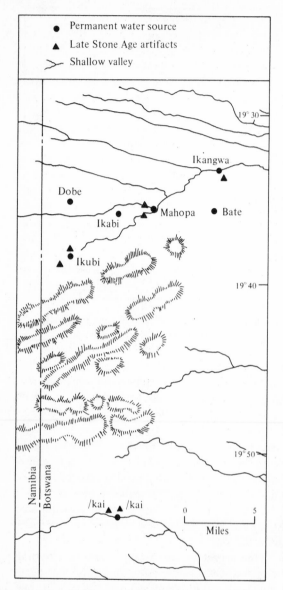

Figure 2. Distribution of Late Stone Age sites and permanent water sources.

the group, the women, of necessity, are as mobile as the men (who hunt), and women and men leave the camp equally often to obtain food. both the women and men who do not seek food on a given day remain in the camp and share in taking care of the children.

The women in sedentary !Kung societies have far less mobility than the men and contribute less to the food supply. The men leave the village to clear fields and raise crops and to care for the cattle of their Bantu neighbors. The women remain in the village where they prepare food and take care of the shelters. Since the men work for the Bantus, they learn the Bantu language. Thus when the Bantus deal with the !Kung, they deal exclusively with the men. This practice, together with the !Kung's emulation of the male dominated Bantu society, contributes to increasingly subservient roles for !Kung women.

Also contributing to a loss of female egalitarianism is the different way that agrarian, as compared to nomadic, !Kung bring up their children. Draper points out that the nomads live in bands consisting of very few people so that a child generally has no companions of the same age. Thus play groups contain children of both sexes and a wide variety of ages. This discourages the development of distinct games and roles for boys and girls.

Unlike the nomadic children, the sedentary children play in groups consisting of children of the same sex and similar ages. The boys are expected to help herd cattle, so they leave the village where they are away from adults and on their own. The girls, according to Draper, have no comparable experience but remain in the village and help the adult women with chores.

In addition to promoting sexual egalitarianism by their child rearing practices, the nomadic !Kung also discourage aggression among children. This is no longer the case when the !Kung become sedentary. The nomadic children observed by Draper do not play competitive games. She attributes this to the wide range of ages of children in a group which would make competitiveness difficult. Moreover, since these children are constantly watched by adults, the adults can and do quickly stop aggressive behavior among children. The children rarely observe aggressive behavior among adults because the nomadic !Kung have no way to deal with physical aggression and consciously avoid it. For example, according to Richard Lee of the University of Toronto, when conflict within a group of adults begins, families leave for other bands. Lee observed that the sedentary !Kung, who cannot easily pick up and leave, rely on their Bantu neighbors to mediate disputes.

In addition to studying social changes taking place when the !Kung settle down, investigators are studying dietary and demographic changes. The !Kung diet is of interest because the nomadic !Kung are exceedingly healthy and are free from many diseases thought to be associated with the diets of people in more complex societies. The sendentary !Kung have substantially altered their diets, thus providing investigators with a unique opportunity to document the effects of diet on the health of these people. The demographic changes taking place among the !Kung are of interest because the settled !Kung seem to have lost a natural check on their fertility rates.

The diet of the completely nomadic !Kung, which has been analyzed by geneticists, biochemists, and nutritionists, consists of nuts, vegetables, and meat and lacks milk and grains. All the investigators agree that the diet is nutritionally well balanced and provides an adequate number of calories. They found very few people with iron deficiency anemia, even when they included pregnant and lactating women in their sample. They also discovered that the nomadic !Kung have a very low incidence of deficiency of the vitamin folic acid and that the concentrations of vitamin B_{12} are higher in their serums as compared to concentrations considered normal for other populations. These findings led Henry Harpending of the University of New Mexico and his associates to suggest that Stone Age people probably had no deficiencies of these vitamins and that deficiencies first appeared when people settled down into agrarian societies.

In addition to being well nourished, the nomadic !Kung are free from many common diseases of old age. For example, Lee and others have found little degenerative disease among elderly !Kung, although it is commonplace for these people to live for at least 60 years and some live for as long as 80 years. A. Stewart Truswell of the University of London also finds that the nomadic !Kung are one of only about a dozen groups of people in the world whose blood pressure does not increase as they grow older.

The medical effects of the altered diet and way of life of the sedentary !Kung are not yet well established. In contrast to the hunter-gatherers, these people consume a great deal of cow's milk and grain. In his studies of a genera-tion of !Kung brought up on such a diet, Lee finds that they are, on the average, taller, fatter, and heavier than the nomadic !Kung. Nancy Howell of the University of Toronto finds that the agrarian women have their first menstrual periods (menarches) earlier than the nomadic women.

The average age of menarche among nomadic !Kung is late—at least age 15.5 according to Howell. Although these women marry at puberty, they have their first children when they are, on the average 19.5 years of age. This late start to reproductive life helps limit the growth of the population. However, a more significant curb on the size of the nomadic populations is the low fertility of the women. Howell finds that the average length of time between giving birth for a nomadic !Kung woman is 4 years. These women have fewer children than any other women in societies that do not practice contraception or abortion. The low fertility of nomadic !Kung contradicts previously held theories that the sizes of hunter-gatherer populatons were limited soley by high mortality rates. The !Kung population size remains stable because there are so few children born. Combining her studies of the fertility and mortality rates of !Kung hunter-gatherers, Howell concludes that the long-term growth rate for such a population is only 0.5 percent per year. This is in sharp contrast to the sedentary !Kung whose population is growing rapidly.

The population growth among the sedentary !Kung results from both a decrease in the age of menarche and a decrease in the average time between births. Lee has found that the birth intervals drop 30 percent when !Kung women become sedentary. The causes of these reproductive changes are unknown, but some investigators suspect that these decreased birth intervals may result from changes in nursing or dietary habits.

Nomadic !Kung women have no soft food to give their babies, and so they nurse them for 3 or 4 years, and during this time the women rarely conceive. Sedentary !Kung women, on the other hand, wean their babies much sooner by giving them grain meal and cow's milk. Irven DeVore of Harvard University believes that a contraceptive effect of the long lactation period is not unexpected, since investigators have observed the same phenomenon in many animals, including monkeys and the great apes. A woman who begins to supplement her infant's diet while the child is very young would not experience this effect because her child would require less and less milk.

Howell and Rose Frisch of the Harvard Center for Population Studies believe that an explanation of the decrease in the age of menarche and in the birth intervals of sedentary !Kung women may involve the diet of the sedentary !Kung. They base this idea on a study by Frisch and Janet McArthur of the Massachusetts General Hospital in Boston. These investigators showed that the amount of body fat must be above a certain minimum for the onset of menstruation and for its maintenance after menarche. Howell points out that the !Kung hunter-gatherers are thin, although well nourished. When women from these bands lactate, they need about 100 extra calories a day. Thus, during the 3 or 4 years that a woman nurses a baby, she may have too little body fat for ovulation to take place. The shorter birth intervals for sedentary !Kung

women would follow from their shorter periods of lactation and larger amounts of body fat. Howell notes that this explanation of the low fertility of nomadic !Kung women cannot be verified until more extensive medical studies are performed with these people.

Although no one claims that the changes taking place in the !Kung society necessarily reflect those that took place when other hunter-gatherer societies became agrarian, studies of the !Kung are providing anthropologists with clues relative to the origins of some features of modern societies. Many findings, such as the social egalitarianism, lack of aggression, and low fertility of nomadic !Kung are leading to new perspectives on the hunting and gathering way of life which was, until 10,000 years ago, the way all humans lived.

Reference

1. R. B. Lee and I. DeVore, Eds., *Kalahari Hunter-Gatherers* (Harvard Univ. Press, Cambridge, Mass., in press).

Part VII

Archaeology Today

As a subfield of anthropology, the prime task of archaeology is to reconstruct extinct cultures. In many respects, the interests of the archaeologist and physical anthropologist converge, as much can be inferred about man's behavior by a study of his artifacts. This is especially true in the case of fossil man and human evolution. Most of the articles contained in the following sections touch on this subject. The articles in this section introduce the reader to some current and important issues in the field of archaeology. For example, in recent years human prehistory is being destroyed at an alarming rate due to the destruction of archaeological sites by often unthinking persons. It is vital that the public develop a commitment to preserve this facet of their human heritage. The article by Hester Davis introduces the reader to the complexity and scope of this problem and attempts some solutions. Ferguson's contribution considers the role that the amateur archaeologist can play as a paraprofessional and conservationist. "The Garbage Project", by William Rathje, illustrates a novel and expanded dimension of archaeology going beyond the traditional scope of the discipline. By excavating contemporary kitchen middens (garbage cans) and refuse heaps useful insights concerning consumer behavioral patterns become apparent. For additional readings in this area the following books and articles are recommended: L. Binford and S. Binford, *New Perspective in Archaeology,* (Aldine, 1968); E. Ralph and H. Michaels' "Twenty-five Years of Radiocarbon Dating", *American Scientist,* Sept. 1974, pp. 551–60; and F. Rainey's "Science and Archaeology", *Archaeology,* 1973, pp. 10–21.

The Crisis in American Archeology

The only sources of adequate information on 20,000 years or more of human occupation of the New World are those data that lie buried in the ground—data that are a nonrenewable resource. When found in their original context, artifacts, remains of houses, fire hearths, storage pits, burials of human beings, and even man's trash and garbage can be used to interpret the way of life of a particular group of people at a particular time and in a particular place. Any disturbance of the original context of these materials destroys the only clues that the archeologist has for interpreting these ways of life. It does not matter whether the disturbance is by a professionally trained archeologist, by a farmer, or by a bulldozer—the original context is destroyed by *any* digging or alteration of the land. The records, observations, and photographs made at the time of the disturbance make the difference between an ability to reconstruct past cultures and their environment and a total loss of information.

Archeological research has, in many respects, become interdisciplinary, calling upon geologists, botanists, zoologists, physicists, engineers, mathematicians, computer scientists, and others to aid in interpreting the past and, in turn, often providing them with data. The current crisis, then, involves not only the preservation of cultural data, but also data concerning the natural environment and how it was used in the past. All these nonrenewable sources of data are disappearing at a rate that has increased almost geometrically since World War II, while the potential for scientific recovery of adequate data, in terms of funds and personnel, has remained—after an initial federal surge—essentially static.

THE NATURE OF THE CURRENT CRISIS

The current crisis has two parallel causes: (i) the

By Hester Davis. Reprinted with permission, from *Science*, 145, 21 January 1972, pp. 267-72. Copyright © 1972 by the American Association for the Advancement of Science.

rate of destruction and the absolute number of sites being destroyed is continuing to increase, and (ii) funds to salvage essential data are not increasing.

The nature of many federally funded activities and federally sponsored programs since World War II has been such that they increase the rate of land alteration; despite the government's publically stated policy of concern, federal funds for the recovery of the archeological resources being destroyed by these programs have not kept pace. Funds for salvage work in reservoirs and some other projects of the U.S. Army Corps of Engineers are available through the National Park Service. However, at a time when the Corps of Engineers is increasing the number and kind of its land alteration projects, the budgets for the Division of Archaeology of the Park Service have been severely curtailed during fiscal years 1970 and 1971. Funds for salvage in areas where highways are being built come through the Bureau of Public Roads and individual state highway departments—in those states that have worked out a cooperative program. There are, however, 24 states in which there is no such cooperative program *(1)*, principally because of state regulations or lack of local concern. In general, other federal agencies have ignored archeology altogether (although the Forest Service is making a beginning) or they have contended that they were not authorized to take any action.

Compounding the problem is the fact that the number of archeological and historical sites adversely affected by federally sponsored projects is equaled, if not surpassed, by activity initiated by states, private businesses, and individuals. By and large, state governments are not providing for the recovery and preservation of information that is being destroyed on state lands, by state projects, or by state-encouraged growth in industry and business. Twelve states provide essentially no funds for archeological research; another 22 spend less than $1000 per year and employ fewer than the equivalent of one full-time person for archeological research. Only 16 states budget state funds specifically for archeology, provide legislative recognition of the archeological program, and employ the equivalent of at least two full-time persons to do archeological research. Six of these 16 have what can be called adequate programs *(2)*. Although 43 states have some form of legislation regulating the excavation of prehistoric sites and materials (either on state land or in the state in general), for the most part this legislation is unrealistic, unenforceable, and sometimes unconstitutional.

Finally, the number of individuals who collect prehistoric and historical objects as a hobby, and consequently dig in sites to obtain their objective, is steadily increasing. The resulting loss of information from indiscriminate digging is tremendous.

In the last decade, the amount of land alteration that adversely affects sites has increased at a rate far in excess of available resources for the rescue of the information; state and federal governments have not provided financial and other legislative support; and archeologists have not come up with programs or leadership to cope with the problem. The result is a crisis.

WHAT HAS BEEN DONE

As early as the 1920's and 1930's, archeologists recognized that much information was being destroyed by collectors and others, for nonarcheological reasons *(3)*. The first massive, coordinated effort to rescue information and material about to be destroyed came just before World War II with projects in conjunction with the federal Work Projects Administration and the Tennessee Valley Authority programs.

After World War II, the Park Service, the Smithsonian Institution, the Corps of Engineers, and the Bureau of Reclamation developed an Interagency Archeological Salvage Program in response to the need to recover and preserve information about prehistoric and early historical sites that would be destroyed or inundated, or both, by federally sponsored reservoirs. Through this salvage program, thousands of sites were located, several hundred were at least tested, and some of this work has been reported on in published papers *(4)*. Although the program began in the early 1950's, the Reservoir Salvage Act of 1960 (Public Law 86–523) made this kind of salvage federal policy.

In the 1950's also, the Bureau of Public Roads, interpreting the 1906 Federal Antiquities Act as applying to land over which it had control, developed a program to salvage archeo-

logical information that might be destroyed by construction of federally aided highways, particularly the then-burgeoning interstate highway system. The Bureau of Public Roads and the highway departments in approximately half of the states are now cooperating on this kind of salvage work.

Federal funding for preservation of information and materials from the past has been largely restricted (except for individual National Science Foundation grants) to areas in which reservoirs and highways are being constructed. Although federal support has remained relatively static or, in recent years, has been considerably reduced, concern in the form of policy statements has increased, particularly with the passage of the National Historic Preservation Act of 1966, the National Environmental Policy Act of 1969, and the President's recent Executive Order *(5)*. An amendment to the Reservoir Salvage Act, now before Congress, would further implement this policy by authorizing all federal agencies to expend funds for archeological investigation, recovery, and publications where that agency's activities are adversely affecting sites or information, or both.

This broader federal concern comes at a time when archeological sites are being destroyed at an alarming rate by myriad forms of land alteration, for which federal agencies, private business and industry, power companies, municipalities, and individuals are all responsible. The resources and techniques of emergency salvage developed by the Interagency Archeological Salvage Program are no longer sufficient.

EXAMPLES OF DESTRUCTION

Because of the size of much modern construction and farming equipment, and because of the needs of modern building and agricultural techniques, land usually needs to be level. Shopping centers, housing developments, airports, and roads are all built on flat land—land that is leveled rapidly by enormous machinery. Farm land upon which eight-row planters or cultivators can be used must also be flat. Even the Mississippi River Valley, which to the casual observer is already flat, has little knolls and levees that must be leveled. These low eminences are precisely the areas in which archeological sites are often located, and the sites are totally destroyed by this land leveling.

Hundreds of thousands of acres of land have been cleared in the last 10 years to create "new" farmland in the Mississippi River Valley alone. But whereas the planning and construction of a huge dam may cover a 10-year period, planning and preparing fields for crops, preparing land for housing developments or shopping centers, and clearing new land may take only a few days or a few months. It is difficult, if not impossible, to plan for the salvage of sites under such circumstances.

A few examples give a vivid picture of the problem *(6)*. Archeologists in Hawaii indicate that 65 percent of the known sites on the island of Oahu have been destroyed, largely because of urban and agricultural development; over half of these sites were destroyed in the last 10 years. Around the northern Great Lakes, resort development is increasing at a tremendous rate. It is in just these areas around natural lakes that Indians lived for several thousand years; many of these sites were destroyed before salvage was possible. When, as occasionally happens, developers actually capitalize on the presence of a site without providing for adequate scientific investigation, the expressed "public" concern for preservation seems a sham. The following is quoted from the *Detroit News*, 21 February 1971 *(7)*: "140 acres, historical Indian grounds, stone carvings, lore, artifacts. Adjoins . . . Michigan's only known petroglyph site. Top-notch land development."

In the Illinois River Valley of Western Illinois, which prehistoric man occupied for several thousand years, industry and the population are both expanding rapidly. A "strip city" from Chicago to St Louis is anticipated. Proper salvage of information from sites in such an area would take years and an army of archeologists. In Vermont a large prehistoric site, rich in information and artifacts, was "bulldozed into oblivion sometime between 1960 and 1965 for a housing development" *(8)*. In Oregon and Florida, sites are being destroyed by the Corps of Engineers and state beach improvement, or "beach nourishment," programs. In Mississippi, a large prehistoric mound was recently removed for road fill. Such itemization could go on for pages, with instances in every state.

Running a close second as a cause of destruction of sites is the hobby of collecting Indian objects and, recently, old bottles and Civil War memorabilia. Digging simply for objects left by Indians or early European settlers destroys the context, of course, and digging by relic collectors has reached alarming proportions. This is partly because it is more difficult to find "nice" pieces on the surface, and partly because there are more people with leisure time to dig. Since most relic collectors and dealers know that the late prehistoric Indians often buried objects with their dead, cemeteries are a prime target. In the Mississippi River Valley, dealers in "Indian relics" *(9)* from Memphis and St. Louis will locate a cemetery, hire laborers, and promise to pay them for each pot they find. Graves are located quickly with a probe, and each is looted of the associated objects, the skeleton itself (and any incomplete vessels or objects) generally being crushed or scattered, or both, in the process. The looting of tombs in the Mediterranean countries is a comparable and equally nefarious activity.

The planned, systematic vandalism described above generally occurs in areas that are known to have rich sites. Perhaps most destructive, simply because of the number of people involved, are the "innocent" collectors—those who find arrowheads or dart points on the surface and dig to find more, without realizing that they are destroying irreplaceable information in the proccess. Other relic collectors, not so innocent, dig to get objects for their collections, but are simply too lazy to make any record.

Again, some examples may help. From New Mexico comes this statement *(10)*.

Confining ourselves strictly to the field of historic preservation, we must place at the top of the list of destroyers the artifact hunter. Armed with detectors, trowels, picks, shovels, whiskbrooms, and even backhoes, these unrestrained agents of destruction have riddled scores of New Mexico sites, ranging from early man hunting camps to nineteenth century ghost towns and military installations, and have almost eliminated any possibility of a thorough archeological investigation of the Mimbres branch of the Mogollon Culture. The principal stimulus is, of course, financial gain.

In Michigan, the archeologists decry the "growing army of treasure hunters armed with metal detectors that are rapidly chewing up every historic site in the State" *(11)*. In Texas, archeologists can enumerate dozens of specific examples of misguided salvage efforts and out-and-out, wanton destruction. One group of incorporated treasure hunters removed tons of invaluable and unique mid–16th century Spanish antiquities from a shipwreck on the Texas-owned tidelands. The chamber of commerce and the historical society in a small town in west Texas persuaded a landowner to donate the site of an early Spanish mission to the town for preservation and development. On a weekend, they gathered at the site and, with county road-building equipment, proceeded to bulldoze the ruins to ground level. They then stacked the rocks and broken adobe bricks, collected what objects they saw, and were ready (they thought) to begin "restoration" of their mission, with local volunteers designing and constructing the buildings.

In undeveloped areas, prime targets of vandalism are rock carvings and paintings. Adding one's own graffiti to such spots is common, but the areas also serve as targets for rifle practice (particularly tempting, I would imagine, when there are buffalo or deer depicted). Sometimes, a diamond saw is ued to cut away the face of the rock. Archeologists and Forest Service personnel in Nevada have recently salvaged a petroglyph site by this method, in order to save it from further destruction by vandals.

There are other causes of destruction. The Park Service indicates that sonic booms over parks in the Southwest are crumbling pueblo stone and adobe buildings that have stood for thousands of years. In the Midwest and West, strip mining does as much damage to sites as it does to the natural environment.

The market for relics and prehistoric art objects provided by private collectors, both large and small, and by many museums as well, is causing an increase in wanton destruction. In the opinion of many archeologists, the buyers or receivers of such objects are as much to blame for the destruction of information as are those who actually do the digging.

These causes of destruction, as well as many others, add up to the loss of massive amounts of information that can never be recovered or re-placed. Without this information, we must remain in ignorance of a significant portion of the human past in the New World.

HOW THE CRISIS IS BEING MET

Some archeologists do little more than wring their hands in despair at the situation, while others try not to think about it. Many, however, are looking for feasible, positive ways to alleviate the crisis.

An obvious way of decreasing the amount of destruction is to enforce the existing state and federal laws that ostensibly were designed to protect and preserve the past. These laws must be examined to see if, when, and how such regulatory measures can be effective. But in point of fact, preservation of information about the past is not something that can be legislated. Laws can be deterrent, but even strictly enforced regulatory legislation is only an aid, not a solution in itself.

Archeologist speak most often of inadequate funding for the job facing them. The amendment to the Reservoir Salvage Act would go a long way toward providing funds to salvage information destroyed as a result of federal programs. Recent cuts in funds have severely crippled the Park Service's archeological salvage program; a marked increase in the budget of the Division of Archeology is vital. A few states are finally providing realistically for the preservation of information and materials within their boundaries, but nearly 90 percent of the states are doing nothing or have inadequate provisions for archeological research.

Other sources of funds for archeological research, such as foundations and educational institutions, are feeling financial pressure from all angles, and the amount of money available from these sources for archeology is not increasing in proportion to the amount of destruction. The result is a widening gap between financial need and supply. As the public becomes aware of what is happening, it is likely that sources of funding may increase. If no one makes the public aware, and if funding is not increased, the crisis will be over, for there will no longer be enough sites remaining to tell us anything about the past.

Many professional archeologists are turning for help to "amateur archeologists"—those persons who study the past in their leisure time. These individuals are in marked contrast to the relic collectors, who simply destroy the past. While the terms "amateur" and "professional" have sometimes been a bone of contention, and while relations between amateurs and professionals have sometimes been strained (with occasional justice on both sides), both groups are beginning to realize that only if they work together is there any hope for American archeology. Almost every state has an organization of amateurs—some with professional leadership, some without. These organizations all have some kind of publication and often sponsor excavations, but turning them into an army of trained allies is almost a full-time job and one that is of concern to an increasing number of professional archeologists. In those states where the amateur organizations and professionals work together, the results have been tremendously encouraging.

It is my opinion that, in the current crisis, the hope for preserving any significant portion of the information about the past lies in cooperation among *all* of those people interested in preserving it. The general public must be made aware of what kinds of things destroy information about the past and, for that matter, that saving some shreds of the past is to their benefit. For each archeologist there are hundreds of individuals who know nothing of what is involved in archeology and probably, at this point, do not care. but just as people have learned about ecology within recent years and have been made aware of the environmental crisis, they can, with effort and organization, be made aware of the archeological crisis. Public education and public relations are full-time jobs; in the case of the archeologist, who generally spends the major portion of his time teaching and doing research, or in the case of the nonprofessional, who generally has some other full-time job, the thought of the time required to educate the public is indeed staggering. Yet, unless more people can be made aware of the fact that archeology is "relevant" and that this nonrenewable resource must be preserved now or never, full interpretation of ways of life in the past and full understanding of our human situation now and in the future will be impossible.

Archeologists must begin and then guide the education of the public. Although most professionally trained archeologists have involved themselves but little in practical politics or the communications media, some of them must learn about practical politics and others must write and speak knowledgably about archeology. Most important, the public must become actively and intelligently concerned and involved.

In addition to arousing and involving the public, archeologists themselves must develop new techniques, new areas of cooperation, and new concepts to deal with the present crisis. It is not realistic to try to salvage sites solely because they are endangered—that is like furiously putting out brush fires while the forest is burning. Archeologists need to review the status of their knowledge of an area, develop regional overviews, formulate research plans to fill existing gaps in information on particular time periods or cultural contexts, or both, and then excavate those sites that will provide the information.

More efforts should be made to preserve some sites and even some large areas (just as has been done with the environment), both for the purpose of interpreting the past to the public and for having these sites or areas available for investigation in the future, when new questions will need to be answered and when new techniques can provide even more precise and specific interpretations of the ways of life in the past.

PROGRESS

Actually, progress is being made in many of the areas discussed above. Some federal agencies, particularly the Forest Service, are hiring archeologists to inventory the archeological resources on their land, to do research, and to educate other personnel in the recognition and preservation of sites and materials. Some private businesses are realizing that it is good public relations to provide for the salvage of information before they destroy a site. The El Paso Natural Gas Company was one of the first to provide funding for survey and salvage along the routes of its pipelines in the Southwest, and other companies are beginning, at long last, to follow suit. In Florida, where resort and housing development are a way of life, the Marco Island

Development Corporation is altering all of Marco Island. For the past 4 years, the company has been aiding the Florida Department of Archives and History and local historical societies in the salvage of information related to the long human occupation of the island.

In Arkansas, the state with which I am most familiar, the Arkansas Archeological Society, an organization made up mostly of nonprofessionals, was largely responsible for the creation of the Arkansas Archeological Survey, a state-supported, statewide research program that coordinates the archeological work of all institutions of higher learning and other concerned agencies in the state. The Survey has provided training sessions in excavation techniques for members of the society for several years, and is inaugurating a program of certification for members as they achieve certain levels of competence in various aspects of archeological research. The societies in Missouri, Texas, and Oklahoma, among others, also are providing members with professionally led training in excavation and research techniques.

Finally, the Society for American Archeology, the foremost professional archeological organization in North America, has recently created the committee on the public understanding of archeology. This committee, made up of one representative from each state, was originally conceived of as a means of providing the public with reliable information about archeology. Its role now is to acquaint all archeologists, the general public, nonprofessional archeologists, and local, state, and federal governmental agencies with the crisis in American archeology, and to suggest ways and means of alleviating the immediate problem of site destruction. The task is an overwhelming one, but one that cannot be postponed.

SUMMARY

The current crisis in American archeology has been brought about by a combination of the greatly increased rate of destruction of unique, irreplaceable archeological information and material, and the lack of adequate funding for salvage of what is being destroyed. Since World War II, land alteration has increased almost

geometrically. Land leveling, urban development, inexperienced or ignorant diggers, commercial dealers in Indian relics—these and many other agents of destruction are obliterating traces of the past. Anything that disturbs the ground where people once lived destroys forever whatever information is left about them and their way of life. Interpretations of man's cultural development through time, of his ability to cope with and use the environment wisely, and of a long, fascinating, and irreplaceable heritage are only possible if the evidence left in the ground is undisturbed and is properly recorded when it is excavated.

The problem of the destruction of archeological sites and information is a complex one, with no single solution. A combination of increased support for archeological research through increased funding, and development of a knowledgeable, interested public will go a long way toward assuring this country that a significant portion of the past will be available for the benefit of future generations. If solutions are not sought and found now, it will be too late—we will have committed ourselves, irretrievably and irreversibly, to the future, without benefit or knowledge of the mistakes and the lessons of the past.

Notes

1. C. R. McGimsey III, *Public Archeology* (Seminar Press, New York, in press).

2. _____, "The present status and future needs of archeological legislation on the state and federal level" (paper presented at the 36th annual meeting of the Society for American Archeology, Norman, Okla., May 1971).

3. M. R. Harrington, *Indian Notes* 1 (No. 2) 37 (1924).

4. J. E. Petsche, *River Basin Surveys* (Publications in Salvage Archeology No. 10, Smithsonian Institution, Washington, D.C., 1968).

5. "Protection and enhancement of the cultural environment" (Executive Order No. 11593, 13 May 1971).

6. Information about specific problems in American archeology was obtained from the members of the Committee on the Public Understanding of Archeology, Society for American Archeology. Quotations and details are from personal correspondence with these individuals, and acknowledgement is made here of their contribution to this article.

7. C. Cleland, personal communication.

8. W. Haviland, personal communication.

9. In my own thinking, a "relic" is an Indian artifact or a historic object that has been stripped of its historic or scientific significance by having been taken out of its original context without an adequate record having been made or kept. It is an object of interest or curiosity for itself only, not for what it might have told us about the culture from which it came.

10. *Historic Preservation: A Plan for New Mexico* (State Planning Office, Santa Fe, N.M., 1971), p. 13.

11. C. Cleland, personal communication.

New Roles for the Amateur Archaeologist

In order to discuss the role of the amateur archaeologist, it is vital to determine just what an amateur archaeologist is. He is not, of course, a relic collector, a dealer in relics, or one of those unfortunate few who supply both of these with their wares—the nefarious pot hunter. Nor is an amateur archaeologist he who digs well but keeps no records. Those who traffic in these valuable materials, who encourage a flow of them for monetary value alone, are not archaeologists—amateur or otherwise.

There are those, however, who do not make their living in the pursuit of scientific archaeology, yet subscribe to the professional tenets of archaeology the science, who may be properly regarded as amateur archaeologists. This small cadre will often be found at the side of professionals eager to learn latest and best techniques, dedicated to the disciplines of archaeology, grounded in local site lore and anxious to contribute.

It is of these, to and about these, that I write. For they are not fully understood by the professional archaeologists, partially because of the difficulty in identifying one among the many, and they are often confused about their own role because it has never been adequately defined. Nor can I fully define it. But there are directions, there are roles. These we can discuss.

An amateur archaeologist can simply record all the sites he can ferret out in his area—adding to his record his opinion of cultural determinations. Such a basic record, shared with the professional, is of untold, lasting value. Buddy Brehm, a serious Nashville amateur, has devoted many hours and many rolls of film to photographing and annotating private collections which would otherwise be lost. Another Nashville amateur, Dick Weesner, amassed an extensive library of archaeological and historical books which he makes available to other amateurs engaged in research.

By Bob Ferguson. Reprinted by permission of Society for American Archaeology, from *American Antiquity*, 37, No. 1, 1972, pp. 1-2.

Each amateur can, of course, contribute the knowledge of his own special field when he joins a local group. I know professional photographers who welcome the opportunity to photograph site or specimen. Newspaper writers can and do take the job seriously of informing the public in archaeological matters when they are members of a group. Each person is a specialist of one kind or another. His daily skill can be his strongest contribution.

The amateur can—especially when a member of a statewide organization—take a very active part in writing and lobbying for state antiquities laws which fundamentally are a demonstration of concern for the archaeological resource. Many of the existing state and federal laws are weak, have loopholes, and are difficult to enforce. All of them do, however, focus the attention of the public on a new concept; for the first time, many people learn that "Indian Rocks" have a value beyond money. The amateur can continue to improve and refine existing laws so that they really reflect the worth of the resource they are intended to protect. In this matter, amateur and professional can work in full harmony and with full appreciation of the contributions each can make. Together they can provide for a State Division of Archaeology and nurse it to full professional quality.

More than anyone, the amateur is the local watchdog. His is the responsibility and the pleasure of safeguarding the archaeological resource. In this sense, the amateur may protect the basis of the science—the cultural residue itself. Ofttimes it lies in a field just outside his door, or in a river bottom just across the county. For the devoted amateur it is sacred ground and he cannot rest when it is threatened. And when it is, he must call upon all his decision-making faculties to decide whether he can handle the site himself, with his fellows, or whether it should be referred to those with more technical and theoretical abilities. In this stewardship role, the amateur is on the front line of archaeology. He is the sentry who often must make a general's decision.

To enumerate a few things the amateur archaeologist can do:

1. Write site reports; assist in publication.

2. Sponsor weekly night courses in archaeo-

logical field technique, anatomy, archaeological theory. In most areas, professionals are available to teach. Learning the new gives new breadth to what the amateur already knows. Knowledge builds confidence.

3. Speak and write on local archaeology and the value of the resource whenever and wherever possible. He should prepare thoroughly because the preparation is itself education.

4. Implement the flow of information between local professional and amateur archaeologists. The time is past for glowering at each other from opposite corners. By seeking to be of value the amateur will be of value.

5. Actively discourage "swap and shop archaeology." It is naught but robbery from the storehouse of knowledge of mankind.

6. Strive to implant the "archaeological ethic" in the minds of all he comes to know. Share with them his knowledge of its worth, reminding them that it is a nonrenewable resource.

7. Sponsor speaking engagements by prominent professional archaeologists in his town. Most are anxious to tell their story and to further amateur efforts. Expenses are generally low.

8. Subscribe to and read one or two leading national publications in archaeology. Improve his towns' archaeology library.

All of the above have been done—or are being done—right now. Alert amateurs, interested in contributing, can discover new roles which will make their work of lasting worth.

The Garbage Project: A New Way of Looking at the Problems of Archaeology

The aim of archaeology is to recover the nature of perished civilizations from imperishables. The archaeologist scrutinizes the material remains which come into his hands in order to reconstruct the behavior involved in their production, acquisition, use and eventual discard. Lately, many professionals have turned their attention to modern "primitive" societies in Africa, Australia and other areas to increase their sensitivity to the interrelationships which exist between materials and human activity; they have studied stone tools, pottery and other material objects in order to understand better how these things fit into different patterns of human behavior. The insights thus gathered add considerable sophistication to their interpretive capacities. So far archaeologists have devoted themselves exclusively to understanding the past in terms of evidence from the past, or to understanding the past in terms of correlates from the present. Now there is an additional use—or better, application—of the science of archaeology. This involves a systematic look at modern society from the archaeological viewpoint, and this is what the University of Arizona's Garbage Project is seeking to provide.

The Garbage Project, initiated in 1972 with the complete cooperation of the Tucson Sanitation Department, has undertaken to study the material culture of Tucson, Arizona, as it is being discarded. The founders of the project, a number of anthropologists at the University of Arizona, were aware from the outset that their ambition to study garbage was a seemingly odd and novel one; accordingly, we sought to give the clearest possible definition to what the study might reveal. First, we believed that assumptions about the way material culture is related to behavior in past civilizations can be tested in a familiar, on-going society. Second, we felt that

applying archaeological methods to such a society can produce valuable insights into that society itself. What follows is a brief description of the project's main activities; it is my principal intention here to outline how such work can serve to expand the social and scientific perimeters of archaeology generally.

As everyone knows, Americans live in an era which is threatened by resource depletion and environmental ruination, and many of today's social-science researchers are examining urbanized society to see how social conditions relate to resource management as it is practiced (or mispracticed) in the contemporary household. The information they seek is information which is badly needed. But the results of the interview surveys being conducted by sociologists may not be entirely adequate; while they provide an understanding of the *beliefs* people have regarding their habits of resource management, they cannot describe satisfactorily the actual resource management these same people practice. For example, owing to present cultural norms, few individuals can be expected to discuss with candor such things as alcohol problems, illicit drug use or large-scale food-waste, especially with interviewers whom they have just met and scarcely know. Even those who are willing to be totally frank are prone to distorted recollection, and so the picture which emerges is a good deal less than accurate.

A more skeptical view is needed of society's habits of material waste, and this is the view which archaeology has to offer. By training, archaeologists maintain a healthy lack of commitment to the accuracy of the written word—or, as in this case, the spoken word. Since their discipline functions to corroborate or disprove historical sources through the analysis of quantifiable materials, they are readily qualified to evaluate modern interview-survey techniques and their results. Waste is the result of human actions and not intentions; therefore waste materials are a telling and honest index of a society's way of life.

The Garbage Project already has some reason to question conclusions derived from verbally-collected data on modern habits of consumption and waste. According to interview surveys, for instance, significantly more vitamins are consumed in Tucson by people with intermediate

By William Rathje. Reprinted with permission, from Archaeology, 27, No. 4, October 1974, pp. 236-41. Copyright © 1974 by Archaeological Institute of America.

incomes than by those with lower ones. Our original garbage data, from 1972, show exactly the opposite: the largest quantities of vitamin containers were discarded by those on a very low income scale.

But the members of the Garbage Project are not so much interested in refuting the findings of others as in complementing them and in discovering what significance the discrepancies have. In fact, we share a mutual interest with our sociological colleagues in refining interviewing techniques, and we are planning a joint venture with an interview-survey project being directed by Dr. Dileep Bal of the University of Arizona; his project, known as ECHO (Evidence for Community Health Organization) deals with patterns of consumption directly related to matters of health. The intention is to record traces of drug, alcohol, cigarette, vitamin and nutrient consumption left in garbage from a selected sample of neighborhoods; after analyzing the garbage from these households for a month, we will make a survey of their occupants using questions designed to enable us to test the answers against the data collected from the garbage. The objective will be to identify and quantify the weaknesses in the two methods of gathering information.

How does one "excavate" modern-day garbage? Our sampling design had to be a little unusual, since Tucson is larger than the sites of Teotihuacán and Nineveh put together. To obtain a representative sample of the households in the city, we resorted to the census reports from 1970: we grouped the 66 census tracts into seven different clusters and then studied the garbage from tracts representative of each cluster. We studied 13 such tracts in the course of 1973 and 19 in 1974. On a biweekly basis last year, and on a weekly basis this year, the Tucson Sanitation Department collected all the refuse from two households chosen randomly in each sample tract. Most of this material came in either plastic or paper bags. In order to cope effectively with the vast array of items, we selected 133 variable categories designed to cover health, nutrition, personal and household sanitation, education and amusement (both for children and adults) communication and pet related materials. The study was conducted in the Sanitation Department's maintenance yard, where student analysts examined and recorded the garbage by item number, volume, cost, material composition, brand and waste weight. Although we examined refuse over an eight-month period, our study could encompass only six hundred out of 110,000 households, or less than one per cent of all the households in Tucson.

To protect the anonymity of the households studied, we recorded garbage samples only by the number of the census tract. Personal items were of no interest since we were looking only for general patterns of resource management; therefore, we did not examine, record or save any names, addresses, photographs, letters or other personal items. The student workers, whose number has now increased to fifty, were given immunizations and provided with lab coats and gloves; happily, to date, none of them has lost any time through illness contracted on the Project.

Our results so far have yielded some interesting conclusions. While considering both the garbage which had been analyzed and the results of survey interviews, we discovered that status-brand items are purchased most regularly in households containing young adults, the aged or members of ethnic minorities. For example, although steak is no more nutritious than hamburger, middle-class families generally bought (and discarded wrappers of) ground round while the other groups mentioned above regularly purchased more costly cuts of beef.

Although some sterotypes were confirmed by the findings, many were disproved. Middle-class white families, for instance, eat proportionately more ham, lamb, pork and chicken than Black, American Indian and Asian households. In addition, the lowest income groups use the most costly educational items for children and the largest quantities of household sanitation items; they also consume the greatest quantity of vitamins, liquor and bread.

Some general patterns of waste have already begun to emerge. As one might expect, there is a high rate of expensive waste of pastry and take-out meals; but the most significant waste is of staples—beef, fruits and vegetables, discarded often in unopened or only half-opened packages. Whereas white middle-class households seem to

KEY   ● Brand
       * Type Needed

Table 1.   Garbage Item Code List.

TISSUE CONTAINER	001
TISSUE SHEETS	002
NAPKIN CONTAINER	003
NAPKIN SHEETS	004
PAPER TOWEL CONTAINER ●	005
PAPER TOWEL SHEETS ●	006
TOILET PAPER PKG. (White)	007
TOILET PAPER SHEETS (White)	008
TOILET PAPER PKG. (Colored)	009
TOILET PAPER SHEETS (Colored)	010
PLASTIC WRAPS	011
BAGS	012
FOIL CONTAINERS	013
FOIL SHEETS	014
LOCAL NEWSPAPERS	015
CIGARETTES (filter)	016
(Pack, Carton)	
CIGARETTES (non-filter)	017
(Pack, Carton)	
CIGARS (Packages, Boxes)	018
PIPE TOBACCO (Pouches, Cans)	019
MEAT-Beef	020
MEAT-Other *	021
POULTRY-Chicken	022
POULTRY-Other	023
FISH-Fresh Water	024
FISH-Salt Water	025
FISH-Crustaceans, Mollusc	026
TV DINNERS *	027
TAKE-OUT MEALS * ●	028
FRESH VEGETABLES *	029
POTATO PEEL	030
CANNED VEGETABLES *	031
CANNED; PACKAGED	032
Soups, Stews, Sauces	
FROZEN VEGETABLES *	033
FRESH FRUIT	034
CITRUS PEEL	035
CANNED FRUIT	036
FROZEN FRUIT	037
VITAMIN SUPPLEMENT *	038
HOUSEHOLD: Sugar	039
HOUSEHOLD: Salt	040
LARD, OIL, MARG.	041
NUTS	042
FOOD DIPS; Whips; Puddings	043
CANDY	044
PASTRY	045
SALAD OIL; Dressing	046

COMMERCIAL DRUGS:	
ASPIRIN	074
STABILIZERS	075
(No Doz, Etc.)	
PHYSICAL	076
(Ex Lax, Contac)	
ILLICIT DRUGS	077
COMMERC. DRUG	078
PARAPHERNALIA	
ILLICIT DRUG, PARA.	079
(Papers, Needle Rigs.	
Bent Spoons)	
INJURY ORIENTED	080
(Iodine, Band-aids)	
BABY SUPPLIES	081
CONTRACEPTIVES:	
MALE *	082
FEMALE *	083
PET VALUES: PET FOODS	084
PET TOYS	085
PET MAINT. (Litter, Combs, etc.)	086
HETERO: PERS. SANITATION. Soap.	087
Mouthwash, Toothpaste, Razor Blades	
MALE: PERSONAL SANITATION	
MOUTH ●	088
BODY ●	089
HAIR ●	090
FEMALE: PERSONAL SANITATION	
MOUTH ●	091
BODY ●	092
HAIR ●	093
HOUSEHOLD CLEANERS	094
HOUSECLEANING TOOLS (Sponges)	095
COOKING & SERVING AIDS	096
AUTO SUPPLIES	097
ELECTRICAL APPLIANCES	098
MECHANICAL APPLIANCES	099
FURNITURE	100
CLOTHING: CHILD MALE	101
ADULT MALE	102
CHILD FEMALE	103
ADULT FEMALE	104
DRY CLEANING	105
ORGANIZATIONAL NEWSPAPER	106
GENERAL INTEREST MAGS.	107
SPECIAL INTEREST MAGS.	108
ENTERTAINMENT GUIDES	109
FLYERS AND JUNK MAIL:	
BOOKS	110

OTHER SPICES	047	RECORDS	111
BABY FOODS ●	048	INSURANCE	112
MILK	049	REAL ESTATE	113
BUTTER	050	FINANCIAL	114
OTHER DAIRY	051	HOUSEHOLD CAT. (Appliances)	115
EGGS	052	FASHION CAT.	116
CHEESE	053	FOOD	117
DECAF. COFFEE ●	054	GIFT SHOP	118
REG. COFFEE ●	055	COMBINATION	119
TEA ●	056	FINANCIAL LETTERS: Money In	120
CHOCOLATE	057	(Paychecks, Bank Balances, Etc.)	
CANNED, BOTTLED	058	FINANCIAL LETTERS: Money Out	121
Fruit Juice		(Bills, Charge, Utilities, Rent)	
FRUIT JUICE CONCEN.	059	KINSHIP LETTERS	122
DIET SODA ●	060	FRIENDSHIP LETTERS	123
REGULAR SODA ●	061	CHILD VALUE:	
CHIPS, CRACKERS	062	EDUC. BOOKS (Nonfic.)*	124
WHITE BREAD	063	EDUCATIONAL GAMES (Toys) *	125
DARK BREAD	064	AMUSEMENT BOOKS *	126
CEREALS: KIDDIE	065	AMUSEMENT TOYS *	127
AVERAGE	066	ADULT VALUE:	
ECOLOGY	067	GATE RECEIPTS *	128
NOODLES	068	EDUC. READING (Nonfic.) *	129
SLOP	069	AMUSEMENT READING (Fic.) *	130
BEER	070	AMUSEMENT GAMES *	131
WINE	071	HOBBY RELATED ITEM *	132
SPIRITS	072	PHOTO SUPPLIES *	133
PROSCRIBED DRUGS	073		

waste such commodities very consistently, ethnic minorities were found to *avoid* this sort of patterned waste. Our data show, moreover, that in their habits of resource management, the young and old are much alike.

The waste in the average household might seem small; but it becomes very costly when it is viewed on a large scale. It is not the occasional whole steak and unopened can of cranberries which are the real contributors to waste; rather, it is the everyday patterns of food purchase, consumption and storage which lead to significant mismanagement. It would seem, given inflation and the national concern over the state of our environment, that there is enough pressure on housewives to conserve; but the facts belie this appearance. The Garbage Project collected much of its beef-waste information at the height of the beef shortage in the spring of 1973—at a time when there must have been pressure not to waste beef products. Perhaps, in a ironic way, the shortage actually compounded waste as shoppers purchased in bulk in order to save a

few pennies and then found themselves unable to properly store the meat they had bought; such errors, in storage and the scheduling of meals, are typical of middle-class households, which regularly buy cheap meats but which also, paradoxically, tend to waste expensive cuts which they buy at random. We estimate that such households average $100 a year in the waste of edible beef alone; this means that at a minimum, the city of Tucson, Arizona, is wasting $500,000 worth of beef each year.

Archaeological research into modern-day garbage will take time to refine. We must reconstruct purchase and consumption patterns with an eye to such variables as garbage disposals, fireplaces, household pets and the recycling of containers, all of which destroy a certain amount of evidence. But then, archaeologists have always been concerned with such factors. The most exciting and fruitful thrust in recent methodological developments, as far as I am concerned, involves the effort to reconstruct the position and importance of material items in on-

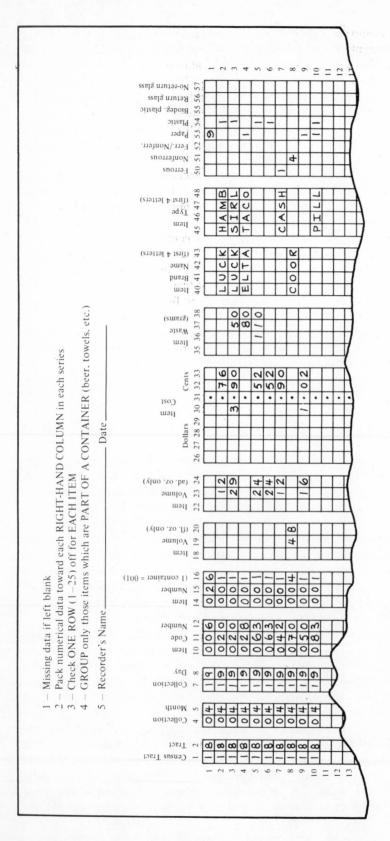

Figure 1. This recording sheet, read in conjunction with the Garbage Item Code List, contains the following information: the data were collected from census tract 18 on April 19. Item 1 consisted of paper towel sheets. 26 in number; the item discarded was made of paper of which more than 9 units were counted (nine is the highest number that can be recorded in column 50–57; if there are more than nine units it is necessary to refer to column 14–16). Item 2 consisted of one container of beef (hamburger); 12 ounces were bought for 76¢ in Luck Supermarket. None was wasted, and only the plastic container was discarded. Item 3 also consisted of beef (sirloin steak): 29 ounces were bought at $3.90 from Luck Supermarket. Fifty grams were wasted; the plastic container was discarded.

going systems from the discard context in which they were found. Put a bit more simply, the concept of *rate* in resource flow is basic to one's ability to extrapolate patterns of sustained behavior from garbage samples. We undertook an investigation in thirty Tucson households to determine the frequency of container discard and to correlate this rate with patterns of purchase and consumption, as determined from information given by the members of each household. The results indicated, as one might expect, that the rates of purchase, consumption and discard were systematically related.

The notion of sustained rate, then, seems to be an accurate characterization of the ongoing process of household consumption, discard and replacement of groups of items during regular periods of accumulation. It also seems to provide a firm basis for inferring patterns of consumption and purchase from discard behavior. Once it is refined, the concept of rate may prove an extremely useful tool for the study of site formations by archaeologists faced with the problem of reconstructing long-term patterns of sustained behavior from garbage middens.

Results of studies such as ours may also prove instructive to archaeologists coping with other traditional problems. It has always been assumed that waste or conspicuous consumption in ancient societies is related to the elites of those social systems. Modern refuse, at least in Tucson, suggests another conclusion altogether. The city's high-income residences are associated with the discard of very little waste of either food or tools. It is the middle-income families, again, which discard large quantities of useful and edible items. This contrast between ancient and modern resource-management correlations may be due to changes in social organization and complexity; but they might also provide archaeologists with new fuel for alternative explanations of past behavior. Either way, the study of garbage can afford an informative view of unfolding cultural processes, both those of the past and the present.

Part VIII

Further Cultural Developments

With the appearance of modern *Homo sapiens sapiens* approximately 40,000 years ago, human groups moved into many previously unoccupied portions of the world. While tracing these movements and activities, this chapter also focuses on subsequent cultural developments culminating in the rise of civilization. The article by Mary Lewin presents data suggesting that the hunting practices of early man in the New World may have contributed to the rapid extinction of several animal species. With the appearance of agriculture, the stage was set for the subsequent rise of civilization and complex socio-political organization of society. Recent archaeological data document a period of experimentation with the early domesticated plants which lasts several thousand years before people settle down to a sedentary way of life based on agriculture. Few authors have had the imagination to suggest, as Darlington does, that certain selective pressures were operating on man—"the domesticator"—as well as his plants and animals. The selection "Dating the British Stone Circles" presents new findings dealing with the age and function of the many megalithic sites found in England. ("Megalithic sites" refers to a western European culture of the neolithic and copper ages, distinguished in part by the presence of monuments made of large stones.) The article is a good example of how chronology can be ascertained by utilizing several techniques available to the archaeologist. Many articles and books have been written dealing with the origin of the state and how it evolved. "The Theory of the Origin of the State" is one such article which attempts to explain why state organization arose in certain areas and not in others. Carneiro argues that one might well consider populations and their relationships to environments. That is, do they occupy an open environment or is their social group marked by being a circumscribed region? The final two selections present examples of cultural developments culminating in the appearance of civilization. The following articles are suggested for additional reading: "The Paleo Indian: Fact and Theory of Early Migrations to the New World", *The Indian Historian*, 1971, pp. 21—6. A recent book dealing with origins of civilization is E. Service, *Origins of the State and Civilization*. (Norton Press, 1975).

Death and Destruction Shows the Path of Early Man

Around 11,000 years ago, in the heart of the Stone Age, many large mammals, happily established many millenia before, suddenly disappeared from the American continent. Geoscientists have been puzzling over this apparent overnight extinction for a long time. Could it in any way be associated with the arrival of Stone Age man on the scene? One person who believes there almost certainly is a connection between the two events is Paul S. Martin, professor of geosciences at the University of Arizona; he has proposed the theory that primitive man, at that time already a proficient big game hunter, was responsible for the obliteration of the megafauna. He and a colleague at the University of Arizona, Austin Long, have now produced a paper in Science (vol. 186, p. 638) providing some firm evidence for his ideas.

They have been looking at organic remains, dung mainly, of the giant ground sloth. So well preserved are these that 19th century palaeontologists were led to believe that the sloth was not extinct at all. Up-to-date radiocarbon dating however has refuted this and allowed a more accurate assessment of ground sloth history. In particular the Arizona researchers wanted to compare the timing of ground sloth extinction in two different areas, one in the Rampart Caves, Arizona, and one much further south, near Puerto Natales, Chile. The new data they came up with shows that in Arizona, the remains were older (by about 300 years) than the Chilean deposits. From their results came no firm evidence for the survival of the giant ground sloth in the Rampart Caves later than 11,000 years ago. Moreover, in the caves, there wasn't a gradual decline in deposition towards the top of the layer; this suggests a sudden extinction rather than an animal population coming under

By Mary Lewin. Reprinted with permission, from *New Scientist,* 16 January 1975. This article first appeared in *New Scientist,* London, the weekly review of science and technology.

gradual stress. And—important for Martin's theory—in both areas, the timing of the ground sloth extinction coincides almost exactly with the arrival of the Stone Age hunters.

These results do tie in very well with Martin's original ideas of the effect of Stone Age man on the New World, that of "explosive overkill" (see Science, vol 179, p. 969). This proposes a brief but devastating coexistence of hunters and large animals, lasting probably no longer than 10 years or so in any one place, which would be largely invisible to palaeontologists. The idea of explosive overkill does much to explain the paradox that has for so long beset geoscientists: the almost total absence of kill sites in the American continent, especially when compared with the more temperate parts of Eurasia, where Palaeolithic remains were found together with large mammalian skeletons. Such a sudden overkill also explains the absence of cave paintings in the New World; the animals were wiped out before there was time to portray the extinct species.

Martin describes his story as the Discovery of America. Some time towards the end of the last Ice Age, big game hunters from Siberia moved into Alaska and then gradually southward. Coming as they did from the frozen tundra of Eastern Siberia and Western Alaska the hunters must have been delighted with the milder climate of their new surroundings. They had also left behind the major endemic diseases of the Old World, unknown in the New. Almost inevitably these two factors alone would have led to a vast population explosion, resulting in a massive band of supremely able and confident hunters, who preferred killing animals as a means of sustenance to any other. This band met an abundance of inexperience innocent prey (mammoths, ground sloths, horses and camels) and a rapid slaughter ensued. Apparently, it only needs one person in four to destroy one animal a week to establish a killing of the biomass in one year. On this basis, extinction would inevitably follow in a decade. There wasn't enough time for the megafauna to learn defensive behaviour, or for more than a very few kill sites to be preserved for the archaeologists.

And so the invading band of hunters swept southwards, from Canada to the Gulf of Mexico in, Martin estimates, 350 years, and then on

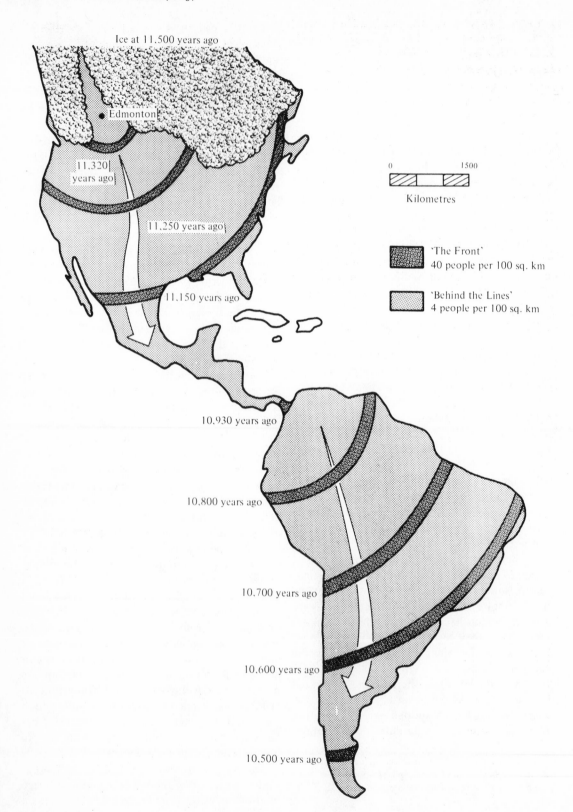

Ice at 11,500 years ago

• Edmonton

11,320 years ago

11,250 years ago

11,150 years ago

10,930 years ago

10,800 years ago

10,700 years ago

10,600 years ago

10,500 years ago

0   1500

Kilometres

'The Front'
40 people per 100 sq. km

'Behind the Lines'
4 people per 100 sq. km

down to the tip of South America in around 1000 years, obliterating the biomass as they went. If this fascinating model is correct, then it will mean, as Martin says, that "the extinction chronology of the Pleistocene megafauna can be used to map the spread of Homo Sapiens throughout the New World".

The Origins
of Agriculture

According to the notions of our forebears, early man first learned to forge and smelt iron to make his weapons and his tools. Then he tamed his beasts and tilled the earth, sowed the seeds of the plants he had collected for food, and so raised his crops. Finally, years of cultivation improved these crops to a standard that came to support agriculture. Man could now provide better fodder for his stock, and could, therefore, breed improved beasts. These developments had occurred in many parts of the world with different kinds of crops and stock on which the different civilizations were based.

This view of agriculture's origins had been reasonably supported by the European discovery of the American civilizations, and it was still generally held at the beginning of the nineteenth century. It showed man progressing almost inevitably by his own efforts, his own skill and intelligence, and in a way that commended itself well to the thought of the nineteenth century.

But in the middle of that century all these ideas were rudely shaken by a series of unforeseen discoveries. It was then that archeology began to show that agriculture had long preceded the smelting of metals. History and language began to indicate that crops had been carried far away from the places where they were first grown. And two naturalists, Darwin and De Candolle, argued that it was not cultivation in itself, but selection by the cultivator—the choice of species and the choice of variations to sow and propagate—that had played the decisive part in improving cultivated plants.

Darwin and De Candolle thus advanced our understanding of the origins of agriculture for the first time in two thousand years. In the hundred years that have followed them, however, a far greater upheaval of ideas has occurred. It has been set off from two directions. One was the study of how plant breeding and selection

By Cyril Darlington. Reprinted with permission, from *Natural History* Magazine, May 1970, pp. 47-56. Copyright © 1970 by The American Museum of Natural History.

actually work among primitive farmers. This we owe largely to the Russian geneticist and plant breeder Nikolai Vavilov. The other was Willard Libby's 1947 discovery of the use of radiocarbon. This led to the physical dating of prehistoric remains and settled the arguments of earlier centuries. What happened when these two fields of inquiry, so utterly remote from one another, came together?

To see how these great advances transformed the problem of the origins of agriculture, we have to look at the world as it was when agriculture began, the world of 10,000 years ago.

First, consider the people. There were about five million people in the world. They were divided into thousands of tribes, all living by various kinds of hunting or collecting, mostly by both. Like their surviving descendants, these people often had special skills for dealing with foods and fibers, drugs and poisons, weapons and boats. The tribes also included some individual artists and craftsmen, as well as men with special knowledge of trade, especially trade in minerals—tools and ornaments, for example, made from obsidian, amber, and precious stones. But, in general, these people had a vast and accurate knowledge of what they could do with the plants, the animals, and the earth on which they depended for their living.

There was, however, one factor in their surroundings on which the main masses of mankind could not depend. This was the climate, for the climate at that time was changing unusually fast. The last Ice Age was in full retreat. The snow was melting all around what is now the temperate Northern Hemisphere. Mountain ranges were becoming passable. The oceans were rising and cutting off islands. Inland seas were drying up. In short, vast new regions were being opened or closed to human habitation.

In these circumstances it is evident that movements of people must have been taking place on a greater scale than ever before. Inevitably the greatest movements of all, and the greatest meeting and mixing of peoples, would be concentrated in those necks of land that join the three continents of the Old World and the two continents of the New. Significantly, therefore, the first evidences of settled agriculture are found close to these necks of land.

Over the last twenty years, radiocarbon dating of the organic remains in a great number of early agricultural settlements has shown beyond doubt that agricuture began at different times in different regions. And it has shown the order in which it actually began in these different regions. The use of radio-carbon has corrected many slight—and a few big—misconceptions.

First, agriculture began, not exactly in what the American Egyptologist James Breasted called the Fertile Crescent, not in the fertile valley bottoms, but rather on the hillsides and tablelands adjoining them. This nuclear zone, as it has been called, is a three-pronged area stretching from the headwaters of the Euphrates, west through Anatolia into the Balkans, south into the Jordan Valley, and east along the foot of the Zagros Mountains toward the Persian Gulf. Later there was a fourth prong crossing Persia south of the Caspian Sea. In other words, the nuclear zone was just at the neck, or the crossroads, of the Old World.

Secondly, we find that this zone of original settlement did not expand—apart from seaside intrusions into Egypt and the Crimea—until about 4000 B.C. There are three or four silent millennia between the beginning of agriculture 10,000 years ago and the great transformation and expansion that followed it. To be sure, during this period pottery was invented. Artists and traders were attracted by the security of the permanent settlements and put their skills and goods at the service of the new, rich, settled communities. But the great technical and biological discoveries of bronze and writing, the wheel and the horse, lay ahead.

These discoveries were made only at the end of the silent millennia, when the great geographical expansion was beginning. In the fourth millennium B.C. the tribes of grain cultivators began to move out of the nuclear zone and to settle or colonize the wild lands of the hunters and collectors, which lay around them. They moved in four main directions: into Europe, into Africa, into India, and into China. They had waited a long time to make these journeys, and they took a long time, more than a thousand years, to accomplish them. Why? The answer depends mainly on the crops they were cultivating. And, as we shall see, these crops give us the answers to several other questions.

That we know exactly what crops were cultivated by the earliest farmers is the result of the work of the Danish botanist Hans Helbaek. The foundation of their agriculture was wheat, and its two main forms continued to live and were cultivated side by side in the nuclear zone for the nine succeeding millennia. The first of these, known as emmer, existed and still exists there wild. The second does not exist wild. It is derived, as we know by experimental breeding and by looking at its chromosomes, from hybridization between emmer and a wild grass also still found growing in this region. This second grain is bread wheat, and today it is still the most important of all man's food crops.

Along with the two wheats, a variety of other food plants were cultivated, a variety that increased with the passing of time: peas and lentils for porridge, barley for beer, linseed for oil, and the vine for wine. Doubtless many unidentified fruits and vegetables were also collected, without at first being bred and cultivated.

But when men passed to the new lands the picture changed. In warmer Egypt linseed began to be grown, not for oil, but for fiber; it was retted and spun for flax and was used to make linen, the first substitute for wool. In colder Europe a new grain, oats, appeared beside the wheat. In India, cotton took the place of wool and flax. In Central Asia the native buckwheat displaced wheat and barley. On the Upper Nile, sorghum displaced the other grains. And almost everywhere various kinds of new light grains, the millets, began to take the place of the heavy-grained wheat and barley.

Some of these later displacements were no doubt due to conscious selection. But some, it seems, were quite unconscious. In 1916 a German geographer, Engelbrecht, attempted to account for these displacements. As a crop is taken into a new territory or habitat, it is apt to be invaded by new weeds. Rye appears as a weed of wheat and displaces the wheat as the crop moves north or moves higher into the mountains. This happens today with cultivated rye, and originally wild rye would have done the same.

No doubt this transformation of crops was exceedingly slow, and indeed its speed was probably the limiting factor in allowing the expansion of agriculture from the nuclear zone. The

Figure 1. The World After Agriculture.

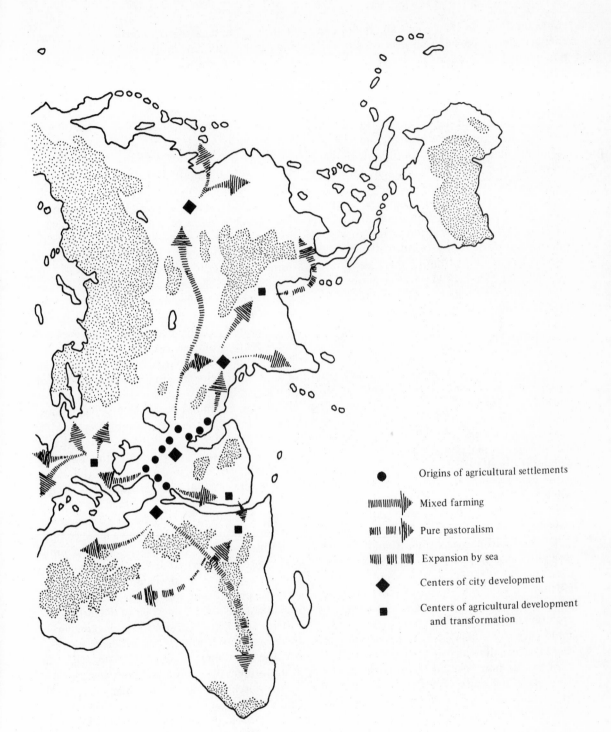

●   Origins of agricultural settlements

||||||||||||||||||▶   Mixed farming

|||| |||| ||||▶   Pure pastoralism

|||| |||| |||| Expansion by sea

◆   Centers of city development

■   Centers of agricultural development and transformation

cultivator had to wait for an evolutionary change, which depended on processes of selection of which he was quite unconscious.

The idea of unconscious selection was Darwin's, but he had no idea how far it would go. It turns out to be the key to the understanding of the development of agriculture. The decisive changes undergone by cultivated plants are not, as one might suppose, in the visible yield, but in properties of behavior which, to the layman or nonfarmer, would seem unimportant.

The discovery of this principle was the main contribution of Vavilov, who found that nearly all cultivated plants had gone through certain parallel transformations. In cultivation they had lost the faculty of distributing their seeds, which was necessary for their survival in nature. And, at the same time, they had acquired a new faculty of submitting to convenient harvesting of fruits and threshing of seed, which was necessary for their survival in the hands of the cultivator.

Take the crowning instance of Vavilov's principle. The ear of wild emmer, when it is ripe, shatters into its separate parts, each containing one grain protected by its coat, the chaff, and armed with a beard that will catch in the coat of any passing animal. When the grain falls to the ground it will dig itself in. But the ear of cultivated emmer or bread wheat does not shatter when ripe. It can be cut and carried unbroken. Only when it is threshed does it gently shed its naked grain into the farmer's bushel or bin.

This extraordinary transmutation, it might be thought, could be the result of conscious selection. It could, if the selector were one who knew all that we know thousands of years later. But how could those first farmers have known what evolutionary changes were possible? And how could they have foreseen how the rich harvests that lay ahead of them might be won?

There is, however, an even more striking example of the scope of unconscious selection. In general, the wild ancestors of crop plants have built-in mechanisms of self-incompatibility: genetic devices that prevent the pollen from growing in the styles and fertilizing the ovules of the same plant. These devices are necessary for the evolutionary success of all wild species for they insure that a proportion of the seed will be crossbred. In cultivation these devices cease to

matter. They confer no immediate advantage; indeed they can only impair the yield. And, sure enough, they are nearly always lost in cultivation. For example, wheat and barley, peas and beans, which all allowed cross-fertilization in their wild ancestors are regularly self-fertilized in their modern cultivated forms. This change was made by selection, but it was not made by conscious selection, for until the last century no one knew it had happened; no one even knew that it could happen.

The cultivator who improved his crops did so, therefore, not by his intelligent practice of plant breeding, but by his intelligent practice of cultivation. And this was a capacity for which, we cannot doubt, the cultivator himself was continually being selected.

The contrast, indeed the conflict, between the tiller of the soil and the keeper of cattle, between the peasant and the herdsman, between Cain and Abel is so ancient and obvious that we naturally think of the domestication of plants and of animals as belonging to separate and opposed problems. But this is misleading. Out of the grain farmer came the ancient civilizations. Around the grain farmer assembled every kind of agricultural and civilized activity. Before grain farming, there was the collecting and even the cropping of roots in many parts of the world. Long before the grain farmer, there was the use of the dog for hunting, for food in time of famine, and later, for herding sheep and goats. But none of these activities led to a more complicated life, which in turn meant a more complicated, a stabler, and ultimately, a more productive society. No great development came about until the grain farmer had, during his four silent millennia, laid the foundations of the future.

The various kinds of stock and stockmen were therefore bound to have had different histories because of their different relations with the grain farmer. What these relations were are still partly obscure. The early settlements mostly contain bones of cattle, pigs, and sheep; but to what extent had these been bred and fed by the farmer and to what extent had he taken them by hunting? Did the early herdsman allow his domesticated female animals to mate with wild males or males that had gone wild? This is the practice of Nagas in India with their gaur cattle today. It is also the practice in mating dogs with wolves. The distinction between what is wild and what is domesticated is therefore harder for the archeologist to draw with stock than with crops.

Allowing for these uncertainties, we may say that sheep and pigs were probably the first to be taken under man's care, probably during the seventh millennium B.C. Later, in the sixth or fifth millennium, came the cattle. Whether their first use was for sacrifice in religious ritual will take us a long time to discover. But certainly this first introduction was quickly followed by their diversified uses for plowing, for milk, for meat, and later, in the salt-hungry regions of Africa, for blood.

When we come to the means of improving domesticated animals along their different lines, we can think of them together and we can see them in contrast with crop plants. The herdsman, it is clear, has from the beginning understood something of the purpose and practice of selection. Indeed we may say that the first herdsmen could never have improved their lot until they understood that better animals could be raised by choosing and setting apart better parents. It is a principle that is suitably and elaborately commemorated by the story of Jacob and Laban in the Book of Genesis.

The processes of animal breeding have thus been more conscious than those of plant breeding, and this has been true at every stage. For example, when the cultivators came into India in the third millennium B.C., they allowed their cattle to hybridize with the native humped cattle. This was no doubt an unconscious and merely traditional practice. But in the Indus city of Mohenjo Daro they also deliberately domesticated new species, notably the native water buffalo. Man's dependence on conscious purpose in dealing with animals as opposed to plants is further indicated by the length of time—five thousand years after the beginning of cultivation—that it took him to acquire the initiative, skill, and audacity to domesticate the most difficult animals, the horse and the camel.

If early farmers were sometimes aware of their effects on crops and stock, it is certain that they were wholly unaware of any effects their crops and stock were having on them (that is, beyond feeding, clothing, or working for them). But those who have observed peasants and pastoralists most closely have seen that between these two great classes of men, there is a genuine and profound contrast, a contrast related to their work. The record goes back, as we saw, to the legend of Cain and Abel, which takes its root in the conflict between the desert and the sown, between the Bedouin shepherds and their peasant neighbors. But on the way, it fills a large part of our history. It is the story of the borderland struggle between the English farmers and the Welsh drovers during the Middle Ages. It is also the story of the struggle between the farming Kikuyu and the grazing Masai in Kenya today.

How are we to describe it? In the first place it should be noted that each class is of many kinds. The nomadic pastoralist may sow crops for a quick harvest during his summer grazing, while the settled peasant may breed cattle or horses to till his land, a practice that has transferred the main labor of farming from the woman with a hoe to the man with a plow. The basic contrast remains however. It is one of character, behavior, and belief.

On the one hand, the peasant is a man who knows and loves his soil and crops. He even worships them. His life, like the lives of his ancestors for two or three hundred generations, has depended on his prudence and industry in handling the soil and crops. He is therefore deeply attached to them, and he and his women will accept serfdom rather than be separated from their land. As a consequence, they are inbred—conservative and traditional, stubborn but peaceful.

How different is the pastoralist! He is correspondingly attached to his animals, but his animals can move and usually have to move in search of pasture. He is therefore mobile, alert, and aggressive. He will steal the cattle and the women of his neighbors. Consequently, he is relatively outbred. And the most mobile of his animals, the horse and the camel, are kept by the most mobile and alert, aggressive and warlike, of herdsmen.

How, then, did this contrast arise? In part, of course, the differences were there in the ancestors, the collectors and the hunters from whom each was partly derived. But it developed during those long silent millennia because the earliest men who chose to adopt these different ways of life were themselves from the beginning dependent for survival on the crops or the stock they were raising. They were therefore dependent on their different abilities to cope with different ways of life. The croppers were in fact being unconsciously selected by their crops, and the stockmen by their stock. Each way of life was tied up together in one related and adapted system.

To put it in another way, man thought himself to be consciously in control of his destiny, but he was in fact unconsciously having his destiny, his evolutionary destiny, thrust upon him. It is a situation from which we can see he has not yet by any means escaped.

The greatest of all human experiments was man's invasion of the New World. Whether it happened fifteen or twenty thousand years ago does not much matter. What matters is that mankind had put himself into two separate boxes between which there was effectively no exchange of people or ideas, of plants or animals, or even of their diseases. That was the situation for over ten thousand years. And during that time, agriculture arose and developed independently in the two boxes. This was, as we may say, an experimental situation, for it goes a long way in showing us what matters and what does not matter for the whole process of developing agriculture.

Looking first at the similarities between the Old World and the New, it can be seen that in the New World, cultivation began around a kind of central or nuclear zone. It began about 7000 B.C., when the ice was melting at its fastest. And it began with a grain crop that the Europeans called Indian corn or maize. A variety of other crops—beans and potatoes, gourds and peppers, cotton and tobacco—slowly assembled around this early crop. But the processes of improvement and distribution show us a number of rule-breaking novelties. Several of these concern maize.

Unlike any of the other important grains, maize has its male and female flowers, the tassels and silks, on different parts of the plant. This has meant that the ordinary evolution toward inbreeding could not occur. Maize remained, and was bound to remain, crossbred. For that reason, it ultimately became the object of the most remarkable of all crop improvements: the American hybrid corn industry of the twentieth century turned an old shortcoming into a controlled advantage.

But maize is also unique with respect to its origin. No botanists would believe that maize was derived from a slender, wild Mexican grass, teosinte. Indeed they had put the two plants into different genera, *Zea* and *Euchlaena*. Yet when the hybridization is tried, the two species are found to cross readily. Their chromosomes pair in the hybrid. And, as Dr. Paul Mangelsdorf found, the hybrid is fertile, yielding the expected recombinations of characters in the second generation. Evidently the selection of mutations, probably conscious selection in this case, has produced the most remarkable evolutionary plant transformation known. All in the course of 9,000 years of cultivation.

There is another American crop, the sweet potato, to which we owe an equally important piece of enlightenment. This plant, coming from Mexico or Peru, was already being cultivated across the Pacific all the way to New Zealand at the time of Columbus. The Maoris had brought it there from the mid-Pacific one or two hundred years earlier, and it had since become the main crop in the North Island. They knew it as *kumara*, the same name that it had borne in Central America. By their languages, their blood groups, their canoes, and their other crops, we know that the Maoris, like other Polynesians, came originally from Indonesia. It is the sweet potato that tells us that at some earlier time other people traveling westward from America had joined them. The two boxes of which I spoke had been almost entirely closed. But not quite.

The great difference between the Old World and the New, however, had nothing to do with these or any other crop plants. In the first place, the nuclear zone of America, instead of being a single, broad, and well-connected area, was split into two by the narrow, twisted 1,500-mile neck that runs from Tehuantepec to Panama, a track that had to befollowed by everyone passing from North to South America. In the second place, stock raising was absent in America. In the previous five millennia the American Indian hunters had killed off what could have been the farmer's stock. Horses and mammoths were no longer available for domestication. All that were left were llamas and turkeys.

These two differences, together with the lesser area and resources of the New World, slowed down the development of agriculture and of civilization. The silent millennia were longer. When the two worlds were brought together in 1492, the civilizations of the New World were found to be about three millennia behind those of the Old World. Mexico and Peru proved to be not unlike the Egypt of Hatshepsut and Thutmose in 1500 B.C. The consequences of this difference in evolution, the submergence of the Amerindians, are with us now, but they are beyond our present inquiry. They show us, however, in a practical way, the overwhelming importance for us today of what happened during the distant years when men and women first began to hoe the earth and sow the seed.

Dating the British Stone Circles

All over the highland regions of the British Isles are remains of stone circles, the gaunt bones of prehistory, offering few clues to their age or purpose. Over nine hundred are known from Cornwall to the Orkneys and from Yorkshire across to Kerry. It is not reasonable to suppose either that they were all contemporary or that they had the same function, but neither is it necessary to assume that they remain as inexplicable as antiquarians found them a century ago. I shall attempt here to construct a broad chronological framework for them and for their different geometrical shapes, based on the examination of 166 megalithic rings (40 circles, 32 flattened circles, 84 ellipses, and 10 egg-shaped rings), or that 17.9 percent of known megalithic rings whose shapes can accurately be established. Methods of construction and reasons for the shapes themselves are only incidentally considered. It may in any case be playing intellectual games to hypothesize on such matters at the moment *(1)*.

Their chronological limits may be defined by C-14 dates, although in themselves these are misleading. Because of past fluctuations in the level of radioactivity, C-14 determinations do not provide the precise dates expected from them and, by the second and third millennia B.C., are too low. Such "dates" can occasionally be tested against historical Egyptian records and tree-ring dating, particularly the long-lived bristlecone pine, and a perceptible widening between C-14 and "real" dates has been realized from about 1000 B.C. backwards. A calibration table correlating these differences *(2)* has been used in Figure 2. In the main, bristlecone-pine, astronomical, and historical dates can be considered as "real" years. So that readers may know which type of date is being used in this paper, all dates based on C-14 determinations are followed by b.c., real years by B.C.

By Aubrey Burl. Reprinted with permission, from *American Scientist*, journal of Sigma Xi, the Scientific Research Society of North America, 61, 1973, pp. 167-74.

Where two dates are available for the same site an average can be calculated, and this is provided with the standard deviation (S.D.) for the differences between the dates, obtained by taking the square root of the sum of the squares of each standard deviation. For Stonehenge II, the second phase of this important monument, the dates are 1720 ± 150 b.c. and 1620 ± 110 b.c., expressed as $100 \pm \sqrt{150^2 + 110^2}$, or S.D. 100 ± 186 years. Standard deviations are given in this form wherever there is more than one date.

With allowance for these caveats one can see the significance of the earliest known date for a stone circle, from New Grange, County Meath, and the latest from Sandy Road, Scone, Perthshire. From the first site come three determinations of 2465 ± 40 b.c., 2475 ± 45 b.c., and 2585 ± 105 b.c., averaging 2533 b.c. (S.D. 120 ± 112 years). Sandy Road has a date of 1200 ± 150 b.c. In recalibrated bristlecone-pine years these represent a span of some 1800 years between about 3300 and 1500 B.C. Such a vast range of time, from the Middle Neolithic almost to the Late Bronze Age, like the wide geographical distribution of the circles, demands a catholic interpretation of their function. No one explanation will account for the complexities of Stonehenge, the claustrophobia of Callanish in the Hebrides, or the architectural eccentricities of recumbent stone circles in Aberdeenshire.

Archaeologists have been concerned with such problems since the early work of John Aubrey (1626–1697) and William Stukeley (1687–1765) on Stonehenge and Avebury. But it has been an engineer, Alexander Thom, who in the last decade has proposed several hypotheses for megalithic settings. It is not generally appreciated that much of his current work on astronomical observatories is concerned more with stone rows than stone circles. His theories have been critically summarized most ably by G. Evelyn Hutchinson *(3)* under the main headings of geometry, mensuration, and astronomy. It is the first of these that is examined further here.

Thom has suggested that among stone circles there are five major shapes: the circle, the flattened circle, the ellipse, the egg, and the complex. Although he did not include them, there are also rectangles known as 4-posters *(4)*, derived from early second-millennium Scottish circles with burials in them. They are approximately contemporary with ellipses but are few and localized and are not considered here. Their existence testifies to the variety of design utilized by the builders of megalithic settings. Thom has put forward no order of development for the shapes, but has theorized that the reason for abandoning the simple circle for more complicated designs was the wish of the planners for circumferences that were multiples of a megalithic "yard" of 2.72 feet.

Cowan *(5)*, in conjecturing methods by which such designs might have been constructed, concluded that the most probable typological order was: circle—flattened circle—ellipse—egg. Hutchinson thought this reasonable, but believed that the evidence from Woodhenge, Wiltshire, presented problems and that the most probable series was: circle—ellipse or egg—flattened circle. It is doubtful whether either sequence could be corroborated without employing archaeological data, and it is fortunate that it is possible to test these theoretical models of development by using artifactual evidence which comes from the circles themselves.

Such evidence includes architectural features, C-14 dates, and finds of pottery and datable implements. From these it appears that Cowan's typology is feasible though oversimplified. The fact that his evolutionary scheme accords with that obtained from archaeological material lends credence to both. It must be emphasized, however, that it is not a single line of growth that emerges but one with two major and several minor strands, often interrelating.

SHAPES

Of the 900+ megalithic rings known in the British Isles *(6)*, the probable proportions are approximately: 600 circles, 150 flattened circles, 100 ellipses, and 50 egg shapes. Before inspecting their chronology it will be useful to make some general remarks.

Circles

These are the easiest to lay out, requiring only a central peg and a length of rope. At some sites like the Lios, County Limerick, a focal stake

hole has been discovered. It is not surprising that most megalithic rings were circular and that the shape was popular from the earliest to the latest period all over Britain. This being so, however, Thom's comprehensive explanation for geometrical designs becomes suspect, for, if he is correct and the planners were indeed trying to set out circumferences as multiples of the megalithic yard, it is puzzling that as many as 66 percent of the settings did not fulfill this requirement.

Flattened Circles

Conversely, it is difficult to provide a reason for these shapes in which a circle has one flattened arc (but see below under the discussion of complex sites). It may be that such an arc is related to the flattened facade of a passage-grave, though in stone circles there is no constant orientation for the flattened side, whereas tomb entrances were nearly always on the eastern side.

Ellipses

The design of these must have a geometrical basis. In general these sites are smaller than the earlier shapes. It is relevant to note that the later development of ellipses in stone circles is paralleled by a similar stage in henges (circular earthen banks, commonly having an inner ditch and one or more entrances), whereby such subcircular Class I henges, like Llandegai I, Caernarvon, were succeeded by ovoid Class II earthworks, like Arbor Low, Derbyshire.

Egg Shapes

Thom suggests two designs for these. Although they appear to be contemporary with the ellipses, they are few in number and apparently unrelated to one another either spatially or culturally. They range from the 135-foot diameter of the stone circle at The Hurlers, Cornwall, to the earthwork enclosure near Woodhenge *(7)* with its Deverel-Rimbury sherds of the middle of the second millennium.

Complex Sites

Despite Thom's contention that perhaps the ultimate development was that of the megalithic ring with several flattened sides, these are not included in this chronological analysis, as it is possible that they have an explanation other than Thom's. Nearly all his complex sites have continuous boundaries either of earth banks, like Avebury, or contiguous stones, like Delfour ring cairn, Inverness, and it is as likely that these are the results of haphazard construction as of precise mathematics.

The form is well exemplified by the flat cairn at Moel ty Uchaf, Merioneth, in which a circle of touching curbstones has three flattened arcs at NW, NE, and SE *(8)*. Similarly, Cairn 1, Chatton Sandyford, Northumberland, is flattened at SE, SW, WSW, NW, and N. Thom's explanation for Moel ty Uchaf is:

They started with a circle 14 yards in diameter. . . . They wanted to have a multiple of 2½ yards in the perimeter [not 44 yards]. So they proceeded to invent a method of drawing flattened portions on the ring which would reduce it to 42½. Later, they had still another external condition to fulfill, if possible. Deneb rose at an azimuth of 173º and they wanted this angle to be shown on the construction so that when the crossaxis pointed to the rising star true north would also be shown.

In contrast to this recondite activity, there is an empirically persuasive argument to explain the construction of a curb of contiguous stones. On the circumference of the projected circle several stones could have been placed diametrically opposite each other. The intervening spaces would then be filled by separate work gangs keeping as near the required curve as their judgment allowed. Deviations which might not be obvious in circles of spaced stones would be very apparent where there was a continuous line, though, of course, only in plan and not to workers on the ground.

This seems to be the explanation at Chatton Sandyford, and it could also explain the irregularities in the shape of the ditch at Avebury. The excavator thought the work must have been carried out by groups working in sections *(9)*. This was likely at the adjacent causewayed camp of Windmill Hill, Wiltshire (ibid., p. 7) and at the analagous camp on Robin Hood's Ball, Wiltshire. Nicholas Thomas wrote *(10)*. "In plan this earthwork is very irregular and seems to have

been designed in a series of straight sections." It is arguable that Thom's complex sites reveal not intricate designs but only long-established practices for laying out earthwork ditches.

Such an explanation for multisided "round" sites had been suspected at the round barrow of Chippenham II, Wiltshire, perhaps dug by six gangs, and at Plaitford, Hampshire, where the central stake hole for the circle was discovered. It would also account for the flattened circles, thus leaving only two basic shapes, the early circle and the later ellipse. This matter could be resolved only by inspection of many accurate plans, and it seems best to accept the four main shapes for the present.

Such an interpretation for complex shapes accords well with Avebury, whose stone circle is likely to be later than the ditch and bank, which otherwise would have been most difficult to construct both because the massive stones would have impeded almost totally the swinging of the axial rope and also because the ditch would have had to be dug perilously close to the shallow-socketed monoliths. Nevertheless, even with the omission of the complex shapes, there remain various designs of geometrical construction whose typology may be determined by the use of traditional archaeological evidence.

DATING

There are several methods by which an archaeological typology of megalithic rings might be composed independently of their shapes. The first is architectural, postulating that the most imposing sites are among the earliest. The second relies on C-14 determinations. The third is based on artifacts found in the circles. Whereas the first has the disadvantage of being only relative with no fixed points in time, the other two come close to an absolute chronology. If all three reveal a similar pattern that coincides with geometrical probability then there is a likelihood that the model is valid.

Architecture

Southern stone circles may well have derived, at least in part, from earthen henges which have average diameters well in excess of 100 feet.

Such an origin makes it likely that many of the primary stone circles would be of a comparable size, and it is not entirely fanciful to consider that the largest stone rings, 100 feet in diameter or more, are among the earliest in the series. Of the 900+ stone circles known to the writer, only just over 600 percent have a diameter of 100 feet or more, and of these 35 are circular. There are 12 flattened circles, 10 ellipses, and 3 eggs.

Another architectural consideration should be the height of the stones. Imposing sites would have tall stones where it was geologically possible. The circle at Almsworthy, Somerset, is 112' × 94' in diameter, but its stones are so small that some might almost be held in one hand, whereas only a few miles north, Porlock, 80 feet in diameter, has stones 6 feet high, weighing several tons. It is a much more impressive circle.

As an arbitrary criterion, where over half the stones are 3 feet tall or more, there are the following settings of over 100-foot diameter: 28 circles, 9 flattened circles, 6 ellipses, and 2 eggs. Circles predominate. But in unimposing sites of over 100-foot diameter with lower stones there are 7 circles, 3 flattened circles, 4 ellipses, and 1 egg. It is manifest that the majority of large, imposing megalithic rings are circular.

In contrast, by far the majority of ellipses are less than 100 feet in diameter (87.5 percent), whereas flattened circles (61 percent) and eggs (66 percent) are more evenly distributed. It is also notable that many ellipses (44 percent) are small in diameter but have tall stones.

If there is any validity in the presumption that large diameters and an early date are correlated, then analysis supports the proposed typology of: circle—flattened circle—ellipse—egg. But it is only with considerable caution that such an argument can be used. There are so many imponderables of geology, size of population, and type of circle that it would be indiscriminate to regard the validity of this criterion as more than tentative.

C-14 Determinations

The most reliable of present dating methods for the archaeologist is that of radiocarbon determinations obtained from sealed material within the circles. Unfortunately, although what dates there are support the hypothetical typology, there are too few for any conclusive scheme. The three earliest are those already cited for New Grange, the gigantic Irish passage-grave, and came from burned material in the passage. Surrounding the chambered cairn are the remains of a 340-foot megalithic ring with stones up to 8 feet high. Cowan believed this to be egg shaped, but his plan came from a faulty reconstruction, and more recent versions show the outer setting to be circular. As both cairn and megalithic ring share a common center, they are likely to be contemporary, and the C-14 date may be extrapolated for the circle.

For Stonehenge II, the uncompleted 86-foot concentric, circular setting of doleritic monoliths, popularly known as the bluestones, up to 6 feet high, there are two dates, 1720 ± 150 b.c. and 1620 ± 110 b.c., averaging 1670 b.c. (S.D. 100 ± 186 years). A slightly later determination of 1500 ± 150 b.c. dates Barbrook II in Derbyshire, a flattened circle, 65 feet in diameter, of small stones within a low rubble bank. One might add Circle 278, Caernarvon, a 40' × 36' ring cairn with stones up to 4½ feet high lining the central space. This circle is flattened on the west. From it came two dates, 1520 ± 145 b.c. and 1405 ± 155 b.c., averaging 1462 b.c. (S.D. 115 ± 214). A final date of 1200 ± 150 b.c. was obtained from a central cremation at Sandy Road, Scone, Perth, an ellipse 24' × 20' of diminutive stones.

From this it can be seen that C-14 dates support both the typology of circle—flattened circle—ellipse and also the supposition that large diameters and tall stones precede small sites of low stones. But even including Circle 278, a total of nine dates from five sites is insufficient to construct a firm framework for the other 900+ circles of Britain. Like architectural considerations, such agreement is helpful but not independently adequate.

Artifacts

It is the third method of dating that provides the most satisfactory data for establishing a probable sequence of geometrical shapes. Many megalithic rings, particularly in the north of Britain, contain burials accompanied by grave goods. Some may be secondary additions to an existing monument, but burials are so common, rising to over 44 percent of sites in northeast Scotland *(11)*, that it is likely that in most cases they were part of the primary ceremonies and therefore reliable for dating.

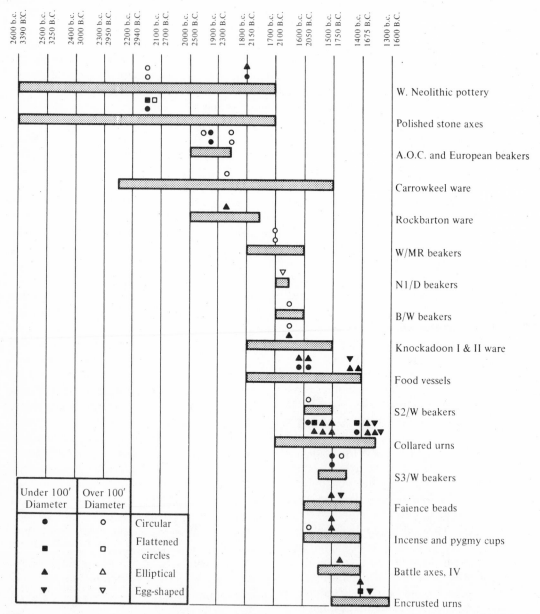

Figure 1. Megalithic rings are plotted on time lines commensurate with the estimated span of production of various artifacts. Radiocarbon dates are followed by b.c.; bristlecone-pine dates by B.C. All rings are placed at the middle point of the artifactual line unless there is evidence that they should be early or late, as is the case with the Western Neolithic pottery from the ellipse at Castle Mahon, County Down, found with a planoconvex flint knife of a later period than the average for the pottery. Most ellipses appear after 1700 b.c.; some circles are 500 years older than this.

Pottery cannot provide the type of precise dating obtained from C-14 determinations. There is much uncertainty about the length of time a particular kind of artifact was being produced, and these periods vary in different parts of the country. Northern beakers in Scotland were produced during three centuries, whereas their counterparts in Wessex began somewhat later and endured for barely a hundred years. It would be naive, consequently, to say that Circle IV, Machrie Moor, Arran, should be dated at around 1600 b.c. because it contained a Hiberno-Scottish food vessel. What can be said is that, if the food vessel was deposited in the central cist at the same time as the surrounding circle was erected, then it is likely that the circle was built at some period between about 1800–1400 b.c., when food vessels flourished in Britain.

Such reasoning is susceptible of refinement by examining specific forms of pottery and the areas in which they were found. This would be necessary were only one site to be considered, but is needlessly rigorous in an overall examination. It is enough to demonstrate the individual floruits of artifacts and the types of megalithic ring in which they have been found. See Figure 1 for a correlation of artifacts, their span of production, and the settings in which they were found.

Some artifacts are not useful for such an analysis because they have too long a period of manufacture. Flat-rimmed ware is a good example. It may have been in use for the larger part of the second millennium. Such sherds, found at Croft Mcraig, Perth, or Loanhead of Daviot recumbent stone circle, Aberdeenshire, do not provide a helpful diagnostic of the age of the circle. Hence this ware is omitted from the diagram, as are lumps of bronze of no definable shape.

Other material is of much greater assistance. Beakers have recently been studied by Clarke *(12);* collard urns by Longworth; Irish Neolithic pottery by Case; battle-axes by Roe; Scottish urns by Morrison; Irish Bronze Age pottery by Harbison; other Bronze Age material by Burgess. It is upon these that the chronology is founded. Datable finds have been discovered at 49 sites—29.5 percent of the 166 rings under consideration, which is a proportion high enough to provide a reliable sample for analysis. Many other circles have yielded artifacts, but eiter the finds cannot be dated or the shape of the ring cannot now be ascertained, and thus it would be misleading to inllude them in this study.

From Fig. 1 it seems that the circular rings really are early in origin and that the ellipses and egg shapes do develop later with a general flourishing from about 1700 b.c. onwards (about 2100 B.C. in the revised chronology). It is also noticeable that the larger sites tend to be earlier, strengthening the hypothesis that imposing rings were among the first to be constructed. Some flattened circles also are early.

If the whole period from 2600 to 1100 b.c. is divided into three equal phases of 500 years, Phase A (2600–2100 b.c.) has only circles, mainly large, and flattened circles. Phase B (2100–1600 b.c.) still has a predominance of circles particularly large ones, with one large egg, and a few small ellipses. Phase C (1600–1100 b.c.) sees a sharp diminution of large circles but a great increase in small diameters, especially ellipses.

The chronological position of the egg-shaped sites remains equivocal inasmuch as the earliest known is Cairnpapple, a circle-henge 115' × 92', in West Lothian. Although this may be dated by the N/NR and N2 beakers found by some stone holes, the stone ring itself must antedate these yet postdate the Group VI and VIII polished stone axes over which it stood. It is possible that Cairnpapple is earlier than 1700 b.c. and may precede the earliest known ellipse, Castle Mahon. The same might be true of Woodhenge *(13).* One can only remark that there are too few datable egg-shaped sites for any dogmatism about their temporal relationships to ellipses.

THE PURPOSE OF MEGALITHIC RINGS

All three analyses appear to confirm that the most probable typology for geometrical shapes is circle and flattened circle, and then a later development of ellipses and egg shapes, which may be contemporary with each other. Yet there is still the possibility that each of the shapes reflects a different origin and that, rather than demonstrating an evolutionary typology, the analyses reveal only the individual time of emergence for each design, all being independent of the others. Such a possibility is diminished somewhat by the presence of the different shapes in monuments of the same type and locality.

This is most clearly seen in the Clava cairns, Inverness. Thom in *Megalithic Sites in Britain* (8) summarized his survey of 19 sites in this close-knit group of tombs with stone circles around them. Among the megalithic rings and cairns there were 13 proper circles, 3 ellipses, 2 flattened circles, and 1 egg. The earliest of these passage-graves and ring cairns (14) were probably built before all the shapes had evolved if the chronology of Figure 1 can be trusted. It is thus just possible that plans of the Clava cairns contain a full sequence of designs and are not just an accretion of shapes received from external sources.

As similar mélanges occur in the south of Britain on Bodmin Moor, Cornwall, at Land's End, and on Dartmoor, Devon, one may conclude either that the layouts are accidental and not geometrical or that the megalithic rings did have specific designs which evolved over the centuries and which it may be possible to disentangle. The archaeological picture is confused because it is not of a single evolution but of separate developments in different regions of Britain, with the majority of ellipses belonging to a cultural group, and it is also perhaps blurred by the near absence of finds from the "ceremonial" sites in the south. Yet some conclusions can still be made.

As Figure 2 shows, circles abound wherever there are megalithic rings. The largest appear to be among the earliest. Of the thirty-five known circles over 100 feet in diameter, 70 percent do not contain burials and 65 percent lie within the Atlantic province along the western coasts from southwest Scotland to Cornwall, especially in the southwest peninsula.

With the exception of an overlap in Cornwall, flattened circles have a distribution distinct from circles. Only two, South Ythsie and Garrol Wood in northeast Scotland, are not of the Irish Sea tradition or influenced by Wessex types of the same cultural pattern. (One might add Tor-darroch and Aviemore ring cairns, Inverness, although the shapes of these Clava tombs are not certain.) Of the remaining thirty there is a remarkable concentration around Cumbria. The larger rings are coastal whereas the smaller tend to be in the later, inland areas like Derbyshire's Peak District, where the C-14 date of Barbrook II—1500 ± 150 b.c.—may be indicative of the later phases.

In contrast, only 15 percent of ellipses are in the Atlantic regions. Nearly two-thirds are in northeast Scotland or in southwest Ireland. Over half certainly contain burials. There are two important size-groups: a minor group of 25 percent whose diameters average 72' × 68', and a major group of 58 percent averaging 27' × 24'. It is noticeable that the proportions are not grossly dissimilar. There is no discernible pattern to the distribution of the larger sites.

From these generalizations tentative interpretations of the function of some stone circles may be made, including the possible astronomical purpose of these sites. Many of the earliest monuments of prehistoric Britain had plans in some way related to the movements of the sun. The majority of earthen long barrows had their burials at the higher end, which was commonly toward the eastern quadrant of the horizon (15). The same astronomical aspect is found in megalithic tombs, whose entrances customarily were built between northeast and southeast. As it is in this part of the horizon that the sun rises, such alignments are unlikely to be fortuitous. Certain groups of henges also have entrances which may be related to solar orientations.

It would be to advance beyond sensible speculation to claim that these orientations, vague and diffuse as they are, were connected with astronomical prediction. Indeed, the closed entrances of megalithic tombs seem to preclude this. Instead, it is more satisfactory to perceive a connection between life and death and the rising and the setting of the sun.

Similar solar positions may exist in some of the earliest stone circles. As well as the rather overtaxed Heel Stone of Stonehenge I, presumptively C-14-dated to 2180 ± 105 b.c., one may refer to the 108-foot flattened Cumbrian circle of The Carles, Castlerigg, Keswick. Here Thom believes there are at least three first-class solar alignments. It is not unlikely that the first stone

Under 100′ Diameter	Over 100′ Diameter	
○	○	Circles
■	□	Flattened circles
▲	△	Ellipses

Figure 2. The distribution of megalithic circle sites shows some interesting patterns. Large circles, probably the earliest in time, are found throughout the British Isles. Flattened circles, with a few exceptions, are found primarily in Cumbria. Most ellipses are in northeast Scotland or southwest Ireland.

circles, sites of ceremony and religion, continued the beliefs inferred from earlier monuments.

If the evolutionary sequence is valid, it could be expected that the large megalithic circular and flattened rings would have conspicuous circumferential stones or outliers in obvious solar positions, for it may be assumed that orientations within such circles would not be for esoteric calculations but more probably for seasonal observances, the summer and winter solstices or the vernal and autumnal equinoxes,

when the sun was midway between its extreme north and south positions on the horizon. Autumnal gatherings are known from causewayed camps, which are the putative ancestors of henges, and the earliest stone circles may have had something of the same purpose, providing a place of meeting for scattered groups at special times of the year. What astronomical alignments they did contain would be calendrical. The large circles and flattened circles could be examined for such lines. Thom, in *Megalithic Sites in Britain*, lists several sites like The Rollright Stones, Oxfordshire; The Hurlers, Fernacre, and Stannon, all in Cornwall; Brats Hill, Cumberland, which are large and considered to have good solar alignments.

Equally, it is feasible that a peasant interest in the movements of the sun might acquire sophistication over several centuries. A facet of this chronological analysis has been to demonstrate the extremely long history of stone circles. A thousand years is time enough not only for the development of ellipses but also for a corpus of astronomical knowledge to be accumulated in some parts of Britain. It is curious that Thom's postulated lunar observatories occupy roughly the same area in Scotland as the ellipses and that his predicated dates of about 1750 B.C. and 1650 B.C. for the observatories *(16)* correspond broadly with the corrected date for the full flowering of the elliptical shape. But this is a matter not to be continued here. There circles are also those that contain burials. Whether the monuments were sepulchral or whether the burial was dedicatory or sacrificial, whether the astronomical alignments were religious and invoked powers of the sun and moon for the dead or whether they were for observation and prediction, or even, after all, illusory, are matters of such complication that they cannot be dealt with here.

What can be added is that many of the large circles, particularly those henge-derived sites in southern Britain, seem to have been associated with the trade in stone axes. The deliberate deposition of two stone axes in mint condition at Llandegai I henge, Caernarvon, led to speculation that the site might have been a meeting place for itinerant axe traders *(17)*. A comparable cache came from Cairnpapple. Concentrations of stone axes have been noted at Avebury and The Ring of Brodgar, Orkney, both circle henges, that is, henges with stone circles in them. Together with the distribution of large stone circles around the axe factories in Cumbria, these discoveries encourage the belief in an early connection between henge, circle, and axe trade.

Several writers have expressed belief in an axe cult *(18)*. It is extraordinary that, even as late as the last century, peasants in Europe believed that prehistoric stone axes found in their fields were thunderbolts and good luck charms. An axe which could be used to till the fields, to clear trees, and which also struck sparks might be considered by Neolithic farmers to represent an extension of the sun. A place where such axes were bartered would thus be not only a market but also a temple in which trade and ritual went hand in hand. The axe might become the symbol of the god, particularly at a sun-important time of the year.

Such a cult would give extra significance to the famous axe carvings at Stonehenge III, with its massive trilithons, as well as the axe carving on the Irish recumbent stone circle of Drombeg, Cork. It would also explain the nonfunctional axes of chalk buried at Stonehenge and Woodhenge, as it would the burial of beautiful jadeite axes at chambered tombs in Brittany like Mané er Hroek and the manufacture of superb minatures with perforations perhaps for use as religious pendants. In this respect discoveries at the two stone circles of Er Lannic in the Gulf of Morbihan, Brittany, become significant. These were large rings, 160 feet and 230 feet in diameter, of tall stones. Their shapes are uncertain because one is a third, the other totally, submerged beneath the sea. They may be analogous to the egg-shaped ring at Le Menec in Brittany. Thom *(19)* suggested a date around 1700 B.C. for megalithic sites near Le Menec. The presence of pottery vase supports at Er Lannic indicates a Breton Early Bronze Age date for these rings, which is not entirely incompatible with Thom's date, though probably earlier.

At these tangential circles there were stone axes deposited beside no fewer than 29 of the 47 stones excavated in the partly drowned north circle. The whole site appeared to be an atelier

for the manufacture of axes *(20)*, an observation in keeping with the hypothesis that stone circles and trade in stone axes were sometimes interconnected. Ritual activity at Er Lannic appears from the fact that stones 10, 12, 14, and 17 were cup-marked. These stones seem very close to important solar and lunar orientations for midsummer setting. Two tall outliers also stand on apparent sun alignments. Er Lannic is a good example of the intermingling of stone axe, sun, and circle.

Woodhenge has already been mentioned for its ritual chalk axes. Near the center of the site was a small grave holding the body of a three-year-old child. It lay facing the midsummer sunrise. Its skull had been split in two. It is probable that a stone axe had been used.

Across the dimmed distance of the past there are glimpses of the activities that took place in the great stone circles of Britain. It must be hoped that we are coming to some understanding of the societies that built them.

Notes

1. This point of view is well expressed by N. Grossman, 1970, *Science* 169: 1228–29. He is skeptical of any "proof" that builders of megalithic settings were aware of the properties of Pythagorean triangles.

2. H. McKerrell. 1971. *Scottish Archaeological Forum* 3: 78.

3. G. E. Hutchinson. 1972. Long Meg reconsidered *Am. Sci.* 60:24–31; 210–19. For A. Thom see: *Megalithic sites in Britain,* 1967, Oxford: Clarendon Press; *Megalithic lunar observatories,* 1971, Oxford: Clarendon Press; The astronomical significance of the large Carnac menhirs, Oct. 1971, *J. Hist. Astron.* 2:147–61; The Carnac alignments, Feb. 1972, *J. Hist. Astron.* 3:11–26.

4. H. A. W. Burl. 1971. Two "Scottish" stone circles in Northumberland. *Archaeologia Aeliana* 49:37–51. This contains a corpus of the known 4-posters in Britain. A recent excavation report of a 4-poster appears in H. A. W. Burl, The excavation of the Three Kings, Northumberland, in press, *Arch. Ael.* Readers interested in rectangular megalithic settings are referred to King Arthur's Hall, a mysterious quadrilateral on Bodmin Moor, and to sites like Crucuno, Morbihan, mentioned by P. R. Giot, *Brittany,* 1960, London: Thames & Hudson, ch. 7.

5. T. M. Cowan. 1969. Megalithic rings: Their design construction. *Science* 168:321–25.

6. H. A. W. Burl. The stone circles of Great Britain and

Ireland, vols. 1 and 2. Unpublished thesis, University of Leicester. Appendix 1 contains a corpus of all known sites. Appendix 4 is a list of all artifacts discovered in these stone circles.

7. This little-known site is mentioned in M. E. Cunnington, *Woodhenge, Wiltshire,* 1929, Devizes, pp. 49–51 and 159. It was possibly a sheep enclosure of the Middle Bronze Age; it is unlikely to have been a ritual site. One wonders if its builders were concerned with the mathematical properties of the perimeter.

8. Thom, *Megalithic sites in Britain,* p. 84. Also see E. G. Bowen and C. A. Gresham, *History of Merioneth,* vol. 1, 1967, Dolgellau, Fig. 37; For Chatton Sandyford, see G. Jobey, 1968 *Arch. Ael.* 46:8.

9. I. F. Smith. 1965. *Windmill Hill and Avebury.* Oxford: Clarendon Press, p. 218.

10. N. Tomas. 1967. The Neolithic causewayed camp at Robin Hood's Ball, Shrewton, Wiltshire. *Wiltshire Archaeological Magazine* 59:1–27.

11. H. A. W. Burl. 1973. Stone circles and ring cairns. *Scot. Archaeol. Forum* 4.

12. Studies containing chronological guidelines to artifacts are: D. L. Clarke, *Beaker pottery of Great Britain and Ireland,* vols. 1 and 2, 1970, Cambridge University Press; I. H. Longworth, The origins and development of the primary series in the collared urn tradition in England and Wales, 1961, *Proc. Prehist. Society* 27:263–306; H. Case, Irish Neolithic pottery: Distribution and sequence 161, ibid., pp. 174–233; F. E. S. Roe, The battle-axe series in Britain, 1966, ibid., 33:199–245; A. Morrison, Cinerary urns and pygmy vessels in southwest Scotland, 1968, *Trans. Dumfriess & Galloway Nat. Hist. & Antiquarian Soc.* 45:80–140; P. Harbison, the relative chronology of Irish early Bronze Age pottery, 1969, *J. Royal Soc. Aniquaries of Ireland* 99:63–82; C. B. Burgess, Chronology and terminology in the British Bronze Age, 1969, *Antiquaries J.* 49.1:22–9.

13. Discussion of Woodhenge, which Thom considers egg shaped, has not been included in the main argument as its dating presents much difficulty. Most of the pottery was grooved ware (G. J. Wainwright with I. H. Longworth, *Durington Walls: Excavations 1966–68,* 1971, London: Society of Antiquaries, pp. 235–306), which is similar to two of the five sherds found at Stonehenge I, dated by C-14 to 2180 ± 105 b.c. This pottery was produced from about 2000–1600

b.c. (ibid., p. 248). Some of Woodhenge's postholes and the ditch also contained W/MR beaker sherds of perhaps 1800–1600 b.c. But a similar pottery mixture in the outer ditch of Windmill Hill causewayed camp was associated with material yielding a C-14 date of 1540 ± 150 b.c. (Smith, *Windmil & Avebury.* p. 11). If a guess were hazarded at a date around 1800 b.c. for Woodhenge, this would not be very different from the pre-1700 b.c. date suggested for Cairnpapple and might indicate that egg-shaped rings had an origin somewhat earlier than ellipses. But two speculative dates are not adequate to support the argument. It is to be hoped that a recent excavation by Dr. Geoffrey Wainwright will make possible the establishment of a reliable series of dates for Woodhenge.

14. A. S. Henshall. 1972. *The chambered tombs of Scotland.* vol. 2, Edinburgh University Press, pp. 283–4. The Clava tombs are considered to belong to her Phase IV (2500–c1700 b.c.) with an origin not later than the end of the third millennium because of the architectural overlap with Orkney-Cromarty tombs in the region. It is hard to accept that ellipses and egg shapes had begun in stone circles as early as this.

15. P. Ashbee. 1970. *The earthen long barrow in Britain.* London: J. M. Dent and Sons, Ltd., pp. 28–30.

16. A. Thom. 1971. *Megalithic lunar observatories,* p. 44. The 1750 B.C. date is based on calculations from three solstitial sites in Argyllshire. A later date of 1650 B.C. (ibid., p. 79) relates to 24 lunar sites in North Britain. These B.C. dates are astronomically based and must be calibrated forwards for their C-14 equivalents.

17. C. Houlder. 1968. The henge monuments at Llandegai, *Antiquity* 43:216–20.

18. For references to the possibility of an axe cult in northern Europe see: M. Gimbutas, Battle axe of cult axe, 1953, *Man* 73:51–54. O. G. S. Crawford, *The Eye Goddess,* 1957, London: Pheonix House, Ltd., pp. 75–78, P. Gelling & H. E. Davidson, *The chariot of the sun,* 1969, London: J. M. Dent & Sons, Ltd., pp. 27–31 ff.; J. B. Calkin. The population of Neolithic and Bronze Age Dorset. 1969. *Proc. Dorset Nat. Hist. & Archaeological Soc.* 90:212.

19. A. Thom. 1971. The astronomical significance of the large Carnac menhirs. *J. Hist. Astronomy* 2:159.

20. Z. le Rouzic. 1930. *Les Cromlechs de Er Lannic.* Vannes: Lafolye & Lamazèlle.

A Theory of the Origin of the State

For the first 2 million years of his existence, man lived in bands or villages which, as far as we can tell, were completely autonomous. Not until perhaps 5000 B.C. did villages begin to aggregate into larger political units. But, once this process of aggregation began, it continued at a progressively faster pace and led, around 4000 B.C., to the formation of the first state in history. (When I speak of a state I mean an autonomous political unit, encompassing many communities within its territory and having a centralized government with the power to collect taxes, draft men for work or war, and decree and enforce laws.)

Although it was by all odds the most far-reaching political development in human history, the origin of the state is still very imperfectly understood. Indeed, not one of the current theories of the rise of the state is entirely satisfactory. At one point or another, all of them fail. There is one theory, though, which I believe does provide a convincing explanation of how states began. It is a theory which I proposed once before *(1)*, and which I present here more fully. Before doing so, however, it seems desirable to discuss, if only briefly, a few of the traditional theories.

Explicit theories of the origin of the state are relatively modern. Classical writers like Aristotle, unfamiliar with other forms of political organization, tended to think of the state as "natural," and therefore as not requiring an explanation. However, the age of exploration, by making Europeans aware that many peoples throughout the world lived, not in states, but in independent villages or tribes, made the state seem less natural, and thus more in need of explanation.

Of the many modern theories of state origins that have been proposed, we can consider only a few. Those with a racial basis, for example, are now so thoroughly discredited that they need not

By Robert Carneiro. Reprinted with permission, from *Science,* 169, 21 August 1970, pp. 733-38. Copyright © 1970 by the American Association for the Advancement of Science.

be dealt with here. We can also reject the belief that the state is an expression of the "genius" of a people *(2)*, or that it arose through a "historical accident." Such notions make the state appear to be something metaphysical or adventitious, and thus place it beyond scientific understanding. In my opinion, the origin of the state was neither mysterious nor fortuitous. It was not the product of "genius" or the result of chance, but the outcome of a regular and determinate cultural process. Moreover, it was not a unique event but a recurring phenomenon: states arose independently in different places and at different times. Where the appropriate conditions existed, the state emerged.

VOLUNTARISTIC THEORIES

Serious theories of state origins are of two general types: *voluntaristic* and *coercive*. Voluntaristic theories hold that, at some point in their history, certain peoples spontaneously, rationally, and voluntarily gave up their individual sovereignties and united with other communities to form a larger political unit deserving to be called a state. Of such theories the best known is the old Social Contract theory, which was associated especially with the name of Rousseau. We now know that no such compact was ever subscribed to by human groups, and the Social Contract theory is today nothing more than a historical curiosity.

The most widely accepted of modern voluntaristic theories is the one I call the "automatic" theory. According to this theory, the invention of agriculture automatically brought into being a surplus of food, enabling some individuals to divorce themselves from food production and to become potters, weavers, smiths, masons, and so on, thus creating an extensive division of labor. Out of this occupational specialization there developed a political integration which united a number of previously independent communities into a state. This argument was set forth most frequently by the late British archeologist V. Gordon Childe *(3)*.

The principal difficulty with this theory is that agriculture does *not* automatically create a food surplus. We know this because many agricultural peoples of the world produce no such surplus. Virtually all Amazonian Indians, for example, were agricultural, but in aboriginal times they did not produce a food surplus. That it was *technically feasible* for them to produce such a surplus is shown by the fact that, under the stimulus of European settlers' desire for food, a number of tribes did raise manioc in amounts well above their own needs, for the purpose of trading *(4)*. Thus the technical means for generating a food surplus were there; it was the social mechnisms needed to actualize it that were lacking.

Another current voluntaristic theory of state origins is Karl Wittfogel's "hydraulic hypothesis." As I understand him, Wittfogel sees the state arising in the following way. In certain arid and semiarid areas of the world, where village farmers had to stuggle to support themselves by means of small-scale irrigation, a time arrived when they saw that it would be to the advantage of all concerned to set aside their individual autonomies and merge their villages into a single large political unit capable of carrying out irrigation on a broad scale. The body of officials they created to devise and administer such extensive irrigation works brought the state into being *(5)*.

This theory has recently run into difficulties. Archeological evidence now makes it appear that in at least three of the areas that Wittfogel cites as exemplifying his "hydraulic hypothesis"—Mesopotamia, China, and Mexico—full-fledged states developed well before large-scale irrigation *(6)*. Thus, irrigation did not play the causal role in the rise of the state that Wittfogel appears to attribute to it *(7)*.

This and all other voluntaristic theories of the rise of the state founder on the same rock: the demonstrated inability of autonomous political units to relinquish their sovereignty in the absence of overriding external constraints. We see this inability manifested again and again by political units ranging from tiny villages to great empires. Indeed, one can scan the pages of history without finding a single genuine exception to this rule. Thus, in order to account for the origin of the state we must set aside voluntaristic theories and look elsewhere.

COERCIVE THEORIES

A close examination of history indicates that

only a coercive theory can account for the rise of the state. Force, and not enlightened self-interest, is the mechanism by which political evolution has led, step by step, from autonomous villages to the state.

The view that war lies at the root of the state is by no means new. Twenty-five hundred years ago Heraclitus wrote that "war is the father of all things." The first careful study of the role of warfare in the rise of the state, however, was made less than a hundred years ago, by Herbert Spencer in his *Principles of Sociology (8)*. Perhaps better known than Spencer's writings on war and the state are the conquest theories of continental writers such as Ludwig Gumplowicz *(9)*, Gustav Ratzenhofer *(10)*, and Franz Oppenheimer *(11)*.

Oppenheimer, for example, argued that the state emerged when the productive capacity of settled agriculturists was combined with the energy of pastoral nomads through the conquest of the former by the latter (*11*, pp. 51–55). This theory, however, has two serious defects. First, it fails to account for the rise of states in aboriginal America, where pastoral nomadism was unknown. Second, it is now well established that pastoral nomadism did not arise in the Old World until after the earliest states had emerged.

Regardless of deficiencies in particular coercive theories, however, there is little question that, in one way or another, war played a decisive role in the rise of the state. Historical or archeological evidence of war is found in the early stages of state formation in Mesopotamia, Egypt, India, China, Japan, Greece, Rome, northern Europe, central Africa, Polynesia, Middle America, Peru, and Colombia, to name only the most prominent examples.

Thus, with the Germanic kingdoms of northern Europe especially in mind, Edward Jenks observed that, "historically speaking, there is not the slightest difficulty in proving that all political communities of the modern type [that is, states] owe their existence to successful warfare" *(12)*. And in reading Jan Vansina's *Kingdoms of the Savanna (13)*, a book with no theoretical ax to grind, one finds that state after state in central Africa arose in the same manner.

But is it really true that there is no exception

to this rule? Might there not be, somewhere in the world, an example of a state which arose without the agency of war?

Until a few years ago, anthropologists generally believed that the Classic Maya provided such an instance. The archeological evidence than available gave no hint of warfare among the early Maya and led scholars to regard them as a peace-loving theocratic state which had arisen entirely without war *(14)*. However, this view is no longer tenable. Recent archeological discoveries have placed the Classic Maya in a very different light. First came the discovery of the Bonampak murals, showing the early Maya at war and reveling in the torture of war captives. Then, excavations around Tikal revealed large earthworks partly surrounding that Classic Maya city, pointing clearly to a military rivalry with the neighboring city of Uaxactún *(15)*. Summarizing present thinking on the subject, Michael D. Coe has observed that "the ancient Maya were just as warlike as the . . . bloodthirsty states of the Post-Classic" *(16)*.

Yet, though warfare is surely a prime mover in the origin of the state, it cannot be the only factor. After all, wars have been fought in many parts of the world where the state never emerged. Thus, while warfare may be a necessary condition for the rise of the state, it is not a sufficient one. Or, to put it another way, while we can identify war as the *mechanism* of state formation, we need also to specify the *conditions* under which it gave rise to the state.

ENVIRONMENTAL CIRCUMSCRIPTION

How are we to determine these conditions? One promising approach is to look for those factors common to areas of the world in which states arose indigenously—areas such as the Nile, Tigris-Euphrates, and Indus valleys in the Old World and the Valley of Mexico and the mountain and coastal valleys of Peru in the New. These areas differ from one another in many ways—in altitude, temperature, rainfall, soil type, drainage pattern, and many other features. They do, however, have one thing in common: *they are all areas of circumscribed agricultural land.* Each of them is set off by mountains, seas,

or deserts, and these environmental features sharply delimit the area that simple farming peoples could occupy and cultivate. In this respect these areas are very different from, say, the Amazon basin or the eastern woodlands of North America, where extensive and unbroken forests provided almost unlimited agricultural land.

But what is the significance of circumscribed agricultural land for the origin of the state? Its significance can best be understood by comparing political development in two regions of the world having contrasting ecologies—one a region with circumscribed agricultural land and the other a region where there was extensive and unlimited land. The two areas I have chosen to use in making this comparison are the coastal valleys of Peru and the Amazon basin.

Our examination begins at the stage where agricultural communities were already present but where each was still completely autonomous. Looking first at the Amazon basin, we see that agricultural villages there were numerous, but widely dispersed. Even in areas with relatively dense clustering, like the Upper Xingú basin, villages were at least 10 or 15 miles apart. Thus, the typical Amazonian community, even though it practiced a simple form of shifting cultivation which required extensive amounts of land, still had around it all the forest land needed for its gardens *(17)*. For Amazonia as a whole, then, population density was low and subsistence pressure on the land was slight.

Warfare was certainly frequent in Amazonia, but it was waged for reasons of revenge, the taking of women, the gaining of personal prestige, and motives of a similar sort. There being no shortage of land, there was, by and large, no warfare over land.

The consequences of the type of warfare that did occur in Amazonia were as follows. A defeated group was not, as a rule, driven from its land. Nor did the victor make any real effort to subject the vanquished, or to exact tribute from him. This would have been difficult to accomplish in any case, since there was no effective way to prevent the losers from fleeing to a distant part of the forest. Indeed, defeated villages often chose to do just this, not so much to avoid subjugation as to avoid further attack. With settlement so sparse in Amazonia, a new area of forest could be found and occupied with relative ease, and without trespassing on the territory of another village. Moreover, since virtually any area of forest is suitable for cultivation, subsistence agriculture could be carried on in the new habitat just about as well as in the old.

It was apparently by this process of fight and flight that horticultural tribes gradually spread out until they came to cover, thinly but extensively, almost the entire Amazon basin. Thus, under the conditions of unlimited agricultural land and low population density that prevailed in Amazonia, the effect of warfare was to disperse villages over a wide area, and to keep them autonomous. With only a very few exceptions, noted below, there was no tendency in Amazonia for villages to be held in place and to combine into larger political units.

In marked contrast to the situation in Amazonia were the events that transpired in the narrow valleys of the Peruvian coast. The reconstruction of these events that I present is admittedly inferential, but I think it is consistent with the archeological evidence.

Here too our account begins at the stage of small, dispersed, and autonomous farming communities. However, instead of being scattered over a vast expanse of rain forest as they were in Amazonia, villages here were confined to some 78 short and narrow valleys (18). Each of these valleys, moreover, was backed by the mountains, fronted by the sea, and flanked on either side by desert as dry as any in the world. Nowhere else, perhaps, can one find agricultural valleys more sharply circumscribed than these.

As with neolithic communities generally, villages of the Peruvian coastal valleys tended to grow in size. Since autonomous villages are likely to fission as they grow, as long as land is available for the settlement of splinter communities, these villages undoubtedly split from time to time (19). Thus, villages tended to increase in number faster than they grew in size. This increase in the number of villages occupying a valley probably continued, without giving rise to significant changes in subsistence practices, until all the readily arable land in the valley was being farmed.

At this point two changes in agricultural techniques began to occur: the tilling of land already under cultivation was intensified, and new, previously unusable land was brought under cultivation by means of terracing and irrigation (20).

Yet the rate at which new arable land was created failed to keep pace with the increasing demand for it. Even before the land shortage became so acute that irrigation began to be practiced systematically, villages were undoubtedly already fighting one another over land. Prior to this time, when agricultural villages were still few in number and well supplied with land, the warfare waged in the coastal valleys of Peru had probably been of much the same type as that described above for Amazonia. With increasing pressure of human population on the land, however, the major incentive for war changed from a desire for revenge to a need to acquire land. And, as the causes of war became predominantly economic, the frequency, intensity, and importance of war increased.

Once this stage was reached, a Peruvian village that lost a war faced consequences very different from those faced by a defeated village in Amazonia. There, as we have seen, the vanquished could flee to a new locale, subsisting there about as well as they had subsisted before, and retaining their independence. In Peru, however, this alternative was no longer open to the inhabitants of defeated villages. The mountains, the desert and the sea—to say nothing of neighboring villages—blocked escape in every direction. A village defeated in war thus faced only grim prospects. If it was allowed to remain on its own land, instead of being exterminated or expelled, this concession came only at a price. And the price was political subordination to the victor. This subordination generally entailed at least the payment of a tribute or tax in kind, which the defeated village could provide only by producing more food than it had produced before. But subordination sometimes involved a further loss of autonomy on the part of the defeated village—namely, incorporation into the political unit dominated by the victor.

Through the recurrence of warfare of this type, we see arising in coastal Peru integrated territorial units transcending the village in size and in degree of organization. Political evolution was attaining the level of the chiefdom.

As land shortages continued and became even more acute, so did warfare. Now, however, the competing units were no longer small villages but, often, large chiefdoms. From this point on, through the conquest of chiefdom by chiefdom, the size of political units increased at a progressively faster rate. Naturally, as autonomous political units increased in size, they decreased in number, with the result that an entire valley was eventually unified under the banner of its strongest chiefdom. The political unit thus formed was undoubtedly sufficiently centralized and complex to warrant being called a state.

The political evolution I have described for one valley of Peru was also taking place in other valleys, in the highlands as well as on the coast *(21)*. Once valley-wide kingdoms emerged, the next step was the formation of multivalley kingdoms through the conquest of weaker valleys by stronger ones. The culmination of this process was the conquest *(22)* of all of Peru by its most powerful state, and the formation of a single great empire. Although this step may have occurred once or twice before in Andean history, it was achieved most notably, and for the last time, by the Incas *(23)*.

POLITICAL EVOLUTION

While the aggregation of villages into chiefdoms, and of chiefdoms into kingdoms, was occurring by external acquisition, the structure of these increasingly larger political units was being elaborated by internal evolution. These inner changes were, of course, closely related to outer events. The expansion of successful states brought within their borders conquered peoples and territory which had to be administered. And it was the individuals who had distinguished themselves in war who were generally appointed to political office and assigned the task of carrying out this administration. Besides maintaining law and order and collecting taxes, the functions of this burgeoning class of administrators included mobilizing labor for building irrigation works, roads, fortresses, palaces, and temples. Thus, their functions helped to weld an assorted collection of petty states into a single integrated and centralized political unit.

These same individuals, who owed their improved social position to their exploits in war, became, along with the ruler and his kinsmen,

the nucleus of an upper class. A lower class in turn emerged from the prisoners taken in war and employed as servants and slaves by their captors. In this manner did war contribute to the rise of social classes.

I noted earlier that peoples attempt to acquire their neighbors' land before they have made the fullest possible use of their own. This implies that every autonomous village has an untapped margin of food productivity, and that this margin is squeezed out only when the village is subjugated and compelled to pay taxes in kind. The surplus food extracted from conquered villages through taxation, which in the aggregate attained very significant proportions, went largely to support the ruler, his warriors and retainers, officials, priests, and other members of the rising upper class, who thus became completely divorced from food production.

Finally, those made landless by war but not enslaved tended to gravitate to settlements which, because of their specialized administrative, commercial, or religious functions, were growing into towns and cities. Here they were able to make a living as workers and artisans, exchanging their labor or their wares for part of the economic surplus exacted from village farmers by the ruling class and spent by members of that class to raise their standard of living.

The process of political evolution which I have outlined for the coastal valleys of Peru was, in its essential features, by no means unique to this region. Areas of circumscribed agricultural land elsewhere in the world, such as the Valley of Mexico, Mesopotamia, the Nile Valley, and the Indus Valley, saw the process occur in much the same way and for essentially the same reasons. In these areas, too, autonomous neolithic villages were succeeded by chiefdoms, chiefdoms by kingdoms, and kingdoms by empires. The last stage of this development was, of course, the most impressive. The scale and magnificence attained by the early empires overshadowed everything that had gone before. But, in a sense, empires were merely the logical culmination of the process. The really fundamental step, the one that had triggered the entire train of events that led to empires, was the change from village autonomy to supravillage integration. This step was a change in kind; everything that followed was, in a way, only a change in degree.

In addition to being pivotal, the step to supra-community aggregation was difficult, for it took 2 million years to achieve. But, once it was achieved, once village autonomy was transcended, only two or three millennia were required for the rise of great empires and the flourishing of complex civilizations.

RESOURCE CONCENTRATION

Theories are first formulated on the basis of a limited number of facts. Eventually, though, a theory must confront all of the facts. And often new facts are stubborn and do not conform to the theory, or do not conform very well. What distinguishes a successful theory from a unsuccessful one is that it can be modified or elaborated to accommodate the entire range of facts. Let us see how well the "circumscription theory" holds up when it is brought face-to-face with certain facts that appear to be exceptions.

For the first test let us return to Amazonia. Early voyagers down the Amazon left written testimony of a culture along that river higher than the culture I have described for Amazonia generally. In the 1500's, the native population living on the banks of the Amazon was relatively dense, villages were fairly large and close together, and some degree of social stratification existed. Moreover, here and there a paramount chief held sway over many communities.

The question immediately arises: With unbroken stretches of arable land extending back from the Amazon for hundreds of miles, why were there chiefdoms here?

To answer this question we must look closely at the environmental conditions afforded by the Amazon. Along the margins of the river itself, and on islands within it, there is a type of land called *várzea*. The river floods this land every year, covering it with a layer of fertile silt. Because of this annual replenishment, *várzea* is agricultural land of first quality which can be cultivated year after year without ever having to lie fallow. Thus, among native farmers it was highly prized and greatly coveted. The waters of the Amazon were also extraordinarily bountiful, providing fish, manatees, turtles and turtle eggs, caimans, and other riverine foods in inexhaustible amounts. By virtue of this concentration of resources, the Amazon, as a habitat, was distinctly superior to its hinterlands.

Concentration of resources along the Amazon amounted almost to a kind of circumscription. While there was no sharp cleavage between productive and unproductive land, as there was in Peru, there was at least a steep ecological gradient. So much more rewarding was the Amazon River than adjacent areas, and so desirable did it become as a habitat, that peoples were drawn to it from surrounding regions. Eventually crowding occurred along many portions of the river, leading to warfare over sections of river front. And the losers in war, in order to retain access to the river, often had no choice but to submit to the victors. By this subordination of villages to a paramount chief there arose along the Amazon chiefdoms representing a higher step in political evolution than had occurred elsewhere in the basin *(24)*.

The notion of resource concentration also helps to explain the surprising degree of political development apparently attained by peoples of the Peruvian coast while they were still depending primarily on fishing for subsistence, and only secondarily on agriculture *(18)*. Of this seeming anomaly Lanning has written: "To the best of my knowledge, this is the only case in which so many of the characteristics of civilization have been found without a basically agricultural economic foundation" *(25)*.

Armed with the concept of resource concentration, however, we can show that this development was not so anomalous after all. The explanation, it seems to me, runs as follows. Along the coast of Peru wild food sources occurred in considerable number and variety. However, they were restricted to a very narrow margin of land *(26)*. Accordingly, while the *abundance* of food in this zone led to a sharp rise in population, the *restrictedness* of this food soon resulted in the almost complete occupation of exploitable areas. And when pressure on the available resources reached a critical level, competition over land ensued. The result of this competition was to set in motion the sequence of events of political evolution that I have described.

Thus, it seems that we can safely add resource concentration to environmental circumscription as a factor leading to warfare over land, and thus to political integration beyond the village level.

SOCIAL CIRCUMSCRIPTION

But there is still another factor to be considered in accounting for the rise of the state.

In dealing with the theory of environmental circumscription while discussing the Yanomamö Indians of Venezuela, Napoleon A. Chagnon *(27)* has introduced the concept of "social circumscription." By this he means that a high density of population in an area can produce effects on peoples living near the center of the area that are similar to effects produced by environmental circumscription. This notion seems to me to be an important addition to our theory. Let us see how, according to Chagnon, social circumscription has operated among the Yanomamö.

The Yanomamö, who number some 10,000, live in an extensive region of noncircumscribed rain forest, away from any large river. One might expect that Yanomamö villages would thus be more or less evenly spaced. However, Chagnon notes that, at the center of Yanomamö territory, villages are closer together than they are at the periphery. Because of this, they tend to impinge on one another more, with the result that warfare is more frequent and intense in the center than in peripheral areas. Moreover, it is more difficult for villages in the nuclear area to escape attack by moving away, since, unlike villages on the periphery, their ability to move is somewhat restricted.

The net result is that villages in the central area of Yanomamö territory are larger than villages in the other areas, since large village size is an advantage for both attack and defense. A further effect of more intense warfare in the nuclear area is that village headmen are stronger in that area. Yanomamö headmen are also the war leaders, and their influence increases in proportion to their village's participation in war. In addition, offensive and defensive alliances between villages are more common in the center of Yanomamö territory than in outlying areas. Thus, while still at the autonomous village level of political organization, those Yanomamö subject to social circumscription have clearly moved a step or two in the direction of higher political development.

Although the Yanomamö manifest social circumscription only to a modest degree, this amount of it has been enough to make a difference in their level of political organization. What the effects of social circumscription would be in areas where it was more fully expressed should, therefore, be clear. First would come a reduction in the size of the territory of each village. Then, as population pressure became more severe, warfare over land would ensue. But because adjacent land for miles around was already the property of other villages, a defeated village would have nowhere to flee. From this point on, the consequences of warfare for that village, and for political evolution in general, would be essentially as I have described them for the situation of environmental circumscription.

To return to Amazonia, it is clear that, if social circumscription is operative among the Yanomamö today, it was certainly operative among the tribes of the Amazon River 400 years ago. And its effect would undoubtedly have been to give a further spur to political evolution in that region.

We see then that, even in the absence of sharp environmental circumscription, the factors of resource concentration and social circumscription may, by intensifying war and redirecting it toward the taking of land, give a strong impetus to political development.

With these auxiliary hypotheses incorporated into it, the circumscription theory is now better able to confront the entire range of test cases that can be brought before it. For example, it can now account for the rise of the state in the Hwang Valley of northern China, and even in the Petén region of the Maya lowlands, areas not characterized by strictly circumscribed agricultural land. In the case of the Hwang Valley, there is no question that resource concentration and social circumscription were present and active forces. In the lowland Maya area, resource concentration seems not to have been a major factor, but social circumscription may well have been.

Some archeologists may object that population density in the Petén during Formative times was too low to give rise to social circumscription. But, in assessing what constitutes a population dense enough to produce this effect, we must consider not so much the total land area occupied as the amount of land needed to support the existing population. And the size of this supporting area depends not only on the size of the population but also on the mode of subsistence. The shifting cultivation presumably practiced by the ancient Maya *(28)* required considerably more land, per capita, than did the permanent field cultivation of say, the Valley of Mexico or the coast of Peru *(29)*. Consequently, insofar as its effects are concerned, a relatively low population density in the Petén may have been equivalent to a much higher one in Mexico or Peru.

We have already learned from the Yanomamö example that social circumscription may begin to operate while population is still relatively sparse. And we can be sure that the Petén was far more densely peopled in Formative times than Yanomamö territory is today. Thus, population density among the lowland Maya, while giving a superficial appearance of spareseness, may actually have been high enough to provoke fighting over land, and thus provide the initial impetus for the formation of a state.

CONCLUSION

In summary, then, the circumscription theory in its elaborated form goes far toward accounting for the origin of the state. It explains why states arose where they did, and why they failed to arise elsewhere. It shows the state to be a predictable response to certain specific cultural, demographic, and ecological conditions. Thus, it helps to elucidate what was undoubedly the most important single step ever taken in the political evolution of mankind.

Notes

1. R. L. Carneiro, in *The Evolution of Horticultural Systems in Native South America: Causes and Consequences; A Symposium.* J. Wilbert, Ed., *Antropológica* (Venezuela), Suppl. 2 (1961), pp. 47–67, see especially pp. 59–64.

2. For example, the early American sociologist Lester F. Ward saw the state as "the result of an extraordinary exercise of the rational . . . faculty" which seemed to him so exceptional that "it must have been the emanation of a single brain or a few concerting minds. . . ." [*Dynamic Sociology* (Appleton, New York, 1883), vol. 2, p. 224].

3. See, for example, V. G. Childe, *Man Makes Himself* (Watts, London, 1936), pp. 82–83; *Town Planning Rev.* 21, 3 (1950), p. 6.

4. I have in my files recorded instances of surplus food production by such Amazonian tribes as the Tupinambá, Jevero, Mundurucú, Tucano, Desana, Cubeo, and Canela. An exhaustive search of the ethnographic literature for this region would undoubtedly reveal many more examples.

5. Wittfogel states: "These patterns [of organization and social control—that is, the state] come into being when an experimenting community of farmers or protofarmers finds large sources of moisture in a dry but potentially fertile area . . . a number of farmers eager to conquer [agriculturally, not militarily] arid lowlands and plains are forced to invoke the organizational devices which—on the basis of premachine technology—offer the one chance of success; they must work in cooperation with their fellows and subordinate themselves to a directing authority" [*Oriental Despotism* (Yale Univ. Press, New Haven, Conn., 1957), p. 18].

6. For Mesopotamia, Robert M. Adams has concluded: "In short, there is nothing to suggest that the rise of dynastic authority in southern Mesopotamia was linked to the administrative requirements of a major canal system" [in *City Invincible*. C. H. Kraeling and R. M. Adams, Eds. (Univ. of Chicago Press, Chicago, 1960), p. 281]. For China, the prototypical area for Wittfogel's hydraulic theories, the French Sinologist Jacques Gernet has recently written: "although the establishment of a system of regulation of water courses and irrigation, and the control of this system, may have affected the political constitution of the military states and imperial China, the fact remains that, historically, it was the pre-existing state structures and the large, well-trained labour force provided by the armies that made the great irrigation projects possible" [*Ancient China, from the Beginnings to the Empire*, R. Rudorff, Transl. (Faber and Faber, London, 1968), p. 92]. For Mexico, large-scale irrigation systems do not appear to antedate the Classic period, whereas it is clear that the first states arose in the preceeding Formative or Pre-Classic period.

7. This is not to say, of course, that large-scale irrigation, where it occurred, did not contribute significantly to increasing the power and scope of the state. It unquestionably did. To the extent that Wittfogel limits himself to this contention, I have no quarrel with him whatever. However, the point at issue is not how the state increased its power but how it arose in the first place. And to this issue the hydraulic hypothesis does not appear to hold the key.

8. See *The Evolution of Society: Selections from Herbert Spencer's Principles of Sociology.* R. L. Carneiro, Ed. (Univ. of Chicago Press, Chicago, 1967), pp. 32–47, 63–96, 153–165.

9. L. Gumplowicz, *Der Rassenkampf* (Wagner, Innsbruck, 1883).

10. G. Ratzenhofer, *Wesen und Zweck der Politik* (Brockhaus, Leipsig, 1893).

11. F. Oppenheimer, *The State*, J. M. Gitterman, Transl. (Vanguard, New York, 1926).

12. E. Jenks, *A History of Politics* (Macmillan, New York, 1900), p. 73.

13. J. Vansina, *Kingdoms of the Savanna* (Univ. of Wisconsin Press, Madison, 1966).

14. For example, Julian H. Steward wrote: "It is possible, therefore, that the Maya were able to develop a high civilization only because they enjoyed an unusually long period of peace; for their settlement pattern would seem to have been too vulnerable to warfare" [*Amer. Anthropol.* 51, 1 (1949), see p. 17].

15. D. E. Puelston and D. W. Callender, *Expedition* 9 No. 3, 40 (1967), see pp. 45, 47.

16. M. D. Coe, *The Maya* (Praeger, New York, 1966), p. 147.

17. See R. L. Carneiro, in *Men and Cultures. Selected Papers of the Fifth International Congress of Anthropological and Ethnological Sciences*, A. F. C. Wallace, Ed. (Univ. of Pennsylvania Press, Philadelphia, 1960), pp. 229–234.

18. In early agricultural times (Preceramic Period VI, beginning about 2500 B.C.) human settlement seems to have been denser along the coast than in the river valleys, and subsistence appears to have been based more on fishing than on farming. Furthermore, some significant first steps in political evolution beyond autonomous villages may have been taken at this stage. However, once subsistence began to be based predominantly on agriculture, the settlement pattern changed, and communities were thenceforth concentrated more in the river valleys, where the only land of any size suitable for cultivation was located. See E. P. Lanning, *Peru Before the Incas* (Prentice-Hall, Englewood Cliffs, N.J., 1967), pp. 57–59.

19. In my files I find reported instances of village splitting among the folowing Amazonian tribes: Kuikuru, Amarakaeri, Cubeo, Urubú, Tuparí, Yanomamö, Tucano, Tenetehara, Canela, and Northern Cayapó. Under the conditions of easy resettlement found in Amazonia, splitting often takes place at a village population level of less than 100, and village size seldom exceeds 200. In coastal Peru, however, where land was severely restricted, villages could not fission so readily, and thus grew to population levels which, according to Lanning [*Peru Before the Incas* (Prentice-Hall, Englewood Cliffs, N.J., 1967), p. 64]. may have averaged over 300.

20. See R. L. Carneiro, *Ethnograph.-archäol. Forschungen* 4, 22 (1958).

21. Naturally, this evolution took place in the various Peruvian valleys at different rates and to different degrees. In fact it is possible that at the same time that some valleys were already unified politically, others still had not evolved beyond the stage of autonomous villages.

22. Not every step in empire building was neccesarily taken through actual physical conquest, however. The threat of force sometimes had the same effect as its exercise. In this way many smaller chiefdoms and states were probably coerced into giving up their sovereignty without having to be defeated on the field of battle. Indeed, it was an explicit policy of the Incas, in expanding their empire, to try persuasion before resorting to force of arms. See Garcilaso de la Vega, *Royal Commentaries of the Incas and General history of Peru*. Part 1, H. V. Livermore, Transl. (Unive. of Texas Press, Austin, 1966), pp. 108, 111, 140, 143, 146, 264.

23. The evolution of empire in Peru was thus by no means rectilinear or irreversible. Advance alternated with decline. Integration was sometimes followed by disintegration, with states fragmenting back to chiefdoms, and perhaps even to autonomous villages. But the forces underlying political development were strong and, in the end, prevailed. Thus, despite fluctuations and reversions, the course of evolution in Peru was unmistakable: it began with many small, simple, scattered, and autonomous communities and ended with a single, vast, complex, and centralized empire.

24. Actually a similar political development did take place in another part of Amazonia—the basin of the Mamoré River in the Mojos plain of Bolivia. Here, too, resource concentration appears to have played a key role. See W. Denevan, "The Aboriginal Cultural Geography of the Llanos de Mojos of Bolivia." *Ibero-americana No. 48* (1966), pp. 43–50, 104–105, 108–110. In native North America north of Mexico the highest cultural development attained, Middle-Mississippi, also occurred along a major river (the Mississippi), which, by providing especially fertile soil and riverine food resources, comprised a zone of resource concentration. See J. B. Griffin, *Science* 156, 175 (1967), p. 189.

25. E. P. Lanning, *Peru Before the Incas* (Prentice-Hall, Englewood Cliffs, N. J., 1967), p. 59.

26. Resource concentration, then, was here combined with environmental circumscription. And, indeed, the same thing can be said of the great desert river valleys, such as the Nile, Tigris-Euphrates, and Indus.

27. N. A. Chagnon, *Proceedings, VIIIth International Congress of Anthropological and Ethnological Sciences* Tokyo and Kyoto, 1968). vol. 3 *(Ethnology and Archaeology)*. p. 249 (especially p. 251). See also N. Fock, *Folk 6*, 47 (1964), p. 52.

28. S. G. Morley and G. W. Brainerd, *The Ancient Maya* (Stanford Univ. Press,. Stanford, Calif., ed. 3, 1956), pp. 128–129.

29. One can assume, I think, that any substantial increase in population density among the Maya was accompanied by a certain intensification of agriculture. As the population increased fields were probably weeded more throughly, and they may well have been cultivated a year or two longer and fallowed a few years less. Yet, given the nature of soils in the humid tropics, the absence of any evidence of fertilization, and the moderate population densities, it seems likely that Maya farming remained extensive rather than becoming intensive.

The Beginning of Chinese Civilization

The origins of man and the beginnings of culture in China were taken for granted in traditional Chinese history. Man was either simply evolved in the creation of the world or created by supernatural beings. In historical times all the peoples of China were recognized as the descendants of Huang-ti, the Yellow Emperor, and the basic cultural practices were attributed to the various rulers in remote antiquity. They formed a continuous sequence with its beginnings in the third millennium B.C., followed by a succession of dynasties for some 5,000 years until the present day.

There is no doubt that the ancient history of China was composed mainly of myths and legends, obviously unacceptable to the modern scientific mind. Reacting against this, some western scholars confidently assumed that China was unpopulated before the first millennium BC and refused to recognize any stone age or history before the Chou dynasty. The field was wide open for new research.

The search for prehistoric China in the present century brought forth a wide variety of speculation. As the theory of human evolution had already been popularly accepted some geologists suggested that, with the rise of the Himalayas, man could have been evolved from the forest apes in Sinkiang or Mongolia. The study of *Gigantopithecus* from Kwangsi led to the conclusions that 'the giants may be directly ancestral to man'. It also happened that the theory of cultural diffusion formed the main stream of anthropological research; archaeologists and art historians in the Chinese fields could not help being engulfed in the tide. So when prehistoric relics began to be unearthed they were conveniently linked up with known cultures in the west; Chinese stone artifacts were described in European terminologies; Chinese painted pottery was recognized as a result of the eastward migration of certain peoples from south-

By Cheng Te-Kun. Reprinted with permission, from *Antiquity*, XLVII, 1973, pp. 197-209.

east Europe; Chinese agriculture and writing were all introduced from the Middle East. All these and much else make fascinating and entertaining reading, freely circulating in western literature. Although they may be regarded as an advancement of knowledge, a large number of them have never been taken seriously by conscientious scholars, who think that they have yet to be substantiated by more widespread discoveries and more thorough excavations. So long as plain archaeological facts are not properly established in their native contexts any comparison with distant parallels would be far-fetched.

We still know very little about the origins of Chinese culture but we have reached a point where we can guess at many things with a certain degree of accuracy. The beginnings of Chinese culture may be traced back to the Lower Paleolithic period and its development continued through the Middle and Upper Palaeolithic up to the Early and Late Neolithic ages. The sequence may be applied as a whole or in parts to various regions and there seems to be a considerable amount of telescoping in the chronology. In some places Palaeolithic cultures survived into Neolithic survivals in historical periods. It is now clear that these ancient cultures had evolved in various geographical surroundings and mixed with one another within the Chinese boundaries. An outline of prehistoric China may now be set out.

GEOLOGICAL BACKGROUND (7, 1 – 13; 3, 18 – 42)

The world as known to the Chinese appeared in her literature as T'ien-hsia, meaning 'Under heaven'. It was conceived of as occupying the eastern land-mass of Asia, with a general west-to-east tilt. A mountain massif is dominated by a series of high ranges, extending eastward like the fingers of a hand from the Tibetan plateau, and most of the rivers flow in the same direction into the sea. The great land mass of China is therefore dissected into numerous areas which remain inter-related with one another.

The physiographical pattern of China was established as early as the Pliocene and has remained unchanged ever since. In general the climate was tropical or sub-tropical, represented by lake deposits and a faunal assemblage essentially similar to that of the present day. The ancient fauna of Yunnan included the K'ai-vaun Forest Ape, which may be regarded as a common ancestor of ape and man. The origins of man in China may have ultimate roots in the coal beds of the Early Pliocene, some 15,000,000 years ago (18, 3).

Hominids in China are assumed to have appeared in the Pleistocene, about 1,000,000 years ago. Although the existence of glaciation has been noted in high mountain areas, none of the valleys and plains in China was actually covered by ice: on stratigraphical evidence the Pleistocene sequence there may be divided into three stages. The Lower Pleistocene is represented by the Sanmenian Series in north China which contain a faunal assemblage dominated by *Equus*, from which they have been known as the 'Horse' Beds, and in general the fauna is essentially a Palaearctic assemblage appropriate to a cool and semi-arid climate. Some 'Horse' Beds have been found as far south as Yunnan, but the fauna in the south is characterized mainly by *Gigantopithecus* as in Kwangsi and Hupei, indicating a tropical climate.

Middle Pleistocene formations are varied, and include the grey conglomerates in the Gobi region, the red conglomerates and thick concretionary clays in the north, the terraces and lateritized fans in the south, as well as the cavities in the limestone massifs. Hence the period is also known variously as the Age of 'Terra Rossa', 'Conglomerates', 'Terraces' or 'Fissures'. The important development at this stage was the rejuvenation of the Ts'ing-ling Range, dividing the Chinese world into north and the south. The northern fauna, characterized by *Euryceros*, is still predominantly Palaearctic, whereas the southern assemblage, characterized by *Stegodon*, is mainly Indo-Malaysian. In addition, some Terra Rossa contain a high percentage of loess-type material indicating that the climate was sometimes cool and semi-arid, and the aeolian dust from the desert to the northwest had begun to invade the region.

The Upper Pleistocene is marked by the intensive deposition of aeolian dust. The climate was cool and semi-arid with a prevailing wind from the north-west. China became in effect divided into two spheres, a semi-arid north and a wooded south, with the semi-arid loess belt between them. The region north of the Ts'ing-ling was finally completely covered with a thick layer of yellow earth, giving rise to the terms of the 'Age of Yellow Earth' or 'Loess Age'.

Holocene formations in China have been described as Black Earths, but this is true only in the north where erosion dominated over sedimentation, for in some regions light coloured sand and consolidated sand-dunes also prevailed. On the other hand in south China the soil was comparatively stable, thanks to protection by vegetation cover.

Viewed as a whole the sedimentary cycles of Late Cenozoic China, which were separated from each other by brief periods of erosion, give the impression that they succeeded 'each other over a constantly rising land platform and under a constantly decreasing temperature'. The result was a unique natural environment which played always a part of cardinal importance in the shaping of man and his culture.

THE LOWER PALAEOLITHIC AGE: 600,000 — 200,000 YEARS AGO (3, 43 — 56; 7, 14 — 24; 8, 3 — 6)

Evidence for man in the Lower Pleistocene is still lacking. Exploration of the earlier caves in Kwangsi has recovered enough fossils to reconstruct the lower mandible of *Gigantopithecus*, giving definite proof that this Giant Ape is not a hominid and has no connexion with the evolution of man (8, 1–2).

By the Middle Pleistocene, around 500,000 years ago, China was populated by the human type formerly known as *Sinanthropus*, but now grouped with *Pithecanthropus* as *Homo erectus*. Three sub-species have been distinguished, *pekinensis*, in the limestone caves in Hopei, *lantienensis* along the river and lake marshes of Shensi, and *yuanmounensis* in the forest regions of Yunnan (unearthed in 1965, 33, 40). *Homo erectus* had a low brain case with prominent brow-ridges and a chin with a profile reminiscent of the anthropoid apes. The capacity of his brain case ranged from 850 to 1,200 cc, as compared with 1,350 cc, the cranial capacity of modern man, and the femur was longer than the humerus, indicating that his limbs were well-developed and his body fully erect. The upper incisors were all shovel-shaped: this is a prominent feature, noticeable in most of the later inhabitants including the majority of the modern Chinese.

Homo erectus was a food gatherer and hunter in China, making tools by pebble-shaping and flake-making. The basic technique, as noted at Locality I in Chou-k'ou-tien, is flaking at an angle of roughly 90° from an unprepared striking platform, but in practice it varies between chipping, alternate flaking and bi-polar hammering. As the most common material is quartz, the flake scars are usually crude and indistinct, but those on the flinty material are sharp and clear. This primitive technique did not produce any standard shapes, and only the suitable pieces were selected for use. A list of the artifacts consists of choppers, chopping-tools, bolas, cores and hammers, which are mainly pebbles; and scrapers, points and beaked implements, which are mostly adapted from flakes. The flat discoidal bolas could be used as missiles in attacking big game, and large triangular points might have served as digging implements.

The lithic industry of *H. erectus* in China was improved as time went on. In the later levels of Chou-k'ou-tien, as at Localities 3, 4 and 15, there is an increase in the use of flint showing a deliberate attempt in the selection of material, and the finished artifacts are generally better defined. The most significant type is a series of small triangular flakes with a straight cutting edge at one end. The larger flakes are usually trimmed at the butt end to facilitate an easier holding.

Primitive pebble and flake tools, similar to those described, have a wide distribution in China. Apart from Chou-k'ou-tien large collections have been found in the northern provinces of Shansi, Shensi and Honan. Scattered finds have also been reported from Liaoning in the north-east and from Kwangsi in south China, suggesting that bands of Palaeolithic hunters wandered far and wide across the land.

These early hominids appear to have lived in groups. In Locality 1 at Chou-k'ou-tien forty-five male and female individuals have been recorded, fifteen of them being children, and more have been unearthed in recent years (15, 29).

Most of the skeletal remains were broken and fragmentary, and as they were found associated with those of other animals in similar conditions, it may be presumed that *Homo erectus* here practised cannibalism. The favoured meat supply was venison, deer being hunted in common with other animals, including gazelle and horse. Extensive traces of fire in the Chou-k'ou-tien cave suggest that food was cooked over the open hearth: fire was a basic item (probably made and kept burning with wood which was gathered around the settlement, providing warmth in the cave and keeping enemies away at night). Thick layers of grain-husks in the cave point to the likelihood of a vegetable element in the diet. Hackberry, a small cherry-like fruit, grew in the vicinity.

THE MIDDLE PALAEOLITHIC AGE: 200,000 — 100,000 YEARS AGO (18, 3, 56 — 59; 7, 29 — 32; 8, 7 — 8)

The fossil remains and stone artifacts which have been recovered from the upper levels of Red Earths, the basal gravel of the loess in north China, and the intermediate caves in south China are regarded as Middle Palaeolithic. The early man of this period is now represented by three groups of fossils in the three river basins of China proper. They are the Ordos Man of Ti-shao-kou in Inner Mongolia at the northern bend of Huangho; the Ch'ang-yang Man of Chao-chia-yen in Hupei in the middle Yangtse; and the Ma-pa Man of Shao-kuan in Kwangtung in the Sikiang valley. Stratigraphical and faunal data show that the Ma-pa Man is the oldest type, dating from late Middle Pleistocene, while Ch'ang-yang Man is the youngest, dating from early Upper Pleistocene. Morphologically they are all recognizable as Neanderthal Man, but having transitional features between typical Neanderthal Man and *Homo sapiens sapiens*. An upper incisor of the Ordos Man is clearly shovel-shaped.

The stone industry of the Middle Palaeolithic peoples is basically in the chopping-tool tradition of *H. erectus*. Some typologically Lower Palaeolithic implements have been found in various regions, but owing to geographical differences and the supply of raw materials, new techniques were evolved, especially in the middle

Huangho. In the Shui-tungkou, Ninghsia, for example, the materials are mainly of red quartzite and of siliceous limestone, and chipping, flaking and retouching were used to fashion choppers, points, scrapers, cores and other tools, mostly still rather large in size, though some are very small. The flake tools are usually broad and short, but not thick and heavy, and long blades are rare; secondary chipping was well-established but was never applied on tiny flakes. In Hou-ke-t'a-feng in Shansi, the pebbles and flakes are mainly coloured quartz and there is a marked increase in the number of scrapers which are mainly medium or small in size. The neat secondary trimming at the cutting edges probably results from an improved technique employing a wooden striker. The appearance of tiny flakes which are described sometimes as 'microliths' seems to suggest that the so-called Gobi microlith tradition was evolved from the advanced chopping-tool culture at this stage: it was destined to become a dominant trait in the semi-arid north.

THE UPPER PALAEOLITHIC AGE: 100,000—25,000 YEARS AGO
(18, 5—7; 3, 56—65; 7, 24—29; 8, 9—13)

Archaeological evidence of man in China during the Upper Pleistocene is relatively abundant and has been recorded in several areas and in various sorts of environment. So far five groups of Upper Palaeolithic man, all *Homo sapiens sapiens*, have been found, three in south China and two in the north. The three southern fossils were in various stages of development, with Liu-chiang Man from Kwangsi as the oldest, followed by Tzu-yang Man from Szechwan (cf. 2, 57–58) and Lai-pin Man also from Kwangsi in chronological order. They all bear primitive mongoloid features which seem to suggest that they were in an evolutionary stage towards racial specialization, and it has been suggested that the Mongoloid race might have its cradle in south China. The Tzu-yang Man is represented by a very complete skull which bears some resemblance to *Homo erectus* on the one hand and *Homo sapiens* on the other, forming a link between the two widely different stages of Chou-k'ou-tien. Recently a radiocarbon date for a piece of wood recovered in the same level as the fossil was obtained of only 5323 + 130 bc (ZK–19) (2 57–8). This date seems to show that objects derived from Level III at Huang-shan-hsi in which the Tzu-yang Man, some *Muntiacus* and *Mammonteus primigenius* and the piece of wood were found, may not be homogeneous or contemporary.

The 'Upper Cave' group of human fossils from near Peking consists of several types of *Homo sapiens* which had been previously classified into three races, but now, with the new materials from south China for comparison, it seems clear that they are all fundamentally Mongoloid but in various degrees of specialization. The fifth group has been found at Ting-ts'un in Shansi, and the fossils include two shovel-shaped upper incisors. Among these five groups of Upper Palaeolithic peoples the 'Upper Cave' community was the youngest, and might have survived into the Holocene, as did some of the Pleistocene fauna of Djalai in Heilungkiang near the Mongolian border.

The Upper Palaeolithic peoples lived in various types of environment and they adapted their cultures accordingly. South China is little known at this stage. Pebble and flake chopping-tools were used and occasionally, as at Tzu-yang, a triangular bone splint was scraped into a point which became blunt and polished through long usage. Some stone artifacts of Palaeolithic types have also been reported from he outlying provinces of Tibet, Chinghai, Sinkiang and Inner Mongolia.

In north China the circumstances of the deposition of the loess on the Yellow Earth were bound up with a very dry climatic phase. The landscape was treeless and the environment was one of dust storms and muddy rain in which man strived to survive, roaming about looking for favourable habitats, especially the oases.

Ting-ts'un Man, who lived in the watersheds in southern Shansi, continued to use pebble and flake chopping-tools, crude flakes being obtained mainly from large hornfels pebbles. The striking platform is only roughly levelled and the flakes removed at an angle less than 90°, making a relatively large and flat bulb of percussion. Secondary trimming is employed to acquire not only a regular shape but also a sharp cutting edge. One of the outstanding types is a thick pointed tool, trimmed at one end into a triangular point and rounded at the other to ensure a better grip, which could have been used for digging up roots. Associated with the loess fauna of the Yellow Earth the Ting-ts'un industry may be regarded as a Middle Palaeolithic survival into the Upper Pleistocene.

The Ordos Man who occupied the oasis of Sjara-osso-gol in Suiyuan practised a different type of industry. The rich fauna shows clearly that the pasture had an abundant supply of water and that early man lived by hunting and collecting freshwater molluscs. Small pebbles of black siliceous stone are flaked and chipped in the Shui-tung-kou fashion, but the cores and flakes are consistently very small, serving as a link between the chopping-tool tradition and the Gobi microlithic industry which began now to flourish in the steppe and desert north, stretching south into Tibet (33, 41; 30).

The early Gobi microlithic implements are made of quartz pebbles, and the industry is basically in the pebble-flake tradition with choppers and 'bolas' as its main output. But new techniques, especially meticulous secondary trimming, were used to produce a typical triangular point with bi-facial chipping. A large number have been collected at Ch'ing-shui-ho in Inner Mongolia, where they are known as 'Ch'ing-shui-ho points'. Mounted on a long shaft such points may have armed javelins for hunting, while a few very small points could have been used as arrowheads. There is also a tendency to use more flinty materials. The Gobi microlithic culture has been reported from An-yang in Honan and Yang-ch'eng in Shansi, confirming the coexistence of two Upper Palaeolithic cultures in middle Huangho.

The most advanced type of Palaeolithic industry may be represented by that of the 'Upper Cave' at Chou-k'ou-tien. In the chopping-tool tradition, secondary retouching is also employed in shaping scrapers and points. Bone and horn implements are also common, including a bone needle 8.2 cm. long, made by grinding and rubbing, with the eye perforated by a sharp stone point. The 'Upper Cave' inhabitants probably wore tailored clothes and strings of bone and stone beads made by grinding, polishing

and perforating. These are strung together with marine shells, fish bones and animal teeth, all perforated and polished and painted with haematite. Burial took place inside the dwelling, and a large quantity of ochre or haematite powder was scattered around the body, a custom which persisted right through historical times. The 'Upper Cave' people either travelled extensively or maintained close communication with other regions, for they imported several 'luxuries': marine shells came from the sea coast to the south-east, pieces of oolitic haematite from Lung-kuan beyond the mountains to the north and big mussel-shells from the south bank of Huangho, all hundreds of kilometres away from their home.

Chou-k'ou-tien was evidently a centre of human activities in this phase. The skeletal remains in the upper cave represent no less than ten individuals, including three complete skulls. They were the weaker members of the family—an old male, a middle-aged and a young woman—who had been killed by their fellow-men, for among these skulls, two had been perforated by a violent blow on the side while a third suffered a fatal blow on the neck.

It is now clear that ancient man in China had reached a marked stage of development by the end of Pleistocene. Some degree of at least seasonal settlement was established, with a recognizable burial rite and a presumed familial social unit. The technique of polishing stone and bone was used, and the bow-and-arrow was presumably in use. These 'neolithic' elements are present early in China as elsewhere, lying behind the cultural development of the following periods.

EARLY NEOLITHIC PERIOD: 25,000—7,000 YEARS AGO (3, 65—77; 7, 38—59; 8, 14—15)

We still know very little about this period. Since a number of 'neolithic' techniques such as polishing and drilling and the use of bow-and-arrow and some advanced arts and crafts in the forms of tailoring of clothes and preparation of metallic red ochre were already practised by the Upper Palaeolithic people towards the end of Pleistocene, it could be quite possible that a 'neolithic' way of life characterized by these traits was evolved right at the very beginning of the Holocene without a transitional Mesolithic stage.

There seems no doubt that the inhabitants of Holocene China were Mongoloid. By this time the land was probably populated by some hunter-fishers who, owing to climatic conditions, were forced to be mobile as in earlier times. Most of the Early Neolithic sites consist of the remains of impermanent settlements along rivers or streams or by the sea, apparently with economies based on fishing. In the south-western provinces similar communities established themselves in forested regions by way of rivers and streams. Among the tool types is a distinct axe-blade known as the 'shouldered axe', an elongated boulder flake-trimmed at one end, with two shoulders and a neck for hafting. This is usually large and heavy, making an efficient tool for felling timber as well as for hollowing out canoes and shaping paddles. The stone industry was otherwise still in the earlier pebble-flaking tradition, surviving from palaeolithic times. In its later development, pecking and polishing were also introduced, but never replaced the older technique completely. In some cases, as in Kwangsi, Kwangtung and Taiwan, coarse gritty pottery decorated with a wide variety of cord impressions has also been found, implying more permanent settlements and the use of various forms of cord. Forest clearing might have paved the way for plant cultivation introduced in Early Neolithic times (6, 51–103).

Along the sea coast the early people seem to have had a more varied economy. This was based on fishing and mollusc collection, and the settlements were usually strewn with shells burnt bones and ashes. In the shell mounds of Ma-lan-chui in Kwangtung, for instance, the stone implements consist of both chippers and polished artifacts together with fragments of bone arrow-heads and awls, and coarse gritty corded ware, mainly decorated with cord-impressions but occasionally with mat impressions and incised patterns, and baked at a low temperature.

Travel by rivers and seaways ensured this early culture a wide distribution. Open settlements or cave sites are always characterized by shell mounds, whether in the Yangtse valley in the north, Indo-China in the south, or on the islands. Some might have been occupied into Late Neolithic and historical times (18, 33–6).

The Early Neolithic of north China is derived from the two earlier Palaeolithic cultures, and still on a hunter-fisher basis. The steppe region of the Gobi, covering Sinkiang and Mongolia, was populated by makers of the Gobi microlithic industries usually found in the consolidated sand dunes of ancient oases. These dune-dwellers were experts in making tiny jasper tools, quite distinct from the typical microliths of western Asia, mainly flakes struck from small cores with a prepared platform and trimmed into sharp points to serve as scrapers, drills and tools, but never geometric. Some were presumably set in wooden or bone shafts to make spears and darts for hunting. Ostrich eggs furnished an important food supply, their shells being used side by side with fossil dinosaur eggs as raw material for a shell industry. The advanced stone and shell industries were sometimes accompanied by corded ware pottery, brownish grey and baked in an open fire, and occasionally with geometric stamped or incised designs.

Some of the oases in the loess region to the south, as those of Ch'ao-yi and Ta-li in Shensi, were also occupied by makers of microlithic tools, apparently living side by side with a large number of pebble-flake-using hunters in the neighbourhood, the settlements of the latter being mostly small and impermanent. The stone industry, though primarily in the pebble-flaking tradition, was predominantly using polishing techniques. The culture also produced a rather coarse pottery, as in Tou-chi-t'ai, Shensi, in three colours, red, grey and black. Some of the sherds are also decorated with cord and basket impressions or incised and dotted patterns.

The same mixture of early cultures occurs in the north-eastern provinces. In Heilungkiang where some Pleistocene fauna survived into the Holocene, were several types of mixed cultures. Near the Mongolian border Djalai Man inhabited a lakeside settlement and had a hunting and fishing economy. He used tiny flint flakes in the Gobi microlithic tradition and some stone artifacts shaped by chipping, rubbing and polishing: the same techniques were also used for tools of bone and antler. In the settlement, a fragment of basketry made of interlaced willow sticks seems to suggest a fish trap. Near Harbin, Ku-hsing-ts'un Man, also a lakeside dweller, did not have a microlithic industry, but his stone artifacts are mainly of Sjara-osso-gol type, and there is an abundant bone industry. Further south in Kirin, Chou-chia-yu-fang Man produced stone tools of palaeolithic forms, somewhat similar to those of the 'Upper Cave' industries near Peking. As a whole these Manchurian cultures may also be regarded as 'Palaeolithic' survivals.

The most advanced Early Neolithic culture in the north-east may be represented by the Ang-ang-hsi culture in Heilungkiang, again with a hunter-fisher economy and permanent settlements. The archaeological material occurs in sand dunes and indicates a mixed tradition. The highly specialized bone industry may be traced to that of the lakeside settlements of Ku-hsiang-ts'un, the microlithic tools are basically in the Gobi tradition and the chipped pebbles and flakes recall the chopping-tools of China proper. These 'palaeolithic-looking' artifacts are found side by side with a large number of 'Neolithic' elements such as polished stone tools, arrowheads, domesticated dogs, corded pottery, and, above all, knives and pestles and flat mealing-stones. The cultural mixture marks the beginning of the Late Neolithic with such prominent features as domestic animals and possible cereal cultivation and village settlement.

The most common cultural element in Early Neolithic China is the cord-marked pottery. It has a wide distribution in East Asia, covering not only China but also the neighbouring regions from Siberia and Japan in the north to Assam and Indo-China in the south. The tradition served as the foundation of the ceramic industry in these regions throughout the ages. No radiocarbon dates for Early Neolithic China are available at present, but for Japan the corded ware (Jōmon) phase is given as 9000 BC (16, 22) and for the Thailand-Burma border 7–8000 BC (12; 13; 28). Considering the early appearance of cord-marked ware and its wide distribution in China, it seems reasonable to propose that the technique was invented not later than 10,000 BC. Being the last phase of the Early Neolithic, Ang-ang-hsi may be dated around 5000 BC.

LATE NEOLITHIC PERIOD: 5000 – 1800BC. (18, 7 – 42; 7, 69 – 156; 8, 16 – 42; 3, 78 – 184)

In this phase China proper seems to have already supported a comparatively large population of agriculturists living in villages and with a subsistence economy based on plant cultivation supplemented by animal husbandry, though hunting and fishing were still practised. Thousands of Late Neolithic sites have been recorded and a number of the more important sites throughly excavated. Some are surprisingly extensive and must imply large social units.

The development of this new economy may be traced to the Central Plain in the Huangho valley, an area occupying a small basin where the Huangho is joined by its two great tributaries, Fen-shui and Wei-shui. Being the most eastern extension of the loess highlands it is bounded by the Shansi plateau in the north, and the Ts'ing-ling mountains in the south, but opened into the flood plain in the east. It constitutes a borderland between the semi-arid highlands to the west and the swampy lowlands in the east, a favoured natural region less susceptible than many to the hazards of drought or flood, and as a result a continuous centre of human settlement, where as we have seen peoples of various cultures have competed for occupation. The economic shift to food production may have been the outcome of specific adjustments to the geographical advantages presented by this terrain, and the population evolved a distinctive culture as it moved to the adoption of plant cultivation and animal domestication. Conditioned by the environment, the Late Neolithic culture assumed from the very beginning a distinctive and in many ways an original pattern (21).

The period witnessed rapid development and intense cultural mixing in the Huangho basin. In the Central Plain it began with a transitional stage which is represented by a cord-impressed pottery level at a number of sites to the southwest of Sian in Shensi, notably Li-chia-ts'un in Hsi-hsiang (1; 14; 26; 29). The pottery forms here are similar to those of Yang-shao, the earliest fully-fledged Late Neolithic stage in north China, but the decoration is still predominantly cord-marked. In some cases this phase has been found overlaid by that of Yang-shao, characterized by red-painted pottery; it is therefore known as the pre-Yang-shao stage.

In the Central Plain the Yang-shao culture underwent several stages of development and expanded in every direction, especially the west. Then rose that of Ch'ü-chia-ling, which expanded southward into the middle Yangtse (19; 15, 29). It was followed by the Lung-shan culture, known from an increasing number of sites extending to the east, and mainly along the coast. Finally came the Hsiao-t'un culture which is identified as Proto-Shang and seen as the foundation for the establishment of the historical Shang dynasty. Historical China certainly had its roots firmly founded in its prehistoric past, as we shall see.

The succession of these four cultures in the Central Plain is confirmed by several stratigraphical sequences (17; 15; 27). They may be alternatively regarded as four stages of the same culture, but together with that of the Gobi they did exist side by side for a considerable length of time. The process of mixing and amalgamation was a long and complicated affair. Late Neolithic sites in different parts of the Huangho basin almost always show a mixture in various proportions of these five cultures, sometimes with traces of 'Palaeolithic' elements as well. The same has been observed also in other parts of China stretching from Heilungkiang in the north-east to Yunnan on the Burma-Thailand border and from Sinkiang in the north-west to Taiwan in the South China Seas.

Physically the Late Neolithic people (sometimes described as Proto-Chinese) were all undoubtedly Mongoloid. It is interesting to note, however, that the group in the Central Plain is similar to those in other parts of the Huangho basin as well as the Indo-Chinese in the south, but relatively distinct from the Lake Baikal A Group in the north. Furthermore, when compared with the branches of modern Mongoloid people it is again closer to the Austro-Asiatic and the Far Eastern Groups than to the Central Asiatic Groups of the continental branch. This fact seems to show that the expansion of the Mongoloid people in the South Seas was an event closely related to the spread of agriculture from China. Remains of the Lung-shan culture are known in Indo-China as well as in the islands off the coast of Fukien and Kwangtung. A few radiocarbon dates have been obtained recently from the Lung-shan level in Taiwan (4, 219). They are in the order of 2500 BC indicating the early spread of the Late Neolithic culture beyond the sea. Since this culture is undoubtedly of mainland derivation it seems reasonable to postulate 3500 BC for the beginning of Lung-shan, 400 BC for the beginning of Ch'ü-chia-ling and 5000 BC for the beginning of Yang-shao in the Central Plain. This last estimate has recently been confirmed by radiocarbon dates derived from the remains at Pan-p'o-ts'un, near Sian. They range from bp 5894 ±110 (ZK 38) to bp 5738 ± 105 (ZK 121), bp 5704 ± 105 (ZK 122) and bp 5427 ± 105 (ZK 127), showing that the site was occupied continuously for about 750 calendar years from 4500 to 3750 BC (23, 2; 20). With its distinctive cultural traits Pan-p'o-ts'un represents an advanced stage of Yang-shao. Its beginning should be placed further back, around 5000 BC.

From the very beginning the Proto-Chinese lived in village communities. The Yang-shao dwelling-site at Pan-p'o-ts'un covers an area of about 70,000 square metres. In the centre of the settlement was a large communal hall with a floor space of about 160 square metres, and round this cluster dwellings and storage pits forming a roughly circular settlement covering about 30,000 square metres, surrounded by a defensive ditch. Beyond this ditch are an ancient cemetery and several kiln sites. The houses, quadrangular or circular in shape and partly subterranean, are uniformly built with wooden posts supporting the roof, the floor and walls being constructed with *hang-tu* (stamped earth) or as wattle-and-daub structures. To avoid the cold wind from the northwest the door faces always the south, with a porch at the entrance which is separated from the rest of the house by low walls. In the centre of the house floor is a fireplace: at Ch'ü-chia-ling (19; 34; 33) the floor is baked or hardened by fire. In the Lung-shan levels the floors and walls are usually plastered with a white limey substance. In the later stage at Ch'ien-shan-yen in Chekiang the houses are on ground level and have standardized rectangular plans with posts at the four corners. A transverse wooden beam was carried centrally on top of the lateral walls, with branches on either side of the beam to carry the roof. The walls were constructed with reed work and clay plaster. These late Neolithic houses represent the most rudimentary form of Chinese architecture, which has always been basically a carpenter's art.

It may be presumed that the Proto-Chinese village was founded on clanship. The inhabitants probably had the same surname and worshipped a common ancestor like most of the Chinese villagers of later and modern times. But as the village grew members of other clans might have been welcomed, and as a result if could have become a large town. The Lung-shan site at Liang-ch'eng-chen in Shantung, for instance, occupies an area of no less than 990,000 sq. m. Sometimes a defensive wall was constructed around the settlement, as at Cheng-tzu-yai in Shantung, making it into a walled city. This was the beginning of a tradition whereby the Chinese became the great wall-builders of the ancient world.

The collection of food-plants among the hunter-gatherer communities of Early Neolithic China might have given rise to an early phase of horticulture based on fruits, nuts and roots, and it may also be presumed that the slash-and-burn technique of forest clearance was employed, for evidence of such activities has been noted in Late Neolithic China and it is still being practised by some minorities in the jungles of southwest China in modern times, where it is known as 'fire farming'. But it was in the Central Plain that typical Chinese agriculture was developed. The loess homeland of the Proto-Chinese was, as it is today, a semi-arid steppe with only a limited annual rainfall in the summer. The yellow earth was homogeneous, fine and soft, and easily tilled with primitive implements. The soil was reasonably fertile and certain indigenous drought-resistant cereal plants were adopted for cultivation (5). The most common were millets; two varieties have been recovered in Shansi, Shansi and Honan. Traces of sorghum and soya bean, and grains of wheat and barley, have also been reported. The last two were both successful crops on the flood plain in Mesopotamia with the help of irrigation, but in China they were adapted to the well-established system of dryland farming.

Wheat has become in time the most important food crop throughout north China. However, in the marshy districts of the Central Plain rice was also planted, and imprints and grains of cereals have been noted in Honan as well as in Shensi. Besides these, seeds of mustard plant and cabbage have also been found, indicating that the people were also engaged in vegetable cultivation. The Yang-shao Chinese were indeed well-furnished with agricultural produce and every household was provided with one or more storage pits for its surplus grain (9).

The expansion of the Late Neolithic culture beyond the Central Plain was responsible for the diffusion of the new pattern of food production to various parts of China, and the cereal crops would naturally have to adapt themselves to variations in soil and climate. Rice found congenial conditions in the wet south, where two varieties, the short and round *keng* and the long and slender *hsien*, have been recognized: south China has continued to be the largest rice producing area ever since. The southern Proto-Chinese also cultivated other food plants to supplement their diet. They include, as in Chekiang, peach, melon, peanut, sesamum, broad bean, sour dates and water chestnut. Under favourable conditions, as in Yunnan on the Burma border, rice, wheat and millet were cultivated side by side (10).

In the beginning the Proto-Chinese kept dogs and pigs in their households, but later on their domesticated animals also included sheep and cattle, horses and chickens. In areas of rice cultivation water-buffaloes were also used to work in the paddy field; bones of this animal have been found at Ch'ien-shan-yen in Chekiang. It may also be assumed that tortoises and fish were raised in ponds in or around their settlements. Apart from providing the population with protein food and sacrificial offerings, the bones, skins, bristle and shell of these animals furnished a constant supply of raw materials for appropriate crafts. In connexion with the ancestral cult, scapulimancy was practised, and it continued to play a part of cardinal importance in the activities of the Shang kings later on.

The Proto-Chinese wore tailored clothes of hemp cloth and silk fabrics. Spindle whorls are common articles in their settlements and loom-weaving may well have been practised. The discovery of textile imprints on Yang-shao pottery and in burials, and an artificially cut cocoon of the *Bombyx mori* in Shansi indicates that the fibre was hemp and that mulberry might have been planted for a silk industry. Sericulture was a monopoly of the Chinese until the sixth century AD.

The spread of agriculture in China was probably responsible for the standard types of agricultural implements throughout the land. There is a wide variety of broad and flat stone axes, adzes, spades and hoes which are characterized by a contracted butt or one or two perforations for hafting, and used for wood-cutting and earth-moving. Most of these served as prototypes for the metal hoes, spades and ploughshares of historic times. A large number of semi-lunar and rectangular stone knives were employed for harvesting crops and cutting grass. They are almost always perforated so as to afford a better grip, but in later types a handle was provided, making a boot-shaped knife which became in time the prototype of the Chinese iron sickle. Some of the sites have also yielded pestles and mortars and grinding stones for preparing grain for food. The homogeneity of agricultural practice in ancient China cannot be over stressed, and this goes to demonstrate that agriculture was a unique and independent development forming the foundation of ancient Chinese civilization (9).

The agricultural Proto-Chinese had no war-like equipment and presumably used arrows of stone, bone or shell more for hunting than for war. The only military weapon seems to be the *ko*, a dagger-axe or halberd which has a tongue-shaped blade with a handle. Hafted at right angles to the shaft it could be used for striking, hacking and cutting. It was the most conspicuous and common armament in metal in Shang and Chou times.

The stone industry of the Proto-Chinese was relatively accomplished. Chipping and pecking were still used, but the standard technique was rubbing and grinding and polishing. In drilling, a sharp point was used with sand as abrasive. Hard substances like jade could be fashioned into effective weapons and beautiful ornaments, and that stone has been regarded as a symbol of Chinese culture ever since.

Another series of technical development may be noted in pottery making. The basic techniques were handed down by the corded-ware potters mentioned above, but many new types of pottery were being developed by the Proto-Chinese. The Yang-shao people specialized in making a red ware, and as some vessels are painted with various designs in red, black and white, it has become known as Chinese Painted Pottery. This pottery style spread widely with the expansion of the Yang-shao culture, and now painted wares of many descriptions have been found throughout the land, from Sinkiang to Taiwan and from Manchuria to Hongkong. Archaeological evidence shows that in Early Yang-shao the painted designs were mainly composed fo zoomorphic elements (animals, birds and human faces), but they degenerated later on into geometric compositions. The design was drawn on to the curved surface of the pot and some of the strokes thin out at the end, indicating that the potter used a brush which was made of soft animal hair tapering to a point like a modern Chinese writing brush. The decoration ranges from simple to complex, with considerable regional and chronological variation. In some cases the brush-strokes are charged with the dynamic tempo characteristic of the rhythmic movement of Chinese calligraphy. It is interesting to note that certain pictorial elements, such as the fish, goat, bat, tortoise, etc., were kept and used as symbols in writing in the following period. Moreover, many Yang-shao pots have inscriptions in simple characters which indicate the existence of an elementary form of writing. The characters are composed of lines and dots and show the beginning of the typical Chinese system of writing which continues to evolve throughout the ages. Furthermore, a number of the characters are recognizable as uniquely Chinese numerals. The first five numbers are simply straight marks written in vertical strokes in a manner similar to numerals used by most ancient peoples, including the early Egyptian. But for five to nine they are each composed of two strokes. Ten is represented by a simple straight stroke, suggesting the use of the decimal system in counting. As a whole this is clearly a unique system of numerals, typically Chinese, with no parallels outside its own cultural sphere, and with most numerals retaining their basic structure until the present day. These facts seem to show that the invention of Chinese writing and of the writing brush took place before 4000 BC, much earlier than as stated in ancient Chinese literature (23; 25, 11).

The Yang-shao potter exploited to the full the plastic qualities of clay. Interesting modelled sculptures appear, the most significant being those in the composite animal form. The head of an owl from Shensi is adorned with a pair of horns and the human heads from Kansu are provided with truncated horns and a coiled serpent, setting the fashion for the Shang and Chou bronzes in which a composite animal style played a leading role.

The Late Neolithic ceramic industry was very inventive, and from the beginning the aim was to produce a ware with two essential qualities, hardness and thinness. The Yang-shao potter was an expert in the construction of kilns (31, 67–85) capable of producing a hard ware at a temperature as high as 1300–1400 C (17, 104; 32). At Ch'ü-chia-ling some pottery vessels are so thin that they are called 'egg-shelled wares' (19, 33–5). The Lung-shan Chinese produced another type of pottery distinctively black in colour, made with a well-prepared fine paste, thrown and polished on the wheel. The ware relies on its form without ornament for its appeal, and typically this black pottery is thin, with an egg-shell delicacy and black and lustrous surface resembling a modern black plastic. Among the basic shapes is a series of tripods, namely the *li* cauldron, *kuei* ewer, and *hsien* steamer, all designed with three hollow legs, which when placed over an open fire would ensure a quicker cooking than a flat or round bottomed pot. A *hsien* steamer is constructed with a *li* as the boiler on which a perforated *tseng* pot may be placed for steaming food: this culinary technique has played an important part in Chinese cooking ever since.

The Lung-shan potter also experimented in making a white ware with the kaolin clay, which paved the way for the production of white porcelain in later times and ultimately made 'china' a product synonymous with its country of origin.

The mixing of the Late Neolithic pottery traditions may be illustrated by the association of red painted and black wares in practically all the later sites throughout the land. In some instances other cultural traits—Gobi, Ch'ü-chia-ling and Hsiao-t'un elements—were also present, existing side by side in various degrees of admixture right into the historical times.

It remains to be noted that it was the art of the Neolithic potter that paved the way for the manufacture of bronze in the following Shang dynasty. Li Chi, the director of the An-yang excavation, has insisted that a proper understanding of Shang bronze-working must include a knowledge of ceramic technology (24, 8). The researches carried out by his colleagues in the Academia Sinica and others confirm that apart from the mining, smelting and refining of the metals, the mixing of the alloy and the retouching of the cast, the entire process of bronze manufacture in Shang China was in the hands of the potter. The basic technique was casting, a unique method in the Chinese ceramic tradition. From the very beginning, the Shang bronze master was proficient in casting, especially by the piece mould-method, and was also aware of the principle of casting-on pre-cast members to the vessel body. The absence of methods such as sheet-metal working, riveting, annealing, tracing, engraving, stamping, repoussé and the *cire perdue* process in Shang times gives clear evidence that Chinese metallurgy had indigeneous origins. Its close relations with the ceramic art may be illustrated by the similar types of vessels and decorative designs inherited by the bronze industry. The whole industrial background shows most eloquently that the Shang bronze industry was a natural development out of the neolithic ceramic tradition. The technical knowledge and skill were both ready for the new adventure. The sudden rise of the dynastic Shang provided an appropriate need and a suitable stimulus for the new invention. Bronze was a new medium with which the traditional shapes and decorations could be expressed. The new output simply continued to manifest the age-old art forms and ceremonial functions with a new kind of material and a new advanced technology (10, 31; 32).

CONCLUSION

The archaeological evidence reviewed above demonstrates beyond any possibility of doubt that all the basic Neolithic cultural traits were the forerunners of those of historical China. In fact, already in Lung-shan times villages were rapidly developing into towns and walled cities, setting the foundation for the rise of the Shang dynasty. The localization of corporate kinship groups would pave the way for the concentration of dominating clans into a metropolis which could impose its rule over a countryside populated by communities in the surviving Neolithic tradition. The Shang people were probably the first to take advantage of this movement, marking the beginning of a dynastic type of political power. The Chinese civilization was created by the Chinese in their homeland and its beginning may be traced way back into prehistoric times.

References

ACADEMY OF SOCIAL SCIENCES, SHENSI

1. Preliminary report of the excavation of a neolithic site at Li-chia-ts'un, Hsi-hsiang, Shensi, in 1961, *Kaogu*, 62.6.290–5,

AN CHIH-MIN

2. Notes on some prehistoric dates in China, *Kaogu*, 72.1.57–9.

CHANG KWANG-CHIH

3. *The archaeology of ancient China* (New Haven), 1968.

4. *Fengpitou, Tapenkeng and the prehistory of Taiwan* (new Haven), 1969.

5. The beginnings of agriculture in the Far East, *Antiquity*, XLIV, 1970, 175–85.

6. *Archaeological studies in Szechwan* (Cambridge), 1957.

7. *Prehistoric China: archaeology in China, I* (Cambridge), 1959.

8. *New light on prehistoric China: archaeology in China*, Supplement to vol. 1 (Cambridge), 1966.

9. Prehistoric agriculture in China, *Encyclopaedia Britannica*, agriculture, History of, 1972.

10. Metallurgy in Shang China, *T'oung-pao*, LIX, 1973, 1–3.

11. Numerals in ancient China, *Journal of the Chinese University of Hong Kong*, 1, 1973.

GORMAN, C.F.

12. Hoabinhian: a pebble-tool complex with early association in South-east Asia, *Science* CLXIII, 1969, 671–3.

13. *Hoabinhian transformation in early South-east Asia: a cultural-chronological sequence c. 10,000 to 5500 BC* (New Orleans), 1969.

HSIA NAI

14. New archaeological finds in the last five years, *Kaogu*, 64.10.485–97.

15. New archaeological finds in China during the great cultural revolution, *Kaogu*, 71.1.29–42

IKAWA, F.

16. The continuity of non-ceramic to ceramic cultures in Japan, *Arctic Anthropology*, II, 1964, 2.95–119.

INSTITUTE OF ARCHAEOLOGY

17. *Miao-ti-kou and San-li-ch'iao* (Peking), 1959.

18. *Archaeology in New China* (Peking), 1962.

19. *Ching-shan Ch'u-chia-ling* (Peking), 1965.

20. Reports on radiocarbon dates, *Kaogu*, 72.1.52–6; 72.5.56–8.

INSTITUTE OF ARCHAEOLOGY AND PAN-P'O MUSEUM

21. *Sian Pan-p'o* (Peking), 1963.

KOTANI, Y.

22. Upper Pleistocene and Holocene environmental conditions in Japan, *Arctic Anthropology*, V, 1969, 2.133.–158.

KUO MO-JO

23. Ku-tai wen-tzu chih pien-cheng ti fa-chan, *Kaogu*, 72.3.2–13.

LI CHI

24. How to study Chinese bronze, *National Palace Museum Quarterly*, I, 1966, 1–9.

LI HSIAO-TING

25. Ch'ung chi-chung shih-ch'ien ho yu-shih tsao-ch'i t'ao-wen ti kuan-ch'a li ts'e Chung-kuo wen-tzu ti ch'i-yuan, *Journal of Nanyang University*, III, 1969, 1–28.

SHENSI INSTITUTE OF ARCHAEOLOGY

26. The neolithic site of Li-chia-ts'un, Hsi-hsiang, Shensi, *Kaogu*, 61.7.352–4.

SHIH CHANG-JU

27. Hsin-shih-ch'i shih-tai ti Chung-yuan, *Ta-lu cha-chih*, IV, 1952, 65–73.

SOLHEIM, W. G. II

28. Re-working south-east Asian prehistory, *Pai-deuma*, XV, 1969, 125–39.

SU PING-CH'I

29. Some problems concerning the Yang-shao culture, *Kaogu Xuebao*, 65.1.51–82.

TAI ERH-CHIEN

30. Stone artifacts found at Nieh-la-mu-hsien, Tibet, *Kaogu*, 72.1.42–3.

WATSON, W.

31. *Cultural frontier in ancient east Asia* (Edinburgh), 1971.

YOSHIDA, M.

32. Metallurgy in ancient China, *Tōhogakuhō*, XXXIV, 1959, 58.

ADDENDUM

33. New finds in archaeology and palaeontology, *China reconstructs*, 72.40–1.

34. A trial digging at the Hsia-wang-kang site in Hsi-ch'nan, Honan, *Wen-wu*, 72.10.6–19.

The Shadow
of the Olmecs

More than one hundred years ago, in 1862, a Mexican scholar named José Maria Melgar set out from a sugar-cane hacienda on the lower slopes of the Tuxtla Mountains, in southern Veracruz, Mexico, to look into a report of a gigantic inverted "kettle" the natives had discovered buried in the soil. Instead of the "kettle," he found a ten-ton basalt head, the "Ethiopic" features of which led him to believe that African Negroes had settled here in remote antiquity. His subsequent article describing this stone, one of a dozen such "Colossal Heads" now known, was the first published account of an object typical of what is called the Olmec civilization.

Just who were the Olmecs?

They were the first American Indians to achieve a level of social, cultural, and artistic complexity high enough for them to be called civilized. As such, they were precursors of the later Mexican and Central American cultures, whose great achievements could not have been realized without them.

Though we are familiar with the Aztec empire, and know something of the Mayas, the name "Olmec" probably means little to most of us. Yet today Olmec archaeology is laying bare one of the most exciting chapters in the history of our continent. Imagine a people capable of carving human heads on a gigantic scale and exquisite figurines from blue-green, translucent jade. Imagine an art style based on the combined features of a snarling jaguar and a human infant. Then transport these people back beyond all known Indian civilizations, to a distance in time of more than three thousand years, and put them down in the inhospitable, swampy jungles of Mexico's Gulf Coast.

The extraordinary discovery Melgar made in these jungles went largely unnoticed until the first decade of this century, when the stone was visited by the German scholar Eduard Seler.

By Michael Coe. Reprinted with permission, from *Horizon* magazine, 13, Autumn 1971, pp. 67-75.

Then it was again forgotten by the archaeological world. Forgotten, that is, until the 1920's, when the pioneer archaeologists Frans Blom and Oliver La Farge discovered the great, swamp-bound site of La Venta. There they found another Colossal Head, along with a number of other great stone sculptures in a style they mistakenly ascribed to the Mayas.

La Venta intrigued several other scholars, who quickly noted that this style, while highly sophisticated, was very different from that of the Classic Mayas, who flourished in the Yucatán Peninsula and farther south from about A.D. 300 to 900. They also noticed that some figurines and ceremonial axes of jade and other fine stones that had been turning up in museums and private collections were stylistically similar to the objects found at La Venta. They christened the unknown, non-Mayan civilization that had produced them "Olmec," after the mysterious tribe (whose name meant "Rubber People" in the Aztec tongue) that dominated the southern Gulf Coast of Mexico on the eve of the Spanish Conquest. But who were the *archaeological* Olmecs? How old was their civilization, and what was its relationship to the other civilizations of Mexico and Central America, for example, the Mayan or Toltec? Only in recent years has enough attention been paid to these questions to provide at least partial answers.

The foundations of scientific archaeology in the Olmec area were laid by Matthew W. Stirling of the Smithsonian Institution during his expeditions between 1938 and 1946. The first task Stirling set for himself was that of excavating Tres Zapotes, the site of Melgar's Ethiopic head. There he came upon an Olmec-type carved stone, the now-famous Stela C, which bore a date in the Mayan system that seemed to match a day in the year 31 B.C.—over three centuries earlier than the most ancient date then known for the Mayas. This and other leads suggested to Stirling, as it did to leading Mexican archaeologists, that the Olmec civilization was probably the most ancient high culture yet known for the New World. After 1940 Stirling moved to La Venta, in neighboring Tabasco, and continued to make spectacular Olmec discoveries, particularly tombs of extraordinary richness.

One group, however, remained skeptical; the Mayan specialists. It seemed heresy to these American and British archaeologists to believe that the upstart Olmec civilization could have predated—and according to Stirling and his Mexican colleagues, even foreshadowed—Classic Mayan culture, which in many respects represented the highest achievement of the American Indian. Since 1840 the world had known and appreciated the splendid achievements of the ancient Mayas in writing, astronomy, calendrical science, art, and architecture. It was inconceivable that the Olmecs could have flourished before A.D. 300. Few Mayan buffs were ready to admit that Stela C at Tres Zapotes was a date to be read in the Mayan system.

The controversy over the Olmecs could not be settled until the advent of radiocarbon dating. In 1955 a University of California team under Dr. Robert F. Heizer opened a series of trenches at La Venta and secured a large number of charcoal samples. Most of the radiocarbon dates turned out to be far older than anyone would then have though possible: 800–400 B.C. Incredibly, Olmec culture seems to have been at its height *seven to eleven* centuries before that of the Classic Mayas. La Venta—with its gigantic basalt monuments, mosaic pavements of serpentine blocks, a hundred-foot-high earthen pyramid, caches of carved jade and serpentine, and other wonders—was not a town or city in the usual sense but a mysteriously remote center for ceremonies and politics, isolated on its swampbound island. Why did it exist at all? And where did its builders come from?

There was no easy answer to the second question. Olmec sculptures had been found along the Gulf Coast as far north as the city of Veracruz, Olmec reliefs carved on a cliff had been located in the state of Morelos, and Olmec jades had turned up in puzzling profusion in the western state of Guerrero. The frequency of such finds prompted Miguel Covarrubias, the talented artist-archaeologist and longtime proponent of Olmec antiquity, to suggest Guerrero as the Olmec homeland, on the theory that they must have learned to carve small figures before moving to Veracruz and Tabasco, where their gigantic monuments are concentrated.

But many archaeologists, including myself, were convinced that Olmec origins would some day be found in the Olmec "heartland," the crescent-shaped, low-lying region along the Gulf Coast. Since the highest development of the culture was surely there, then why couldn't its beginnings, perhaps as far back in the pre-Classic period as 1500 B.C., also be there?

My own quest for Olmec origins—and for the conditions, ecological or otherwise, that may have stimulated the rise of native American civilization—led me, in December, 1964, on a trip of exploration up the sluggish, meandering Coatzacoalcos River, which drains the northern part of the Isthmus of Tehauntepec, to a riverside village called Tenochtitlán. A few miles south of the village lies a jungle-covered mesa known as San Lorenzo. In 1945 Matthew Stirling had been taken there by local Indians who had seen a great stone eye staring up from the dirt of a trail crossing the mesa. The eye turned out to belong to a new Colossal Head, one of a number of basalt monuments that Stirling found and excavated that season and the next. Some of these multiton heads, with their "football" helmets, flat faces, and staring eyes, have traveled as far afield as Leningrad and are the best-known examples of Olmec achievement in sculpture.

Two mysteries had immediately presented themselves to Stirling at San Lorenzo. First, the basalt from which the heads and other stones were carved did not occur anywhere around the site, the nearest source lying some fifty miles to the northwest.

The second mystery concerned the final disposition of the sculptures. Almost all of them were found either lying on the bottoms or the slopes of the deep, jungle-filled ravines that cut into the San Lorenzo mesa. Stirling guessed that some non-Olmec invaders had smashed or otherwise mutilated the monuments and then pushed them into the ravines. If so, there would be little chance of dating the Olmec occupation of San Lorenzo by associating the sculptures with archaeological layers.

The idea of mounting a major archaelogical effort at San Lorenzo came to me during my trip in 1964. By the end of the next year I found myself, aluminum camera case in perspiring hand, standing in the grass-covered "street" of Tenochtitlán looking in vain for a sympathetic face. The natives were decidedly *not* friendly. Those Colossal Heads that had gone around the world had been removed by Veracruz archaeologists without the villagers' approval, and they were angry. Even so, I felt sure that a little diplomacy would make it possible to work there, and my optimism proved to be justified. We eventually claimed the majority of the local villagers as our friends and colleagues.

In 1966 Yale University, with financial backing from the National Science Foundation, began three years' work at the site. Our first step was to build a camp. In southern Mexico there are supposed to be two climatic seasons: a winter dry season, when it almost never rains, and the very wet summer. But in southern Veracruz some kind of moisture—drizzle, rain, or torrential downpour—is almost always falling. Shivering in our leaky tents, we found that fierce northers sweep down the Gulf Coast in winter, bringing cold drizzle and rain for days at a time. Until we put up houses with thatched roofs, we were a very soggy camp.

Our next job was to get San Lorenzo mapped. The picture that emerged after two seasons of surveying was very different from the one we had first imagined: San Lorenzo turned out to be one of the world's strangest archaeological sites.

The mesa, rising some 150 feet above the surrounding grass- and swamp-covered plains, was originally considered to be a naturally formed plateau, the ravines being the result of erosion. Indeed, it must in large part be the result of geologic uplift by tectonic forces, most likely one of the deeply buried salt domes that are common in the northern half of the Isthmus of Tehauntepec. But San Lorenzo as we see it today has clearly been altered by the hand of ancient man. Reaching out like fingers on its north, west, and south sides are long, narrow ridges divided by the ravines. A pair of ridges on the western side exhibit bilateral symmetry, that is, every feature on one ridge is matched mirror-fashion by its counterpart; another such pair, divided by an asymmetric ridge, can be seen on the south side. This is hardly consistent with a natural origin.

Our excavations over three years demonstrated that the ridges are artificial, consisting of fill and cultural debris to a depth of at least twenty-five feet. Presumably, the first inhabitants—the Olmecs or their predecessors—took advantage of an already existing sand-and gravel-covered hill to carry out their plans. What could they have had in mind? As our map began to take shape, my first thought was that they might have been trying to construct a running or reclining animal on a titanic scale, three-quarters of a mile long, with its legs stretching north and south. But a subsequent mapping of the entire zone by aerial photography revealed much more of the total plan of San Lorenzo than our field map did. It showed a gigantic bird flying eastward, its extended wing feathers forming the ridges on the north and south, with its tail trailing to the west.

This may sound like poppycock, since such a grandiose plan could only have been appreciated from the air. Yet similar effigy mounds were erected by the early Adena and Hopewell cultures of our own midwestern states, and the tremendous hilltop markings above the Peruvian deserts cannot be fully grasped from ground level either. My own guess is that some ancient Olmec ruler or priest (or both), inspired by cosmological ideas, ordered this construction on such a scale to impress the gods and men but that the plan was never completed.

There are several hundred earth mounds on the flat surface of San Lorenzo, but the site is not very impressive compared with such Mesoamerican giants as Teotihuacán or Tikal. At the center stands a very modest pyramid, probably once the substructure for a thatched-roof temple. Extending north and south of it are pairs of long mounds with narrow plazas between them. Presumably this was the focal point of San Lorenzo.

But was it an "empty" site, as we guess La Venta to have been, inhabited only by priestly bureaucrats and their entourages? Apparently not, for most of the two hundred structures are what we call house mounds: low, rectangular or ovoid platforms of earth designed to raise the pole and thatch houses of the commoners above the discomforts caused by summer (and winter) rains. A reasonable estimate of the ancient population might be a thousand persons, thus making Olmec San Lorenzo far from "empty."

When we arrived, there was no archaeological chronology for San Lorenzo, and we had to work one out for ourselves. This meant digging at least a dozen statigraphic trenches and pits, peeling off layer by layer as we descended and segregating all broken pottery, stone tools, and other artifacts from each stratum. Having done this before at pre-Classic sites in coastal Guatemala, I was familiar with very early Mesoamerican pottery, but I was appalled by the number of potsherds—several hundred thousand in all—that acumulated in our three seasons at San Lorenzo. This material has now been analyzed, and I have worked out a pre-Classic sequence consisting of seven distinct phases, or cultures, followed by a long period of abandonment (from around the time of Christ to about A.D. 900), and finally, a very late reoccupation by another, Toltec-like people.

But it is the pre-Classic period that concerns us here, for in that time span lies the story of the Olmecs at San Lorenzo. This is a story with dates, too, for we were fortunate enough to find well-preserved hearths or cooking fires with ample charcoal for radiocarbon analysis. It now seems that the first people to inhabit the San Lorenzo plateau arrived about 1500 B.C. They were not Olmecs, since their finely made pottery showed no signs of Olmec influence, but they may have been their ancestors. Two and a half centuries later, around 1250 B.C., there are signs that the people at San Lorenzo were beginning to take on Olmec characteristics: beautiful figurines of white clay show the unmistakable baby faces of the Olmecs,and there is much of the white-rimmed black pottery distinctive of the culture. Most important, we found a stone fragment that must have been part of a monumental carving of basalt.

The height of civilization in the area was reached in what we call the San Lorenzo phase, reliably dated to 1150–900 B.C. Here we are faced with remains that are undeniably Olmec, and it is also apparent that the site itself had reached its present form by that time. Olmec figurines of all sorts are found, some showing ball players wearing the heavy, padded belts and gloves typically used in that sacred game. Neither we nor Stirling found jade at San Lorenzo, which is curious since the Olmecs of La Venta were master jade carvers.

We are confident that the bulk of the fifty-eight known monuments at San Lorenzo were carved during the San Lorenzo phase. How do we know this? Remember that Stirling found most of his stones lying in or near the ravines, obviously not in their original positions. One morning in March, 1967, I spotted a rough stone slab, or stela, sticking out of the ground in one of the western ridges and ordered that it be dug up. It was this modest excavation that enabled us to date the Olmec sculptures of San Lorenzo and to solve the riddle of their final disposition.

The stela in question appeared to be in its original position, and I wanted to establish its relationshp to whatever strata might exist in the ridge. It soon became clear, however, that the workman I had set at this task could not do his job within the limited excavation square I had measured off. Slightly to the north on the east-west ridge we started a new square, with the idea of enlarging the total work area. To my astonishment and delight we hit upon another sculpture, totally buried.

This turned out to be Monument 34, a magnificent, larger than life-size statue of a half-kneeling man in pure Olmec style. Like almost all other known Olmec monuments, this one had been mutilated before burial, in this case by having its head knocked off. At each shoulder was a disk, perforated in the center, to which movable arms could be attached; whether they were of wood or stone we had no way of knowing.

Here, then, were two monuments, one just north of the other. If we continued to excavate along the ridge in the same direction, mightn't we find a whole line of buried monuments? My guess was right. For weeks we dug on, uncovering one mutilated sculpture after another. And while following the same kind of lead west along another ridge, a second line of stones appeared, this time oriented east-west. Both "collections" produced a great variety of representations, ranging from a gigantic column embellished with a relief of a horrific werejaguar-god to a tiny carving of a fantastic spider. We now had strong evidence that a single monumental act of destruction had been inflicted on the Olmec sculptures of San Lorenzo. The iconoclasts had begun by smashing some monuments and pitting the features of others, sometimes by grinding axes on them. They had then dragged the objects of their fury onto specially prepared floors running along the ridges of the site, placed them carefully in long lines, and covered them with a special fill. Clearly, the stones found by Stirling in the ravines had *not* been pushed there by ancient hands but had slipped down, as the slope eroded, from their original positions in the ridges. This opened up the posibility that there might be a great many more stones still to be discovered.

Once we could associate the sculptures with archaeological strata, we were able to date them—or rather, date their final placement. From our study of the pottery and other artifacts lying on the floors and in the covering fill we learned that the great act of destruction took place no later than 900 B.C. But here again, we had settled one problem only to raise another: until now no archaeologist would have believed the Olmec sculptural style to be any older than 800 B.C. In the period 1150–900 B.C., when we are positive our monuments were carved, the rest of Mesoamerica had not yet shown the first glimmerings of civilized life. Only at San Lorenzo did civilization burn brightly, with no antecedents yet discovered. Where did these people come from, with their culture already in full development?

The mysteries of San Lorenzo were tied up with more than the monuments. In one of the ridges we uncovered a troughlike stone, U-shaped in cross section. In his 1946 explorations Stirling had found a number of these lying jumbled at the bottom of one of the ravines, along with a like number of flat, rectangular stones, also of basalt. He surmised that the latter were covers for the troughs, which had once been fitted end to end to form a drain. He was right. On the edge of that same ravine, on the southwestern border of the San Lorenzo plateau, one of my laborers pointed out to me the end of just such a drain, still in place and deeply buried.

We excavated the drain completely during the final season, no simple task as it was covered with twelve to sixteen feet of overburden. A very remarkable system it was: a "main line" sloping down in an east-west direction and measuring 558 feet in length, with three subsidiary lines, totaling 98 feet, meeting the main line at a steep angle. From loose stones lying on the surface elsewhere, we are reasonably sure that another

system, the mirror image to this one, lies on the southeast edge of the site.

What was the purpose of this drain, which represents no less than thirty tons of hard basalt? At its upper end there are openings for water to enter. Nearby, on the surface of the site, are several artificial ponds constructed by the Olmecs. We have good reason to believe that during the San Lorenzo phase, when the drain system was put down, its starting point lay beneath the center of a large pond that was later covered up. Thus, it appears that the drain had no other function than to draw off water from the pond.

Since irrigation is unnecessary in the wet local climate, the ultimate function of this strange water-control system must have been purely ceremonial, perhaps connected with ritual bathing by the ancient Olmec leaders. Near the head of the drain we uncovered a remarkable statue of the Olmec rain god, complete with snarling, werejaguar face, while near its other end was a curious stone receptacle in the shape of a duck. The latter, discovered by Stirling, has an opening into which a trough-stone would fit perfectly.

What kind of world did the Olmec leaders of San Lorenzo look out upon from their lofty plateau? Who owed them allegiance? Was theirs a tribal polity, ruled by chiefs, or a pristine state, dominated by kings? Since the Olmecs of those times left no writing, we must rely on other lines of inquiry to answer these questions. But first let us consider the magnitude of the Olmec achievement at San Lorenzo three thousand years ago.

The site itself represents hundreds of thousands of tons of material—gravel, soil, sand, and rock—carried in by basketloads on men's backs. Similarly, the monuments must have required an army of laborers. Geological analysis has shown that the source of the basalt used in almost all the San Lorenzo monuments is the Cerro Cintepec, an extinct volcano some fifty miles north-northwest of San Lorenzo. The Colossal Heads average about eighteen tons, and one of the so-called altars weighs even more than that.

The Olmecs must have selected boulders of a suitable shape from the slopes of the volcano, somehow transporting them to the nearest navigable stream (no small distance) and then floating them to the mouth of the Coatzacoalcos

River on balsa rafts. From there they would have been poled and pulled up the river to a point near San Lorenzo. Finally, each boulder would have been hauled up 150 feet, probably with ropes and simple rollers, to their final destination. We ourselves had some experience using simple materials and methods to move the monuments, and I can attest to the enormous effort required to move a ten-ton stone just one foot! It took fifty men with ropes and poles to set one Colossal Head upright. Thus, moving the larger monuments must have involved using more than a thousand workmen at a time.

Then there is the testimony of the persons represented by the stones. Scholars seem to agree that the Colossal Heads are portraits of Olmec rulers. Likewise, the seated figures in the niches of the "altars," shown either with ropes holding captives or carrying the characteristic were-jaguar infants, seem to depict real men. Great leaders, or their descendants, must have ordered the carving and setting up of these monuments—at what cost can only be imagined. Surely, then, we can postulate the existence of a polity that was more powerful than a mere tribal state.

But there is more. The existence of a political state implies a government with territorial jurisdiction not over a single tribe but over many. Whether an Olmec state can be postulated under this definition can never be fully determined, any more than it can be for *any* of the later civilizations of Mexico, other than the documented civilization of the Aztecs. Nevertheless, there is good reason to believe that the San Lorenzo Olmecs exerted an influence, political or otherwise, upon regions as distant as the highlands of central and western Mexico, where Olmec pottery and even Olmec rock paintings have been discovered during the past few years.

But the most compelling evidence for San Lorenzo's high cultural and political status under the Olmecs comes from what at first glance might be thought an unlikely line of inquiry: ecology. Working within a sample area of about thirty square miles, centering on San Lorenzo, we are now trying to arrive at some idea of what the upper limit of human population may have been three thousand years ago. The extent of the sample area is probably that which would have been controlled by an agricultural tribe. If our population figure turns out to

be much lower than the number of persons presumably involved in the construction and maintenance of the Olmec center, then San Lorenzo would have to have drawn labor and tribute from an area far greater than that of our sample.

Our calculation is based on the number of mouths that native systems of cultivation could have fed. It is not an easy one to make. Our preliminary studies strongly suggest, however, that the local population could never have constructed the artificial plateau and set up the monuments unaided. We may assume, then, that the Olmec rulers held sway over more than one tribe, and that they may, indeed, have exercised authority over much of southern Mexico.

One significant outgrowth of our study has been the work of Dr. Elizabeth S. Wing of the Florida State Museum, who has managed to identify scraps of bone contained in our Olmec rubbish heaps. The Olmecs were more finicky in their culinary habits than the present-day natives, who eat almost any kind of fish or game they can get their hands on. Olmec preferences, however, are curious, since the most common animals represented are snook (a large and good-tasting fish), man, marine toad, and turtle! We are not particularly bothered by the human remains, since cannibalism is well attested for the rest of Mesoamerica, but the toads are a puzzle, as they cannot be skinned without an extremely dangerous poison getting into the meat. We are now looking into the possibility that the Olmecs used them for a hallucinogenic substance called bufotenine, which is one of the active ingredients of the poison.

Far more significant, however, has been our research into local farming practices. The Olmecs, like all Mexican Indians, were basically corn eaters. Here we think that we may have hit upon the secret of the very early rise of native civilization in the San Lorenzo area. As in most of the world's tropical lands, the basic system of agriculture is of the shifting, or slash-and-burn, type, which means that a farmer will fell the trees or bush on a plot of land, burn them when dry, and continue to plant and harvest on the plot until declining yields or other factors force him to abandon it and search for another patch of forest.

One must also remember that there is a dry season and a rainy one. Most Mesoamerican farmers have only one major crop, planted with the first rains and harvested in the fall. On the gently rolling upland soils of the San Lorenzo area, however, there are *two* major crops, thanks to the winter northers, which keep the soil moist. Furthermore, in summer, when the rainstorms sweep daily across southwest Mexico, the winding, sluggish Coatzacoalcos River rises rapidly and covers all of the low-lying land with great sheets of water. San Lorenzo becomes a world afloat. As the rains taper off and the floods recede, the gift of the river is revealed: fresh mud and silt, deposited along the broad natural levees that flank the river.

These levees are classed by the natives as "prime land." While the upland areas tend to be communally owned, the levees are pretty much in private hands. Even though it is possible to cultivate only one crop on them, during the dry season, their production is incredibly high for indigenous corn farming. As might be expected, those who bid for economic—and political—power in the village must gain effective control of the levee lands.

Was this, then, how the Olmecs rose to power and civilization more than three millenniums ago? We are reminded of ancient Egypt, so obviously tied to the rise and fall of its one great river. It is hardly a coincidence that most of the world's early civilizations have arisen in major river basins, and our Olmecs of San Lorenzo seem to have been no exception.

Every story has an end, or at least an epilogue. Olmec civilization did not come to a close after the massive destruction of San Lorenzo around 900 B.C. Curiously enough, La Venta seems to have reached the summit of its achievement immediately *after* this brutal event, and it may be that the overthrow of San Lorenzo's rulers was instigated by the leaders of that island citadel. Thereafter, the Olmec character of San Lorenzo was lost, for the pre-Classic reoccupations that continued until the beginning of the Christian Era lack the art style that is the Olmec hallmark.

Eventually, even La Venta was destroyed, and perhaps its successor, Tres Zapotes. But Olmec civilization became transformed into some of the other brilliant civilizations of Mesoamerica's Classic period. The farther back we trace the Classic cultures of Mexico and Central America, the more characteristic of the Olmecs they seem to become.

The most clear-cut case for an Olmec heritage is presented by the famous Mayan civilization of the Classic period. It may seem a far cry from the earth or adobe constructions of the Olmecs to the towering pyramid-temples of the Mayas, but a closer look at Mayan art and learning reveals much in common. Take the day-to-day calendar system called the Long Count. Although for many decades scientists considered this a Mayan invention, Stirling and others have shown that it had far earlier roots in Olmec country. There is now good reason to believe that the well-known writing system of the Mayas may be of Olmec origin as well. Based on what we know of the earliest Classic Mayan art and culture, the Mayas themselves may, indeed, once have been Olmec, moving in the centuries before the Christian Era eastward into the jungles of Yucatán and Guatemala.

Strong Olmec influence may also be detected in the Oaxaca highlands of Mexico, where the Zapotec people held sway. Kent Flannery of the University of Michigan has recently identified a local Oaxaca culture that was either importing Olmec products or making very good imitations of them, and Olmec artistic traits are to be found in the well-known Danzante reliefs, the strange stone carvings of slain men erected at the great Zapotec site of Monte Albán.

The list could be expanded to encompass most early civilizations of Mexico and Central America. The Olmecs seem to be behind all of them—an ancient, shadowy, "mother culture" whose own origins remain shrouded in mystery even to this day.

Part IX

Epilogue

The final segment will hopefully convey to the reader a message about the future — a final thought concerning the "Study of Man" and its relevance and implications for the future. Prescott's article suggests a correlation between violence and lack of body pleasure. He argues strongly for the promoting of bodily pleasure, especially during the formative years. Such insights derived from examining behavioral patterns cross-culturally may effect some positive changes in our society of the future. Stover's 2001 article provides an interesting ending, recapitulating the rise and demise of the human animal in this space odyssey.

Body Pleasure and the Origins of Violence

Human violence is fast becoming a global epidemic. All over the world, police face angry mobs, terrorists disrupt the Olympics, hijackers seize airplanes, and bombs wreck buildings. During the past year, wars raged in the Mideast, Cyprus, and Southeast Asia, and guerrilla fighting continued to escalate in Ireland. Meanwhile, crime in the United States grew even faster than inflation. Figures from the Federal Bureau of Investigation show that serious crimes rose 16% in the first six months of 1974—one of the largest crime increases since FBI record-keeping began.

Unless the causes of violence are isolated and treated, we will continue to live in a world of fear and apprehension. Unfortunately, violence is often offered as a solution to violence. Many law enforcement officials advocate "get tough" policies as the best method to reduce crime. Imprisoning people, our usual way of dealing with crime, will not solve the problem, because the causes of violence lie in our basic values and the way in which we bring up our children and youth. Physical punishment and violent films and TV programs teach our children that physical violence is normal. But these early life experiences are not the only or even the main source of violent behavior. Recent research supports the point of view that the deprivation of physical pleasure is a major ingredient in the expression of physical violence. The common association of sex with violence provides a clue to understanding physical violence in terms of deprivation of physical pleasure.

Unlike violence, pleasure seems to be something the world can't get enough of. People are constantly in search of new forms of pleasure, yet most of our "pleasure" activities appear to be substitutes for the natural sensory pleasures

By James W. Prescott. This article appeared in *The Futurist*, April 1975, pp. 64-74. Permission to reprint granted by *The Futurist*, published by the World Future Society, P.O. Box 3069 (Bethesda) Washington, D.C. 20014. The article was also reprinted in *The Bulletin of the Atomic Scientists*, November 1975.

of touching. We touch for pleasure or for pain or we don't touch at all. Although physical pleasure and physical violence seem worlds apart, there seems to be a subtle and intimate connection between the two. Until the relationship between pleasure and violence is understood, violence will continue to escalate.

As a developmental neuropsychologist I have devoted a great deal of study to the peculiar relationship between violence and pleasure. I am now convinced that the deprivation of physical sensory pleasure is the principal root cause of violence. Laboratory experiments with animals show that pleasure and violence have a reciprocal relationship, that is, *the presence of one inhibits the other*. A raging, violent animal will abruptly calm down when electrodes stimulate the pleasure centers of its brain. Likewise, stimulating the violence centers in the brain can terminate the animal's sensual pleasure and peaceful behavior. When the brain's pleasure circuits are "on," the violence circuits are "off," and vice-versa. Among human beings, a pleasure-prone personality rarely displays violence or aggressive behaviors, and a violent personality has little ability to tolerate, experience, or enjoy sensuouly pleasing activities. As either violence or pleasure goes up, the other goes down.

The reciprocal relationship of pleasure and violence is highly significant, because certain sensory experiences during the formative periods of development will create a neuropsychological predisposition for either violence-seeking or pleasure-seeking behaviors later in life. I am convinced that various abnormal social and emotional behaviors resulting from what psychologists call "maternal-social" deprivation, that is, a lack of tender, loving care, are caused by a unique type of sensory deprivation, *somatosensory* deprivation. Derived from the Greek word for "body," the term refers to the sensations of touch and body movement which differ from the sense of sight, hearing, smell, and taste. I believe that the deprivation of body touch, contact, and movement are the basic causes of a number of emotional disturbances which include depressive and autistic behaviors, hyperactivity, sexual aberration, drug abuse, violence, and aggression.

These insights were derived chiefly from the

controlled laboratory studies of Harry F. and Margaret K. Harlow at the University of Wisconsin. The Harlows and their students separated infant monkeys from their mothers at birth. The monkeys were raised in single cages in an animal colony room, where they could develop social relationships with the other animals through seeing, hearing, and smelling, but not through touching or movement. These and other studies indicate that it is the deprivation of body contact and body movement—not deprivation of the other senses—that produces the wide variety of abnormal emotional behaviors in these isolation-reared animals. It is well known that human infants and children who are hospitalized or institutionalized for extended periods with little physical touching and holding develop almost identical abnormal behaviors, such as rocking and head banging.

Although the pathological violence observed in isolation-reared monkeys is well documented, the linking of early somatosensory deprivation with physical violence in humans is less well established. Numerous studies of juvenile delinquents and adult criminals have shown a family background of broken homes and/or physically abusive parents. These studies have rarely mentioned, let alone measured, the degree of deprivation of physical affection, although this is often inferred from the degree of neglect and abuse. One exceptional study in this respect is that of Brandt F. Steele and C. B. Pollock, psychiatrists at the University of Colorado, who studied child abuse in three generations of families who physically abused their children. They found that parents who abused their children were invariably deprived of physical affection themselves during childhood and that their adult sex life was extremely poor. Steele noted that almost without exception the women who abused their children had never experienced orgasm. The degree of sexual pleasure experienced by the men who abused their children was not ascertained, but their sex life, in general, was unsatisfactory. The hypothesis that physical pleasure actively inhibits physical violence can be appreciated from our own sexual experiences. How many of us feel like assaulting someone after we have just experienced orgasm?

The contributions of Freud to the effects of early experiences upon later behaviors and the consequences of repressed sexuality have been well established. Unfortunately time and space does not permit a discussion of his differences with Wilhelm Reich and this writer concerning his "Beyond the Pleasure Principle."

The hypothesis that deprivation of physical pleasure results in physical violence requires a formal systematic evaluation. We can test this hypothesis by examining cross-cultural studies of child-rearing practices, sexual behaviors, and physical violence. We would expect to find that human societies which provide their infants and children with a great deal of physical affection (touching holding, carrying) would be less physically violent than human societies which give very little physical affection to their infants and children. Similarly, human societies which tolerate and accept premarital and extramarital sex would be less physically violent than societies which prohibit and punish premarital and extramarital sex.

CROSS-CULTURAL STUDIES OF PHYSICAL VIOLENCE

Cultural anthropologists have gathered exactly the data required to examine this hypothesis for human societies—and their findings are conveniently arranged in R. B. Textor's *A Cross-Cultural Summary* (HRAF Press, 1967). Textor's book is basically a research tool for cross-cultural statistical inquiry. The survey provides some 20,000 statistically significant correlations from 400 culture samples of primitive societies.

INFANT NEGLECT AND ADULT VIOLENCE

Certain variables which reflect physical affection (such as fondling, caressing, and playing with infants) were related to other variables which measure crime and violence (frequency of theft, killing, etc.). The important relationships are displayed in the tables accompanying this article. The percent figures reflect the relationships among the variables, e.g. high affection/low violence plus low affection/high violence. This procedure is followed for all tables.

Societies ranking high or low on the Infant

Table 1. High Infant Physical Affection.

Adult Behaviors	Percent %	N	Probability P
Invidious display of wealth is low	66	50	.06
Incidence of theft low	72	36	.02
Overall infant indulgence high	80	66	.0000
Infant physical pain low	65	63	.03
Negligible killing, torturing or mutilating the enemy	73	49	.004
Low religious activity	81	27	.003

The coded scales on infancy were developed by cultural anthropologists Barry, Bacon and Child; on sexual behavior by Westbrook, Ford and Beach; and on physical violence by Slater.

Physical Affection Scale were examined for degree of violence. The results (table 1) clearly indicated that those societies which give their infants the greatest amount of physical affection were characterized by low theft, low infant physical pain, low religious activity, and negligible or absent killing, mutilating, or torturing of the enemy. These data directly confirm that the deprivation of body pleasure during infancy is significantly linked to a high rate of crime and violence.

Some societies physically punish their infants as a matter of discipline, while others do not. We can determine whether this punishment reflects a general concern for the infant's welfare by matching it against child nurturant care. The results (table 2) indicate that societies which inflict pain and discomfort upon their infants tend to neglect them as well.

Adult physical violence was accurately predicted in 36 of 49 cultures (73%) from the infant physical affection variable. The probablility that a 73% rate of accuracy could occur by chance is only four times out of a thousand.

Show how the physical affection—or punishment—given infants correlates with other variables. For example, cultures which inflict pain on infants appear to be more likely to practice slavery, polygyny, etc. In the tables, *N* refers to the number of cultures in the comparison while *P* is the probability that the observed relationship could occur by chance and was calculated by the Fisher Exact Probability Test.

SEXUAL REPRESSION AND ADULT VIOLENCE

Thirteen of the 49 societies studied seemed to be exceptions to the theory that a lack of somatosensory pleasure makes people physically violent. It was expected that cultures which placed

Table 2. Pain Inflicted by Parent or Nurturing Agent.

Adult Behaviors	Percent %	N	Probability P
Slavery is present	64	66	.03
Polygyny (multiple wives) practiced	79	34	.001
Women status inferior	78	14	.03
Low infant physical affection	65	63	.03
Low overall infant indulgence	77	66	.000
Developing nurturant behavior in child is low	67	45	.05
Supernaturals (gods) are aggressive	64	36	.01

a high value upon physical pleasure during infancy and childhood would maintain such values into adulthood. This is not the case. Child rearing practices do not predict patterns of later sexual behavior. This initial surprise and presumed discrepancy, however, becomes advantageous for further prediction. Two variables that are highly correlated are not as useful for predicting a third variable as two variables that are uncorrelated. Consequently, it is meaningful to examine the sexual behaviors of the 13 cultures whose adult violence was not predictable from physical pleasure during infancy. Apparently, the social customs which influence and determine the behaviors of sexual affection are different from those which underlie the expression of physical affection toward infants.

When the six societies characterized by both high infant affection and high violence are compared in terms of their premarital sexual behavior, it is surprising to find that five of them exhibit premarital sexual repression, where virginity is a high value of these cultures. It appears that *the beneficial effects of infant physical affection can be negated by the repression of physical pleasure (premarital sex) later in life.*

The seven societies characterized by both low infant physical affection and low adult physical violence were all found to be characterized by permissive premarital sexual behaviors. Thus, *the detrimental effects of infant physical affectional deprivation seem to be compensated for later in life by sexual body pleasure experiences during adolescence.* These findings have led to a

Table 3. Relationship of Infant Physical Affection Deprivation to Adult Physical Violence.

High Infant Physical Affection	Low Infant Physical Affection	High Infant Physical Affection	Low Infant Physical Affection
Low Adult Physical Violence	High Adult Physical Violence	High Adult Physical Violence	Low Adult Physical Violence
Andamanese	Alorese	Cheyenne	Ainu
Arapesh	Aranda	Chir-Apache	Ganda
Balinese	Araucanians	Crow	Kwakiutl
Chagga	Ashanti	Jivaro	Lepcha
Chenchu	Aymara	Kurtatchi	Pukapuka
Chuckchee	Azande	Zuni	Samoans
Cuna	Comanche		Tanala
Hano	Fon		
Lau	Kaska		
Lesu	Marquesans		
Maori	Masai		
Murngin	Navaho		
Nuer	Ojibwa		
Papago	Thonga		
Siriono			
Tallensi			
Tikopia			
Timbira			
Trobriand			
Wogeo			
Woleaians			
Yahgan			

Derived from: R. B. Textor. A Cross-Cultural Summary. HRAF Press. New Haven, Connecticut, 1967. Infant behavior ratings from Barry, Bacon & Child. Adult violence ratings from P. E. Slater.

revision of the somatosensory pleasure deprivation theory from a one-stage to a two-stage developmental theory where the physical violence in 48 of the 49 cultures could be accurately classified. In short, violence may stem from deprivation of somatosensory pleasure either in infancy or in adolescence. The only true exception in this culture sample is the headhunting Jivaro tribe of South America. Clearly, this society requires detailed study to determine the causes of its violence. The Jivaro belief system may play an important role, for as anthropologist Michael Harner notes in *Jivaro Souls,* these Indians have a "deep-seated belief that killing leads to the acquisition of souls which provide a supernatural power conferring immunity from death."

The strength of the two-stage deprivation theory of violence is most vividly illustrated when we contrast the societies showing high rates of physical affection during infancy *and* adolescence against those societies which are consistently low in physical affection for both developmental periods. The statistics associated with this relationship are extraordinary: The percent likelihood of a society being physically violent if it is physically affectionate toward its infants *and* tolerant of premarital sexual behavior is 2% (48/49). The probability of this rela-tionship occurring by chance is 125,000 to one. I am not aware of any other developmental variable that has such a high degree of predictive validity. Thus, we seem to have a firmly based principle: Physically affectionate human societies are highly unlikely to be physically violent.

Accordingly, when physical affection and pleasure during adolescence as well as infancy are related to measures of violence, we find direct evidence of a significant relationship between the punishment of premarital sex behaviors and various measures of crime and violence. As table 4 shows, additional clusters of relationships link the punishment and repression of premarital sex to large community size, high social complexity and class stratification, small extended families, purchase of wives, practice of slavery, and a high god present in human morality. The relationship between small extended families and punitive premarital sex attitudes deserves emphasis, for it suggests that the nuclear family structure in contemporary Western cultures may be a contributing factor to our repressive attitudes toward sexual expression. The same can be suggested for community size, social complexity, and class stratification.

Not surprisingly, when high self-needs are

Table 4. Premarital Sex is Strongly Punished.

Adult Behaviors	Percent %	N	Probability P
Community size is larger	73	80	.0003
Slavery is present	59	176	.005
Societal complexity is high	87	15	.01
Personal crime is high	71	28	.05
Class stratification is high	60	111	.01
High incidence of theft	68	31	.07
Small extended family	70	63	.008
Extramarital sex is punished	71	58	.005
Wives are purchased	54	114	.02
Castration anxiety is high	65	37	.009
Longer post-partum sex taboo	62	50	.03
Bellicosity is extreme	68	37	.04
Sex disability is high	83	23	.004
Killing, torturing and mutilating the enemy is high	69	35	.07
Narcissism is high	66	38	.04
Exhibitionistic dancing is emphasized	65	66	.04
High god in human morality	81	27	.01

combined with the deprivation of physical affection, the result is self-interest and high rates of narcissism. Likewise, exhibitionistic dancing and pornography may be interpreted as a substitute for normal sexual expression. Some nations which are most repressive of female sexuality have rich pornographic art forms.

ACCEPTANCE OF EXTRAMARITAL SEX MAY REDUCE VIOLENCE

I also examined the influence of extramarital sex taboos upon crime and violence. The data clearly indicate that punitive-repressive attitudes toward extramarital sex are also linked with physical violence, personal crime, and the practice of slavery. Societies which value monogamy emphasize military glory and worship aggressive gods.

These cross-cultural data support the view of psychologists and sociologists who feel that sexual and psychological needs not being fulfilled within a marriage should be met outside of it, without destroying the primacy of the marriage relationship.

These findings overwhelmingly support the thesis that deprivation of body pleasure throughout life—but particularly during the formative periods of infancy, childhood, and adolescence—are very closely related to the amount of warfare and interpersonal violence. These insights should be applied to large and complicated industrial and post-industrial societies.

SEXUAL PLEASURE VS. SEXUAL VIOLENCE

Crime and physical violence have substantially increased over the past decade in the United States. According to FBI statistics, both murder and aggravated assault increased 53% between 1967 and 1972, while forcible rape rose 70%.

These figures again raise the question of the special relationship between sexuality and violence. In addition to our rape statistics, there is other evidence that points to America's preference for sexual violence over sexual pleasure. This is reflected in our acceptance of sexually explicit films that involve violence and rape, and our rejection of sexually explicit films for pleasure only (pornography). Neighborhood movie theaters show such sexually violent films as *Straw Dogs, Clockwork Orange,* and *The Klansman,* while banning films which portray sexual pleasure *(Deep Throat, The Devil in Miss Jones).* Attempts to close down massage parlors are another example given of our anti-pleasure attitudes. Apparently, sex with pleasure is immoral and unacceptable, but sex with violence and pain is moral and acceptable.

A questionnaire I developed to explore this question was administered to 96 college students whose average age was 19 years. The results of the questionnaire support the connection between rejection of physical pleasure (and particularly of premarital and extramarital sex) with expression of physical violence. Respondents who reject abortion, responsible premarital sex, and nudity within the family were likely to approve of harsh physical punishment for children and to believe that pain helps build strong moral character. These respondents were likely to find alcohol and drugs more satisfying than sex. The data obtained from the questionnaire provide strong statistical support for the basic inverse relationship between physical violence and physical pleasure. If violence is high, pleasure is low, and conversely, if pleasure is high, violence is low. The questionnaire bears out the theory that the pleasure-violence relationship found in primitive cultures also holds true for a modern industrial nation.

DRUGS, SEX, AND VIOLENCE: THE UNHOLY TRINITY

Another way of looking at the reciprocal relationship between violence and pleasure is to examine a society's choice of drugs. A society will support behaviors that are consistent with its values and social mores. U.S. society is a competitive, aggressive, and violent society. Consequently, it supports drugs that facilitate competitive, aggressive, and violent behaviors and opposes drugs that counteract such behaviors. Alcohol is well known to facilitate the expression of violent behaviors, and, although addicting and very harmful to chronic users, is acceptable to American society. Marijuana, on the other hand, is an active pleasure-inducing drug which enhances the pleasure of touch and actively inhibits violent-aggressive behaviors. It is for these reasons, I believe that marijuana is rejected in American society. For similar reasons heroin is rejected and methadone (an addicting drug minus the pleasure) is accepted.

The data from my questionnaire support this view. As table 5 shows, very high correlations between alcohol use and parental punishment indicate that people who received little affection

Table 5. Somatosensory Index of Human Affection Factor 1: 66.6%.

Violence Approved
.85 Hard physical punishment is good for children who disobey a lot.
.81 Physical punishment and pain help build a strong moral character.
.76 Capital punishment should be permitted by society.
.75 Violence is necessary to really solve our problems.
.74 Physical punishment should be allowed in the schools.
.69 I enjoy sadistic pornography.
.54 I often feel like hitting someone.
.43 I can tolerate pain very well.

Physical Pleasure Condemned
.84 Prostitution should be punished by society.
.80 Abortion should be punished by society.
.80 Responsible premarital sex is not agreeable to me.
.78 Nudity within the family has a harmful influence upon children.
.73 Sexual pleasures help build a weak moral character.
.72 Society should interfere with private sexual behavior between adults.
.69 Responsible extramural sex is not agreeable to me.
.61 Natural fresh body odors are often offensive.
.47 I do not enjoy affectional pornography.

Alcohol and Drugs Rated Higher than Sex
.70 Alcohol is more satisfying than sex.
.65 Drugs are more satisfying than sex.
.60 I get hostile and aggressive when I drink alcohol.
.49 I would rather drink alcohol than smoke marijuana.
.45 I drink alcohol more often than I experience orgasm.

Political Conservatism
.82 I tend to be conservative in my political points of view.
.77 Age (Older).
.51 I often dream of either floating, flying, falling, or climbing.
.45 My mother is often indifferent toward me.
.42 I often get "uptight" about being touched.
.40 I remember when my father physically punished me a lot.

In Prescott's experiment, students rated a series of statements on a scale of 1 to 6, where 1 indicated strong agreement and 6 strong disagreement. Through a statistical technique (factor analysis), Prescott developed a personality profile of the violent person.

Table 5 shows the degree of relationship among the various statements which reflect social and moral values. The figures at left, known as "loadings," are treated like correlation coefficients. They indicate the strength with which each variable contributes to the overall personality description of the respondent as defined by this specific profile.

The collaboration of Douglas Wallace, Human Sexuality Program, University of California Medical School, San Francisco, in the questionnaire study is gratefully acknowledged.

from their mothers and had physically punitive fathers are likely to become hostile and aggressive when they drink. Such people find alcohol more satisfying than sex. There is an even stronger relationship between parental physical punishment and drug usage. Respondents who were physically punished as children showed alcohol-induced hostility and aggression and were likely to find alcohol and drugs more satisfying than sex. The questionnaire also reveals high correlations between sexual regression and drug usage. Those who describe premarital sex as "not agreeable" are likely to become aggressive when drinking and to prefer drugs and alcohol to sexual pleasures. This is additional evidence for the hypothesis that drug "pleasures" are a substitute for somato-sensory pleasures.

PHILOSOPHICAL AND RELIGIOUS ROOTS: THE MIND/BODY PROBLEM

The origins of the fundamental reciprocal relationship between physical violence and physical pleasure can be traced to philosophical dualism and to the theology of body/soul relationships. In Western philosophical thought man was not a unitary being but was divided into two parts, body and soul. The Greek philosophical conception of the relationship between body and soul was quite different than the Judeo-Christian concept which posited a state of war between the body and soul. Within Judeo-Christian thought the purpose of human life was to save the soul, and the body was seen as an impediment to achieving this objective. Consequently, the body must be punished and deprived. In St. Paul's words: "Put to death the base pursuits of the body—for if you live according to the flesh, you shall die: but if by the spirit you mortify the deeds of the flesh, you shall live" (Romans 9:13). St. Paul clearly advocated somatosensory pleasure deprivation and enhancement of painful somatosensory stimulation as essential prerequisites for saving the soul.

Aristotle did not view a state of war between the body and soul, but rather envisioned a complimentary relationship in which the state of the soul or mind was dependent on the state of the body. In fact he stated that " . . . the care of the body ought to precede that of the soul" *(Politica).*

Aristotle also appreciated the reciprocal relationship between pleasure and pain, and recognized that a compulsive search for bodily pleasure originates from a state of bodily discomfort and pain:

Now, excess is possible in the case of the goods of the body, and it is the pursuit of excess, but not the pursuit of necessary pleasures, that makes a man bad. For all men get some kind of enjoyment from good food, wine, and sexual relations, but not everyone enjoys these things in the proper way. The reverse is true of pain: a bad person does not avoid an excess of it, but he avoids it altogether. For the opposite of an excess is pain only for the man who pursues the excess. . . .

Accordingly, we must now explain why the pleasures of the body appear to be more desirable. The first reason, then, is that pleasure drives out pain. When men experience an excess of pain, they pursue excessive pleasure and bodily pleasure in general, in the belief that it will remedy the pain. The remedial (pleasures) become very intense—and that is the very reason why they are pursued because they are experienced in contrast with their opposite.

Nichomachean Ethics, Book 7

In his discussion of the highest good, Aristotle was quite explicit: "Therefore, the highest good is some sort of pleasure, despite the fact that most pleasures are bad, and, if you like, bad in the unqualified sense of the word." *(Nichomachean Ethics,* Book 7).

It is evident that the Judeo-Christian concept of body pleasure is quite the opposite of that outlined by Aristotle, particularly, the relief of body pain and discomfort through somatosensory pleasure. This denial of somatosensory pleasure in Pauline Christian doctrine has led to alternate forms of "relief" through such painful stimulations as hairshirts, self-scourgings, self-mutilations, physical violence against others, and in the non-sensory pleasures of drugs.

Experimental animal studies have documented counterparts to these phenomena. For example, animals deprived of somatosensory stimulation will engage in mutilations of their own bodies. Animals deprived of touching early in life develop impaired pain perception and an aversion to being touched by others. They are thus blocked from experiencing the body-pleasure therapy that they need for rehabilitation. In this condition, they have few alternatives but physical violence, where pain-oriented touching and body contact is facilitated by their impaired ability to experience pain. Thus, physical violence and physical pain become therapies of choice for those deprived of physical pleasure.

BIBLICAL ORIGINS OF THE IMMORALITY OF PLEASURE

The question arises as to how Christian philosophy and theology, which borrowed heavily from Aristotle, managed to avoid, if not outright reject, Aristotle's teachings regarding the morality of pleasure. The roots to this question can be found throughout the Old Testament, beginning with the account in Genesis of the expulsion of Adam and Eve from the Garden of Eden. The first consequence of Eve's transgression was that nudity became shameful. This event may well be the beginning of man's hostility toward women and the equating of woman with evil, particularly the evils of the body. This is vividly portrayed in Zechariah (5:5–8) in an angel's description of the flying bushel: " 'This is a bushel container coming. This is their guilt in all the land.' Then a leaden cover was lifted and there was a woman sitting inside the bushel. "This is wickedness, he said, and he thrust her inside the bushel, pushing the leaden cover into the opening.' "

Violence against sexuality and the use of sexuality for violence, particularly against women, has very deep roots in Biblical tradition, and is spelled out very early on. The nineteenth chapter of Genesis, the first book of the Old Testament, holds that the rape of woman is acceptable but the rape of man is "a wicked thing." This chapter about the destruction of Sodom and Gomorrah describes Lot's hospitality to two male travelers (actually two angels) who were housed with him. In the evening the townsmen of Sodom came to Lot's house and said to him:

"Where are the men who came to your house tonight? Bring them out to us that we may have intimacies with them." Lot went out to meet them at the entrance. When he had shut the door behind him, he said, "I beg you, my brothers, not to do this wicked thing. I have two daughters who have never had intercourse with men. Let me bring them out to you, and you may do to them as you please. But don't do anything to these men, for you know they have come under the shelter of my roof." They replied, "Stand back! This fellow," they sneered, "came here as an immigrant, and now he dares to give orders! We'll treat you worse than them!" With that, they pressed hard against Lot, moving in closer to break down the door. But his guests put out their hand, pulled Lot inside with them, and closed the door; at the same time they struck the men at the entrance of the house, one and all, with such blinding light that they were utterly unable to reach the doorway.

As the story continues, the two angels escort Lot and his family to safety and then destroy Sodom and Gomorrah for their great sinfulness. Yet not a word of reproach is given to Lot for his willingness to hand over his two virgin daughters to be gang raped. This same story is repeated in the books of Ezekiel (23:1–49) and Judges (19:22–30).

Given such a tradition, it is understandable that during the Inquisition only women were charged with having intercourse with the devil and put to death for this crime of pleasure. What man has died at the stake for having slept with Satan? This tradition is maintained in modern cultures where women are punished for prostitution but their male customers are not.

The historical and Biblical acceptance of rape down through the ages has brutalized the psyche of males brought up in this tradition. This is well illustrated in the account of Michael McCusker, a Marine sergeant who witnessed a gang rape in Vietnam. McCusker tells of a rifle squad of nine men who entered a small village.

They were supposed to go after what they called a Viet Cong whore. They went into the village and instead of capturing her, they raped her—every man raped her. As a matter of fact, one man said to me later that it was the first time he had ever made love to a woman with his boots on. The man who led the platoon, or the squad, was actually a private. The squad leader was a sergeant but he was a useless person and he let the private take over his squad. Later he said he took no part in the raid. It was against his morals. So instead of telling his squad not to do it, because they wouldn't listen to him anyway, the sergeant went into another side of the village and just sat

and stared bleakly at the ground, feeling sorry for himself. But at any rate, they raped the girl, and then, the last man to make love to her, shot her in the head.
The Winter Soldier Investigation:
An Inquiry into American War Crimes
(Beacon Press, Boston, 1972)

What is it in the American psyche that permits the use of the word "love" to describe rape? And where the act of love is completed with a bullet in the head!

MODERN ORIGINS
OF SEXUAL VIOLENCE

Why do men rape women? Researchers report that most rapists have a family background of paternal punishment and hostility and loss of maternal affection. I interpret rape as man's revenge against woman for the early loss of physical affection. A man can express his hostility toward his mother for not giving him enough physical attention by sexually violating another woman.

Another explanation may be that the increasing sexual freedom of women is threatening to man's position of power and dominance over women which he often maintains through sexual aggression. Rape destroys sensual pleasure in woman and enhances sadistic pleasure in man. Through rape, man defends himself from the sensual pleasures of women which threaten his position of power and dominance.

It is my belief that rape has its origins in the deprivation of physical affection in parent-child relationships and adult sexual relationships; and in a religious value system that considers pain and body deprivation moral and physical pleasure immoral. Rape maintains man's dominance over woman and supports the perpetuation of patriarchal values in our society.

NEW VALUES FOR
A PEACEFUL WORLD

It is clear that the world has only limited time to change its custom of resolving conflicts violently. It is uncertain whether we have the time to undo the damage done by countless previous generations, nor do we know how many future generations it will take to transform our psychobiology of violence into one of peace.

If we accept the theory that the lack of sufficient somatosensory pleasure is a principal cause of violence, we can work toward promoting pleasure and encouraging affectionate interpersonal relationships as a means of combatting aggression. We should give high priority to body pleasure in the context of meaningful human relationships. Such body pleasure is very different from promiscuity, which reflects a basic inability to experience pleasure. If a sexual relationship is not pleasurable, the individual looks for another partner. A continuing failure to find sexual satisfaction leads to a continuing search for new partners, that is, to promiscuous behavior. Affectionately shared physical pleasure, on the other hand, tends to stabilize a relationship and eliminate the search. However, a variety of sexual experiences seems to be normal in cultures which permit its expression, and this may be important for optimizing pleasure and affection in sexual relationships.

Available data clearly indicate that the rigid values of monogamy, chastity, and virginity help produce physical violence. The denial of female sexuality must give way to an acceptance and respect for it, and men must share with women the responsibility for giving affection and care to infants and children. As the father assumes a more equal role with the mother in child-rearing and becomes more affectionate toward his children, certain changes must follow in our socioeconomic system. A corporate structure which tends to separate either parent from the family by travel, extended meetings, or overtime work weakens the parent-child relationship and harms family stability. To develop a peaceful society, we must put more emphasis on human relationships.

Family planning is essential. Children must be properly spaced so that each can receive optimal affection and care. The needs of the infant should be immediately met. Cross-cultural evidence does not support the view that such practices will "spoil" the infant. Contrary to Dr. Benjamin Spock, it is harmful for a baby to cry itself to sleep. By not answering an infant's needs immediately and consistently, we not only teach a child distrust at a very basic emotional level, but also establish patterns of neglect which harm the child's social and emotional health. The discouragement of breast feeding in favor of bottle feeding and the separation of healthy newborns from their mothers in our "modern" hospitals are other examples of harmful child rearing practices.

About 25% of marriages in the U.S. now end in divorce, and an even higher percentage of couples have experienced extramarital affairs. This suggests that something is basically wrong with the traditional concept of universal monogamy. When viewed in connection with the cross-cultural evidence of the physical deprivations, violence, and warfare associated with monogamy, the need to create a more pluralistic system of marriage becomes clear. Contemporary experiments with communal living and group marriage are attempting to meet basic needs that remain unfulfilled in the isolation of a nuclear marriage. We must seriously consider new options, such as extended families comprised of two or three couples who share values and lifestyles. By sharing the benefits and responsibilities of child rearing, such families could provide an affectionate and varied environment for children as well as adults, and thereby reduce the incidence of child abuse and runaways.

The communal family—like the extended family group—can provide a more stimulating and supportive environment for both children and adults than can the average nuclear family. Communal living should not, of course, be equated with group sex, which is not a sharing, but more often an escape from intimacy and emotional vulnerability.

OPENNESS ABOUT THE BODY

No matter what type of family structure is chosen, it will be important to encourage openness about the body and its functions. From this standpoint, we could benefit from redesigning our homes along the Japanese format, separating the toilet from the bathing facilities. The family bath should be used for socialization and relaxation, and should provide a natural situation for children to learn about male-female differences. Nudity, like sex, can be misused and abused, and this fear often prevents us from accepting the honesty of our own bodies.

The beneficial stimulation of whirlpool baths should not be limited to hospitals or health club spas, but brought into the home. The family bath should be large enough to accommodate parents and children, and be equipped with a whirlpool to maximize relaxation and pleasure. Nudity, openness, and affection within the family can teach children and adults that the body is not shameful and inferior, but rather is a source of beauty and sensuality through which we emotionally relate to one another. Physical affection involving touching, holding, and caressing should not be equated with sexual stimulation, which is a special type of physical affection.

TEACHING CHILDREN TO LOVE, NOT COMPETE

The competitive ethic, which teaches children that they must advance at the expense of others, should be replaced by values of cooperation and a pursuit of excellence for its own sake. We must raise children to be emotionally capable of giving love and affection, rather than to exploit others. We should recognize that sexuality in teenagers is not only natural, but desirable, and accept premarital sexuality as a positive moral good. Parents should help teenagers realize their own sexual selfhood by allowing them to use the family home for sexual fulfillment. Such honesty would encourage a more mature attitude toward sexual relationships and provide a private supportive environment that is far better for their development than the back seat of a car or other undesirable locations outside the home. Early sexual experiences are too often an attempt to prove one's adulthood and maleness or femaleness rather than a joyful sharing of affection and pleasure.

SEXUAL EQUALITY OF WOMEN

Above all, male sexuality must recognize the equality of female sexuality. The traditional right of men to multiple sexual relationships must be extended to women. The great barrier between man and woman is man's fear of the depth and intensity of female sensuality. Because power and aggression are neutralized through sensual pleasure, man's primary defense against a loss of dominance has been the historic denial, repression, and control of the sensual pleasure of women. The use of sex to provide mere release from physiological tension (apparent pleasure) should not be confused with a state of sensual pleasure which is incompatible with dominance, power, aggression, violence

Karlsonn är mormor i familjen Jönsson, (som du tidigare fått som klippdocka i Vi Barn). Hon bor ibland hos Jönssons. Särskilt när det är jul eller sommarlov eller när mamma och pappa vill fara bort alldeles själva några dagar och inte tycker att barnflickan Sara skall behöva vara ensam med alla barnen. Mormor har korsett, det är en sorts underkläder. Barnen i familjen tycker mycket om den, för den ser så spännande och annorlunda ut. Och ovanpå, till vardags, har mormor långbyxor och envid skjorta. Till fint har mormor blå kappa med hatt i samma tyg och skor med rosett. Mormors hund Mimmi är alltid med mormor. Mormors man hette Ture, men han är död sedan många år.

Figure 1.   Swedish paper doll exemplifies the frankness about the human body that is needed in the struggle to substitute physical pleasure for physical punishment, author Prescott says. In this paper doll, no attempt is made to idealize or de-sexualize the body: the body is simply accepted as it is. The Swedish text describes the doll as Ruth Karlsson, the grandmother in the Johnson family.

and pain. It is through the mutual sharing of sensual pleasure that sexual equality between women and men will be realized.

THE PSYCHOBIOLOGY OF MORAL BEHAVIOR

The sensory environment in which an individual grows up has a major influence upon the development and functional organization of the brain. Sensory stimulation is a nutrient that the brain must have to develop and function normally. How the brain functions determines how a person behaves. At birth a human brain is extremely immature and new brain cells develop up to the age of two years. The complexity of brain cell development continues up to about 16 years of age. Herman Epstein of Brandeis University has evidence that growth spurts in the human brain occur at approximately three, seven, 11, and 15 years of age. How early deprivations affect these growth spurts has yet to be determined; however, some data suggest that the final growth spurt may be abolished by early deprivations.

W. T. Greenough, a psychologist at the University of Illinois, has demonstrated that an enriched sensory environment produces a more complex brain cell in rats than an ordinary or impoverished sensory environment. His studies show that extreme sensory deprivation is not necessary to induce structural changes in the developing brain. Many other investigators have shown that rearing rats in isolation after they are weaned induces significant changes in the biochemistry of their brain cell functioning. Other investigators have shown abnormal electrical activity of brain cell functioning in monkeys reared in isolation. I have suggested that the cerebellum, a brain structure involved in the regulation of many brain processes, is rendered dysfunctional when an animal is reared in isolation and is implicated in violent-aggressive behaviors due to somatosensory deprivation. It has been shown that cerebellar neurosurgery can change the aggressive behaviors of isolation-reared monkeys to peaceful behavior. Predatory killing behavior in ordinary house cats can be provoked by stimulating the cerebellar fastigial nucleus, one of the deep brain nuclei of the cerebellum.

Abnormally low levels of platelet serotonin have been found in monkeys reared in isolation and also in institutionalized, highly aggressive children. These findings suggest that somatosensory deprivation during the formative periods of development significantly alters an important biochemical system in the body associated with highly aggressive behaviors. A number of other investigators have documented abnormalities in the adrenal cortical response system in rodents who were isolation-reared and who developed hyperactive, hyperreactive, and hyperaggressive behavior. Thus another important biochemical system associated with aggressiveness is known to be altered by somatosensory deprivation early in life.

Clearly, if we consider violent and aggressive behaviors undesirable then we must provide an enriched somatosensory environment so that the brain can develop and function in a way that results in pleasurable and peaceful behaviors. The solution to physical violence is physical pleasure that is experienced within the context of meaningful human relationships.

CHANGING THE PATTERNS OF DEPRIVATION AND VIOLENCE

For many people, a fundamental moral principle is the rejection of creeds, policies, and behaviors that inflict pain, suffering and deprivation upon our fellow humans. This principle needs to be extended: We should seek not just an absence of pain and suffering, but also the enhancement of pleasure, the promotion of affectionate human relationships, and the enrichment of human experience.

If we strive to increase the pleasure in our lives this will also affect the ways we express aggression and hostility. The reciprocal relationship between pleasure and violence is such that one inhibits the other; when physical pleasure is high, physical violence is low. When violence is high, pleasure is low. This basic premise of the somatosensory pleasure deprivation theory provides us with the tools necessary to fashion a world of peaceful, affectionate, cooperative individuals.

The world, however, has limited time to correct the conditions that propel us to violent con-

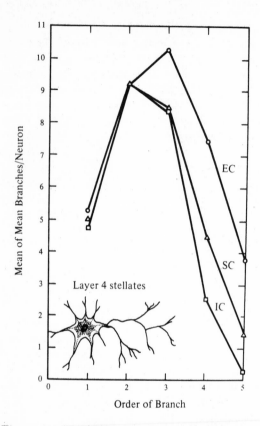

Figure 2. This figure shows the effects of the rearing environment upon a type of nerve cell found in the fourth layer of a rat's visual cortex. The number of branches of the dendrites (a part of the nerve cell which receives input from other nerve cells) is much greater in animals reared in groups in a toy-filled environment (EC) than occurs in rats reared socially (SC) or individually (IC) in small laboratory cages.

Reprinted from *Science*, 30 June 1972, vol. 176, p 1445. F. R. Volkmar & W. T. Greenough.

frontations. Modern technologies of warfare have made it possible for an individual or nation to bring total destruction to large segments of our population. And the greatest threat comes from those nations which have the most depriving environments for their children and which are most repressive of sexual affection and female sexuality. We will have the most to fear when these nations acquire the weapons of modern warfare. Tragically, this has already begun.

References

Bacon, M. K., Child, I. L. and Barry, III, H. A.: "Cross-Cultural study of Correlates of Crime." *J. Abnormal and Social Psychology*, 1963. *66*, 291–300.

Barry, H., Bacon, M. K. and Child I. L. "Definitions, Ratings, and Biblio-Graphic Sources for Child-training Practices of 110 Cultures." In *Cross-cultural approaches: Readings in Cooperative research* (Ford, C. S., Ed) New Haven: HRAF Press, 1967.

Berman, A. J., Berman, D. and Prescott, J. W.: "The Effect of Cerebellar Lesions on Emotional Behavior in the Rhesus Monkey." In *The Cerebellum, Epilepsy, and Behavior*. (Cooper, I. S., Riklon, M. V., Snider, R. S., Eds.). Plenum NY, 1974 pp. 227–284.

D'Angelo, R. *Families of Sand*. A Report Concerning Flight of Adolescents From Their Families. School of Social Work. The Ohio State University, 1974.

Epstein, H. T. S.: "Phrenoblysis: Special Brain and Mind Growth Periods. II. Human Mental Development." *Develop. Psychobiol*. 1974, *7*, 217–224.

Greenough, W. T.: "Experimental Modification of the Developing Brain", *American Scientist*, 1975, *63*; 37–46.

Harlow, H. F.: "Early Social Deprivation and Later Behavior in the Monkey." In *Unfinished tasks in the behavioral sciences*. 1964, 154–173.

Heath, R. G.: "Maternal-social Deprivation and Abnormal Brain Development: Disorders of Emotional and Social Behavior." In *Brain Function and Malnutrition: Neuropsychological Methods of Assessment*. (Prescott, J. W., Read, M. S., and Coursin, D. B., Eds.). NY, John Wiley 1975.

Mitchell, G. "What Monkeys Can Tell Us about Human Violence." *The Futurist*, April 1975, pp. 75–80. (See Part III.)

Naroll, R. "Deterence in History." In *Theory and Research and the Causes of War*. (Pruitt, D. G. and Snyder R. D., Eds.) Prentice Hall: Englewood Cliffs., N.J. 1969, pp. 150-164.

Naroll, R.: "Cultural Determinants and the Concept of the Sick Society." In *Changing Perspectives in Mental Health*. Plog and Edgerton (Eds.). Holt, Rinehart and Winston, NY, 1969. 128–155.

Prescott, J. W.: "Early Somatosensory Deprivation as an Ontogenetic Process in the Abnormal Development of the Brain and Behavior." In *Medical Primatology*, 1970. (Goldsmith, I. E. and Moor-Jankowski, Eds.). Karger, Basel: 1971. pp. 357–375.

Prescott, J. W.: "Before Ethics and Morality." In *The Humanist*. Nov/Dec. 1972.

Prescott, J. W. "Abortion or the Unwanted Child: A choice for a Humanistic Society." The *Humanist* March/April, 1975.

Riesen, A. H. (Eds.).: *The Developmental Neuropsychology of Sensory Deprivation.* Academic Press, NY, 1975.

Rohner, R. P. *They Love Me, They Love Me Not: A World Wide Study of the Effects of Parental Acceptance and Rejection.* HRAF Press. New Haven 1975.

Rosenzweig, M. R.: "Effects of Environment on Development of Brain and of Behavior." In E. Toback (Ed) *Biopsychology of development.* NY: Academic Press, 1971, pp. 303–342.

Russell, E. W. "Factors of Human Aggression: A Cross-Cultural Factor Analysis of Characteristics Related to Warfare and Crime." *Behavior Science Notes:* HRAF Quarterly Bulletin. HRAF Press 1972, 1, 275–312.

Saltzberg, B., Lustick, L. S., and Heath, R. G.: "Detection of Focal Depth Spiking in the Scalp EEG on Monkeys." *Electroencephal. Clin. Neurophysiol.* 1971, *31,* 327–333.

Slater., P.E. and Slater, D. A."Maternal Ambivalence and Narcissism: A Cross-cultural Study." *Merrall-Palmer Quarterly of Behavior and Development.* 1965, *11,* 241–259.

Slater, P. E. Unpublished coding guide for the cross-cultural study of narcissism. Walthom, MASS. 1964. Source for code on "Killing, Torturing or Mutilating the Enemy." R. B. Texten (1967).

Steele, B. F. and Pollack, D. B.: "A Psychiatric Study of Parents Who Abuse Infants and Small Children." In *The Battered Child.* Helfer, R. E. and Kempe, C. H. (Eds.). University of Chicago, 1968. 103–148.

Steinmetz, S. and Strauss, M. (Eds.): *Violence in the Family.* Dodd Mead, 1974.

Soumi, S. J. and Harlow, H. F." Social Rehabilitation of Isolate-Reared Monkeys." *Developmental Psychology,* 1972, *6,* 487–496.

Texter, R. B. *A Cross-cultural Summary.* New Haven HRAF Press, 1967.

Whiting, J. W. M. and Child, I. L.: *Child Training and Personality.* Yale University Press, New Haven, 1953.

Whiting, B. B.: "Sex Identity Conflict and Physical Violence: A Comparative Study." American Anthropologist, 1970 72, 1227–1288.

Apeman, Superman—
or 2001's Answer
to the World Riddle

Nobody who can identify the opening and closing bars of music in *2001* need puzzle long over the film's meaning.

At the start the eye of the camera looks down from barren hills, under the rising sun at dawn, into a still valley below. As the sun mounts, the eye advances into the valley. Zarathustra is come forth out of his cave; hailing the sun—"Thou great star!"—he descends from the hills once more to invest himself in humanity and go at man's progress again. Zarathustra's cosmic mission is given out in the great blast of trumpets which pronounces the World Riddle theme (C-G-C) from *Thus Spake Zarathustra,* by Richard Strauss.

Richard Strauss wrote of this music that it was his homage to the philosophical genius of Nietzche:

I meant to convey by means of music an idea of the human race from its origins, through the various phases of its development, religious and scientific, up to Nietzche's idea of the Superman.

Down there in that awesome valley human destiny is on the starting line with the apemen, members of the genus *Australopithecus,* discovered for anthropology in South and East Africa. The savannah-land in the opening scenes is authentic East African landscape, which today is exactly as it was when the apemen roamed there during Lower Pleistocene times. The apemen are shown to be peaceful and vegetarian. They spend all day eating and chewing plant foods.

But one morning a great, black monolith appears in the midst of their usual feeding place. The sheer perfection and improbability of this artifact arouses in the dim chambers of one apeman's preadamite brain some sense of form, and

By Leon Stover. Reprinted with permission, from *Above the Human Landscape: An Anthology of Social Science Fiction,* Willis E. McNelly and Leon E. Stover, pp. 337-82. Copyright © 1972 by Goodyear Publishing Company.

he reaches out to touch—fearfully at first, then with great yearning—the smooth surfaces and smart edges of this magnificently artificial thing. He is inspired to artifice himself. He discovers the principle of the lever, an extension of his arm, in a long bone picked out of a crumbled tapir skeleton. He bashes this club around experimentally in a pile of old bones from which he lifted it out, in a slow motion sequence of his great hairy arm lifting up and crashing down, causing debris to flower outward in floating arcs, intercut with visions of a falling tapir.

This insightful apeman leads his kind to hunting and meat eating. Meat eating takes less time than plant eating, and with it comes the leisure for tool making which in turn leads, eventually, to science and advanced technology. This first triumph of artifice, the hunting club, is underlined by the C-G-C World Riddle theme, climaxing in full orchestra and organ. The weapon is tossed to the air in a fit of religious exaltation the while the apemen dance around the monolith, and. . . .

. . . In a wipe that takes care of 3 million years of evolutionary history, the bone in its toss is replaced by a spaceship in flight. The camera comes upon a great wheel-shaped orbital station that turns slowly and majestically to the tune of the Blue Danube, which waltzes for man's easy, technological virtuosity. The audience, accordingly, is treated to a long appreciation of the docking maneuvers, in three-quarter time, of a shuttle craft come up from Earth. Its single passenger is an American scientist on a secret mission to the crater Clavius on the moon, where mystery awaits.

The space platform is fitted out with Hilton, Pan Am and Bell Telephone services. The audience always ohs and ahs to see these familiar insignia in the world of the future, which goes to confirm what anthropologists have learned from disaster studies, that people really love their culture. It is part of them. People are thrown into a state of shock when floods, tornadoes or other destructive events remove large chunks of their familiar material environment.

The scientist from Earth continues the last leg of his journey in a low flying moon bus, the while its occupants eat ham and cheese sandwiches. The juxtaposition of the eternally banal picnic lunch with the fantastic lunar landscape zipping by below serves to re-emphasize the confident virtuosity of space technology. But this confidence is shattered by the mystery at Clavius: the monolith again, this time excavated out of lunar soil. While the suited party examines it, a stinging, ringing beam of shrill sound penetrates their helmets. The camera looks up from the very base of the monolith to the sun in a wide angle shot duplicating the one that brought the apemen sequence to a close with the bone club soaring high.

The wipe from the screaming monolith to a ship headed for deep space covers several months. The energy emitted from the monolith fled toward Jupiter, the ship's destination. A crew of five (three in hibernation) and a talking, thinking IBM 9000 series computer, occupy an enormous, sperm-shaped craft: man seeding the cosmos.

During the outward voyage the two men acting as caretakers on the ship display flatter personalities than the spirited computer, HAL, which is plugged into everything and runs everything. Man's technology has advanced so far that it is overwhelming. Technology, basically, is an artificial means of extending human organs. Clothes are an extension of the skin, a computer is an extension of the brain, a wheeled vehicle is an extension of the legs, a telephone is an extension of the ear and mouth, and so on. The more such extensions are elaborated by man, the more they seem to take on a life of their own and threaten to take over. A simple example of extensions getting out of hand is the urban congestion and air pollution created by use of the automobile in great numbers. Another is big organization, made possible by electronic extensions of the speech functions, which makes for suffocating dehumanization in the "organization man." To paraphrase Hamlet, "How like a cog is man!" The two men aboard ship are exactly that. HAL runs the ship and they act like low grade robots, passively eating colored paste for food that comes out of a machine, passively watching TV broadcasts from Earth, passively receiving birthday greetings from home.

HAL symbolizes that point of no return in the development of technology when man's extensions finally take over. They possess the more life the more man is devitalized by them. It will be suicide for man to continue in his love for material culture. Dependence on an advanced state of technology makes it impossible to revert to a primitive state of technology. And it is too late to solve the problem with a "technological fix."

HAL reports an imminent malfunction in the directional antenna of the ship. One of the men, Astronaut Frank Poole, leaves the ship in a space pod in order to replace the unit. The old unit is brought back, tested, and found to be without defect. The two men worry about HAL's lapse of judgment. HAL insists the unit will fail on schedule. So Poole replaces the unit by way of testing HAL. But HAL tested is HAL irritated. When Poole steps out of the space pod to reinstall the unit, HAL works one of the pod's mechanical arms—a runaway extension of the human arm—to snip off his oxygen line. Poole's partner, Mission Commander David Bowman, goes after the body in another space pod and returns to the ship. But HAL won't obey the command to open the port. The only way into the ship now is through the emergency air lock, providing the entrant is fully suited. Bowman, in his haste to rescue Poole, forgot to bring his helmet into the pod.

Meanwhile, HAL had turned off the life-support systems for the three men in hibernation. The blinking lights which register their deaths say, LIFE PROCESSES TERMINATED, a fitting obituary for technomorphic man.

But at bottom, Bowman is a real hero. He triumphs over the technomorphism that turns men into dull machines. He manipulates the pod's waldo arm to open the airlock on the ship, then aligns the pod's hatch with it. Bowman calculates that if he blows the hatch bolts, the air exploding outward from the pod will blast him into the evacuated airlock; perhaps he can survive half a minute in hard, cold vacuum. In a realistic sequence of human daring and bravery, Bowman is exploded into the ship with a silent frenzy that does not pick up sound until the lock is closed and air pressure is restored.

Bowman's next move is to lobotomize HAL, who pleads sorry for the four murders in a parody of a guilty human trying to get off the hook: "I admit I've made some pretty bad decisions lately." The humor of this line conceals an affirmation of HAL's autonomy. Removal of his higher control centers is a significant act forecasting things to come. It looks forward to the time when man shall be able to cut himself loose from his extensions altogether. The solution to a runaway technology is not mastery over it but abandonment of it. The liabilities of human dependence on material means are to be left behind in the conquest of some higher form of existence.

The monolith appears outside the cabin windows at this juncture to indicate the direction of that conquest. Bowman follows it in his space pod, but the monolith vanishes in a purple glow. Straining his eyes on the spot he suddenly is led down a rushing corridor of computer-generated effects that represent his translation through a fourth dimensional experience.

During this sensational ride, Bowman is given a god-like vision of whole galaxies in full form, turning wheels of hot gasses and their embedded star clusters. Through this cosmic whirlpool shoots a symbolic representation of the parent ship: a fiery, sperm-shaped comet thing that drives across the screen and into a pulsing, luminous gas cloud. A delicate point of theology is raised here. In that novel of theological science fiction, *Perelandra* (N.Y.: Macmillan, 1944; 1961) C. S. Lewis argues that man is evil; space travel will only spread the blight. He is out to rebut the idea that

humanity, having now sufficiently corrupted the planet where it arose, must at all costs contrive to seed itself over a larger area: that the vast astronomic distances which are God's quarantine regulations, must somehow be overcome.

The viewpoint of *2001*, however, is that man's seeding of the cosmos is a positive good. For the men who will go out to quicken the universe with the human presence will be supermen, lifted beyond the evil they did on Earth as captives of their technology. Man's extensions always carried a built-in margin of wickedness, beginning with the apeman's weapon of the hunt that could be used also as a weapon of war. But the supermen will be fully emancipated from material extensions as from the material body that is extended by technology. The universe will be made full with the essential goodness of a disembodied humanity.

The transition for Bowman takes place in a hotel suite, mocked up beyond Jupiter by the kind of super beings he and the rest of mankind are destined to join. There Bowman ages rapidly and takes to bed, living out the childhood of man to the end. When the end comes, the great monolith stands before his bed, that recurrent symbol of the great yearning that prompted the apemen millions of years ago to reach for tool making and that now prompts Bowman to reach out for something beyond artifice. He struggles upward from his sheets, unrecognizable in his stupendous oldness, yet reaching painfully for that ineluctable goal waiting beyond the mysterious form standing before him. He reaches forward to touch it, reaching for rebirth. . . .

Cut to a view of planet Earth as seen from outer space. The camera moves aside from the great green disc in the sky to include another luminous body nearby. It is an enormous transparent globe that contains an alert, watchful embryo of cosmic proportions, looking down on Earth with the eyes of Bowman, as he prepares to liberate all humanity from the disabilities of material existence and promote it to the status he has attained to. This giant embryonic figure is a symbolic show, for the sake of something to visualize on the screen, of Bowman's leadership in attaining to a state of pure, incorporeal intellect.

Such a destiny is predicted not alone by science fiction writers. It is to be found also in *The Phenomenon of Man* (N.Y.: Harper 1959) by the late Pierre Teilhard de Chardin, the Catholic priest and anthropologist, who explains that the gathering force of mind that has come to envelope the surface of the planet Earth out of prehuman beginnings must eventuate in a projection into space as a purely spiritual component that will converge ultimately at the Omega point in one single intellectual entity, the very stuff of God. But once all the consciousness of the universe has accumulated and merged in the Omega point, God will get lonely in his completeness, and the process of creation must begin again by way of arousing conscious creatures to reach out once more for closure in one collective identity.

2001 comes to an end on a great trumpeting blast of the World Riddle theme, C-G-C, the shimmering globe of Bowman's pure mind stuff staring the audience in the face. Soon the whole population of Earth will join him. But the story of man is not complete with the evolution from apeman to superman. When the curtain closes, the superman is still one step away from evolving into God.

But even then the story is not finished. For the universe is cyclical. God will come down from the hills again. Thus spake Zarathustra:

Lo! I am weary of my wisdom. I need hands reaching out for it. For that end I must descend to the depth, as thou dost at even, when sinking behind the sea thou givest light to the lower regions, thou resplendent star! Zarathustra will once more become a man.

Now that the theologians tell us that God is dead, it appears that the burden of theology is upon SF.

Index

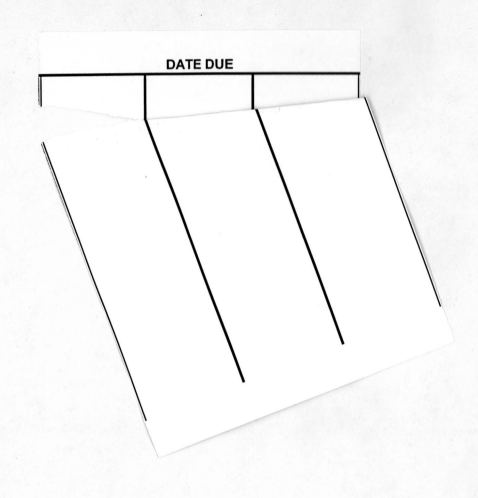

DATE DUE